THE RED BOOK

OF

MICHIGAN;

A

CIVIL, MILITARY AND BIOGRAPHICAL HISTORY.

BY

CHARLES LANMAN,

AUTHOR "DICTIONARY OF CONGRESS," ETC.

DETROIT:
E. B. SMITH & COMPANY.
WASHINGTON:
PHILP & SOLOMONS.
1871.

CORRIGENDA.

A few typographical errors have been discovered since this volume went to press, which the reader will please correct as follows:

Page 9. For La Honton read *La Hontan.*
" 88. " Greenley " *Greenly.*
" 91. " Robert McClellan read *McClelland.*
" 101. " Mahew read *Mayhew.*
" 106. " this table of population substitute that on page 507.
" 416. Transfer names of J. J. & L. B. Adams to preceding page.
" 436. For Labodee read *Labadee.*
" 475. " Zini Pitcher read *Zina.*
" 497. " G. L. Whiting read *Whitney.*
" 515. " Mharles M. Cooley read *Thomas.*

PREFACE.

THE Compiler of this volume is a native of Michigan, and although long an exile from its borders, he has never lost his affection for the beautiful country. He has revisited it a number of times, and in a former publication did what he could to make known its physical attractions and aboriginal lore. Whilst cognizant of the fact that an admirable History of the Territory was in existence, and that one or two good Gazetteers of the State had been published, he felt convinced that there was still needed, for the use of the general public, a more comprehensive volume, and that want he has now endeavored to supply. His leading object has been to prepare an authentic book of reference, rather than to make any display as a writer; and while he has been contented to perform the duties of a literary scout, the success of his present enterprise has been assured by the effective artillery of James H. Lanman and General John Robertson. To the first, who is a relative of the Compiler, he is indebted for the history of the Territory, from its earliest settlement down to the organization of the State; and the latter, who was the able and indefatigable Adjutant-General of Michigan during the War for the Union, has contributed a complete account of the important part which the State took in subduing the Rebellion. Not only has he chronicled the action of the Legislature, but he has taken special care to place upon the record, in compact form, the heroic achievements of the Officers and Soldiers who have honorably identified their names with the State of their nativity or adoption.

With regard to the biographical part of this volume, the Compiler alone is responsible. Although most of this information has been obtained from original sources, he did not deem it advisable to amplify his records more than was absolutely necessary. He regrets, however, that a few of his notices are more brief than they should have been; and, if any persons have been omitted altogether, who deserved notice on account of their association with Michigan, it is because his efforts to obtain the proper data were unsuccessful. His leading intention has been merely to give the salient points in the lives of the persons who pass under consideration, referring the reader, who may desire further information, either to the historical narratives in the present volume, or to the more elaborate biographies hitherto published. Indeed, so far as the numerous officers are concerned, who acquired reputation during the Rebellion, or died the death of heroes, their services were found to have been so well depicted by General Robertson, that the Compiler has generally omitted their names altogether in his department of the work. To the many friends who have kindly assisted him, by their correspondence, he would tender his grateful acknowledgements. And, to the People of Michigan, he now dedicates this Historical Record, as an expression of his regard for their superior intelligence, persevering enterprise and exalted patriotism.

CHARLES LANMAN.

GEORGETOWN, D. C., *November*, 1870.

CONTENTS.

FIRST PART.

CIVIL HISTORY OF MICHIGAN.

PAGE

General Description of the State.—Its Soil and Scenery; Heavily Timbered Land; Oak Openings; Burr Oak Plains; Prairies; Rivers; Lakes; Wild Animals; Birds and Fishes 9

First Advance of the French Missionaries and Travellers.—Brebœuf; Daniel; Pijart; Raymbault; First Arrival of White Men at Saut de Ste. Marie; Father Jacques Bressani; Chaumonotot; Claude Dablon; Mesnard; Lallemand; Dreuillette; Gareau; Mesnard Advances to Che-goi-ne-gon; Allouez; Marquette; Indian Council at Saut de Ste. Marie; Marquette's Explorations and Death; La Salle; His Explorations; Michilimackinac Founded; Death of La Salle; Saut de Ste. Marie; Fort St. Joseph; Detroit Founded by Cadillac; Early Condition; Attacked by Ottawas and Foxes; Hennepin; La Hontan; Charlevoix; Their Operations on Lakes Erie, Huron, Michigan, and Superior 14

Colonial Pioneers.—Merchants; The Rangers of the Woods; The French Peasantry; The Jesuits; French Soldiers; French Policy; Indian Mythology; Frontier Posts, and the Fur Trade at Michilimackinac and Detroit.......... 30

Struggle Between France and England for Possession —The Iroquois and Algonquins; British Troops Advance into Canada; Battle of Quebec; Death of Wolfe and Montcalm; British Detachment under Rogers takes Possession of Michigan; Rogers traverses Lake Erie; Pontiac makes his First Appearance; Bellestre; Surrender of Detroit........ 35

Condition of the Country under the English.—Pontiac forms a Confederacy to attack the English Posts; War breaks out; Siege of Detroit; Battle of Bloody Bridge; Indians assemble around Michilimackinac; Minavavana; Alexander Henry; Wawatam; Michilimackinac destroyed; General Bradstreet arrives; Peace concluded; Death of Pontiac........ 43

The Fur Trade and American Independence.—Hudson's Bay Company; English Administration of the Law; Criminal Trial; Quebec Act; Mineral Rock on Lake Superior; North-west Company; American Revolution; Expeditions from Detroit; Indian Council held at Detroit; American Independence established........ 52

Organization of the North-western Territory.—Arthur St. Clair appointed Governor; English refuse to surrender the Posts: Indian Disaffection; Indian Coun-

PAGE

cil at Detroit; Message from the Spanish Settlements on the Banks of the Mississippi; Campaign of General Harmar; Campaign of General St. Clair; Campaign of General Wayne; Extension of French Settlements; Michigan surrendered to the United States; Condition of the Territory in connection with the Fur Trade; Currency employed in the Fur Trade...... 58

Condition after the Surrender of the Posts.—Michigan erected into a Territory; General Hull appointed Governor; Detroit destroyed by Fire; Administration of the Law; Third Indian Confederacy under Tecumseh and the Prophet; Le Marquoit; Land Office established; Walk-in-the-Water; Population in 1811; Memorial from Michigan praying Aid from the General Government; Savage Outbreak; Operations on the Wabash; American Fur Company........ 64

War between Great Britain and the United States.—Defenceless condition of Michigan; Representations of William Hull; Appointed to Command the Western Army; Crosses to Sandwich and Addresses the Canadians; Policy of Prevost; Surrender of Detroit; Tecumseh; Conduct of Hull; Expedition to the River Raisin; Capture of Chicago; Battle of the River Raisin; General Harrison's Campaign; Commodore Perry; His Victory on Lake Erie; General Harrison arrives at Malden; Marches to Detroit; Battle of the Thames; Death of Tecumseh; His Character; Attack on Mackinaw; Peace concluded........ 69

Transition from Territory to State.—Lewis Cass appointed Governor of the Territory; Its Condition at that Time; Public Lands brought into Market; First Steamboat on the Lakes; University Founded; Expedition to Explore the Lakes; The Clinton Canal; G. B. Porter appointed Governor; Mode of making Surveys; Controversy with Ohio; State Organized........ 79

History as a State and Present Condition.—Admission of Michigan into the Union as a State; Stevens T. Mason the first elective Governor; Act passed for establishing University of Michigan; Other Events of his Administration; Organization of the Militia; Administration of William Woodbridge and J. Wright Gordon; Branches of University Established; Grand Lodge of Free Masons; John S. Barry Elected Governor; Administration of Alpheus Felch and William L. Greenly; Epaphroditus Ransom elected Governor; Progress of Agriculture; Re-election of Governor Barry; Great Railroad Conspiracy Case; Commercial Advantages of Michigan; Administration of Robert McClelland and Andrew Parsons; Election and Re-election of Kinsley S. Bingham; Ship Canal at the Falls of St. Mary; Moses Wisner elected Governor; Election to the same Office of Austin Blair, Henry H. Crapo, and Henry P. Baldwin; and Complete List of Governors under French, English, and American Rule........ 85

Education.—University of Michigan; Its Professors and Instructors; General Features; Homeopathic Controversy; Action on the Admission of Women as Students: Possessions and Advantages; Observatory; Adrian College; Albion College; Kalamazoo College; Michigan Female College; State Agricultural College; Hillsdale College; Public Schools of the State; State Normal School; State Reform School; Asylum for the Deaf, Dumb and Blind; Superintendents of Public Instruction; Asylum for the Insane; State Prison; Public School Statistics; Union School System, and List of Incorporated Literary Institutions........ 91

PAGE

Agriculture.—Population and Statistics; Government Lands; Value of Crops; Fruit Culture; Counties of the State; Increase of Population 103

Mineral Wealth.—Copper Interest of Lake Superior; Iron Interest of the Same; Salt Springs of Saginaw; Plaster Beds of the Grand River; Magnetic Waters of Eaton Rapids; Chronological History of Geological Explorations in Michigan 107

Railroads.—Michigan Central Railroad and its Branches; Michigan Southern Railroad and Branches; Detroit and Milwaukee Railroad; Flint and Pere Marquette Railroad; Amboy, Lansing and Traverse Bay Railroad; Condition of New Railroads 115

Lumbering Interest.—The Pine Forests; The Hard-wood Forests; Amount of Lumber Manufactured; Climate of the Lumber Region; Various Attractions 120

The Fisheries.—Their Commercial Value; Variety of Fish Taken; Principal Localities where the Business is Carried on 124

Commerce.—The Great Lakes; Their Coast Line and Area; The Steamboat and other Shipping; European Consumers of Grain; The Northern Peninsula; The Southern Peninsula; Resources of the State; Ship Canal of St. Mary; Indebtedness of the State; Banking Institutions 126

The Indians and Antiquities of the State.—The Number of Indians in the State; Their Annuities and Condition; Ancient Gardens and Mounds; Ancient Mining on Lake Superior; The Mound Builders; Indian Names of Michigan 130

Recent Developments.—The Grand Traverse Region; The Sand Dunes on Lake Michigan; The Saginaw Valley, Its Lumber, Salt Springs and Gypsum Beds; The Straits of Mackinaw; Mackinaw City; The Cheboygan Region, its Lumbering and Agricultural Interests 133

Notes.—Order of Odd-Fellows; Nativities of Population 140

SECOND PART.

HISTORY OF MICHIGAN DURING THE REBELLION.

Military Department of Michigan from 1861 *to* 1871 143

Prefatory Notes.—Love of Michigan for the Old Flag; Necessity of an Historical Record; Origin of the Information 144

Introductory.—The American Rebellion; Unprepared condition of Michigan; Valedictory Message of Governor Moses Wisner; Sentiments of Governor Austin Blair; War Meeting in Detroit; Flag Song of Michigan Troops; Organization of Troops and provision for Ways and Means; Special Session of the Legislature and its Action; Curious Telegram 146

Raising of Troops.—The First Regiments; The Secretary of War to the Governor of Michigan; Camp of Instruction; Progress of Recruiting; Message of Governor Blair; Action of the Legislature; Re-inforcements Demanded; Action of the Adjutant General; Patriotism of the Churches; Additional

PAGE

Troops sent to the Front; Particulars of the Draft; Military Census; Appeal from Governor Blair; Report from Adjutant General Robertson; Gratitude of the Legislature; Michigan Cavalry; Enrollment of Districts; A new Draft; Another Report from the Adjutant General; Veteran Troops; Another call for Troops; Proclamation of Governor Blair; Continued Organization; Troops furnished by Counties; Action of Legislature; Valedictory Message of Governor Blair; Legislature thank the Retiring Governor; Governor Crapo's Inaugural; Soldiers thanked by Legislature; Total number of Michigan Troops by Counties; Conscription; End of the War; Proclamation of thanks from Governor Crapo; Governor Baldwin comes into Office; Nativities of Michigan Volunteers; Analysis of Volunteers; Table of Casualties; Table of Dates and Places when and where the Troops of the State were mustered in, and mustered out of the Public service........ 150

Financial Statistics.—Amount of the money expended by State for Enlisting Troops; Amounts paid by Counties; Appropriation by Legislature for Soldier's Home; Disbursements by Colonel George W. Lee........ 195

Sanitary Operations.—Michigan Soldier's Relief Association; Report of James M. Edmunds; Operations of the Association; The Christian and Sanitary Commissions; The Ladies' Aid Society of Kalamazoo; State Sanitary Fair; Appeal from Citizens to the Ladies; Response of the Ladies, and their Appeal to the People; Success of the Fair; The Christian Commission and Delegates to the Commission........ 197

Volunteer Surgeons.—Bright Array of Names........ 208

Soldier's Vote in the Field.—Letter of the Executive; Commissions for Army of the Potomac; For Army of the Cumberland; For Army of the Tennessee; and for Army of the Gulf; Result of the Vote for Presidential Electors and Governor........ 210

Reception of Troops.—Committee of Reception; Committee of Finance; Courtesies of Railroad and Steamboat Companies........ 212

Presentation of Colors.—Adjutant General's Report; Letter of Major John H. Knight; Attendance of Soldiers; A War Poem; Number of Flags Presented........ 213

The Harper Hospital.—Its Success and final Transfer into a Soldier's Home........ 217

The Soldier's and Sailor's Monument.—Measure Inaugurated; Board of Directors; Officers and Committees, Adoption of Design by Randolph Rogers; Plan of Monument; Corner Stone laid by the Masonic and Odd Fellow Fraternities; Oration by Governor Blair........ 218

Cemeteries at Gettysburg, Sharpsburg, and Andersonville.—Appropriation by Legislature; Appointment of T. W. Ferry as Commissioner; Appointment of John I. Bagley as Trustee; Andersonville........ 221

Rebel Raid from Canada.—Adjutant General's Report; Action of the Confederate Secretary of the Navy; Manifesto of the Confederate President; Telegrams and Letters from Lieutenant-Colonel B. H. Hill and Commander J. C. Carter; The Steamers Philo Parsons and Michigan........ 222

The Michigan Contingent.—Heroism of Michigan Troops; Various Campaigns; Their Motto........ 231

PAGE

Regiment of Engineers and Mechanics.—Colonel William P. Innes; Engagement at Lavergne; Opinions of Greeley and Rosecrans; Services in the Atlanta Campaign; Colonel John Yates...... 233

The Cavalry Brigade.—First Regiment; Colonel T. F. Broadhead; Colonel Charles H. Town; Fifth Cavalry, Colonel J. T. Copeland, Colonel Freeman Norvil, Colonel R. A. Alger; Sixth Cavalry, Colonel T. W. Kellogg, Colonel George Gray; Seventh Cavalry, Colonel W. D. Mann; General A. S. Williams; Operations of the Michigan Cavalry Brigade; Justice granted by Congress; Michigan Senators and Representatives; Report on Conduct of Michigan Troops at Gettysburg by General Custer; The Michigan Cavalry in Maryland; Report of Colonel C. H. Town; Report of General Kilpatrick; Report of Colonel Alger; Report of General Custer on Virginia Campaign; Raid of General Kilpatrick; Another Report by General Custer on operations around Richmond; Losses during Campaign; Additional Reports of Colonels Alger and Kidd; Report of Colonel Peter Stagg; Gen. Custer's Report of Winchester Campaign; Services of Staff Officers; Captors of Battle Flags; Heroic Deaths; Final Actions of the Brigade........ 235

The Second Cavalry.—Colonel F. W. Kellogg; Colonel Gordon Granger; Point Pleasant in Missouri; Colonel P. H. Sheridan, Boonville; Operations in Mississippi, Kentucky, and Tennessee; Colonel Archibald Campbell; Battle of Chicamauga; Further Operations; Colonel Thomas Johnson; Continued Engagements...... 265

The Third Cavalry.—Colonel J. K. Mizner; New Madrid, in Missouri; Battle of Iuka; Report of Captain L. G. Wilcox; Tribute of General Rosecrans; Services in Kentucky, Tennessee and Mississippi; Arkansas Cattle; Michigan City; Escort to General Canby; On duty in Texas...... 270

The Fourth Cavalry.—Colonel R. H. G. Minty; First Battle at Stanford, in Kentucky; Numerous Engagements in Tennessee and Mississippi; Its Fighting Reputation; Major F. W. Mix; Battles of Chicamauga and Missionary Ridge; Minty's Report; Lieutenant J. H. Simpson; Major Horace Gray; Death of Lieutenant Edward Tucker; Death of Lieutenant Randolph; Rebel Testimony; Death of Lieutenant T. W. Sutton; General Kilpatrick's Raid; Operations near Jonesboro; Famous Charge Under Minty; Private William Bailey's Exploit; Operations Around Atlanta; Corporal C. M. Bickford; Colonel B. F. Pritchard; Attack on Selma and its Capture; Capture of Jefferson Davis; Official Notes and Names of Officers and Men at the Capture; Distribution of the Reward...... 273

The Eighth Cavalry.—Colonel John Stockton; Its Bright Record; Lieutenant-Colonel G. S. Wormer; Capture of General Morgan; Major Edgerly; Lieutenant-Colonel Mix; Operations Against the Forces of General Hood...... 287

The Ninth Cavalry.—Colonel James I. David; Pursuit of General Morgan and his Further Fighting Operations in Tennessee and Kentucky; With General Sherman on his March from Atlanta to the Atlantic; Morgan's Escape..... 289

The Tenth Cavalry.—Colonel Thaddeus Foote; Colonel L. S. Trowbridge; Affair at Watauga River; Death of Captain Weatherwax; Service with General Stoneman; Affair at Abbott's Creek; Incident at Strawberry Plains; Further Operations in that Vicinity...... 292

PAGE

The Eleventh Cavalry.—Colonel S. B. Brown; Operations at Saltville and Marion, in Virginia; Captain E. C. Miles; Death of Colonel Mason and Lieutenant Davis; Lieutenant-Colonel Charles E. Smith; Subsequent Services in North Carolina........ 296

The "Merrill Horse" Cavalry.—Captains James B. Mason, Jabez H. Rogers and Almon E. Preston; Services in Missouri, Arkansas, and Georgia 298

The Light Artillery.—Colonel C. O. Loomis; The Brave Boy McIntire; Report of General Rousseau; Guenther's Battery; Death of Lieutenant Van Pelt; Captain W. S. Bliss; Pittsburgh Landing; With General Sherman at Atlanta; Murder of Lieutenant Bliss; Siege of Corinth; Captains A. W. Dees; George Robinson; L. R. Smith; John C. Schultz; J. W. Church; John J. Dennis; John S. Andrews; Paddock and C. H. Lamphere; Operations in the South-west; Charles J. Thompson; Edward J. Hillier; Death of Captain S. De Gobyer at Vicksburg; Captains J. J. Daniels, C. H. O'Riordan, Charles Dupont, and Charles Heine........ 299

The Sharp-shooters.—Colonel C. V. DeLand; Battle of the Wilderness; Civilized Indians; Major Levant C. Rhines; Corporal B. F. Young; Death of T. H. Gaffney; of Lieutenant G. A. Graveraet; Captain G. C. Knight and Lieutenant Martin Wager; Before Petersburg; Operations in Front of Petersburg; Colonel W. A. Nichols; The Fall of Petersburg and Richmond; Michigan Troops the First to Enter Petersburg; Report of General O. B. Wilcox........ 305

The First Infantry.—Colonel O. B. Wilcox; Opportune Arrival in Washington; Colonel John C. Robinson; Colonel H. S. Roberts; Death of Captain O. C. Comstock; Second Battle of Bull Run; Report of Chaplain Arthur Edwards; Death of Captains Wendell, Alcott, Whittlesey and Pomeroy; and Lieutenants Arnold, Garrison and Bloodgood; Colonel Franklin W. Whittlesey; Operations in Maryland and Virginia; Death of J. B. Kennedy; At Gettysburg; In the Wilderness under Colonel W. A. Throop; Death of Captain James H. Wheaton; Major George Lockley; Death of Captain L. C. Randell and Lieutenant W. S. Woodruff; Report of General Wilcox on Operations in Virginia........ 310

The Second Infantry.—Colonel J. B. Richardson; Colonel O. M. Poe; In Peninsula Campaign; Bull Run; Colonel Louis Dillman; In Mississippi Campaign; Report of Colonel W. Humphrey; Battle of the Wilderness and Army of the Potomac; Order of General R. G. Berry; Testimony of Correspondents; Rebellion Record; Death of Lieutenants Sherman, Fletcher, and Williams; Report of General Wilcox; Colonel Ralph Ely........ 316

The Third Infantry.—Colonel Daniel McConnell; In Battles of the Peninsula; Report of Colonel A. A Stevens; Colonel B. M. Pierce; His Report of Operations; Colonel M. B. Houghton; In Virginia and at Gettysburg; In the South-west........ 323

The Fourth Infantry.—Complimented by General McClellan; Death of Colonel Woodbury; Report of Captain J. F. Randolph; Colonel H. H. Jeffords and his Death; Colonel Lombard; His Death; Death of Captain W. H. Loveland; Reorganized and again in the Field under Colonel J. W. Hall; General Griffin........ 326

PAGE

The Fifth Infantry.—Colonel H. D. Terry; Numerous Officers killed in the Virginia Campaign; Death of Colonel John Gilluly; Colonel E. T. Sherlock; His Death; Colonel Pulford; at Gettysburg and in Virginia; Numerous Casualties among Officers and Men; Testimony of General Berry and General Kearney; Letter from Colonel Sherlock 328

The Sixth Infantry.—Its Isolation; Colonel F. W. Curtenius; Services at Baltimore and New Orleans; On Lower Mississippi; Captain Charles E. Clark; General T. Williams at Baton Rouge; Colonel Thomas S. Clark; His Report; Exploit of Private Charles Dustin; Complimented by Generals Butler and Banks; Transfer to Artillery arm of Service; March on Mobile and its Surrender; Reports of General Butler and Weitzel; Miscellaneous Testimony 333

The Seventh Infantry—Colonel Ira R. Grosvenor; Heavy Losses at Antietam; Including Captains A. H. Zacharias and J. H. Turrill, and Lieutenants J. P. Eberhard and John A. Clark; Death of Baxter; His Heroism at Fredericksburg; Pennsylvania Campaign; Death of Colonel A. E. Steele and Lieutenant Slafter; In Command of Major S. W. Curtis; Operations in Virginia; Sergeant A. Smith's Exploit and Reward; Colonel Lapointe; Particulars respecting Captain A. H. Zacharias; Death of Lieutenant John J. Brown 336

The Eighth Infantry.—Colonel W. M. Fenton; Called the Wandering Regiment; Death of Adjutant N. M. Pratt and Lieutenant F. M. Badger; Nine Battles in four States; James Island; Death of Captains S. C. Gould and B. B. Church; At Bull Run; In Maryland; Mississippi and East Tennessee; Siege of Knoxville; Wilderness; Death of Colonel F. Graves; Colonel R. Ely; Cold Harbor; Death of Lieutenant E. A. Nye, Major W. E. Lewis, and Lieutenant T. Campbell; Weldon Road; Death of Major Belcher at South Mountain; Major R. N. Doyle at Petersburg; Report of Colonel W. M. Fenton of Operations at Wilmington Island; Report of General Stevens; Tribute to Major Belcher by General J. D. Cox 340

The Ninth Infantry—Colonel W. W. Duffield; Defence of Murfreesboro; Death of Lieutenant A. Chase; Battle of Stone River; Colonel W. Wilkinson; Operations in Georgia; Death of Lieutenant C. F. Fox 345

The Tenth Infantry.—Colonel C. M. Lum; Services in Georgia; Buzzard's Roost; Jonesboro; Bentonville 347

The Eleventh Infantry.—Colonel William L. Stoughton; His Report of Stone River; Colonel Melvin Mudge; Chicamauga; Death of Captain C. W. Newbern; Mission Ridge; Death of Major B. G. Bennett; Loss of a Leg by Colonel Stoughton; Death of Lieutenant E. Catlin 350

The Twelfth Infantry.—Colonel W. H. Graves; His Report of Operations at Middleburg; Complimented by General Grant; Services in Arkansas 352

The Thirteenth Infantry.—Colonel Charles E. Stuart; Colonel Michael Shoemaker; Operations in Tennessee; Report of Colonel J. B. Culver; Death of Captain C. C. Webb; Report of Colonel Shoemaker; Report of Colonel Harker; Services in Georgia; Exploit of Julius Lillie, Orderly Sergeant 354

The Fourteenth Infantry—Colonel Robert P. Sinclair; In Alabama and Georgia; Jonesboro; Bentonville; Colonel H. R. Mizner; Colonel G. W. Drummond; March to Savannah; Capture of Flags 357

PAGE

The Fifteenth Infantry.—Colonel J. M. Oliver; At Shiloh; Death of Captain G. A. Strong and Lieutenant M. W. Dresser; Corinth; In Mississippi; Alabama; In Georgia Campaign; Colonel F. S. Hutchinson; Numerous Engagements and extensive Marching; Death of Captain C. H. Barnaby at Atlanta 360

The Sixteenth Infantry.—Colonel T. B. W. Stockton; Gaines' Mill; Major N. E. Welch; Death of Captain T. C. Carr and Lieutenants B. McGraw and R. Williams; Captain R. W. Ransom; Death of Lieutenants M. Chittick and J. Ruby at Malvern Hill; Colonel N. E. Welch at Middleburg; Death of Captain J. M. Mott and Lieutenants Brown, Jewett, and Borden at Gettysburg, and R. T. Elliott at the Wilderness; Captains G. H. Swan and Guy Fuller; Major B. F. Partridge; Death of Colonel Welch; Incidents 362

The Seventeenth Infantry.—General James E. Pittman; Colonel W. H. Withington; South Mountain; Death of Lieutenant George Galligan; Report of Colonel F. W. Swift; Colonel C. Luce in Mississippi; Death of L. L. Comstock; Army of the Potomac; Death of Captain J. S. Vreeland and Lieutenant A. E. Canfield; Reports of General Wilcox and General McClellan 365

The Eighteenth Infantry.—Organized by Hon. Henry Waldron; Colonel Charles C. Doolittle; In Kentucky, Tennessee, and Alabama; Colonel Hulbard; Captain Moore; Exploit 369

The Nineteenth Infantry.—Colonel Henry C. Gilbert; In Department of the Cumberland; A Surrender; Tribute from a Confederate Officer to Colonel Gilbert; In Atlanta Campaign; Death of Colonel Gilbert and Captain C. H. Calmer; Major E. A. Griffin; His Death, and that of Lieutenant Charles Mandeville, and Captains C. W. Bigelow and John J. Baker; Atlanta to the Sea; Report of Colonel David Anderson; Death of Captain L. Gibbon and Lieutenant C. G. Purcell; Note respecting Lieutenant Baldwin 372

The Twentieth Infantry.—Tidus Livermore, Commandant; Colonel A. W. Williams; Services in Kentucky; Colonel W. H. Smith; Interview with General Morgan; Death of Lieutenant W. M. Green; Commended by General Burnside; In Tennessee; Death of Colonel Smith; Major Byron M. Cutcheon; At the Wilderness; Major George C. Barnes; Casualties at Spottsylvania; Alexander Bush and Frank Philips; Colonel C. B. Grant; Casualties in Peninsula Campaign 374

The Twenty-first Infantry.—J. B. Welch, Camp Commandant; Colonel Ambrose A. Stevens in Kentucky; Colonel W. B. McCreery at Stone River; Report of General Sheridan; Death of Colonel McCreery; Colonel L. K. Bishop in Georgia and South Carolina; Captain A. C. Prince 379

The Twenty-second Infantry.—Hon. and Colonel Moses Wisner; Colonel Heber Le Favour at Chicamauga; Brave Sergeant and Corporals; Death of Captains W. A. Smith and E. Snell; In Note; Story of Johnny Clem 382

The Twenty-third Infantry.—Colonels David Jerome and M. W. Chapin; In Kentucky and Tennessee; Colonel O. S. Spaulding; Hard fought Battles; Major W. W. Wheeler; At Campbell's Station; Spaulding's Report; Death of Lieutenant W. C. Stewart at Resaca; Death of Captain David M. Averill at Franklin; Service in North Carolina 384

The Twenty-Fourth Infantry.—The "Iron Brigade;" Colonel Henry A. Morrow; Battle of Gettysburg; Heroism of Privates William Kelly and Silburne

PAGE

Spaulding; Captain Albert M. Edwards; Nine Standard Bearers killed or Wounded; Report of Colonel Morrow complimenting Heroic Officers; Speed, O'Donnell, Wallace, Safford, Grace, Humphreville Dickey, and Shuttuck; On the Rappahannock; In the Wilderness; Death of Captain George Hutton and Lieutenant William B. Hutchinson; Colonel Morrow Wounded; Death of Seville Chilson; Siege of Petersburg; In Note; Patrick Maloney 388

The Twenty-Fifth Infantry.—Hon. H. G. Wells Commandant of Camp; Colonel O. H. Moore; In Kentucky; Battle with General Morgan; Touching interview between Union and Confederate Officers; General Hartsuff; Legislature of Kentucky; The Rebel General Morgan on Colonel Moore's Generalship; Various Operations in Georgia; Colonel Benjamin F. Orcutt; Death of Adjutant E. M. Brutzman; With the Army of General Sherman, 392

The Twenty-Sixth Infantry.—The Skirmish Regiment; Colonel Judson S. Farrar; Death of Captain John C. Culver; In the Army of the Potomac; Major L. Saviers; A Tree cut down by Bullets at Spottsylvania; Complimented by Generals Barlow and Miles; at Cold Harbor; Death of J. A. Lothain; Captain A. G. Dailey; Captain S. H. Ives; Present at Surrender of Lee's Army 397

The Twenty-Seventh Infantry.—Colonel D. M. Fox; In Kentucky and Tennessee; Major Samuel Moody; Services at Spottsylvania; Death of Lieutenants Charles H. Seymour, Charles T. Miller, and Major Moody; Captain E. S. Leadbetter; Death of Lieutenant J. W. Brennan; Captain Charles Wait at Petersburg; Death of Lieutenants Mason Vosper and Theodore S. Meade; Gallantry of Captain Wait and his War Cry of "*Fort or Nothing;*" Heroism of Major Moody 400

The Twenty-Eighth Infantry.—Hon. S. S. Lacy Commandant of Camp; Colonel Delos Phillips; Colonel W. W. Wheeler; Battle of Nashville; Joins the Army of General Sherman; Death of Lieutenant Matthew Holmes; Death of Lieutenant John E. Kenyon 405

The Twenty-Ninth Infantry.—Hon. J. F. Driggs; Colonel Thomas F. Taylor; Colonel Charles C. Doolittle in Command of Decatur; Its Successful Defence; Nolansville; Death of Lieutenant F. Van Vliet; Colonel G. S. Wormer; Service in Michigan 406

The Colored Regiment—Colonel Henry Barns; Lieutenant-Colonel W T. Bennett; Colonel H. S. Chipman; In Florida; In South Carolina; Death of Captain A. E. Lindsey; Operations at Georgetown, S. C.; and Mustered out at Charleston 408

The Militia Guards.—The Scott Guard; The Detroit Light Guard; The Lyon Guard; Report of the Adjutant General on the Militia of Michigan, and conclusion of the History of Michigan during the Rebellion 410

THIRD PART.

BIOGRAPHICAL HISTORY OF MICHIGAN.

The Names alphabetically arranged 415

PAGE

FOURTH PART.

MISCELLANEOUS RECORDS.

The Census of Michigan in 1870, (officially furnished for this work by the Census Bureau) 507
State Officers of Michigan from 1836 to 1870 508
The Judiciary of Michigan in 1870 509
Presidential Electors of Michigan from 1837 to 1869 510
Officers of the University of Michigan from 1837 to 1870 510
Trustees of Michigan Colleges in 1870 515
Books connected with the Territory and State of Michigan 517
Newspapers of Michigan with their Publishers in 1870 518
The Post Offices of Michigan in 1870 521
Constitution of the State of Michigan 526
Amendments to the Constitution 548

FIRST PART.

CIVIL HISTORY OF MICHIGAN.

CIVIL HISTORY OF MICHIGAN.

GENERAL DESCRIPTION OF THE STATE.

The name of Michigan is derived from the Indian word *Michsawgyegan*, the meaning of which is the Lake Country. It is bounded on the north by Lake Superior; on the east by Lakes Huron, St. Clair, and Erie; on the south by Ohio and Indiana; and on the west by Wisconsin and Lake Michigan; and the extent of its dominion is fifty-six thousand two hundred and forty-three square miles.* Along the shores of Lake Erie there stretches a belt of level and heavily-timbered land, bearing a growth of large and noble forest trees upon a low and level soil. The land gradually rises towards the centre of the State, presenting a variegated scenery composed of tracts of dense wilderness, alternated with prairies, natural parks or oak openings, copses of burr-oak, marshes, barrens, and pine groves, each watered by small streams, lakes, or springs. That part of the State which borders Lake Superior is more bold and primitive, and is broken by mountains and plains, hills and valleys. The Porcupine Mountains, which are the dividing ridge, and separate the waters of Lake Superior and Lake Michigan, are about two thousand feet high and abound in the charms of Alpine and imposing coast scenery. Many parts of this northern peninsula exhibit a bold, rocky, and sterile prospect, which caused one of the early French travellers—La Honton—to call this region "the fag end of the world." It abounds with forests of white and yellow pine, and will probably never be favorable for agricultural production, although it is a rich mineral region. The northern part of the lower peninsula, generally speaking, is flat and swampy; the central and southern portions are gently rolling, covered with groves of oak, alternated with tracts of heavily-timbered land, are peculiarly favorable for the production of wheat, which is the staple product, and present the most picturesque points of scenery, and resources for even a dense population.

The soil of Michigan is various in its character. It is in general much more level than that of New York and New England, being of alluvial formation, and comparatively free from rocks. The different species of soil consist of heavily-timbered land, oak openings, burr-oak plains, prairies, and pine groves, each of which will be considered.

The heavily-timbered land consists of tracts which are densely wooded with a variety of large forest-trees, the principal of which are the black and

---

* Additional information on the topography of the State will be found in subsequent pages of this volume.

white walnut, oaks of different species, maple, ash, elm, linden, sycamore, hackberry, cottonwood, aspen, locust, butternut, box or dogwood, poplar, whitewood, beech, cherry, sassafras, white, yellow, and Norway pine, hemlock, spruce, tamerack, cedar, chestnut, and pawpaw; as well as the smaller trees and shrubs, such as willow, alder, sumach, and honeysuckle, together with the different kinds of undergrowth which are found in the Middle States. This timbered land is often found upon the borders of the streams, upon what are called *bottoms*, and also upon the ridges which border them. It is discovered along the shores of the lakes from Monroe to Detroit, and thence to Lake Michigan, in a belt varying from five to fifteen miles in breadth. But a small proportion of the peninsular part of the State is, however, densely wooded.

There are various other species of soil which constitute a beautiful variety, and which will be described in their proper order. The heavily-timbered soil is generally composed of a deep vegetable mold, sometimes commingled with clay, and produces a dense and luxuriant vegetation. Compared with the other sections of the State, it is gloomy, being generally more low and level, and it is more difficult to clear from the thick and tangled mass of trees which covers it; but these disadvantages are made up by its fertility, and it yields in great abundance the grasses, oats, buckwheat, potatoes, rye, and large crops of corn. Perhaps it is not so favorable to wheat, being damp, from the fact that it is shut out from the sun, and also cold in its nature.

In advancing into the interior of the State, across the narrow belt before described, we arrive upon a more dry and undulating soil—a species of land which swells into little hills like artificial mounds, and is called *oak openings*. This land is composed of a sandy loam, mingled sometimes with limestone pebbles, and appears light upon the surface, but, when laid open by the plough, turns black from the intermixture of lime in its composition. The trees, consisting chiefly of whiteoak, scattered over the ground generally from ten to sixty feet apart, and extending for miles like cultivated parks, now sweeping down to a clear stream, a fertile prairie, or the brow of a transparent lake, impress one with the idea that he is travelling through an old, rather than a newly-settled country. These openings constitute a feature which distinguishes this from most of the adjoining States. The land, although not as productive as some other kinds of soil, yields heavy crops of oats and abundant harvests of wheat, besides the ordinary products of the Middle States. Although containing apparently but a thin covering of decomposed vegetable matter, the absence of that material is made up by the admixture of lime in its composition, which is favorable to vegetation; and in summer the surface is almost entirely covered with red, yellow, white, and purple flowers, which, in their richness and beauty, are not known in the older-settled portions of the country, spreading a gorgeous carpet through the forest as far as the eye can reach. The surface of the oak openings also presents a turf of matted grass, which requires three or four yoke of oxen to break it up; and, as you can ride for miles in a carriage under the trees that are thus widely separated, it does not need so great an amount of labor in clearing it as the timbered land. The trees, however, are usually girdled in order to effect their decay. These oak openings extend throughout the greater part of the lower peninsula.

Another species of soil of very great value is found in the State, commencing at the county of Jackson and studding the timbered land and oak openings from the head of the Kalamazoo river to the shores of Lake Michigan. It is called *burr-oak plains* or openings; a soil which consists of tracts spread over with groves of trees of a small size, called the burr-oak, with a rough bark and deep green foliage. They closely resemble cultivated orchards of pear trees, springing from a soil which is composed of a brown loam mingled with clay; yet they are highly productive, and are deemed by the settlers of the greatest value, yielding in abundance the crops of the Middle States—corn, oats, potatoes, buckwheat, rye, and all the products of the other kinds of soil. As the trees, like those of the whiteoak openings, are widely separated, this land requires but little clearing; but four or five yoke of oxen are generally used to break it up for seeding. Corn to the amount of forty, and sometimes eighty, bushels to the acre is produced from these openings, and from forty to fifty bushels of oats. Thirty bushels of wheat to the acre are also frequently obtained from this land; but the average amount may be placed at about twenty-five bushels.

Scattered through the south and southwestern part, particularly upon the borders of the Kalamazoo, the Grand, and St. Joseph rivers are, what are called *prairies*. These consist of a soil destitute of trees, and covered with a deep surface of black sand and vegetable mold. It is more productive than any other species, yielding very large crops of corn and potatoes, as well as wheat, which is, however, apt not to be as clean as that on the openings. All other crops that are produced in this climate it yields in great profusion. These prairies throughout the State are comparatively small, but in Illinois they stretch out beyond the horizon like a sea. Being comparatively easy to cultivate, and producing so abundantly, they are always selected by the farmers before any other kind of soil. The dry prairies on the banks of the Kalamazoo and St. Joseph rivers furnish a soil equal to any other in the West, and frequently from thirty to fifty bushels of corn have been raised upon them the first season, without being ploughed or hoed; and when the mold has been once subdued, from thirty to eighty bushels of corn, or forty of wheat, have been obtained to the acre; they are also very favorable for grass.

Another species of soil found in the State is called *wet prairies* or *marshes*, tracts which are generally in part or in whole covered with water; and they produce a long coarse grass that is only favorable for winter stock, and make a fine ranging ground for horses and cattle in the spring. When drained, these wet prairies may be converted into valuable meadow land.

Another species of soil that we meet with in the interior is termed *barrens*. They consist of tracts which are sparsely scattered over with stunted oaks or bushes, that would seem to indicate that the land is not favorable to vegetation. It is found, however, that by cultivation it produces well.

The kind of soil which is called *swamp* or *marsh land* is found in considerable tracts in the greater part of the State. It is in winter covered with water, and has a deep mire, which is dangerous to the traveller, and is sprinkled here and there with a few scattering trees or groves of tamerack, which resemble pine. In many places these marshes are caused by beaver-dams.

The mineral productions of the State are various, and some of great value. Although the soil of the lower peninsula is, as has been before remarked, of alluvial formation, yet there are occasionally seen ledges of sandstone, which abounds in parts of the counties of Hillsdale, Jackson, Calhoun, Kalamazoo, Livingston, Ingham, Eaton, Barry, Shiawassee, Clinton, and other portions of the State. Gray limestone is also found; and on the immediate shore of Lake Huron a greenish-colored clay has been discovered. Indications of coal are apparent in the counties of Eaton, Ingham, and Shiawassee. On the banks of Grand river, near the Grand Rapids, beds of gypsum or plaster occur, which are of considerable importance. Salt-springs, used for the manufacture of salt, are scattered throughout a considerable portion of the interior; and clay, sand, marl, bog-iron ore, with other kinds, and springs tinctured with mineral qualities, especially sulphur, have been discovered in the eastern part of the peninsula, that will be of advantage for medicinal purposes.

The shores of Lake Superior are rich in mineral wealth, especially copper, and a large mass of that metal, near the mouth of the Ontonagon river, of many thousand pounds' weight, excited the interest of travellers from the earliest period. Among the rocks on this part of the coast are to be found iron ore, prase, jaspar, carnelian, agate, sardonyx, and other rare stones of some value.

The greater part of the State is also well watered by numerous rivers and small streams, which variegate the landscape, and flow into the surrounding lakes. The principal of these are the Raisin, Grand river, the Kalamazoo, the St. Joseph, the Huron, the Clinton, the Saginaw, and the Ontonagon. The Detroit, the St. Clair, and the St. Mary's cannot be properly called rivers, as they are only straits which connect the lakes in the eastern and more level portions. Upon the eastern border of the State the rivers are sluggish, but as you advance into the interior they become more clear and rapid. The St. Joseph is a transparent and beautiful, though shallow stream, which meanders through the western part of the State over a bed of limestone rock and pebbles, and watering counties of great fertility, consisting of oak lands and prairies, flows into Lake Michigan. The Kalamazoo is also a clear but narrow river, that runs over a surface of sand, limestone rock, or pebbles, and, watering extensive and productive tracts of the State, empties into the same lake. The Grand river is the largest stream in the interior, and, after furnishing a convenient channel for navigation and large manufacturing advantages, empties into Lake Michigan at Grand Haven. There are various other streams of less importance, which furnish sites for manufacturing establishments, and eligible points for settlement on their banks.

The little lakes scattered over the soil are another peculiar point in the scenery. These are clear, and abound with fish; and in summer, when the vegetation upon their banks is in full bloom, appear like mirrors, where Nature, dressed in green and flowery robes, may admire her own beauty amid the solitude.

But the great lakes which wash its shores are the most prominent feature of the State. These constitute much the largest body of fresh water on the face of the globe. To the eye they appear like oceans, and water the borders of the forest for thousands of miles, from the State of New York to the regions of Canada lying along the shores of Lake Superior, which are now ranged chiefly by tribes of Indians, fur traders, and miners. Their surges roll like those of the sea, and the mariner obliged to navigate them often encounters as dangerous storms as upon the ocean. Their waters, however, are not, like those of the open sea, of a blue color, but have a tinge of green, from the fact that they are fresh. They were formerly explored only by the bark canoes of the Indians, and were the theatre of the fur trade, which will be described hereafter; but are now crossed by steamboats of large tonnage, as well as vessels and ships of all sizes.

The origin of the names of the great lakes is not wanting in interest. Lake Ontario was formerly called Lake Frontenac, while that of Erie is derived from a nation of Erries, who roamed along the northern borders of Ohio, and were destroyed by the Iroquois. Lake Huron was termed Karegnondi, and also Lake of Orleans. Lake Michigan was called Lake Michigonong, and also Lake of Puans and Illinese, and Lake of the Dauphin. Lake St. Clair was named by La Salle's expedition, from the day on which he entered the river. The length of Lake Superior is estimated at five hundred miles, and its breadth at one hundred and ninety. This lake is as clear as crystal, and the polished stones upon the bottom, as well as numerous shoals of fish, can be seen at a great depth. Lake Michigan is believed to be three hundred and thirty miles long, and sixty miles broad. Lake Huron is two hundred and sixty miles long, and, coastwise, three hundred and sixty; its breadth is one hundred and sixty miles. Lake Erie is two hundred and eighty miles long, and its widest part is about sixty-three miles. Lake St. Clair is thirty miles long and twenty-eight miles broad. It is thus seen that this chain of lakes must furnish an important channel of navigation in the future commerce of the country.

The wild animals of this as well as the other portions of the Northwest are various. The mammoth or mastodon once roamed through its forests, and its skeletons are now found below the surface.* Herds of buffaloes roved over the prairies upon the borders of Lake Erie as late as 1720, and we have a full account of that fact from the early French travellers; but these have been driven, by the progress of emigration, to the plains which sweep along the base of the Rocky Mountains. The elk and moose and troops of deer formerly fed on the green herbage upon the banks of the Detroit; but these have now retired to the more unsettled portions of the State. The wolverine, the black or brown bear, the wolf, the elk, the deer, moose, lynx, wild-cat, panther, fox, marten, raccoon, porcupine, opossum, weasel, polecat, gopher, the black, red, gray, and striped squirrel, marmot or woodchuck, rabbit, hare, and various other species of animals, are now found in the interior. The beaver, the otter, the muskrat, and the mink inhabit the rivers and small streams, and furnished a valuable article of commerce during the early French, English, and American fur trade. Of birds, the robin, the blackbird, the thrush, the lark, the bluebird, different species of the sparrow, the wren, the woodpecker, the brant, and the loon, the jay, and the cuckoo, are the most common. The forests shelter flocks of the wild turkey and the partridge. The grouse or prairie-hen swarms on the prairies. Pigeons appear in large flocks at particular seasons of the year, and the snipe and the white partridge are not uncommon. The eagle, the brant, the buzzard, and others of the vulture kind, the crow, the raven, the heron, and owls of different species, the most distinguished of which is the great white owl, are among the carnivorous birds. The streams and lakes abound with numerous species of wild ducks, of various and beautiful plumage. They fly in large flocks along the shores of the lakes, and feed in the marshes which fringe them, sometimes blackening the surface by their numbers. The swan may sometimes be seen floating upon the waters; and flocks of wild geese, in the season of summer, collect around the small interior lakes, after their winter migrations, where they obtain their food from the wild rice, which is the peculiar product of this region.

The rivers, interior lakes, and surrounding waters of the country abound with fish. These are of various species and of delicious kinds. In the strait of St. Mary and Lake Superior they are of a more valuable sort, from the

---

* In the collection of geological specimens owned by the compiler of this volume is a very large and perfectly-preserved *mammoth tooth*, which was found near the mouth of the St. Joseph river in Michigan.

fact that the water of the latter lake is clear and very cold. The quantity in the last-named lake is very great. The sisquovette, which are not found in other portions of the lake waters, are seen in great abundance in Lake Superior. They sometimes grow to the weight of eight or ten pounds.

The principal fish which are found in the surrounding lakes and interior waters of the country are the sturgeon, whitefish, Mackinaw trout, salmon trout, common trout, muskalunge, pickerel, pike, perch, herring, the rock bass, the white and black bass, catfish, pout, common eel, bullhead, roach, sunfish, dace, sucker, carp, mullet, billfish, swordfish, bullfish, stone-carrier, sheep's-head, the gar, and many other kinds. The muskalunge, Mackinaw trout, and whitefish are deemed most valuable. The former is sometimes caught weighing forty pounds. The Mackinaw trout resembles in lustre and appearance the salmon. The whitefish, a very delicious fish, is similar to the shad, with brighter scales, which appear like burnished silver. This fish has been celebrated by the French travellers from the earliest period, and Charlevoix, who travelled through this region in 1720, once declared that "nothing of the fish kind could excel it." Great numbers of trout and whitefish are taken upon the lakes and shipped to Ohio, New York, and Pennsylvania, besides those which are consumed in the State.

The northern part of the lower peninsula of Michigan, bordering on Lake Huron, has not yet been thoroughly surveyed and brought into market. The soil of this section of the State is not so favorable for agriculture as that of the southern portion. It is more wet and marshy, abounds with pine, and is broken by sandhills and swamps. It has been remarked that the portion of the State bordering on Lake Superior is broken and rocky; and, although containing some elevated table-lands which may be adapted to cultivation, it may be considered unfavorable to agriculture. It has, however, been ascertained to be a rich mineral region. The most settled portion of the State has been organized into counties, as the advance of population has required.

From the brief view which has been taken of the productions of the soil, it is clearly perceived that it affords a variety of resources. The low and densely-wooded land upon the immediate shore of the lower lakes, where the streams run sluggishly over beds of clay, is strikingly contrasted with the more rolling character of the oak lands, extending from this belt towards the centre, dotted as they are by natural ponds of pure water, and coursed by more rapid streams, which have their beds upon sand or gravel; and these in turn are entirely distinct from the more primitive, rocky, and rugged portion lying in that part of the upper peninsula bordering on the shores of Lake Superior. Exhibiting different degrees of fertility, the southern part, from its undulating character and its clear streams, affords a greater inducement for present settlement than the level strip to which allusion has been made, or the more primitive and rocky region of the north. It happens, accordingly, that emigration has in a great measure crossed this strip and sought the more rolling country, leaving the marshes and the mouths of the streams which flow into the eastern side; a section of the State somewhat unfavorable to settlement from the configuration of the land, but from the fact that it has been productive of the class of bilious disorders prevailing in the greater portion of our new country.

FIRST ADVANCE OF THE FRENCH MISSIONARIES AND TRAVELLERS.

The wide region stretching away in a luxuriant expanse of forest, river, and prairie, from the shores of the great lakes westward to the banks of the

Mississippi, was first explored and colonized by the French. That portion of the French territory now comprised in the Canadas, the original point of French settlement, was long the centre of its trade, commerce, and religion; yet the government claimed the country, both by right of discovery and appropriation, that extended far beyond the boundaries of their actual colonization. Nor were the settlers who had established themselves upon the banks of the St. Lawrence at any time wanting in zeal and enterprise in extending their explorations. It was early the avowed object of that government to carry the cross of the Roman Catholic Church to the remotest bounds of the Western territory, and thus to secure the advantages of its great resources. The principal directors of the ecclesiastical establishments that were collected at Quebec, found it their policy to become informed of the condition of the domain upon the great lakes; and as early as 1634, the Jesuits, Brebœuf and Daniel, joined a party of Hurons who were returning from that walled city, and, passing through the Ottawa river, raised the first hut of the Society of Jesus upon the shore of Lake Iroquois, a bay of Lake Huron, where they daily rang a bell to call the savages to prayer, and performed all those kind offices which were calculated to secure the confidence and affection of the tribes on the lake shores. In order to confirm the missions, a college was founded in Quebec during the following year; and a hospital was established at the same place for the unfortunate of every class, both civilized and savage. Three nuns of Dieppe, in France, were selected to advance into the Canadian wilderness in 1639; an Ursuline convent, for the education of girls, was also erected; and at Silleri a small band of the Hurons was trained to the civilization and faith of the French, for the purpose of spreading the religion and influence of their colonies through the Western wilderness. A plan for the establishment of missions, not only among the Algonquins of the North, but also south of Lake Huron and in Michigan, was formed, indeed, within six years after the discovery of Canada.

The French were at this period excluded from the navigation of Lake Ontario by the hostility of the Mohawks, and their canoes had never ruffled the waters of Lake Erie. The Ottawa, in consequence, was the only avenue to the West; and in 1641, Pijart and Charles Raymbault were found roaming as missionaries among the tribes of Lake Nipissing.

In September, 1641, the first bark canoe, laden with French Jesuits, was paddled through the Ottawa river for the Falls of St. Mary, and, passing by the islands of Lake Huron, they reached these falls after a navigation of seventeen days. At this place they found a large collection of Indians from the neighboring tribes, many of whom had never seen civilized men, and had never heard of the true God. The white men were invited to dwell among them; for, said the savages, "We will embrace you as brothers; we will derive profit from your words." Raymbault, the first missionary to the tribes of Michigan, feeble with consumption, during the next year returned to Quebec. Thus the French at this early period had advanced their missionary posts beyond the shores of Lake Huron and to the outlet of Lake Superior. Father Jaques and Bressani, Jean de Brebœuf, Chaumonotot, Claude Dablon, Mesnard, and others, while carrying the cross through the forests of the Northwest, were not to be impeded by tortures and burnings, nor death even, from their darling projects. They toiled and suffered, were struck down with the tomahawk; they lived the life of beggars, and died the death of martyrs; were covered with burning bark, and scalded with boiling water, and scarred with hot iron, until the gentle Lallemand cried out amid his tortures, "We are made a spectacle unto the world, and to angels, and to men;" but with the zeal of ancient martyrdom the Jesuits pressed on from the strongholds of Quebec, filling the ranks of the dead as one after another fell, advancing to the remote boundaries of the lake shores the cross and the lilies of the Bourbons.

During the month of August, 1654, two young fur-traders having joined a band of the Ottawas or Algonquins, in their bark canoes, upon an exploration of five hundred leagues, reappeared after two years before St. Louis with a fleet of fifty canoes. Describing the territory stretching around the great lakes in glowing colors, and the savage hordes which were then scattered through the forests, they sought to effect a wider extension of French commerce into that region. Their request was granted; and in 1656, Gabrielle Dreuillette and Leonard Gareau, former missionaries among the Hurons, were selected for the mission; but just below Montreal a band of Mohawks attacked their fleet, Gareau was mortally wounded, and the expedition prevented. The traders of the lakes, seeking the furs which abounded in those forests, and backed by the Western Indians, who desired a league by which they might resist the Iroquois, soon advanced to Green Bay, and in 1659 two of them passed the winter on the shores of Lake Superior. During the following year they returned to Quebec, escorted by sixty canoes, laden with peltry, and paddled by three hundred Algonquins.

The zeal of Francis de Laval, the bishop of Quebec, appears to have been kindled, by their accounts of the country, with a desire to enter upon the mission, but to Rene Mesnard was allotted this task, so full of hazard. Charged with the duty of exploring the territory around Green Bay and Lake Superior, and of establishing at some convenient point a place for the general assembly of the neighboring tribes, this aged man, in August, 1660, with but few preparations, departed on his mission, trusting, to use his own words, "in the Providence which feeds the little birds of the desert, and clothes the wild flowers of the forest." During the month of October he reached a bay on the south shore of Lake Superior, which he named St. Theresa; writing to a friend, "in three or four months you may add me to the memento of deaths." After a residence there of eight months, in the year 1661, he complied with the invitation of the Hurons, who had taken refuge in the isle of St. Michael, and, leaving his converts, advanced with one attendant to the Bay of Che-goi-me-gon. Lost in the forest, he was never afterward seen; and among the amulets of the Sioux were discovered his breviary and cassock.

But the rude missionary posts around the lakes struggled on, and were in danger of falling, when the Canadian colonies were re-enforced in 1665 by a royal regiment, with Tracy as viceroy, Courcelles, a veteran officer, as governor, and Talon, a man of business and perseverance, as intendant, and the representative of the King in civil matters. French enterprise now pressed forward to the West with increased vigor, and in August, 1665, Father Claude Allouez, following the old course of the Ottawa, on the 1st day of October reached the principal village of the Chippewas in the Bay of Che-goi-me-gon. A chapel dedicated to the Holy Spirit soon arose amid the green luxuriance of the forest, and the passions of the rough tribes were subdued by paintings which the missionary displayed of the horrors of hell and the terrors of the final judgment. The dwellers around St. Mary flocked to his station; the Hurons and Ottawas, upon the deserts north of Lake Superior, secured his presence at their wigwams; and the Pottowatomies, from the borders of Lake Michigan, invited him to their homes, while the Sacs and Foxes travelled from their villages, and the Illinois came to gather counsel and to describe the beauties of their quiet river. The Sioux, also, from the west of Lake Superior, in a land of prairies, living on wild rice and skin-covered cabins, welcomed the stranger. After residing for nearly two years upon the southern margin of Lake Superior, in August of 1667 he returned to Quebec, and urged the establishment of permanent missions, to be accompanied by colonies of French emigrants upon the lakes; but in two days after reaching that post, with another priest, Louis Nicholas, he returned to the mission of Che-goi-me-gon.

The condition of Canada at that time was favorable to the progress of the missions of this portion of the West. The monopoly of the West India Company, organized for the purpose of prosecuting the fur-trade, had been yielded up. Peace was enjoyed, and a new recruit of missionaries had arrived from France. Aided by such advantages, Allouez, Claude Dablon, and James Marquette in 1668 repaired to the Chippewas and established the mission of St. Mary, the first settlement commenced by Europeans within the boundaries of Michigan. During the following years these missionaries were employed in strengthening the power of France over the possessions which she claimed, from Green Bay to the head of Lake Superior, and in collecting information respecting the region extending toward the Mississippi. They resolved in the year 1669 to attempt its exploration, and selected as a companion a young Illinois, for the purpose of becoming acquainted with the dialect of that tribe.

The commerce of the fur-trade between the Algonquins and the French secured the protection of their tribes and their deep attachment, while a desire of strengthening the power of France over the Western territory pervaded the mind of Louis of France and Colbert, his minister. Talon, the intendant-general, moreover, desired to advance the same object, and for this purpose despatched his agent, Nicholas Perrott, in order to call a general congress of the lake tribes at the Falls of St. Mary. Procuring at Green Bay a guard of Pottowatomies, he reached the settlement of the Miamis at Chicago, the first of civilized men who had ever visited that point.

The desired Congress of the Indian tribes convened at the falls of St. Mary in May of 1671, was composed of prominent delegates from the head waters of the St. Lawrence, the Mississippi, the lakes, and even the Red river; and of veteran officers from the armies of France, intermingled here and there with a Jesuit missionary. A cross having been raised, and also a cedar post marked with the French lilies, the representatives of the savage hordes were informed that they were under the protection of the French King. During that year Marquette gathered a branch of the Hurons at Point St. Ignace, upon the continent north of the peninsula of Michigan, an establishment that was long a convenient resting-place for the savages and the fur-trade.

In 1672, Allouez and Dablon, who were the active agents of the French Government in carrying the cross through the eastern part of Wisconsin and the north of Illinois, seeking by mild means to secure the good offices of the Kickapoos upon the Milwaukie and of the Miamis of Lake Michigan, explored the countries to the south of the village that had been thus founded by Marquette, and had even extended their explorations to the tribes of the Foxes, then scattered along the banks of the Fox river. But the power of the French in this quarter was mainly confined to the immediate shores of the lakes and their connecting waters. Beyond these was a river flowing thousands of miles into the sea, which had never been traced to its outlet, of which Allouez had reported the name to be *Messipi*, or the

Great river. This stream, long the object of curious inquiry, was now to be sought, in order that the French power might be spread along its banks.

Thus labored Marquette, a solitary missionary upon the lakes, until 1673, when M. Talon, the intendant-general of the colony, ambitious to close his career in that region with something of honor, despatched M. Joliet, a citizen of Quebec, to this man, and unfolded, at the same time, a project for the exploration of the country along the line of the *Michisepee*, or the Great river, to its mouth, which current reports declared flowed into a large sea. Nor was Marquette unwilling to aid the enterprise. Upon the thirteenth of May, everything being ready, this adventurer, together with Joliet and five other Frenchmen, left Michilimackinac in two bark canoes, supplied with Indian corn and jerked meat, and commenced their voyage to the unknown country. They soon arrived at an Indian village which was familiar to Marquette, and made known to the savages their plan. These savages, however, seemed to be horror-struck at the boldness of the project to explore the great river. There were Indians in that quarter, they told the whites, who would destroy them; monsters who would swallow up them and their canoes; a demon who would ingulf all who ventured near his watery and boiling domain, and heats that would parch them. "I thanked them for their good advice," says Marquette, "but informed them I could not follow it, since the salvation of souls was at stake, for which I should be overjoyed to give my life."

The navigators now passed through Green Bay, from the mud of which there arose, says the voyager, "mischievous vapors, which cause the most grand and perpetual thunders I ever heard." They entered the Fox river, and, dragging their canoes through the rapids, and cutting their feet with the stones, they soon arrived at a village where there lived together a band of the Miamis, Mascoutens, and Kickapoos. Here they found a cross hung with skins, because the Great Spirit had given to the Indians a successful chase. Father Allouez had been here, and had taught them that the cross was the only visible emblem of the true religion. This village was at that time the remote boundary of western exploration, and beyond it no Frenchman had before gone. They were now journeying through a country before unknown to white men. On the 10th of July the adventurers left these savages amazed at the hardihood of the whites, and, aided by two guides, started for the stream, which was believed to run but three leagues distant from the Mississippi, and to flow into that river. The Indian guides, having conducted them to the portage without any mishap, left them "alone amid that unknown country, in the hand of God." Advancing with prayers, they soon arrived at the Wisconsin, a stream abounding with sand-bars, but studded with islands and bordered by banks green with vegetation, and variegated by groves and pleasant slopes. Floating down the stream in their canoes, they arrived, on the 17th of June, at the Mississippi, "with joy," says Marquette, "that I cannot express."

The adventurers had now reached the main channel, which they were to explore to its mouth; and, after having admired the herds of buffalo and deer which roamed along its borders, and the swans which floated upon its surface, as well as some great fish which nearly dashed their canoes to atoms, they at length came to the footprints of human beings on the sand, and a trail leading to a meadow. Leaving their canoes in charge of the crew, Joliet and Marquette now advanced towards what seemed to them an Indian village, sufficiently near to hear the voice of the savages. With prayers they made known their presence by a loud cry, and were soon received by an embassy of four old men, who presented them the pipe of peace, and informed them at the same time that they were in a village of the Illinois. The French voyagers were here entertained with a grand feast, accompanied with much smoking. The feast consisted of four courses; the first was of hominy, the second of fish, the third of dog, and the fourth of roasted buffalo. When the feast had been concluded, they were marched through the town with much ceremony; and, having passed the night quietly, they were escorted by six hundred Indians to their canoes. The Illinois, says Marquette, were handsome, kindly, and effeminate. They used guns, and were feared by the savages of the South and West, where they made many prisoners, and sold them as slaves.

Having left the Illinois, the voyagers passed the rocks on which were painted the monsters of whose existence they had heard at Lake Michigan, and reached the mouth of the Missouri. Leaving the Missouri, they encountered the demon against which they had been warned, that was nothing more than a great rock in the stream, and soon arrived at the Ohio. From the Ohio, although somewhat troubled by the mosquitoes, they passed in safety to the region of the Arkansas.

At this place they were attacked by a crowd of warriors, and would have been overpowered had not Marquette presented the pipe of peace, which softened the rough savages; for, says the Jesuit, "God touched their hearts." On the succeeding day they proceeded on their way, and were feasted by the hospitable savages upon corn and dogmeat cooked in earthenware, the Indians being amiable and ceremonious, passing the dish from one to another. Here the voyagers determined to return to the North, as they were now confident of the place where the Mississippi was discharged, that being the principal object of the expedition. In consequence, they left Akamsca on the 17th of July, retracing their track; and, amazed at the numbers of "grounds, meadows, woods, buffaloes, stags, deer, wildcats, bustards, swans, ducks, paroquets, and beavers" upon the Illinois river, they arrived at Green Bay in September of that year, where they reported what they had seen.

Father Marquette returned to the Illinois, and performed his clerical offices by their request until the year 1675. On the 18th of May, as he was passing through Lake Michigan in his canoes, he proposed to land at the mouth of a small stream running from the peninsula to perform mass, and retired a little distance to pray. Not returning, his men went in pursuit of him, and soon discovered the missionary, but he was dead; and they made a grave and buried him in the sand, upon the western part of the peninsula of Michigan, on the borders of a stream which now bears his name, and where the place of his interment was recently to be seen. Thus passed away this quiet man in the wilderness, after a long life spent in doing good. Yet he left the impression of his virtues behind him, and his name the world has embalmed and will perpetuate.

At length the enterprise of Robert de la Salle, a native of Normandy, in France, a young man of strong passions, but great energy, entered upon a project which had for its object the perpetuation of the power of France by the permanent colonization of the West. La Salle was, according to Charlevoix, brought up among the Jesuits, and, having lost his patrimony in France, and being of an adventurous and enterprising spirit, he turned his mind to the French colonies on this side of the Atlantic about the year 1670. Having arrived at the Canadian port, he occupied himself with a project, popular in that day, connected with a short passage to China, and had already planned an expedition across the great lakes to the banks of the Pacific when Father Marquette returned from the Mississippi. The highly colored views which this missionary gave of the country, and its extensive channels of interior communication westward, kindled the sanguine mind of La Salle, and induced him to redouble his exertions to carry out his object. With that view he resorted to M. de Frontenac, then the governor-general of Canada, and at once laid before him the dim but gigantic outline of his project, having for its end the extension of the French power, by constructing a chain of fortifications at the most prominent points along the lakes and rivers of the West. The first step towards this favorite scheme was to rebuild Fort Frontenac, which lies on Lake Ontario, of stone; and the politic adventurer deemed this an important point to win the favor of the governor-general, as that fort was called after his name. Frontenac entered warmly into his views. Believing that the French power would be greatly strengthened by carrying out the design, he advised La Salle to apply directly to the King of France; and, to aid his application for royal patronage, he gave the adventurer letters to Seigneilay, who, as minister of marine, had succeeded his father, the well-known Colbert.

With glowing hopes, La Salle now resorted to the French King, and made known his wants. His plan was approved by the minister, who received his letter, and he was invested with the title of chevalier, and also with the seignory of Fort Frontenac, on the condition that he would rebuild it. From all the nobility of that country he received also assurances of full countenance and aid. Encouraged by these assurances, La Salle, with his lieutenant, Tonti, an Italian, and thirty men, sailed from Rochelle on the 14th of July, 1678, reached Quebec on the 15th of September of the same year, and soon after proceeded to Fort Frontenac. Here he found laboring in the missionary cause Louis Hennepin, a friar of the Franciscan order, daring, vain, and determined, ambitious to reap the glory of discovery, and not too scrupulous as to the means. Hennepin had been appointed by his religious superiors acting missionary, to accompany the expedition of La Salle, and arrived at this point, in readiness to meet him, in October of 1678.

The chevalier having no means to carry out his project, and being at that time somewhat involved in debt, was obliged to cast about for money to advance his enterprise. He commenced operations, accordingly, by sending forward a party of his men along the shores of the lakes to collect skins, from which he might accumulate something to pay his winter expenses, for he had an exclusive right from the French monarch to trade in that region. The advantages of this course were two-fold: for, while the Frenchmen whom he should despatch were collecting the furs, they could, at the same time, prepare the minds of the Indians for his coming. In the first place it was made a part of his duty to alter and repair Fort Frontenac; Lake Ontario was to be navigated; a fort was to be built on Lake Erie, and a bark of extraordinary size for those inland seas was to be constructed. All these duties devolved upon himself; and, with the small funds which he had to accomplish them, they would, to a man of moderate soul, have appeared formidable. But to the stout heart of the French chevalier they were as nothing, for his perseverance was unconquerable, and his ambition looked forward to the time when his name should be covered with glory as the benefactor of France, and the Columbus of its colonies in the West.

Having despatched his men for the objects which have been mentioned, La Salle embarked upon Lake Ontario, with his followers, on the 18th of November, 1678, in a little vessel of ten tons, "the first ship that had ever sailed on that fresh-water sea." Against strong winds the vessel was finally, after having occupied four weeks in beating up from Kingston to Niagara, pushed as near the falls as could be done with safety, and the adventurers landed. Here some magazines were built with great difficulty, as the ground was frozen, and the posts could be driven down only by pouring boiling water upon the surface, and thus thawing the earth. Here also they formed their first acquaintance with the Iroquois of Niagara Village upon Lake Erie, and founded a second fort; but, impeded by the jealousy of the Iroquois, they relinquished the project, and merely erected a temporary work to secure the magazines. Leaving orders for his men to build another vessel, La Salle returned to Fort Frontenac to procure anchors, cables, chains, and other outfits for his new ship. Through the winter days, when Lake Erie lay before them covered with ice, like "a plain paved with fine-polished marble," his men hammered upon the ship, while others gathered furs and peltry in the forest, or strove to gain the good-will of the Iroquois, who claimed the country through which they were to pass, and who had never shown themselves the special friends of the French. On the 20th of January, 1679, the chevalier returned. The vessel in which his outfits had been embarked was wrecked; and, although the most valuable part of her cargo was saved, the greater portion of her provisions went to the bottom. This, however, did not dishearten the stout-hearted adventurer. A considerable quantity of furs was collected during the winter, with which the commander, in the spring of 1679, returned to Fort Frontenac, and Tonti was sent out upon the shores of the lakes to muster his men, who had been before despatched into that region. The vessel, however, was at length built, in spite of all these obstacles, rigged and manned, and made ready to sail.

The chain of fortifications thus projected by La Salle was afterward constructed upon the water-line of the Northwest, and its remains are still to be seen stretching from the shores of Lake Ontario to the mouth of the Mississippi.

On the seventh day of the month of August, 1679, the bark of sixty tons burden having at length been built, she started on the first voyage which had ever been made upon that inland sea, amid the sound of *Te Deums* and the discharge of arquebuses. This vessel was named the *Griffin*, and the image of that animal was carved on her prow. Robert de la Salle was her commander; and Louis Hennepin, the missionary, burning with ardor to make new discoveries, and also the journalist of the expedition, was on board. The crew consisted of fur-traders taken from the Canadian colonies. They sounded while they ploughed along the waves of Lake Erie, as they did not know the depth of the water, and on the tenth of the same month they arrived near the islands which are grouped at the entrance of the Detroit river, where they anchored. Hennepin says of these islands: "They make the finest prospect in the world. The strait (of Detroit) is finer than Niagara, being one league broad, excepting that part which forms the lake *that we have called St. Clair.*"

The explorers, passing up the river and advancing across Lake Huron, soon landed on the shore of the northern part of the peninsula of Michigan, and in August they built the old Fort of Michilimackinac. The descriptions of the country by these early travellers, although not entirely accurate, are interesting, and they will be regarded as of great value when the shores of the lakes shall be crowded with a dense population. Of the scenery Hennepin remarks: "The country between the two lakes (Erie and Huron) is very well situated, and the soil very fertile. The banks of the strait (Detroit) are vast meadows, and the prospect is terminated with some hills covered with vineyards, trees bearing good fruit, groves and forests so well disposed that one would think Nature alone could not have made, without the help of art, so charming a prospect. That country is stocked with stags, wild goats, and bears, which are good for food, and not fierce as in other countries; some think they are better than our pork. Turkey-cocks and swans are there very common; and our men brought several other beasts and birds, whose names are unknown to us, but they are extraordinary relishing.

"The forests are chiefly made up of walnut, chestnut, plum, and pear trees, loaded with their own fruit, and vines. There is also abundance of timber for building; so that those who shall be so happy as to inhabit that noble country cannot but remember with gratitude them who have led the way."

From Michilimackinac the French explorers went to Green Bay. Here La Salle collected a cargo of furs, and dispatched them in the Griffin back to Niagara, in order to pay the debts which he owed in that quarter. But the vessel was never heard of afterward. With fourteen of his Frenchmen he now paddled down Lake Michigan in canoes, marking the shoals of that lake by bear-skins stuck on poles, and feeding on the flesh of that animal. On the first of November, having reached the St. Joseph river of Lake Michigan, he built another rude fort at its mouth, called fort Miami. Tonti, the Italian, La Salle's lieutenant, had been sent out upon the borders of the lake with some of his men to procure venison and to collect the straggling Frenchmen, and the party remained at St. Joseph awaiting the return of the Griffin.

But winter now came on, and the Griffin did not appear. The party of La Salle, therefore, on the 1st of September, occupied themselves in driving palisades near the mouth of the St. Joseph river of Lake Michigan, in order to warn off the French bark from the shoals upon the borders of that lake. If the lakes should be frozen before the vessel returned new obstacles would be thrown in his way; for the wilderness presented but few friendly inhabitants and cultivated fields, the shores of the lakes no hospitable ports, so that he determined to proceed upon "his great voyage and glorious undertaking;" and, collecting his crew, and leaving in the rude fort of St. Joseph a few men, he set out with the remainder and three monks. Passing to the Illinois, the party descended that river "by easy journeys, the better to observe that country," which abounded with marshes, where no safe footing could be obtained. Through these swamps the adventurers proceeded until they arrived at a village of the Illinois Indians, which contained about five hundred untenanted cabins. Here the party of the Sieur de la Salle, being worn down with hunger, provided themselves with a quantity of corn, which was found hidden in holes in the ground under the Indian wigwams, and placed it on shipboard. This point is supposed to have been the present site of Rock Fort, upon the Illinois.

On the 4th of January, 1680, the ship being ready and the voyagers prepared, they proceeded into a lake believed to be Peoria, where they caught some good fish with which they might season their corn, when bands of savages appeared on both sides of the river, to which they had now returned. When, however, the startled Frenchmen supposed that, having been engaged in depredation, their season of fighting had arrived, they were agreeably surprised by being asked who they were, the savages "being naturally inclined to peace." The question having been answered, they were received by the Indians with much kindness, who, not as savages are used to do, but "as men well-bred and civilized," spread out before the needy voyagers "beef, and stag, and all sorts of venison and fowls." This hospitable reception was repaid by discharges of firearms, and by presenting them large draughts of brandy. A feast, continuing three days, was at length concluded, and the Frenchmen discovered in the Illinois great humanity, and a "good disposition to civil society." They were "flatterers complaisant and cunning," and, although they paid a sort of respect to virtue, they were still effeminate and dissolute. In the midst of this nation La Salle concluded to build another fort, for the pacific character of the Indians in that quarter induced him to select this as its most favorable site. A point upon the rising ground, near the river, was chosen for that object, and here a rude fortification was built, which La Salle named *Crevecœur*, the Broken Heart: a touching name, indicating his disappointment, occasioned by the loss of the Griffin and the consequent wreck of his hopes, the jealousy of a portion of the savages, who had been persuaded that he was a friend of the Iroquois, and the mutiny of his men, which had already begun to show itself by administering to him poison: misfortunes which sunk him in poverty, casting a gloom over his burning but iron heart, beclouding his glorious vision, and plunging him in doubt and despair.

The winter was passed, and La Salle remained in the wilderness until the vegetation began to spring up on the prairies. Bereft of property, with his men, who even sought his life, fast deserting him, with Indians around him, instigated by capricious and uncertain motives, he still had left his own determined spirit: a spirit fearless of obstacles, which burned the brighter amid the gloom that encompassed it. He found it necessary, therefore, to return to the Canadian colonies to raise men and money, and to prepare another outfit, for he was still firmly resolved to persevere in his original project. In accordance with this determination, he employed M. Dacan and Father Louis Hennepin to proceed from that point on an expedition for the discovery of the sources of the Mississippi, with a party consisting of eight persons, and on the last day of February, 1680, he started them on their voyage. At Fort Crevecœur the chevalier remained until the succeeding November, leaving Tonti and his men among the Illinois, and then departed from that fort for Canada. On his passage along the river, being struck with the position of a high rock upon the bank, he at once determined to construct a fort at that point, and, marking out a plan, sent it to Tonti at Fort Crevecœur. Tonti immediately proceeded to the execution of the project, but had hardly commenced when a revolt broke out among the men whom he had left at Fort Crevecœur, and he was obliged to return. This new fort was named St. Louis, and was placed under the command of Tonti when La Salle returned to France. Its site was probably the spot that is now called Rock Fort, in La Salle county, Illinois.

Tonti, thus left in the woods with a garrison of undisciplined Frenchmen, lived on with little quietude until September of 1681, when, to his horror, a body of the Iroquois appeared in this region, having been irritated during a journey along the borders of the lakes. What was the policy of Tonti in reference to these two hostile savage nations does not clearly appear, yet it is evident that he must have preserved neutral ground, acting as a mediator between them. But succor did not come; and at length he was obliged to return to Canada with five men, in the middle of September of the same year, reaching Lake Michigan in October, and spending the winter upon its borders. Thus ended this expedition for discovery along the shores of the great lakes, under the auspices of an individual who should be known as the first navigator of Lake Erie.

But let La Salle be followed to the close of his adventurous career. He had returned to Canada, where he busied himself in raising recruits, constructing vessels, and gathering funds; and the spring of 1682 found him again upon the Illinois, manning Crevecœur, rebuilding Fort St. Louis, and soon after returning to Fort Frontenac to prepare for his second voyage, which commenced on the Illinois river in 1683, when the mouth of the Mississippi was descried. But La Salle soon departed for France, to lay before the throne the record of what he had done, and also his project for the exploration and settlement of the far-famed Louisiana. A fleet was provided by the agency of Seigneilay, consisting of twenty-four vessels, four of which were destined for Louisiana, carrying two hundred and eighty persons, soldiers, artificers, and " women." Starting on his voyage across the ocean, on the 24th of July, 1684, he reached his destined point, where he was assassinated by his own men. Thus fell La Salle; a man of energy, accomplished, virtuous, ardent, and self-sacrificing; one of a class who ruin themselves while they benefit the world, neglect the means of happiness, and raise up for themselves a lasting remembrance.

No settlement had at this time been made at Detroit, because the traders and Jesuit missionaries had a more direct and safer route to the upper lakes, from Montreal to Michilimackinac, by the way of the Ottawa river. But this point had long been regarded an eligible position for a settlement, as it commanded a broad tract of country, and stood, as it were, at the gate of the upper lakes, in a direct route from these lakes to the English colonies of New York, by the way of Lake Erie.

The French and English both desired to obtain possession of this post. But while the English were looking to its acquisition, they were anticipated by their rivals. Taking counsel from the movements of their opponents, the French called a grand meeting of the Iroquois, or Five Nations, at Montreal. The chiefs of the different tribes from the St. Lawrence to the Mississippi attended this meeting; also the principal men and the Governor-General of Canada. Here the establishment of a post at that place was discussed, and the grounds on which the two nations based their claims to it weighed. The Iroquois, however, said that, understanding the French were about to make a settlement at that point, they were opposed to the measure, as they had already prohibited the English from doing the same. The Governor-General of Canada replied that the land belonged neither to the Iroquois nor to the English, but to the King of France, and that there was already an expedition on the march for the purpose of erecting a colonial establishment at that place. In accordance with this plan, Antoine de la Motte Cadillac, lord of Bouaget, Mont Desert, having been granted a tract of fifteen acres square by Louis XIV, left Montreal, accompanied by a Jesuit missionary and one hundred men, and arrived at the point of the wilderness which is now the site of Detroit, in the month of July, 1701, where they commenced the foundation of the first permanent settlement in Michigan. Before it had only been known by the French missionaries as a trading-post, and in 1620 it was occupied by an Indian village, which was called Teuchsa Grondie. The Saute de St. Marie, as we have seen, had at that time been founded, and a rude post was also erected at Fort Gratiot, which was a resting point for the fur-trade.

This chain of fortifications was all the defence which was constructed upon the lake shores for nearly a century and a half, and it comprised a part of that line of forts that was projected by La Salle, extending from the St. Lawrence down the Mississippi to New Orleans. Their object was to furnish outposts by which the territory of Canada on the borders of the lakes could be held, the English settlements hemmed in, the Jesuit missionaries and settlers protected against the numerous and capricious tribes of savages in this quarter, and by which the fur-trade might circulate, with full success, along the lakes and streams of the Northwest. The forts of Detroit, Michilimackinac, St. Joseph, and Green Bay were of rude construction, and the chapels erected by their side were used for the religious assemblies of the French settlers, who were from that time collected around the posts, and also of the Indians who were under the special guardianship of the Jesuit missionaries. These structures, minute points on the borders of the forest, were either roofed with bark or thatched with straw, and on their top was generally erected the cross. Tribes of friendly Indians that could be induced to settle near them had their villages or wigwams around these posts, and also their planting-grounds, in which they cultivated Indian corn, not only for the French settlers, but also for the persons connected with the fur-trade. They derive their principal importance from the fact that they were the only outposts of the French Government in this country before the English conquest, and, consequently, the theatres of the most interesting frontier operations.

About three years after Detroit was founded, the Ottawa Indians in that vicinity were invited to Albany, in New York, upon what was supposed to be a friendly visit. As St. Joseph was surrounded by villages of the Hurons, Pottowatomies, and Miamis, so also was Detroit at that time guarded by parts of the friendly tribes of the Hurons and Pottowatomies near the settlements, and an Ottawa village had been erected on the opposite bank of the river. It would appear that while the Ottawas were in Albany they had been persuaded by the English, who even then wished to obtain possession of the post of their rivals, that it was the design of the French to wrest the dominion of the country from their hands; and they accordingly set fire to the town, but without success, as the fire was soon extinguished. At this time, also, groups of savages of the same tribe, having made a successful expedition against their enemies the Iroquois, and warm with victory, were seen paraded in hostile array in front of the fort; but M. Tonti, who was the commandant of the post, despatching the Sieur de Vincennes against them, he dispersed their bands, and rescued the Iroquois prisoners whom they left behind them in their flight.

The progress of operations on the lake shores was not at this period marked with any very great interest, as the settlements were few; but they reflect, nevertheless, the spirit which prevailed in France during their continuance. The lands lay sleeping in their original silence and solitude, undisturbed by the plough. Occasionally the settlers may have been surprised by their ancient enemies the Iroquois, but the appearance of parts of these nations excited a surprise which soon settled down into peace. But in 1712 the Ottagamies or Foxes, who had been before but little known, but who were probably in secret alliance with the Iroquois, projected a plan for the destruction of Detroit. They made their arrangements in secret, and sent their bands to collect around the new French settlement, which was then garrisoned by a force of twenty soldiers, of whom M. Du Buisson was the commandant. The occupation of the three French villages of Indians, the Ottawas, Pottowatomies, and Hurons, were then absent on a hunting excursion. A converted Indian, however, under the influence of a Jesuit missionary, disclosed their plot before it was ripe for execution, and Du Buisson immediately sent despatches through the forest to call in the aid of the friendly Indians, and prepared for an effective defence.

On the 13th of May of that year the Foxes made their onset upon Detroit with fiendish yells. No sooner, however, was the attack commenced, than portions of the friendly Indians were seen through the wilderness, painted for battle as is their custom, and the gates of the fort were opened to receive them. A consultation was now held at the council-house, and they renewed their league with Du Buisson, and expressed their determination, if necessary, to die in the defence of the post. On the arrival of the friendly Indians, the Foxes retreated to the forest which until lately adjoined the boundary of Detroit, and intrenched themselves in their camp.

The French then sallied out from the fort, and, backed by their savage allies, erected a blockhouse in front of their camp, in order to force the enemy from their position. Here the latter were closely besieged; being cut off from their supply of water, and, driven to desperation by thirst and famine, they in turn rushed out from their strongholds upon the French and the friendly Indians, and succeeded in getting possession of a house near the village. This house they fortified, but they were here attacked by the French cannon, and driven back to their former intrenchment.

Finding that their league was likely to prove unsuccessful, the Foxes now sent despatches to the French commandant asking for peace, which was denied them. Upon this they considered themselves insulted, and, burning with revenge, they discharged showers of blazing arrows upon the fort. The lighted matches they had affixed to their arrows coming into contact with the dry roofs of the houses, kindled them into flame, when the precaution was taken to cover the rest with wet skins, and by this means they were preserved. The desperation of the Foxes almost discouraged the French commandant, and he had nearly determined to evacuate Detroit and to retire to Michilimackinac, when his Indian allies promised to redouble their efforts for his defence; and the war-songs and dances of their bands, heard through the solitude of the forest, assured him that a more desperate effort was about to be made in his behalf. The preparations having been finished, the French and Indians advanced upon the Foxes with more determined courage, and, pouring upon their intrenchments a deadly fire, they were soon filled with the dying and the dead. Once more the Foxes demanded peace. Before any capitulation, however, was completed, the enemy retreated towards Lake St. Clair during a storm at midnight, on the nineteenth day of the siege.

The French and their Indian allies, as soon as they discovered their flight, prepared for a pursuit, and soon came upon their camps. An action began, which at the outset was in favor of the Foxes, the French and Indians being repulsed. But a different plan of operation was soon after adopted, and with better success. At the end of three days a field battery was completed, and the intrenchment of the Foxes fell before the French cannon.

The Foxes may be considered the Ishmaelites of the wilderness, for they were at enmity with all the tribes on the lakes. They collected their forces on the Fox river of Green Bay, where they commanded the territory between the lakes and the Mississippi, so that it was dangerous for travellers to pass through that region except in large bodies and armed, while their warriors were sent out to seek objects of plunder and devastation. So great was the danger apprehended by the missionaries and traders of passing through that territory, as well as by the French settlers, and so great the injury already done by those tribes, that an expedition was fitted out against them by the French, backed by their Indian allies, who were rankling under a sense of repeated wrongs. This warlike nation had stationed itself on the banks of the Fox river, at a place then and now called by the French *Butte des Morts*, or the Hill of the Dead, defending their position by a ditch and three courses of palisades. Here they collected their women and children, and prepared for a desperate resistance. M. de Louvigny, the commandant of the expedition, perceiving the strength of their works, determined not to expose his men by a direct attack, but entered upon a regular siege, and was preparing for the final crisis when the Foxes proposed a capitulation.

This was accepted; and the pride of the Foxes being thus humbled, they sank into obscurity during the remainder of the French war.

Thus it is seen that, although the few French forts upon the lakes were rudely constructed, and but poorly adapted to make a serious and effective defence, they were nevertheless competent, with their small garrisons, to protect the emigrants against the disaffected tribes which were from time to time arrayed against them. The pickets which surrounded them, composed of upright stakes, furnished a line of concealment rather than strong bulworks, and, together with the light cannon with which they were mounted, enabled the French to suppress the disturbances that occasionally sprang up around their posts.

The early missionaries and French travellers who journeyed through the region of the lakes exhibit a peculiar form of character. Tinctured with the spirit which prevailed in France at the period of their immigration, the novel scenes around them impressed them with those sentiments of romance so peculiar to the French. They show the spirit under which the missionaries and soldiers travelled, and the eloquence with which the scenes around them tended to inspire their minds.

The forests amid which their lot was cast were calculated to fill them with wonder and admiration. A vast chain of inland seas, which appeared to them like oceans, stretched a watery horizon along the borders of the wilderness. Flocks of water-fowl of varied plumage streamed along the shores of the lakes, and the waters swarmed with fish. The face of nature, fresh in the luxuriance of a virgin soil, was everywhere clothed with magnificent vegetation. Did they travel through the Indian trails or bridle-paths which wound through the forest, extensive tracts of oaklands, that seemed like cultivated parks, met their eye, studded with little crystal lakes and streams and covered with flowers. Herds of buffaloes wandered over the prairies, trampling down the flowers which blushed in their track as they rushed on in clumsy motion. Great numbers of moose and elk, which in the size of their horns almost rivalled the branches of the trees, bounded through the thickets. Deer were here and there seen feeding upon the margin of the water-courses. Flocks of wild turkeys and other game filled the woods; the prairies were alive with grouse, and pigeons swept along like clouds above the forest, in numbers which sometimes almost hid the sun.

But more than this, they beheld in the luxuriance of the soil a prize which, if judiciously managed, would be a source of inexhaustible wealth to their nation. Rich clusters of grapes hung from the trees, which reminded them of the champaign districts of France from which they emigrated; and apples and plums, crude to the taste, but that by culture might be much improved, abounded in the groves.

"Lake Erie," says La Honton, who commanded a fort upon it in 1688, "is justly dignified with the illustrious name of Conti; for assuredly it is the finest upon earth. You may judge of the goodness of the climate from the latitude of the countries that surround it. Its circumference extends to two hundred and thirty leagues, but it affords everywhere a charming prospect, and its shores are decked with oak trees, elms, chestnut trees, walnut, apple, plum trees, and vines which bear their fine clusters up to the very tops of the trees, upon a sort of ground that lies as smooth as one's hand. Such ornaments as these are sufficient to give rise to the most agreeable idea of a landscape in the world. I cannot express what quantities of deer and turkeys are to be found in these woods, and in the vast meadows that lie upon the south side of the lake. At the foot of the lake we find wild beeves (buffaloes,) upon the banks of two pleasant streams that disembogue into it without cataracts or rapid currents. It abounds with sturgeon and whitefish, but trouts are very scarce in it, as well as the other fish that we take in the Lakes of Hurons (Huron) and Illinese (Michigan.) It is clear of shelves, rocks, and banks of sand, and has fourteen or fifteen fathoms water. The savages assure us that it is never disturbed by high winds except in the months of December, January, and February, and even then but seldom, which I am very apt to believe, for we had very few storms when I wintered in my fort in 1688, though the fort lay open to the Lake of Hurons. The banks of this lake are commonly frequented by none but warriors, whether the Iroquese, the Illinese, the Oumamies, &c., and it is very dangerous to stop there. By this means it comes to pass that the stags, roebucks, and turkeys run in great bodies up and down the shore all around the lake. In former times the Errironons and the Andastogueronons lived upon the confines of the lake; but they were extirpated by the Iroquese, as well as the other nations marked on the map."

Charlevoix, who travelled through the region of the lakes in 1720 as an accredited agent of the French government, gives an account equally interesting respecting the condition of the country at the time when he wrote. "The first of June being the day of Pentecost," says he, "after having travelled up a beautiful river for the space of an hour, which has its rise, as they say, at a great distance, and runs between two fine meadows, we passed over a carrying-place of about sixty paces in breadth, in order to avoid turning round a point which is called the Long Point. It is a very sandy spot of ground, and naturally bears a great quantity of vines. The following days I saw nothing remarkable, but coasted along a charming country, hid at times by very disagreeable prospects, which, however, are of no great extent. Wherever I went ashore I was enchanted by the beauty and variety of a prospect which was terminated by the noblest forests in the world. Add to this, that every part of it swarms with water-fowl. I cannot say whether the woods afford game in equal profusion, but I well know that on the south side there is a prodigious quantity of buffaloes. Were we all to sail as I then did, with a serene sky, in a most charming climate, and in water as clear as that of the purest fountain; were we sure of finding everywhere secure and agreeable places to pass the night in, where we might enjoy the pleasure of hunting at a small expense, breathe at our ease the purest air, and enjoy the prospect of the finest countries in the universe, we might possibly be tempted to travel to the end of our days. I recalled to mind those ancient patriarchs who had no fixed place of abode; who lived in tents; who were, in a manner, the masters of all the countries they passed through; and who enjoyed in peace and tranquillity all their productions, without the plague inevitable in the possession of a real and fixed estate. How many oaks represented to me that of Mamre! How many fountains put me in mind of that of Jacob! Each day a new situation, chosen at pleasure; a neat and commodious house, built and furnished with all necessaries in less than a quarter of an hour, and floored with a pavement of flowers continually springing up on a carpet of the most beautiful green; on all sides simple and natural beauties, unadulterated and inimitable by any art."

Charlevoix at that early period visited Detroit for the purpose of viewing the young colony, where he recommended that an accession should be made to the strength of the infant settlement from Montreal. This addition to their power was approved of by the French, on the ground that it would secure them the fur-trade, then too much within reach of the English of New York. He also attended, while here, a council of the chiefs of the three villages near Detroit, where the question was discussed whether it was proper to introduce brandy among the Indians, a practice which the Jesuits finally succeeded in abolishing. In alluding to Detroit, he says, "It is pretended that this is the finest part of all Canada; and really, if we can judge by appearances, nature seems to have denied it nothing which can contribute to make a country delightful: hills, meadows, fields, lofty forests, rivulets, fountains, rivers, and all of them so excellent in their kind, and so happily blended as to equal the most romantic wishes. The lands, however, are not equally proper for every kind of grain; but most are of a wonderful fertility, and I have known some produce good wheat for eighteen years running without any manure; and, besides, all of them are proper for some particular use. The islands seem placed on purpose for the pleasure of the prospect, the river and lake abound in fish, the air is pure, and the climate temperate and extremely wholesome."*

The Jesuit being requested by Tonti to visit the great council at Detroit, consented to do so on the day of his arrival; and his account of that council is here transcribed:

"On the 7th of June, which was the day of my arrival at the fort, (Detroit,) Mons. de Tonti, who commands here, assembled the chiefs of the three villages I have just mentioned, in order to communicate to them the orders he had received from the Marquis de Vaudreuil. They heard him calmly and without interruption. When he had done speaking, the orator of the Hurons told him in a few words that they were going to consult about what he had proposed to them, and would give him their answer in a short time. It is the custom of the Indians not to give an immediate answer on an affair of any importance. Two days afterward they assembled at the commandant's, who was desirous I should be present at this council, together with the officers of the garrison. Sasteratfi, whom the French call King of the Hurons, and who is, in fact, hereditary chief of the Tionnontatez, who are the true Hurons, was also present on this occasion; but as he is still a minor, he came only for form's sake: his uncle, who governs in his name, and who is called regent, spoke in quality of orator of the nation. Now the honor of speaking in the name of the whole is generally given to some Huron, when any of them happen to be of the council. The first view of their assemblies gives you no great idea of the body. Imagine to yourself, madame, half a score of savages almost stark naked, with their hair disposed in as many different manners as there are persons in the assembly, and all of them equally ridiculous; some with laced hats, all with pipes in their

* These travellers were not, nor could they be expected to be, in all cases accurate, from their rapid passage through the Western territory; but in their accounts of their own experience we derive much valuable information of its actual condition during the time when they wrote. Glimpses of wild beasts which they had never before seen, vegetable productions whose names they did not know, fragments of facts collected from the accounts of the Indians, always exaggerated and seldom authentic, passed in rapid succession before their minds, while they journeyed onward in bewildered amazement, through rivers, lakes, forests, and Indian camps; and their impressions, thus colored and distorted, found their way into their books. But, taken as a whole, their accounts are as accurate as could be expected, considering the circumstances under which they wrote. If, for example, the zealous Marquette depicts "wingless swans" as floating upon the Mississippi; if Hennepin describes "wild goats" upon the shores of Lake Erie; if La Honton discourses upon the "Long River," and Charlevoix alludes to the "citrons" as growing upon the banks of the Detroit, we are disposed to attribute their inaccuracies less to intentional misrepresentation than to natural and obvious mistake. Accurate observation and minute care are required to establish with perfect correctness the facts connected with any country, and he who should look to early records for historical matter will find much chaff to be winnowed from the genuine and golden wheat.

mouths, and with the most unthinking faces. It is, besides, a rare thing to hear one utter so much as a single word in a quarter of an hour, or to hear any answer made even in monosyllables; not the least mark of distinction, nor any respect paid to any person whatsoever. We should, however, be apt to change our opinions of them on hearing the result of their deliberations."

This, as is described by Charlevoix, was the general mode in which the Indian councils were held with the French upon the lakes when questions of importance were to be decided. It was necessary to secure the concurrence of the savages in every measure of policy, so that these tribes should co-operate with them in carrying it into effect.

COLONIAL PIONEERS.

The posts of the French upon the lakes, while the Western Territory was under their government, exhibit a peculiar form of character, combined with institutions no less singular. The few feeble colonies that were scattered through this territory had emigrated principally from Britanny and Normandy, provinces of France. Working men, drawn from the more dense settlements around Quebec and Montreal, the seats of the bishops, the seigneurs, and the Jesuits, were sent out for the purpose of building up the posts, and of protecting the fur-trade carried on through the chain of the great lakes. Despatched for these objects, they were expected to endure cheerfully the hardships they would be called on to encounter in their establishment. The population assembled at these posts consisted of the military by which they were garrisoned, Jesuits, priests, merchants, traders, and peasants. But a small portion of this population, however, was stationary. It was moved from place to place, as the interests of the French government seemed to require.

The French commandants at these posts were the most prominent individuals, and, with their garrisons, constituted a little monarchy within themselves. Their power was arbitrary, extending to the right of doing whatever they might deem expedient for the welfare of the settlements, whether in making laws or in punishing crimes. Under this simple and imperfect form of government, the oldest merchants residing at the several posts were reverenced as the head men of their particular colony. Careful and frugal in their habits, without much of what we should call rigid virtue, it was their policy to exercise their influence among the settlers with paternal mildness, that they might secure their obedience, to keep on good terms with the Indians in order to retain their trade, and they often fostered a large number of half-breed children around their posts, who were the off-spring of their licentiousness.

The *Coureurs des Bois*, or rangers of the woods, were either French or half-breeds, a hardy race, accustomed to labor and privation, and thoroughly conversant with the character and habits of the savage tribes from which they obtained their furs and peltry. They could, with no less skill than the Indians, ply the oar of the light canoe upon the waters of the lakes, were equally dexterous in hunting and trapping, and, as they pointed their rifles at the squirrel on the top of the tallest tree, they could confidently say to their ball, like the ancient warrior, "to the right eye." These half-breeds generally spoke the language both of their French and Indian parents, and knew just enough of their religion to be alike regardless of that of each. Employed by the French companies as voyageurs or guides, their forms, which were models of manly beauty, were developed to great strength by propelling the canoe along the lakes and rivers, and by carrying heavy packs of merchandise for the fur-trade across the portages, by means of leather straps, suspended from their shoulders or resting against their foreheads. From having travelled through numerous points of the wilderness, they became familiar with the trails of the most remote Indian tribes, and with the depth of the water in every inlet and stream of the lakes, as well as with every island, rock, and shoal. Their ordinary dress was a "moleton" or blanket-coat, a red cap, a belt of cloth passed around the middle, and a loose shirt. Sometimes, in their voyages through the lakes they wore a brown coat or cloak, with a cape which could be drawn up from their shoulders over their heads like a hood. At other times they had on elkskin trowsers, the seams of which were ornamented with fringes, a surtout of coarse blue cloth reaching to the calf of the leg, a scarlet-colored worsted sash fastened about the waist, in which was stuck a broad knife, employed in dissecting the animals taken in hunting, and moccasins made of buckskin. Affable, gay, and active, these men were employed by the French merchants either as guides, canoemen, carriers, or traders, to advance into the wilderness and procure their furs from the Indians, to transport them along the lakes and streams, and lodge them in the several depots or factories which were established in connection with the French forts.

The peasants, or that class of the lake settlers who cultivated small patches of ground within the narrow circle of their picket-fences, were few. Their dress was peculiar and even wild. They wore surtouts of coarse blue cloth, fastened at the middle with a red sash, a scarlet woollen cap containing a scalping-knife, and moccasins made of deerskin. Civilization and barbarism were here strangely mingled. Groups of Indians from the remotest shores of the lakes, wild in their garb, would occasionally make their appearance at the settlements with numerous canoes laden with beaver-skins, which they had brought down to these places of deposit. Among them were intermixed the French soldiers of the garrison, with their blue coats turned up with white facings, and the Jesuits, with their long gowns and black bands, from which were suspended by silver chains the rosary and crucifix, who, with the priests, had their stations around the forts, and ministered in the chapels.

Agriculture was but little encouraged by the policy of the fur-trade or the character of the population. It was confined to a few patches of Indian corn and wheat, which they rudely cultivated, with little knowledge of correct husbandry. They ground their grain in windmills, which were scattered along the banks of Detroit river and the St. Clair lake. The recreations of the French colonists consisted in attending the religious services held in the rude chapels on the borders of the wilderness, in adorning their altars with wild flowers, in dancing to the sound of the violin at each other's houses, in hunting the deer through the oak-land openings, and in paddling their light canoes across the clear and silent streams. The women employed themselves in making coarse cotton and woollen cloths for the Indian trade. In their cottages were hung rude pictures of saints, the Madonna and child, and the leaden crucifix supplied the place of one of silver. Abundance of game strayed in the woods, and the waters were alive with fish.

As these immigrants were sent out by the French Government, they were provided by its direction, through the commissariat department, with canvass for tents, hoes, axes, sickles, guns, so many pounds of powder, and meat, with the stipulation that these should be paid for when a certain quantity of land had been cleared.

The Jesuits, who were the most active agents in the exploration of these regions, were, as a class, persons of highly-cultivated and intelligent minds and of polished manners. The narratives of their wanderings through the wilderness throw a coloring of romance around the prairies, and forests, and lakes, which amounts almost to a classic spirit; yet they have left upon the lake-shores but few monuments either of their benevolence or their enterprise. The success of the Jesuits among the Indians was small compared with the extent of their labors. By the savages these Catholic missionaries were regarded as medicine-men and jugglers, on whom the destiny of life and death depended; and, although they were greatly feared, they succeeded in making but few converts to their religious faith, excepting young children or Indians just about to sink into their graves.

The administration of the law around these scattered posts was founded on no compact and settled system. The *Coutume de Paris*, or custom of Paris, was the law of Canada; but this code, although it was received and practised upon in the older and more populous settlements of the lower province, was not adopted and enforced with any degree of uniformity or strictness among the more distant colonists. The commandants of the posts had the principal cognizance of the population around them, and exercised their authority in a mild though arbitrary manner. Indeed, such was the feudal character of this law, that the French paid a willing and implicit obedience to their commandants, who, being invested with unlimited power, were styled the "governors of the posts." A perfect system of law can exist only where there is sufficient intelligence to mark out and determine the rule of right, and sufficient moral power to enforce it. A register was kept, in which the character and circumstances of the colonists were recorded, and in which the Jesuit or the commandant of the post might inspect the condition of each one as upon a map. There was here no system of education like that which prevailed in New England; and all the knowledge acquired by the children of the colonists was obtained from the priests and related to the tenets of the Catholic Church.

A singular form of character was also thrown around the territory by the mythology of the savages. The Indians had not only their good *Manitos*, but their evil spirits; and the wild features of the lake scenery appears to have impressed their savage minds with superstition. They believed that all the prominent points of this wide region were created and guarded by monsters; and the images of these they sculptured on stone, painted upon the rocks, or carved upon the trees. Those who obeyed these supernatural beings, they thought, would after death range among flowery fields filled with the choicest game, while those who neglected their counsels would wander amid dreary solitudes, stung by "gnats as large as pigeons."

The plan of distributing the land was calculated to prevent the settlement of the country. A law was passed requiring the houses of the inhabitants to be placed upon ground with a front of only one acre and a half and running forty acres back. This kept the settlements in a close line along the banks of the streams. A feudal and aristocratic spirit also controlled the grants of land. The commandants of the forts had the power to convey lands, with the permission of the governor-general of Canada, subject to the confirmation of the King of France, the right of shooting hares, rabbits, and partridges being reserved to the grantor. The grantee was bound to clear and improve the land within three years from the date of his deed. The timber that might be necessary for the construction of fortifications or vessels was reserved; and no person was permitted to work upon his land at the trade of a blacksmith, gunsmith, armorer, or brewer but on pain of forfeiture. He was forbidden the trafficking in spiritous liquors with the Indians; and, what was the most singular requisition of all, he was bound to plant or assist in planting a long Maypole at the door of the principal manor on the first of May in each year. Such were the feudal features of this system, equally opposed to the increase of the settlements, to freedom, and independence. How striking is the contrast between this system and the policy of our American laws now acting on the soil, which, by furnishing land cheap, offer every encouragement to agriculture, and thus freely open the treasures of the earth to the labors of our hardy and enterprising citizens.

As early as 1749, the post of Detroit and the others upon the Northwestern lakes, Michilimackinac, Ste. Marie, and St. Joseph, received an accession of immigrants. The last two were called after the saints of those names in the Catholic calendar. Michilimackinac derives its name from the Indian words *Michi-mackinac*, meaning a great turtle, from its supposed resemblance to that animal, or from the Chippewa words *Michine-maukinonk*, signifying the place of giant fairies, who were supposed by Indian superstition to hover over the waters around that beautiful island. The origin of the name of Detroit is the French word *Detroit*, signifying a strait, because the post was situated on the strait connecting Lake Erie with Lake St. Clair.

During the whole period of the French domination, extending from the first settlement of the country down to the year 1760, the traffic of Michigan was confined principally to the trade in furs. This interesting traffic upon the great lakes was carried on by the French under peculiar circumstances. As the forests of the lake region abounded with furs which were of great value in the mother-country, it became an important object with the Canadian government to prosecute that trade with all the energy in its power. The rich furs of the beaver and otter were particularly valuable, from the great demand for them in Europe. Large canoes made of bark and strongly constructed were despatched annually to the lakes laden with packs of European merchandise, consisting of blankets, printed calicoes, ribbons, cutlery, and trinkets of various kinds, which the Indians used, and Detroit, Michilimackinac, and Ste. Marie were their principal places of deposit.

To secure the interests of the large companies, licenses for this trade were granted by the governor-general of Canada to the merchants, who sometimes sold them to the coureurs des bois. The possessor of one of these licenses was entitled to load two large canoes, each of which was manned by six men. The cargo of one of these canoes was valued at about a thousand crowns. This merchandise was sold to the traders on a credit, and at about fifteen per cent. advance on the price it would command in ready money. But the voyages were very profitable, and there was generally a gain of about one hundred per cent. on the sum invested in the enterprise. The traders endured most of the fatigue and the merchants received most of the profit. On the return of one of these expeditions, six hundred crowns were taken by the merchant for his license; and as he had sold the thousand crowns' worth of goods at their prime cost, from this sum he also deducted forty per cent. for bottomry; the remainder was then divided among the six coureurs des bois, who were thus left with but a small compensation for all their perils and hardship.

The *coureurs des bois* were the active agents of the fur-trade. Thoroughly acquainted with the navigation of the lakes, they fearlessly swept along the waters of these inland seas, encamping at night upon its shores. Of mixed white and Indian blood, they formed the connecting link between civilization and barbarism. Their dress was also demi-savage. Lively and sanguine, they were at all times ready to join the Indians in the dance, or pay respect to their ceremonies. Their French fathers had familiarly associated with the native tribes, and their mothers and wives were the inmates of Indian camps. In many respects their character resembled that of mariners upon the ocean, for the same general causes might be said to operate upon both. Instead of navigating the high seas in ships tossed by storms, and ploughing the waves from port to port, it was their lot to propel their light canoes over the fresh-water seas of the forest; where, hurried from one Indian village to another, like the mariner on the ocean, they acquired all those habits which belong to an unsettled and wandering life.

Advancing to the remote shores of Lake Superior or Lake Michigan, and following the courses of the rivers which flow into them, as soon as they reached the points where the Indians were in the habit of resorting, they at once encamped. Here they opened their packages of goods, exhibited them to their savage customers, and exchanged them for furs; and, having disposed of all their merchandise, and loading their canoes with the peltries it had procured, they bade adieu to their Indian friends, and started on their voyage back, with feathers stuck in their hats, keeping time with their paddles to the Canadian boat-song.

La Honton, in his Journal, which was published in France, and a translation of which was afterward published in this country, gives an interesting account of the fur-trade, showing the general course of that traffic while the Canadas were under the French. The author resided at Montreal. At this time (1688) Michilimackinac was the principal stopping place for the traders on their way from Montreal or Detroit to the forests bordering on Lake Superior. Here their goods were deposited, and here the furs were collected for their return freight. Sometimes, however, the traders, accompanied by numerous canoes of the Ottawas, would proceed directly to the older settlements on the St. Lawrence, where they supposed they might be able to dispose of their cargoes to greater advantage than at the interior posts.

The following is La Honton's account of the fur-trade at the period referred to:

"Much about the same day," says he, "there arrived twenty-five or thirty canoes, being homeward bound from the great lakes, and laden with beaver-skins. The cargo of each canoe amounted to forty packs, each of which weighs fifty pounds, and will fetch fifty crowns at the farmer's office. These canoes were followed by fifty more of the Ottawas and Hurons, who come down every year to the colony in order to make a better market than they can do in their own country of Michilimackinac, which lies on the banks of the Lake of Hurons, at the mouth of the Lake of Illinese (Michigan). Their way of trading is as follows:

"Upon their arrival they encamp at the distance of five or six hundred paces from the town. The first day is spent in ranging their canoes, unloading their goods, and pitching their tents, which are made of birch bark. The next day they demand audience of the governor-general, which is granted them that same day, in a public place.

"Upon this occasion each nation makes a ring for itself. The savages sit upon the ground with pipes in their mouths, and the governor is seated in an arm-chair; after which there starts up an orator or speaker from one of these nations, who makes an harangue importing that his brethren are come to visit the governor-general, to renew with him their wonted friendship; that their chief view is to promote the interest of the French, some of whom being unacquainted with the way of traffic, and being too weak for the transporting of goods from the lakes, would be unable to deal in beaver-skins if his brethren did not come in person to deal with them in their own colonies.

That they knew very well how acceptable their arrival is to the inhabitants of Montreal, in regard of the advantage they reap from it; that, in regard to the beaver-skins, they were much valued in France, and the French goods given in exchange were of an inconsiderable value; and that they mean to give the French sufficient proof of their readiness to furnish them with what they desire so earnestly.

"That, by way of preparation for another year's cargo, they are come to take in exchange fusees, and powder and ball, in order to hunt great numbers of beavers, or to gall the Iroquese in case they offered to disturb the French settlements; and, in fine, in confirmation of their words, that they throw a porcelain collar (belt of wampum), with some beaver-skins, to the kitchi-okima (so they call the governor-general), whose protection they laid claim to in case of any robbery or abuse committed upon them in the town. The spokesman having made an end of his speech, returns to his place and takes up his pipe, and the interpreter explains the substance of the harangue to the governor, who commonly gives a very civil answer, especially if the presents be valuable, in consideration of which he likewise makes them a present of some trifling things. This done, the savages rise up and return to their huts, to make suitable preparation for the ensuing truck.

"The next day the savages make their slaves carry the skins to the houses of the merchants, who bargain with them for such clothes as they want. All the inhabitants of Montreal are allowed to traffic with them in any commodity but rum and brandy, these two being excepted upon the account that when the savages have got what they want, and have any skins left, they drink to excess, and then kill their slaves; for when they are in drink they quarrel and fight, and if they were not held by those who are sober, would certainly make havoc one of another. However, you must observe that none of them will touch either gold or silver. As soon as the savages have made an end of their truck, they take leave of the governor, and so return home by the river Ottawas. To conclude, they do a great deal of good, both to the poor and rich, for you will readily apprehend that everybody turns merchant upon such occasions."

To the question what was the condition of the Northwest territory when it was claimed and occupied by France, we can furnish a ready answer. It was a vast ranging-ground for the numerous Indian tribes, who roamed over it in all the listless indolence of their savage independence; of the Jesuit missionaries, who, under the garb of their religious orders, strove to gain the influence of the red men in behalf of their Government as well as their Church, by their conversion to the Catholic faith; the theatre of the most important military operations of the French soldiers at the West; and the grand mart where the furs, which were deemed the most valuable products of this region, were collected for shipment to France, under a commercial system which was originally projected by the Cardinal de Richelieu.

The condition of a country, although often in some measure modified by the nature of the climate and the soil, is more generally founded upon the character of the people and that of its laws. This is clearly exhibited in the case of the Northwest; for while that domain was rich in all the natural advantages that could be furnished by the soil, it was entirely barren of all those moral and intellectual fruits springing from bold and energetic character, directed by a free, enlightened, and wholesome system of jurisprudence.

STRUGGLE BETWEEN FRANCE AND ENGLAND FOR POSSESSION.

While the forests were thus reposing in the silence of nature, broken only by the peaceful operations of the fur-trade, more important events were transpiring beyond their eastern boundary. From the Atlantic to Quebec, France and England, who seemed to have transferred their hereditary hatred from the Old World to the New, had been long struggling to obtain undivided dominion over the northern portion of the latter. Backed by Indian allies, who leagued themselves with one or the other, as they were influenced by caprice or a desire to prostrate some hostile tribe, these two great powers engaged in a desperate struggle for supremacy. The whole of Canada, Illinois, and the territory thence to the borders of the Mississippi were then claimed by the French, while the English occupied most of the country east of the Alleghany Mountains.

Both nations found efficient auxiliaries among the Indian tribes. On the side of the English were the Iroquois, called by them the Six Nations. These combined tribes formed the most powerful savage confederacy then existing on the continent. It consisted of the Onondagas, the Cayugas, the Senecas, the Oneidas, and the Mohawks, and in 1712 the Tuscaroras of North Carolina were received into the league. Their domain embraced a very extensive tract of country, and from time to time it was enlarged by new conquests. They were robust and muscular, and delighted in ornamenting their persons with the finery so highly prized by the Indians, such as medals, ribbons, the skins of wild beasts, and porcupine quills dyed of various colors. They possessed great energy, decision, and perseverance, and, when excited, were remarkable for the force and eloquence with which they spoke. Towards the west they claimed supremacy over the country as far as the Mississippi, and towards the northwest as far as Hudson's Bay; in short, all that was not occupied by the Southern Indians, the Sioux, the Knisteneaux, and the Chippewas. Their affairs were conducted with more system than those of the more western tribes. Every year they held a grand council, consisting of representatives from each nation, at Onondaga, in the present State of New York. Their youth were taught to bend the bow before their muscles were sufficiently strong to propel the arrow to its mark, and to grapple with the wild beasts of the forests as they would with the French, or their enemies the Algonquins. The cause of their attachment to the English is not known; but it was probably in part caprice, and partly a desire to overthrow the power of their rivals who have been mentioned. When their naked and painted warriors appeared on the edge of the forest, it was always a signal that mischief was at hand. "We are born free: we neither depend on Onondio nor Corlaer" (France nor England), said Haaskouan to De la Barre in 1684, and the course they pursued was the performance of this declaration.

The Algonquins, on the other hand, were the allies of the French. The territory of this nation extended from Lake Erie along the whole chain of the upper lakes to Lake Winnepeg and Hudson's Bay on the north, and to the mouth of the Ohio river on the south. They were connected with the tribes immediately east of the St. Lawrence, and with those in the interior of New England. There were two powerful tribes, however, which were not connected with this league, the Hurons and the Foxes. The Hurons were of Iroquois origin; but, from causes which are not known, they had severed from that confederacy, and taken part with the French; while the Foxes, who were of the Algonquin race, sided with the English. The causes of the Friendship entertained by the Algonquins residing on the borders of the lakes for the former are obvious. The French mingled familiarly with them, and endeavored by all possible means to secure their good-will. The traders visited their villages and took to themselves Indian wives. The Jesuit missionaries erected chapels in their camps, presented to them sculptured images, styling them their patron saints, held the crucifix before the dying, offered up their devotions with them before the picture of the Virgin, and planted the cross upon their graves. The French and Indians hunted together, lodged in the same wigwam, and drank from the same cup. On the contrary, the English were cold, distant, and forbidding in their manners: how, then, could the Algonquins be friendly to them, or how the enemies of the French?

For a long time these savages had been sent out into the neighboring wilderness to attack the feeble settlements upon their borders, and to bring back the scalps of their murdered victims. Many a spot was made wet with the blood of its unfortunate inhabitants, and many a red column of British regulars wavered before the rifles of the combined French and Indians, covered by some swamp, or fighting from behind a breastwork of fallen trees. The forests were often lighted up by the conflagration of burning villages, and the midnight solitude was startled by the shrieks of females under the tomahawk or scalping-knife, and mocked by human fiends, whose horrid thirst for blood was no less insatiable than that of the wolves which howled about their camps.

It was at length determined by the British Government to make a powerful effort to possess themselves of the French colonies. Both France and England, it will be recollected, claimed these countries on the same grounds: that is, original discovery, conquest, and appropriation.

In 1757 the Earl of Chatham projected a campaign of a very formidable character against the French colonies, and the last great struggle soon commenced. Twelve thousand British soldiers arrived in this country, under the command of General Amherst; and, at the same time, bodies of rangers, trained to the mode of fighting peculiar to the French and Indians, and also to the hardships of the forest, or what was called the "woods service," were brought into the field under the command of a citizen of New Hampshire, Major Robert Rogers, to co-operate with the British regulars and the colonial troops.

Numerous positions having been occupied along the lake shores and the borders of the French colonies, in 1759 it was determined to bring the question to a speedy and decisive issue. It was proposed to divide the English army into three parts, and to penetrate to the very heart of Canada in three different directions, with a view to overthrow the French power at a single blow. Brigadier General Wolfe, a young and gallant officer, was ordered to ascend the St. Lawrence and lay siege to Quebec. The duty assigned to General Amherst was to seize on Ticonderoga and Crown Point, and thence to proceed by the way of Lake Champlain and the St. Lawrence river to Quebec, to co-operate with General Wolfe in the siege of that place. The third division of the army, under the command of General Prideaux, was destined to attack Niagara, and, after obtaining possession of it, to be embarked on Lake Ontario, and proceed against Montreal. If that city should surrender before Quebec, General Prideaux was to unite his forces with those of General Wolfe, under the walls of the latter. General Amherst, after making great exertions, was obliged to retire into winter quarters without accomplishing his object. General Prideaux, as he had been directed, advanced against Niagara, which was garrisoned by a body of French troops from Detroit, Venango, and Presque Isle, and succeeded in capturing that post.

The most difficult and important branch of the attack had been entrusted to Wolfe. The English fleet, having on board eight thousand men, under the command of this general, soon reached the Island of Orleans, opposite to Quebec, in the St. Lawrence river. The French force amounted to nine thousand men. The English were led on by a young officer, whose war-cry, like that of Nelson at a later period, was "Victory or Westminster Abbey." The first attack made by him was upon Montmorenci, where his troops were landed under cover of a fire from the ships-of-war. Here at last, then, on the broad St. Lawrence, were unfurled the hostile banners of these great rival nations. The glory of the two crowns was at stake. The cross of England glowed brightly upon its crimson ground, amid martial music, and floating above thousands of muskets glittering in the beams of the morning sun. Nor was the French force wanting in the gallantry which distinguished their opponents. The lilies embroidered upon the folds of their flag were borne aloft in triumph above hearts as brave as ever beat in human bosoms. Tribes of savages were seen armed and painted for the struggle which was to decide the destinies of these mighty rivals. The French force was commanded by a gallant and chivalrous officer, the Marquis de Montcalm. Before them lay the great river of Canada; beside them were the walls of Quebec, the stronghold of their power; and at a distance were seen the Falls of Montmorenci, glittering like a sheet of molten silver as they tumbled from the cliffs.

The effective force under Montcalm consisted of about ten thousand men, and his position was defended by floating batteries and armed vessels. Wolfe, by way of stratagem, sailed nine miles up the river, in order to distract the attention of the French army: when the French commander detached M. Bougainville with a strong force to that point to prevent the English from landing. But about midnight the boats of the British ships floated silently down the St. Lawrence, and, being hailed by the French sentinels who were stationed on its banks with the cry of "Who comes there?" the English, who knew their watchword, replied "*La France*," and were suffered to proceed unmolested to their point of debarcation.

At about four o'clock in the morning the British troops began to land, not having been discovered in their progress down the river. Soon after they commenced ascending the precipitous declivity which leads to the Heights of Abraham. They were protected by two field-pieces, and their front was covered by the Royal Americans, a corps raised in New York and New England, as also by a reserve of one regiment and the light infantry. They soon gained the heights and prepared for battle. The Marquis de Montcalm, the moment he discovered the English troops in possession of these important heights, sallied from Beauport with only a single field-piece. The two hostile armies soon met. The Canadian marksmen and Indian allies, no less expert with the rifle, were detached by the French commander to conceal themselves among the bushes and corn-fields, from which they could most effectually annoy the enemy. The French troops advanced with great firmness, although composed for the most part of raw and undisciplined militia. As soon as they had reached within about two hundred yards of the British line, they commenced a sharp but irregular fire, supported by the Indians and the Canadian marksmen, who with their rifles did great execution. But they were met by that unshaken courage and obstinate determination which are characteristic of British soldiers: and the Scotch Highlanders, with their broadswords, making terrible havoc in their ranks, the French columns began to waver. General Wolfe, in the commencement of the action, received a bullet in his wrist while gallantly leading his men to the charge; but, winding a handkerchief about the wound, he continued to fight on as though nothing had occurred. A second ball soon after struck him in the breast, and he fell. While leaning his head on the shoulder of his officers, he was startled from the lethargy of death by shouts from his ranks: "They fly! they fly!" "Who fly?" he faintly inquired. "The French," was the reply. "Then," said he, "I die happy;" and his spirit departed amid the thunders of the battle. The Marquis de Montcalm, the commander of the French army, was also mortally wounded, and died a few days after the engagement. Monuments have been erected to these two heroes in the city of Quebec. The remains of the French army, retiring to Montreal, demanded a capitulation, which was granted. Accordingly, in November, 1760, articles of agreement were entered into between General Amherst and the Marquis de Vaudreuil, by which the latter surrendered to the Crown of England Detroit, Michilimackinac, and all the posts within the government of Canada that were in possession of the French.

A few days after the signing of this capitulation, Major Rogers was detached by General Amherst, at the head of a competent force, to take possession of the distant posts on the frontier, to administer to the French inhabitants there the oath of allegiance, and effectually to establish the power of England in place of that of France. He was ordered to embark his troops in boats, on Lake Erie, stopping on his way at Presque Isle, to make known to the officer of that post the instructions he had received. He was also the bearer of despatches to Brigadier General Monkton, which he was to deliver and receive from that officer his final orders as to the manner in which he should proceed to take possession of Detroit, Michilimackinac, and the other French posts. Having accomplished the objects of the expedition, he was to return in compliance with the orders that might be given him by General Monkton, transport his boats across the portage of Niagara Falls into Lake Ontario, where they were to be delivered into the hands of his commanding officer, and thence he was to march his detachment by land to Albany.

In obedience to these instructions, Major Rogers embarked the force assigned him in fifteen whale-boats at Montreal. On arriving at Fort Frontenac he met with a party of Indians who were out upon a hunting excursion, and communicated to them the first news of the capitulation. They found these savages friendly, and were supplied by them with wild fowl and venison. Soon after they fell in with another body of about fifty Indians, on a stream which flows into Lake Ontario, where they were taking salmon. They all appeared to be gratified with the intelligence that the French had surrendered the country. After arriving at Toronto, the detachment were not long in reaching Niagara, where they provided themselves with moccasins, blankets, and such other articles as were necessary for the expedition. Proceeding on their way to Detroit they soon reached Presque Isle, from which point Rogers embarked in a canoe and proceeded to the old site of Fort Duquesne, now called Pittsburg. Here he found Brigadier General Monkton, and delivered to him the despatches he had brought from General Amherst. A detachment of Royal Americans, or colonial troops, under Captain Campbell, were marched from this post for the purpose of aiding him in so hazardous an expedition. At the same time an officer was ordered to drive forty fat cattle from Presque Isle to Detroit, where it was supposed they would be wanted by the troops. Captain Wait was also sent back to Niagara for provisions, and directed on his return to coast along the northern shore of Lake Erie and encamp about twenty miles east of Detroit. Thus started the first English military expedition that had ever ventured upon the western shore of Lake Erie for the purpose of wresting from the French their possessions in these distant regions.

At this time appeared Pontiac, a chief who was destined to figure largely in the history of this territory at a subsequent period. His residence was

Pechee Island, which looks out upon the waters of Lake St. Clair, about eight miles above the city of Detroit. An Ottawa by birth, and belonging to a tribe which claimed to be the oldest in this quarter, he was greatly esteemed both by the English and French. Thus his influence was greater than that of any other individual among the lake tribes. His personal qualities, indeed, were such as to ensure respect; and he possessed, moreover, hereditary claims to authority, according to the customs of the Indians. His form was cast in the finest mould of savage grace and strength, and his eye seemed capable of penetrating at a glance the secret motives which actuated the tribes around him. Such was Pontiac, the daring chief who was about to dispute the English claims to the territory of the lakes. He could not endure the sight of this people driving the game from his hunting-grounds, and his old friends and allies, the French, from the lands they had so long possessed. Accordingly, when he was apprized that an English detachment was advancing along the lakes to take possession of the country, he could not restrain his indignation. Forthwith he despatched a body of Ottawas from Detroit, with a message to the English, who were then encamped at the mouth of Chogage river, informing them that Pontiac, the King of the country where they were, was approaching, and requesting them to stop until he should arrive. Pontiac, on reaching the English camp, demanded of Rogers the business on which he had come, and how he dared to enter his country without his permission. Major Rogers replied that he had no designs against the Indians, and that his only object was the removal of the French, who had hitherto been the means of preventing all friendly relations between his tribes and the English. Pontiac then gave him to understand that he should stand in his path until the morning, and at the same time presented him with a small string of wampum, signifying that he forbade the English detachment from advancing any farther without his permission. He also told Major Rogers that if he was in want of any food he would send his warriors, and they should procure it for him.

A council having in the meantime been held, Pontiac made his appearance in the English camp the next morning, saying that he had the most friendly disposition towards the English, and he smoked the pipe of peace with their commander. At the same time, he informed Rogers that he would protect him against a party of Indians who had stationed themselves at the mouth of the Detroit river; and he sent also several of his warriors to assist Captain Brewer in bringing on the cattle which he was driving to Detroit. In addition to this, he despatched messengers to the Indians encamped on the Detroit river, and to those on the north and west shores of Lake Erie, to inform them that he had given the English permission to pass through his territory; and, still farther to evince his friendship, he supplied them with venison, wild turkeys, and several bags of parched corn.

Encamping at some distance from the mouth of the Detroit river, Rogers despatched the following letter to M. Bellestre, the French commandant at Detroit:

"*To Captain Bellestre, or the Officer Commanding at Detroit:*

"SIR:—That you may not be alarmed at the approach of the English troops under my command when I come to Detroit, I send forward this by Lieutenant Brheme, to acquaint you that I have General Amherst's orders to take possession of Detroit and such other posts as are in that district, which, by capitulation agreed to and signed by Marquis de Vaudreuil and General Amherst, the 8th of September last, now belong to Great Britain. I have with me the Marquis de Vaudreuil's letters to you, directed for your guidance on this occasion, which letters I shall deliver you when I am at or near your post, and shall encamp the troops I have with me at some distance from the fort, till you have reasonable time to be made acquainted with the Marquis de Vaudreuil's instructions and the capitulation, a copy of which I have with me likewise.

"I am, sir, your humble servant,

"ROBERT ROGERS."

After this he encamped with his detachment on a stream which empties into Lake Erie. Here he found a number of Huron chiefs, who inquired of him whether the reports which they had heard in regard to the surrender of the territory were true; apprizing him, at the same time, that they had been sent out by M. Bellestre for the purpose of defending the country, and to obtain information as to the events which had transpired below. Rogers confirmed the fact of the capitulation, and made a speech to the Hurons of the most conciliatory character; after which he encamped at the west end of Lake Erie with his detachment. The next day he met with a party of Indians, who told him that Bellestre was "a strong man," and that he intended to fight the English. Not long after, sixty Indians, who said that they had come from Detroit the previous day, arrived at his camp. They offered to conduct the English detachment to that place, and informed Rogers that M. Brheme, who had been sent by him with the letter, had been imprisoned by the French commandant.

While the English were thus advancing towards Detroit, the French commandant was not idle. He had collected round his post numerous tribes of savages, and, knowing that they were strongly impressed by symbols, he had caused a pole to be erected, with the image of a man's head on the top, and upon this was placed a crow. He told the Indians that the head represented the English, and the crow himself, and that the meaning of it all was, that the French would scratch out the brains of their enemies. The Indians, however, would not believe it, and expressed their apprehensions that the reverse would be the fact, and that the English at Detroit would scratch out the brains of the French.

About this time Rogers received the following letter from the commandant of Detroit:

"SIR:—I received the letter you wrote me by one of your officers, but, as I have no interpreter, cannot fully answer it. The officer that delivered me yours gives me to understand that he was sent to give me notice of your arrival to take possession of this garrison, according to the capitulation made in Canada; that you have likewise a letter from Monsieur Vaudreuil directed to me. I beg, sir, you will halt your troops at the entrance of the river till you send me the capitulation and the Marquis de Vaudreuil's letter, that I may act in conformity thereto.

"I have the honor to be, &c., &c.,

"DE BELLESTRE."

Shortly after, on the 25th of November, the English commander received the letter inserted below from M. Bellestre:

"DETROIT, 25th Nov., 1760.

"SIR:—I have already, by Mr. Barrager, acquainted you with the reasons why I could not answer particularly the letter which was delivered me the 22d instant by the officer you sent to me. I am entirely unacquainted with the reasons of his not returning to you. I sent my Huron interpreter to that nation, and told him to stop them should they be on the road, not knowing positively whether they were inclined to favor you or us; and to tell them from me they should behave peaceably; that I knew what I owed to my general, and that, when the capitulation should be settled, I was obliged to obey. The said interpreter has orders to wait on you and deliver you this.

"Be not surprised, sir, if along the coast you find the inhabitants upon their guard. It was told them you had several Indian nations with you, to whom you had promised permission to plunder; nay, that they were even resolved to force you to it. I have therefore allowed the said inhabitants to take to their arms, as it is for your safety and preservation as well as ours; for, should those Indians become insolent, you may not, perhaps, in your present situation, be able to subdue them alone.

"I flatter, myself, sir, that, as soon as this shall come to hand, you will send me, by some of the gentlemen you have with you, both the capitulation and Monsieur de Vaudreuil's letter.

"I have the honor to be, sir,

"Your very humble and obedient servant,

"De Bellestre."

After advancing five miles farther up the Detroit river, Rogers the next day sent a second letter, of which the following is a copy, by Captain Campbell:

"Sir:—I acknowledge the receipt of your two letters, both of which were delivered to me yesterday. Mr. Brheme has not yet returned. The enclosed letter from the Marquis de Vaudreuil will inform you of the surrender of all Canada to the King of Great Britain, and of the great indulgence granted to the inhabitants, as also of the terms granted to the troops of his most Christian majesty. Captain Campbell, whom I have sent forward with this letter, will show you the capitulation. I desire you will not detain him, as I am determined, agreeable to my instructions from General Amherst, speedily to relieve your post. I shall stop the troops I have with me at the hither end of the town till four o'clock, by which time I expect your answer. Your inhabitants will not surprise me: as yet I have seen no other in that position but savages waiting for my orders. I can assure you, sir, the inhabitants of Detroit shall not be molested, they and you complying with the capitulation, but be protected in the quiet and peaceful enjoyment of their estates; neither shall they be pillaged by my Indians, nor by yours that have joined me.

"I am, &c., Robert Rogers.

"To Captain Bellestre,
Commanding at Detroit."

After despatching this letter he pushed his boats up the Detroit river to within half a mile of the fort, and encamped his detachment in a field.

The English camp was soon visited by Captain Campbell and a French officer, who presented to Major Rogers M. Bellestre's compliments, stating that he was instructed by that officer to inform him that the post had been surrendered. Lieutenants Lefflie and McCormick were then sent with thirty-six Royal Americans, who immediately took possession of the fort; when the Indians, to the number of seven hundred, who had been collected there by the French commander, set up a tremendous yell, exulting that their prophecy concerning the crow had been verified.

Major Rogers now formally took possession of this important post, receiving at the same time a plan of the fort, and a list of the warlike and other stores. The French commandant and the troops forming the garrison were placed under the charge of Lieutenant Holmes, with thirty Rangers, to be conducted to Philadelphia. Twenty men were also sent to escort the French soldiers from the posts of Miami and Gatanois, and the command of the fort was given to Captain Campbell. Rogers, having made a treaty with the neighboring Indians, set out with a party to Lake Huron for the purpose of taking possession of Michilimackinac; but the ice in the lake so obstructed his passage that he could not proceed by water, and the Indians told him that it would be impossible for him to reach that place by land without snow-shoes. Accordingly, having replaced the ammunition and stores which he had taken with him at Detroit, he left that post on the 21st of November, 1760, after intrusting to Captain Campbell its command. With the change of jurisdiction thus effected, a new scene will now open upon us.

CONDITION OF THE COUNTRY UNDER THE ENGLISH.

No material change took place in the condition of the country in consequence of its surrender to the English. The capitulation of Montreal permitted the French emigrants to remain in the territory and to enjoy undisturbed their civil and religious rights. Agriculture was no more encouraged than before, and the same general plan continued to be pursued in conducting the fur-trade. No land was allowed to be purchased directly of the Indians, nor were the English commandants, styled governors, permitted to make any grants of land except within certain prescribed limits. The settlements of the French, however, continued to extend, and their long, narrow farms, surrounded by pickets and fronted by houses of bark or logs and their roofs thatched with straw, were seen stretching along the banks of all the principal streams. There were as yet no schools, and the instruction of the children continued to be confided entirely to the Catholic priests. Before that time peltries had constituted almost the only medium of traffic, but now English coin began to be introduced. Horses were for a long time unknown at Detroit, the first having been brought there, it is said, from Fort Duquesne after Braddock's defeat.

Although the English had acquired possession of the country, it had been against the will of the Indians. The design of Pontiac probably was to lead the English into his territory only that he might have a better opportunity to destroy them. He believed that it was their intention to drive him from his lands, and he therefore considered them as dangerous intruders. His spacious domain, its waters abounding with fish and its woods with game, had now fallen into the hands of a people whom he had always looked upon as his enemy. Some of the Indians had been struck by the British officers in the garrison, an indignity which their savage natures could not endure, and they readily joined with their chief to expel these hated strangers from their country.

Pontiac was not long in circulating war-belts among all the principal tribes on the borders of the lakes, and he formed a chain of operations extending more than a thousand miles along their waters. He flattered himself that if the British garrisons could be destroyed or driven away he should afterward be able effectually to defend the country against farther intrusion by means of his own strength combined with that of his savage allies. A grand council of the Indians was accordingly soon assembled at the River Aux Ecorce, and Pontiac addressed them in person. He told them that it was the design of the English to drive the Indians from their country, and that they were their natural and inveterate enemies. He also assured them that the Great Spirit had appeared to a Delaware Indian in a dream and thus addressed him: "Why do you suffer these dogs in red clothing" (the English) "to enter your country and take the land I gave you? Drive them from it: and then, when you are in distress, I will help you." He also exhibited to them a war-belt, which he said the French King had sent over from France, ordering them to drive out the British and make way for the return of the French.

The shores of the lakes were soon alive with bodies of Indian warriors, who had abandoned their hunting-grounds and camps and were repairing to the posts on the frontier. Among these were seen the Ottawas, the Chippewas, the Miamis, the Pottowatomies, the Missisagas, the Shawanese, the Ottagamies, and the Winnebagoes, besides parties from numerous other tribes. At about the same time they attacked the Forts of Le Bœuf, Venango, Presque Isle, Michilimackinac, St. Joseph, Miami, Green Bay, Ouiatonon, Pittsburg, and Sandusky. Their military operations, indeed, extended along the entire line of the waters of the lower lakes.

This general and simultaneous attack was made in the month of May, 1763, and was so sudden and wholly unexpected that the garrisons were all taken by surprise. Detroit was then the most important station upon the lakes, and was garrisoned by one hundred and twenty-two men and eight officers, Major Gladwin being the commandant. Three rows of pickets surrounded the fort in the form of a square. Most of the houses of the French were situated within these pickets, that they might be protected by the guns of the fort. The inhabitants were provided with arms and ammunition. Within the pickets there was also a circular space, which was named by the French *Le chemin du Ronde*, from its being a place of deposit for arms; and over the gates of the fort, and at each of its corners, there were small dwellings. The town was defended in front by an armed schooner named the Beaver, moored in the river, which at this point is about three-quarters of a mile wide. The post commanded the great channel of communication from Lake Michigan to Buffalo and Pittsburg; its possession, therefore, was an object of great importance; and Pontiac, who was the chief director of the confederacy, undertook its reduction in person.

His plan was one which strikingly exhibits the cunning which is so characteristic of the Indians. He intended to take the fort by surprise; and for this purpose he ordered a party of his warriors to saw off their rifles so short that they could conceal them under their blankets, and, under a feigned pretence, to gain admission into the fort, and massacre the garrison. To carry out his design, he encamped at a short distance from the post, and sent word to the commandant that he was desirous of holding a council with him, that "they might brighten the chain of peace." On the evening of that day, an Indian woman, by the name of Catharine, brought to Major Gladwin a pair of moccasins which she had been employed to make for him, and he was so much pleased with them that he gave her an elk-skin, and told her to take it home and make from it several pairs more. She took the skin, but continued to linger about the gate of the fort as if her business were unfinished; and the singularity of her conduct attracted attention. Major Gladwin accordingly ordered her to be called back, and inquired of her why she did not hasten home, that she might finish the moccasins by the time he had required them to be done. The woman remarked that she did not like to take the skin away, as he seemed to prize it so much, since she feared "*she could never bring it back.*" Her mind seemed to be struggling with some secret, and, after being pressed, she developed the whole plot. Major Gladwin immediately ordered the guards to be doubled, and sentinels to be stationed on the ramparts.

As night approached, fires were seen in the Indian camp, and their war-songs were distinctly heard, so that the English commandant was convinced that something important was contemplated by them, and that the woman had told the truth, as the savages always excite themselves in this manner preparatory to any great enterprise they are about to undertake.

The next morning, according to previous arrangement, Pontiac and his warriors repaired to the fort. As he was advancing, he noticed that there was an unusual number of soldiers upon the ramparts, and that the officers all had pistols in their belts. Having entered the council-house, or the place assigned for the meeting, he opened the discussion with a speech, in which he made great professions of friendship for the English. As the time approached when, as the woman had stated, the belt was to be delivered and a fire upon the garrison commenced, his gestures became more vehement. At this moment the governor and his officers drew their swords, and the English soldiers made a clattering upon the ground with their muskets. Pontiac himself was now the party surprised, but he continued perfectly calm and unmoved.

The commandant soon commenced his reply, but, instead of thanking the chief for his professions of friendship, he charged him with being a traitor, and, to convince him of his knowledge of the plot, he stepped forward to the Indian who sat on his skin nearest to him, and, opening his blanket, exposed the shortened rifle. At the same time, addressing himself to the warriors, he told them instantly to leave the fort, as his men, should they discover their treachery, would show them no mercy. He also assured them that they would be permitted to go out in safety, as he had promised them his protection.

The warriors accordingly sallied out of the fort; but, as soon as they had passed the gates, they turned about and fired upon the garrison. They then proceeded to the commons, where they murdered an English woman who resided there, and, horrid to relate, cooked and feasted upon her remains. After this they went to Isle de Cochon, (Hog Island,) and barbarously destroyed a whole family.

The savages had now sufficiently evinced their hostile intentions. Collecting around the fort, they fired upon the garrison from the nearest houses, and even from behind the pickets. Measures were soon taken, however, to burn such buildings as they could avail themselves of for this purpose, by throwing shells. But, as soon as the shells fell, the savages ran up to them, with loud yells, and extinguished the matches before they had time to explode. Still, in spite of all their efforts to prevent it, the buildings were soon demolished, and the Indians then withdrew to a low ridge which overlooked the pickets, and from this they kept up a constant fire upon the fort.

Although Pontiac, as the acknowledged head of the confederacy, was the leader in the attack upon Detroit, he was aided by several chiefs, who had placed themselves under his direction. Among these were the Ottawa chiefs *Mahigam*, or the Wolf, *Wabunemay*, or the White Sturgeon, *Kittacomsi*, and *Agouchiois;* and the Chippewa chiefs *Pashquois*, *Gayashque*, *Wasson*, and *Macatay-wasson*.

The influence of Pontiac had for a long time been very great, not only with the French, but also with the remotest tribes upon the borders of the lakes. In 1746 he defended Detroit against a combined force under Mackinac, the Turtle, aided by a portion of his own tribe, the Ottawas. While he was thus assisting the French, they were no less warm in their attachment to their allies. "When the French arrived at these falls" (the Saute de Ste. Marie), said a Chippewa chief, "they came and kissed us. They called us children, and we found them fathers. We lived like brethren in the same lodge. They never mocked our ceremonies; they never molested the places of our dead. Seven generations have passed away, but we have not forgotten it. Just, very just, were they towards us."

The siege of Detroit by Pontiac continued. Sometimes blazing arrows were launched from the bows of his warriors upon the chapel for the purpose of burning it; and this they would have effected had they not been deterred from farther attempts by a Jesuit, who persuaded them that such an act would call down the vengeance of the Great Spirit. A breach was now attempted to be made in the pickets, and in this Major Gladwin co-operated with them, by ordering his men to cut them away from the inside, so that it was soon accomplished; but no sooner was it filled with the Indians than a small brass cannon, which had been brought to bear upon this point, was discharged upon them, and made terrible havoc. After this the fort was simply blockaded and its supplies cut off, by which means great suffering was occasioned to the garrison. Among the killed on the side of the English was Sir Robert Devers, whose body was boiled and eaten by the savages. Captain Robertson experienced a similar fate, and off the skin of one of his arms a tobacco-pouch was made.

Major Campbell, it will be recollected, had been appointed to the command of the fort by Major Rogers, and it was a great point with the savages to get possession of the person of this officer, as he was much esteemed, not only by the French and English, but by the Indians also, for his chivalrous character, and, therefore, the more valuable as a hostage. Pontiac accordingly solicited an interview with this officer, that, as he stated, "they might smoke the pipe of peace together." Two French citizens recommended this interview, and were, in fact, made the agents of Pontiac to effect it. The Indian chief, in the meantime, solemnly promised that the English commandant should be permitted to return in safety to the fort. The proposal was acceded to; but no sooner had Pontiac got his enemy into his hands, than his promise was entirely forgotten, and he told him that his life even should not be spared but on the condition that the fort was surrendered. The conduct of Pontiac in this transaction had been such as to destroy all confidence in his word. The fate of this brave and generous officer was truly melancholy. An Ottawa chief had been killed in the siege of Michilimackinac, and his nephew hastened to Detroit to seek for revenge. Here meeting with Major Campbell, he instantly killed him with a blow of his tomahawk. The murderer fled to Saginaw to escape the vengeance of Pontiac.

The Beaver, the armed vessel to which allusion has been made, had been sent to Niagara for the purpose of hastening the arrival of a re-enforcement of men, and to procure a supply of provisions. Lieutenant Cuyler, with ninety-seven men, was sent from that post with supplies, and, apprehending no danger, they had landed at Point Pelee and encamped. Here they were discovered by the Indians, and at dawn the next morning they were attacked, and the whole party either cut off or taken prisoners, with the exception of one officer and thirty men, who succeeded in gaining a barge, in which they crossed Lake Erie and reached Sandusky Bay. The savages placed their prisoners on board the boats, and compelled them to manage them, escorting them in triumph to Detroit, along the Canadian bank of the river. When they were near this place, four British soldiers determined to make their escape, and for this purpose changed the course of the boat they were in, setting up at the same time a loud cry. After some resistance their Indian guards leaped overboard, one of them dragging a soldier along with him, and they both were drowned. The remaining three were now fired on by the Indians in the other boats, and also by those on the bank of the river, though without any other effect than wounding one of their number. In the meantime the armed schooner on the Detroit side opened a fire upon the savages, which dispersed their boats, and likewise the guard upon the opposite shore. The rest of the prisoners were taken by the Indians to Hog Island, and there put to death.

The French residents themselves did not escape wholly unharmed amid these scenes of savage violence. Maintaining a neutral position in the war, they were regarded with no little jealousy by their former allies of the Algonquin race. Their houses were in several instances broken open, and their cattle plundered by Pontiac's warriors, though the Ottawa chiefs gave to the sufferers certificates of indemnity for all such losses, formed of pieces of bark, on which was drawn the figure of an otter, the emblem of his tribe, and these pledges were all faithfully redeemed at a subsequent period.

The savages, finding that all their attempts to destroy the fort were unavailing, endeavored to engage the French in the alliance; and for this purpose Pontiac assembled a council of his warriors and of the French inhabitants at the river Aux Ecorce, on which occasion he addressed to them the following speech:

"My Brothers:—I have no doubt that this war is very troublesome to you, and that my warriors, who are continually passing and repassing through your settlements, frequently kill your cattle and injure your property. I am sorry for it, and hope you do not think I am pleased with this conduct of my young men; and, as a proof of my friendship, remember the war you had seventeen years ago, (1746,) and the part I took in it. The Northern nations combined together and came to destroy you. Who defended you? Was it not myself and my young men? The great chief Mackinac (the Turtle) said in council that he would carry to his native village the head of your chief warrior, and that he would eat his heart and drink his blood. Did I not then join you, and go to his camp and say to him, that if he wished to kill the French, he must pass over my body and the bodies of my young men? Did I not take up the tomahawk with you? aid in fighting your battles with Mackinac, and in driving him home to his country? Why do you think I would turn my arms against you? Am I not the same French Pontiac who assisted you seventeen years ago? I am a Frenchman, and I wish to die a Frenchman.

"My brothers," continued Pontiac, throwing a war-belt into the midst of the council, "I begin to grow tired of this bad meat which is upon our lands, but I see that this is not your case; for, instead of assisting us in our war with the English, you are actually assisting them. I have already told you, and I now tell you again, that when I undertook this war, it was only your interest I sought, and that I knew what I was about. I yet know what I am about. This year they must all perish; the Master of Life so orders it. His will is known to us, and we must do as He says. And you, my brothers, who know Him better than we do, wish to oppose His will. Until now I have avoided urging you upon this subject, in the hope that, if you could not aid, you would not injure us. I did not wish to ask you to fight with us against the English, and I did not believe that you would take part with them. You will say you are not with them. I know it; but your conduct amounts to the same thing. You tell them all we do, and you carry our counsels and plans to them. Now, take your choice. You must be entirely French, like ourselves, or entirely English. If you are French, take this belt for yourselves and for your young men, and join us. If you are English, we declare war against you."

Previous to this, and on the third of June, 1763, news had been received of the conclusion of peace between France and England; and one of the French inhabitants, holding up a copy of the treaty in answer to this harangue, replied: "My brother, you see that our arms are tied by our great father, the King of France; untie this knot, and we will join you; but, till that is done, we shall sit quietly on our mats."

The vessel which had been despatched to Niagara now returned with a supply of provisions and arms. To prevent her reaching the fort, a great number of Indians had left the siege and repaired to Fighting island, a short distance below. After annoying her from their canoes at the mouth of the river, they at length resolved to get possession of her by boarding, and were approaching her with all their force for that purpose, when she opened upon them a destructive fire, which wounded and killed a large number, and put the rest to flight. She then dropped down the river to wait for a fair wind, and a few days afterward reached Detroit without farther molestation.

Pontiac now endeavored to destroy the vessels which were anchored opposite to the fort, as they greatly aided in its defence. He, for this purpose, demolished the barns of several of the French settlers, and from the materials, which were of a resinous nature and perfectly dry, he constructed rafts, and, setting them on fire, committed them to the current of the river, which is here quite rapid, in the expectation that they would float down against them and burn them. The English, however, perceiving his object, anchored small boats above the vessels, fastened to each other with iron chains, to intercept and turn away these dangerous masses, in which they were perfectly successful, and the blazing rafts passed harmlessly by.

It was not long, however, before efficient aid was received by the English garrison. A fleet of gun-boats made its appearance, strongly armed, and having on board a detachment of three hundred regular troops, under the command of Captain Dalyell, one of the aids of Sir Jeffry Amherst. Supposing that Pontiac might be surprised in his camp, they landed a force of two hundred and forty-seven men, and marched up the river with that object. But this chief, apprised of their intentions, had removed his women and children, and prepared for a vigorous defence. A party of his warriors were concealed behind the pickets of the neighboring farms, others lay hid in the long prairie grass, which grew here to a great height, and others again were concealed behind heaps of wood. The British force had no sooner reached the point now called Bloody Bridge, than they received a destructive fire from the rifles of the savages. For a moment their columns wavered, as their commander, Captain Dalyell, had fallen at the first discharge; but, soon rallying, they fought with great bravery, and charged upon the enemy with the bayonet. The Indians, however, without being seen, continued to pour forth a destructive fire upon the English, and could only be dislodged from their places of concealment by driving them from house to house, and from field to field. Perceiving that their numbers were diminishing, and that they were fighting under great disadvantages, the English now commenced a retreat to the fort, protected by the armed gun-boats, after a loss of nineteen men killed and forty-two wounded.

While these scenes were passing at Detroit, events of a still more tragical character were taking place on the upper lakes. Michilimackinac, which is distant nearly four hundred miles from Detroit, has been already described.

This fort was surrounded with pickets of cedar, and its stockade was washed by the waves of the strait. At that time the fort was protected by several pieces of brass cannon, taken from the trading-posts of Hudson's Bay. There was a chapel in which mass was regularly performed by a Jesuit missionary. At this post there were about thirty families, and it was garrisoned by ninety-three men. The savages here were still more inveterate in their hostility to the English than at Detroit. Alexander Henry, the English trader, had been obliged to wear the garb of a coureur des bois on his way to that post, where there were then but four English merchants residing. The hostile disposition of the savages was, indeed, clearly manifested on his first arrival. He had been there but a very short time when he was visited by a body of Chippewas, painted and dressed in the most warlike style, with feathers thrust through their noses. Their chief, Minavavana, thus addressed him:

"Englishman, it is to you that I speak, and I demand your attention.

"Englishman, you know that the French King is our father; he promised to be such, and we, in return, promised to be his children: this promise we have kept.

"Englishman, it is you that have made war with this our father. You are his enemy, and how then could you have the boldness to venture among us, his children? You know that his enemies are ours.

"Englishman, we are informed that our father, the King of France, is old and infirm, and that, being fatigued with making war upon your nation, he has fallen asleep. During this sleep you have taken advantage of him, and possessed yourselves of Canada. But his nap is almost at an end: I think I hear him already stirring, and inquiring for his children, the Indians; and when he does awake, what must become of you? He will destroy you utterly.

"Englishman, although you have conquered the French, you have not yet conquered us. We are not your slaves. These lakes, these woods and mountains, are left to us by our ancestors; they are our inheritance, and we will part with them to none. Your nation supposes that we, like the white people, cannot live without bread, and pork, and beef, but you ought to know that He, the Great Spirit and Master of Life, has provided food for us in these spacious lakes, and on these wooded mountains.

"Englishman, our father, the King of France, employed our young men to make war upon your nation. In this war many of them have been killed, and it is our custom to retaliate until such time as the spirits of the slain are satisfied. But the spirits of the slain are only to be satisfied in one of two ways: the first is by spilling the blood of the nation by which they fell; the other, by covering the bodies of the dead, and thus allaying the resentment of their relations. This is done by making presents.

"Englishman, your King has never sent us any presents, nor entered into any treaty with us, wherefore he and we are still at war; and, while he does these things, we must consider that we have no other father or friend among the white people than the King of France. But for you, we have taken into consideration that you have ventured among us in the expectation that we should not molest you. You do not come armed with an intention to make war. You come in peace to trade with us, and supply us with necessaries of which we are much in want. We shall regard you, therefore, as a brother, and you may sleep tranquilly, without fear of the Chippewas. As a token of our friendship, we present you this pipe to smoke."

But, although no attack was made upon him, it was perceived that the spirit of the savages was anything but friendly. He was afterward visited by a chief who was at the head of a party of Ottawa warriors, who also made him a speech, and compelled him to deliver a part of his goods to the Indians on a credit.

Thus affairs were here speedily coming to a crisis. The warriors in the wilderness around this post had also received from Pontiac the war-belt, and were now busy in collecting their bands for the purpose of joining his confederacy, the object of which was to blot out the English power from the territory bordering on the lakes. No serious suspicions were awakened at Michilimackinac, although large bodies of Indians had been noticed collecting around the post, some of them apparently for the purpose of purchasing European merchandise, trinkets, and silver ornaments which Henry had for sale, but for the most part without any apparent object.

On the seventh of June, Wawatam, a Chippewa chief, called on this trader, who had recently come from the Saute de Ste. Marie, telling him that he was sorry that he had left the Saute, and requesting that he would go back with him to that post the following day. He also desired to know if Major Etherington had not received some bad news; for, said he, "I have been disturbed with the noise of evil birds." The following day he repeated his request, and urged his suspicions anew. The trader conceived it to be his duty to inform Major Etherington of what had taken place: but, unfortunately, this officer paid no attention to it, considering it as mere idle apprehension.

The number of savages having greatly increased, it was proposed the next day to celebrate the anniversary of the King's birth by a game which is called *Baggatiway*. This is a common game among the Indians, and is played with bats and ball. A ball is placed in the centre of an open piece of ground: the players divide themselves into two parties, and a struggle then takes place between them to knock the ball to the post of the opposite party. It had been agreed among the savages to throw the ball, as if by accident, over the pickets; and, when this had been done, to rush after it, possess themselves of the fort, and massacre the garrison.

The game was accordingly commenced, and Major Etherington, who was present as a spectator, laid a wager on the success of the Chippewas, the greater part of the garrison being at the same time collected outside the fort to witness the sport. Suddenly the ball, according to their previous understanding, was thrown over the pickets, and, as appeared very natural, the Indians all rushed after it. But almost instantly the war-cry of the savages rose from the interior of the fort, and a dreadful scene commenced. The trader, who had been prevented from being present at the game, hearing the tumult without, and finding the savages, about four hundred in number, in possession of the post, crawled over a low fence which separated his house from that of M. Langlade, a French Canadian, and entreated him to afford him some place of concealment. But Langlade, shrugging up his shoulders, hastily turned away from the window where he had been looking out, coolly saying that he knew of no such place. At this moment a Pawnee slave belonging to Langlade beckoned to Henry to come to a door which she pointed out to him, conducted him to the garret of the house, and, having concealed him there, locked the door and took away the key.

Henry gazed through the crevices of the wall upon the scene below, and it was a scene of horror. A great number of the English soldiers lay dead around the fort; some were seen struggling between the knees of the savages, who were scalping them while yet alive. Others were cut in pieces, and their blood was drank by the warriors from the hollows of their hands joined together, while they were shrieking most hideously, like so many demons. At length there was a profound silence, an awful suspense, which denoted that, for want of more victims, the work of death was done.

The Indians now gathered about the house of Langlade, and asked him if any of the English had taken shelter there. Langlade replied that none had to his knowledge, but that they might examine for themselves. Two or three of the savages coming to the garret door, demanded the key, and, unlocking it, went in.

By this time Henry had concealed himself behind a heap of birch-bark vessels which were used in the making of maple-sugar, where the dark color of his clothes, aided by the absence of light in the room, prevented him from being seen, so that the Indians, satisfying themselves that there was no one there, soon went away. There was a mat in the room, and Henry, laying himself down on it, soon fell asleep. It was not long, however, before he was awakened by the wife of Langlade, who informed him that most of the English had been despatched, but that he might hope to escape. The shades of night now came on, and the trader sought again in slumber to forget the horrors of the scene.

He was not, however, so easily to escape. Langlade's wife, notwithstanding the encouragement she had held out to him, determined to make known his place of concealment, saying that the Indians would murder her if the trader was found secreted in her house. Accordingly, she took the key and gave it to Wenniway, a chief of the most hideous appearance. This warrior was more than six feet in height, and his naked body was painted all over with a mixture of grease and charcoal, as was his face, with the exception of a circular ring around each of his eyes. Accompanied by a body of savages, he entered the garret, and approaching the trembling trader, grasped him by the collar, and fixing his eyes steadfastly upon him, raised his knife, as if about to plunge it into his breast; but, suddenly checking himself, he dropped the fatal weapon and said, "I won't kill you. I have lost a brother, whose name is Musinigon. You shall be called after him."

But the sufferings of the trader were not yet at an end. He was stripped of his clothes and carried to L'Arbre a Croche as a prisoner. Here, however, his friend Wawatam, faithful to his promise of protection, appeared in his behalf, ransomed him, and accompanied the trader to the island of Mackinaw, where he concealed him from a band of drunken savages in what is now called the Scull Rock.

The fort of Michilimackinac was now burned to the ground. Seventy of the English soldiers had been massacred, and, to complete the sanguinary deed, the bodies of many of them were boiled and eaten by the savages. The lives of the remainder, as well as of the prisoners taken at St. Joseph and Green Bay, were spared, and on the return of peace they were all released, either with or without ransom. At the close of these tragical events a number of Indian canoes arrived with English traders, who were beaten, insulted, and marched to the prison lodge.

After the work of devastation had been finished, many of the Indians retired to the island of Mackinaw, while others repaired to Detroit, to aid Pontiac in the siege of this post. This chief, however, soon found that his enemies were too formidable for him. General Bradstreet now arrived to relieve the fort, at the head of an army of three thousand men. On his way he had destroyed the villages of the hostile savages, laid waste their corn-fields along the rich bottoms of the Maumee, dispersed the natives in every direction, and reached Detroit without opposition. The Indians, perceiving that they could no longer contend against so powerful a foe, laid down their arms, and thus the war was brought to a close. Of Pontiac, after his discomfiture, but little is certainly known. Disappointed and mortified at the failure of his plans, he retired to Illinois, where he was assassinated about the year 1767 by an Indian of the Peoria tribe. The character of this chief was bold and strongly marked. Excelled by none of his race in courage, strength, and energy, he possessed traits which pointed him out for a leader. To have had sufficient influence to bring the numerous tribes of the West, along a frontier of a thousand miles, to co-operate with him in his desperate undertaking, must have required much more than ordinary talents. Although destitute of those principles of honor which prevail among civilized nations in the operations of war, he possessed a larger share of humanity than is commonly found among savages. Undismayed by difficulties, and far-seeing and comprehensive in his plans, he fought from a sense of justice and in defence of the rich domain which had been bequeathed to him by his ancestors.

THE FUR-TRADE AND AMERICAN INDEPENDENCE.

From the year 1679, when La Salle and Hennepin crossed Lake Erie with the first vessel that had ever disturbed the waters of that lake, the face of the country had been, down to the time of the English occupation, but little changed. During the period of the French power in this quarter, the fur-trade had been vigorously carried on along the great chain of lakes, and through every channel in which it could be made to circulate, either by companies chartered for that object, or by individual enterprise. The *coureurs des bois,* who acted, says La Honton, "like East Indiamen and pirates," returning periodically from their inland voyages to swell the population at the different posts, brought with them in bark canoes the furs and peltry which they had collected, and deposited them at the factories erected to receive them; from thence they were at regular seasons transported to the headquarters of the trade at Montreal and Quebec, where they were shipped for Europe.

The principal channels through which this traffic was carried on between the upper and lower provinces continued to be the Ottawa river or Lake Erie, the packs, when the latter course was adopted, being transported across the portage of Niagara Falls upon the backs of the traders.

The condition of this trade under the French, although depending much on the peculiar character of the people, was essentially modified by the positive operation of the laws. The government of the colony was, it is true, exercised with apparent mildness, but still it was impressed with those harsh principles which characterized the most aristocratic period of the Bourbons. Even the form of land distribution, founded on the *Coutume de Paris,* was extended to the French colonies of the West. Its operation was exceedingly oppressive, and greatly retarded the growth of the settlement. It confined the energies of the people to narrow tracts of land, granted under burdensome conditions, placing them in the power of *seigneurs,* which was but another name for masters, instead of opening the broad and fertile bosom of the West to free and unencumbered industry, such as is now effecting such extraordinary changes in that region under the equal laws of our own Republic. The people under this system were but the mere appendages of large corporations, parts of a vast machine which was planned and kept in motion solely for the benefit of royal monopolies.

It has been remarked that the aspect of things in these remote regions was but little changed after they came into the possession of the English

The chapels and the forts continued in much the same state; the little farms of the French, surrounded by pickets, stretched along the banks of the streams as before; and the country presented a variegated aspect of French, English, and Indian manners. The red coats of the British regulars contrasted very strikingly with the peasant garb of the French farmers, and with the wild and fantastic dress of the natives.

The insurrection being quelled, a system of conciliatory measures was adopted to secure the good-will of the disaffected tribes; small grants of land were made around the posts, and the Indians themselves were induced to cede portions of their territory for a trifling consideration to the French colonists. These grants were made, however, without any authority from the British Government. The French settlements extended along the banks of the Detroit and St. Clair rivers to the distance of about twenty miles above and below the town, with here and there a lonely hut of some French trader at a favorable point in the interior. Detroit continued to be the most prominent post, and three years after the Pontiac war the town contained not less than a hundred houses, independent of the barracks. On the west side of the town lay the commons, which received the name of the *King's Garden.* The fort was surrounded by pickets and mounted with small cannon, was garrisoned by two hundred men, and the commandant exercised a sort of arbitrary power under the general supervision of the governor-general of Canada.

Meanwhile the Hudson's Bay Company, which had been long a rival of the old French companies, extended its operations through the wilderness which had been the ranging ground of the French traders. This company had been chartered in 1669 by Charles II. That charter, granted to a company of English merchants, authorized them to occupy a very extensive region north of Canada for the prosecution of the fur-trade, to establish military posts for the defence of their persons and property, and to traffic with the native tribes.

From 1763 to the close of the three following years, the trade from Montreal with the interior had been greatly diminished, the Indians carrying on most of their traffic with the agents of the Hudson's Bay Company. In 1766 individual adventurers began to extend their operations along the lake shores in the same track that had formerly been pursued by the French, and soon came in collision with the large companies which were striving to occupy for their exclusive benefit this extensive region. Thus the course of the trade continued to present the same wild features which had characterized it under the former *regime*.

The English made but little change either in the laws or in their administration, and pursued the same general policy as had their predecessors the French. The commandants of the posts, although responsible to the governor-general at Quebec, were still possessed of a discretionary power which was all but absolute, and which they exercised in a highly arbitrary manner, as perhaps was necessary among such a population as they had to deal with. Whenever any crime was committed, however, which required a formal trial, it was customary for these officers to summon a jury of the most respectable inhabitants, and to abide by their decision.

A semblance of the criminal laws of England was, it is true, introduced, but these laws were administered without any regard to fixed principles or to established rules. A single example will suffice to show the manner in which legal proceedings were conducted in 1776.

Governor Hamilton, at that time the commanding officer at Detroit, being informed of a theft committed by a Canadian Frenchman, directed

Philip Dejean and twelve jurors to hear and adjudge the case: they accordingly proceeded to the trial, and convicted the individual of the crime alleged against him. The record of this trial has come down to us, and it is a most singular document. Lord Dorchester, however, then governor of Canada, was no sooner made acquainted with the proceedings in this case, so contrary to every principle of law, than he issued a warrant for the arrest of Hamilton and Dejean, though, unfortunately, they had both previously left the country.

In 1774 an act was passed, called the Quebec Act, establishing the boundaries of Canada, including Michigan, and extending thence to the Mississippi and Ohio rivers on the south, and north from the St. Lawrence to the latitude of 52°, or to the lands of the Hudson's Bay Company. This act granted to the Catholic inhabitants the free exercise of their religion, the undisturbed possession of their Church property, and the right in all matters of litigation to demand a trial according to the former laws of the province. But this right was not extended to the settlers on lands granted by the English crown. The criminal laws of England were introduced into Canada, and the crown reserved to itself the right of establishing courts of civil, criminal, and ecclesiastical jurisdiction.

The enterprise of the people was not wholly confined to the fur-trade. The mineral region upon the shores of Lake Superior had been visited as early as 1773; a project was formed for working the copper ore discovered there, and a company in England had obtained a charter for that object. This company consisted of the Duke of Gloucester, Mr. Secretary Townshend, Sir Samuel Tutchet, Bart., Mr. Baxter, consul of the Empress of Russia, Mr. Cruikshank, Sir William Johnston, Bart., Mr. Bostwick, and Alexander Henry, the English fur-trader who figured so conspicuously in the fall of Michilimackinac. A sloop was accordingly purchased, and the miners commenced their operations. They soon found, however, that the expenses of blasting and of transportation were too great to warrant the prosecution of the enterprise, and it was abandoned. Previous to this, a company of English adventurers had embarked in the same project, but they also gave it up on account, as they said, "of the distracted state of affairs in America."

In 1783 several influential merchants, who had been individually engaged in the fur-trade, entered into partnership for its more vigorous prosecution, though without any charter, and established what was styled the Northwest Company. The stock of this company was divided into sixteen shares. No money was paid in, but each of the partners engaged to furnish his proportion of the goods necessary to carry on the trade.

In 1787 the shareholders appointed from their number special agents to import from England such goods as might be required, and to store them at Montreal. The plan they adopted for conducting the trade was similar to that which had been pursued by the French. The European goods were, by the orders of the agents, made into such articles as were wanted by the traders and Indians, and packed up and forwarded, and the money for the outfits was also supplied by them.

Storehouses were erected in convenient and accessible situations on the borders of the lakes, and the posts formerly occupied by the French were employed for the same purpose. Connected with these there were also trading-houses and places where the various persons employed in carrying on the trade might be accommodated. Agents were sent to Detroit, Mackinaw, the Saute de Ste. Marie, and the Grand Portage near Lake Superior, where the furs were deposited when brought from the interior, and whose business it was to have them packed and sent to Montreal for shipment to England.

The most important point of the fur-trade was the Grand Portage of Lake Superior, situated in a remote region to the northwest, where the greatest quantity of furs could be collected. Here the proprietors of the establishment, the guides, clerks, and interpreters, messed together in a large hall hung round with elk-horns, ornamented pipes, hatchets, and other implements used by the Indians in war and peace, while the canoe-men, or *coureurs des bois*, were allowed nothing but a dish which they called "hommony," consisting of Indian corn boiled in a strong alkali and seasoned with fat.

The persons employed in this traffic were a motley and very peculiar race. Besides the clerks, interpreters, and guides, there was a numerous body, half Indian and half French, which had been constantly increasing in this quarter from the frequent intermarriages between the traders and the native women. The canoes employed by them were of large size, each one being capable of containing ten men and about sixty-five packages of furs.

The European goods purchased for this traffic consisted of blankets, cutlery, glass beads, and other trinkets, besides different articles that were obtained at Montreal.

These goods were ordered from England the season before they were wanted, shipped from London the following spring, and arrived in Canada early in the summer. Here they were made up into packages of a convenient size, weighing each about ninety pounds, sent to the interior the next spring, exchanged for furs during the succeeding winter, and the following autumn these furs were received at Montreal and shipped for London.

Thus this interesting trade, which had been carried on for more than a century, still continued to circulate in its ordinary channels along the waters of the lakes. But the spirit of mercantile rivalry was carried to a great extent, and, unhappily, excited all the worst passions in the human breast. The Hudson's Bay and Northwest Companies, the respective boundaries of which were not very clearly defined, came into active and desperate collision, and made repeated attacks upon the trading-posts of each other. Lord Selkirk, however, having placed himself at the head of the Hudson's Bay Company, succeeded at length in uniting the stock of the two companies, and thus put an end to the strife. These two companies held dominion over the territory bordering on the lakes, and studied only to keep it a barren, howling waste, that they might the better fill their own coffers.

The American Revolution was now about to break forth. The people of the English colonies at the East had declared that they would not submit to be taxed by the mother-country unless they were represented in the British Parliament. A duty having been imposed upon tea, a vessel lying in Boston harbor with a quantity of it on board had been taken possession of by a party of the inhabitants, and the obnoxious article was thrown into the sea. From this may be dated the commencement of a struggle which, in the desperation with which it was fought and the magnitude of its results, is scarcely paralleled in history.

During this eventful struggle, the wilderness then comprising the territory of the present State of Michigan, with but a small population, consisting principally of British soldiers and persons connected with the fur-trade, from its remote situation was but little affected by the war, though the Indians within its borders were employed to harass the American settlements upon the frontiers of New York, Pennsylvania, and Virginia.

Detroit and Michilimackinac were, during this period, the points of greatest interest. At these posts the Indian warriors were assembled and furnished with arms and ammunition, and from thence they were despatched against the nearest American settlements, to pillage, burn, and destroy, and to massacre and scalp the defenceless inhabitants. On their return from their murderous expeditions, these savage allies were met by the British commanders in the council-houses of Mackinaw and Detroit, and there received the stipulated price for the scalps which they brought.

It is not to be wondered at that the European inhabitants of Michigan and Canada should have been opposed to the doctrines of the American Revolution. The French population had been accustomed to a despotic government, and from habit were little inclined to any other; while the English colonists were mere adventurers, and had come to the country for no other reason than to benefit their fortunes by its trade. They were, therefore, actuated by a totally different spirit from that which animated the inhabitants of the original English colonies, who were fixed in their habits, and who had fled from the persecutions of the people of England, that they might enjoy, undisturbed, the right of self-government in matters of religion.

Not only were parties of Indians sent out against the American settlements, but in some instances they were supported by the regular troops and the local militia. One of these joint expeditions, commanded by Captain Byrd, set out from Detroit to attack Louisville. It proceeded in boats as far as it could ascend the Maumee river, and from thence crossed over to the Ohio; but the high water here preventing them from reaching the place for which they started, they marched to what is called Ruddle's Station. The formidable force which they presented intimidated the garrison at this post, and it immediately surrendered, under the promise of being protected from the Indians. This promise, however, was violated, and the prisoners were all massacred. A small stockade, called Martin's Station, was likewise taken by the same commander, and his advance threw the whole region into the utmost consternation, when he suddenly withdrew.

Another expedition started from Detroit under the command of Henry Hamilton, the commandant of the post. At that time the feeble settlements in what now comprises Kentucky were much exposed to the hostile inroads of the savages, and General Clarke, an officer of great bravery and experience, had been sent by the Governor of Virginia for their defence. Supposing that he could better accomplish his object by reducing Kaskaskia, Kahokia, and other small French settlements in this region, which were believed to be friendly to the British cause, he descended the river and took possession of them.

Governor Hamilton was no sooner informed of these proceedings than he collected a force of regulars, militia, and Indians and proceeded to St. Vincent, where he halted to make arrangements for active operations as soon as the season would permit. His design was to recover the posts which had been captured by General Clarke, to attack and defeat the force under his command, and destroy the infant settlements of the Americans in this region.

General Clarke was soon advised of the movements of Hamilton. A Spanish merchant informed him that this officer was extremely careless in his operations, and that he had sent a part of his force to the Ohio river to destroy the settlements along its banks. The American general accordingly despatched an armed boat to the Wabash, with orders to her commander not to permit anything to pass that river, while he himself set out with one hundred and thirty men for the same point, although in the depth of winter. Sixteen days were occupied in crossing the country, the soldiers sometimes marching up to their breasts in water along the shores of the Wabash, that stream having overflowed its banks. As soon as they arrived at St. Vincent, the soldiers were drawn up in order of battle, and, with the trunk of a tree formed in the shape of a cannon, they boldly advanced to attack the British post. Governor Hamilton, supposing that he was about to be assailed by artillery, immediately surrendered. The British were suffered to return to Detroit; but their commander, who was known to have been active in instigating the Indians to commit the greatest barbarities, was placed in irons and sent to Virginia as a prisoner of war.

Still some of the savages were not well affected to the British cause. As early as 1776 the Delawares had received a message from the Hurons of Detroit, requesting them to "*keep their shoes in readiness* to unite with their warriors." Netawatwees, however, the chief of the Delawares, who wished to remain neutral, would not listen to this proposal, but sent to the Huron chief in return several belts of wampum, admonishing him at the same time to keep quiet, and to remember the misery which the Hurons had formerly brought upon themselves by engaging in wars on the side of the French. The reply of the Delawares was delivered in the presence of De Peyster, the English commandant, who cut the belts of wampum in pieces, threw them on the ground, and commanded the messengers who brought them instantly to quit the country.

Certain Moravian missionaries, who were engaged in their peaceful and pious labors on the banks of the Muskingum, did not escape the suspicions of the English in this quarter. These disinterested and charitable men were accused of holding a secret correspondence with the Congress at Philadelphia, and of contributing their influence, as well as that of their Indian congregation, to aid the American cause.

The Indian agent was therefore sent to Niagara, and a grand council of the Iroquois was assembled, at which those tribes were urged to break up the Indian congregation collected by the Moravians. Not wishing, however, to have anything to do with it, they sent a message to the Chippewas and Ottawas, with a belt, stating that they gave the Indian congregation into their hands "to make soup of."

In 1781 the Moravian missionaries arrived at Detroit, where they were immediately brought before De Peyster, the English commandant. A war council was held at the same time, when the council-house was completely filled, the different tribes being arranged on either side. The assembly was addressed in a long speech by Captain Pipe, the principal chief of the Wolf tribe, who had committed the most savage barbarities upon the scattered American settlements. He told the commandant "that the English might fight the Americans if they chose: 'it was their cause, and not his; that they had raised a quarrel among themselves, and that it was their business to fight it out. They had set him on the Americans," he said, "as the hunter sets his dog upon the game." By the side of the British commander stood a war-chief, with a stick in his hand four feet in length strung with American scalps. "Now, father," said he, presenting the stick and addressing himself to the commandant, "here is what has been done with the hatchet you gave me. I have made the use of it that you ordered me to do, and found it sharp."

It was by such influences that these savage tribes were instigated to commit the most atrocious cruelties against the defenceless American settlements on the frontiers during the whole course of the Revolutionary war.

Every avenue was closed whereby a different influence might be introduced among them, and they were made to believe that the Americans were only seeking to possess themselves of their lands, and to drive them away from the territory they had inherited from their forefathers.

But, after the country from Maine to Florida had been drenched with blood in this great contest for freedom, the American cause was at last triumphant; and by the treaty of peace concluded at Versailles in 1783, an end was at last temporarily put to these barbarities; the distant settlers were permitted once more to resume their labors and to sleep without alarm.

ORGANIZATION OF THE NORTHWESTERN TERRITORY.

But, although the war was at an end, the posts and trading stations along the lakes, within the acknowledged limits of the United States, were not given up. Of the real causes which induced the British Government, in violation of all the principles of good faith, to retain these posts, we have no means of judging. It may, however, be fairly inferred from the conduct of individuals, that if that Government did not actually and by direct means promote the Indian war which broke out at this time, it did not, to say the least, discountenance it.

There is ample evidence to show that British emissaries were sent to the remote Indian tribes on the borders of the lakes to instigate them to take up arms, and that, after they had done so, they looked for aid from the English garrisons within the American territory. In the treaty of peace of 1783, there was no express stipulation in regard to the surrender of the northwestern posts; but by the second article of Jay's treaty, in 1794, it was agreed that the British troops should be withdrawn from all the posts assigned to the United States by the former treaty (of 1783) on or before the first day of June, 1796.

The conduct of England in so long persisting in retaining possession of a country which did not belong to her, we shall not pretend to account for; but the value of this country, from the richness of its soil and its other advantages, soon began to attract attention.

Measures were accordingly taken for its temporary government. The circumstance which had more particularly directed the public attention to this western domain was a memorial from the soldiers and officers of the Revolutionary army, presented to General Washington in 1783, setting forth their claims to a portion of the public lands. Nothing, however, was granted to them at that time.

The country had been completely exhausted by the terrible struggle in which it had been so long engaged, and, heavily burdened with debt, it was now seeking for some means by which it could secure its liquidation; and, as the war had been prosecuted for the general good, it was held that the States claiming lands in this quarter were bound to grant portions of them for this object. The territory northwest of the Ohio was claimed by several of the Eastern States, on the ground that it was included within the limits indicated by their charters from the English Crown. In answer to the wishes of the Government and people, these States, in a patriotic spirit, surrendered their claims to this extensive territory, that it might constitute a common fund to aid in the payment of the national debt.

To prepare the way for this cession, a law had been passed in October, 1780, that the territory so to be ceded should be disposed of for the common benefit of the whole Union; that the States erected therein should be of suitable extent, not less than one hundred nor more than one hundred and fifty miles square; and that any expenses that might be incurred in recovering the posts then in the hands of the British should be reimbursed.

New York released her claims to Congress on the 1st of March, 1781; Virginia on the 1st of the same month, 1784; Massachusetts on the 19th of April, 1785; and Connecticut on the 4th of September, 1786.

Meanwhile, the Iroquois, in 1784, conveyed to the United States all their right to any lands west of Pennsylvania; and on the 1st of January, 1785, by the treaty of Fort McIntosh, the Ottawas, Chippewas, Delawares, and Wyandots surrendered all the lands claimed by them south of the Ohio, a belt of territory six miles broad, commencing at the River Raisin and extending along the strait to Lake St. Clair, a tract of twelve miles square at the Rapids of the Maumee, together with the Islands of Bois Blanc and Mackinaw, and also a tract six miles by three on the mainland, to the north of the last-mentioned island. These different cessions having been obtained from the native tribes, in 1787 a government was organized for this extensive region, which received the name of the *Northwest Territory.*

It is unnecessary here to examine particularly the details of this ordinance: it was based on the principles of civil liberty maintained in the Magna Charta of England, re-enacted in the Bill of Rights, and incorporated into our different State constitutions. This ordinance, it is well known, was drawn up by Nathan Dane, of Beverly, Massachusetts, a benevolent and excellent man, and a distinguished lawyer, who was the compiler of a very valuable abridgment of American Law, and the founder of the Dane Law School in the University of Cambridge.

On the 7th of April, 1788, a company of forty-seven individuals landed at the spot where Marietta now stands, and there commenced the settlement of Ohio. The first code of laws for this territory was published by nailing them to the body of a tree upon the banks of the Muskingum, and Return Jonathan Meigs was appointed to administer them, the Governor, Arthur St. Clair, not having yet arrived.

We have seen that the Western posts were still retained by the British Government, notwithstanding the peace concluded in 1783. Several questions of no little interest had sprung up, which excited unfriendly feelings between the two nations and governed their policy. Debts due by Americans to British subjects, the payment of which had been guaranteed by the treaty, were not paid; and, on the other hand, the slaves belonging to American citizens, and who had been taken away by the British officers, were not restored. In consequence of this unsettled state of things, when the Baron Steuben was sent by General Washington to Sir Frederic Haldimand at Quebec to arrange matters for the occupation of these posts, with instructions to proceed to Michigan and along the line of the lake frontier for the purpose of taking possession of them, he was informed that they would not be given up, and was refused passports to Niagara and Detroit.

Combined with the retention of the posts, a new confederacy among the savages was evidently organizing in the West. As early as December, 1786, a grand council of the different tribes was held near the mouth of the Detroit river. At this council were delegates from the Six Nations, from the Hurons, the Ottawas, the Miamis, the Shawanese, the Chippewas, the Cherokees, the Delawares, the Pottowatamies, and from the confederates of the Wabash. The principal subject of discussion at this council appears to have been a question of boundary. It was contended by the Indians that the United States had no right to cross the Ohio river, but they advised a pacific line of policy so long as there was no actual encroachment upon their territory. The design of this discussion undoubtedly was to create a belief that the Americans intended to drive them from their lands, and, as was said, to "kindle their council fires wherever they thought proper, without consulting the Indians." The American Government, indeed, considered that the treaty of 1783 vested in them jurisdiction over the Indian territory, a claim which the native occupants were by no means disposed to admit. At this time, also, the United States were at issue with a foreign Power respecting the right of navigating the Mississippi.

Among other things, as a plea for still retaining the Western posts, it was pretended by the English that the extensive and valuable country in which they were situated had been ceded away through some oversight on the part of the commissioners, or from their ignorance of the geography of the country. But the real motives by which they were actuated are sufficiently manifest. They had already succeeded in exciting hostile feelings among the Indian tribes, and this they were determined to take advantage of for the purpose of preventing this broad and fertile region from passing out of their hands.

Many of the half-breeds were also active in seconding the views of the English, not only by inflaming the minds of the Indians, but by promising to take up arms in their cause, from a belief that if they did not thus side with them they would not afterward be suffered to trade in their territory. Meanwhile Alexander McKenzie, an agent of the British Government, visited Detroit, painted like a savage, and stated that he had just returned from the remote tribes of the upper lakes, who were all in arms, and prepared to oppose the claims of the Americans to the Western lands; that large bodies of warriors had already assembled, and that they were about to attack the infant settlements of Virginia and Ohio. The artifice practised by McKenzie succeeded to his wish; and he could the better operate upon the prejudices and passions of the Indians as he spoke their language perfectly well. Elliot and the notorious Simon Girty were no less active in exciting the savages to war.

In 1794 an agent was sent from the Spanish settlements on the banks of the Mississippi for the same object, and to hasten the organization of the Indian confederacy against the United States. "Children," said he to his savage auditors, "you see me on my feet grasping the tomahawk to strike them, (the Americans.) We will strike together. I do not desire you to go before me in the front, but to follow me. Children, you hear what these distant nations have said to us, so that we have nothing to do but to put our designs into immediate execution, and to forward this pipe to the three warlike nations who have been so long struggling for their country. Tell them to smoke this pipe, and to forward it to all the lake Indians and to their Northern brethren. Then nothing will be wanting to complete our general union from the rising to the setting of the sun, and all the nations will be ready to add strength to the blow we are going to strike." Excited by these various means, bands of savage warriors, armed with the tomahawk and scalping-knife, were seen hastening towards the lake posts, and another great Indian confederacy was formed, consisting of the Ottawas, the Pottowatamies, the Wyandots, the Miamis, the Chippewas, and the Delawares.

As early as 1785 and 1786 the hostile Indians had occasionally sent their war-parties against the feeble frontier settlements in Kentucky and along the banks of the Ohio, where a few enterprising emigrants from Virginia and New England had erected their little clusters of log-cabins.

These border incursions, which most clearly appear to have been countenanced by the British, induced the American Government in 1790 to send into that quarter General Josiah Harmar, an accomplished and able officer, to put a stop to them. He advanced against the hostile tribes with a force amounting to fourteen hundred men; but, imprudently dividing his army, he was taken by surprise and defeated by a body of Indians led on by that sanguinary and desperate warrior, the Little Turtle.

General Harmar, having failed in his enterprise, was succeeded by Major General St. Clair, the Governor of the Northwestern Territory; and in October, 1792, this officer advanced into the Indian country with a force of about two thousand men. Warned as he was by the disaster that had proved so fatal to his predecessor, he fell into an ambuscade that had been laid for him, where the Indians, firing from behind their breastwork of fallen trees, carried destruction into the American ranks, and soon covered the ground with their dead. So sudden and unexpected was the attack, and so murderous the fire of the enemy, that the general was compelled to order a retreat, leaving his artillery in the hands of the savages.

On account of these repeated disasters, it became necessary to increase the army by enlistments, and to push a still stronger force against the hostile Indian tribes. General Washington therefore made the most strenuous efforts to effect this object; but, owing to the panic produced by the disastrous defeats of Harmar and St. Clair, with but little success. There was, moreover, no small opposition to the war; and additional measures were deemed necessary to bring it to a close.

In 1793 General St. Clair was succeeded by General Anthony Wayne in the command of the Western army. Advancing through the forests to the spot which had been rendered memorable by the defeat of St. Clair, he there constructed a fort upon the site of the old fortification, and called it Fort Recovery. Situated in the midst of the scene of former carnage, there might then have been seen around it, under the trees and amid the fallen logs, the bleached bones of those who had been slain.

General Wayne soon reached the confluence of the Au Glaze and Maumee rivers, and found the villages spread along the bottoms of the latter completely deserted. A short time afterward he arrived at the Rapids of the Maumee, and erected there a fort about four miles above the British post, which he called Fort Deposite, in which he placed his stores and baggage. This British post, established on American ground, had been fortified by a detachment sent from Detroit the preceding spring, and the Indians appeared to look upon it as their last refuge in case they were attacked.

The British Government had demanded, before the treaty of 1783, as one of the conditions of peace, the complete independence of the savage tribes, with, of course, the power to grant their lands to whomsoever they pleased. The Americans having refused to accede to this condition, that post was established on the banks of the Miami for the purpose, it was believed, of countenancing the Indians, and of actively supporting them should they gain the ascendancy. General Wayne therefore felt it necessary to advance with the utmost caution, as everything depended not only upon his courage, but his prudence. He had been directed, however, in case he was opposed by the British, to treat them according to the usages of war.

The American commander was not long in coming up with his savage foe. The Indians regarding him with great fear from his supposed cunning, calling him the *Blacksnake* on that account; while the American army, consisting of three thousand men, no doubt presented a truly formidable appearance to them.

The Indian force, their whole strength being collected at this point, was in point of numbers about the same. Most of the savages were naked and painted for battle. Stationed in a dense forest, and protected by the rocky bank of the river and a breastwork of fallen trees, they were disposed in three lines within supporting distance of each other.

Wayne's Legion consisted of two thousand regulars and one thousand mounted militia, under General Scott, of Kentucky. The right flank of his army rested on the river, a brigade of mounted volunteers under General Todd occupied the left, and General Babee, with his division, formed the rear. Major Price was ordered to advance with a select battalion of riflemen to reconnoitre, and, if attacked, to retreat in pretended confusion, in order to entice the enemy towards the main body. The stratagem proved successful; and while the savages were rushing forward and startling the wilderness with their yells of triumph, the American army advanced against them with trailed arms, being ordered to press them with the bayonet, to rouse them from their lurking-places, and deliver a close fire upon their backs, so as to allow them no opportunity to escape. The Indians now began to break, and retreated towards the walls of Fort Maumee. While these events were taking place, the gates of the fort had been shut, and the English within gazed with apparent indifference upon the scene. In the action there was actually engaged on the side of the savages a force from Detroit, headed by a prominent individual of that place. General Wayne destroyed the Indian villages and the cornfields on the banks of the Maumee, and proceeded towards Fort Defiance.

Before he left the battle-ground, however, he paraded his force in front of the British post, that they might see its strength, while he advanced with his staff towards the glacis to examine the character of the position, and to ascertain, as far as was possible, what were the intentions of the garrison. The American officers, as they drew near, could discover the British soldiers, with matches lighted and standing by their guns, ready for any emergency that might arise. Some attempts were made by his officers to persuade the British commander to revenge this insulting parade before his post by allowing them to salute the Americans with a discharge from their artillery. Nothing of this kind, however, was permitted, though a correspondence of no very friendly character took place. General Wayne finally succeeded in concluding a treaty with the Indians at Greenville, which effectually broke up the confederacy.

The settlements in Michigan up to this period had advanced but slowly. The French Canadians had extended their farms to a considerable distance along the banks of the St. Clair; and on the Detroit river there were a few straggling French settlements, as also on Otter Creek, and on the rivers Rouge, Pointe aux Tremble, and other small streams flowing into Lake Erie. Agriculture and the fur-trade constituted nearly the entire occupation of the inhabitants.

Detroit and Frenchtown, both in the eastern part of the peninsula, were at this time the only places of much importance. The former was merely a small cluster of rude wooden houses, defended by a fort, and surrounded by pickets, and formed, as it had long done, the principal depot for the fur-trade. The population, independent of the soldiers of the garrison, consisted principally of Scotch, French, and English merchants, who had removed here after the conquest of the country, for the prosecution of that traffic. The goods required here were obtained from Montreal, and bills of credit for small sums, payable at that place or at Quebec, were allowed to be issued by the merchants, on condition of their giving security to double their amount. Frenchtown, on the river Raisin, now a place of considerable importance, consisted at that time of only a few log cabins, erected by the French on either bank of the river. Two Indian villages, one occupied by the Ottawas, the other by the Pottowatamies, stood on the present site of the city of Monroe. Being a depot for the Northwestern Company, the surrounding Indians periodically resorted there to exchange their furs and peltry for cloths, beads, silver ornaments, fire-arms, ammunition, and such other articles as they required. The French settlers in the vicinity also disposed of their corn here in exchange for goods, and from thence it was transported to the upper lakes for the use of the traders.

About this time a project was started, which, had it been successful, would have been highly injurious to the interests of this part of the West. In 1795, Robert Randall, of Pennsylvania, and Charles Whitney, of Vermont, in connection with several merchants of Detroit, entered into a compact, the object of which was to appropriate to themselves a tract of territory comprising nearly twenty millions of acres, situated between Lakes Erie, Huron, and Michigan. This was to be done by securing to themselves the pre-emption right. The land was to be divided into forty-one shares, five of which were to be apportioned among the traders of Detroit who were parties to the agreement, six were to be given to Randall and those associated with him, and the remainder were to be distributed among members of Congress who should exert their influence in procuring the passage of the necessary law. The amount proposed to be paid for this vast tract was from half a million to a million of dollars; and it was believed that the merchants of Detroit had sufficient influence with the Indians to induce them to part with the land. In opposition to the measure, it was represented that, under the treaty of 1783, the right of purchase belonged exclusively to the United States; while, on the other hand, it was urged that the Indians were dissatisfied with this treaty, and did not consider themselves bound by it, and that the plan proposed would alone establish tranquility among them, and secure peace to the country. But, as soon as the corrupt character of the plan was discovered, the two principal projecters were brought before the bar of the House of Representatives, when, on the hearing of the evidence, Randall was discharged, but Whitney was fined to the amount of the costs which had accrued, and received a severe reprimand.

The Indian power having been broken by Wayne's victory, and the treaty of Greenville binding the savages from farther aggression, the island of Mackinaw was at last surrendered, and Detroit also given up, the retiring garrison, to show their spite, locking the gates of the fort, breaking the windows in the barracks, and filling the wells with stones, in order to annoy the new occupants as much as was in their power. The latter post was soon after taken possession of by a detachment of troops under the command of Captain Porter, and the American flag hoisted on its ramparts for the first time. Thus Michigan at last passed quietly into the possession of the United States.

While the English held this country, Mackinaw was the chief place of rendezvous for the Indians and the traders of the Northwest Company. Starting from this picturesque island in huge canoes, propelled by the *voyageurs*, the merchants would at times sweep across the sparkling waters of those inland seas, provided with the means of the most luxurious revelry, and, encamping on their shores, would there hold their feasts, surrounded by half-bred dependants, traders, and Indians.

While the French were in possession of this country, as there was but little coin for general circulation, accounts were kept in beaver-skins or other furs reduced to their current value. The price of beaver at Michilimackinac in 1765 was two shillings and sixpence the pound, Michilimackinac currency; otter-skins were six shillings each, and marten-skins one shilling and sixpence. Ten beaver-skins were given for a stroud blanket, eight for a white blanket, two for a pound of powder, one for a pound of shot or ball, twenty for a gun, two for an axe of one pound weight, and one for a knife. The notes and coin of Quebec were sometimes seen at the lake posts, but not in sufficient quantity to be relied on for a uniform currency.

CONDITION AFTER THE SURRENDER OF THE POSTS.

It was a long time after this fertile but uncultivated territory came into the possession of the United States before its character was materially changed. The Canadian French continued to form the principal part of its population. The interior of the country was but little known except by the Indians and the traders, who explored it in the pursuit of furs. As the effect of transferring the jurisdiction from France to England had been little more than to change the garrisons from French to English, and to give to the Hudson's Bay Company a monopoly of the fur-trade, so its surrender to the United States produced but little alteration in its general features. As the Indian title was not fully extinguished, no lands were brought into market, and, consequently, the settlements proceeded but very slowly.

In the division of the Northwestern Territory, what is now the State of Michigan constituted a single county, which received the name of Wayne. It sent one representative to the Legislature of the Northwestern Territory, which was held at Chilicothe. A Court of Common Pleas was organized for the county, and the general court of the whole territory sometimes met at Detroit. No roads had as yet been constructed through the interior, nor were there any settlements except on the frontiers. The habits of the people were essentially military, and but little attention was paid to agriculture except by the French peasantry. In winter they drove their carrioles over the ice with their Canadian ponies that were of Norman stock, many of which are now to be seen in this country; and in summer they employed small wooden carts, well adapted to the state of the roads, for the carriage of their goods—vehicles that are still used.

The county continued to send a representative to the General Assembly of the Northwestern Territory at Chilicothe until 1800, when Indiana was erected into a separate territory; and two years afterward it was annexed to this new-formed territory, and remained under its jurisdiction until 1805. In the month of January of that year it was erected into a separate territory, and William Hull was appointed the first governor. The system of government was somewhat peculiar, the executive power being confided in the governor, the judicial in three judges, who were authorized to "adopt and publish" laws suited to the territory, and not incompatible with the ordinance of 1787, and the legislative power was exercised by the two jointly. On the 25th of July of that year the territory was divided into three districts, namely, Erie, Huron, and Michilimackinac, for each of which a court was established, to be held by one of the judges of the Supreme Court of the territory, with exclusive jurisdiction in criminal matters, and also in all civil cases above the sum of twenty dollars, those below this sum being cognizable by justices of the peace. A few years afterward it was divided into counties, in each of which was organized a county court. The laws thus introduced were, as might be expected, crude and ill-digested, as is abundantly attested by the records of the courts at that period, which are still preserved.

General Hull, when he arrived at Detroit to assume his official duties as governor of the territory, found the town in ruins, it having been destroyed by fire. Whether this disaster had been occasioned by accident or design was not known. However this may have been, as the town was very compact, covering only two acres of ground, and the materials were of the most combustible nature, it was soon entirely consumed, and the unfortunate inhabitants were obliged to encamp in the open fields, almost destitute of food and shelter. Still they were not discouraged, and soon commenced rebuilding their houses on the same site. The General Government also took their case into consideration, and an act of Congress was passed, granting to the sufferers the site of the old town of Detroit, and ten thousand acres of land adjoining it.

A judiciary system was now adopted, and the territorial militia were organized. In October of the same year a report was made to Congress of the condition of the territory, and in May of the following year a code of laws was adopted similar to those of the original States. This code was signed by Governor Hull, Augustus B. Woodward, and Frederick Bates, judges of the territory, and was called the "Woodward Code." The bounds of the territorial government, as then established, embraced all the country on the American side of the Detroit river, east of a north and south line drawn through the centre of Lake Michigan.

The Indian land-claims had been partially extinguished previous to this period. By the treaty of Fort McIntosh in 1785, and that of Fort Harmar in 1787, extensive cessions had either been made or confirmed, and in the year 1807 the Indian titles to several tracts became entirely extinct.

In consequence of the settlements which had been made under the French and English Governments, some confusion sprang up in regard to the titles to valuable tracts that were claimed by different individuals under the French laws. Congress accordingly passed an act establishing a board of Commissioners to examine and settle these conflicting claims; and in 1807 another act was passed, confirming to a certain extent the titles of all such as had been in possession of the lands then occupied by them from the year 1796, when the territory was surrendered, down to the date of that act. Other acts were subsequently passed, extending the same conditions to the settlements on the upper lakes.

In addition to their settlements along the shores of the Detroit and St. Clair rivers, and the lake of the latter name, where there was a continued line of cottages, with farms adjoining, containing orchards of pear and apple trees, planted, probably, in the reign of Louis XIV., and the old posts on the island of Mackinaw, at Ste. Marie and at St. Joseph, the French colonists had a line of cabins on the river Raisin, where the city of Monroe (then called Frenchtown) now stands. The interior of the country was but little known except by those who were engaged in the fur-trade, and these were interested in representing it in as unfavorable a light as possible. The Indian titles to the land had been but partially extinguished, and no portion of the public domain had yet been brought into market. But few American settlers had therefore ventured into this region, though the adjoining State of Ohio had already acquired a considerable population.

The distance of this territory also, and the unsettled state of affairs along the western borders of the lakes, necessarily prevented immigration. On the opposite shore there was a jealous foreign power, and the interior of the country was occupied by different savage tribes. The territory, too, had but just emerged from an Indian war, and another was evidently preparing. This third Indian confederacy was not only countenanced by the English, but directly instigated by them. The motives which led to it, and the means employed to bring it about, were the same as had proved successful in exciting the former insurrections under Pontiac and the Little Turtle. The old story was revived, that the Americans were about to drive the Indians from their lands that they might occupy them themselves. The chief projectors of this savage league were Tecumseh and his brother the Prophet.

The warlike leader of the enterprise was Tecumseh, while the Prophet, whose Indian name was Elkswatawa, was to operate on the minds of the savages by means of superstition, and to excite in them a spirit of fanaticism still more to inflame their natural ferocity.

The disaffection of these tribes was certainly what might have been expected. They saw a new power encroaching upon the inheritance that had been handed down to them from their ancestors, introducing their hated cultivation upon their soil, and rudely disturbing the graves of their dead. It was not difficult, therefore, to unite them in one last desperate struggle to resist this aggressive and threatening power.

Their titles had been only very partially extinguished, and they complained, that where this had been done, the treaties had been unfairly conducted; that the Indians had been deceived; that they were in a state of intoxication at the time they signed away their lands, and that, even under these circumstances, only a part of the tribes had given their consent. The dissatisfaction thus existing among them was artfully fomented by the agents of the Northwest Company, who foresaw that if the Americans were permitted to occupy this country they would be cut off from a valuable portion of their trade; while the English Government, which had ceded away this extensive tract without any very definite notions of its importance or extent, looked with complacency on any attempts made by the savages to retain it in their hands. An overreaching spirit had doubtless actuated many of the pioneer settlers of the West, and wrongs had been inflicted upon the Indians which required correction. Taking advantage of this, the traders, and the English generally, were indefatigable in sowing the seeds of discontent among the savage tribes; and it was contended that they should hold the undisturbed possession of the Northwestern Territory, without surrendering the right of pre-emption to the United States.

The Prophet commenced his mission among the tribes in 1806. Taking advantage of the superstitious notions of the Indians, he told them that the Great Spirit had appeared to him in a dream, and appointed him his agent upon the earth; and that, as such, his own tribe, the Shawanese, being the oldest tribe of the West, he was commanded to direct them to form a general confederacy against the United States. He had been instructed also, he said, to proclaim to the red men that it was the will of the Great Spirit that they should throw away the arts of civilization, return to their skins for clothing, and to their bows and war-clubs for arms, renounce the intoxicating drinks of the white men for pure water, and, in a word, resume all the customs of their ancestors. The Americans, he said, had driven the Indians from the seacoast, and were now preparing to push them into the lakes, so that they had no alternative but to make a stand where they were, and drive back these insatiable intruders to the other side of the Alleghany Mountains.

The plan of this league was in many respects similar to that formed by Pontiac. Tecumseh's intention was to surprise the posts of Detroit, Fort Wayne, Chicago, St. Louis, and Vincennes, and to unite all the tribes from the borders of New York to the banks of the Mississippi.

As early as the year 1807, the Shawanese chief and his brother, the Prophet, were actively engaged in sending their emissaries, with presents and war-belts, to the most distant tribes, to induce them to join in the confederacy; and when the comet appeared in 1811, the latter artfully turned it to account, by practising on the superstitions of the savages. Thus the fame and the influence of the Prophet spread rapidly among the tribes of the Northwest.

On the 4th of May, a special mission, consisting of deputies from the Ottawas, was sent to a distant post upon the borders of Lake Superior, and a grand council being there assembled, it was addressed by Le Marquoit, or Trout. He told the Indians that he had been sent by the messenger and representative of the Great Spirit, and that he was commissioned to deliver to them a speech from the "first man whom God had created, said to be in the Shawanese country."

He then informed them what were the instructions of the Great Spirit in the succeeding address: "I am the father of the English, of the French, of the Spaniards, and of the Indians. I created the first man, who was the common father of all these people as well as of yourselves, and it is through him, whom I have awaked from his long sleep, that I now address you. But the Americans I did not make. They are not my children, but the children of the Evil Spirit. They grew from the scum of the great water when it was troubled by the Evil Spirit, and the froth was driven into the woods by a strong east wind. They are numerous, but I hate them. My children, you must not speak of this talk to the whites; it must be hidden from them. I am now on the earth, sent by the Great Spirit to instruct you. Each village must send me two or more principal chiefs, to represent you, that you may be taught. The bearer of this talk must point out to you the path to my wigwam. I could not come myself to L'Arbre Croche, because the world is changed from what it was. It is broken and leans down, and as it declines the Chippewas and all beyond will fall off and die; therefore, you must come to see me and be instructed. Those villages which do not listen to this talk will be cut off from the face of the earth."

It was by such means that the savages were roused to attack the frontier settlements of the West, and afterward to unite with the English in their war with the United States. In consequence of these menacing movements of the Indians, it was considered advisable to construct a stockade around the town of Detroit for its defence. The population was as yet small. There had been, indeed, up to that time but little to encourage the settlement of the country. The land had not been offered for sale, and a great portion of Western New York was still unoccupied: not a single steamer navigated the lakes, nor had any roads been made into the interior.

Nor was the neighborhood of Detroit without symptoms of Indian disaffection. In September, 1809, a special council of the Hurons was called near Brownstown, and, at the instigation of their principal chief, Walk-in-the-Water, they freely spoke of their grievances to Governor Hull. The speech addressed by this chief to the governor, setting forth the title of his tribe to a large tract of territory near the mouth of the Detroit river, which was claimed by the United States under the treaty of Greenville, shows how much dissatisfied they were with this treaty, and with the encroachments of the Americans upon their soil. In the midst of all these evidences of discontent on the part of the Indians, Michigan remained in a comparatively defenceless state. There were at this time in the whole territory but nine settlements of any importance; nor was the character of the population at these points such that it could be expected to oppose any very active resistance in the conflict which seemed to be approaching.

These settlements were situated on the rivers Miami and Raisin, on the Huron of Lake Erie, on the Ecorce, Rouge, and Detroit rivers, on the Huron of St. Clair, the St. Clair river, and the island of Mackinaw; and, in addition to these, there was here and there a group of huts belonging to the French fur-traders. The villages upon the Maumee, the Raisin, and the Huron of Lake Erie contained a population of about thirteen hundred; the post of Detroit and the settlements on the rivers Rouge and Ecorce and on the Huron of St. Clair numbered two thousand two hundred; the island of Mackinaw, with the small detached log-houses, about a thousand; Detroit was garrisoned by ninety-four men, and Mackinaw by seventy-nine. Thus the entire population of the State was only about four thousand eight hundred, four-fifths of whom were Canadian French, and the remainder chiefly Americans, with a few English and Scotch.

As there was no longer any doubt of the hostile intentions of the savages, it was deemed prudent to present a memorial to Congress, setting forth the defenceless condition of the territory and praying for aid from that body. Accordingly, on the 27th of December, 1811, such a petition was drawn up, signed by the principal inhabitants of Detroit, and forwarded to Washington.

The joint efforts of Tecumseh and the Prophet were successful in drawing a large body of Indians, probably not less than eight hundred, from the shores of Lake Superior to the station of the latter at Tippecanoe, though it is supposed that one-third of their number died of want and hardship on the way. Their plans were now nearly ripe for action, and parties of the Ottawas, the Miamis, the Chippewas, the Wyandots, the Mississagies, the Shawanese, and the Winnebagoes were to be seen with their bodies painted for war, and again seizing the hatchet.

The first hostile demonstrations were made against the French settlements, where bands of strange warriors made their appearance, armed for battle, and painted in the most hideous manner, with feathers stuck in their hair, and strings of bears' claws about their necks, entering the houses by force, taking whatever they chose, and wantonly destroying with their tomahawks the beehives in the gardens of the settlers. Near the banks of the Kalamazoo, in the county of the same name, a smith's forge had been set up, where hatchets and knives were made for the approaching contest: and at no great distance from it, in a retired spot, surrounded by a dense forest, the Indian women, with their children, had collected, for the purpose of raising corn to furnish a supply of food for the warriors.

Still more flagrant acts of aggression were perpetrated in the State of Indiana, where numerous murders were committed, and horses and other property stolen. It had been for some time noticed that the savages were collecting about the Prophet's station, apparently with no friendly design. A conference was therefore held, in which it was insisted that these hordes should be made to return to their homes, that the property which had been stolen from the Americans should be restored, and that the murderers should be given up.

Tecumseh, on his part, denied that any league, such as was complained of, had been formed, and protested that he and his brother had no other object in collecting the tribes together but to strengthen the amicable relations between them, and to improve their moral condition. In regard to the murderers of the whites, who were alleged to have taken refuge among his tribe, he denied that they were there, saying, at the same time, that even if they were they ought to be forgiven, as he had forgiven the whites who had murdered his own people in Illinois.

All their plans having been fully matured, the contest at length began in earnest, on the banks of the Wabash, at the Prophet's town; and, while the battle was raging, the Prophet was seen on an adjoining eminence singing a war-song to inflame with greater desperation the savage combatants. It was now no longer doubtful that another fierce and obstinate struggle was to be encountered. The Indian warriors, excited by fanaticism and a thirst for blood, in opposition to their chiefs, hastened from all sides towards the lake frontier to join Tecumseh. Meanwhile, the English on the opposite shores were looking with no small interest upon what was passing, regarding the savages as important allies to their own cause in the conflict in which they expected shortly to be engaged. "My son," said one of their agents to an Indian chief, "keep your eyes fixed on me. My tomahawk is now up; be you ready, but do not strike till I give the signal."

The statement of the fact should not be omitted that about this time the American Fur Company was formed, under the auspices of Mr. John Jacob Astor, of New York. Its operations were carried on much after the manner of the old French and English companies, by establishing chains of posts along the lake shores. This company annually collected a great quantity of furs, which were sent by the way of the Mississippi or the lakes to New York, from whence a large part of them were exported to foreign countries. They had also an extensive fishery on Lake Superior, where they took great quantities of trout and whitefish, which were salted, packed in barrels, and sent to the different ports of the adjoining country. But the company is now virtually extinct.

WAR BETWEEN GREAT BRITAIN AND THE UNITED STATES.

In June, 1812, war was declared between Great Britain and the United States. Without entering into particulars as to the causes of this war, suffice it to say that it was chiefly provoked by the continued impressment of American seamen, the unjust capture of American vessels, and the enforcement of illegal blockades.

Governor Hull, the year before, had represented to the General Government the exposed and defenceless condition of Michigan. That the posts at Detroit, Mackinaw, and Chicago were badly fortified and with insufficient garrisons, while at no great distance from them there was a large body of British subjects, who could, in case of war, be brought against them; that the whole American force consisted of but about five thousand men, whereas the militia of Canada amounted to more than one hundred thousand; and that the forests about Detroit were filled with hostile savages, who were secretly pledged to the confederacy of Tecumseh. This post he represented as of great importance, inasmuch as it commanded a wide extent of country, and furnished a point of support for operations against the Indians of the upper lakes. He proposed, therefore, that a powerful naval armament should be equipped on Lake Erie, sufficient to command that inland sea, and to co-operate effectively with the force at Detroit; or, if that were not done, that a strong detachment of troops should be marched from Niagara, to act in conjunction with those under his command in the invasion of the British provinces.

A body of troops was soon collected at Dayton, in Ohio, consisting of about twelve hundred men, raised by order of the President of the United States, and their number was somewhat increased by volunteers. These troops were formed into three regiments, under the command of Colonels McArthur, Finelly, and Cass, and a fourth regiment, about three hundred strong, under Colonel Miller, afterward joined them, the whole being under the command of General Hull, the governor of Michigan.

With this force the general marched from Dayton towards Detroit, and soon arrived at the Maumee of the lakes. The dense forests through which they had to pass, wholly without roads, opposed formidable obstacles to their progress. At the rapids of the Maumee a vessel was procured for the transportation of the sick soldiers, and of such bulky articles as would encumber the army. As this vessel was proceeding for Detroit by the way of the channel leading to Malden, she was captured by the British, who communicated to the Americans the first news of the declaration of war.

On the fifth of July General Hull arrived at Detroit, where his troops immediately set themselves to work to prepare for the coming contest. Four days afterward he received a communication from the Secretary of War, investing him with discretionary power either to seize Malden and advance into Canada, or to remain on the defensive. That place formed the most prominent and commanding position upon this part of the lake coast, and its possession would give him advantages in any future operations against the provinces of Canada.

He therefore crossed the Detroit river with his army, and established himself at Sandwich. From his headquarters at this place he issued a proclamation* addressed to the Canadians, setting forth his object in invading their country, and inviting them to place themselves under the protection of the United States; protesting, at the same time, against the barbarity of employing the savages, and threatening indiscriminate retaliation against all who should be found fighting by their side. It was hoped that by this means the French Canadians would be induced either to join the Americans or remain neutral.

Many of the American officers were anxious to proceed immediately to the attack of Malden, but it was determined to wait for heavy artillery to be brought from Detroit. The army, therefore, remained quietly at Sandwich, merely sending out occasional foraging parties to procure provisions.

General Hull wished to ascertain what was the actual state of things at Malden, and he accordingly detached Colonel Cass, with two hundred and eighty men, to reconnoitre that position. On reaching the river Canard, he dislodged a picket-guard of the enemy, killing ten of their number, and seizing the bridge which they had been stationed there to defend. This bridge was only about four miles from Malden, and Colonel Cass was anxious to keep possession of it, to aid them in their contemplated attack upon that place. This, however, was thought inexpedient by General Hull, as such a course, he said, would bring on a general engagement, which he wished at that moment to avoid, as his artillery had not yet arrived, and a considerable detachment had been sent away from his army.

While the Americans were thus stationary at Sandwich, a British force was despatched from the Canada side to take possession of the island of Mackinaw. The whole garrison of this post was only fifty-seven men, under the command of Lieutenant Hanks; and the first intimation which this officer received of the declaration of war was the arrival of a body of British troops, supported by more than a thousand Indian warriors, consisting of Sioux, Winnebagoes, Talleswain Ottawas, and Chippewas. The savages, it appears, had been directed, in case of resistance, to show no quarter, and

* This energetic and well-written address is said to have been from the pen of Governor, then Colonel Cass.

the odds being so fearfully against him, the American officer immediately surrendered. A detachment, under the command of Capt. Brush, had been sent by Governor Meigs, of Ohio, to escort a quantity of provisions destined for the American army, and General Hull, being informed that a body of Indians had left Malden to intercept this convoy, despatched Major Van Horn, with two hundred men, for its protection. On arriving at Brownstown this detachment was suddenly attacked by the savages, who, from behind a breastwork of logs and the trunks of trees, opened a deadly fire upon the American troops. Major Van Horn, finding himself unable to contend against the superior numbers of the enemy, retreated to Detroit, leaving eighteen of his men dead on the field.

The ordnance he was waiting for from Detroit not having arrived, on the 8th of August General Hull convened a council of war for the purpose of deciding what should be done, when it was determined to remain two days longer, and at the expiration of that time to make an attempt upon Malden at all hazards. Information, however, having been received in the meantime that the garrison at Malden had been re-enforced, General Hull changed his resolution, withdrew his army from the British territory, and retired to Detroit. The reasons he assigned for so unexpected a movement were, that General Brock was on his way to Malden with a considerable body of fresh troops; that his communication with Detroit was in danger of being cut off; and that the savage bands from the upper lakes, having no farther occupation in that quarter, would soon be pouring down upon him.

As it was important to open a communication with the River Raisin, that the army might receive the supplies sent from Ohio, six hundred men, under Lieutenant-Colonel Miller, had been detached to Frenchtown by General Hull for that object, the day that he crossed the Detroit river. Scarcely had this body reached Monguagon, when they were attacked by a superior force of British and Indians, the latter led on by Tecumseh, who opened upon them a destructive fire from their usual lurking-places behind trees and fallen timber, and in thickets of brushwood. The enemy being protected by a dense forest on the left, Colonel Miller advanced into it with his whole line, ordering his men to deliver a single fire, and then charge with the bayonet. This was gallantly done, and the British, as well as their savage allies, gave way before the fury of the onset. But, though thrown into confusion and broken, they still continued to fight with the utmost desperation. Tecumseh, although wounded, was seen in the thickest of the battle, and his shrill warcry was heard above the fire of the musketry. An Indian, whose leg had been broken by a musket-ball, while writhing with the agony of his wound, loaded his rifle and shot an American horseman. Many of the savages had stationed themselves in the tops of the trees, from which they discharged their rifles and arrows with deadly aim. The British force was commanded by Major Muir, of the forty-first regiment, and was four hundred strong without the Indians. The American loss in the action was ten non-commissioned officers and privates killed and forty-five wounded of the regular troops, and eight killed and forty-five wounded of the Ohio and Michigan volunteers. The British retreated under the cover of their armed vessels, which were anchored in the Detroit river, while the savages scattered themselves in the woods.

It was now determined to bring in the supplies needed for the army by a more circuitous route, and Colonels McArthur and Cass, with three hundred and fifty of the best troops, were detached from Detroit on the 13th of August for that object.

On the 14th the British General Brock arrived at Malden, and, advancing immediately to Sandwich with all his forces, the following day he summoned General Hull to surrender. "It is far from my intention," he said, "to join in a war of extermination, but you must be aware that the numerous bodies of Indians who have attached themselves to my troops will be beyond my control the moment the contest commences." To this menace the American general answered, "I have no other reply to make than that I am prepared to meet any force which may be at your disposal."

The character of General Hull seems to have been well understood by the British commander. Indeed, in addition to the evidence he had given of indecision in not advancing against Malden, it was alleged that a portion of his correspondence, found on board an American vessel captured near that place, but too clearly evinced a want of those qualities which should distinguish a military commander.

Tecumseh, with his warriors, was at this time with the British general, to aid him in his projected attack upon the American post; and the latter, being anxious to acquire some knowledge of the country around Detroit, that he might avail himself of it in case he should from any cause be obliged to retreat into the neighboring forest, applied to this chief for information. Tecumseh took a strip of elm bark, stretched it upon the ground, and placed a stone upon each corner. Then with his scalping-knife he delineated upon it an accurate representation of the country, with its swamps, woods, and rivers. Pleased with this display of ingenuity, and to show his gratitude for the important services which this renowned chief had rendered to the British cause, Brock took his sash from his waist and presented it to him. The savage, however, would not wear it, but gave it to the Wyandot chief, Round-Head, "because," said he, "he is an older and better warrior than I am." Before the British crossed to the American side, their commander expressed a hope that the Indians, in case Detroit was taken, would not massacre the defenceless inhabitants. "No," answered Tecumseh; "I despise them too much to have anything to do with them."

As soon as he received the refusal to capitulate, Brock commenced a cannonade upon the American fort from across the river. This was answered from the opposite shore with considerable effect. An armed vessel being now seen about a mile below Detroit, it was supposed that the British intended to cross there, and Captain Snelling was detached with a body of troops to prevent it. It was suggested at the same time that a single piece of heavy ordnance would compel the British armed vessel to remove from her position, and keep the enemy from landing. This advice, however, was disregarded, and Captain Snelling was recalled to the fort by break of day.

Very early on the morning of the 16th the whole British force was seen slowly crossing the river under cover of their armed vessels, and they soon landed and advanced to Springwells without opposition. Here they halted, while the British general sent a second summons to the commander of the American post to surrender. It was not long, however, before the enemy was again seen advancing, his force being composed of regulars and of volunteers dressed in British uniforms, approaching nearer and nearer, as they moved deliberately through the forest bordering on the river, supported by their Indian allies under Maissot, Walk-in-the-Water, and Tecumseh. The American soldiers were impatiently waiting for orders to fire upon the advancing column, when all at once a white flag was hoisted upon the walls of the fort. General Hull, with cannon planted and poised to carry destruction into the ranks of the enemy, with a force which, to say the least, could have successfully resisted any immediate attack, suddenly gave orders that the detachments posted outside of the pickets and those on the ramparts should retire within the fort. Detroit, in a word, was given up without a shot being fired. The American soldiers dashed their muskets upon the ground in an agony of mingled shame and indignation. The regular troops were surrendered as prisoners of war, all the public property was given up, and no stipulations were made in behalf of the Canadian allies. The honor of the American arms was tarnished, and General Hull was disgraced forever. The detachments under Colonel Cass and Captain Brush had been included in the capitulation, but they fortunately escaped the disgrace that had been prepared for them.

General Hull was tried for treason and cowardice before a court-martial, and, though acquitted on the first charge, was convicted on the second, and sentenced to be shot: but, in consideration of his former services in the war of the Revolution, he was pardoned by the President. There seems to be no doubt in some minds that the conduct of General Hull was not that of a brave and efficient officer. He neglected to advance into Canada when he might have done so with a fair prospect of success; he evinced a want of firmness in resisting the enemy; and, finally, he gave up an important post that was prepared for a siege without firing a gun in its defence; surrendering, at the same time, the entire territory under his charge.

On the other hand, it has been said in his defence that he was in the midst of an immense wilderness, filled with savages, where he was cut off from all aid from the East. It has been alleged, too, that a spirit of insubordination prevailed among the militia, and that party strife among them ran high. But we would draw a veil over the subject. This much is in his favor, that the verdict of the court exonerated him from the guilt of treason, whatever might have been the verdict of his country.

Meantime the military post of Chicago also capitulated. Influenced by a fear of the hostile Indians on the borders of Lake Michigan, General Hull had, on the first breaking out of the war, ordered Captain Heald, the commander of this post, to abandon it and retire to Fort Wayne. A large body of savages had collected around it, and they were promised all the surplus stores if they would abstain from harassing the detachment on its withdrawal from the fort. There was among these stores a quantity of powder and whiskey, either of which it was thought imprudent to relinquish to the Indians; the former was accordingly deposited in a well and the latter thrown away. The savages, however, found out what had been done, and they were perceived collecting around the fort, apparently with hostile intentions. The garrison, consisting of fifty-four regulars and twelve militiamen, accompanied by twelve families who had fled there for protection, retired from the post, and had not proceeded more than half a mile when they were attacked by the savages. Having imprudently destroyed the means of defending themselves, they were soon compelled to surrender, which they did not do, however, until about half their number had been killed and several of the women and children. The prisoners were distributed among the neighboring tribes, and on the following morning the fort was set on fire and burned to the ground.

Being now in possession of Michigan, the British established a provisionary government at Detroit, the savages meanwhile being permitted at pleasure to ravage the frontier settlements and insult the defenceless inhabitants.

But, although the British arms had been thus far successful, it was determined to wrest from them the advantages they had gained. Accordingly three separate armies were assembled: that of the north, stationed upon the shores of Lake Champlain, and under the command of General Hampton;

that of the centre, between Lakes Ontario and Erie, under General Dearborn; and that of the west, under General Harrison, to take up its position at the head of Lake Erie. The protection of the Michigan frontier, therefore, devolved more immediately upon the latter. The defence of Upper Canada was at this time committed to Colonels Proctor and Vincent, and that of the lower province to General Sheaffe, under the direction of the governor-general of the provinces.

General Harrison lost no time in marching his army towards the lake frontier. He sent forward a detachment of his forces to Presque Isle, to wait there for the arrival of the main body; and General Winchester, with eight hundred Kentuckians, was ordered to advance to Frenchtown, on the River Raisin, where he arrived on the 13th of January.

This officer took up a position on the Frenchtown side of the river, close to its banks. Sentinels were placed around the encampment, and the night being cold, the troops spent the greater part of it in ranging about the village. During the evening, a French Canadian from Malden gave information that a body of British and Indians, amounting in all to about three thousand men, were preparing to start from that place for the River Raisin soon after he left. No notice, however, was taken of this intelligence, from a belief that it was without any foundation, and, consequently, no precautionary measures were adopted, the main road by which alone the enemy could pass being left entirely unguarded. So completely unapprehensive, indeed, was the American commander of any danger, that he had taken lodgings on the opposite bank of the river, at the house of a Frenchman.

Early on the morning of the 22d of January, just after the *reveille* had been beaten, a rapid fire of musketry was heard from the sentinels. The enemy, it appears, had arrived without being observed during the night, and taken up a position behind a small ravine, from which he now opened a tremendous fire of shells, and of grape and cannon shot, upon the American camp. The consternation of the Americans was greatly increased by the advance of the British troops under Proctor, and by the fiendish yells of the savages. A general panic ensued, and great numbers were cut down. In the meantime, General Winchester arrived from the opposite shore, and attempted to rally his retreating soldiers; but, exposed as they were to a heavy fire from the enemy, they continued to fall back. Orders were then given to incline towards the centre, and retire within the pickets of their camp. These orders, however, appear not to have been heard, and the troops, pressed by the bayonets of the British regulars, and attacked by the savages on their right, retreated in great confusion upon the ice across the river.

An attempt was now made to re-enforce the right wing, but without success. Owing to the suddenness of the attack, and the want of all preparation to meet it, there was neither system, discipline, nor obedience. The savages had posted themselves along the edge of the surrounding forest, at every point where there was any chance for retreat. They also completely commanded the long narrow lane leading to the village, and here great numbers of the Americans were killed. On the borders of the wood, the two chiefs, Round-Head and Split-Log urged on their warriors to the commission of the most frightful cruelties, and here the tomahawk and scalping-knife were dyed in blood. Colonel Allen was shot down, but Majors Graves and Madison continued gallantly to maintain their position within the pickets against all the attacks of the British, supported by their savage allies. General Winchester had in the meantime been taken prisoner; and not long after a flag arrived from the British lines with orders addressed to Major

Madison from that officer to cease hostilities, and surrender his troops prisoners of war. To this the former replied, that, as the Indians were in the habit of massacring their prisoners, he would agree to no capitulation unless the safety of his men was first expressly guaranteed. The surrender was finally adjusted upon the conditions that the lives of the soldiers should be protected; that individual property should be held sacred; that sleds should be sent the next morning with the wounded to Amherstburg, and that the sidearms of the officers should be restored at Malden. The battle-field was covered with the lifeless forms of the brave Kentuckians, who but a few hours before were seen full of hope, and glowing with all the ardor of patriotism. The painted savage and the British regular, the ardent and chivalrous son of high promise, who had been nursed in the lap of luxury, and the hardy yeoman, with his sleeves bared for battle, as they had been before rolled up while guiding the plough across his peaceful prairies, lay side by side on this field of death.

Shortly after the action, Colonel Proctor marched away with his regular troops and most of his savage allies, the remainder being left to guard the prisoners. At about sunrise the next morning, however, most of the Indians were seen coming back, painted in the most hideous manner, and in a state of intoxication. It was not long before they set up their horrid yells, and, rushing into the houses where the wounded prisoners were lying, they tore from them their blankets, and then despatched them with their tomahawks. Among these unhappy men there was a young Kentuckian of extraordinary beauty. Struck with his perfect proportions and manly grace, a chief claimed him as his prize, and led him in triumph, and in seeming admiration, through the village. But this was only in mockery of his victim; the tomahawk was commissioned to do its horrid work, and his clustering ringlets were soon seen waving from the scalp-stick of the merciless savage.

Most of the prisoners were confined in two houses. These the savages set on fire, and, as their victims attempted to escape from the windows, they pushed them back into the flames. Major Woolfolk, General Winchester's secretary, was shot dead in the street; and, to complete the atrocity of this bloody transaction, the bodies of those who were slain were left where they fell to feed the wolves of the neighboring forest. The condition of such of the prisoners as escaped immediate death was not much better. These were marched towards Malden; and as soon as, from fatigue and exhaustion, they were unable to proceed farther, they were immediately despatched, and their bodies left unburied.

Meantime General Harrison was in Ohio, making every effort in his power to overcome the difficulties by which he was surrounded. Michigan, from the nature and position of the country, separated as it was by a dense forest from the inhabited portions of the United States, and occupied by savage tribes hostile to their cause, was a conquest of great value to the British. It gave them the command, too, of the posts on the upper lakes, and thus they were enabled to control the resources of the vast tract of territory along those inland seas and of the country extending from the western borders of Indiana and Illinois to the mouth of the Maumee.

Thus completely in the possession of the British and Indians, and protected by the intervening forests, Lake Erie seemed to be the only channel by which Michigan could be approached with a prospect of recovering it from the enemy. It became, therefore, an object of great importance to obtain the mastery on that lake, which was then commanded by an English fleet under Commodore Barclay.

At this conjuncture, Oliver Hazard Perry, a young officer twenty-eight years of age, then in charge of a flotilla of gunboats at Newport, anxious to obtain more active service, turned his attention to this lake; and his views having been approved by the Naval Department, he proceeded without loss of time to the port of Erie, for the purpose of building and equipping a fleet there sufficiently powerful to give him the command of its waters. A braver or more efficient officer could have been nowhere found. He was in the prime of early manhood, active, vigorous, and intelligent, generous, and self-sacrificing even to a fault, and possessed of those fine moral traits which gave a finish to his character, and admirably harmonized with the manly beauty of his person. He labored with indefatigable zeal to hasten the construction and equipment of his vessels, and, after encountering and overcoming every kind of discouragement, he at length found himself in the command of a sufficient force to meet the enemy. As, however, there was a difficulty in crossing the bar at the mouth of the harbor, and he was closely watched by the British commander, he remained quietly at anchor in port until a favorable opportunity should occur to sally forth. At length the fortunate moment arrived, and the American fleet was got safely over the bar, and made its way towards the upper end of the lake. On reaching Put-in Bay, Captain Perry there came to anchor, impatient for an opportunity to measure his strength with the enemy, and to wrest from him the superiority on this inland sea.

On the 10th of September, at dawn of day, as their anchors were apeak, and the crews of the different vessels were shaking out their topgallant-sails, the enemy were seen bearing down, under light sail, in order of battle, with their hulls newly painted, and the crimson flag of England waving at their mastheads. The British fleet, consisting of the ships Detroit, carrying nineteen guns, the Queen Charlotte, of seventeen guns, the schooner Lady Prevost, of thirteen guns, the brig Hunter, of ten guns, the sloop Little Belt, of three guns, and the schooner Chippewa, of one gun and mounting two swivels, was commanded by a veteran officer of tried skill and valor.

The British vessels no sooner made their appearance than the American fleet prepared for action and stood out upon the lake. It consisted of the brigs Lawrence, of twenty guns; Niagara, of twenty guns; Caledonia, of three guns; the schooners Ariel, of four guns, Scorpion, of two guns, Somers, of two guns; the sloop Trippe, of one gun; and the schooners Tigress and Porcupine, each of one gun.

While the two fleets were thus approaching each other the savages were not idle. Tecumseh had stationed himself with a band of warriors upon the island at the mouth of the Detroit river, waiting with intense interest the issue of the contest. No sooner was any change made in the movements of the hostile squadrons than he paddled swiftly over to Malden to communicate the fact. From the first roar of their guns he predicted the success of the English, and was greatly surprised when the news was brought to him that they had struck their colors to the Americans.

The order of battle decided on by Commodore Perry was to attack the Detroit, the British flag-ship, himself with the Lawrence, to oppose the Niagara to the Royal Charlotte, and the rest of his fleet was ordered to act as circumstances might require, and assail the enemy as they should be directed by signals, while the Ariel and Scorpion were instructed to take a position on the weather-bow and ahead of the Lawrence, in order to draw off a portion of the fire from that ship.

As the two fleets neared each other, the action was commenced by the enemy's flag-ship, the Detroit, she being mounted with long guns, while the American vessels had only short pieces. The American commander resolved to capture the hostile fleet or perish in the attempt, bore down directly for the Detroit, making signals at the same time for all his vessels to come into close action. Owing to causes which are not very clearly understood the Niagara did not bear down to his aid. Still he was undaunted, although alone and exposed to nearly the whole of the enemy's fire. Ranging along the front of their squadron, single and unsupported, he successively poured upon their ships from the battery of the Lawrence tremendous broadsides of ball and grape, while he received from them in return a no less destructive fire, which shivered his spars and covered his decks with wounded and dead. Such a fire no single vessel could long withstand. The hull of his ship was pierced in every direction, twenty-one of his men had been killed, sixty-one were wounded, and only fifteen remained who were capable of duty. All of his cannon except one had been dismounted, and this he continued to work with his own hands.

His ship being thus a complete wreck, and incapable of being longer defended, he determined to abandon her; and ordering his boat, amid a shower of shot, he proceeded to the Niagara, which vessel then lay at a considerable distance and had not been yet brought into close action. Meeting Captain Elliott at the gangway, he requested him to take the boat in which he had come and bring up the rest of the vessels, while he himself would bear down upon the enemy with the Niagara. The flag of the Lawrence now came down, amid the cheers of the British sailors, who supposed that the American fleet had struck. Ordering every sail on board the Niagara to be set, he was not long in closing with the enemy's ships; and passing along their line he poured upon them, in quick succession, tremendous broadsides. Having driven the Royal Charlotte out of line, he next attacked the Detroit, and by the severity of his fire drove her men from their quarters. Captain Elliott now came up with the smaller vessels, and, taking a raking position under the stern of the Detroit, assisted to complete the victory. The slaughter on board this ship was dreadful: twenty-seven of her men had been killed and ninety-six wounded. At length a white handkerchief was hung out on the end of a boarding-pike as a signal of surrender; the triumph was complete, and all the vessels of the enemy were taken. The dead of both fleets were buried on an island in the lake.

The conduct of Perry was no less distinguished by humanity after the action than it had been by skill and bravery while the battle was raging; and the British commander long afterward expressed his grateful recollection of the generous courtesy of his youthful conqueror. It is thus that the horrors of war are in some degree softened by a display of the kindlier feelings of our nature.

This brilliant success gave to the Americans the uncontrolled command of the lake, and on the 23d of September their fleet landed twelve hundred men near Malden. Colonel Proctor, however, had previously evacuated that post, after setting fire to the fort and to the public store-houses. Commodore Perry in the meantime passed up to Detroit with the Ariel to assist in the occupation of that town, while Captain Elliott, with the Lady Prevost, the Scorpion, and the Tigress, advanced into Lake St. Clair to intercept the enemy's stores.

Thus General Harrison, on his arrival at Detroit and Malden, found both places abandoned by the enemy, and was met by the Canadians asking for his protection. Tecumseh proposed to the British commander that they should hazard an engagement at Malden; but the latter foresaw that he should be exposed to the fire of the American fleet in that position, and therefore resolved to march to the Moravian towns upon the Thames, near St. Clair Lake, above Detroit, and there try the chance of a battle. His force at this time consisted of about nine hundred regular troops and fifteen hundred Indians commanded by Tecumseh. The American army amounted to two thousand seven hundred men, of whom one hundred and twenty were regulars, a considerable number militia, about thirty Indians, and the remainder Kentucky riflemen, well mounted, and mainly young men, full of ardor, and burning with a desire to revenge the massacre of their friends and relatives at the river Raisin.

The American general lost no time in seeking the enemy, whom he found drawn up in order of battle and prepared to receive him. On his right, in a swamp, was posted Tecumseh with his Indian warriors, while the space between them and the river was occupied by the regular troops. The American general extended his line to the same length with that of the British infantry, his small body of regulars he ordered to seize the enemy's artillery, and the few friendly Indians were directed to act on his flank.

It had been determined to penetrate the swamp and turn the right of the Indians, as they could not cross the river, and the infantry were on the point of making this movement, when it was ascertained that the British were drawn up in a double line, and that, to enable them to occupy the whole space between the swamp and the river, they had been obliged to open their files. The plan of attack was therefore changed, and Colonel Johnson, with his mounted Kentuckians, was ordered to charge the enemy in front. These brave volunteers rushed upon the British column with such impetuosity that, unable to resist the fierceness of the onset, it broke and fled. Cleared of the regular force of the enemy, the battle-field now exhibited a series of personal encounters between the Kentuckians and Indians. Tecumseh, being wounded, it is said, and exasperated to desperation by the flight of his allies, resolved to sell his life as dearly as possible. Rushing, therefore, into the hottest of the conflict, he soon fell, pierced by a pistol-ball, and instantly expired.

This renowned chief deserves a passing notice. He possessed a noble figure, his countenance was strikingly expressive of magnanimity, and he was distinguished by moral traits far above his race. He was not remarkable for eloquence, or even for intellect, but he was a warrior in the broadest Indian sense of the word. Without the far-reaching views of Pontiac or his hereditary rank, still, in sudden action and desperate valor, he showed himself superior to that chief; and, though a new man, he acquired unbounded influence, and placed himself above all competitors as the great champion of Indian rights. While his brother, the Prophet, was the principal manager of the confederacy in all that related to its organization and plans, he was its executive arm in the field. There were other peculiarities by which he was no less distinguished. Like Pontiac, he manifested a deep interest in regard to the manners and customs of the whites; he would not sanction the barbarities practised by the Indians, and he disdained the personal adornments in which they so much delight. Although holding the rank of a brigadier-general in the British service, he pertinaciously adhered to his Indian garb; a deerskin coat, with leggins of the same material, was his constant dress, and in this he was found dead at the battle of the Thames. During the latter years of his life he was almost incessantly engaged either in the council or at the head of his warlike bands, and he sunk at last on the field of his glory, with tomahawk in hand and the cry of battle upon his lips.

"Like monumental bronze, unchanged his look,
A soul which pity touch'd, but never shook;

> Train'd, from his tree-rock'd cradle to his bier,
> The fierce extremes of good and ill to brook;
> Unchanging, fearing but the shame of fear,
> A stoic of the woods, a man without a tear."

With the death of Tecumseh the confederacy was dissolved, and a peace was concluded with the Ottawas, Chippewas, Miamis, and Pottowatamies.

The American fleet was now employed in removing the ammunition and stores from the captured British posts; and on the 18th of October General Harrison and Commodore Perry issued a joint proclamation at Detroit for the better government of the territory of Michigan, and guarantying to the inhabitants their rights of property, and the enjoyment of their ancient usages and laws.

The island of Mackinaw was now the only part of the territory remaining in the possession of the enemy. This being a post of great importance, from its commanding the upper lakes, and being the centre of the fur-trade, a fleet under Commodore Sinclair, with a body of land forces under Colonel Croghan, the gallant defender of Sandusky, was despatched in July, 1814, for the purpose of capturing it. After reconnoitering the coast near the island, the commodore proceeded to the neighboring island of St. Joseph, where he destroyed a few trading-posts and then returned.

Meanwhile, the British commandant was actively employed in strengthening his defences, and in summoning to his aid the nearest savage tribes. It was at first proposed to attack the post near the village, as that part was the most free from trees, and, consequently, afforded less covert to the Indians. This, however, was objected to by Sinclair, as his fleet would be here exposed to the fire of the fort. It was finally concluded to land on the northeastern side of the island, although from this point they would be obliged to traverse its whole breadth, through a dense forest, in order to reach the British position. After marching some distance through the wilderness, on arriving at a small clearing, the detachment was fired on from all sides by the savages stationed in the surrounding woods. Major Holmes, at the head of a considerable force, was directed to charge the enemy; but, as he was gallantly executing the order, he was shot down by a rifle-ball. The fire, indeed, was so destructive, that the advanced party was obliged to retreat to the main body, upon which the whole force retired to their boats, abandoned the enterprise, and returned to Detroit. In consequence of this failure, the British retained possession of Mackinaw until the conclusion of peace.

The victory of Commodore Perry having secured the command of Lake Erie, Proctor's army having been routed, and the Indian confederacy broken up, nothing of special interest transpired in Michigan during the remainder of the war. Colonel Cass was left with a brigade for the protection of the territory, which he effectually accomplished, until the treaty of peace, concluded at Ghent on the 17th of February, 1815, put an end to all farther hostilities.

TRANSITION FROM TERRITORY TO STATE.

Michigan now emerged into a new existence. Colonel Cass, who had served with great credit during the war, was appointed governor of the territory, and under his administration it gradually advanced in prosperity.

Hitherto there had been but little inducement for immigration from the East: the public lands had not been brought into the market, and recently the country had been suffering under the devastation of war. The beautiful oak-openings on the Kalamazoo, the fertile tracts on the borders of Grand River, the prairies of the St. Joseph, and the rich and inviting slopes along the shores of Lake Michigan, were traversed only by the wild beast and the savage, and the streams navigated only by the bark canoe. The feeble settlements on the frontier had been converted into scenes of desolation; no roads through the interior had been constructed; and the only access to the country by land from the East was through the trackless wilderness distinguished by the name of the Black Swamp, and by the military road along the Detroit river. Everything, therefore, was to be done to develop the resources of the territory, and to secure to it the advantages which, from its position and the fertility of its soil, it was entitled to enjoy.

It would appear, however, that the character of the country in regard to the latter particular was at that time but little understood, as is shown by the following fact: In 1812, Congress had passed an act providing for the survey of the bounty-lands to be granted for the soldiers enlisting for the war which had then just commenced, and this survey was directed to be made in the territory of Michigan. The persons employed for this object, however, made so unfavorable a report in regard to the soil, representing it as marshy and everywhere sterile, that in 1816 the act was repealed, and the quantity of land required for this purpose was ordered to be surveyed in Arkansas and Illinois. The surveyors either did not make a thorough examination of the soil, or, what perhaps is more probable, they were deceived by the sandy nature of the oak-lands, which have a yellowish color before they are brought into cultivation, but which, from the quantity of lime they contain, turn black after they are exposed to the action of the sun and air by the plough.

During that year, however, and the two following, the country was more fully explored, and numerous tracts of fertile land, with a rolling surface, variegated by groves and lakes, were discovered. These lands were forthwith surveyed, and in 1817 and 1818 portions of them were offered for sale, showing the superiority of our enlightened and liberal laws, contrasted with the narrow policy of the former possessors of the soil. A great change now took place in public opinion in regard to the value of these lands, and subsequent surveys more fully confirmed the inaccuracy of the impressions which had hitherto prevailed in relation to them.

With the introduction of steam navigation upon its vast inland seas, a new era may be said to have commenced in the history of the progress of the West. This was in 1819, when the first steamboat, the Walk-in-the-Water, made her appearance on Lake Erie, crossing that lake and passing up to Mackinaw.

By the census taken about that time, the population of Michigan was ascertained to be eight thousand eight hundred and ninety-six. Detroit contained two hundred and fifty houses, and fourteen hundred and fifteen inhabitants, independent of the garrison. The island of Mackinaw, which continued to be a central mart for the fur-trade, had a stationary population of four hundred and fifty, which was at times increased to not less than two thousand by the Indians and traders who resorted there from the upper lakes. The settlement at the Saute de Ste. Marie contained only fifteen or twenty houses, occupied by French and English families.

Although, by the ordinance of 1787, lot number 16 was directed to be reserved in every township for the support of common schools, no measures had yet been taken to introduce a system of public instruction, if we except the act passed by the governor and judges in 1817 for the establishment of what was styled in it the *Catholepestemiad*, or University of Michigan. This act, which was drawn up by Augustus B. Woodward, Chief Justice of the Territory, is a very curious document. He was a gentleman possessing extensive acquirements, but was not a little eccentric in his character, and the views he entertained on this and some other subjects were certainly not very practical. The phraseology of the act is not its least singular feature, and would seem better suited to the age of my Lord Coke than to the understanding and condition of a race of new settlers engaged in clearing away the forest. This university was to have thirteen *didaxia* or professorships, each of which was to be liberally endowed, and it was designed to lay broad and deep the foundations for a thorough education.

Indeed, all Judge Woodward's projects seem to have been upon no very moderate scale. Detroit is indebted to him for a plan of the city laid out in the form of a *cobweb*, with public squares, a circus, a *Campus Martius*, streets, cross-streets, avenues, &c., more vast in its conception and more complex in its design than ancient Rome, and requiring a longer period to fill it up than from the time of Romulus to our own day. The utilitarian tendencies of his successors, however, have made strange havoc with this magnificent plan, the traces of which are now nowhere visible but on the map.

On the admission of Illinois into the Union in 1818 all the territory lying north of that State and Indiana was annexed to Michigan; and the following year Congress passed an act authorizing the election of a delegate from the Territory to the National Legislature, who should have the right of speaking, but not of voting. This was of great advantage to the inhabitants, as they were thereby provided with a representative through whom they could make known their wants to the General Government.

Michigan, meanwhile, gradually continued to advance in population. The settlers extended themselves along the banks of the rivers Raisin, Huron, and St. Clair, and cleared away the forest from the spots where now stand the villages of Ann Arbor, Ypsilanti, Pontiac, Jackson, and Tecumseh.

That portion of the Territory, however, situated upon the borders of the upper lakes was then but little known; and in 1820 an expedition was set on foot for the purpose of exploring it, to ascertain the number and condition of the Indian tribes in that quarter, and to select such positions as might be most favorable for its defence. This expedition, which was under the direction of Governor Cass, was accompanied by a mineralogist, a topographical engineer, and a physician; was provided with an escort of soldiers, and the commanding officers of the posts along the lakes were ordered to afford it every facility in their power. The party started from Detroit on the 24th of May in bark canoes manned by *voyageurs* and Indians.

Passing up the river St. Clair, they proceeded along the shores of Lake Huron, visited the island of Mackinaw, then maintained as a trading-post by the Northwest Company, and soon arrived at the Saute de Ste. Marie.

This was considered a favorable point for the establishment of a military post. By the treaty of Greenville, concluded in 1795, the Indians had agreed that all the lands which they had granted to the French or English should be transferred to the United States. This place they had ceded to the French, who had formerly maintained a garrison here: it was clear, therefore, that it came within the provisions of that treaty. A council was therefore called, at which the Indian chiefs attended, dressed in fine broadcloths and decorated with trinkets of British manufacture. The savages opposed the occupation, and sought to prevent it by denying all knowledge of the original cession; and when it was fully explained to them they still persisted in withholding their consent, though in less positive terms, suggesting that their young men might prove unruly and kill the cattle which should stray from the post. This being understood as intended for a threat, Governor Cass replied that he would give himself no farther trouble to confer on the subject, but that so sure as the rising sun would set in the west, so sure should an American garrison be established at that place, whatever might be their decision.

The chiefs, who appear to have been under British influence, now spent several hours in discussion. Some of them were willing that the Americans should occupy the post if there were no troops stationed there. At length a chief, who held the rank of a brigadier general in the British service, seized his war-lance and struck it furiously on the ground, intimating thereby that the place would not be given up except to superior force, and the council soon afterward dispersed in a hostile spirit.

The expedition under Governor Cass consisted of sixty-six men, of whom thirty were regular soldiers, and the savages numbered about eighty warriors. The latter occupied the site of the old French fort and the Americans were drawn up upon the bank of the river St. Mary, a ravine separating the two at a distance of five or six hundred yards.

While the Americans were waiting to see what would be the issue of the affair, the British flag was hoisted from the midst of the Indian encampment by the chief who had shown so hostile a disposition in the council. On discovering this, Governor Cass ordered his men to stand by their arms, and, taking an interpreter, proceeded directly to the Indian camp. Here he indignantly tore down the obnoxious flag, telling the chief who had hoisted it that it was an insult of the grossest kind; that the flag was the emblem of national sovereignty; that the ensigns of two different nations could never float on the same soil; that they would not be permitted to raise any other than that of the United States; and that if they attempted it again that Power would set a strong foot upon their necks and crush them to the earth. When he had said this the governor returned to his encampment, and a few minutes after he arrived there the Indian women and children were seen quitting their lodges and getting on board their canoes. No act of hostility, however, was committed; and some of the older chiefs, who had not been present at the council, came forward and made overtures of peace. At seven o'clock the same evening a treaty was concluded with them, by which they ceded to the United States a tract of four miles square around the Saute, including the portage, the site of the old French fort, and the village, reserving to themselves the right of fishing at the falls and of encamping upon the shores. The calumet was smoked, and blankets, knives, silver trinkets, and broadcloths were distributed among them.

Everything having been settled, the expedition started again, and proceeded along the shores of Lake Superior. Here they were struck with the appearance of the Pictured Rocks, which extend for miles along the shores of the lake, stained with a variety of hues by the washing of mineral waters, and which exhibit to the delighted beholder the most singular scene imaginable of Nature's painting. They visited also the Doric Rock, which presents the appearance of a rude though magnificent piece of architecture chiselled from the solid stone, and examined other curiosities on this part of the coast. The Copper Rock, at the mouth of the Ontonogon river, which has from time immemorial been the subject of Indian superstition in this wild, sequestered region they found particularly worthy of notice.

Having completed its survey, the expedition returned to Detroit by the way of Lake Michigan. The results were a more accurate knowledge of the geography of the country and of the operations of the Northwest Fur Company, the selection of sites for a line of military posts, and several important treaties with the Indian tribes, ceding valuable tracts of land to the United States. Mr. Henry R. Schoolcraft, who accompanied the expedition, afterward published his journal, giving a particular account of the country, and of the incidents which occurred along their route.

Soon after this an important change took place in the government of the territory. In 1823 Congress passed an act abrogating the legislative powei of the governor and judges, and establishing a legislative council, to consist of nine members, limiting also the judges' term of office to four years. Two years afterward all county officers, excepting those of a judicial character, were made elective by the people; all executive appointments were required to be approved by the legislative council; and an act was passed empowering the governor and council to divide the territory into townships, to incorporate the same, and to define their rights and privileges.

The Erie Canal, which had been commenced in 1817, was in 1825 opened for navigation from the Hudson to Buffalo; and this event forms an important epoch in the progress of Michigan. The effect of this great public improvement on the interests of the West was twofold; it cheapened the foreign merchandise of which it stood in need, and in the same or a still greater proportion enhanced the value of its agricultual products. Its lands therefore increased in value, new facilities and new motives were offered for settlement, and from this period those vast and fertile regions advanced rapidly in population and general prosperity.

To meet the claims of the increasing population of the territory, new privileges were granted. In 1827 the legislative council was made elective by the people, with the power of enacting laws, subject to the approval of Congress and the veto of the local executive; and upon this footing things remained until the territory was admitted into the Union.

Governor Cass, meanwhile was indefatigable in his efforts to have roads constructed through the interior, and, warned by the experience of the past, to provide effectually for the public defence. His whole administration, indeed, was characterized by a persevering zeal to promote the prosperity of Michigan; to improve its institutions, and to develop its resources.

A new impulse, as we have already remarked, had been given to the progress of the West. It offered a boundless field for enterprise, and began to be considered the proper asylum and retreat for all who would better their fortune by industry. It was emphatically "the poor man's country," where his labor was sure to be rewarded by competence, and eventually by wealth. Hence population flowed in rapidly from the East. The hardy settlers, scattering over the country, made the woods resound with the stroke of the axe; and everywhere the smoke of their cabins was seen ascending from the depths of the forest. The lakes presented a no less animated scene: the white wings of commerce were spread out upon their waters, and the cloud from the distant steamer was seen stretching along the horrizon. The reign of Nature in these hitherto silent and secluded solitudes was at an end, and that of man, with all its life, and bustle, and activity, had begun.

In 1831, General Cass, having been appointed secretary of war, was succeeded by Mr. George B. Porter in the government of the territory, the population of which at this time amounted to about thirty-five thousand. During his administration, Wisconsin, which had before been annexed to Michigan, was erected into a separate territory. Meantime the commerce on Lake Erie was rapidly increasing. A road, which was, to say the least, passable at some seasons of the year, was constructed across the Black

Swamp, and numerous avenues were opened into the interior. In consequence of these improvements, the country became better known, a spirit of speculation was awakened, and, in addition to the actual settlers, the woods were traversed by numbers in search of desirable tracts, which they purchased at the Government price, in the expectation of realizing large profits from their rapid increase in value.

The method adopted by the Government in making their surveys is one of great accuracy. Two straight lines were drawn across the territory, the one running north and south, the other east and west. The north and south line was denominated the principal meridian, and the east and west line was called the base line. The territory was then divided into townships six miles square, and these were subdivided into thirty-six sections of a square mile each, the townships being numbered in regular order, commencing at the meridian and base lines and increasing as they receded from them. The mathematical accuracy of this method, and the farther circumstance that each section and township, and also the lines of the sections, were blazed or marked upon the trees, enabled the emigrant, even in the depths of the forest, to find clear landmarks to guide his course and to ascertain the actual boundaries of each tract. The smallest lot which could be purchased was one of eighty acres, or a fractional lot made by a township line or by the course of a stream.

Prior to the year 1820, the established Government price for land was two dollars an acre, one-fourth of which was required to be paid at the time of purchase, and the remainder in three annual instalments, the land being subject to forfeiture if these were not punctually paid, while a discount of eight per cent. was allowed if the whole amount was paid in advance. This system, however, was found to be productive of serious evils. The expectation of gain induced many to make large purchases, and while some realized fortunes, perhaps, from their investments, others, who were less successful, were without the means of paying their instalments, and thus the whole became liable to forfeiture. These results led to a total change of the system. The price of the public lands was reduced from two dollars to one dollar and a quarter the acre, the whole of which was required to be paid down at the time the purchase was made. This was attended with the best effects, preventing a vast deal of trouble and loss to the Government, discouraging reckless speculation, and enabling the industrious settler with moderate means to acquire for himself a clear and unencumbered title to his land.

Meanwhile, a controversy sprang up which came near terminating in serious collision with a neighboring State. By the ordinance of 1787 it was provided that any one of the grand divisions within the limits of the Northwest Territory should be entitled to admission into the Union whenever its population amounted to sixty thousand; and Michigan having already that number of inhabitants, claimed the right thus granted. The controversy alluded to was in relation to the boundary-line between the latter and Ohio, as established by the ordinance of 1787. Each government claimed a rich and extensive tract as falling within its limits, which was made still more valuable from the proposed terminus of the Wabash and Erie canal, a work of great promise, being included within it. So much excitement, indeed, prevailed that both parties sent a military force to the disputed frontier.

The people of Michigan, having called a convention and formed a State constitution, petitioned Congress to be admitted into the Union, claiming as a part of their territory the tract in dispute with Ohio. Congress, however, decided in favor of the latter State, and assigned to Michigan, in place of the fertile strip along her southern border, about twenty-five thousand square miles of barren, mountainous country on the shores of Lake Superior.

We here conclude our brief account of Michigan as a territory. We have seen it in the infancy of its settlement, under the blighting effects of feudal institutions similar to those existing in France at that period, being then little more than a mere ranging-ground for the Jesuit missionary and the fur-trader, a waste roamed over by the wild beast and the savage, and designedly kept in this state as a shelter for the fur-bearing animals. We have seen the French banner supplanted by the red cross of England without producing any material change in the condition of the country. And, finally, we have seen the stars and stripes of our own Republic planted on the soil, and witnessed in the extraordinary improvements which have since taken place the wonder-working energies of our free institutions.

HISTORY AS A STATE AND PRESENT CONDITION.

In the foregoing pages the reader has been presented with a picture of Michigan in her youth; it now becomes our duty briefly to consider her attractions and condition as a prosperous matron. From the time when she entered the Union as a State, until she became a distinguished defender of the United States against the assaults of the Great Rebellion, the story of her career is without any peculiar incidents of misfortune or renown. In what manner, and with whose help, she defended the nation in its period of danger, will be fully set forth by another hand, in the succeeding part of this volume, while the present writer will content himself in this and the following chapters with a concise compilation from official documents of the civil affairs of the State down to the present time, together with a glance at some of its later developments.

The act of Congress which finally admitted Michigan into the Union with her constitution of September, 1835, was approved January 26, 1837, and Stevens T. Mason entered at once upon his duties as the first elective governor. Although a Virginian by birth, he had been six years identified with the territory as secretary and acting governor. He was elected governor of the prospective State, however, in October, 1835, and continued in that position until January, 1840. The estimated population of the State in 1837 was about two hundred thousand; and its area was then estimated at forty thousand square miles, which was divided into thirty-six counties. From the very start the genius of her people was exemplified by the enactment of laws, for the building of not less than four railroads, several of which, under new names, were destined to be eminently successful. And then the special attention of her legislators was turned to the cause of education. An act was passed in March of that year for the organization and support of the primary schools, thereby keeping pace with the will of Congress in setting aside for school purposes one thirty-sixth part of the public lands in the State; and, within the same month, the other important act was passed which gave existence to the University of Michigan. It was to be located at Ann Arbor, placed in charge of a board of twelve regents, originally appointed by the governor, but subsequently elected by the people, with the governor, lieutenant-governor, judges of the Supreme Court, and the chancellor of the State, as *ex officio* members. It was to have three departments, one of literature, science, and art; the second of law, and the third of medicine. It was to have not more than twenty-six professorships; and its support was to be derived from a grant of seventy sections of land, which the superintendent of public instruction, then in office, valued at nearly nine hundred and twenty-two thousand dollars. Special attention was also directed to the mineral resources of the State; an appropriation of twenty-nine thousand dollars made for a geological survey; and the appointment of State geologist was conferred upon Dr. Douglass Houghton, who did more than any other man to make known to the world the mineral riches of Michigan. Nor were the pioneer legislators of the new State unmindful of the cause of internal improvement, for they at once passed an act establishing a board of seven commissioners for that purpose, of which the governor was made president, and that board authorized a number of surveys for railroads. For the central route, from Detroit to the mouth of the St. Joseph, they appropriated four hundred thousand dollars; for the southern route, from Monroe to New Buffalo on Lake Michigan, one hundred thousand dollars; for the northern route, from Black to Grand river, fifty thousand dollars; and at the same time legislative acts were also passed incorporating the roads between Detroit and Shiawassee, and Gibraltar and Clinton. The commendable spirit of enterprise thus manifested by the public authorities was seconded by the people at large, as may be seen by glancing at the agricultural statistics published in 1838. The rye crop, for example, amounted to 21,944 bushels; oats, 1,116,910; buckwheat, 64,022; flax, 43,826 pounds; hemp, 524 pounds; neat cattle, 89,610; horses, 14,059; sheep, 22,684; and swine, 109,096. When compared with the present, these figures seem almost insignificant, and yet they told a "flattering tale," and the absence of any allusion to the great staple of wheat will strike the reader as remarkable. It was also in 1838 that appropriations were made for the survey of the St. Joseph, Kalamazoo, and Grand rivers, with a view to the improvement of their navigation.

In 1839 the militia of the State was regularly organized, and eight divisions, with two brigades of two regiments each, were assigned to the following generals: John R. Williams, George Miles, Charles C. Hascall, John Stockton, Joseph W. Brown, Isaac E. Crary, Edwin M. Bridges, and Horace H. Comstock. Another event of this year was the completion of the Penitentiary at Jackson, which was built on the plan of the famous prison at Auburn, New York: and as to the progress of education throughout the State, the official reports gave the number of nearly thirty thousand pupils in the common schools, and the amount of money expended during the year as more than eighteen thousand dollars. With this year also terminated the administration of Governor Mason, who, besides having had the honor of inaugurating the new State, proved himself to be not only a man of ability, but a faithful friend of Michigan. He had emigrated from Virginia to the Territory in 1831, when he was appointed its secretary, in his nineteenth year, and he only lived about three years after retiring from the office of governor of the State, to which he was twice elected, and which he filled with credit and ability.

The second Governor of the State was William Woodbridge, who served in that capacity from January, 1840, to February, 1841, when he resigned to accept a seat in the United States Senate. His advent to the Territory dated as far back as 1814, when he was appointed to the post of secretary; after which, in 1819, he was elected a delegate to Congress, made a judge of the Supreme Court in 1828, took an active part in the Constitutional Convention of 1835, and was chosen in 1837 to the State Senate. After leaving the executive chair, the then lieutenant-governor, J. Wright Gordon, became the acting governor, and served as such for the balance of the term. In looking over the records, we find the leading events of this joint administration to have been as follows: The railroad from Detroit to Ann Arbor, a distance of forty miles, was completed; and branches of the State University were established at Detroit, Pontiac, Monroe, Niles, Kalamazoo, Grand Rapids, Jackson, White Pigeon, and Tecumseh. The population of the State had now risen to more than two hundred and twelve thousand, and the leading towns claimed the following numbers, viz: Detroit, nine thousand one hundred and one; Ypsilanti, two thousand four hundred and nineteen; Pontiac, nineteen hundred and four; Marshall, seventeen hundred and sixty-three; and Monroe, seventeen hundred and three. And after what manner the State was progressing in material wealth may be gathered from the subjoined figures. In 1841 the average price of wheat was seventy cents per bushel, and the crop amounted to $2,100,000: corn was sold for thirty cents, and amounted to $810,000; oats twenty cents, and the yield $800,000; hay five dollars per ton, and the amount $750,000; pork was sold for two cents per pound, and the profit was $900,000; the fur-trade amounted to $425,000: the potato crop to 2,051,000 bushels; whiskey and high-wines, $400,000; maple sugar, $83,151; fish trade, $192,000; wool, $70,000; dairies, $300,000; and home-made goods, $100,000. The exports for that year amounted to nearly four millions of dollars; and as the result of the distribution act of Congress the State became possessed of five hundred thousand acres of public land, many portions of which were selected with great care and were to become the foundation of an important revenue. Associated with the administration of Governor Gordon was the reorganization of the Grand Lodge of Freemasons, with the constitutional number of lodges. Of the early introduction of this order into the Territory of Michigan we have no satisfactory data. The Grand Lodge was first organized at Detroit June 24, 1826; was incorporated by the Legislative Council in 1827; and by a formal resolution, adopted in 1829, masonic labor was suspended. A general meeting of the Masons of the State was called for inquiry in 1840, and in 1841 the former grand officers granted dispensations for several lodges. The first grand master under the original organization was General Lewis Cass. The Grand Royal Arch Chapter was organized in 1848; the Grand Council of Royal and Select Masters was organized in 1858; and the Grand Commandery, Knights Templar, was organized January 15, 1857.

In November, 1842, commenced the administration of John S. Barry as Governor of the State, and he continued in that position until November, 1845. He was an emigrant from New England, and had been a resident of Michigan for many years; and the town in which he settled was Constantine, where he occupied a high position. During the first year of his term he had the satisfaction of seeing the university opened for the reception of students, when the charge for tuition was fixed at ninety-four and a half dollars per annum, or three hundred and seventy-eight dollars for the full course of four years. The Central and Southern Railroads were now progressing rapidly, the former having been finished to Marshall, one hundred and ten miles, and the latter to Hillsdale, sixty-eight miles. The private roads from Toledo to Adrian, and twenty-five miles of that from Detroit to Pontiac were also completed. The number of pupils reported as attending the common schools was nearly fifty-eight thousand, and the school tax for the year amounted to fifty-four thousand six hundred and forty dollars. In 1843 a State land office was established at Marshall, which was invested with the charge and disposition of all the lands belonging to the State, and to Digby V. Ball was assigned the duty of conducting the affairs of the office. In 1844 the taxable property of the State was found to be $28,554,282, the tax being at the rate of two mills on the dollar; the expenses of the State amounted to seventy thousand dollars; the income from the two railroads was about three hundred thousand dollars; the University had now become so prosperous that its income was ample to pay the interest on the University stock; and the amount of money which the State was able to loan to the several progressing railroads was one hundred and twenty thousand dollars. Renewed efforts were now made to increase the efficiency of the common schools, and those who were acquainted with them were beginning to see that the schools of Michigan would be but little behind those of the Eastern States. In 1845 the population of the State had nearly reached three hundred and five thousand, which was a gain in five years of not less than ninety-two thousand; and in his message to the Legislature Governor Barry stated that the indebtedness of the State amounted to $4,077,177, while its resources reached $4,150,000.

The successor of Governor Barry was Alpheus Felch, who took the executive chair in November, 1845, and continued in it until March 3d, 1847, when he resigned to accept a seat in the United States Senate. He emigrated from Maine to Michigan when quite young, and as early as 1836 became identified with public affairs, first as a member of the Legislature, then as a bank commissioner, as auditor-general of Michigan, and also as a judge of the Supreme Court. The leading incidents of his administration was the sale to private corporations of the two railroads belonging to the State, the Central having brought two millions of dollars and the Southern road five hundred thousand dollars. It was in 1846 that the University library was enriched with a choice collection of about five thousand volumes purchased in Europe; the exports for that year amounted to $4,647,608; the tonnage of vessels enrolled in the collection district of Detroit was 26,928 tons; the steam-vessels numbering 8,400 and the sailing vessels 18,527, the whole of them giving employment to eighteen thousand seamen. In 1847 the counties in the State numbered thirty-nine, and the townships four hundred and thirty-five, of which two hundred and seventy were supplied with good libraries, containing in the aggregate thirty-seven thousand volumes. Indeed the common schools seem to have prospered beyond all expectations, for now the scholars numbered about ninety-eight thousand pupils, and in the 2,869 districts were employed twelve hundred male teachers and nearly two thousand female teachers. During the unexpired nine months of Governor Felch's term, the Lieutenant Governor, William L. Greenly, performed the duties of governor. It was while this administration existed that the war with Mexico was commenced and terminated; and in answer to the requisition from the War Department Michigan furnished to the cause one regiment of volunteers, commanded by Thomas W. Stockton, and one independent company, at a cost of about ten thousand five hundred dollars. The people were willing to volunteer, but owing to the imperfection of the militia laws the troops were obtained with some difficulty.

In November, 1847, Epaphroditus Ransom became the Governor of Michigan, and served out his term of two years to November, 1849. He was a New England man, and had served in the Michigan Legislature. It was his privilege to sign the bills for establishing the Asylum for the Insane at Flint, and also the Asylum for the Deaf, Dumb, and Blind at Kalamazoo, both of which institutions were liberally endowed with lands, and each of them placed in charge of a board of five trustees. The appropriation in 1869 for the deaf and dumb and blind amounted to $81,500. On the first of March, 1848, the first telegraph line was completed from New York to Detroit, and the first despatch transmitted on that day.

With regard to the agricultural interests of the State, their progress was quite unprecedented; and for the benefit of comparison with previous as well as subsequent years we submit the following figures bearing upon 1849. The land reported to be under cultivation at that time amounted to 1,437,460 acres, and of wheat there were produced 4,739,300 bushels; other grains 8,179,767 bushels; wool, 1,645,756 pounds; maple sugar, 1,774,369 pounds; horses, 52,305; neat cattle, 210,268; swine, 152,541; sheep, 610,534; and while the flour mills numbered two hundred and twenty-eight, the lumber mills amounted to seven hundred and thirty. In 1847 the act was passed removing the seat of government from Detroit to Lansing, and temporary buildings for the use of the Legislature were at once erected at a cost of $12,450.

In November, 1849, John S. Barry was again and for a third term called upon to take charge of the State as its governor. He continued in office until November, 1851. Among the first acts of the Legislature to which he appended his name was one for the establishment at Ypsilanti of a Normal school, which was endowed with lands and placed in charge of a board of education consisting of six persons. But the two great events which transpired during his administration were, first, the removal of the seat of government from Detroit to Lansing, and, secondly, the adoption of the present Constitution of the State, an authentic copy of which will be found at the conclusion of this volume. As late as 1846 the site of the new capital was occupied by only one log-cabin, and it derived its name from one of its earliest settlers. It is located on Grand river, in Ingham county, was organized as a city in 1859, and, in addition to an important water privilege, it enjoys the advantages of a rich agricultural country which surrounds it on every side. Another event of importance which transpired during the administration of Governor Barry was that known as the "Great Railroad Company Case." A series of lawless acts had been committed on the property of the Michigan Central Railroad Company along the line of their road and especially at Leoni and Michigan Centre, in Jackson county; and, finally, their depot in Detroit was burnt in 1850 by an infernal machine. Thirty-seven men were brought to trial in 1851, and of these twelve were convicted. The conspirators were defended by William H. Seward, of New York, and the prosecution was conducted by Alexander D. Fraser, of Detroit, and the judge who presided on this occasion with great ability was Warner Wing.

In view of the fact that the commercial advantages of Michigan are quite peculiar, and unequalled by any other of the interior States of the Union, we may, with propriety, at this point, take a glance at her immediate surroundings. The five great lakes with which she is so closely connected drain an area of 335,515 square miles, and the navigable waters extending from Lake Erie downward will admit the passage of vessels not exceeding 130 feet keel, 26 feet beam, and 10 feet draught. The total traffic of these great waters in 1851 was estimated at 326,000,000, employing 74,000 tons of steam and 138,000 tons of sail. In 1839 the twenty-five largest steamers on these lakes had an average of 449 tons burthen, while the average of those which flourished in 1851 was about 1000 tons. In the former year, the first-class steamers took ten days to make the round trip from Buffalo to Detroit, but in the latter year the swiftest steamers only required three days to perform the same trip. The total number of steamers on Lakes Erie and Michigan and the straits was 140, and the numbers belonging to the districts of Detroit 47, Mackinaw 12, and Chicago 4. And in this connection, the fact is worth stating that during the nine years preceding 1851 the steamboat tonnage of the Mississippi valley had only doubled, but that during the same period the tonnage of the great lakes more than quadrupled itself, whereby we obtain an idea of the remarkable increase of the lake country, in population, production and trade.

In November, 1851, Robert McClelland became the governor of the State and his administration lasted until March, 1853, when he resigned to accept a seat in the Cabinet of President Pierce as Secretary of the Interior. He had become a citizen of Michigan as far back as 1833, and had served not only in the State legislature, but also as a Representative in Congress. On his retirement, the lieutenant-governor, Andrew Parsons, became the acting governor, and continued to act until the close of the term in November, 1854. Perhaps the most significant fact connected with that year was, that the pupils throughout the State who attended the common schools, were not less than one hundred and seventy-five thousand, an increase in four years of forty-three thousand. Such victories of peace are what Michigan has always prided herself upon, and are in perfect harmony with the victories of war, in behalf of the Union, upon which she justly prided herself ten years afterwards.

From November, 1854, to November, 1858, the executive chair was filled by Kinsley S. Bingham. He emigrated to Michigan in 1833, and, prior to his election as governer, he had served with honor both in the State legislature and as a Representative in Congress. All the material interests of the State progressed with rapidity during his administration, but the most notable event of his first official term was the completion of the Ship Canal at the falls of St. Mary. In 1852, August 26, an act of Congress was approved granting to the State of Michigan seven hundred and fifty thousand acres of land, for the purpose of constructing a Ship Canal between Lakes Huron and Superior. In 1853, February 5, the legislature of Michigan accepted the grant made by Congress, and provided for the appointment of commissioners to select the donated lands, and to arrange for building the canal. A company of enterprising men was formed, and a contract was entered into, by which it was agreed that the canal should be finished in two years, and the work proceeded. Every article of consumption, machinery, working implements and materials, timber for the gates, stone for the locks, as well as men and supplies, had to be transported to the site of the canal from Detroit, Cleveland, Chicago, and other lake ports; the stone for finishing the locks having been brought from Marblehead near Sandusky City, Ohio, and from the Detroit river. The rapids or *Saute* which had to be surmounted have a fall of seventeen feet and are about a mile long. The length of the canal is less than one mile, its width one hundred feet, depth twelve feet, and it has two locks of solid masonry. The contracting parties had many drawbacks to contend with in their operations, a sickly season having been one of them, but they persevered, and in May, 1855, the work was completed, accepted by the commissioners and formally delivered to the State authorities. The disbursements on account of constructing the canal and selecting the lands, amounted to $999,802, while the lands which were assigned to the company and selected through the agency at Saute Ste. Marie, as well as certain fine lands in the upper and lower peninsula, filled up to an acre the full measure of the Government grant. In consideration of its national character, as a highway between the lower lakes and Lake Superior, and in view of the sound character of the work, the originators and builders of this canal deserve the gratitude of the country. With regard to the laws of Michigan, it should be mentioned here that in 1857 two volumes containing all the statutes down to date were compiled by Thomas M. Cooley, and published in two volumes at Lansing under the authority of the State legislature.

The successor of Governor Bingham was Moses Wisner, and his term extended from November, 1858, to November, 1860. He emigrated from New York to Michigan in 1839; was a lawyer by profession, and a true patriotic citizen of the State. Soon after his retirement, the mutterings of the Great Rebellion began to be heard, and he, together with his two successors, Austin Blair and Henry H. Crapo, each of whom was twice elected, were so identified with the military operations of the State during the war, that we shall leave their services to be considered by our colleague in the second part of this volume; while our own biographical notices of all the territorial and State governors of Michigan will be reserved for the concluding part of the volume. In the meantime, however, we may in this place introduce with propriety the names of the several governors and administrators, under whose jurisdiction Michigan has been placed since the erection of the royal government, more than two hundred years ago. Under French rule they were Sieur de Mesy, appointed in 1663; Sieur de Courcelle, 1665; Sieur de Frontenac, 1672; Sieur de Barre, 1682; Sieur Marquis de Nouville, 1685; Sieur de Frontenac, 1689; Sieur Chevalier de Callieres, 1699; Marquis de Vaudreuil, 1703; Marquis de Beauharnais, 1726; Sieur Compte de la Gallisoniere, 1749; Sieur de la Jonquiere, 1749; Marquis du Quesne de Menneville, 1752; and Sieur de Vandreuil de Cavagnal, 1755. Under English rule the governors were James Murray, 1765; Paulus Emelins Irving, 1766; Guy Carleton, 1766; Hector T. Cramahe, 1770; Guy Carleton, 1774; Frederick Haldemand, 1774; Henry Hamilton, 1774; Henry Hope, 1775; Lord Dorchester, 1776; Alured Clarke, 1791; and Lord Dorchester, 1798. The American governors, by appointment and election, have been William Hull, 1805; Lewis Cass, 1814; George B. Porter, 1832; Stevens T. Mason, 1834; John S. Horner, 1835; Stevens T. Mason, 1836; William Woodbridge, 1840; J. Wright Gordon, 1841; John S. Barry, 1842; Alpheus Felch, 1845; Epaphroditus Ransom, 1847; John S. Barry, 1849; Robert McClelland, 1851; Andrew Parsons, 1853; Kinsley S. Bingham, 1854; Moses Wisner, 1858; Austin Blair, 1861; Henry H. Crapo, 1865; and Henry P. Baldwin, 1869. And for purposes of reference, we also insert at this point the progress of population for the half-century preceding the year 1860; as follows:—Population in 1810, 4,762; 1820, 8,765; 1830, 31,639; 1840, 212,267; 1850, 397,654; and 1860, 749,113. At our present writing the result of the current census, for 1870, is not officially known; but should the last decade be equal to that which preceded it, the population of Michigan might be set down at about fourteen hundred thousand.

Having thus taken a brief chronological view of the leading events in the history of Michigan as a State, we now propose to lay before the reader a more comprehensive account of her condition at the close of Governor Crapo's administration, with some particulars of a later date, and what we propose to submit shall be arranged under the several heads of Education, Agriculture, Mineral Wealth, Railroads, Lumbering Interest, Fisheries, Commerce, The Indians and Antiquities of the State, and Recent Developments.

EDUCATION.

Among the very first laws enacted by the Legislature of Michigan after its organization as a State was one for the establishment of the State University, founded on the act of Congress of 1826, which appropriated two entire townships of wild land for the special purpose. That action on the part of its original legislators, suggested by a clause in the constitution enjoining upon the legislature the "encouragement of learning and the general diffusion of knowledge among the people," was highly creditable to their intelligence, and was the key-note to the subsequent prosperity of the State. A prime mover in this enterprise was the Rev. John D. Pierce, the first superintendent of public instruction; and among the professors first chosen were Asa Gray and Douglass Houghton, the first as professor of botany and zoology, and the second of geology and mineralogy. By careful and judicious management the University has progressed so rapidly that it is now awarded a prominent place among American institutions, and in foreign countries the mother State is more widely known through the fame of her University than through any other means. In July, 1868, Mr. Pierce read a paper before the association of county superintendents, at Marshall, in which he recounted the interesting history of the University, and from which we make the following extract:

"It was reserved to Michigan to rear up, within thirty years from its inception and the location of its site, an institution rivaling, not only Yale and Harvard, but outstripping them both. This now is universally acknowledged. Men from the oldest institutions in the United States concede the great fact. The best authorities say that the University of Michigan is a marvel. Thirty years ago the land—the forty acres that it now occupies—was an unfurrowed plain, whose soil the plough had never chafed, never disturbed—where, but as yesterday, the deer roamed free as air, the wolf howled, and the Indian pitched for the night and kindled his camp-fires. You will find in all the history of the past nothing to compare with it in the rapidity of its development and growth."

It was not until 1850 that the University had any recognized head. In 1842 it had four professors; in 1850 the medical department was organized; in 1859 the law department; and in 1860 the professorships numbered twenty-eight and the students six hundred. The total disbursements from 1837 to 1851 amounted to $286,928; but since that time the receipts and expenditures have greatly increased. For five years preceding 1868 the number of students averaged more than one thousand, and in the latter year the receipts amounted to $62,772.82, derived from the following sources; interest from the University fund, $37,086.22, and from students' fees, $25,686. The buildings in which it is domiciled are the chief attraction of the beautiful city of Ann Arbor, are handsome and imposing, commandingly situated and surrounded by tastefully laid out grounds, bordered with beautiful shade trees. In its organization, the university conforms to the Prussian system which is regarded as the most perfect in the world. According to the thirtieth report of the board of regents, the names of the professors, instructors, and other officers of the institution were at that time as follows, the first chancellor or president, elected in 1852, having been Dr. Henry Tappan:

Rev. Erastus O. Haven, D.D., LL.D., President of the University, and Professor of Logic and Political Economy; salary $2,000.

Rev. George P. Williams, LL.D., Professor of Physics; salary $1,500.

Abram Sager, M.A., M.D., Professor of Obstetrics and Diseases of Women and Children; salary $1,000.

Silas H. Douglass, M.A., M.D., Professor of Chemistry and Mineralogy, Pharmacy and Toxicology; salary $1,500.

James R. Boise, LL.D., Professor of the Greek Language and Literature; salary $1,500.

Alonzo B. Palmer, M.A., M.D., Professor of Pathology, the Practice of Medicine, and of Hygiene; salary $1,500.

Alexander Winchell, LL.D., Professor of Geology, Zoology, and Botany; salary $1,500.

Corydon L. Ford, M.A., M.D., Professor of Anatomy and Physiology; salary $1,000.

Henry S. Frieze, M.A., Professor of the Latin Language and Literature; salary $1,500.

De Volson Wood, C. E. M. A., Professor of Civil Engineering; salary $1,500.

Hon. James V. Campbell, LL.D., Marshal Professor of Law; salary $1,000.

Hon. Charles I. Walker, Kent Professor of Law; salary $1,000.

Hon. Thomas M. Cooley, Jay Professor of Law; salary $1,000.

James C. Watson, M.A., Professor of Astronomy and Director of the Observatory; salary $1,500.

Samuel G. Armor, M.A., M.D., Professor of Institutes of Medicine and Materia Medica; salary $1,000.

Edward P. Evans, Ph. D., Professor of Modern Languages and Literature; salary $1,500.

Rev. Lucius D. Chapin, M.A., Professor of Moral and Intellectual Philosophy; salary $1,500.

Edward Olney, M.A., Professor of Mathematics; salary $1,500.

Rev. Andrew Ten Brook, M.A., Librarian; salary $1,500.

Ashley Pond, M.A., Fletcher Professor of Law; salary $1,000.

William W. Greene, M.D., Professor of Civil and Military Surgery; salary $1,000.

Adam K. Spence, M.A., Professor of the French Language and Literature; salary $1,500.

Charles K. Adams, M.A., Professor of History; salary $1,500.

Moses C. Tyler, M.A., Professor of Rhetoric and English Literature; salary $1,500.

Allen J. Curtis, M.A., Assistant Professor of Rhetoric and English Literature; salary $1,500.

Albert B. Prescott, M.D., Assistant Professor of Chemistry and Lecturer on Organic Chemistry and Metallurgy; salary $1,000.

George B. Merriman, M.A., Assistant Professor of Mathematics; salary $1,000.

Stillman W. Robinson, C. E., Assistant Professor of Mining, Engineering, and Geodery; salary $1,000.

Martin L. D'Ooge, M.A., Assistant Professor of the Ancient Languages; salary $1,000.

Henry S. Cheever, M.A., M.D., Demonstrator of Anatomy and Curator of the Medical Museum; salary $500.

Geo. E. Frothingham, M.D., Prosector of Surgery and Assistant Demonstrator of Anatomy; salary $500.

John H. Burleson, Secretary and Stewart; salary $1,000.

Hon. D. McIntyre, Treasurer; ——.

Preston B. Rose, M.D., Assistant in Chemistry; salary $300.

Albert E. Foote, M.D., Assistant in Chemistry; salary $250.

William J. Cocker, Assistant in General Library; salary $400.

Silas H. Douglass, M.A., M.D., Dean and Secretary of Medical Faculty; salary $200.

William C. Durkee, LL.B., Law Librarian; salary $110.

W. J. English, Keeper of the Museum; salary $150.

John Carrington, Janitor; salary $400.

Gregory Naglee, Janitor; salary $400.

James Ottley, Janitor; salary $400.

Robert Howard, Janitor; salary $400.

Although some changes have taken place in this list it is given in full for future reference.

The whole number of professors in 1869 was thirty-six and the students in attendance during that year numbered twelve hundred and twenty-three, of whom 418 were in the department of science, literature, and arts; 418 in the department of medicine and surgery, and 387 in the department of law. The total number of graduates was three hundred and five, a larger number than were ever before graduated; of whom eighty were doctors of medicine, one hundred and fifty-two bachelors of law, and seventeen mining and civil engineers. The receipts from various sources for the year amounted to about seventy-seven thousand dollars, the whole of which was expended. The University, in view of its vital and intimate connection with the general school system of the State, has aimed to lay a foundation sufficiently broad to satisfy all just demands. It has laid out the work of the department of science, literature, and arts in six parallel courses of study, not taking any other American or foreign college for its model, but endeavoring to meet the exact and just demands of the school system of the State. By an act of the Legislature, passed in 1855, it was provided that there shall always be at least one professor of homœopathy in the University, and yet the board of regents from that time to 1868, notwithstanding the numerous changes in its membership, had never appointed a professor with that title. In 1867 the Legislature granted further aid to the University on condition that the law should be executed; and with this law before them the regents determined to appoint such a professor, but made it incumbent upon him to lecture in some place outside of Ann Arbor. It was thought this would be a compliance with the law, and prevent any unhappy conflicts in the regular medical school. The Supreme Court of the State decided against this action, and so the gift of the Legislature was not available. At this point of the controversy the President of the University, E. O. Haven, discussed the question at issue in a calm and judicious manner, taking the ground that no partisan professorships of any kind or name should be established, and, after making an earnest appeal to the Legislature to reverse their action, concluded by saying that the Regents ought to respect the will of the people, and must in the end accept the aid tendered by the State on the conditions insisted upon. Another subject of vital interest to the cause of education, which has created a diversity of opinion in Michigan, is the admission of women to the University. In 1867 the Legislature adopted a resolution to the effect that the high objects for which the University was organized will never be fully attained until women are admitted to all its rights and privileges. The President then in office noticed this subject in his annual report, and set forth his objections to the demand made, and recommended that no change at that time should be made in the policy of the University; but the President subsequently gave it as his opinion that the best method for Michigan would be to make provision for the instruction of women at the University on the same conditions as men. He came to this conclusion slowly. "A few objections," he argued, "have sometimes seemed to me strong, but the most of what is urged against it is fanciful and partakes of the nature of the thoughtless opposition made to what is new. The standard of education would not be changed. The habits of study would not be affected. The honor of the University would rather be increased than diminished. It does not injure the young men of the Sorbonne in Paris that ladies also can listen to the lectures. The demand that women would enjoy the same advantages as men grows out of Christian civilization, and if difficulties arise we must not shrink from them, but overcome them. Responsibility makes strength." But, notwithstanding the President's argument and the existing law, the question is still in abeyance.

With regard to the museum attached to the University, all are agreed in pronouncing it interesting and valuable. The natural history collection embraces six thousand European minerals, purchased of the late Baron Ledever; a large collection of minerals from Lake Superior, the fruit of geological surveys and expeditions, and of the liberality of Professors Houghton and Winchell; also a very large zoological collection, consisting of birds which visit Michigan, with most of the mammals of the State; nearly a complete series of the reptiles found east of the Rocky Mountains; two thousand species of molusca, embracing all the land and fresh-water forms of the Northern and Western States; a considerable collection of fishes and radiata; the Winchell collection of land and fresh-water shells, from all parts of the State and from Jamaica; two thousand specimens of insects; the Trowbridge collection of animals from the Pacific coast; and more than two thousand species illustrative of the flora of the State. To all of which collections important additions are annually made.

That part of the museum connected with the medical department has been selected and prepared with direct reference to teaching. Besides containing a number of adult skeletons, articulated and separate, of the most perfect description, there are preparations illustrating the various stages of development and change, from the first rudiments of fœtal life to extreme old age; and a variety of partial or complete skeletons of inferior animals, to exhibit the various modifications. It contains, likewise, beautifully prepared skulls and teeth, to illustrate first and second dentition, and others showing many of the diseases to which they are subject. Various *arterial preparations*, complete and partial, afford good facilities for studying the vascular system. Several hundred alcoholic preparations of healthy and diseased structures—human and comparative—furnish important aid in illustrating physiology and pathology; while models in plaster and *papier-mache*, with a valuable collection of plates, splints, and surgical instruments, meet the wants of the more practical branches. An important addition to these means of illustration has recently been made by an importation from Europe, of great beauty and value; among which are a collection of bones of the head, disarticulated and mounted, and an extended collection of wax models, illustrative of various anatomical and pathological conditions, including representations of the anatomy of the pelvis and its contents, of several varieties of hernia, of specimens of small-pox and the vaccine disease, and of a large number of cases in ophthalmic surgery, etc. The department of the museum illustrative of materia medica consists of a very complete suite of crude organic medicinal substances, embracing between five and six hundred specimens imported from Paris, put up in beautiful glass-covered half-gallon jars of uniform appearance, finely displayed, arranged according to their order in natural history, and labeled in both French and English; besides about one thousand other specimens of simple mineral and vegetable substances and pharmaceutical and officinal preparations, active principles, etc., arranged in groups convenient for study; and altogether comprising a collection which, in amount, variety, and adaptness to the purposes of instruction, it is confidently believed is not equaled by any of a similar character even in the older institutions in this country. Besides these actual specimens, medical botany is illustrated by between one and two hundred large and finely-colored plates, framed and glazed, and displayed for observation. A full suite of instruments used in diseases of females is deposited in the museum, illustrating the surgical processes required in this class of cases; and the magnificent portraits of cutaneous diseases, by Dr. Erasmus Wilson, and the no less useful collection by Dr. Robert Willis, illustrate very fully this department of Pathology.

The collection in that part of the museum devoted to the fine arts and history was commenced in the year 1855 by Professor Frieze, and at present comprises—1. A gallery of casts, in full size and in reduction, of the most valuable ancient statues and busts. These were mainly executed at the imperial modeling establishment of the Louvre, by Desachy, of Paris, and by the brothers Micheli, of Berlin. 2. A gallery of more than two hundred reductions and models, in terra cotta, and other materials. These represent the principal statues, portrait busts, vases, and other antiquities in the Museo Borbonico, and other European museums. They were executed at Naples. 3. A gallery of engravings and photographic views, executed in Italy and Greece, illustrating especially the architectural and sculptural remains of ancient Rome, Pompeii, Paestum, Athens, and Corinth. 4. The Horace White collection of historical medallions, comprising, first, four hundred and fifty casts from antique gems in the Royal Museum at Berlin, illustrative of ancient history; second, over five hundred casts illustrative of mediæval history and of the Renaissance period; third, about four hundred medallion portraits of leading personages in modern history. These portraits were derived from authentic sources, and reduced with fidelity, and the whole were cast by Eichler, of Berlin. Not included with the above are several busts and reliefs, copied from Thorwaldsen, Canova, Powers, and others, and also a copy of the Laocoon, presented by the class of 1859.

From the foregoing particulars it will be seen that the University meets the wants of the people in all the higher degrees of education. Having been endowed by the General Government, it now affords education almost without money and without price. There is no young man so poor that industry, diligence, and perseverance will not enable him to obtain an education. While the sons of the rich are educated here, a considerable number of those who are not rich are enjoying the same advantages. Many young men, accustomed to work on the farm, or in the shop of the mechanic, have been smitten with the love of knowledge, and are manfully working their way through a liberal education, by appropriating a part of their time to the field or the workshop; and thus it is that the institution is proving itself a blessing to the people at large. The expenditures in its behalf for 1869 have already been stated. We may also add that there is connected with this University a well-conducted observatory; and that in 1868, during the months of July, August, September, and October, Professor James C. Watson discovered six new asteriods, which is the largest number ever discovered by one man in the same period of time. Besides its noble University, it is to the credit of Michigan that she is the supporting mother by her influence of not less than seven or eight distinct colleges, as well as a Normal school, a Reform school, and her Common schools, which we will now proceed to describe:

The first to be mentioned is Adrian College, located in the town whose name it bears. It was incorporated March 23, 1859, and its first term for instruction commenced December 1, 1859. It was formerly under the immediate patronage and direction of the Wesleyan Methodist denomination, but was transferred to the Methodist Church in 1867, and is based upon a liberal policy, and embraces in its board of trustees, which is self-perpetuating, and in its faculty, members chosen for their educational interest and power, from other religious denominations. Its departments of instruction are open to both sexes, and include thorough classical and scientific courses, to which there is joined instruction in commercial studies and the arts of teaching, painting, and music. Its buildings, numbering four, three stories high, are all handsome and spacious, and have been erected and furnished at a cost of not less than two hundred thousand dollars. It also has an endowment fund of one hundred thousand dollars; and it is the only college formally recognized by the General Conference of the Methodist Church in the United States. Its faculty in 1868 was as follows:

Rev. A. Mahan, D.D., President, and Professor of Mental and Moral Science.

Rev. G. B. McElroy, A.M., Professor of Mathematics and Astronomy.

Rev. I. W. McKeever, A.M., Professor of Natural Philosophy and Natral History.

A. H. Lowrie, A.M., Professor of History and Political Economy, and Principal of the Preparatory Department.

I. W. Cassell, A.B., Professor of the Latin and Greek Languages.

(Unfilled,) Professor of Chemistry and Geology.

Miss Ada A. Alvord, A.B., Principal of the Ladies' Department.

J. M. Thompson, Professor of Vocal and Instrumental Music.

Miss Sallie E. Rose, Assistant Teacher of Music.

Miss Alice Van Slyke, Teacher of Painting.

Augustus F. Bruske, Teacher of German.

In the village of Albion is located another college belonging to the Methodist Episcopal denomination. In 1835 this institute was located at Spring Arbor, under the name of the Wesleyan Seminary; but in April, 1839, it was removed to Albion, and in the following year a collegiate department was added for women, with the power of conferring degrees upon such persons pursuing a scientific and classical course of instruction. In 1860 the institution was incorporated, with full college powers, and adopted a higher grade of studies. The institution is under the patronage of the Michigan and Detroit Annual Conferences of the Methodist Episcopal Church. They elect the board of trustees. The officers of the Board are: James W. Sheldon, Esq., Albion, President; Rev. William H. Brockway, Albion, First Vice President; S. W. Walker, Esq., Detroit, Second Vice President; George B. Joycelyn, Albion, Secretary; Rev. A. M. Fitch, Albion, Treasurer; and Rev. M. A. Dougherty, Financial Agent.

The board of instruction is as follows:

George B. Joycelyn, President, and Professor of Mental and Moral Science.

Rev. W. H. Perrine, A.M., Professor of Natural Science and Fine Arts.

William H. Shelley, A.M., Professor of Latin Language and Literature.

Rev. John McEldowney, A.M., D.D., Professor of Greek Language and Literature.

Miss Rachel Carney, M.S., Preceptress, and Professor of Modern Languages.

Miss Sallie A. Rullison, B.S., Professor of Mathematics.

Miss Kate A. Joycelyn, Teacher of Instrumental Music.

Henry C. Northrup, Teacher of Phonography.

Fay C. Pierson and William Harper, Assistant Teachers in Preparatory Department.

Mrs. Maria H. Cushman, Stewardess.

The endowment fund amounts to ninety thousand dollars; the number of pupils for 1868 was three hundred and fifty; but the buildings, which are handsome, will accommodate five hundred pupils.

The next institution that we notice is Kalamazoo College. It embraces several departments, each, to a considerable extent, distinct from the others, and is, properly speaking, a university. It embraces a college proper, designed to furnish instruction to young men in a four years' course of study similar to that adopted in the best institutions of other States. It also embraces a female department, with a four years' course, including all the higher branches usually taught in colleges of this class. Also a preparatory department, open to the youth of both sexes who wish to fit themselves for a college course, or to pursue English or classical studies to only a limited extent. A commercial department, with a thorough, practical, and comprehensive course of study, designed to fit the student for any situation of commercial or business life. Lastly, there is a normal department where students are instructed by the regular college professors and teachers provided for that purpose, in the theory and practice of the profession.

This college was chartered in 1833, and is consequently the oldest literary institution in the State. The first building erected was burned in 1844. The present main building—male department—situated on "Mt. Carmel," in the western part of the village, was erected in 1848, and is 104 by 46 feet, and four stories high. The Ladies' College, a beautiful architectural structure, situated on South street, was erected in 1858, and is truly an ornament to the State. The location of the Kalamazoo College leaves nothing to be desired, it being in one of the healthiest and most beautiful situations in the country.

The members of the faculty in 1868 were as follows:

Kendall Brooks, D.D., President and Professor of Mathematics.

Silas Bailey, D.D., Professor of Moral and Intellectual Philosophy.

H. L. Wayland, A.M., Professor of Rhetoric and Logic, and Instructor in Greek.

J. A. Clark, A.M., Professor of Latin.

Miss H. P. Dodge, Principal of the Female College, and Professor of English Literature.

Mrs. Martha L. Osborne, Professor of Modern Languages.

Miss M. H. Blakeslee, Instructor in Music.

Miss E. D. Wood, Instructor in Drawing and Painting.

With regard to the institution called Olivet College, and located in that village, we gather from official sources the following particulars: This college is under the fostering care of the Presbyterians and Congregationalists, and its resources amount to one hundred and eighty-two thousand dollars. The faculty in 1868 was as follows:

Rev. Nathan J. Morrison, D.D., President, and Drury Professor of Moral Philosophy.

Rev. Oramel Hosford, A.M., Professor of Mathematics and Natural Philosophy.

Rev. John M. Barrows, A.M., Professor of Botany and Geology.

R. C. Kedzie, A.M., M.D., Lecturer on Chemistry and Anatomy.

John H. Hewitt, A.M., Rutan Professor of the Latin Language and Literature.

Joseph L. Daniels, A.M., Professor of the Greek Language and Literature.

Alexander B. Brown, A.B., Professor of Vocal and Instrumental Music.

Rev. H. O. Ladd, A.M., Instructor in Rhetoric and Mental Science.

Merritt Moore, Principal of the Preparatory Department and Instructor in Mathematics.

Edward S. Elmer, A.B., Instructor in the Ancient Languages.

Miss Henrietta P. Dennis, Principal of the Ladies' Department and Instructor in French.

(Unfilled), Instructor in drawing and Painting.

Miss Anna M. Bennedict, Assistant Teacher in the Preparatory Department.

Miss L. A. Willard, Assistant Teacher of the Piano.

Another flourishing and important institution is favorably known as the Michigan Female College. It was founded at Lansing in 1855, and its object was to provide for the education of the daughters of the State, although by a late report we learn that a thousand pupils have been received from nine other States. The courses of study are both classical and scientific. But an institution of greater importance and reputation, also located in the vicinity of Lansing, is the State Agricultural College. It is located on Cedar river; and although the act creating it was passed in 1855 it was not organized until 1857; and it is the first institution of the kind which has ever succeeded in this country. The tract of land which it occupies was purchased by the State Agricultural Society, (whose annual reports are valuable and interesting,) and contains six hundred and seventy-seven acres of choice land. Its object is to give to students a thorough practical and theoretical education to fit them for the occupation of farming. It is well supplied with all the appliances for such an institution, and its herbarium is one of the largest in this country, numbering more than twenty thousand specimens. Students residing in Michigan are admitted free, while those from other States are charged only twenty dollars per annum for instruction. The students are obliged to perform farm labor three hours every day, and are paid for their earnings. It has been endowed by the General Government with a gift of public lands, which have been placed in the market for the benefit of the college; and in 1857 the faculty was: President and Director of the Farm, Joseph R. Williams; Professor of Mathematics, Calvin Tracy; Professor of Chemistry, Lewis R. Fisk; Professor of Physiology and Entomology, Henry Goadby; Professor of Natural Science, D. P. Mayhew; Professor of Farm Economy and Secretary, Robert D. Weeks; and Professor of Horticulture and Treasurer, John C. Holmes.

We now come to speak of Hillsdale College, which is located in the beautiful town whose name it bears, and which is under the jurisdiction of the Free-will Baptist Church. Its buildings are spacious and handsome, and the institution is quite celebrated. Its faculty is as follows:

Rev. Edmund B. Fairfield, D.D., LL.D., President.

Rev. Ransom Dunn, A.M., Burr Professor of Biblical Theology.

Rev. Henry E. Whipple, A.M., Professor of Rhetoric and Belles Letters.

Spencer J. Fowler, A.M., Professor of Mathematics and Natural Philosophy.

George McMillan, A.M., Professor of the Greek and Latin Languages.

Hiram Collier, A.M., Professor of Natural Science.

Cyrus Jordan, A.M., Assistant Professor of the Languages.

Mrs. Julia M. Jordan, Principal of the Ladies' Department.

Miss Ellen Smith, A.B., Assistant Principal.

Eugene Haanel, A.M., Teacher of French and German.

From colleges to schools the transition is natural, and our first notice in this connection shall be of the State Normal School at Ypsilanti. The act creating this institution was passed in 1849, and appropriated for its support twenty-five sections of salt spring lands. It was commenced in 1852, boasts of a large and handsome edifice, and is intended to prepare teachers of both sexes; and, according to the last report of its principal, the school has gained much in the last two years from the co-operation of the county superintendents of common schools, who are credited with having done much for the cause of education. It is conducted at an annual expense generally speaking of about ten thousand dollars, but the outlay for 1869 was $18,500. More extensive than the above is the State Reform School, established at Lansing in 1856. It is designed to afford to homeless boys an opportunity to escape from the career of crime, which would otherwise await them, in such a manner that they may be enabled to gain an honest livelihood. It occupies a beautiful building which overlooks the Grand river at Lansing. The inmates are chiefly employed in farming and gardening, but a portion of them work at various trades, and all the branches of the common school are systematically taught. There is a chapel attached to the school, and everything is done to reform and elevate its inmates. The cost of carrying on the institution amounts to between forty and fifty thousand dollars per annum, although the expenditures for 1869 amounted to $56,025.

We come now to a brief consideration of the educational work accomplished by the public schools of Michigan, and the exhibit made by the Superintendent of Public Instruction in his annual report for 1868 reflects the highest credit upon all who have participated in the important work. The total number of school districts is 4,843, and these are located in 778 towns and cities and in all of the fifty-nine organized counties of the State. The number of children attending school was 249,920; male teachers, 2,086; female teachers, 7,522; school-houses, 4,694; and their value, $4,285,627. The two classes of teachers received respectively $47.78 and $21.92 per month, and the total amount paid to them for the year 1868 was $1,038,131; the total expenditures on account of the schools amounting to $2,449,356. The number of books in the district libraries was 86,901 and in the town libraries 45,322. For over thirty years, writes the worthy Superintendent of Public Instruction, Rev. Oramel Horsford, the cause of education in Michigan has been constantly onward. In 1837—thirty-one years ago—the venerable John D. Pierce, first Superintendent of Public Instruction, and still an active worker in the cause, reported 14,297 children between five and seventeen years of age in the State. Now we report, between five and twenty years, 354,704. He then reported $21,375.91 expended for school purposes. In 1868 the aggregate exceeds two millions. The University fund was then about one hundred and fifty thousand dollars. Now it is $559,978. The University reports 1,223 students; the normal school, 262; and the local colleges nearly two thousand. The total expenditures for education in the State during the past year can be hardly less than three millions.

But we must not, in this connection, forget to mention the purely benevolent institutions of the State, and first the Michigan Asylum for the Deaf, Dumb, and Blind, located in Flint. This institution began operations in 1854, and has a large number of inmates. To teach the deaf to hear, the dumb to speak, and the blind to see, would have been deemed a miracle but a few years ago, but who that has visited our modern asylums can doubt that all this has practically been accomplished by the exertions of philanthropic men.

Through this public beneficence, the unfortunate inmate of the asylum, which, by the way, has been re-named, and is called an institution, as in better keeping with its purpose, is in many respects more fortunate than many in less favored lands who enjoy every sense in perfection. He is taught to manufacture wagons, paper boxes, etc., to weave mats and carpets, and to manufacture a variety of useful articles. Above all, he is enabled to acquire a liberal education, and is thereby placed in a higher sphere than those who, in years past, looked on him with pity and contempt. Self-reliant, fully competent to obtain by their own hands an honest livelihood, the inmates of this institution go forth into the world. And who, but those families possessing an unfortunate member, bereft of the sense of speech and hearing, can appreciate the joyful emotions felt by his friends when the deaf and dumb pupil is first enabled to communicate with them in an intelligent manner.

The asylum *is free* to all the deaf and dumb, and the blind, in Michigan, between the ages of ten and thirty years. All are entitled to an education without charge for board or tuition. The time for admission is about the first of October.

Thus we see, that in little more than twenty years, Michigan has adopted a system of education unexceled in older communities; nor is the hand of progress to cease its zealous efforts. An improvement in the school law is now being agitated, by which all children shall be compelled to attend school for a certain length of time, unless parents shall adequately provide for their education elsewhere. The State imposes a heavy tax on its citizens for the support of the public schools, and is it not bound to secure to society the full benefit of these schools? The child has a sacred and indefeasible right to so much education as society can provide. Society embraces all men in its bosom, and its safety and well-being are essential to the safety and well-being of all. If there be any parent who interferes with the education of his child, his views must be sacrificed to the greater interests of the multitude.

With regard to the men who have hitherto held the office of Superintendent of Public Instruction, and under whose guidance so much good has been accomplished, their names are as follows: John D. Pierce, Franklin Sawyer, O. C. Comstock, Ira Mahew, Francis W. Shearman, Ira Mahew again, J. M. Gregory, and the present incumbent, Oramel Hosford.

We come now to speak of the Michigan Asylum for the Insane. We can say that the edifice is spacious and beautiful, and that in its furnishing and adaptedness to the purpose for which it was established, it is not one whit behind the other institutions of the country in efficiency and high character. The number of patients treated in 1867 and 1868 was 373, and the number remaining at the commencement of 1869 was 229. According to the latest reports for 1869 the annual expenditures amounted to $63,500, and it has capacity for three hundred patients.

As to the State Prison, its condition has lately been improved, but it is not yet a self-sustaining institution. The number of inmates in 1868 was 622; the earnings amounted to $85,238, and disbursements $94,136. We regret to say that the usual liberality and wisdom of the State authorities have not been manifested in the general management of this institution; but we are glad to know that through the influence of Governor Baldwin there is a fair prospect of improvement. Appropriation for its support in 1869, only $2,000.

As a fitting paragraph in this chapter we may append the following particulars, respecting the number of students reported in the higher institutions of the State, for the year ending with 1868:

University, 1,223; Agricultural College (many rejected for want of room,)

92; Normal School (average attendance,) 223; Adrian College (Methodist,) 242; Albion College (Episcopal Methodist,) 263; Hillsdale College (Free-Will Baptist,) 235; Kalamazoo College (Baptist,) 102; Hope College (Dutch Reform,) 96; and Olivet College (Congregational,) 295.

The following facts are given concerning the primary schools and educational funds:

The average length of the schools during the year 1868 was six and two-tenths months. To capitulate: there were employed 2,086 male teachers, and 7,522 females, at average wages per month, to the former, $47.78, and to the latter, $21.92. To this should be added the board of a large portion of the whole number. There were 72 stone school-houses, 416 brick, 3,609 frame, and 618 of logs; the whole, including sites, valued at $4,384,081. The amount expended on buildings during the year was $805,706. The total resources of the schools amounted in all to well nigh three millions; and about three-fourths of this was by the voluntary action of the several districts.

The school fund amounted to $2,550,337, most of which pays 7 per cent. It will ultimately reach nearly four millions. The University fund is $559,978, and draws 7 per cent. The Normal School fund was $66,697, and drew 6 per cent. All parties have at all times sacredly regarded the educational fund. Other State funds have been sometimes squandered, and sometimes stolen, but rogues have ever left the school funds unharmed, and we think we can challenge any State to show a better appreciation of popular education than has the State of Michigan during its brief but splendid career.

With regard to the Union School system of the State, it has been pronounced commendable in the highest degree: Two or more districts, according to the law, may vote on the question of uniting for a Union School District; those that give a two-thirds vote majority in favor of it may unite if the whole number of scholars is two hundred. Immediately after the vote is taken the several district boards notify the school inspectors, who shall unite said districts, giving five days' notice of a meeting to be held to elect officers, six in number, who constitute the Union School Board, and are called trustees.

The district may then proceed to raise funds to build a school-house, which may be by direct tax or by bonds. In a country growing as rapidly as ours, it has been thought advisable to issue bonds; this method equalizes the tax so that those who may settle in the district five, ten, or fifteen years after the house is built, and have the benefit of the schools, have their proportion of the tax to pay, so that in proportion to the increase of property and inhabitants, the tax is lessened, that it might not be more than one-tenth, or even one-twentieth, what it would be to raise a direct tax. This is one of the best features in the law. Funds raised on bonds are restricted, or limited, as follows:—Districts thus united, having 50 scholars, may raise not to exceed $3,000; 100 scholars, $10,000; 200 scholars, $20,000; 300 scholars, $30,000; 400 scholars, $50,000.

And now, in further illustration of the avidity with which the people of Michigan have always fostered the idea of mental culture, we submit a list of the literary institutions which were incorporated by the Legislature during the fifteen years intervening between the adoption of its two State Constitutions, viz: Marshall Academy, White Pigeon, date of incorporation, 1836; Central College, Spring Arbor, 1845; Spring Arbor Seminary, 1835; Wesleyan Seminary, at Albion, 1841; Michigan and Huron Institute, 1837; Tecumseh Academy, 1838; Grand River Theological Seminary, 1839; Lake Academy and Teachers' Seminary 1839; Marshall College, 1839; Marshall Female Seminary, 1839; St. Phillip's College, 1839; Allegan Academy, 1843; Grand Rapids Academy, 1844; Utica Female Seminary, 1844; Ann Arbor Female Seminary, 1845; Ypsilanti Seminary, 1845; Adrian Seminary, 1846; Clinton Institute, 1846; Vermontville *Academical* Association, 1846; White Pigeon Academy, 1847; Raisin Institute, 1847; Howell Academy, 1848; Leoni Institution, 1848; Leoni Seminary, 1848; Olivet Institute, 1848; Woodstock Manual Labor Institute, 1848; Oakland Female Seminary, 1849; Tecumseh Literary Institute, 1849; Clarkson Academical Institute, 1850; Clinton Institute, 1850; Young Ladies' Seminary, at Monroe, 1850; St. Mark's College, Grand Rapids, 1850; and St. Mary's Academy, at Bertrand, 1850. Surely, of such an educational record as we have now briefly sketched, the State of Michigan may well be proud; and the results are every day developing in the happiness and prosperity of her people.

AGRICULTURE.

In 1860 the population of Michigan was about seven hundred and forty-two thousand, but at the present time it is supposed to exceed a million and two hundred thousand. This is an increase of more than thirty-three per cent. in ten years. Now, in the absence of accurate data connected with the present year of 1870, we can only suggest an approximation to the present condition of agriculture in the State, and this may be ascertained by adding the above per centage to the figures contained in the census reports of 1860, which, with regard to the most important particulars, are as follows:

Improved farm lands, 3,476,296 acres.
Unimproved farm lands, 3,554,538 acres.
Cash value of farm lands, $160,836,495.
Number of horses in the State, 137,917.
Number of cattle, 478,344.
Number of sheep, 1,271,743.
Number of swine, 372,386.
Value of live stock, $23,714,771.
Bushels of wheat, 8,336,368.
Bushels of Indian corn, 12,444,676.
Bushels of oats, 4,036,980.
Pounds of wool, 3,960,888.
Bushels of potatoes, 5,261,245.
Value of orchard productions, $1,122,074.
Pounds of butter, 15,503,482.
Pounds of cheese, 1,641,897.
Pounds of maple sugar, 4,051,822.
Gallons of sorgham molasses, 86,953.
Gallons of maple molasses, 78,988.
Pounds of honey, 769,282.
Value of slaughtered animals, $5,093,362.

In 1860 the value of the live stock in the State was $23,714,791, and at the beginning of the year 1869 it had increased to $54,426,109. The wheat crop for 1867, a good average year, amounted to 16,000,000 bushels of what is known as winter wheat; the clip of wool reached 10,500,000 pounds; and the apple crop amounted to 410,000 barrels, the estimated value of which was $1,500,000. But the latest authentic figures by which we can exhibit the wealth of Michigan in leading agricultural products are for the years 1866, 1867, and 1868, as follows:

Products.	Amount of crop.	Average yield per acre.	Number of acres in each crop.	Value per bushel or pound.	Total valuation.
1866.					
Indian corn, bushels	16,118,680	32	503,709	82	13,217,318
Wheat, bushels	14,740,639	13.8	1,068,162	2.55	37,588,630
Rye, bushels	413,150	15.5	26,655	1.05	437,939
Oats, bushels	8,293.877	34.7	236.135	.47	3,898,122
Barley, bushels	418.971	25	16,759	1.02	427,350
Buckwheat, bushels	1,306,819	20	65,341	.98	1,280,683
Potatoes, bushels	5,037,298	110	45,793	.56	2,820,877
Tobacco, pounds	278,786	1200	232	.15	48,818
Hay, tons	1,218,959	1.3	937,651	13.75	16,760,682
Total	......	......	2,900,447	......	76,473,423
1867.					
Indian corn, bushels	15,118.000	31.4	481.464	.96	14,513.280
Wheat, bushels	15,250,000	12.4	1,229,838	2.34	35,685,000
Rye, bushels	600.000	17.2	34.883	1.30	780,000
Oats, bushels	8,045,000	29.5	272,711	.68	5,470,600
Barley, bushels	418,000	20.9	20,000	1.36	568,480
Buckwheat, bushels	1,293.000	17.2	75,174	1.04	1,341.720
Potatoes, bushels	5,750,000	97.5	58,974	.93	4,197.500
Tobacco, pounds	3,500.000	1000	3,500	.21	735.000
Hay, tons	1,377,000	1.3	1,059,230	16.14	22,224,780
Total	......	......	3,235,774	......	85,519,360
1868.					
Indian corn, bushels	18,815.000	33	570,151	.76	14,299,400
Wheat, bushels	16,012,000	12 5	1,280,960	1.64	26,259.680
Rye, bushels	606,000	18.1	33,480	1.09	660,640
Oats, bushels	7,562.000	30.1	251,229	.50	3,781,000
Barley, bushels	430,000	23.3	18,454	1.56	670,800
Buckwheat, bushels	1.267,000	19.4	63,309	.82	1,638,940
Potatoes, bushels	5,650,000	94	60,106	.56	3,164,000
Tobacco, pounds	3,430,000	1100	3,118	,21	720,360
Hay, tons	1,473,000	1.25	1,178,400	15.00	22,095,000
Total	......	......	3,461,207	......	72,689,660

The several incorporated bodies to whose care the farming interests have been assigned are the State Board of Agriculture, the Michigan Agricultural Society, and the Agricultural College, already noticed in these pages. According to R. F. Johnstone, who holds the position of secretary of the society just named, "the general system of agriculture in Michigan has been largely governed by the necessity which has compelled each farmer to apply all his abilities to the clearing and amelioration of the surface of the land. But the time has come when this system must be changed, the necessity for which is indicated by the decreased production of fields longest under cultivation. Farms that formerly produced thirty to forty bushels of the choicest wheat to the acre now seldom yield over twenty-five, and in many cases the quality is inferior; and where this yield is exceeded it is upon the new and recently cleared lands, where the soil is yet rich in the elements of fertility with which nature has supplied the surface."

Of government lands undisposed of, lately lying in the State of Michigan, there were more than four and a half millions of acres; and, in view of that fact, the following particulars are worth reproducing: That part of the southern peninsula known as the "Grand Traverse Country" has recently been attracting the attention of actual settlers and parties speculating in lands. In this district the State Agricultural College has located over one hundred thousand acres. The climate and soil are favorable to the growth of peaches, pears, grapes, and other fruits. Wheat of the best quality, comparing favorably with any raised in other parts of the State, is successfully cultivated. Its sheep-walks are highly commended. Concerning the timber there, the secretary of the State Board of Agriculture remarks as follows: "The prevailing growth over a large portion of the country, embracing the best soil for cultivation, is the sugar-maple. Having considerable acquaintance with this species of tree, from the Penobscot to the Potomac and Ohio, the writer can safely say that he never saw such grand specimens as are to be met with in countless numbers in the Grand Traverse Country. They are frequently found of a height of sixty to seventy feet, without a limb, of a diameter of three feet or more at the ground, and very straight. Of course, such large trees cannot stand as closely together as smaller ones; they hold possession of the ground, however, which in many cases is free from undergrowth, so that the forest presents the appearance of an artificial plantation or park through which the people on horseback may readily pass in any direction."

With regard to the condition of the public lands of Michigan, we gather from the records in the office of the Secretary of State the subjoined information. Of the primary school land, during the year 1869, there were sold 25,940 acres for $103,936, against 28,848 for $115,393 in the year preceding. Swamp lands sold, 7,369 acres, for $11,253; University land, 88 acres, for $1,053; Agricultural School land, 13,480 acres, for $43,000; Asylum land, 80 acres, for $640; State Building land for $260; Salt Spring land, 196 acres, for $945; Internal Improvement land, 559 acres, for $699; and Normal School land for $160, making a grand total of 45,475 acres for $161,948. According to the State census of 1865 the public lands amounted to 35,995,520 acres; of which 3,647,645 were improved, and 12,086,660 were liable to pay taxes.

The grant to the State, under the act of Congress known as the Swamp Land Act, was about six millions of acres. The lands were located in all parts of the State. Though known as swamp lands, a large proportion of them were well adapted to agricultural purposes, and many of them were covered with valuable forests. The appropriations made by the State Legislatures prior to 1868 amounted to more than 4,000,000 of acres.

With the above figures before him, taken in connection with the general descriptions in the first part of this volume, the reader will obtain a fair idea of the condition of agriculture in the State of Michigan in 1868.

Another statement which may be added in this connection is that of the aggregate cash value per acre of the farm products of the State for the year 1869; which is as follows: Corn, $25.08; wheat, $20.50; rye, $19.72; oats, $15.05; barley, $36.34; buckwheat, $15.90; potatoes, $52.64; tobacco, $231; hay, $18.75; and aggregate of all crops per acre, $21.

With regard to the fruit culture, we submit the following returns for 1869: From 12,000 to 15,000 acres of land are devoted to fruit culture in Western Michigan, the greater portion of which is planted in trees not yet bearing. The average prices of fruit during the season were about as follows: Strawberries per quart, 10 cents; raspberries, 12 cents; blackberries, 8 cents; apples ber bushel, 80 cents; pears, $3; cherries, $4; plums, $3; quinces, $4; peaches, per box or basket, 75 cents; grapes per pound, 10 cents. The value of the fruit crop of the season is estimated as follows: Apples, $113,392; peaches, $563,722; pears, $11,262; cherries, $2,520; grapes, $7,110; blackberries, $107,705; raspberries, $50,617; strawberries, $12,737; and plums, $1,100; total, $870,165. The total shipments from twelve ports in the region named are stated as follows: Apples, bushels, 141,740; peaches, baskets, 751,630; quinces, baskets, 446; pears, baskets, 3,754; plums, baskets, 490; cherries, baskets, 630; grapes, pounds, 71,100;

blackberries, quarts, 1,346,324; raspberries, quarts, 421,812; strawberries, quarts, 127,372; cranberries, bushels, 370; cider, barrels, 660; tomatoes, baskets, 145.

The appropriations made by the State for the support of the Agricultural College in 1869 amounted to $45,000.

Having elsewhere spoken of the total area of the State of Michigan, we insert in this place a summary of the counties in which it is divided. Of course, in the extent of their population, there is great difference, and while some of them are not fully organized, we find the number to be seventy-five, and their names as follows, with the population according to the census of 1870, excepting those marked with a star, which are from the census of 1864, there being no later returns at this date:

Alcona, population, 693; Allegan, 18,831; Alpena, includes "Thunder Bay," of Lake Huron, 2,756; Antrim, Grand Traverse Region, 1,985; Barry, 22,070; Bay, on Saginaw Bay, 15,900; *Berrien, 25,856; Benzie, 2,184; Branch, 26,244; Calhoun, 36,172; *Cass, 17,776; Cheboygan, includes island of Mackinaw, 2,197; Chippeway, includes Saute St. Marie, 1,690; Clare, —; Clinton, 22,886; Crawford, ——; Delta, 2,421; Eaton, 25,196; *Emmet, extreme northern part of Lower Peninsula, and includes Mackinaw City, 1,211; Genessee, 33,910; Gladwin, 14; Grand Traverse, Grand Traverse Region, 4,332; Gratiot, 17,869; Hillsdale, 31,705; Houghton, includes Copper Region and Porcupine Mountains, 13,905; Huron, on Saginaw Bay, 9,053; Ingham, includes Lansing, State capital, 25,281; Ionia, 27,682; Iosco, on Saginaw Bay, 3,155; Isabella, 4,479; Jackson, 36,082; Kalamazoo, 32,068; Kalcasca, Grand Traverse Region, 424; Kent, 50,330; Kewenaw, includes Copper Region, Porcupine Mountains, and Isle Royal, 4,206; Lake, 548; Lapeer, 21,355; Leelenaw, Grand Traverse Region, 4,569; Lenawee, 45,635; Livingston, 19,339; Macomb, on Lake St. Clair, 27,617; Manistee, 6,084; Manitou, 1,043; Marquette, Iron Region, 14,982; *Mason, 844; Mecosta, 5,645; Menominee, on Green Bay, 1,892; Macinac, head of Lake Michigan, 1,716; Midland, 3,021; Missaukee, 130; Monroe, on west end of Lake Erie, 27,486; Montcalm, 13,351; Montmorency, ——; Muskegon, 14,899; *Newaygo, 3,481; Oakland, 40,898; *Oceana, 2,379; Ogemaw, 12; Ontonagon, includes Copper Region and Porcupine Mountains, 2,895; Osceola, 2,105; Oscoda, 70; Otsego, ——; Ottawa, 26,558; Presque Isle, 355; Roscommon, ——; Saginaw, includes Salt Region, 38,902; Sanilac, 14,564; Schoolcraft, includes "Pictured Rocks" of Lake Superior, 52; Shiawassee, 20,856; St. Clair, on Lake St. Clair, 36,837; St. Joseph, 26,669; Tuscola, on Saginaw Bay, 13,715; *Van Buren, 17,830; Washtenaw, includes "University of Michigan," at Ann Arbor, 41,449; Wayne, includes City of Detroit, and partly on Lake St. Clair, 119,685; Wexford, 950.

As the general census for 1870 is not likely to be published for one or two years, our only way to study the recent progress of Michigan is by mentioning such statements as may happen to come, in an isolated form, to our knowledge. For example, here is a significant paragraph bearing upon the city of Detroit. In 1860 the total population was about 46,000, and the number of families in the city was 8,963. In 1870 it contained about 80,000 inhabitants and 14,698 families; and to these figures may be added of mercantile shops 718, groceries 381, offices 446, hotels 63, boarding-houses 196, churches 54, public halls 13, public schools 108, machine shops 893, and restaurants 669. Barring one or two items, these results are certainly creditable to the people, whose progress in material prosperity is remarkable.

Every intelligent and thoughtful man occasionally looks forward to the future, and wonders what his State and country are to be in years to come. Of course we cannot lift the veil and view the State as it will be a generation or a century hence. But we can look back and see what it was a half century since. We can trace its progress from that time to the present, and from its growth in the past we may form a tolerably correct idea of what it may be in the future.

The first census of Michigan was taken in 1810, and showed a population of 4,618 whites, 120 free colored, and 24 slaves. Total, 4,762.

In 1820 there were 8,591 whites, 174 colored. Total, 8,765.

In 1830, 31,346 whites, 261 colored, 32 slaves. Total, 31,639.

In 1840, 211,560 whites, 707 colored. Total, 212,267.

In 1850, 395,071 whites, 2,583 colored. Total, 397,654.

In 1860, 742,314 whites, 6,798 colored. Total, 749,213.

In 1864, according to the State census, the population was 805,379.

The vote of the State at the election of 1869 was over 220,000. This, allowing one voter to every five persons, would indicate a population in 1870 of over 1,100,000. There is scarcely a doubt that the census of 1870 will show a population in the two peninsulas of more than 1,200,000.

The ratio of increase from 1840 to 1850 was 87⅓ per cent. From 1850 to 1860, 88⅓. A fraction over 60 per cent. increase from 1860 to 1870 would make the population of the State at the latter date 1,200,000, as above estimated. And the same ratio of increase from 1870 to 1880 would swell the population to about two millions.

We confidently expect that the above figures will be found none too high ten years hence. We see no reason why we may not expect an increase of sixty per cent. during that time. No part of the State can yet be said to be densely populated, while large portions of it are yet covered with primeval forests, in which the sound of the settler's axe has never been heard.

Only at one time since the first settlement of the State, and then but for a brief period, has the advance been as rapid as at present. Everywhere, in city, village, and country, there is a substantial and healthful progress. With judicious legislation, both State and National, this progress should continue. Such legislation it is proper to expect; and hence, if made the recipient of such, the continued prosperity and rapid development of Michigan, is undoubtedly assured.

MINERAL WEALTH.

The copper interest of Michigan was first brought into public notice by the speculation excitement of 1845. The large spur of country which projects into Lake Superior, called Keweenaw Point, became the El Dorado of that day. In that year the first active operations were commenced near Eagle Harbor, and the Cliff mine was developed; in 1848 the mines on the Ontonagon were first opened; and in 1855 operations were commenced in what is known as the Pewabic mine. For several years after these mines were discovered the Falls of St. Mary were a great stumbling-block in the way of success, but the opening of the canal between the waters of Lakes Huron and Superior gave a wonderful impetus to the whole business, which steadily increased from a yield of about twenty-five hundred tons of pure copper in 1853 to eighty-five hundred tons in 1861. During the twenty years succeeding 1845 there were not less than one hundred and twenty copper-mining companies organized under the laws of Michigan. The amount of capital invested was not less than twelve millions of dollars. What is known as the copper region, extending about one hundred and thirty-five miles in length and from one to six in width, is divided into three districts, each one of which has some peculiarities of product; the Ontonagon or western district developing more masses; while the other two, the Keweenaw Point and Portage Lake districts, are more prolific in the vein rocks, the copper being generally scattered. The copper product of Michigan from 1845 to 1868 amounted to 128,275 tons, the total value of which has been put down at more than seventy-three millions of dollars.

Another mineral interest of Michigan, which promises to become an important source of revenue, is that of iron. The first shipment of pig-iron of any consequence was made in 1858, although the mines were opened in 1857 by the "Pioneer Iron Company." The centre of this business is Marquette, on Lake Superior, and from that county is obtained one-fifth of all the iron ore used in the United States. In the village and vicinity are several shafts more than a hundred feet deep, a number of blast furnaces, and several machine-shops where various kinds of castings and iron manufactures are turned out. It has been demonstrated that there is no better iron to be found anywhere than among the hills of Lake Superior, and shipments of ore are now regularly made to the States of Ohio, Pennsylvania, and New York. The ore is found in a slate formation, and is granular, specular, and hermatite, yielding 75 per cent. of pure iron. For car-wheels, gearing, shafting, for cranks and flanges nothing has been found to surpass or even equal the iron of Michigan. The whole region lying back of Marquette is said to contain an inexhaustible supply of iron ore, and there are people who believe that Lake Superior is surrounded with a belt of the same ore.

These facts, as it has been truly said by another, exhibit the untold wealth of Michigan in iron ore alone, and point with certainty to an extent of business that will add millions to the invested capital of the State, dot it with iron manufactories of all kinds, and furnish regular employment to thousands of citizens, while the wares of the State and the raw material will be found in all the markets of the country. The product of Michigan iron for 1869 was in advance of all previous years, was sold at the rate of two dollars per ton, and gave employment to about two hundred vessels, the demand having been greater than the supply. For purposes of reference we subjoin the value of the product annually for a term of years: 1858, $249,202; 1859, $575,529; 1860, $736,496; 1861, $419,401; 1862, $984,977; 1863, $1,416,935; 1864, $1,867,215; 1865, $1,590,430; 1866, $2,405,960; 1867, $3,475,720; 1868, $3,676,705; 1869, $5,296,315.

We now come to the salt interest of the State. It was demonstrated by the late Douglass Houghton that the Salt Springs of Michigan would prove to be valuable, but it was not until 1859 that salt became a staple article of merchandise for home consumption. It was in that year that certain enterprising citizens of East Saginaw petitioned to the Legislature for the passage of laws to protect the salt interest; and an act was at once passed allowing a bounty of ten cents per bushel and an exemption from taxation on real and personal property used in the manufacture, the bounty to be paid when five thousand bushels had been made by the manufacturers. This gave an impulse to the business, and operations were commenced at Grand Rapids and East Saginaw. The law allowing a bounty was amended in 1860 greatly reducing the amount, and providing that all companies which commenced manufacturing previous to the first of August, 1861, should be allowed five cents per barrel, until they received one thousand dollars, after which all bounties ceased. The property was exempt from taxation for five years, and none of the companies formed since 1861 received any bounty.

In 1869 the Saginaw Valley turned out not less than 596,873 barrels of salt, and the Legislature provided by law for the appointment of a State inspector of salt, the first man appointed having been Dr. S. S. Garrigues. At that date there were in the Saginaw Valley 59 companies, 119 salt blocks, 4,198 covers, 4,045 kettles, 123 grainers; 3,000 men were employed in the business, and the cost of producing was thirty cents per bushel, and the capital invested amounted to $2,632,500. At Port Austin the yield for 1869 was 14,000 barrels.

In 1833 certain plaster beds were discovered in Kent county, in the vicinity of Grand Rapids, which have been found to be inexhaustible. They were first brought to market through the enterprise of De Garmo Jones, of Detroit. The mineral is found imbedded in slate, and is cut out clear; and the demand for it having been great in all parts of the western country, it finds a ready market, to which it is transported by the Detroit and Milwaukee railroad. The amount annually manufactured in this locality varies from ten to twenty thousand tons.

It is worthy of mention, in this connection, that during the summer of 1870 there was quite a rush of people to the town of Eaton Rapids, seeking health from the magnetic waters of that place. These waters are very copious, and certain properties have been discovered in them which are said to upset many of the old opinions of scientific men. That they are of great value in curing certain types of disease, seems to have been fully demonstrated. But the town of St. Louis, in Gratiot county, claims to be equally supplied with magnetic waters with Eaton Rapids, and a report made by Professor Samuel P. Duffield claims for them a variety of valuable qualities. In a paper which Professor Alexander Winchell read before the association, for the advancement of science on the magnetic wells of the State, he submitted many interesting particulars. The wells are widely separated in position, and their waters are derived from different geological formations. Some are supplied from the bottom of the coal measures, and others from geological positions five hundred and one thousand feet lower. Nor is there any greater correspondence in the chemical constitution of the waters. They are all, however, more or less alkaline, and some of them saline and chalybeate. The conclusions arrived at by the professor are as follows: 1. Nearly all pieces of iron and steel are found possessed of permanent and varying polarity. 2. Neutral iron is polarized by being placed in the magnetic meridian or in a vertical position. 3. This induced polarity can be detected in its effects upon a permanent magnet. 4. The mineral waters of Michigan tend to induce polarity (i. e., the same as the south end of the needle) in the outer end of a rod of soft iron passed through a cork into a bottle of the water. 5. This property is retained by the water for weeks and months. 6. A rod of steel, or a knife blade, immersed in the water from twenty minutes to ten hours acquires very sensible polarity, though practically neutral before immersion. 7. No satisfactory evidence exists that the water itself is polarized or that magnetism can be bottled up in it. 8. The phenomena are more likely to arise from some chemical action between the water and the iron; and this supposition is strengthened by the fact that they arise equally when the rod is simply moistened, when it is immersed in water rendered artificially alkaline or salt, and when the surface of the steel is unpolished, and, or *not*, arise when pure rain water is employed. 9. Should it be shown that the magnetism is *not* excited by chemical action, and that the water itself possesses a feeble polarity, we may recall to mind the mountains of magnetic oxyd of iron near Lake Superior, the disintegration of which, in former ages, has supplied an enormous amount of magnetic iron sand, which is strewn along the shores of the great lakes, and enters largely into the constitution of the palæozoic strata, forming sometimes, it may be, real lodestone strata, as alleged, and that particles of this magnetic oxyd may float, polarized, in water flowing from subterranean reservoirs in any part of the lower peninsula of Michigan.

Vast coal beds underlie nearly the whole central portion of Michigan, most of it of very good quality, yet nearly all the coal consumed in the State is brought from Pennsylvania and Ohio, at a very heavy cost in the way of lake and railroad freight charges. In view of these facts it is a matter of individual interest to nearly all the people of the State to have the coal veins of Michigan opened and worked. The developments thus far in mining it have not reached important results, although beds of it have been worked in Shiawassee and Jackson counties with success; but it is gratifying to state that a very great improvement is soon to take place in the development of this important element of wealth. The coal-field of Michigan, according to Professor J. W. Foster, is about one hundred feet thick, and extends over an area of five thousand square miles.

In 1869 the Governor of Michigan, Henry P. Baldwin submitted to the Legislature the importance of a thorough and complete geological survey of the State, and an interesting report made by the joint committees of the two houses, and signed by Lyman D. Norris and John Q. McKernan, was made the basis of farther legislation. From that report we are permitted to extract the subjoined summary of geological exploration and legislation in Michigan from the earliest to the present times:

1659.—First mention of copper in the Upper Peninsula, in the Relations of the Jesuit Fathers concerning their mission in the New World.

1771.—First mining enterprise, near the forks of the Ontonagon river, by Alexander Henry. (See, farther on, the speech of an Indian chief of Ontonagon, at the treaty of Fond du Lac.)

1789.—Explorations of Alexander McKenzie, on the shores of Lake Superior.

1800.—Under the elder Adams, Congressional resolution providing for an agent to collect information of the copper mines of Lake Superior.

No results extant.

1819.—Expedition of Governor Cass and H. R. Schoolcraft along the south shore of Lake Superior.

Results meager; published in Schoolcraft's "Journal of Travels," etc., 1821.

1823.—Expedition of Major Long, with several scientific gentleman, who, on their return from the Red River of the North, coasted the north shore of Lake Superior.

Reports of the War Department.

1823.—Expedition of Governor Cass and Colonel McKenney, of the Indian Department, to Fond du Lac, to negotiate the treaty with the Chippewas.

The Governor, in his speech in the Council, says: "We also wish that you would allow your Great Father to look through the country, and take such copper as he may find. This copper does you no good, and it would be useful to us to make into kettles, buttons, bells, and a great many other things."

The replies of the chiefs are quite characteristic and piquant, and are models of brevity and point, quite suggestive to legislative councils of later day.

Shin-gaw-ba W'ossin, Chief of Saute St. Marie band, says:

"If you have any copper on your lands I advise you to sell it. It is of no advantage to us. * * * If any of you have any knowledge, bring it to light."

Yellow Thunder.—"In my country there is no copper. If I said there was I should lie."

Plover, (of Ontonagon.)—"I have no knowledge of any copper in my country. There is a rock there. I met some of your people in search of it. I told them if they took it, to *steal* it, and not let me catch them."

Another chief, (of Ontoganon,) name not known.—"You have heard the words of the Plover on this rock. This, Fathers, is the property of no one man. It belongs alike to us. It was put there by the Great Spirit, and it is ours. In the life of my father, the British were busy working it. It was then big, like that table. They tried to raise it to the top of the hill, and they failed. They then said the copper was not in the rock, but in the banks of the river. They dug for it by a light, working under ground. The earth fell in and killed three of their men. It was then left until now. Fathers, at the time of which I speak, a great price was paid by the English for our permission. We expect no less from you. If you take this rock, Fathers, the benefit must be to our children who are now but this high (a foot.) For ourselves we care but little. We are old and nearly worn out."

Another chief, (name not known.)—"*Fathers*, the copper I brought here was taken from the bed of the river. I will point out the place."

Maw-gaw-gid.—"There is no metal in our part of the country. I have heard neither our old nor young men speak of any."

This copper rock was found by Captain Porter, lying on the west bank of the Ontonagon, about thirty-four miles from its mouth, weighing about one ton, and two-thirds pure copper; but as three cataracts, with a descent of seventy feet, was between the rock and the lake, the captain did not "steal" the copper. Touching the land that the Great Spirit had given the red men, the commissioners were more successful.

"Sketches of a Tour to the Lakes," by Thomas L. McKenney, Baltimore. 1827.

1831.—Dr. Houghton was with Schoolcraft in an United States expedition to find the sources of the Mississippi, and in his reports refers to the aid received from this exploration.

State of Michigan.—1837.—Session laws, page 14, provides for a geological, zoological, botanical, and topographical survey. Dr. Douglass Houghton as chief, and five assistants, were appointed. These assistants were Dr. Abram Sager, (botany and zoology,) S. W. Higgins, (tôpographer,) C. C. Douglass, Bela Hubbard, William P. Smith, and later, Dr. John Wright, botanist, was added.

1838.—Session laws, page 119, is a new and enlarged act.

The reports made under these acts were as follows:

1838, January 26th.—General Geology. 37 pp.

1839, February 4.—A report of 153 pp., devoted to Geology, Zoology, Botany, Topography, and to the local geology in Eaton, Ingham, Jackson, Wayne, and Monroe. This year the department of Zoology and Botany were suspended.

1840, January 6.—A special Report on Salt Springs.

1840, February 3.—A report of 109 pp. upon Geology and Topography, and local examination of the geology and coal measures of Jackson, Calhoun, Kalamazoo, Ionia, and Kent, Lenawee, Hillsdale, Branch, St. Joseph, Cass, Berrien, Washtenaw, Oakland, and Livingston counties.

1841, February 1.—Came the fourth annual report, 169 pp., (89 pp. devoted to Geology, etc., of Lake Superior country,) Latitudes and Magnetic Variations, rise and fall of lake water, and general geology of the organized counties, and "furs, fish, and harbors of Lake Superior."

1841, February 4.—A brief report relative to State and county maps. Four county maps were published and sold. Ten were finished and ready for the engravers. They are waiting yet, if extant.

1842, January 25.—Dr. Houghton sends in his last (5th) Annual Report of only 6 pages, with notices of the geology of the western portion of the Lake Superior country.

By the act of 1837 $29,000 were appropriated, $3,000 for 1837, $6,000 for 1838, $8,000 for 1839, and $12,000 for 1840.

By the act of 1838 this appropriation was so modified as to give $12,000 a year for three years, with a conditional drawback upon the University fund of $4,000.

The financial pressure of the times cut short the labors of Dr. Houghton, and while he was in the active prosecution of a plan for connecting the linear surveys of the public lands with a geological survey, his death, by drowning, near Eagle river, on the night of October 13th, 1845, put an end to his usefulness, and all the people of our young State are mourning over his untimely death. His was truly a sad loss to the State and nation.

An enthusiastic lover of science for itself and for no selfish ends, with a constitution that seemed never to know fatigue or fear, labor or danger, he had withal a kindly, loving heart, that drew to itself all who were brought within his circle. Simple as a child and as unassuming as he was scholarly, he wrote his name in the history of this State, there to remain forever.

The influence that such men have lives after them, and if there is anything of unsensational enthusiasm in the advocacy of the writer of this report of such thorough geologic work as would most gratify the spirit of that great and good man of science, (if he is permitted "to participate in the cares and concerns of this mortal life,") it springs from the recollection of many months of intimate personal intercourse had with him in the earliest days of our University. His low, compact, sinewy figure, crowned with a dome-like brain, always bent downward like a full head of wheat, as he sauntered across the college campus, surrounded by the baker's dozen of the students of those days—always welcome companions to him—is one of memory's pictures never to be effaced. With his forward and downward look he seemed ever to be interrogating mother Earth and asking for her secrets, while no rare bug, or beetle, or blade of grass, or stone escaped his notice, but was seized and examined and taken as the text for many pleasant and instructive lectures to the loving group that stood around.

"Peace to the just man's memory." He is at rest from his labors in the bosom of that common mother whose secrets he sought so earnestly to explore. We may confidently believe that his title to the *six feet* finally to be allotted to us all is under the good old common law tenure: "Cujus est solum, ejus est usque ad cœlum." He who owns the soil, owns it to the Heavens.

And what were the results of his labors? Necessarily fragmentary and incomplete, they were not inconsiderable. His discoveries and developments of the Gypsum, Marl, Mineral Springs, Bog Iron Ore, Coal, Iron, Copper and Brine Springs, (of which latter many analyses and locations are given now fully verified,) in various localities in this State, disclosed a world of undeveloped wealth, the rapid returns from which were many years delayed by the financial troubles of his day, the sparseness of settlements, the want of surplus capital, and the necessities among the pioneers of every State, to labor first for bread and a foothold.

1847, March 1.—Reference should here be made to an act of Congress of this date, under which Dr. C. T. Jackson spent two seasons in an exploration of the Lake Superior region, and in 1849–50 made a report thereon of 801 pages.

This work was continued by Foster and Whitney, in their two reports, "Copper Lands" (224 pages) and "Iron Regions," (406 pages,) given to the world, the first 1850, April 15, and the second 1851, November 12.—*See Ex. Doc., No. 69, First Sess. XXXI Cong., vol. 9, and Ex. Doc. No. 4, Special Sess. XXXII Cong., vol. 3.*

Since then, a period of almost twenty years of unexampled development of mines and minerals in the upper peninsula, nothing has been done there by government, State or national, and but small expenditures have been authorized on the lower peninsula, as hereinafter detailed.

1859.—By act No. 206, the Governor was authorized to appoint a geologist and assistants to finish the survey; and $2,000 for that year, $3,000 for the following were appropriated.

Professor A. Winchell was commissioned by Governor Wisner, and sent in his first report December 31, 1860, of 330 pages, devoted wholly to the lower peninsula, setting forth the progress of the work for the years 1859 and 1860. Of this report, 210 pages are geological, 30 pages zoological, (Professor Miles',) and 85 pages botanical.

During the first year fully one-half the appropriation was absorbed in zoological work. The geological results, then, are properly chargeable with only $4,000. The whole two years' work was, at the request of Governor Wisner, kept in the lower peninsula, principally because the means provided were not sufficient to inaugurate effective work in the upper.

The work indicated from this report is a general survey of the settled counties, and of the entire lake shores of the lower peninsula, with detailed examinations, with a view of settling questions as to coal, gypsum and brine, and other questions connected with economic geology.

The practical results of Dr. Houghton's survey are too far from our day to estimate; but those of Professor Winchell are nearer our time, and can be found, more or less, in the current and contemporary news of the day.

A few of these results, addressed to those members of both houses, who will hinge their vote upon the question, "Will it pay?" your committee beg leave to refer to. Operations for coal in Hillsdale were arrested. The citizens of Grand Rapids were informed that if they would find brine, they must go lower, to the salina formation. The deepest and most productive salt basin was located beneath the Saginaw Valley, and as the result of pure geological induction in remote portions of the State, before the first brine was seen, 850 feet was fixed as the depth at which good brine would be found—a prophesy verified almost to a foot by Dr. Lathrop in the Saginaw Valley. A complete table of geological formations of the lower peninsula, and their equivalencies with recognized groups in other States, was for the first time constructed. The existence of gypsum beneath a ridge of clay on the shore of Tawas Bay was insisted on, and the discovery of that deposit, the commercial value of which is now a matter of notoriety, was made under the direction of Professor Winchell. Projected borings for artesian water, searches for coal, gypsum, and petroleum, have been favored or discouraged, and large outlays of money saved.

The existence of *three* salt basins was established, the upper of which supplies Bay City and vicinity, (except the deep wells;) the middle, the Saginaw; and the lower, the wells at St. Clair, Mt. Clemens and Port Austin. The wells at the three last named places were undertaken under the advice of the State Geologist, purely upon geological calculations, according to the methods of rigorous science. In the case of the St. Clair well, the communications of the Geologist with Colonel Whiting, as to depth, supply and strength of brine, are instructive indications of the value of science in business enterprises.

The special survey and report upon the geology and climatology of the Grand Traverse Region, 1866–7, has been the means (though wholly a private work) of turning the attention of the people to that country, and has largely increased its population, particularly of those interested in fruit culture, under the tempering influence of the waters of Lake Michigan.

More might be added, but this ought, in the opinion of your committee, to secure a liberal appropriation.

1861.—By joint resolution No. 7, provision was made for printing and distributing five thousand copies of the report made in 1859.

1861.—By act No. 64, two thousand dollars for the year, and a like sum for the next, were appropriated for continuing the geological survey, with direction to restrict labor to geology exclusively, except so far as the collection of specimens in botany and natural science may not materially interfere with the same.

Under this act but one thousand dollars was drawn and expended. Governor Blair failed to draw his warrant for the remainder, rather procrastinating than refusing, and the season for field work passed, and the country was soon involved in the tumult of war, and the continuance of the survey was not pressed by the officers in charge.

1863.—By act No. 212, a special appropriation of fifteen hundred dollars for that year, and a like sum for 1864, was appropiated to provide that a suitable person (presumably a geologist) should visit the salt localities of the State, and make a special survey thereof, with direct reference to the feasibility of salt boring; also, to collect and arrange suitable specimens of the different strata obtained from salt borings, and the same to arrange in a cabinet suitable for the same, in some room of the Capitol, (possibly the library room, as the *least* crowded and most capacious.)

Your committee are unable to find any public report showing the expenditure of this appropriation.

In the same year, by joint resolution No. 10, Professor Winchell, designated as "late" State geologist, is required to turn over to the board of State auditors all instruments, material, and property of any description, of the State, used by him and his assistants; also, all specimens, and the geological survey was closed—leaving, as your committee believe, six thousand dollars of unexpended appropriations, and a considerable amount of geological labor and material half done, but yet extant, and in condition to be saved and made of practical use to the people of this State.

It will be seen from this condensed review that, aside from the 89 pages of the reports of February 1, 1841, and a few brief notices subsequent thereto, a period of *twenty-eight years* of general growth, prosperity, and development has been allowed to pass, and the richest mineral territory in iron and copper in the world has been left wholly unaided by State appropriations in the development of its gigantic possibilities. Is it any wonder that the enterprising people of that far away region, who have accomplished so much with such little means, grow restive in a connection that brings them no share of the public money derived from a common taxation, that has been profusely scattered over the lower half of the State, in the shape of Prisons,

Reform Schools, Insane, Deaf, Dumb, and Blind Asylums, Normal School, Agricultural College, University, geological surveys, and internal improvements, and all the thousand and one ways that those *nearest* to the public treasury *reach* for its contents?

In the meanwhile, those hardy pioneers have labored and waited, until now, with a population of nearly 35,000, a capital invested in 112 companies for developing copper of $16,250,500, upon which has been paid dividends of $5,880,000, and an iron interest which, in the twelfth year of its commercial life, produced over one-fifth of all the iron mined in the United States, they have rights, and the State has duties—long-neglected duties—toward them, which it were wise to no longer neglect.

Your committee are of opinion that the State is fully able, and ought to be willing, to enter now upon an enlarged and liberal geologic survey of both peninsulas; that if but one can be undertaken, the Lake Superior country is entitled to the preference; and that the survey there, in addition to the duties usually assigned to such officials, should also include the statistics and history of the mineral, mining, smelting, manufacturing, and transportation interests; the compilation of accurate maps, showing the topography, geology, and timber, and the position of all mines, furnaces, and roads of the iron and copper region. Your committee would further note the fact that within the limits of the proposed survey, the State owns a large amount of swamp and school land, reserved from market on account of its supposed mineral value, the determination of which value is a matter of common interest to all the people, while the United States are also holders of large tracts of supposed mineral land, whose value is wholly unknown, as much of the data given by Foster and Whitney, nearly twenty years ago, is shown by private examination to have been erroneous and imperfect.

RAILROADS.

We have already alluded to the origin and building of the principal railroads of the State, and we now propose to speak of their success and present condition. The oldest and most successful is the Michigan Central. After passing into the hands of a private company it was extended to Chicago, a distance of 284 miles from Detroit; and in regard to its equipment, management, and general success it occupies a first-class position.

In May, 1849, it was completed and in operation from Detroit to New Buffalo. New Buffalo was a small village at the southern extremity of Lake Michigan, a few miles east of the present Michigan City. It has now entirely disappeared from the map. The Michigan Central Railroad terminated there, and from this point two daily lines of steamers ran to Chicago, a distance of nearly forty-five miles. The time between Chicago and New York became thus reduced to two and a half days. The Galena Railroad of Illinois was at that time completed and in operation from Chicago to Elgin, a distance of forty-two miles. The Galena Railroad Company for a time entertained the design of completing the Michigan Central road from New Buffalo into Chicago, but that was finally done by the Michigan Central Railroad Company themselves. On its line have sprung up a large number of beautiful towns and villages; the older places along the route have greatly increased, and the country through which it passes exhibits a degree of thrift and prosperity that will compare favorably with the most flourishing sections of the country. Its business arrangements are such that goods may now be shipped from Chicago to Portland, in Maine, with only one change of cars, and four passenger trains leave the two cities of Chicago and Detroit daily. The eastern terminus being at the latter city, it has full advantage of the various connections at that point, viz: The Great Western and Grand Trunk Railways, the important steamboat routes to Cleveland, Buffalo, and Lake Superior, and the different freight routes to the different lake ports of which Detroit is the nucleus. By means of what is called the "Joliet cut-off" it is connected with St. Louis by the "Chicago, Alton, and St. Louis Railroad." As this is the leading railroad artery of the State we submit the following particulars furnished from an official source:

In reference to connections with other roads in the State of Michigan, it is evident that the managers are pursuing the wise policy of assisting such new lines as must increase the local business, and whose friendship must be permanently beneficial. In furtherance of these views, aid was given to the Jackson, Lansing, and Saginaw Railroad, which has now become a valuable ally; and also to the Grand River Valley Railroad, extending from Jackson to Grand Rapids, a distance of ninety-four miles. The latter road is now operated as the Grand River Valley Division of the Michigan Central Railroad, under terms of an agreement whereby certain money was advanced to complete and equip it, the lessees covenanting to pay the interest on its bonds, and a maximum rental after three years, equivalent to five per cent. upon its capital stock. Although this road has only been in working order for a short period it is earning a fair revenue and contributing a large and remunerative business to the main line. Arrangements have also been made with the directors of the Michigan Air-line Railroad for a lease of that portion of their road between Niles and Jackson, at a rental which should be equal to the interest on bonds which might be used in completing it, not exceeding $18,000 per mile, at eight per cent. interest. The distance by this line between Niles and Jackson is sixteen miles shorter than the one now in use, and renders the business of a rich section of country lying in many places twenty-five or thirty miles south of the Michigan Central Railroad directly tributary to it. The *Peninsular Railway*, extending from Battle Creek to Lansing; the *Kalamazoo and South Haven Railroad*, running from Kalamazoo to Bloomingdale; the *Fort Wayne, Jackson, and Saginaw Railroad*, and the *Chicago and Michigan Lake Shore Railroad*, are all valuable tributaries to the Michigan Central Railroad, especially the latter, which opens up the finest fruit-growing section of the State. Arrangements were made in 1869 conducing to more harmonious relations and greater unity of action between the Great Western Railway of Canada and the Michigan Central Railroad; and on January 1st, 1870, the eastern and western agencies of both roads were consolidated. The benefits of this consolidation are apparent in the reduction of expenses and in a more active co-operation for securing business; but the North Shore Route will be able to compete for traffic on much better terms when the projected line from Glencoe to Buffalo is built, and when it is able to obtain at the latter place benefits which are now only conceded to the South Shore Route in consequence of the rivalry existing between the New York Central and Erie Railroads. The new line from Glencoe to Buffalo will be nearly an air-line from Detroit, with easy grades, and can be operated very economically at a high rate of speed. It is estimated that the distance between New York and Chicago via Buffalo, Glencoe, Detroit, and the short cut-off between Niles and Jackson, alluded to before, will not exceed 900 miles, and that much faster time can be made over the new route than over the present short line via Pittsburg.

The Michigan Southern is another of the great lines of travel and freight transportation to which the State owes much of its prosperity. The history of this road, for which we are indebted to Henry M. Flint, Esq., afford another example of the benefits of railroad consolidation:

The Michigan Southern and Northern Indiana Railroad Company was formed on the 25th of April, 1855, by the consolidation of two railroads which had existed for some time previously, namely, the Michigan Southern railroad, and the Northern Indiana railroad. The Northern Indiana railroad, as it existed at the time of its consolidation with the Michigan Southern Railroad Company in 1855, originated in a company formed in Indiana, as early as 1835, under a charter from the State, as the Buffalo and Mississippi Railroad Company. The Northern Indiana Railroad Company commenced its operations in the year 1852, under the provisions of a charter from the State of Ohio, which was granted on the 3d of March, 1851. The Northern Indiana and Chicago railroad had also commenced its operations about the same time, under a charter from the State of Illinois. The three roads last named became merged into one about the year 1854, under the name of the Northern Railroad Company.

The Michigan Southern Railroad Company was formed under a charter from the State of Michigan, on the 9th of May, 1846, and in pursuance of an act authorizing the sale to them of the existing Michigan Southern railroad and the Jackson and Tecumseh Branch thereof, which were both owned and operated by the State of Michigan. The organization was completed, and the conditions of the act were complied with in December, 1846, so that the Michigan Southern Railroad Company entered into possession of the railroad and its branch that year. The railroad from Monroe westward was commenced by the State of Michigan about 1838, but it was only finished as far as Hillsdale at the time of its sale to the Michigan Southern Railroad Company in 1846. It was extended by that company in 1852 to the Indiana State line, near Middlebury, and was connected there with the Northern Indiana railroad. The latter road was completed to Chicago in June, 1852.

The Jackson and Tecumseh Branch was extended to Jackson in 1855, and a branch was built from Constantine, which was the terminus of the old Michigan Southern railroad, to Three Rivers, in Michigan, in 1853. The Goshen Branch forms part of the Goshen air-line from Toledo to Elkhart, where it makes connection with the old line from Chicago to Monroe.

The Erie and Kalamazoo railroad from Toledo to Adrian, leased from the Erie and Kalamazoo Railroad Company, is run and used as part of the main line of the Michigan Southern railroad from Chicago to Toledo. Part of the Detroit, Monroe, and Toledo railroad, which was mostly built by the Michigan Southern Railroad Company, and is exclusively controlled and operated by them, is used as far as Monroe as part of the Michigan Southern railroad from Chicago to Detroit. The Detroit, Monroe, and Toledo road is also used as a line from Detroit to Toledo, connecting at Toledo with roads to Cincinnati and Cleveland.

The number of miles of road now owned and operated by the Michigan Southern and Northern Indiana Railroad Company is as follows:

Toledo to Chicago via old line, 243; Toledo to Elkhart, air-line, 132; Detroit to Toledo, 65; Monroe to Adrian, 33; Jackson Branch, 42; Three Rivers Branch, sub-leased, 12. Total miles, 527.

In September, 1849, soon after the organization of the Michigan Southern Railroad Company, a statement was submitted to the stockholders by the Board of Directors, exhibiting the condition of the road and the finances of the company, and soliciting a new subscription of a quarter of a million of dollars to provide means for extending the road west from Hillsdale. A portion of the stock was subscribed, and in the spring of 1850 the line from Hillsdale to Coldwater, a distance of twenty-two miles, was put under contract. The road then in operation from Monroe to Hillsdale, a distance of sixty-nine miles, was that which had been originally constructed by the State of Michigan. It had a wooden rail covered by a flat bar of iron. The company had released the Erie and Kalamazoo road, extending from Adrian to Toledo, thirty-three miles in length, making a total of one hundred and eleven miles then operated by the company.

In the original grading of these roads the crossing of the valleys was effected, for the most part, by bridges of timber. Since that time, however, the whole extent of the tracks on these roads has been relaid with heavy rails, and the valleys on the route have been filled with permanent embankments, with new bridges and culverts for the streams and water-courses. Heavy expenses have also been incurred in providing abundant station accommodation all along the line.

In the summer of 1850 the line was put under contract from Coldwater to Sturgis, a distance of twenty-three miles, and in March, 1851, this portion of the road was completed and opened. Some delay was experienced in determining upon the location of the line west of Sturgis, and contracts for the remainder of the road in Michigan were not made until May, 1851. During the winter and spring of 1851 the Indiana road was put under contract. The Michigan Southern road was opened to White Pigeon in the latter part of July, 1851. The Northern Indiana road was opened in successive stages: During the fall of 1851, to South Bend, and on the 9th of January, 1852, to La Porte. In February, 1852, the road was opened from Michigan City to Ainsworth, in Illinois, and to Chicago in March, 1852. On the 22d of May, 1852, the entire line was opened, and a passenger train went through from Toledo to Chicago. Thus, in the space of twenty months, embracing two severe winters, the company constructed one hundred and sixty miles of new road, and relaid and nearly rebuilt fifty miles of old road.

The last act of legislation necessary to the consolidation of the companies owning the Michigan Southern and the Northern Indiana lines of railroad, was passed by the Michigan Legislature on the 13th of February, 1855; full authority therefor having previously been given by the States of Illinois, Indiana, and Ohio. Immediately after the passage of the last-mentioned act, the necessary measures were taken to carry the same into effect, and on the 26th of April, 1855, the articles of consolidation were finally sanctioned and approved by the unanimous vote of the stockholders of the respective corporations.

Improvements of every kind at once sprang up in all directions, through the region in which the roads run. At Toledo, the new depot grounds were soon brought into use, and the whole business of that terminus was transferred to them. These grounds were situated on the Maumee river. At this point the Cleveland and Toledo railroad unites with the Michigan Southern. The inconvenient ferry which formerly existed at this point has long since been dispensed with, and in place of it a handsome bridge has been erected. This point is also the eastern terminus of the Toledo, Wabash and Western railroad, whose trains run into the passenger depot of the Michigan Southern road.

In February, 1868, a contract was entered into with the Erie railway, of New York, by the terms of which that company guarantees the building a broad gauge railroad from a point on the Atlantic and Great Western railway, near Akron, Ohio, to Toledo, Ohio, less than one hundred miles. The

Michigan Southern and Northern Indiana railroad agree to lay a third rail on their line to Chicago, thus to perfect a broad gauge route from Chicago to New York by one of the shortest lines. The new road will be completed within a year, and will effect a revolution in travel between New York and Chicago, as the wide and comfortable cars of the Erie road can then carry passengers from one city to the other without change.

The next road which we have to mention is the Detroit and Milwaukee Railroad, with which was incorporated the Detroit and Pontiac and the Oakland and Ottawa Railroads. It was first opened its entire distance, one hundred and eighty-eight miles, from Detroit to Grand Haven, in November, 1858. It has been the means of opening up one of the best farming regions of the State. The principal cities and towns upon its line are Pontiac, Fentonville, St. John's, Ionia, Grand Rapids, and Grand Haven, and the growth of these places has received a great impetus since its completion; while numerous villages have also sprung into being, as if by magic, at numerous points along the line. These changes are plainly visible in the improved trade of Detroit, and the increase from the same cause must continue to be strongly marked. In 1858 the company completed one of the finest railroad wharves in the world: it is fifteen hundred feet long by ninety broad, the west end of which is occupied by the freight house, the dimensions of which are four hundred and fifty by one hundred and thirty-two feet. In connection with this road, at its western terminus—Grand Haven—splendid steamships ply regularly between that place and the city of Milwaukee, having the most sumptuous accommodations for passengers, together with ample room for all classes of freight.

The population of that section of Michigan which is directly tributary to or dependent upon the Detroit and Milwaukee Railroad as a means of outlet is at the present time more than 250,000, having upward of one million acres of improved land. At Corunna, in Shiawassee county, the road crosses the immense bituminous coal bed, which stretches throughout the central portion of the State, and which is undoubtedly destined, at no very distant day, to prove a source of immense business to the road and of wealth to the mine owners. Opening, as it does, a road through the very heart of the State, and intersecting for two hundred miles much good farming land, the local business alone is now, and is destined to be, truly immense. The cost of this road was a little more than nine millions of dollars.

Although isolated and not extensive the Flint and Pere Marquette Railroad deserves a brief notice for what it has accomplished for the Saginaw valley. In 1856, when Congress adopted a general system of donations of the public lands in the Western States to aid in constructing railroads, lands were granted to Michigan for a similar purpose. In 1857 these lands were conferred by the Legislature upon the Pere Marquette Company, which surveyed the route of its road from Flint to Pere Marquette, in the county of Mason, upon the eastern shore of Lake Michigan, a distance of one hundred and seventy-two miles, and located the line in the summer of 1857. In September of that year, the commercial world was fearfully convulsed, and, owing to the constant disasters, the work of construction was not commenced until the fall of 1858. In the following year some thirteen miles of road were graded, and five miles of track was laid with Michigan iron manufactured at Wyandotte. The next year, 1858, the work of grading was continued, but the financial difficulties of the times were such as to preclude the company from obtaining their iron that season so as to extend the track. In 1860 the time had expired wherein the company were to complete the first twenty miles of the road, so as to entitle it to the benefit of the law of the State conferring upon the companies the lands granted by Congress to aid in its construction. In this dilemma, with the apprehension of a possible forfeiture being declared by the State, the company received from the governor and other influential officers and citizens of the State, such assurances of good will, that no advantage or exception would be taken if the company would prosecute the enterprise in good faith, and the contractors were induced to proceed and complete the first twenty-six and a half miles of the route.

Another State railroad is that of Amboy, Lansing, and Traverse Bay, which is designed to connect the great northern lumber region of the State with the markets of Indiana, Ohio, and Illinois. Although not belonging to Michigan, the great Canadian railways have exerted an important effect upon its prosperity, and the official intercourse between the managers of the Great Western and Grand Trunk roads and those of Michigan has been honorable as well as profitable to all the parties concerned.

The condition of the new railroads in the State on the first of January, 1870, was, in substance, as follows: The Allegan and Holland road, twenty-two miles long, was completed. The Flint and Pere Marquette road is expected to be finished as far as Henry, one hundred and twenty miles, before the year 1871. The Grand Rapids and Indiana road is expected to be completed before the close of 1870. The Michigan Air-line road is finished from Three Rivers to Centreville; and the Grand Rapids and Lake Shore road is progressing with despatch to Pentwater. In June, 1870, the Lake Superior and Mississippi Railroad was completed; it is one hundred and fifty miles in length, and is the connecting link between Duluth and St. Paul. Steamers of a large class now leave Cleveland and Detroit almost daily for Duluth, a distance of one thousand miles, making landings at all the American ports on Lakes Huron and Superior; and this new route to the far Northwest not only promises to be eminently popular with summer tourists, but will become a favorite line of travel for all emigrants bound to the head-waters of the Mississippi. On the 1st of August, 1870, it was announced that the State of Michigan had in operation not less than thirteen hundred and twenty-five miles of railroad, the cost and equipment of which was estimated at about $60,000,000; but with this fact we have to chronicle the following information: In the spring of 1870 the Supreme Court of Michigan decided that a certain act of the Legislature, passed in 1864, authorizing municipalities to issue bonds in aid of railroad companies was unconstitutional, and the bonds issued under said act invalid. On the 27th of July following the Legislature met in extraordinary session for the purpose of considering this question; and although the Governor in his message proposed that the said bonds should be made good, the Legislature by a decided vote refused to entertain the proposition. The debt thus set aside was stated to amount to $5,367,175.50, equivalent to a tax of $27.44 per capita on the total vote of the State at the preceding Presidential election. In September, 1870, the Fort Wayne, Jackson, and Saginaw railroad was completed, the distance from Jackson to Fort Wayne being 95 miles; at the latter place it is connected with the Jackson, Lansing, and Saginaw road, of which it virtually forms a part, the two lines making a distance of 211 miles. The lines of railroad which have been surveyed, but are not yet completed, amount to 968 miles.

LUMBERING INTEREST.

The pine forests of Michigan are a leading feature of its undeveloped wealth, and yet it has been estimated that its hard-wood forests are equally extensive and valuable. The pine lands are so located and distributed as to bring almost every portion of the State, sooner or later, in connection with the commerce of the lakes. The pine timber is generally interspersed with many other varieties, such as beach, maple, white ash, oak, cherry, etc., and in most cases the soil is suited to agricultural purposes. This is particularly the case on the western slope of the peninsula, on the waters of Lake Michigan, and along the central portion of the State. On the east and near Lake Huron, the pine districts are more extensively covered with pine timber, and generally not so desirable for farming purposes. There are good farming lands, however, all along the coast of Lake Huron, and extending back into the interior.

A large portion of the pine lands of the State are in the hands of the St. Mary Canal Company and individuals, who are holding them as an investment, and it is no detriment to this great interest, that the whole State has been thus explored and the choicest of the lands secured. The developments which have thus been made of the quality and extent of the pine districts, have given stability and confidence to the lumbering interest. And these lands are not held at exorbitant prices, but are sold upon fair and reasonable terms, such as practical business men and lumbermen will not usually object to.

It is a remarkable fact that almost every stream of water in the State, north of Grand river, penetrates a district of pine lands, and the mouths of nearly all these streams are already occupied with lumbering establishments of greater or less magnitude. These lumber colonies are the pioneers, and generally attract around them others who engage in agriculture, and thus, almost imperceptibly, the agricultural interests of the State are spreading and developing in every direction. The want of suitable means of access alone prevents the rapid settlement of large and fertile districts of the State, which are not unknown to the more enterprising and persevering pioneers, who have led the way through the wilderness, and are now engaged almost single-handed in their labors, not shrinking from the privations and sufferings which are sure to surround these first settlements in the new districts.

The Grand Traverse region, with its excellent soil, comparatively mild climate, and abundance of timber of every description, is attracting much attention, and extensive settlements have already commenced in many localities in that region. The coast of Lake Michigan, from Grand river north, for upwards of one hundred miles to Manistee river, presents, generally, a barren, sandy appearance, the sand hills of that coast almost invariably shutting out from the view the surrounding country.

North of the Manistee, however, this characteristic of the coast changes, and the hard timber comes out to the lake and presents a fine region of country, extending from Lake Michigan to Grand Traverse Bay, and beyond, embracing the head waters of the Manistee river. This large tract of agricultural land is one of the richest portions of the State, and having throughout its whole extent extensive groves of excellent pine timber interspersed, it is one of the most desirable portions of the peninsula. Grand Traverse Bay, the Manistee river, and River Aux Becs Scies are the outlets for the pine timber, and afford ample means of communication between the interior and the lake for such purposes. The proposed State roads will, if built, do much towards the settlement of this region. A natural harbor, which is being improved by private enterprise, is found at the mouth of the River Aux Becs Scies, and a new settlement or town has been started at this point. This is a natural outlet for a considerable portion of the region just described. The lands here, as in other localities in the new portions of the State, are such as must induce a rapid settlement whenever the means of communication shall be opened.

The valley of the Muskegon embraces every variety of soil and timber, and is one of the most attractive portions of the peninsula. The pine lands upon this river are scattered all along the valleys in groups or tracts containing several thousand acres each, interspersed with hard timber, and surrounded by fine agricultural lands.

The Pere Marquette river and White river, large streams emptying into Lake Michigan, pass through a region possessing much the same characteristics. This whole region rests on a lime rock, has a rich soil, and is well watered with living springs, resembling, in many features, the Grand river valley. Beds of gypsum have been discovered on the head waters of the Pere Marquette.

The unsettled counties in the northern portion of the State, the northern portion of Montcalm and Gratiot, Isabella, Gladwin, Clair, and a portion of Midland, are not inferior to any other portion. There is a magnificent body of pine stretching from the head of Flat river, in Montcalm county, to the upper waters of the Tittabawassee, and growing upon a fine soil, well adapted to agriculture. This embraces a portion of the Saginaw valley, and covers the high ground dividing the waters of Lakes Huron and Michigan.

The eastern slope of the peninsula embraces a variety of soil and timber somewhat different, in its general features, from other portions of the State. The pine lands of this region are near the coast of the lake, and lie in large tracts, but with good agricultural land adjoining.

There are in the lower peninsula, in round numbers, about twenty-four million acres of land. Taking Houghton lake, near the centre of the State, as a point of view, the general surface may be comprehended as follows: The Muskegon valley to the southwest, following the Muskegon river in its course to Lake Michigan. The western slope of the peninsula directly west, embracing the pine and agricultural districts along the valleys of several large streams emptying into Lake Michigan. The large and beautiful region to the northwest, embracing the valley of the Manistee and the undulating lands around Grand Traverse Bay. Northward, the region embraces the head waters of the Manistee and Au Sauble, with the large tracts of excellent pine in that locality, and beyond, the agricultural region extending to Little Traverse Bay and the Straits of Mackinaw. To the northeast, the valley of the Au Sauble and the pine region of Thunder Bay. To the east, the pine and hard timber extending to Saginaw Bay. To the southeast, the Saginaw valley; and to the south, the high lands before described in the central counties.

Thus we have yet undeveloped over half of the surface of this peninsula, embracing certainly twelve to fifteen millions of acres, possessing stores of wealth in the timber upon its surface, reserving the soil for the benefit of those who, as the means of communication are opened, will come in and possess it, and thus introduce property into the region. It is estimated that one-tenth of the area north of the Grand river is embraced in the pine region. The swamp lands granted to the State will probably cover nearly double the area of the pine lands proper, the remainder, for the most part, being covered with a growth of hard timber suited to the necessities of the increasing population. It has been estimated that in good years the pine lumber of the State yields not far from ten millions of dollars, and yet it is thought that the various hard woods might be made to yield a larger income. For example, the region around Saginaw Bay is perhaps the most remarkable locality in the world in regard to the quality and variety of its hard-wood timber. There, for nearly a hundred miles in extent, upon streams debouching into the bay, are dense forests of the choicest oak, with a great profusion of hickory, black walnut, white ash, white wood, bird's-eye maple, red elm, and other valuable varieties. The manufacture of agricultural implements will probably, in the future, be extensively carried on in this region. The profusion of this growth is only equalled by its accessibility to market, by the streams upon which it abounds. But hard-wood forests are found in other parts of the State, which are nearly as valuable as those of the Saginaw region. And to crown all, it has been demonstrated that the lumber manufactured in Michigan, including all its varieties, is unsurpassed in its soundness and durability by that of any other in the country. In the lumber districts of the eastern shore there are 212 saw-mills with an invested capital of $6,822,000, which in 1869 cut 738,641,700 feet of lumber, 149,901,000 laths, and 243,820,000 shingles. Number of men employed at mills, 5,204. In the lumber woods it is estimated that 10,250 men were employed at wages varying from $20 to $25 per month with board; mill labor, $2 and $2.50 per day. The western shore lumber region includes the districts of Muskegon, Manistee, Ottawa, and Oceana. About 1,000 men are employed in the mills at Muskegon, exclusive of men in the woods. In that district 260,000,000 feet of lumber were cut in 1869. The products of the other districts in 1869 are not given, but they produced in 1869 480,000,000 feet of lumber and 250,000,000 laths. The season's work on the Black river, it is estimated, was about 100,000,000 feet of logs, including a few million feet left over from the previous season. The progress which the lumber trade is making in the northern part of the southern peninsula is said to be remarkable.

In concluding this chapter, we may with propriety make an allusion to the climate of the State. As the presence of the ocean tends to mitigate the excessive temperature of the Atlantic slope, so do the great lakes exercise a similar influence over the two peninsulas of Michigan, lessening the winter's cold and the summer's heat. The temperature of the State has been fixed as follows:

Ann Arbor.—Spring, 45.5; summer, 66.3; autumn, 48.4; winter, 25.3; year, 46.4.

Fort Brady.—Spring, 37.6; summer, 62.0; autumn, 43.5; winter, 18.3; year, 40.4.

The annual precipitation of rain is as follows:

Ann Arbor.—Spring, 7.30; summer, 11.20; autumn, 7.00; winter, 3.10; year, 28.60.

Mackinac.—Spring, 4.67; summer, 8.88; autumn, 9.01; winter, 3.31; year, 23.87.

Fort Brady.—Spring, 5.44; summer, 9.97; autumn, 10.76; winter, 5.18; year, 31.35.

With these facts before us, and remembering what has been recorded respecting the soil and vegetable productions of Michigan, and its peculiar position, it would seem that so far as the climate of the State is concerned, we are warranted in coming to the conclusion that it is a most fortunate region of country. If the more southern portions, in this respect, are found to be on a par with the neighboring States of Ohio and Indiana, when we come to look at the northern peninsula we find it abounding in charms which are peculiarly its own, unless we admit northern Wisconsin into the partnership. Those portions of the State which are washed by the northern part of Lake Michigan, Lake Huron, and Lake Superior, and where the pine forests abound, have but two seasons, summer and winter. In September the wild geese and other water-fowl commence their migrations; in October the first snows appear, and these, with the dense woods, retain a warmth in the soil until the opening of spring; and, although the thermometer may fall to —30°, the dry, cold, and elastic winds rob the temperature of its intensity, so far as it relates to the human system. And then, during the long winter nights, the wonderful Northern Lights come forth in all their pomp; and after they have delighted and bewildered us with their beauty and splendor, would seem to say to the dwellers in Southern Michigan, who are wont to boast of their bright skies, brilliant sunsets, and matchless Indian summer, that to the North belong the chief glory of these phenomena of the seasons. It is in winter, too, and in the North, that the wild animals attain their greatest perfection—the beaver his coat of velvet, and the partridge and owl their snow-white plumage. In April the lakes and streams are released from their icy fetters, and summer, without oppressive heat, but with charming influences and associations, then comes forth like a queen, and spreads a quiet gladness from lake to lake and from shore to shore, and when once enjoyed, can never be forgotten.

THE FISHERIES.

Hemmed in, as is the State of Michigan, by four of the largest lakes in the world, and all of them filled with the purest water, it is not to be wondered at that its fisheries should have become an important item in its commerce. We have not the data to give an accurate account of the yield of fish, but we can safely say that they bring in a revenue of more than a million of dollars per annum, give employment to many hundred men and boats, and find a ready market in the States of Ohio and Indiana, as well as Michigan itself. The most important fish taken in these waters is the white fish, and while the largest proportion of them are salted, large numbers of them are sold in a fresh state, and are popular in markets as distant as Washington city, whither they are sent, neatly packed in ice. They are found in the straits and all the lakes; are taken with seines, gill nets, trap nets, and with spears, but never with the hook. They are celebrated for their edible qualities, and in the Western States occupy a similar position to that of the shad along the Atlantic coast. Their average weight is from three to five pounds, but specimens are occasionally taken weighing fifteen pounds.

The Detroit river white fish—in the capture and shipment of which Mr. George Clark has become celebrated—are more juicy and better flavored than those caught in the upper lakes, probably from the fact that they feed on more delicate food, but those found in Lake Superior surpass all others in size. They were once so numerous that eight thousand were taken at a single haul. At present a haul of one or two thousand is thought a very good one. In all the rivers they are growing scarce very gradually, but surely. The ratio of decrease cannot be arrived at with any degree of precision. A few years ago they were mostly taken with gill nets, and when they fell off in one place, a corresponding increase would be found in another. Now they are taken with trap nets along the shore. The trap nets are a decided advantage over gill nets. They allow the fish to be kept alive, and then are taken out at leisure; they are, therefore, of better quality.

Pickerel.—This variety is also held in high esteem. They are good, either fresh or salted and dried, and for packing rank next in value to white, although held nominally at the same price as trout when packed. They generally run up the rivers and lakes in the spring to spawn, where they are caught in considerable numbers. Average weight, two pounds, although occasionally weighing ten pounds.

Lake or Mackinaw Trout.—This species are as voracious as pickerel. They are chiefly caught in Lake Huron with gill nets and hooks. Saginaw bay appears to be a favorite resort with them. Some winters, large quantities are caught in the bay through the ice, with a decoy fish and spear. They spawn in the fall, generally in the bays and inlets. Average weight, five pounds; large specimens reaching seventy-five pounds.

Siscowit.—These are mostly found in Lake Superior, and are preferred by some to any other kind. They are of the trout family, and for fat are unequalled; they are mostly taken in gill nets. They spawn in the fall, and are very superior for packing. They are also of some value for their oil. Common weight, four pounds.

Large Herring.—These are very good fish, found only in the straits and large lakes. They spawn in the fall; but few are caught. Average weight, one pound and three-quarters.

In addition to the above, the muscalonge—a large and delicious variety—black and white bass, rock bass, perch, sturgeon, catfish, eels, gar, mullet, sucker, perch, sunfish, as well as the lovely and valuable common trout, and many other kinds abound in the waters of Michigan.

White fish are taken both in the spring and fall, chiefly the latter; spring is the season for pickerel; trout are taken at all seasons.

The localities where the commercial fish abound are numerous, but the following are the most important, and we mention them in the order of their importance: Mackinaw, Detroit river, Au Sauble, Thunder Bay, Saginaw Bay, Beaver Islands, Grand Haven, St. Joseph, Michigan City, Green Bay, Saugatuck, Point Sauble, White Lake, and Port Huron. The total proceeds, as already mentioned, of all the Michigan fisheries is estimated at more than one million of dollars per annum.

That the fishing business of the great lakes is yet in its infancy must be apparent to all who reflect upon the inexhaustible supplies to be found in these lakes and their tributaries; and for this kind of food the surrounding market is almost without a limit. The barrels for packing constitute no inconsiderable item of this vast and constantly growing trade. Their manufacture is a regular branch of business in some localities, but large numbers are also made by the fishermen themselves when not engaged upon the waters. The nets employed come chiefly from Massachusetts, and the large item of salt used is obtained from within the limits of the State. Of the men who originated the trade on Lake Huron, perhaps none have been more successful than Mr. Harvey Williams, of Saginaw. Around Mackinaw, on Lakes Superior and Michigan, the more successful men engaged in the business have been the Canadian French and Norwegians, the last of whom are wont to perform exploits upon the stormy waters which sometimes astonish the natives of the surrounding shores. It has been estimated by the more sanguine citizens of Michigan that the value of her fisheries, when fully developed, will exceed the product of all the interior States of the Union added together; but however that may be, the fact remains that Michigan has been bountifully treated by the hand of Nature in this particular, as well as in many others, and it should not falter in its duty as a faithful steward.

COMMERCE.

As nearly all the interests hitherto touched upon in this compilation are directly connected with the commerce of the State, there is but little to add in further illustration of that subject. It is admitted on all sides that there is not a State in the Union which surpasses Michigan in her commercial advantages, and if her natural resources are properly fostered and developed they will keep her for a long time to come in the van of prosperous commonwealths. She is also unequalled among the States in the extent of her coast line, which measures about fourteen hundred miles, and her natural harbors are numerous, and, generally speaking, so favorably located as to require but little expense or labor to make them available in all seasons for all classes of shipping.

The combined area of all the great lakes, according to Professor J. W. Foster, is approximately estimated to exceed 90,000 square miles, and the depression in most of them is sufficiently profound to reach below the sea-bed. The following table, though not strictly accurate, is believed to embrace their prominent features, and are the latest conclusions arrived at by scientific men:

	Length.	Breadth.	Depth.	Height above sea.	Area in miles.
Superior	355	164	900	605	32,000
Michigan	310	84	600	383	22,000
Huron	168	120	600	578	20,400
Erie	246	60	300	564	9,600
Ontario	190	50	800	233	6,300
Total area	....	....	....	....	90,300

In the absence of minute and authentic statistics respecting the shipping of the State, we can only draw conclusions from isolated particulars. For example, the commercial value of wheat passed through the St. Mary canal in 1856, the year after it was completed, was not less than five millions of dollars. In 1854 Lake Superior boasted of two steamboats and five sailing vessels, but at the end of two years from that date there were forty steamers and sixteen sail vessels upon its waters. In 1839 the number of steamboats which navigated the great lakes was fifty-four, and in splendor of equipments many of them, such as the Michigan and Illinois, the Detroit, the Western World, Plymouth Rock, Buckeye, and Sandusky, the Cleveland, and the Buffalo, were at that time unsurpassed by any other vessels of their kind in the United States, the burthen of several of them measuring two thousand tons. In 1827 there were only three steamers running from Detroit to Buffalo during an entire week, but in 1855, when that class of ships was mostly popular, there were from eight to ten departures from Detroit every day. The *Walk-in-the-Water*, Captain Jedediah Rogers, the celebrated pioneer steamer, arrived at Detroit May 20, 1819, and she occupied a whole week in making one trip to Black Rock, advertising to touch at all the towns on the American side of Lake Erie. She was wrecked near Buffalo in 1821. In 1855 the two miles of wharf at Detroit were hardly sufficient to accommodate the shipping of that port, but the steamboat business has of late years been materially interfered with by the numerous lines of railroad. In 1859 the total number of vessels navigating the waters of the five great lakes, which all paid some tribute to Michigan, was more than sixteen hundred, and their aggregate burthen was over four hundred thousand tons. They were manned by over thirteen thousand seamen, navigating over five thousand miles of lake and river coast, and transporting over six hundred millions of exports and imports. To use the language of W. P. Strickland, the State of Michigan is the greatest lumber region in the world, not only on account of its interminable forests, but for getting its lumber product to market. With a lake coast, on the lower peninsula alone, of more than one thousand miles—with numberless water-courses emptying at convenient distances into her inland seas—she enjoys advantages which many empires might envy. Her white-winged carriers are sent to almost every point of the compass with the product of her forests, which, wherever it may go, is the sign of improvement and progress; while by the large expenditures involved in the manufacture of lumber and the employment of thousands of hardy laborers, the general prosperity is materially enhanced and a market opened within her own borders for a considerable share of the productions of her own soil. In 1867, or two years after the rebellion, the total tonnage of the United States was 3,957,514, and the total amount assigned to the State of Michigan was 112,797, or to the district of Detroit 87,999, Mackinaw 2,703, Port Huron 14,662, and the district known as Michigan 9,433.

Within the last few years the European consumers of grain and other products have been convinced that their wants can be supplied with promptness, and to a large extent from the State of Michigan alone. Her resources are amply sufficient to afford employment for half a century to a tenfold larger number of vessels than have hitherto been employed. The foreign ports to which shipments of lumber and staves have been made are Liverpool, Cork, Greenock, Glasgow, London, Hamburg, Cadiz, and Calais; and to many of them large shipments have been made of flour and grain, but chiefly to Liverpool. Surrounded as it is on three sides by navigable waters, the State of Michigan is favorably situated for carrying on an extensive commerce. The total lake trade of the State, valued at $30,000,000 in 1851, was in 1863 estimated at $65,000,000, notwithstanding the fact that the development of the gigantic railroads of the West has absorbed a large portion of the trade that would otherwise have been conducted through the lakes. The great mining district of the northern peninsula, to which as yet no railroad has been constructed, finds an outlet for its productions only through the lakes, and yearly adds a large quota to the already heavy commerce of the State. The shipping, estimated in 1850 at 38,144 tons, was in 1863 increased to upwards of 100,000 tons. The internal and transit trade of the State, by means of its railroads, etc., is also immense, and has been largely increased since the completion of the great Canadian lines of railroad.

As bearing directly upon the commerce of Michigan, the following general remarks respecting the later developments in the aspect of the country are worthy of consideration:

That section of the State known as the "Northern Peninsula," lying between Lake Superior and Lake Michigan is three hundred and sixty miles long, and from thirty-six to one hundred and twenty miles wide. This portion of the State is as yet comparatively unsettled, though its advantages are such as to induce a rapid immigration. The general surface is much diversified by mountains, hills, valleys, and plains. The eastern portion to the "pictured rocks," is undulating, rising gradually from the lakes to the interior, where it assumes the character of an elevated table-land. Westward the country becomes broken into hills, with intervening plains, until it is interrupted by the Porcupine Mountains, which form the dividing ridge separating the waters of Lake Superior from those of Lake Michigan. The highest peaks toward the western boundary are from one thousand eight hundred to two thousand feet high. The ridge is often broken through by the larger streams, bordered by extensive valleys. The spurs of these mountains project in different directions, often exhibiting their denuded cliffs upon the northern shores. The greater portion of the peninsula, the sand plains excepted, is covered with immense forests, principally of white and yellow pine. Of the pine lands, there are millions of acres stretching between the Saute de Ste. Marie and the Ontonagon and Montreal rivers. The country is abundantly supplied with water, and though none of the streams are large, yet they furnish immense power, and the means of internal navigation. The head branches of those flowing in different directions frequently interlock. The lake coast of this section of the State is estimated at between seven hundred and eight hundred miles in length, and it is believed that five-sevenths of the entire peninsula may be reached by the common lake vessels.

The "Southern Peninsula," which is four hundred and twelve miles long by from fifty to three hundred in width, has generally a level or rolling surface, in some parts broken and hilly. The eastern portion, for a distance varying from five to twenty-five miles from the shore, is almost a dead level, but westward the land rises into an irregular ridge, in some parts attaining the height of six hundred or seven hundred feet above the level. This ridge has much greater proximity to the eastern than to the western shore, and serves to separate the waters flowing into the lakes on each side. The portion of the southern part of the State denominated hilly, branches off from the principal ridge in different directions through the adjoining country. The hills consist of an irregular assemblage of somewhat conical elevations, occasionally attaining the height of one hundred and fifty or two hundred feet, but ordinarily of not more than from thirty to forty feet. The main portion of the table-land passing westward to Lake Michigan, with the exceptions noted, assumes a very gradual descent, exhibiting a gently undulating and very rarely broken surface. The ridge of land before spoken of again takes a rise near the mouth of Au Sauble river, and is seen from the lake to stretch on for many miles along and beyond the coast. It has been considered the highest land of the region, and is certainly the most rugged part of the lower peninsula. Taking the great extent of this peninsula into consideration, however, it may, in a comparative point of view, be said to possess a great evenness of surface, with a sufficient declivity, nevertheless, to allow the waters to drain off in lively and healthy streams. The coasts, both towards Lakes Michigan and Huron, are sometimes exhibited in high, steep banks, and those of the former are frequently seen in bluffs and sand hills, varying from one hundred to three hundred feet in height.

Among the citizens of Michigan who have long been paying special attention to the geographical and other interests of the State of Michigan is Albert D. Rust, editor of the Michigan *Advance;* and he has divided the resources of the State into five classes, as follows:

1st. Mining. 2d. Fruit culture. 3d. Manufacture of salt. 4th. Manufacture of lumber. 5th. Agriculture. He believes that the cultivation of the soil will eventually be the most independent and remunerative of all occupations.

As the ship canal of St. Mary is now performing an important part in developing the commerce of Michigan, the subjoined facts, taken from the inaugural message of Governor Baldwin, will be read with interest:

The gross earnings of the canal for 1867 were $33,515.54. This was $10,446 more than was received in 1866. Of this increase, $4,666.96 were the result of the increase of the rate of tolls from 4½ to 6 cents per ton upon the tonnage of steamers.

The entire receipts for tolls for the year 1868 were $25,977.14; being $7,538.40 less than the year before. This falling off was owing, in a great degree, to the exceedingly depressed condition of the copper mining interest.

The canal had been in operation fourteen seasons prior to 1869. Very considerable repairs had been made during the two preceding years, which, with those now being prosecuted, will place it in as good condition as the wear and tear of this length of time would allow.

The board of control in 1868 authorized it to be dredged, to clear it of the mud and stone which had been borne down by the ice and current. Three hundred feet of a new pier were to be built on the north side, at its western terminus. The valves of the lock gates and the slope walls were to be repaired and improved. These improvements to be made under the charge of the superintendent, during the winter months.

This canal, though located in Michigan and under State control, is a national work, and of great national importance. At the time of its projection it was supposed to be of sufficient capacity for the transit of any vessels which the trade of Lake Superior would ever require, or which could pass through the shallow waters of the St. Clair Flats or the St. Mary river.

For the removal of these river and lake obstructions Congress has made large appropriations, and the work is now in progress.

Already the commerce which has been developed along the shores of Lake Superior has become so extended that the class of vessels which has been found most advantageous to be used in this trade cannot be loaded to their full capacity, for the lack of sufficient depth of water in the canal.

The great Northwest is yet in its infancy. Population is pressing into the States and Territories with wonderful rapidity. A railroad is already being constructed from the Mississippi, at St. Paul, to the head of Lake Superior, (completed in 1870,) which, during the season of navigation, must make this canal the great outlet for the products of northern Wisconsin, Minnesota, and the Territories beyond. Should the Northern Pacific railroad be constructed, Lake Superior would become emphatically the key to the Northwest, and thus this canal, as its outlet, of still greater national importance.

Although this is a national work, Michigan—not alone the upper peninsula, but the whole State—is deeply interested in its improvement, and in all that will tend to make it the great avenue of the trade of Lake Superior and the Northwest. Since its construction, other avenues have been opened, through which no small portion of the trade and wealth of this region is being diverted to other States.

As not out of place in this connection, we submit a few particulars respecting the indebtedness of the State. On the first of January, 1867, the debt of Michigan amounted to $3,976,185, and in July, 1870, it had been reduced to $2,444,528. Besides this, the county and municipal debts of the State incurred during the late war, have been greatly reduced. There have also been large reductions in the rates of taxation. In 1867, the apportioned taxes amounted to $880,739, but before the close of 1868 they had been reduced to $713,747; and in 1869 the apportionment had been reduced to $465,264. The State derives its revenues from direct taxation, and also from specific taxes. The specific taxes are paid by railroads, mining companies, Masonic lodges, banks, insurance, and express companies, etc. These taxes yield annually an increasing revenue, which does not come directly from the pockets of the people, but from rich corporations; and these taxes are devoted to paying the interest and principal of the State indebtedness. The revenue from these specific taxes, in 1866, was $101,606.88; in 1867, it was $251,325.42; 1868, $280,952.07; in 1869, the law taxing National bank shares having been pronounced by the courts illegal, it fell to $268,530.51. As the wealth of the State increases, the revenue from these sources must constantly grow, unless the rates are diminished. And the last report of the Auditor-General shows that, within another year, it is likely the specific taxes alone will yield sufficient revenue to provide for the State debt, so that the people may be entirely relieved of direct taxation on that account. With regard to the Banking institutions of the State, we may mention that the National Banks number forty-two, and have a capital of $5,535,000; State Banks two, with a capital of $200,000; and the private Banking Houses and Savings Institutions also number forty-two; and there are in the State thirty Insurance Companies.

THE INDIANS AND ANTIQUITIES OF THE STATE.

As a matter of convenience, we submit in this place a few particulars respecting the Indians and the antiquities of Michigan. The total number of the former, consisting of Chippewas, Ottawas, and Pottowatamies, is about twelve thousand, among whom are located a few schools, supported by the Methodist, Presbyterian, and Roman Catholic denominations.

The Government pays to these Indians annually, in cash annuities, about $40,000, and in goods $3,000. It also pays for the support of schools, for smiths and smith-shop supplies, and for agricultural and mechanical purposes, some $20,000, and for agency expenses, including salary of agent and assistant, pay of interpreters, etc., nearly $8,000. Thus, the annual disbursments for Indian purposes in the State amount to something over seventy thousand dollars.

The Chippewas of Lake Superior mostly reside in Houghton county, near the head of Keweenaw bay. The Ottawas and Chippewas are principally in the counties of Oceana, Mason, Grand Traverse, Emmet, Cheboygan, Mackinaw, and Chippewa. The Chippewas of Saginaw, Swan creek, and Black river, are mostly in the counties of Isabella and Bay. The Chippewas, Ottawas, and Pottowatamies are in Cass and Van Buren counties, and the Pottowatamies of Huron are in Calhoun county.

The early history of the State is replete with accounts of the labors of the old French missions. Many were the lives sacrificed and privations encountered by these men to win the native tribes to the standard of the cross. So long as the missionary was in their midst and superintended their labors, they yielded to his guidance and adopted his recommendations, so far, at least, as conduced to their comfort; but when he withdrew, with equal facility they glided into their former habits. The superstructure raised with so much care fell to the ground the moment the sustaining hand was withdrawn. At present, with the exception of a few points in the upper peninsula, there are to be found few traces of the Catholic religion among the Indians of the State.

As a general thing, it is impossible to induce them to conform to the usages of civilized life, and, except in the manufacture of a few baskets and the supply of a few furs, we see no evidence of their industry.

The effect of the contact of the two races has been to afford the Indian additional incentives to vice, while his intellectual and moral elevation has been little advanced; and at this day, it cannot be said that he stands higher in the scale of civilization than when first known by the white man.

With regard to the antiquities of the State of Michigan, it affords us pleasure to submit the following, which has been supplied to us by the writer:

In common with her sister States of the great West, Michigan can boast of her antiquities, the undoubted remains of a great people, who claimed for their land, long anterior to the so-called "aborigines"—a people of whom the earliest known Indians have no traditions. Of a precisely similar character with the "tumuli," "forts," and "mounds" of the Ohio valley, are the ancient remains in Michigan, and in addition to these are the remains of ancient "gardens"—traces of which are found in no other portion of the continent so distinctly marked as those of southern Michigan. The ancient "mounds," the probable use of which has given rise to more controversy than any of the other antiquities of the country, are of quite frequent occurrence in Michigan, being found in all parts of the State, especially upon or near the banks of the large rivers—the St. Joseph, Kalamazoo, Grand, Raisin, and Huron. The so-called "forts" are but seldom met with, and are uniformly of small dimensions, the principal ones being in the southeast, along the shores of the Detroit, Huron, and Raisin rivers, and occasionally upon Lake Erie, between the Detroit and Maumee rivers. The gardens are found principally in the rich prairies and "oak-openings" of southern Michigan, where their antiquity is clearly evinced by the fact that in the centre of the garden beds immense oak trees, evidently several hundred years old, are found growing. In the counties of St. Joseph, Cass, and Berrien, there are many of these ancient gardens still in excellent preservation, and having undoubted traces of their original uses.

In addition to the remains above alluded to, there are to be found in the great iron and copper mining regions of the northern peninsula, the most indisputable evidences that this region was once inhabited by a race superior in every respect to the American Indians of the present day—a race that understood the mode of working and the value of metals. The high antiquity of the evidences of ancient mining discovered by the present copper and iron miners of the Keweenaw, Ontonagon, and Marquette districts is inferred not only from the fact that the existing race of Indians were in perfect ignorance of the locality of the mines until pointed out by the whites, but that the ancient stone and metal tools discovered are entirely unlike anything now in use by the Indians in any part of the country. Still another evidence is had, as is the case with the gardens of southern Michigan, in the fact that trees of the largest size, evidently at least five hundred years old, are found growing upon the piles of rubbish that must have been thrown from the mines by the ancient miners. In the winter of 1847, while passing over a portion of the location now occupied by the Minnesota Mining Company, Mr. Samuel Knapp, the intelligent agent of the company, observed a continuous depression of the soil, which he rightly conjectured was caused by the disintegration of a vein. There was a bed of snow on the ground three feet in depth, but it had been so little disturbed by the wind that it conformed to the inequalities of the surface. Following up these indications along the southern escarpment of the hill, where the company's works are now erected, he came to a longitudinal cavern, into which he crept. He saw numerous evidences to convince him that this was an artificial excavation, and at a subsequent day, with the assistance of two or three men, proceeded to explore it. In clearing out the rubbish they found numerous stone hammers, showing clearly that they were the mining implements of a past race. The following spring he explored another excavation in the neighborhood, which was twenty-six feet deep, filled with clay and a mass of decayed vegetable matter. When he had penetrated to the depth of eighteen feet he came to a mass of native copper, ten feet long, three feet wide, and nearly two feet thick, weighing over six tons. On digging around it the mass was found to rest on billets of oak, supported by sleepers of the same wood. The ancient miners had evidently raised the mass about five feet, and then abandoned it as too laborious. The vein was wrought in the form of an open trench, and where the copper was most abundant the excavation extended deepest. The rubbish taken from the mine is thrown out in mounds, which can easily be distinguished from the surrounding ground, and upon which large trees are now growing. In various other localities of the northern peninsula the most convincing traces are discovered, that go to prove that the mines were extensively worked by an intelligent race—at least far more intelligent than the present Indians. The workings appear to have been effected by the use of stone hammers and wedges, specimens of which are to be found in the greatest abundance in the vicinity of the mines. In some instances there are traces of fire, and pieces of charcoal have been discovered, showing that fire was used as an agent to destroy the cohesion of the copper with the surrounding stone. Metallic hammers and knives have been discovered in the mines, though the instances are very rare, the copper being evidently carried to a distance, where it was fashioned into the rings and ornaments frequently found in the tumuli of the Ohio. The immense labor required to sink these ancient mines—frequently through several feet of solid rock—is another evidence that the present race of Indians, or any race of men possessing their characteristics, could not have performed the work, for no amount of personal benefit could induce the Indian to undergo such physical exertion. According to Professor J. W. Foster, these ancient miners were none other than the Mound Builders, whose works are known to be scattered throughout the entire Northwestern States. The specimens of their genius which we find in Michigan are generally small, varying in height from six to ten feet, and in rare instances reaching a height of twenty feet. Some of the most remarkable that have been noticed are in Girard township, Branch county, and in Raisin township, in the county of Lenawee. One of the latter was opened many years since and found to contain a mass of human bones. On the north side of Grand river, ten miles from its mouth, there is an ancient mound about ten feet high, with an immense pine tree, nearly one hundred feet high, growing from its apex. A mound in the vicinity was opened, and nothing found until the ground below was penetrated to the distance of about three feet below the original level, where were discovered a quantity of human bones, several pieces of iron three or four inches long, several arrow heads, some pieces of brass, and the remnant of a brazen vessel much mutilated. In the southwest corner of the county of Calhoun, on the north side of the St. Joseph river, is a semicircular fort two hundred feet in diameter, and another in the southeast corner of the county, of the same dimensions, with an embankment from one to three feet high. In the county of Wayne, in Springwells township, on the north bank of the Detroit river, is a fort of the circular or elliptical kind, with an embankment two or three feet in height, and encompassing perhaps one acre, situated on firm land and surrounded by a swamp. On the east side, in approaching the fort, there are two parallel embankments of earth, within a few feet of each other, rising four or five feet, and crossing the swamp in a direct line towards the fort. Forts of the square or the rectangular kind are sometimes found. There is said to be one two miles below the village of Marshall, one in the township of Prairie Ronde, several on the Kalamazoo, and in some other places. In Bruce township, in the county of Macomb, on the north fork of the Clinton, are several. The latter consist mostly of an irregular embankment, with a ditch on the outside, and including from two to ten acres, with entrances, which were evidently gateways, and a mound on the inside opposite each entrance. In the vicinity there are a number of mounds. Several small mounds have been found on a bluff of the Clinton river, eight miles from Lake St. Clair. In sinking the cellar of a building for a missionary, sixteen baskets full of human bones were found of a remarkable size. Near the mouth of this river, on the east bank, are ancient works representing a fortress, with walls of earth thrown up similar to those in Ohio and Indiana.

In this connection, after mentioning the fact that the popular name of Michigan is the Hoosier State, it may interest the reader to look at the meanings of the following Indian names associated with the State of Michigan: Kalamazoo, which means *Looming, or Wuragi river;* Numma-sapee, or River Raisin, *River of Sturgeons;* Minosa-goink, or River Rouge, *Singeing Skin River;* Waweawtonong, or Detroit, *Place where you go round the sun in approaching;* Getchigomme, or Lake Superior, *Sea Water;* Equabaw, *End of deep water;* Wassawassepee, *River where fish are speared by torchlight;* Iosco, *Water of Light;* Keewenaw, or *The canoe is carried back;* Muskegon, or *Marshy River;* Moskego-sepee, or Moskegon, *Marshy River;* Pocagonk, *The Rib River;* Titebawassee, *River that runs alongside;* Ottawa, or *The Traders;* Tuscola, or *Warrior's Prairie;* Nundee Norgon, or Ontonogon, *Hunting River;* Wrockumiteogoc, or Huron river, *Clear Water;* Owosso, *Person warming himself;* Cheboygan, or *A place of metals;* Nagaikur-Sebee, or River Ecorce, *Bark River;* Sac-e-nong, or Saginaw, *Sac Town;* Michisawgyegan, or Lake Michigan, *Great Lake;* Manistee, or *River with Islands;* Chippewas, or Ojibways, *The Ruling People;* Mackinaw, *Place of Giant Fairies, or Great Turtle;* Washtenaw and Washtenong, or Grand River, *Running over Shining Pebbles;* Shiawassee, or *Strait Running;* Powetink, or Grand Rapids, *Falling Waters;* Powating, the Saute Ste. Marie, or *Water Shallow on the Rocks;* Yondotia, or Detroit, *Great Town;* and Cowthenake-Sepee, or Au Glaize river, *Falling Tree River.* According to J. H. Lanman, the Indian names which marked the prominent points of Michigan exhibit the mode in which the savages defined the topography of the country, and were used as land marks to guide them in their migrations. A general term, founded on a certain feature of natural scenery, was often used to designate a wide tract of territory.

RECENT DEVELOPMENTS.

Under this heading we propose to speak of several distinct localities, which have been, and are at the present time, attracting the special attention of the public, viz—the Grand Traverse Region, the Saginaw Valley, the Straits of Mackinaw, and the Cheboygan Region. With regard to the first, Professor Alexander Winchell has declared it to be the most remarkable and desirable section of country in the Northwest, and as he is the only man who has thoroughly explored it, the value of his opinion cannot be questioned. In 1866 he published a report on its geological and industrial resources, and it is from that production that we gather the following particulars:

Grand Traverse Bay is a bay of Lake Michigan, about thirty-four miles long and of ample depth, and received its name from the French *voyageurs.*

The region to which it has given its name is divided into five counties, viz: Antrim, Leelanaw, Grand Traverse, Benzie, and Kalkasca, the first three alone being contiguous to the Bay. The mean elevation of this country is two and thirty feet above Lake Michigan, and it is intersected with a great number of small and beautiful lakes and rivers of the purest water, and its surface is undulating and picturesque, and its low or swamp lands are not worthy of mention. Patches of clayey soil are not unfrequent, but a well-mixed sandy loam is the dominant soil on the hills, and their productiveness is said to be unsurpassed. Generally speaking, the region is covered by a magnificent growth of hard-wood timber, the sugar maple being the most abundant species, although the beech, the white elm, the oak, poplar, birch, the hemlock, the cedar, white pine, and arbor vitæ are found to a considerable extent in certain localities. For the most part, these forests present an endless colonnade of majestic pillars, and, but for the prostrate forms of the fallen patriarchs of the wood, a vehicle could be driven through the unbroken forest from one end of the region to the other. All the quadrupeds and birds peculiar to the State are found in this particular section, and the common trout is abundant in its beautiful lakes and streams. Its geological formations are said to be unusually interesting to scientific men, and consist of lignite, drift, shales, various limestones, and salt—the last of which underlies the whole region. With regard to the farm products, Professor Winchell asserts that this region is capable of producing any crop which flourishes in the Northwestern States and as far south as the latitude of Cincinnati. Winter wheat is the staple crop, and the yield varies from twenty-five to thirty bushels per acre. Corn grows well, and, generally speaking, reaches perfection. Oats are very profitable, yielding fifty bushels to the acre. Buckwheat also flourishes luxuriantly. The potatoes of the region cannot be excelled—will grow without cultivation, and the yield is frequently three hundred bushels to the acre; and timothy hay is always a successful crop. As a fruit-growing region it is doubtful whether any other part of the United States will compete with this—the apple, peach, pear, plum, cherry, grape, and all the more common berries attaining the greatest perfection. According to the latest estimates, the population of the region is not far from ten thousand; and, although ample access is had to it by propellors from all the lake ports, it cannot be long before it will be easily reached by means of all the usual land communications. Beyond all controversy, writes Professor Winchell, the Grand Traverse Region offers stronger attractions to capital and settlement than any other portion of the State, or of the entire Northwest. Even the mighty forest, which has to be felled before the farmer can avail himself of the soil, is probably less of a detriment than an advantage. Besides insuring him an inexhaustible supply of fuel, for the labor of cutting; besides furnishing him with a merchantable commodity in the form of cord wood, upon which he can realize for each day's work; besides protecting him and his stock and crops from the severity of the wintry blast—the forest itself is a source of food to horses and cattle, both in summer and winter. And it is a cheering fact that the religious and educational accommodations have kept pace with the development of the region.

Professor Winchell, in his report, makes an allusion to the Sand-Dunes, which form conspicuous landmarks along the western coast of southern Michigan, although not a prominent feature in the Grand Traverse Region. They consist of irregular heaps of sand which have been accumulated by the winds blowing in a certain direction upon specific shores. While the dunes of Cape Cod seldom measure more than eighty feet, those of Michigan sometimes measure more than a hundred feet. It is generally found, too, that they assume a *lee* and *strike* side,—the gentle and long slope being to the windward, and the steep acclivity towards the sheltered portion. The Sleeping Bear and Pointe Aux Chenes, near the foot of Lake Michigan, are conspicuous examples of these dune-like formations, while at the head, at New Buffalo and Michigan City, they are equally conspicuous. All these dunes are found to be moist to within a few feet of the surface, and hence become clothed with vegetation, of which the peric tribe is the most observable. If, down to the present time, the ingenuity of man has not been able to make them useful, it is a source of thankfulness that they have not done, and are not doing, any particular harm.

With regard to the Saginaw Valley, we may begin by saying that its inhabitants claim it to be the largest and most valuable tract of timbered country in the world. The bay and river which bear the same name have long been distinguished for their natural attractions, and have an abundance of water to satisfy all the demands of navigation. From the earliest time the surrounding region has been famous as a seat of the fur-trade, and its earliest white inhabitants were two Indian traders, named Louis Campau and John B. Cushway. It was first settled by agricultural emigrants about the year 1836, but did not make any advances in enterprise until 1850, when, under the leadership of Charles Little and his son Norman Little, an extensive lumber trade was commenced, and all the steps taken to secure the manifold advantages born of active business and high ideas of education. Its leading town, originally named Buena Vista, but now called East Saginaw, was incorporated as such in 1859, and is already known as a ship-building place of importance, giving profitable employment besides to large numbers of men connected with the lumber-trade and various kinds of wood and iron manufactures; and it is connected with Detroit by steamboat lines and a well conducted railway. The next town in importance is Saginaw City, which is mainly dependent for its prosperity upon the salt interest, which has its centre here. The packing and shipping of salt has progressed so rapidly that a large proportion of the Northwestern States look to Michigan for their supply; and by several of the highest authorities of the country, the salt manufactured in the Saginaw Valley has been pronounced of the most superior quality, forty gallons of brine yielding fifty-six pounds of salt, which is a larger per centage than the yield of the Syracuse salt works. There is, perhaps, no region in the State where there is less actual waste land than in Saginaw. Wherever it is cleared and properly cultivated it proves to be of unsurpassed fertility. The proximity of the heavy timbered lands to a ready market for lumber, affords a rich reward for the toil and labor of clearing. The immense oak and pine timber finds a ready sale, while the less valuable varieties, when cut up for fuel, are needed by the salt manufacturers, who pay remunerating prices. The demand for this purpose alone is immense, and must increase until the country is stripped of its forests. These advantages are not overlooked by those who are in search of new homes in Michigan, and the consequence is that there is an active demand for lands for farming purposes.

We may add, in this connection, that the gypsum beds located on the Bay of Saginaw are being rapidly developed, and becoming of great value to the State. In 1868 there were shipped from that locality twenty thousand tons of crude gypsum, and two thousand barrels of calcined gypsum, while the yield of the Grand Rapids bed amounted to 41,720 tons of the crude and 116,630 pounds of calcined gypsum.

From Mr. Albert D. Rust, who resides in the Saginaw Valley, and is devoting his energies as an editor and citizen to the development of that portion of the State, we have received the subjoined information:

This region is quite well adapted to agricultural purposes, but will ultimately be more of a grazing country, than one for raising grain.

It is a very remarkable circumstance that Michigan did, a good many years ago, get the reputation of being sterile and unhealthy, and so general was the impression that this reputation was given in the descriptive geographies; but, so far from this being the fact, the case is, that for the last five or eight years Michigan has increased in population and celebrity more rapidly than ever before. Amongst the best wheat in the New York market may be found Michigan wheat; the best quality and greatest abundance of fruits is from Michigan. No State is less subject to fatal diseases. To be sure, the fever and ague did prevail there in some parts several years ago; but that disease is scarcely known there now, save in a few localities; as in other new States, it has come and gone forever.

The winter is not severe; it is much less so than in other States in the same latitude east. Sleighing does not appear usually until January, and lasts about three months. There is snow enough to make it pleasant and good for business. The rivers break up the first of April. The mercury seldom ever goes below ten degrees below zero, and frequently not as low as zero. We think that this part of the State is better adapted for comfortable homes than other Western States. Almost all kinds of business found in any country may be followed in Saginaw Valley.

We come now to speak of the Straits of Mackinaw. This locality is certainly remarkable, and its early history has already been touched upon in the first part of the present volume. It is the centre of that great chain of lakes and rivers, which well-nigh divides the continent. The three largest lakes of the system, Superior, Michigan, and Huron, are spread around, pointing to this spot, while between them, three vast peninsulas of land press down upon the waters until they are compressed into a river only four miles in width. On the north is the peninsula of Canada, on the south that of Michigan, and on the west that of the Copper Region. Here they are divided only by the Straits of Mackinaw. Land and water, by an inevitable necessity, seem to centre here, the navigable waters covering an area of eighty thousand square miles, and surrounded by a continuous coast of five thousand miles. The climate has been found to be as favorable as that of most civilized States, either for the production of food or the pursuits of commerce; and as to the productive wealth of the vast country which they drain it has been fully demonstrated by a number of scientific writers to be unsurpassed in any other quarter of the world. With these facts before us, we can begin to comprehend the remarkable enterprise of Edgar Conkling in attempting to found a commercial emporium on the Straits of Mackinaw, which, if carried out, will perpetuate his name, as a man of mind and commercial courage, for ages to come. At this point, according to that able and sound reasoner, Edward D. Mansfield, as well as at the upper end of Lake Superior, there must be large cities to supply the demands of commerce. It is not a matter of speculation, but a necessity of nature. The same necessity has already created Buffalo, Toledo, Detroit, Chicago, and St. Louis. The demand for such towns on the shores of Lakes Huron and Superior, and especially at the Straits of Mackinaw, whose Bay and Lake Michigan flow together, are obviously far greater than those which have already caused the growth of Buffalo and Chicago. They have grown to supply the commerce of comparatively limited districts. One means of testing this is to apply *radial lines* to the site of any city existent or proposed, so as to include what naturally belongs to them, and thus compare them with one another. The *radial lines* of New York and Philadelphia extend across the ocean to Europe on one hand, and across the mountains to the Valley of the Mississippi on the other. In looking to this fact we are no longer surprised that New York has its million of inhabitants, and Philadelphia its six hundred thousand.

If we look to the radial lines of Chicago we find that they are limited on the south by the competition of St. Louis and on the north by Milwaukee. Yet Chicago, at the southern end of Lake Michigan, has risen to be a large city by a sudden and extraordinary growth, arising from the rich though limited country about it. Apply these radial lines to Mackinaw and we find that they naturally include all of Michigan, a large part of Wisconsin, and a large part of Canada West; but in reference to water navigation no interior site in America is equal to that of Mackinaw. Here concentrate the navigation of eighty thousand square miles of water surface, which has no common centre but that of the Straits of Mackinaw. Two facts must be observed: that a commercial point which concentrates the trade of Lakes Superior and Michigan must lie within the circuit of their coasts; but there is no such point but Mackinaw. The other is that the point of commerce which offers the shortest distance, and therefore the cheapest to the great markets of the Atlantic will be preferred. Mackinaw is five hundred miles nearer to Buffalo than is Fond du Lac, and three hundred miles nearer than Chicago. So it is the same distance nearer to the Gulf of St. Lawrence or the city of New York. It is on the south side only, through the peninsula of Michigan, and toward the States of Indiana and Ohio, that the position of Mackinaw seems deficient in communications. But we no sooner see this than we see also two great lines of railroad progressing from the South through the peninsula toward Mackinaw. The one passes on the west side from Fort Wayne (Indiana) through Grand Rapids and Traverse Bay; the other through Lansing and Amboy, both terminating on the north at Mackinaw, and both, by connection with Indiana and Ohio roads, at Cincinnati on the south; thence they will soon be carried to the orange-growing shores of Florida. Thus may some future traveller be borne in a few hours from the soft air of the southern Atlantic to the keen breezes of the North and bathe his languid limbs in the clear cold waters of Michigan.

These, together with many others of like character, are the considerations which induced Mr. Conkling (formerly a citizen of Cincinnati) to undertake his gigantic enterprise. It was in 1853 that he purchased a large tract of land, consisting of the extreme northern point of the southern peninsula of Michigan, where he has laid out a town and seaport which he named Mackinaw City; and although the financial troubles of 1857 and the subsequent war for the Union did much to retard his various plans, he is now devoting his best energies and ample means, under the most efficient and liberal policy that it is possible to devise, for the varied interests, moral and material, of all who may settle there. The city has three safe and commodious harbors, and everything is being done to make it a profitable and agreeable place of residence; and a leading idea of the proprietor is to establish at this point an educational institution equal to the wants of the country. On this point he has communicated to us the following:

"In view of the increasing population of this country, and their needed increased intelligence to rightly develop it, and to promote their intellectual and moral happiness, the proprietor takes great pleasure in carrying out a long-cherished purpose of recognizing his obligation to forego the usual merely selfish accumulation and appropriation of personal gains, and to participate in the future glory of this the grandest country and Government of the world, by pledging the principal avails of this large and valuable property of near 5,000 acres to provide for the building up and endowment of a superior 'University,' with common school branches, for the free education of the present and future generations of this locality, who must take part in ruling the destinies of the world.

"He has determined that the free educational facilities of Mackinaw City shall not be excelled by any other city of this country, and shall be worthy of the State and a commercial centre so highly endowed by nature, second only to Detroit within Michigan, and equalled but by few lake cities.

"Thus the proprietor, in voluntarily becoming a mere trustee for the citizens of Mackinaw City, presents the most powerful incentive to invite an intelligent, enterprising, and wealthy population not only to enjoy all the superior natural advantages of the city and its surroundings, but also to enjoy the educational fund arising from the purchase of their homes and the value of the property resulting from their own enterprise and capital in building up an important city."

Another of the later developments which have taken place within the limits of the State is that of the Cheboygan region, and for the only satisfactory account of it that can be had, we are indebted to Professor N. H. Winchell, of Ann Arbor. A report that he published of this region in 1869 is so full of interest that we subjoin a large proportion of it, as follows:

The Indian word (Chab-wa-e-gun) of which Cheboygan is a corruption, signifies *place of ore*, but it is not known why the Indians so named this region, the river or the lake. No ore to justify the name has yet been discovered.

The Cheboygan and its tributaries comprise the most northern river system of the lower peninsula, its outlet into Lake Huron being within nine miles of the latitude of the Straits of Mackinac. Several of the tributaries rise as far south as the mouth of Thunder Bay river, in the heighth of land of Otsego county, where also rise the Sauble and the Manistee, two of the largest rivers of Michigan, while from east to west this system spans the whole peninsula, its most western source being within a quarter of a mile of the head of Little Traverse Bay. There is not a more beautiful cluster of connected inland lakes to be found in the State, or in any other State, than those which find outlet through the Cheyboygan. Mullett Lake, within ten miles of Lake Huron, covers about thirty square miles, or 19,200 acres; Burt's Lake, extending twelve miles further west, covers about the same area; Crooked Lake, eight miles still farther west, about ten square miles, or 6,400 acres; Douglass Lake, with the small lakes adjoining, about twelve square miles, or 7,680 acres, and Cheboygan Lake, about twenty-five square miles, or 16,000 acres. The water of these lakes is clear and pure, and contains an abundance of excellent fish. The famous "speckled trout" finds its favorite haunts in these waters, and for sporting fishermen there is no more attractive region in the United States. The district occupied by these lakes, stretching from the head of Little Traverse Bay eastward across the State, is dry, elevated, and covered with hard wood timber; and hence the shores of the lakes are rarely low or marshy. The streams which connect them generally flow with a smooth and steady current. There are rapids, however, in Cheboygan river, about a mile above its mouth, where water-power mills for lumbering and for flouring purposes have been erected. A substantial canal and lock at this place, constructed by permission of the State Legislature, to aid in the passage of these rapids, and the dam above, somewhat impede the navigation of the river, as they are regulated by the local convenience of the managers. Yet their capacity is sufficient to permit the passage of tugs and scows of any size capable of navigating the river. In Black river, below Cheboygan lake, occurs a series of rapids, which extend for three miles, having an aggregate descent of between fifty and sixty feet. This water power has not yet been improved. The country adjacent is somewhat settled by farmers, but it is generally an unbroken wilderness. Black river, above Cheboygan lake, also contains rapids in which there is a perpendicular fall, in some places of four or five feet. These occur from six to ten miles above the lake. At this place the bed of the river consists of limestone rock *in situ*, but at the rapids below Cheboygan lake, few rocks are visible, except metamorphic boulders.

The soil and timber of the Cheboygan region are such as promise to make it, when cleared, one of great agricultural resources. The soil varies within short intervals, so that a single farm may possess such a diversity of soils as to adapt it to the culture of a large variety of products. The prevailing feature of the soil of the region is a silico-calcareous sand; yet there are places, especially along the branches of the river below Mullett and Cheboygan Lakes, and extending to the site of the village of Cheboygan, where the clayey element is most prominent. The soil in some places is a copper-colored clayey loam; in others it is a black vegetable loam, resembling the prairie soil of Illinois. Where the sandy constituent and the clay or loam become mixed, as they frequently do, a very superior soil for agricultural purposes results. Much of the country is rolling, especially where the clayey soil predominates, while the sandy tracts are generally level. There is occasionally also a patch of marly soil, which when plowed crumbles in the atmosphere. Soil of this kind occurs on the east and north shores of Mullet Lake. Calcareous marl is often found also in the bed of the lakes, sometimes in the form of pebbly reefs or islands. The carbonate of lime is deposited from the water on little fresh water shells, (*Planorbis*,) and as they are rolled by the ripples they increase in size till they become as large as walnuts. Sometimes they become crushed and form a calcareous sand, or eventually a calcareous marl, which is useful not only as a fertilizer of the soil, and for making lime, but is sometimes mixed directly with sand to form an inferior mortar, or with water to form a whitewash.

The most common trees, off the river margins and the low lands, are beech, maple, pine, and hemlock, with occasional oaks and elms. The white pine occurs principally along the streams, where it is mixed with other timber, most frequently with hemlock or Norway pine. The Norway pine alone often forms extensive orchard-like tracts on the sandy plains. Another common but worthless species of pine, known among the lumber-men as "pitch pine" or "spruce pine," is a scattered, straggling tree, never exceeding ten inches in diameter, properly called Bank's pine, (*Pinus Banksiana*.) The beech and maple, as well as the elm, sometimes grow to stately dimensions, while the oaks are generally small. Of course, the country furnishes other less noticeable species of timber, as iron-wood, poplar, balm of Gilead, white birch, ash, and bass, while the ever-present cedar, larch, and spruce, of the northern latitudes, fill up the low lands. There is no butternut, hickory, or black-walnut; no whitewood or chestnut.

The settlement of such a region, of course, is not entirely dependent on or controlled by the lumber interest. Although initial impulse may have been due to this interest, yet the settlement of the Cheboygan region has outgrown it, and has developed other and more permanent elements of prosperity.

Permanency in a new settlement must be based upon some lasting and important resource. In the Cheboygan region, strangely enough, that resource is, or will soon become, chiefly agricultural. The country is rapidly filling up with farmers.

The farmers raise oats, potatoes, corn, wheat, in short, almost anything that can be raised in southern Michigan, though not always with the same certainty. Having but recently settled on their farms, their efforts are mainly expended in the improvement of them, and in the production of a winter's subsistence for themselves and their stock. Some of the farmers told the writer that they had raised wheat, even forty bushels to the acre, and that it was always a sure crop. One old settler of sixteen years ago, Mr. E. A. Dodge, on Mullet Lake, raises, together with the products of the farm, garden vegetables for the Cheboygan market. In his garden were strawberries, lettuce, cucumbers, cabbage, onions, etc., and in an adjoining field he had young apple and cherry trees, and several choice varieties of grapes.

Another farmer said he raised from three-fourths of a bushel of winter wheat a crop of forty bushels; and from ten bushels of spring wheat he received two hundred and sixty-three bushels. The cultivation of wheat has not been carried on heretofore, owing to the lack of a flouring-mill; and it was not until the past season that such a mill was supplied.

Cheboygan village contains about 800 inhabitants; stands on a clayey soil; has several stores, two churches, and three hotels. Above the village, fields of wheat, grass, potatoes, oats and peas line the river banks, the land on both sides being well cleared. In the channel of the river are twelve feet of water, but the entrance to the river is choked by a bar of clay and boulders. This obstruction for a number of years impeded the growth of the place, by shutting off communication with passing steamers. The officers of the lake survey have made preliminary examination and estimates for the dredging of a channel through this bar.

Should this improvement be carried out, nothing can prevent the Cheboygan region from becoming one of the most wealthy and important portions of the Lake Huron shore.

NOTE FOR PAGE 87.

After the brief allusion to the Masonic order, it was intended, as a matter of historical courtesy, to mention the Order of Odd-Fellows in connection with Michigan, and we do it in this place. The date of introduction in the State was the year 1844; the first and second lodges having been instituted at Detroit; the third at Pontiac; the fourth at Jackson; and the fifth at Marshall. The various patriarchal branches were also established in the same year. The Order has progressed rapidly in the State, many of its best citizens taking an interest in its success; so that at the present time the total number of lodges is 107; the number of members, 7,207; amount of receipts during the last year, $41,749; and the amount expended for brothers and widows, $7,221.

NOTE FOR PAGE 107.

It is too soon as yet to give the result of the census for 1870, but for purposes of reference the following facts are submitted respecting the nativities of the population of Michigan in 1860: Michigan, 294,828; New York, 191,128; German States, 38,787; British America, 36,482; Ohio, 34,000: Ireland, 30,049; England, 25,743; Pennsylvania, 17,460; Vermont, 13,779; Massachusetts, 9,873; Connecticut, 7,639; New Jersey, 7,531; Holland, 6,335; Scotland, 5,705; Indiana, 4,482; New Hampshire, 3,482; France, 2,446; Maine, 2,214; Virginia, 2,176; Illinois, 2,167; Wisconsin, 1,908; Switzerland, 1,269; Rhode Island, 1,122; and Kentucky, 1,054; the difference between the above figures and the total population of 749,113 having been born in a great variety of States and countries. It is supposed that the census of 1870 will exhibit the same ratio, but a total population nearly twice as large.

SECOND PART.

HISTORY OF

MICHIGAN DURING THE REBELLION,

BY

GENERAL JOHN ROBERTSON.

HISTORY OF

MICHIGAN DURING THE REBELLION.

MILITARY DEPARTMENT OF MICHIGAN—1861 TO 1871.

			FROM	TO
Austin Blair,	Jackson,	Gov.C'm-in-Cf	Jan. 1, 1861	Dec. 31, 1864
Henry H. Crapo,	Flint,	" "	Jan. 1, 1865	Dec. 31, 1868
H. P. Baldwin,	Detroit,	" "	Jan. 1, 1869	In office.
John Robertson,	Detroit,	Adj. General,	Mar. 15, 1861	In office.
J. H. Fountain,	Manchester	Q. M. General,	April 1, 1861	Mar. 25, 1863
Wm. Hammond,	Tekonsha,	" "	Mar. 25, 1863	Mar. 20, 1865
Orrin N. Giddings,	Kalamazoo,	" "	Mar. 21, 1865	Mar. 25, 1867
Friend Palmer,	Detroit,	" "	Mar. 26, 1867	In office.
James E. Pittman,	Detroit,	Paymaster,	May 21, 1861	Nov. 1, 1862
James E. Pittman,	Detroit,	Insp. General,	Nov. 1, 1862	Mar. 21, 1867
Russell A. Alger,	Detroit,	" "	Mar. 21, 1867	In office.
DeWitt C. Gage,	E. Saginaw,	Judge Adv.	Mar. 10, 1865	April 17, 1869
L. S. Trowbridge,	Detroit,	" "	April 17, 1869	In office.
Heber Le Favour,	Detroit,	Ass. Adj. Gen.	April 1, 1861	June 14, 1861
DeGarmo Jones,	Detroit,	" "	June 15, 1861	May 5, 1862
Fred. Morley,	Detroit,	" "	May 6, 1862	Mar. 11, 1865
Friend Palmer,	Detroit,	A. Q. M. Gen.	May 17, 1861	Mar. 26, 1867
Eb. O. Grosvenor,	Jonesville,	Aid-de-Camp,	May 15, 1861	Mar. 10, 1865
Wm. Hammond,	Tekonsha,	" "	May 15, 1861	Mar. 25, 1863
John F. Miller,	Ann Arbor,	" "	May 15, 1861	Mar. 10, 1865
Jerome Croul,	Detroit,	" "	May 15, 1861	Mar. 10, 1865
James A. Dwight,	Ypsilanti,	" "	Oct. 1, 1863	Mar. 10, 1865
David H. Jerome,	Saginaw,	" "	Mar. 10, 1865	May 10, 1867
H. A. Newland,	Detroit,	" "	Mar. 10, 1865	April 17, 1869
Ch. J. Dickerson,	Hillsdale,	" "	Mar. 10, 1865	In office.
Jas. W. Romeyn,	Detroit,	" "	May 6, 1865	April 17, 1869
William Phelps,	Detroit,	" "	May 10, 1867	April 17, 1869
Milo E. Gifford,	Plainwell,	" "	April 17, 1869	In office.
Alfred B. Wood,	E. Saginaw,	" "	April 17, 1869	In office.
G. S. Wormer,	Detroit,	" "	April 17, 1869	In office.
Wm. K. Gibson,	Jackson,	Mil. Secretary	May 15, 1861	Sept. 13, 1862
Eugene Pringle,	Jackson,	" "	Sept. 13, 1862	Mar. 10, 1865
Isaac Delano,	Flint,	" "	Mar. 10, 1865	Sept. 16, 1865
Thomas J. Cobb,	Flint,	" "	Sept. 16, 1865	Dec. 31, 1868

			FROM	TO
F. G. Russell,	Detroit,	Ste.Mil.Board	April 17, 1869	In office.
A. S. Williams,	Detroit,	" "	Mar. 11, 1859	Sept. 19, 1861
A. W. Williams,	Lansing,	" "	Mar. 11, 1859	April 25, 1861
H. M. Whittlesey,	Detroit,	" "	Mar. 11, 1859	Sept. 19, 1861
C. W. Leffingwell,	Gr. Rapids,	" "	Mar. 11, 1859	Sept. 19, 1861
John Robertson,	Detroit,	" "	Mar. 15, 1861	Jan. 18, 1862
J. H. Fountain,	Manchester	" "	April 1, 1861	Jan. 18, 1862
Wm. M. Fenton,	Flint,	" "	June 17, 1861	Aug. 7, 1861
E. H. Thomson,	Flint,	" "	Aug. 13, 1861	Dec. 6, 1862
Eb. O. Grosvenor,	Jonesville,	" "	Sept. 19, 1861	Mar. 11, 1865
John F. Miller,	Ann Arbor,	" "	Sept. 19, 1861	Jan. 31, 1862
James E. Pittman,	Detroit,	" "	Sept. 19, 1861	Dec. 6, 1862
Wm. Hammond,	Tekonsha,	" "	Jan. 31, 1862	Mar. 25, 1863
Jerome Croul,	Detroit,	" "	Jan. 31, 1862	In office.
N. B. Eldridge,	Lapeer,	" "	Jan. 31, 1862	Dec. 6, 1862
Omar D. Conger,	Port Huron,	" "	Dec. 6, 1862	Jan. 19, 1869
A. T. Crossman,	Flint,	" "	Dec. 6, 1862	In office.
James A. Dwight,	Ypsilanti,	" "	May 23, 1864	Mar. 11, 1865
David H. Jerome,	Saginaw,	" "	Mar. 11, 1865	In office.
Henry L. Hall,	Hillsdale,	" "	Mar. 5, 1867	In office.
S. M. Cutcheon,	Ypsilanti,	" "	Jan. 19, 1869	In office.
J. H. Edwards,	Detroit,	Cl'kA.G.office	Dec. 1862	Dec. 1864
David Wallace,	Detroit,	" "	April, 1863	Aug. 1865
Geo. G. Wilcox,	Detroit,	" "	June, 1863	In office.
Edw. M. Simons,	Detroit,	" "	June, 1863	May, 1866
Frank G. Baker,	Detroit,	" "	July, 1864	Sept., 1865
Phillip M. Crapo,	Flint,	" "	Feb'y, 1865	Dec., 1867
David S. Snow,	Flint,	" "	March, 1865	March, 1867
Wm. R. Noble,	Detroit,	" "	August, 1865	June, 1867
Wm. J. Handy,	Detroit,	" "	Jan'y, 1866	April, 1869
William Hart,	Adrian,	Clk Q.M.Dept	June, 1861	March, 1864
Darwin W. Pratt,	Detroit,	" "	Sept. 1863	Nov., 1863
Frank S. Clark,	Detroit,	" "	Jan. 1864	April, 1867
J. T. Hammond,	Tekonsha,	" "	Mar. 1864	May, 1865
J. A. Fairfield,	Detroit,	" "	Feb'y, 1864	April, 1864
Frank G. Baker,	Detroit,	" "	May, 1864	July, 1864
T. F. Giddings,	Kalamazoo,	" "	Sept., 1865	Nov., 1865
Thomas Kiley,	Detroit,	State Armorer	April, 1862	In office.

PREFATORY NOTES.

Michigan, by her love for the "Old Flag," by her loyalty and patriotism, by her great and bloody sacrifice, and by the unbounded zeal and liberality of her people in the cause of the Union, especially by the bravery, efficiency, and great prowess of her troops in the field, has acquired an exalted position among her sister States, and is justly the recipient of much credit for her part in suppressing the rebellion.

The propriety and duty of having an authentic historical record of the part borne in that sanguinary struggle by her soldiers and people, and which has made her fame so national in this respect, will be universally admitted.

The great necessity for a published work embracing as much as possible of the subject had impressed the mind of the compiler so long and so forcibly, and the matter failing to receive the attention of others, induced, and it may be said, compelled him, from a sense of duty to the State and her troops in the late war, to attempt its production.

In undertaking it, he is fully aware that much more responsibility has been assumed than is successfully or satisfactorily met, and he is very sensible of the fact that the subject ought to have fallen in more capable hands.

For the defects, errors, or omissions, which unavoidably occur in a work of this description, the compiler trusts that he will be excused or pardoned, in consideration of an honest and anxious desire, and a most earnest endeavor to effect the purpose he had in view.

In its arrangement, it has been deemed best, for several reasons, to refrain from the introduction of biographical matter, and from referring to any of the causes to which the war is chargeable, as neither could have been included without extending the work beyond the proposed limit, or reducing much the narrative of special services of regiments, which was not desirable.

The compilation has, in the main, been made from the records of the State military departments, the written reports of commanding officers of regiments, and other official papers, consequently the work is presumed to be substantially accurate and reliable, and is as full as circumstances would permit.

It is necessarily a condensed and very brief narrative of the operations of Michigan in the war of the rebellion, and giving only very limited sketches of a few of the engagements of her brave regiments in the field, merely glancing at some of the more prominent encounters with the enemy in their long and varied service. To include more at this time has been deemed impracticable; yet, as these special selections are truthfully characteristic of their entire conflicts in the war, conclusions may easily be arrived at as to what they were in general.

They are sketches of the part taken by the regiments in encounters with the enemy, in which they were specially or heavily engaged, or conspicuously distinguished, illustrating in a degree their fighting qualities and general efficiency. In their selection, commandants of regiments have uniformly been consulted, and the data from which the sketches are drawn were mostly supplied by them, to whom, and the Michigan officers generally, the compiler is under many obligations for reports and other documents covering particular operations of their respective regiments, which have aided much in their preparation.

No attempt is made to claim for Michigan, or for her troops, any particular or special merit, or more than an equal credit with all other States and their troops for the part taken by them in the war for the Union. For it must be conceded that in all the times that shall come claims cannot be successfully sustained by any particular State for any special portion of the honor of preserving the Union. All that any can reasonably undertake and accomplish in this respect will be to truthfully represent as far as possible their own action, and the services rendered by their troops, there leaving the matter.

If any particular battle could be selected and designated as the action in which the backbone of the rebellion was broken and finally suppressed, then, on a comparison of the services of the troops of the various States in that engagement, a verdict might possibly be rendered; but no such selection can be made nor any such conclusion arrived at. For all time it must be decided that the Rebellion was not destroyed in any single battle, but by the continued hammering of the entire Union armies during the four long years of fearful and bloody war; and the accursed and hideous monster was beaten, baffled, starved, worn to a helpless skeleton, and then, while in the act of begging for bread and quarter, was toppled over into its selected resting place, to die an unwilling and humiliating death.

But it is claimed, in all candor, that no State evinced more loyalty to the Union, or more determination to maintain its life and honor, than did Michigan; that no troops in all the Union armies gave better or more conclusive evidence of true courage, efficiency, and patriotism, or exhibited a more supreme love for the great cause in which they were engaged, or rendered more valuable or gallant service than did hers.

INTRODUCTORY.

The outbreak of the American Rebellion in 1861, and the formidable onset of the rebels in arms, which, unfortunately, found all departments of the National Government unprepared for its fearful emergencies, came unanticipated and unprovided for upon all the States whose authorities were not participants in or privy to the conspiracy.

The people to whom war was then only a name, and not a dreadful fact, and who had for years been garnering the rich harvests of peace, amid great commercial prosperity and social tranquility, refused to credit the predictions and threatenings of a coming eclipse on the peace of the nation, until its terrible shadow had fallen upon them.

The disruption of the Union had been threatened so often and so causelessly, that busy men regarded it only as a common rallying cry of unscrupulous politicians, and rarely or never admitted, even in thought, that it might suddenly become a fearful reality. It was only when the guns of rebel batteries were fired at Fort Sumter, and shot and shell riddled the national flag, that the self-deception of the patriots of the land ceased; that the dreadful responsibilities of the crisis were acknowledged and accepted; and that the people determined upon the action that was instantly needed.

The manner in which existing deficiencies were supplied, the necessities of the times met, the constantly augmenting burdens of the struggle borne, and the whole problem solved so triumphantly at last, furnishes some of the imperishable pages of history.

Michigan, in common with her sister States of the North, never actually nor impliedly conceded the possibility of a civil war until the first blow was struck and the light of treason burst from Sumter's walls. Her people, thoroughly loyal in all the fires of their being, did not expect it in others; and in politics, as in law, they proposed to hold all innocent until guilt was indisputably proven. Thus there was no preliminary arming for the terrible conflict, no antecedent training, no husbanding of resources, no abatement of encumbrances, no occupancy of advantageous position, and the enemy vigorously assailed the walls while the unthinking garrison were yet engaged in the avocations of peace, and the rusty weapons were yet stacked in their quiet places of years past.

The census of Michigan for 1860 showed a population of 751,110. The number of able-bodied men capable of military service was estimated in official documents of that date at 110,000. The State debt at the close of that year was $2,228,842.79, besides $100,000 in canal bonds, which the State had guaranteed, and the actual value of the taxable property of the

State was estimated at $275,000,000. The financial embarrassments of our Commonwealth were, however, neither few nor unimportant, and an annual tax of $226,250 was deemed a grievous burden.

The militia department of the State was in a very feeble condition, caused by lack of the necessary pecuniary aid to encourage its numerical strength and efficiency. Yet feeble as it was, it formed a nucleus from which were rallied the first regiments sent to the field in defense of the Union, and from it germed much of the *esprit de corps* and superior military appearance, coupled with the general efficiency, which characterized the earlier Michigan troops, and, indeed, which pervaded all the Michigan regiments throughout the war.

For what was valuable in the militia at that time the State was more indebted to Colonel F. W. Curtenius, of Kalamazoo, who had been Adjutant-General for several years, and up to 1861, than to any provisions of her laws.

The companies then organized, and which constituted the entire available militia force, were twenty-eight in number, and their aggregate strength was 1,241 officers and men. For the support of this military establishment the State annually spent the enormous sum of three thousand dollars, appropriated for that purpose by the Legislature.

Notwithstanding these physical disadvantages, the *morale* of the people was true as steel. On retiring from the Gubernatorial chair, at the close of his term in 1860, the lamented Moses Wisner addressed a cogent and eloquent valedictory message to the new Legislature.

After presenting, in careful summaries, all the essential facts in reference to the manifold and important material interests of the State, he then proceeded to a discussion of the grave situation of national politics, over which an unprecedented sombre hue had been cast, by the recent passage in various Southern States of ordinances of secession. In the language used at that critical moment by our Executive there was no shadow of faltering, no tinge of disaffection, no uncertain sound. It breathed devotion to the Union in every sentence, and for the maintenance thereof at all hazards every paragraph was a stirring argument. We quote these inspiring utterances which then fell upon the ear of patriots, amid doubt, disloyalty, and danger, like tidings of better days and harbingers of future glory: "This is no time for timid and vaccillating councils, when the cry of treason and rebellion is ringing in our ears." "The Constitution as our fathers made it is good enough for us, and must be enforced upon every foot of American soil." "Michigan cannot recognize the right of a State to secede from this Union. We believe that the founders of our Government designed it to be perpetual, and we cannot consent to have one star obliterated from our flag. For upwards of thirty years this question of the right of a State to secede has been agitated. It is time it was settled. We ought not to leave it for our children to look after." "I would calmly but firmly declare it to be the fixed determination of Michigan that the Federal Constitution, the rights of the States, must and shall be preserved." These glowing words, this noble advice, were enforced by the personal and patriotic services of their author and giver, and fidelity to the national interests, and the great love of country which prompted them, added the honored name of Moses Wisner to the long lists of martyrs to the cause of the Union offered by our State.

Simultaneously with the valedictory of Governor Wisner, the Legislature of 1861 listened to the inaugural of his successor, Austin Blair. The mantle of Elijah had fallen upon a fitting Elisha; and a profound and philosophical discussion of the true nature of our complex system of government, and of the real signification of the existing and impending issues, was closed with these emphatic and telling utterances: "We are satisfied with the Constitution of our country, and will obey the laws enacted under it, and we must demand that the people of all the other States do the same; safety lies in this path alone. The Union must be preserved, and the laws must be enforced in all parts of it at whatever cost. The President is bound to this by his oath, and no power can discharge him from it. Secession is revolution, and revolution in the overt act is treason, and must be treated as such. The Federal Government has the power to defend itself, and I do not doubt that that power will be exercised to the utmost. It is a question of war that the seceding States have to look in the face. They who think that this powerful Government can be disrupted peacefully have read history to no purpose. The sons of the men who carried arms in the seven years war with the most powerful nation in the world, to establish this Government, will not hesitate to make equal sacrifices to maintain it. Most deeply must we deplore the unnatural contest. On the heads of the traitors who provoke it must rest the responsibility. In such a contest the God of battles has no attribute that can take sides with the revolutionists of the slave States.

"I recommend you at an early day to make manifest to the gentlemen who represent this State in the two Houses of Congress, and to the country, that Michigan is loyal to the Union, the Constitution, and the laws, and will defend them to the uttermost; and to proffer to the President of the United States the whole military power of the State for that purpose. Oh! for the firm, steady hand of a Washington, or a Jackson, to guide the ship of state in this perilous storm. Let us hope that we shall find him on the 4th of March. Meantime, let us abide in the faith of our fathers—'Liberty and Union, one and inseparable, now and forever.'"

Marshalled by such leaders, and also inspired by its own invincible *amor patræ*, the Legislature was neither timid nor slow in unfurling its colors to the breeze, and in joint resolutions offered on February 2d, 1861, it declared its adherence to the Government of the United States, pledged to and tendered it all its military power and material resources, and declared that concession or compromise was not to be entertained or offered to traitors. Still nothing definite was done—no actual defensive or aggressive military steps were taken—until rebel foolhardiness precipitated the struggle that had become inevitable by converging upon Fort Sumter the fire of the encircling batteries of Charleston Harbor.

On April 12, 1861, the news was received at Detroit that the rebels at Charleston had actually inaugurated civil war by firing upon Fort Sumter. This intelligence created much excitement, and in view of the uncertainty of coming events, the people, much alarmed, commenced looking around to estimate how united they would be in the cause of the Union. On the following day a meeting of the Detroit bar, presided over by the venerable Judge Ross Wilkins, was held, and resolutions were adopted pledging that community to "stand by the Government to the last," and repudiating the treason of the South. By the following Monday, (April 15th,) when the surrender of the South Carolina fortress was known throughout the land, and the call of the President for 75,000 volunteers had been received, the entire State was alive to the emergencies and duties of the hour, and the uprising of the people was universal. Public meetings were held in all the cities and in most of the towns—even in the Christian churches—pledges of assistance to the nation in its hour of peril made, and volunteering briskly commenced. In all portions of the State the watchfires of patriotism were kindled, blazing with an inspiring brightness, and the cheering illumination spread all over the land, as this lyric will testify:

Trumpet, and ensign, and drum-beat are calling,
From hillside and valley, from mountain and river,
"Forward the flag!" e'en though heroes are falling,
Our God will His own chosen standard deliver.

"Union and Freedom!" our war-cry is rolling,
Now o'er the prairie, now wide o'er the billow,
Hark! 'tis the battle, and soon will be tolling
The knell of the soldier, who rests 'neath the willow.

Banner triumphant! though grand is thy story,
We'll stamp on thy folds in this struggle to-day,
Deeds of our armies, transcending in glory,
The bravest yet chanted in poesy's lay.

Wise were our fathers, and brave in the battle,
But treason uprises their Union to sever.
Rouse for the fight! shout loud 'mid war's rattle,
The Union must triumph, must triumph forever!

Trumpet, and ensign, and drum-beat are calling,
From hillside and valley, from mountain and river,
"Forward the flag!" e'en though heroes are falling,
Our God will His own chosen standard deliver.*

Fortunate in her Executive and Legislative departments, and equally so in the management of her interests at the National Capital, having men of influence connected with several Departments who loved the reputation of their State, and ever ready and anxious to advance her cause, especially so in her representatives in both houses of Congress, Michigan fearlessly launched her bark on the turbulent sea of rebellion and war.

On Tuesday, April 16th, Governor Blair arrived in Detroit, and in the afternoon met a large number of leading citizens and capitalists of that city at the Michigan Exchange. The State had been called upon to immediately furnish to the General Government one infantry regiment, fully armed, clothed, and equipped.

It was estimated that $100,000 would be immediately required to defray the necessary expense of organizing the regiment, but the treasury was empty, and State finances so situated, that this pressing call could not be immediately met. Upon the laying of these facts before the meeting by the Hon. John Owen, State Treasurer, a resolution was passed pledging Detroit to loan the State $50,000, and calling upon the people throughout the State to make a like advance. A subscription paper was also circulated upon the spot, and the sum of $23,000 pledged by those present.

Commitees were also appointed to solicit further subscriptions in the city, and to aid the Governor in his undertaking. This liberal and prompt action at this opportune moment furnished the sinews of war for the time being. With these pledges of the people in hand, and his own good credit, Mr. Owen succeeded in raising a sum sufficient to enable the Executive to commence the clothing and equipment of troops, which sum, and all others obtained in like manner for this purpose, were assumed by the State on the assembling of the Legislature. During the same day a proclamation was issued by the Governor, calling for ten companies of volunteers, and ordering

* Flag song of Michigan troops in 1861.—By D. Bethune Duffield.

the Adjutant-General to accept the first ten companies that should offer, and making it the duty of that officer to issue all the necessary orders and instructions in detail. The movement thus inaugurated did not slacken in impetus nor lessen in ardor. The State responded to the call of its authorities most promptly. The patriotism of the people was in a blaze. War meetings were held in every town, and the tenders of troops from all points in the State far exceeded the requisitions yet made by the General Government. The necessary loan was readily taken, mostly by our own people, and all the duties of the hour were promptly met and discharged.

On April 23d the Governor issued his proclamation convening the Legislature in extra session at Lansing, on the 7th of May. On the following day, April 24th, the order was issued from the Adjutant-General's office for organizing the 1st regiment of infantry and appointing its field officers; its rendezvous was fixed at Fort Wayne, and the immediate assembling there of its various companies ordered. Authority had also been given for the raising of the Coldwater Battery, afterwards known as Loomis's. The battery was rapidly recruited, and the horses therefor were purchased with funds loaned to the State by the citizens of Coldwater. It was at once ordered to Fort Wayne, where its equipment was completed. The 2d regiment was also hurriedly recruited, and its companies concentrated at Cantonment Blair, Detroit. On May 2d the companies of the 1st regiment were mustered into the service of the United States. Meanwhile two other regiments, the 3d and 4th, had been formed, and were accepted by the State conditionally, it being apprehended that they would not be needed. The 3d went into camp at Grand Rapids, and the 4th at Adrian.

The Legislature met, pursuant to call, on the 7th, and the Governor addressed to them a stirring message, in which he detailed the work already accomplished, and asked the Legislature to legalize what had already been done, and invest the State authorities with sufficient power for the future.

Within a session of four days laws were passed, clothing the Governor with power to raise ten regiments and a war loan of one million dollars.

Fully aware of the valuable and patriotic services to be required of the soldiers of the State, and of the great sacrifices which must be made by their families in their absence, and, at the same time, anticipating that some might be left unprovided for, or might be brought to want by the contingencies or casualties of war, the Legislature wisely enacted the "Soldiers' Relief Law" for the relief of their families by counties, allowing more or less, according to their circumstances, but not exceeding fifteen dollars per month. This allowance, in case of the death of the soldier, to continue for one year after such death.

On May 13th the first regiment left for the seat of war fully armed and equipped.

Under the new legislation the organizing of regiments was rapidly pushed and the various requisitions upon the State for men promptly and expeditiously met.

The troops were ordered to be clothed, equipped and subsisted under the direction of the Quartermaster-General of the State on contracts made by the Military Contract Board, organized May 15th bv legislative authority. This Board was composed of Colonels E. O. Grosvenor of Jonesville, Jerome Croul of Detroit and William Hammond of Marshall. Their duties were accomplished with much individual ability, great energy, coupled with an exemplary economy, and relieving the Quartermaster-General from much responsibility and labor.

The State Military Board was then composed of General A. S. Williams and Colonel H. M. Whittelsey of Detroit, Col. A. W. Williams of Lansing, and Col. C. W. Leffingwell of Grand Rapids, together with the Adjutant-General and Quartermaster-General of the State, members *ex officio*.

In June following Col. Wm. M. Fenton was appointed a member of the Board in place of Col. Williams, who had gone to the field with the 2nd Infantry. Col. Fenton having entered the service, Col. E. H. Thomson succeeded him, and on the 13th of August was elected President of the Board.

J. H. Fountain of Manchester had been appointed Quartermaster-General in March, and was a faithful and energetic officer. He was ably aided in his arduous duties by Friend Palmer of Detroit who was appointed his assistant in May following. This officer, now Quartermaster-General, having served several years in the U. S. Quartermaster's Department, rendered invaluable services to the State during the entire war, and to him the State is greatly indebted for the efficient and economical direction given to the administration of that Department.

General Fountain was succeeded as Quartermaster-General by General William Hammond of Marshall March 25th, 1863, who served until March 21st, 1865, when he was relieved by Gen. O. N. Giddings of Kalamazoo. Both these officers served with marked ability and faithfulness.

General Palmer, the present Quartermaster-General, followed General Giddings.

Colonel James E. Pittman of Detroit was appointed State Paymaster on the 21st of May, 1861, for the purpose of paying such Michigan troops as received pay from the State, a duty which he most faithfully executed. He also served as a member of the State Military Board, from September 19th, 1861, until November 1st, 1862, when he was commissioned as Inspector-General of the State.

When the war commenced General John Robertson held the appointment of Adjutant-General, and still acts in that capacity.

On April 1st, 1861, Captain Heber Le Favour was appointed Assistant Adjutant-General, and served until June 15th following, when he volunteered for field service, being relieved by Captain De Garmo Jones, who resigned May 6th, 1862. Both of these officers served with marked efficiency. Colonel Frederick Morley immediately succeeded Captain Jones, and served with eminent ability and distinction until the close of the war, rendering arduous and valuable services as Assistant Adjutant-General of the State.

NOTE.—The following telegram was sent over the wires, in the form given below, and delivered to the Adjutant-General of Michigan with great secrecy. It is inserted for the purpose of showing the agitation and distrust manifested among the Western people in the early days of the war. The Illinois Central Railroad Company, at whose instance the dispatch was made, feared a raid on their line, and were preparing to meet it:

CHICAGO, April —, 1861.

Others and, Chicago Mayor, Governor our by signed Blair Governor to directed message have, secret profound a this keep to and, want immediate in are we, us to them bring will Central Michigan, Adjutant-General tell, once at, them have they if, Michigan from arms of stand thousand five or one wants Governor our. Guns no but, ready are troops. Borders own our on invasion suppress to troops send to orders have State our. * * *

RAISING OF TROOPS.

The President's first call upon Michigan for troops to aid in suppressing the rebellion was, as previously stated, for one regiment only, and was most promptly met by the muster into service of the 1st infantry, under Colonel O. B. Wilcox, and its early movement to the seat of war in Virginia. This regiment was soon followed by the 2d infantry, in command of Colonel Israel B. Richardson, while at the same time many companies were recruited throughout the State without authority in the hope of obtaining places in some regiment; being disappointed in this respect they sought and found service in regiments of other States. In the meantime the organization of the 3d and 4th regiments had been commenced on the responsibility of the governor; and while they were in process of recruitment a letter was received from the Secretary of War limiting the force required from Michigan to four regiments only including the three months' regiment, covering only authority for those already in the field and those being organized in the State. The letter referred to is inserted for the purpose of showing the estimate made at that time of the magnitude of the rebellion then fully inaugurated:

WAR DEPARTMENT, WASHINGTON, *May* 11, 1861.

Governor AUSTIN BLAIR, *Lansing, Michigan :*

DEAR SIR :—I have the honor to forward you, enclosed herewith, the plan of the organization of the volunteers for three years, or during the war. Three regiments are assigned to your State, making, in addition to the one regiment of three months' militia already called for, four regiments. It is important to reduce rather than enlarge this number, and in no event to exceed it. Let me earnestly recommend to you, therefore, to call for no more than four regiments, of which only three are to serve for three years, or during the war; and if more are already called for, to reduce the number by discharge.

SIMON CAMERON, *Secretary of War.*

This policy was extremely at variance with the views entertained by the State executive regarding the necessities of the country at that time, and deeming an immediate preparation to meet coming emergencies his duty, assumed the responsibility of establishing a camp of instruction at Fort Wayne, near Detroit, for the officers of the 5th infantry, Col. H. D. Terry; 6th infantry, Col. F. W. Curtenius; and the 7th infantry, Col. Ira R. Grosvenor. On the 21st of May companies were assigned to those regiments, and their officers and non-commissioned officers were ordered to assemble at Fort Wayne on the 19th of June. The camp was organized and commanded by General A. S. Williams, assisted by Colonel J. E. Pittman, Major W. D. Wilkins, and Captain Henry M. Whittelsey. A course of instruction followed with much success until August 1st, when the camp was broken up, and the force sent to various localities to recruit their men and organize the regiments. This was accomplished with astonishing promptness, the 6th being mustered in August 20th, the 7th August 22d, and the 5th August 28th, and all had left for the field prior to the 12th of September.

The camp of instruction attracted much attention in other States, and received the favorable comments of public journals. It has always been considered in Michigan as a most judicious and eminently successful effort; its value becoming more and more apparent as the war progressed, not only in the efficiency of these particular regiments, but in many others, having the benefit of officers who had received the instruction of the camp.

Soon after the breaking up of the camp General Williams was appointed a brigadier general of volunteers and left for the field in Virginia, with Major Wilkins and Captain Whittelsey on his brigade staff.

About the time the camp was established the pressure for appointments as commissioned officers had reached its maximum, and men were being forced upon the consideration of the governor by influential citizens of both political parties to a most unbearable degree, and often with an utter disregard of fitness or qualification for the position. This pressure continued during the entire earlier portion of the war; and it might well be presumed that under such circumstances some improper appointments were likely to be made. Yet much care was uniformly exercised in the selection and promotion of officers, and always with qualification for the office and loyalty to the Government as the tests, more than personal friendship or political status.

The law of Congress of August 3d had authorized the President to receive into service 500,000 volunteers; the proportion of Michigan was understood at the time to be 19,500, but in the adjustment of credits 21,337 was charged against the State.

In addition to this force were Captain Duesler's company (C) 1st U. S. sharpshooters, (Berdan's,) raised at large, equipped and armed by the State, mustered at Detroit on the 21st of August, with an aggregate strength of a hundred of the best picked riflemen in the State, and Captain A. B. Stuart's company (B) 2d U. S. sharpshooters, raised at Lansing and mustered at Detroit on the 4th of October, with an aggregate of seventy-eight on its muster-rolls.

Also, two companies of cavalry for the "Morrill Horse," a Missouri regiment. These companies were recruited at Battle Creek, "H" by Captain J. H. Rogers, and "I" by Captain J. B. Mason, and both left the State on the 3d of September.

The "Jackson Guard," a Detroit company, composed of Irishmen, raised by Captain John McDermott, failing to get a position in the early Michigan regiments, offered their services to Colonel James Mulligan, then recruiting a regiment in Illinois. They were accepted, and the company joined his command in June, and were with him in his gallant defence of Springfield, Missouri.

Several other Michigan companies, not obtaining places in Michigan regiments, getting impatient at the delay in finding an opportunity to serve their country, accepted service in regiments of other States. It would have afforded much pleasure to have been able to notice them more fully at this time, but sufficient data cannot be obtained for that purpose. These companies, so far as ascertained, were "E," "F," and "H," 42d, and "B" and "H," 44th regiments Illinois infantry, company "C," 70th New York infantry, (Sickles Brigade,) from Paw Paw, mustered on the 21st of June in command of Captain W. H. Hugo; company "K," 1st New York cavalry, raised at Grand Rapids and mustered on the 12th of August under command of Captain Anson N. Norton. The regiment was raised and organized by Col. A. T. McReynols, and was commanded by him in the field. Company "D," 66th Illinois infantry, commonly designated as the "Western Sharpshooters," mustered November 9th in command of Captain John Piper, of Battle Creek.

Under this call, Colonel T. F. Brodhead, of Detroit, received authority to raise the 1st regiment of cavalry, and a like authority was given to the Hon. F. W. Kellogg, of Grand Rapids, member of Congress from this State, to organize the 2d and 3d cavalry, while Colonel T. B. W. Stockton, of Flint, obtained authority to recruit and organize the Stockton regiment, afterwards designated as the 16th infantry.

In response to this requisition, the State continued recruiting, sending regiment after regiment to the field, and down to December, 1861, had sent the following organizations to the front:

The 1st regiment infantry, 3 months, from Detroit, May 15, 780 strong—Colonel O. B. Wilcox commanding.

The 1st regiment, from Ann Arbor, September 16, 751 strong—Colonel John C. Robinson commanding.

The 2d regiment infantry, from Detroit, June 5, 1020 strong—Colonel J. B. Richardson commanding.

The 3d regiment infantry, from Grand Rapids, June 13, 1042 strong—Colonel D. McConnell commanding.

The 4th regiment infantry, from Adrian, June 25, 1024 strong—Colonel D. A. Woodbury commanding.

The 5th regiment infantry, from Detroit, September 11, 900 strong—Col. H. D. Terry commanding.

The 6th regiment infantry, from Kalamazoo, August 30, 1020 strong—Col. F. W. Curtenius commanding.

The 7th regiment infantry, from Monroe, September 5, 1020 strong—Col. Ira R. Grosvenor commanding.

The 8th regiment infantry, from Detroit, September 27, 900 strong—Col. W. M. Fenton commanding.

The 9th regiment infantry, from Detroit, October 25, 943 strong—Col. W. W. Duffield commanding.

The 16th regiment infantry, from Detroit, September 16, 960 strong—Col. T. B. W. Stockton commanding.

The 11th regiment infantry, from White Pigeon, December 9, 1000 strong—Col. W. J. May commanding.

The 1st regiment mechanics and engineers, from Marshal, December 11, 1000 strong—Col. W. P. Innes commanding.

The 1st regiment cavalry, from Detroit, September 29, 1150 strong—Col. T. F. Brodhead commanding.

The 2d regiment cavalry, from Grand Rapids, November 14, 1170 strong—Lieut. Col. W. C. Davis commanding.

The 3d regiment cavalry, from Grand Rapids, November 28, 1180 strong—Lieut. Col. R. H. G. Minty commanding.

The 1st battery, from Detroit, June 1, 123 strong—Captain C. O. Loomis commanding.

The 2d battery, from Grand Rapids, December 17, 110 strong—Captain W. S. Bliss commanding.

The 3d battery, from Grand Rapids, December 17, 80 strong—Captain A. W. Dees commanding.

The 4th battery, from White Pigeon, December 9, 126 strong—Captain A. F. Bidwell commanding.

The 5th battery, from Marshal, December 17, 76 strong—Captain J. H. Dennis commanding.

Ten of these regiments were clothed and subsisted by the State under the direction of the Quartermaster-General.

On the 2d of January, 1862, Governor Blair delivered his message to the Legislature, then in extra session. The following extract therefrom was accepted at the time as the expression of the people of the State on the war question:

"I cannot close this brief address without an allusion to the great object that occupies all men's minds. The Southern rebellion still maintains a bold front against the Union armies. That is the cause of all our complications abroad and our troubles at home. To deal wisely with it is to find a short and easy deliverance from them all. The people of Michigan are no idle spectators of this great contest. They have furnished all the troops required of them, and are preparing to pay the taxes and to submit to the most onerous burdens without a murmur. They are ready to increase their sacrifices, if need be, to require impossibilities of no man, but to be patient and wait. But to see the vast armies of the Republic, and all its pecuniary resources, used to protect and sustain the accursed system which has been a perpetual and tyrannical disturber, and which now makes sanguinary war upon the Union and the Constitution, is precisely what they will never submit to tamely. The loyal States having furnished adequate means, both of men and money, to crush the rebellion, have a right to expect those men to be used with the utmost vigor to accomplish the object, and that without any mawkish sympathy for the interest of traitors in arms. Upon those who caused the war, and now maintain it, its chief burdens ought to fall. No property of a rebel ought to be free from confiscation—not even the sacred slave. The object of war is to destroy the power of the enemy, and whatever measures are calculated to accomplish that object, and are in accordance with the usages of civilized nations, ought to be employed. To undertake to put down a powerful rebellion, and, at the same time, to save and protect all the chief sources of the power of that rebellion, seems to common minds but a short remove from simple folly. He who is not for the Union, unconditionally, in this mortal struggle, is against it. The highest dictates of patriotism, justice, and humanity combine to demand that the war should be conducted to a speedy close upon principles of the most heroic energy and retributive power. The time for gentle dalliance has long since passed away. We meet an enemy, vindictive, bloodthirsty, and cruel, profoundly in earnest, inspired with an energy and self-sacrifice which would honor a good cause, respecting neither laws, constitutions, nor historic memories, fanatically devoted only to his one wicked purpose to destroy the Government and establish his slaveholding oligarchy in its stead. To treat this enemy gently is to excite his derision. To protect his slave property is to help him to butcher our people and burn our houses. No. He must be met with an activity and a purpose equal to his own. Hurl the Union forces, which outnumber him two to one, upon his whole line like a thunderbolt; pay them out of his property, feed them from his granaries, mount them upon his horses, and carry them in his wagons, if he has any, and let him feel the full force of the storm of war which he has raised. I would apologize neither to Kentucky nor anybody else for these measures, but quickly range all neutrals either on the one side or the other. Just a little of the courage and ability which carried Napoleon over the Alps, dragging his cannon through the snow, would quickly settle this contest, and settle it right. If our soldiers must die, do not let it be of the inactivity and diseases of camps, but let them at least have the satisfaction of falling like soldiers, amid the roar of battle, and hearing the shouts of victory; then will they welcome it as the tired laborer welcomes sleep. Let us hope that we have not much longer to wait."

Following this patriotic and bold stand assumed by the Governor in his message, the Legislature, equally appreciating the great emergencies of the country, with firmness and pluck worthy of the people whom they represented, passed the following well-timed and highly appropriate joint resolution in reference to the rebellion:

Whereas the Government of the United States is engaged in putting down a causeless and wicked rebellion against its authority and sovereignty, inaugurated by ambitious men to obtain political power—a government, the safety and perpetuity of which must ever rest upon the loyalty of its citizens and an adherence to the Constitution;

And whereas the welfare of mankind, the usefulness and power of the nation, are involved in the events and issues of the present conflict; therefore, be it

Resolved, (the House concurring,) That Michigan, loyal to herself and to the Federal Government, reaffirms her undying hostility to traitors, her abiding love for freedom, and her confidence in the wisdom and patriotism of the national administration.

Resolved, (the House concurring,) That the people of Michigan deem it the imperative duty of the Government to speedily put down all insurrection against its authority and sovereignty, by the use of every constitutional means, and by the employment of every energy it possesses; that Michigan stands firm in her determination to sustain, by men and treasure, the Constitution and the Union, and claims that the burthen of loyal men should be lightened, as far as possible, by confiscating to the largest extent the property of all insurrectionists; and that as between the institution of slavery and the maintenance of the Federal Government, Michigan does not hesitate to say, that in such exigency, slavery should be swept from the land, and our country maintained.

Resolved, That the Governor be requested to forward a copy of the foregoing preamble and resolutions to each of our Senators and Representatives in Congress.

Approved January 18, 1862.

At the commencement of the year 1862 recruiting was being vigorously prosecuted under most favorable circumstances, brought about in part by a brisk competition, often leading to various schemes for inducing recruits to change regiments, both before and after muster, neither legitimate nor honest, but still considered by some as having the ring of a certain kind of smartness; and although there was much complaint and many protests made against this mode of operating, leading to the publication of prohibitory orders on the subject, it was found impossible to prevent the practice.

At the various recruiting depots in the State there were being hastily organized and rapidly equipped five regiments of infantry and three batteries of artillery. Their completion was most industriously pushed by the officers charged with their recruitment, and they left for the field as follows:

13th infantry, from Kalamazoo, February 12th, 925 strong, Col. M. Shoemaker commanding.

12th infantry, from Niles, March 18th, 1,000 strong, Col. Francis Quinn commanding.

15th infantry, from Monroe, March 27th, 869 strong, Col. J. M. Oliver commanding.

14th infantry, from Ypsilanti, April 17th, 925 strong, Col. R. P. Sinclair commanding.

10th infantry, from Flint, April 22d, 997 strong, Col. C. M. Lum commanding.

7th battery, from Kalamazoo, February 12th, 145 strong, Capt. C. H. Lamphere commanding.

6th battery, from Coldwater, March 3d, 158 strong, Capt. J. S. Andrews commanding.

8th battery, from Monroe, March 13th, 156 strong, Capt. Saml. De Golyer commanding.

A lancer regiment, composed of a fine body of men, principally from Canada, had been raised by Col. Arthur Rankin, of Windsor, an English Canadian. It had been mustered into service with the maximum number and equipped, with the exception of horses. It would have left the State with those named, but was disbanded by an order of the War Department, contrary to the repeated protests of the Governor, and without giving any reason for such a procedure, losing to the service of the Union a remarkably fine appearing regiment.

Two more companies for the 1st U. S. sharpshooters also left the State for the field; "I" in command of Capt. A. Milan Willett and "K" under the command of Spencer J. Mather, the former company mustered on the 4th and the latter on the 20th of March.

There was also a company of sharpshooters raised in Detroit by Capt. Kin S. Dygert for the 16th Michigan, which was mustered on the 3d of February and joined the regiment in the field without delay.

In the month of April Capt. G. S. Wormer, of Detroit, was authorized to raise and equip a company of infantry to serve as a guard over Generals Burrows and Harding and Judge Hill, all influential citizens of Nashville, Tennessee, then rebel prisoners on the island of Mackinac, and who had been arrested by Andrew Johnson for treason. This company was designated the Stanton Guard. It was mustered into the service May 10th and immediately took transport for Mackinac, where it served until the 25th September following, when it was disbanded, the necessity for the service having passed away by the release of the prisoners.

The reports made in July by the several regiments, batteries, and independent companies gave an addition of 2,028 recruits to their original strength since their organization, showing a total of 24,281 officers and men enrolled from the commencement of the war to July 1st, and an estimated number of 1,453 enlistments in regiments of other States, giving 25,734 as the grand total. Add to this the lancer regiment disbanded, and a battalion of cavalry raised at Coldwater by Major Hughes, designated the "Chandler Horse Guard," which was mustered out of service under an order of the War Department for irregularities in organization, and we have an aggregate of nearly twenty-seven thousand men enrolled and mustered into service previous to the first of July. Furnishing over six thousand more than had been called for by the requisition of the Government, exhibiting a degree of patriotism and promptness unsurpassed by any other State, and men too whose loyalty, patriotism, and courage had been tried and proved on almost every battle-field.

During McClellan's disastrous peninsula campaign in May and June the Michigan regiments had become much depleted by the usual casualties of service and by wounds, disease, and death, whilst recruiting had entirely failed in the State. The 17th infantry was then organizing, and it was found almost impossible to obtain men for its completion, and recruits for regiments in the field could not be enlisted under any circumstances.

The following letter was post-marked Albion, Michigan, and addressed to the Adjutant-General of the State, and received in May, 1862:

Mr. Robertson:

Sir:—In the name of God Almighty, the Government of the United States, and the people of the State of Michigan, send me by special train to Kalamazoo forthwith five corporals and forty privates, with forty rounds of fixed ammunition and two days cooked rations each. I have work for them. I have holed an old and big secesh den of traitors and want to dig them out.

BRONSON,
Independent Detective and Acting U. S. Marshal.

P. S.—Telegraph to me about what time they will get there.

"B"——

I. D. & U. S. M.

GALESBURG, *May* 26.

This fearful condition of affairs had assumed so formidable a shape as to make it necessary to hold public meetings in some localities of the State to stimulate the people to more energy in the cause of the Union, and especially in recruiting for the regiments in the field. A public meeting for that purpose was called in Detroit, to be held in the afternoon of Tuesday, the 15th July, and on assembling on the Campus Martius in accordance with the call, and while the business in view was being proceeded with, the gathering were surprised by a mob of men, who furiously interrupted the deliberations and entirely broke up and dispersed the meeting, driving the officers from the stand, and compelling some of them to seek shelter and safety in the "Russell House," a hotel adjacent to the Campus Martius. The exhibition of this rebel spirit in our midst proved of immediate and lasting advantage to the cause of the army in the field, for it aroused such a feeling of indignation at these disloyal and treasonable operations, and such utter contempt for the ruffians who had been thus engaged, that the masses of the respectable citizens of both political parties determined that such proceedings should not be tolerated in Detroit, and therefore next day a meeting was appointed for Tuesday, the 22d of July, to carry out the objects of the previous meeting, and for the further purpose of maintaining the right of citizens to hold such meetings without interference or molestation. An immense gathering assembled under the call, severely rebuking the disloyal element, and with unbounded enthusiasm avowing a most faithful and persistent support of the war, and pledging, with prodigal liberality, means and personal encouragement, and adopting instant measures for the recruitment of the regiments of the State, and urging the immediate re-enforcements of the armies of the Union.

This prompt action of the citizens had the desired effect, giving recruiting new life and energy, and led to the immediate proffer of the gallant 24th regiment to the cause of freedom and humanity, and served to end all open demonstrations in favor of rebellion in the metropolis of the State.

The general alarm for the cause of the Union, resulting from the reverses of McClellan, flashed over the State and brooded over her loyal people, being shared in for a short time by Michigan, in common with the other loyal States; but she soon rallied from a despondency which was but temporary, and burst forth with a renewed degree of unsurpassed vigorous energy and enlarged patriotism.

President Lincoln, advised by the Governors of the loyal States, who had consulted together regarding the emergency,* issued a proclamation on July

---

*BY TELEGRAPH FROM NEW YORK, *June* 30, 1862.

TO THE GOVERNOR OF MICHIGAN:

"*Private and Confidential.*"—In view of the present state of military movements, and the depleted condition of our efficient forces in the field, resulting from the usual and unavoidable causes of the services, together with the large numbers of men required to garrison the numerous cities and military positions that have been captured, as well as to protect our avenues of supplies in the enemy's country, it is proposed to address a memorial to the President to-day, to be signed by all the Governors of all the loyal States, and some other officials of the country, requesting him at once to call upon the several loyal States for such number of men as may be required to fill up organizations in the field, and add such increased numbers of men to the army heretofore authorized a may in his judgment be necessary to speedily crush this rebellion and restore our

2d for 300,000 men, the War Department assigning to Michigan a quota of 11,686. On the 15th of July orders were published from the Adjutant General's Department of the State urgently appealing to the people for a prompt and effective response, and prescribing regulations for a system of organization. The following is an extract from the order referred to:

"The Governor has confidence in the loyalty, patriotism, and courage of the people, that they will cheerfully respond to the President's call, firmly believing that this force will be quickly raised to aid in speedily putting an end forever to this unjustifiable and cruel rebellion.

"The time has now arrived for men who love their country and desire its perpetuity as a nation to make sacrifices in its defence. Without resort to drafting, let the ranks be speedily filled, let every heart be nerved, and every man welcome the hour that calls him to his country's rescue; let him be self-sacrificing, patriotic, and courageous; let him make the camp his home, and the brave soldiers of the Union his companions, until this national struggle be ended, and show that the privations, hardships, and dangers endured by the noble sons of the State who have fought their country's battles, and that the bloody battle grounds so recently trodden by them have not drained the State of its patriots nor lessened the love of her people for the national flag, nor their determination that its folds shall float over them unimpaired forever."

In addition to the 17th infantry in process of organization by recruits from the State at large, six regiments of infantry were ordered, and apportioned respectively to the six Congressional districts, confining the recruitment of each regiment to its own district, establishing a camp for each, and appointing commanders of camp, who were charged with the raising of the regiments. These regiments, having the following gentlemen as commanders of camp, were the 18th, at Hillsdale, Hon. Henry Waldron; 19th, at Dowagiac, Col. Henry C. Gilbert; 20th, at Jackson, Hon. Fidus Livermore; 21st, at Ionia, Hon. J. B. Welsh; 22d, at Pontiac, Col. Moses Wisner; and the 23d, at East Saginaw, Hon. D. H. Jerome.

The Adjutant General of the State, in his report for 1862, says of the action of the people regarding this call:

"The response of the people of the State to the President's call was patriotic and prompt almost beyond expectation. Individuals of every degree of prominence forthwith began to interest themselves in the business of filling the regiments. Communities gave to it their time and their almost exclusive attention, while, better than all, the substantial masses of the people offered themselves in person. War meetings were held in almost every village and township in the State. Representatives of all classes converted themselves either into recruits or recruiting officers, and among the most efficient of the latter were ministers of the Gospel, some of whom led the men they had enlisted into the field."

The Christian Church in this State generally proved by its pronounced patriotism, and manifest devotion to the cause of the country, an element of immense success. All true patriots commend its noble cause, all faithful Christians endorse its glorious action. From the time that Sumter was fired

---

Government. The decisive moment to accomplish this end, it is believed, has arrived. Shall we add your name to the memorial?

(Signed,) E. D. MORGAN, *Governor New York.*
R. G. CURTIN, *Governor Pennsylvania.*

They were immediately telegraphed by Governor Blair to use his name on the memorial.

on until Lee and Johnston laid down their rebellious arms, and Davis fled for his life, it encouraged and nerved by word and deed the soldier in the field, aided much in the recruitment of men by its approval of the cause, and its openly avowed abhorrence of rebels and those who sympathized with them and opposed the war. Where it did not, cowardice most mean and grovelling, disloyalty gross, and blackest treason, prevented its being included in the Providence of God among the instrumentalities to save the nation, and hence, neither deserves nor can expect any better fate than the certain condemnation of every true lover of his country and of his race, and the disapproval of the God of nations.

The valuable services rendered at this time by the loyal Press throughout the State can never be over-estimated; for its successful efforts in strengthening the hands of public officers, in moulding public opinion in favor of loyalty to the Government, in encouraging patriotism among the masses, and inspiring those at the front with a heroism leading to gallant deeds.

The Adjutant-General further says in his report:

"Immediately following the issue of this order, applications reached the Adjutant-General's office, by telegraph and otherwise, from all sections of the State, urging authority to recruit, and desiring instructions and forms for the enlistment of companies. Facilities to promote this purpose were promptly furnished, and as soon as the camp grounds could be provided with suitable quarters, men began to flock in by companies and detachments. The gentlemen who had been charged with the duty of supervising the organization of the regiments performed their labors with diligence and success, and in little over a month from the date of the President's call, men enough had been raised in the State, and nearly enough were in camp, to fill all the regiments which the War Department had asked for as the number first needed under the President's requisition.

"In the meantime, while the patriotism of the people was thus zealously manifesting itself in all portions of the State, the people of Detroit and of Wayne county desired an opportunity to put in the field a regiment of their own citizens, in addition to those already in progress. Authority was promptly given by the Governor for this purpose, and the 24th regiment was ordered, organized under the direction of Colonel H. A. Morrow, and placed in rendezvous at Detroit, making the eighth infantry regiment then in course of completion."

The Executive of the nation, Abraham Lincoln, was looking anxiously into the future and calling earnestly upon the States for information as to what he might expect to sustain him in meeting coming emergencies. Under date of July 28th, he telegraphed to Governor Blair:

"It would be of great service here for us to know as fully as you can tell, what progress is made and making in recruiting for old regiments in your State. Also, about what day the first new regiment can move from you, what the second, what the third, and so on. This information is important to us in making calculations. Please give it as promptly and accurately as you can."

To this dispatch the Governor instantly replied as follows:

"Very little can be done in recruiting old regiments until the new regiments are filled up; although every exertion will be made to do so. The new regiments will commence to take the field about the 1st September, or sooner, if possible, and will all be in service in the field during that month."

In providing for the immense reinforcements to the national armies under this call, some delay in arming and equipping the troops unavoidably occurred, and the Michigan regiments were ready before their field equipment. With great dispatch, however, they were put in readiness for the field, and left the State fully armed, clothed, and equipped, in the order hereafter mentioned.

On the completion of the eight regiments referred to, it was ascertained that in the rush to the rescue more companies had been raised than could be placed in the district regiments, and on the 20th of August an order was issued from the Adjutant-General's office directing the recruitment of the 25th and 26th regiments of infantry, and assigning the surplus companies thereto.

The 25th rendezvoused at Kalamazoo, under the direction of the Hon. H. G. Wells, commandant of camp, and the 26th at Jackson, in command of Colonel Judson S. Farrar. They were put in condition for active service with much promptness, and left the State immediately thereafter.

About the time that the President's last call for volunteers appeared, the Governor had permission from the War Department to send into the field another regiment of cavalry, and authority was given to Colonel R. H. G. Minty, then lieutenant-colonel of the 3d cavalry, to proceed at once to raise the 4th cavalry. Appointments to recruit were eagerly sought for, and the regiment was rapidly raised to the maximum, and on the 29th of July was ordered into rendezvous at Detroit. On the 29th of August it was mustered into the United States service, and was only awaiting its horses and equipments. As soon as these were provided, it left the State on the 26th of September.

Soon after the organization of the 4th, Colonel J. T. Copeland, late of the 1st cavalry, sought and obtained the permission of the War Department, approved by the Governor, to raise another regiment for the same branch of service; and still later—when the President had issued an order providing for the draft of a further force of 300,000 men, Hon. F. W. Kellogg, member of Congress from this State, secured authority (also subject to approval by the Governor) to raise two additional regiments for the same arm. The 5th and 6th cavalry, comprising two of the three regiments thus authorized, were recruited with great rapidity, and would have been in the field by the 1st of October had horses, arms, and equipments been provided as fast as the men were ready for them. They left the State in the early part of December.

The 9th battery of light artillery was raised in connection with the 5th cavalry, by Captain I. I. Daniels, and left for the field with that regiment, fully equipped and mounted.

The bodies of troops thus referred to comprise all the district organizations that were sent from the State into active service since the requisition of the President, made on the 2d of July, and are as follows:

The 17th regiment infantry, from Detroit, August 27, 982 strong—Colonel W. H. Withington commanding.

The 24th regiment infantry, from Detroit, August 29, 1027 strong—Colonel H. A. Morrow commanding.

The 20th regiment infantry, from Jackson, September 1, 1012 strong—Colonel A. W. Williams commanding.

The 18th regiment infantry, from Hillsdale, September 4, 1002 strong—Colonel C. E. Doolittle commanding.

The 22d regiment infantry, from Pontiac, September 4, 997 strong—Col. M. Wisner commanding.

The 21st regiment infantry, from Ionia, September 12, 1007 strong—Col. A. E. Stevens commanding.

The 19th regiment infantry, from Dowagiac, September 14, 995 strong—Col. H. C. Gilbert commanding.

The 23d regiment infantry, from East Saginaw, September 18, 883 strong—Col. M. W. Chapin commanding.

The 4th regiment cavalry, from Detroit, September 26, 1223 strong—Col. R. H. G. Minty commanding.

The 25th regiment infantry, from Kalamazoo, September 29, 896 strong—Col. O. H. Moore commanding.

The 9th battery, from Detroit, December 4, 168 strong—Captain J. J. Daniels commanding.

The 5th regiment cavalry, from Detroit, December 4, 1305 strong—Col. J. T. Copeland commanding.

The 6th regiment cavalry, from Grand Rapids, December 10, 1220 strong—Col. George Gray commanding.

The 26th regiment infantry, from Jackson, December 13, 903 strong—Col. J. S. Farrar commanding.

The quality of the men, physically, mentally, and morally, forming the material of these regiments, has never been and can never be excelled in the armies of any State or nation, and it may well be questioned if it was ever equaled outside of the limits of the Union.

The infantry regiments went to the field thoroughly armed and equipped, the arms furnished being of a superior quality. The cavalry were equally well equipped; but a portion of the arms of some of them were not furnished until after reaching the seat of war.

At the time the call was made by the President, and on which the above designated regiments were raised, much anxiety as to coming events and results existed throughout the land, and great despondency pervaded the masses, prevailing to an alarming extent in the army. The disasters of Bull Run and Ball's Bluff, and Bank's retreat from the Valley of the Shenandoah were fresh in the memory. McClellan's fruitless peninsula campaign had just terminated. Gloom covered the Union cause throughout the North, and loyal hearts were sad. But with these disasters and discouragements patriotism seemed to grapple, and strong and loyal men flocked to service under the standard of their country, without money or price, and with laudable determination. The regiments referred to were recruited in these memorable days, the darkest of the rebellion. Fighting had produced much suffering, and bullets, death, and war had proved a fearful reality; yet patriotism in Michigan was at its maximum, and her people demonstrated their indomitable pluck.

While great activity prevailed among the people and in the State Military Departments, in meeting the call of July 2d, strong hopes were entertained that the final requisition for additional volunteers had been reached. The President issued an order on the 4th of August for a draft to be made without delay of 300,000 militia to serve for nine months. On the 9th of the same month general orders were promulgated by the War Department, assigning the quotas of the several States, that of Michigan being 11,686, same as under the last call.

Special instructions of a later date directed that if volunteers for old and new regiments mustered from July 2d exceeded the number called for (11,686) the excess might be deducted from the number drafted.

Accepting the exigency, the Governor issued his proclamation to the proper civil officers of each township and ward to make a complete census of the citizens of proper age and forward returns to the county clerk of their respective counties on or before the 10th day of September following. This new demand upon the resources and patriotism of the people was assented to with great unanimity, and its propriety and necessity generally accepted, but the desire was to obviate a draft, and strong efforts were being put forth to furnish the quota in volunteers.

The commissioners appointed by the Governor to superintend the draft, together with the sheriffs and clerks of counties, were constituted recruiting officers.

General orders were issued from the Adjutant-General's Department of the State, apportioning the quota to be raised on the basis of the census of 1860, (the military enumeration being yet incomplete,) and accrediting each county with the number of men which had been furnished by each since the 2d of July, as shown by special returns made from the regiments themselves, and appointing the following-named persons to carry the draft into effect in their respective counties:

Allegan county, Henry Dumont, commissioner; L. Foster, surgeon. Branch county, Geo. A. Coe, commissioner; Phineas P. Nichols, Henry B. Stillman, surgeons. Berrien county, Charles R. Brown, commissioner; John M. Roe, Morgan Enos, surgeons. Bay county, Henry Raymond, commissioner; Chas. H. Reynolds, surgeon. Barry county, Norman Bailey, commissioner; John Roberts, surgeon. Calhoun county, J. B. Greenough, commissioner; Z. T. Slater, W. H. Johnson, surgeons. Cass county, Chas. W. Clisbee, commissioner; Alonzo Garwood, surgeon. Clinton county, R. Stickland, commissioner; Dr. Topping, surgeon. Cheboygan county, ——; Eaton county, Joseph M. Hazlett, commissioner; Alden B. Sampson, surgeon. Emmet county, ——. Genessee county, Warner Lake, commissioner; Daniel Clarke, surgeon. Gratiot county, ——, commissioner; John B. Cheeseman, surgeon. Grand Traverse, Morgan Bates, commissioner; ——, surgeon. Hillsdale county, E. O. Grosvenor, commissioner; A. Cressy, surgeon. Huron county, W. D. Luddington, commissioner. Ingham county, Lemuel Woodhouse, commissioner; Dr. Hill, surgeon. Ionia county, Albert Williams, commissioner. Isabella county, ——. Jackson county, Eugene Pringle, commissioner; Gordon Chittack, surgeon. Kent county, P. H. L. Pierce, commissioner; Almon M. Ellsworth, surgeon. Kalamazoo county, Charles S. May, commissioner; Wm. Mottram, surgeon. Lapeer county, Virtulon Rich, commissioner; Oliver T. Strowbridge, surgeon. Livingston county, William Riddle, commissioner; Chas. W. Haze, surgeon. Lenawee county, Perley Bills, commissioner; Dr. Pearsoll, Edwin P. Andrews, surgeons. Leelanaw county, ——. Macomb county, Dexter Muzzy, commissioner. Mecosta county, ——. Midland county, Lorenzo F. Taylor, commissioner. Manitou county, ——. Mason county, ——. Manistee county, ——. Monroe county, Edwin P. Dorch, commissioner and surgeon. Montcalm county, R. K. Divine, commissioner. Muskegon county, Chauncey Davis, commissioner. Newaygo county, John A. Brooks, commissioner; A. D. Leonard, surgeon. Oceana county, ——. Ottawa county, C. B. Albee, commissioner; J. D. North, surgeon. Oakland county, Clark Beardslee, commissioner. Shiawasse county, Iona Fuller, commissioner; David F. Alsdorf, surgeon. Saginaw county, Addison Brewer, commissioner; Hiram C. Driggs, surgeon. St. Clair county, Marcus H. Miles, commissioner; C. M. Stockwell, surgeon. St. Joseph county, John W. Frey, commissioner; Francis J. Morse, surgeon. Tuscola county, Charles B. Mills, commissioner; Wm. Johnson, surgeon. Van Buren county, O. T. Welch, commissioner; John W. Emery, Eugene Bitely, Decatur, surgeons. Wastenaw county, James McMahon, commissioner; D. A. Post, Ebenezer Mills, surgeons. Wayne county, Christian H. Buhl, commissioner; E. M. Clark, J. M. Swift,

Louis Davenport; Dr. Keiffer, surgeons. C. H. Buhl of Wayne resigned after serving a considerable time, and was succeeded by Joseph Warren.

In counties where commissioners and surgeons were not appointed by this order, the Sheriffs thereof were authorized to designate commissioners, with power to appoint surgeons.

On account of the want of preparation in most of the States for an immediate draft, the Government found it expedient to postpone the period for it to take place and to extend the time for the completion of the regiments in process of organization.

In the meantime the most strenuous and effective measures were being continued by most of the townships and wards then behind to furnish the number required of them without recourse to draft, and to aid in this, large local bounties were offered and the most efficient means of recruiting employed.

The results of the military census are presented in the following table taken from the Adjutant-General's report for 1862. Where the figures are omitted in the first column, the counties failed to make returns.

Table showing the number of persons between the ages of 18 *and* 45 *enrolled by Assessors, September* 10, 1862, *the number exempted, and the number subject to draft; together with the number returned in June, under a law of the State.*

COUNTY.	No. of men enrolled by Assessors.	No. exempted.	No. subject to draft.	No. returned in June, under State law.
Allegan			1,844	2,721
Barry	2,264	*818	1,446	1,814
Bay	1,061	315	746	
Berrien			2,534	3,172
Branch			2,713	
Calhoun	5,126	1,123	4,003	4,499
Cass			1,824	2,217
Cheboygan	109	†72	37	104
Clinton	2,126	748	1,378	
Eaton	2,672	790	1,882	
Emmet			25	
Genesee			2,627	2,513
Hillsdale	4,392	1,238	3,154	3,708
Huron	642	103	539	
Ingham			1,773	2,563
Ionia	2,850	1,234	1,616	
Isabella			276	
Jackson	4,527	‡618	3,909	3,885
Kent			3,934	2,160
Kalamazoo	4,369	738	3,631	3,527
Lapeer	2,530	795	1,735	1,897
Lenawee	6,544	1,067	5,477	5,095
Livingston			2,248	2,782
Mackinac	223		§223	188
Macomb	3,485	819	2,666	2,976
Mason	111	76	35	
Midland			132	152
Mecosta	229	97	132	200
Monroe	3,069	675	2,394	1,936
Montcalm			573	240
Newaygo	650	161	489	
Ottawa			1,760	2,085
Oakland	5,901	968	4,933	4,967
Shiawassee			1,305	
Sanilac	1,294	436	858	
Saginaw	2,951	821	2,130	2,497
St. Clair	4,006	972	3,034	4,042
St. Joseph			3,089	3,276
Tuscola			776	750
Van Buren	2,734	544	2,190	2,355
Washtenaw	5,879	984	4,895	
Wayne	12,538	2,432	10,106	11,224
Subject to draft			91,071	

*Of these 797 were exempted by the surgeon. †Most of these are Indians, whom hitherto the War Department has refused to muster into service. ‡ Exempted by surgeon, 419. §There was no surgeon in this county, and these figures show the total enrollment.

In the same report of the Adjutant-General is found the following statement regarding the population of counties and the number of persons subject to draft on the basis of the census of 1860:

"The total population of the counties above enumerated at the census of 1860 was 715,595. The proportion of persons residing therein who are subject to draft is as 1 to 857-1000. The counties which have made no returns are Alcona, Alpena, Chippewa, Delta, Gratiot, Grand Traverse, Houghton, (included with Keweenaw in 1860,) Iosco, Leelanaw, Marquette, Manitou, Manistee, Muskegon, Osceola, Oceana, Ontonagon, Presque Isle, and Schoolcraft, and their aggregate population in 1860 was 35,415. The same ratio which rules in the counties from which returns have been received would produce in the counties last mentioned a military strength of 4,507, making the aggregate of persons yet remaining in the State between the ages of 18 and 45, and subject to draft for military purposes, 95,578, less the number of volunteers who have enlisted since September 10, 1862."

The War Department, now fully aware of many obstacles in the way of making a draft at that time and hoping that the necessary additional troops could be raised by volunteer enlistments, left the time for drafting to the discretion of the governors.

Early in September three companies of men, nearly full, had been offered from the Upper Peninsula, and there was reason to believe that three more would be filled in the same section of country. The 27th infantry was, therefore, with the assent of the Government, organized and put in rendezvous at Port Huron in command of Lieut. Col. Thomas S. Sprague. The authority given by the War Department to Col. Kellogg to raise the 7th cavalry was confirmed by the Governor, and that regiment was thereupon organized and ordered, under date of October 29th, to rendezvous at Grand Rapids.

At the same time the Governor accorded permission, (the same having been previously given by the General Government, subject to his approval,) to Col. John Stockton, of Mount Clemens, and to Capt. James J. David, of Trenton, then in the U. S. Quartermaster's Department, to raise an additional regiment of cavalry, and the 8th was thereupon ordered, with its camp at Mount Clemens, and the 9th, which had its rendezvous at Coldwater.

An urgent desire having been manifested to organize another infantry regiment, Col. Edward Doyle, of Detroit, received authority, with the assent of the War Department, to raise the 28th; and on application the Department also consented to the raising of a regiment of sharpshooters, the organization of which had been placed in the charge of Capt. C. V. DeLand, of the 9th infantry. The Government had specially authorized advanced bounty and one month's pay to volunteers in either of these regiments, and vigorous efforts were very generally entered upon to fill their ranks.

It was supposed by many citizens that were an opportunity offered for men to enlist for the same term as the law provided for drafted levies—nine months—larger numbers would avail themselves of it to volunteer for that period who declined to accept a longer service. Willing to afford every reasonable encouragement to the disposition so generally manifested to furnish all the men required without resorting to draft, and fully mindful, also, of his obligations to the National Government, His Excellency, on the 29th of November, issued a proclamation which so clearly represents the situation at the time, and is so intimately connected with the State military record, that we take the liberty of presenting it in full:

To the People of the State of Michigan :

It is essential to the maintenance of the honor of the State, by meeting its obligations to the Federal Government, that the quota of the troops required of Michigan under the call for 600,000 men should be speedily furnished. I have felt great confidence that this might be done without resort to a draft, but it will be impossible at the rate enlistments have been making for the last month and more. The number required of each town and ward in the State has been assigned upon the principle of giving credit for all recruits furnished since the first of July last. Substantial justice in this respect has been done toward all. To be exact was impossible, and to go back of the first of July was impracticable, both because the order of the Secretary of War did not authorize it, and because there was no reliable record by which such credit could be made up with any chance of fairness.

It is, therefore, indispensable that the several towns and wards of cities should furnish the number of recruits assigned to them, and I take this occasion to assure the people that unless the men are furnished by voluntary enlistment they will be taken by the draft.

For the purpose of still giving abundant opportunity to fill the quota of the State by voluntary enlistment, recruiting will be continued as follows:

1st. Recruits will be received for new regiments now forming in the State, and for all the old regiments now in the field, until and including the 29th day of December next. These must be enlisted for the term of three years or during the war.

2d. From the 1st to the 16th day of December next volunteer recruits will be received for the old regiments only *to serve for nine months*, in pursuance of the act of Congress.

3d. On the 30th day of December next the draft will commence and proceed until the requisite number is obtained in all those towns and wards which shall then be found delinquent.

Less than four thousand men are now required to fill the entire quota of the State, and I earnestly hope that they will be found to come forward cheerfully and *enlist for the war*, as all our troops thus far have done. And I desire this not so much because there is anything discreditable in a draft, as because it is exceedingly desirable that all the troops from Michigan should stand on the same footing in the army. Let the people of Michigan make one more loyal and vigorous effort, and the entire number required can be obtained, and the high reputation of the State for patriotism and promptness will be maintained.

AUSTIN BLAIR.

Dated Jackson, November 29, 1862.

The aggregate number of troops enlisted and mustered up to December 23d, 1862, as reported by the Adjutant-General, was as follows:

Total, including recruits, sent to the field before July 1st, 1862, 24,281; "Lancers" and "Hughes' Horse Guards," regularly mustered into the service, but disbanded without leaving the State, 987; three regiments of cavalry, ten of infantry, and one battery, sent since July 1st, 13,739; recruits (including six for nine months) received from July 1st to December 23d, 2,162; estimated strength of three regiments of cavalry, two of infantry, one of sharpshooters, and two batteries, organizing in the State, 4,400. Total, 45,569.

This does not include volunteers from this State who have gone into the regiments of other States, to a number known to exceed 1,400.

A considerable number of recruits had also been enlisted in the State during the summer and fall for the regular army, probably three or four hundred at least.

These troops, with the exception of a few of the earlier regiments that were mustered into service by the late Lieut. Col. E. Buckus, Capt. J. C. Robinson, and Capt. H. R. Miner, U. S. army, were mustered under the direction of the late Gen. J. R. Smith, U. S. army, a citizen and resident of Michigan, who was United States military commander in the State and chief mustering officer until the adoption of the provost marshal's system when he was detailed as commissary of musters, in which capacity he served until the close of the war. The energetic and faithful services rendered by him aided much in facilitating the speedy despatch of troops to the front.

The report of the Adjutant-General of the State for 1862 closes with the following extract, which undoubtedly expressed the estimation in which the Michigan troops were held, and did not by any means over-estimate their services, and certainly was correct as to the loyalty and patriotism of the people at that period of the war:

"At the time of making the last annual report from this department, covering only a small portion of the force now in the service from this State, it was thought that the regiments then reported would be all that would be required to suppress the rebellion; but another year is nearly closed, and regiment after regiment has been raised, until a large army has gone from the State, and still the rebellion goes on. Notwithstanding all this, the loyalty and patriotism of the people is unexhausted. The same determination seems to exist as at the commencement of the war, that it must be put down, and the nation redeemed at any sacrifice. The promptness and cheerfulness with which every call made by the General Government upon the State has been responded to bespeaks the intelligent loyal patriotism of its people. The people of Michigan are intelligently loyal on the subject of the war, and her soldiery are intelligently brave and patriotic, true to the honor of their State and their nation, preferring on all occasions death before dishonoring either.

"The troops from the State of Michigan have gained a prominent position in the armies of the nation. They have done their duty faithfully, fully, and fearlessly, and borne the brunt of many well-fought fields. Some of them have proved an anomaly in modern warfare; suddenly called from the common avocations of life, and within a very few days of the time of leaving their native State, they have been pitted against the veteran troops of the enemy of their country in superior numbers, and completely routed them. It has been the fortune of some of them voluntarily and successfully to lead the 'forlorn hope,' regardless of opposing numbers. Their scars and thinned ranks now attest their services to their country. The honor of their nation and their State has been safe in their hands, and both will cherish and reward them. Monuments to the memory of the brave dead are now erected in the hearts of the people, and national monuments to their memory will be erected by a grateful country."

The military operations in the field in 1862 had not been much in favor of the Union cause. In December the Union army in Virginia had failed in its attack on Fredericksburg, the Western army had been successful at Stone River in the same month, both important engagements, and in effect nearly balancing. Yet the people of the country seemed not to be discouraged nor to falter in their determination to press on to ultimate success by putting down the nefarious rebellion. In good old Michigan loyalty and patriotism seemed in the ascendant.

Governor Blair, in his message to the Legislature, in January, 1863, in speaking to the Michigan soldiers in the field, alludes to their services as follows:

"Gentlemen, I commend the Michigan troops to your active sympathy and support. By their heroic endurance of the hardships of war, and by their splendid bravery in battle, they have crowned the State with glory. Their battle-cry is 'Michigan! remember Michigan,' and Michigan must remember them. We have already a long list of immortal heroes dead in battle. I hope you will in some appropriate way place upon the enduring records of the State your appreciation of the valor and patriotic devotion of these brave men. Let us hand down their names to posterity upon an illuminated page, that they may be revered as examples for all time to come. They belong to history now. We must take care that it is rightly written. Your hearty thanks are also due to the gallant men who still uphold the flag of our country in the field, and have lately borne it on to victory over bloody ground. Let us send them warm words of cheer from home. May God give them other and greater victories, and bring them speedily back in peace and triumph. Then, indeed, shall Heaven's arches ring with glad shouts of welcome."

In February following, the Legislature expressed in the following joint resolution the sentiments of the Michigan people on the war question:

"That we are unalterably opposed to any terms of compromise and accommodation with the rebels while under arms and acting in hostility to the Government of the Union, and on this we express but one sentiment—unconditional submission and obedience to the laws and Constitution of the Union."

In March, the following preamble and resolutions were passed by the Legislature in compliment to the Michigan soldiers in the field:

Whereas the citizen soldiers of Michigan have responded cheerfully to their country's call, have never hesitated or faltered when duty prompted or danger threatened, and by their indomitable fortitude under the fatigues and privations of war, their heroic bravery and brilliant achievements upon the battle-field, have crowned themselves with glory, and given to Michigan imperishable renown; therefore,

Resolved by the Senate and House of Representatives of the State of Michigan, That, tendering to them the thanks of the State for their valuable services, we also assure them that while Michigan thus holds them forth as examples of emulation to the soldiers of other States, she is also proudly grateful to them for the renown which their noble deeds have shed upon her name, and claiming them for her own, she points to them with feelings of maternal pride, and in the language of the noble Roman mother exclaims, "These are my jewels."

Resolved, That the Governor be, and he is hereby, required to forward a copy of the foregoing preamble and joint resolution to each of the regiments and batteries of Michigan soldiers now in the field.

An act was passed by this Legislature authorizing the payment by the Quartermaster-General of $50, State bounty from March 6, 1863, which was continued until November 20th following. The Legislature also legalized the action of the townships, cities, and counties in raising bounties for volunteers.

In compliance with a recommendation of the Governor, the Legislature generously appropriated $20,000 to assist sick and wounded soldiers in the field, and likewise to aid those in the State, and in payment for services of agents to properly carry into effect the measure. In 1865 an additional amount of $25,000 was set apart for that purpose.

Under the law referred to six agents were appointed, and entered upon this duty: Benjamin Vernon, at Detroit; Dr. J. Turonicliffe, Jr., at Washington, D. C.; Luther B. Willard, at Nashville, Tenn.; J. B. Gillman, at Louisville, Ky.; Weston Flint, at St. Louis, Mo.; and Darius Clark, in New York city. During the latter part of the war D. A. Millard was employed at the Washington agency.

The necessity for these agencies became more and more apparent every day as the war progressed, proving of immense benefit to the Michigan troops in general, and particularly to those who found it necessary to accept pecuniary assistance. The agencies were managed by gentlemen much in sympathy with the cause of the soldiers, taking much interest in their welfare, consequently laboring faithfully in their behalf.

At the commencement of 1863, three regiments of cavalry, two of infantry, one of sharp-shooters, and two batteries were in process of recruitment within the State.

During January, the company known as the "Provost Guard," raised by Captain E. D. Robinson, under authority from the War Department, for duty at the Detroit Barracks, was mustered into service. Also company "L," "Merrill Horse," recruited at Battle Creek by Captain Almon E. Preston.

The 7th cavalry, recruiting for which had commenced in September previous, remained in rendezvous at Grand Rapids until the 20th of February following, when eight companies, which had been completed, were ordered to report at Washington, and a few days thereafter took up their march for that purpose, under command of Colonel W. D. Mann. The remaining battalion was left in camp to recruit, and joined the regiment in the field during the month of May.

The 8th cavalry, at its rendezvous at Mt. Clemens, enlisted a force in officers and men of 1,117, as is shown by its muster-in rolls, and two battalions moved towards Kentucky on the 12th of May, under command of Colonel John Stockton, the remaining companies following two weeks thereafter.

The 9th cavalry, under command of Colonel James J. David, took up its line of march from Coldwater to Cincinnati on the 18th, 20th, and 25th of May, leaving two incomplete companies to be filled. These soon after joined the regiment in the field. The muster-in rolls show the original strength of the regiment as 1,073.

Recruiting for the two regiments of infantry forming, in December—the 27th and 28th—proceeded so slowly that it was determined, in view of the exigencies of the service, to consolidate them, and on the 1st of February the 27th was ordered to break camp at Port Huron and proceed to the rendezvous of the 28th, at Ypsilanti. The process of consolidation was there completed, the united regiments becoming known as the 27th Michigan Infantry. On the 12th of April, eight companies being filled, began their movement to Cincinnati, under command of Colonel D. M. Fox, their muster-in rolls showing an aggregate of 865. The completion of the regiment was afterwards effected.

The 1st regiment of Michigan sharp-shooters, which had its first rendezvous at Kalamazoo, was afterward transferred to Dearborn, and on the 8th of July, six companies only being filled, was ordered to Indianapolis, under command of Colonel C. V. DeLand. The completed muster-in rolls of the regiment show an aggregate of 963.

The 10th battery, under command of Captain J. C. Schultz, left Grand

Rapids with the 7th cavalry, destined to Washington, its muster-in roll containing the names of 104 officers and men.

The 11th battery, under Captain Charles J. Thompson, raised in connection with the 9th cavalry, left Coldwater with the regiment, having 108 names on its muster-in rolls, and reported at headquarters of the Department of Ohio, at Cincinnati.

The 12th battery, Captain E. G. Hillier, which had a somewhat informal origin in connection with the 8th cavalry, was ordered to Dearborn after the departure of the latter regiment. It proceeded thence to Indianapolis in July. The muster-in roll of the battery shows that up to its completion 219 officers and men had been mustered in.

The quota of the State, under the President's call of August 4, 1862, for 300,000 militia remaining unfilled, a draft was made in February following, on the basis of the census of 1860, in the counties then in arrear for the small deficiency then existing. The number of men drafted was 1278. Of this number (either of themselves or by substitutes) 710 were delivered at the United States barracks at Detroit, 545 of whom were sent to various regiments and batteries in the field, a few of the remainder deserting, while others were discharged for alienage, disability, or other causes, by United States authorities. Of the 545 men thus realized from the draft for a service of nine months each, 430 were induced to enlist for three years, 115 only going into the field for the shorter term. These facts are exhibited in clearer detail in the subjoined table, showing the result of the draft:

Counties in which draft was made.	Number drafted.	Delivered at barracks	Accounted for at barracks or sent to regiments.		
			For 3 ye'rs	For 9 mos.	Total.
Allegan	45	33	20	2	22
Barry	47	37	10	21	31
Calhoun	8	2	2	—	2
Cass	56	44	34	1	35
Clinton	41	28	17	11	28
Genesee	76	60	36	8	44
Hillsdale	68	39	15	16	31
Ingham	65	36	20	5	25
Jackson	49	24	12	8	20
Lapeer	158	92	56	14	70
Livingston	84	42	31	4	35
Macomb	127	64	44	2	46
Monroe	74	39	26	6	32
Oakland	59	19	13	1	14
Saginaw	19	4	3	1	4
Shiawassee	45	25	11	10	21
St. Clair	178	72	47	1	48
St. Joseph	16	14	11	1	12
Tuscola	7	2	—	1	1
Van Buren	56	34	22	2	24
Total	1,278	710	430	115	545

On the 23d of June Col. F. W. Kellogg was authorized by the War Department to raise two additional regiments of cavalry and two more batteries of artillery, to be completed within forty days. The authority was upon the direct and urgent requests of the Secretary of War endorsed by the Governor, although he had determined to raise no more new regiments, but to receive volunteers only for the wasted regiments in the field. Having thus consented to the proposed increase, the 10th cavalry and 13th battery were thereupon, under the personal management of Col. Kellogg, placed in rendezvous at Grand Rapids, and the 11th cavalry and 14th battery were also organized under the same direction, with headquarters at Kalamazoo. It was found impracticable, however, to complete these bodies within the time originally limited, and the 10th cavalry, in command of Col. Thaddeus Foote, of Grand Rapids, left its camp for Lexington, Kentucky, on the 1st of December, and the 11th, in command of Col. S. B. Brown, of St. Clair, for the same destination on the 17th, the former numbering 912 and the latter 921 on their muster-in rolls. The two batteries remaining in the State in the process of organization.

The Michigan cavalry had been so uniformly celebrated in the Union armies that the War Department gave the State a preference regarding that arm of service; consequently Michigan furnished eleven regiments, a larger proportion of her troops in cavalry than did any other State. To Col. Kellogg unusual credit should be awarded, having by indefatigable and persistent energy, with great ability and tact in that direction, raised six of these fine regiments, an achievement unparalleled in the recruitment of troops in this or any other State.

In July the Secretary of War commissioned Henry Barns, of Detroit, a colonel in the United States army, with authority to recruit a colored regiment in Michigan. With the approval of the Governor he at once commenced this arduous task, and the 1st Michigan colored infantry were placed in process of recruitment. The organization was completed on the 17th of February following, when it was mustered into the service of the United States, with 895 names on its rolls. The designation of the regiment was afterwards changed by the War Department, with the consent of the Governor of the State, to the 102d United States colored troops. It left its rendezvous at Detroit on the 28th of March to join the Ninth Army Corps, then at Annapolis, Maryland.

In March, 1863, the Congress of the United States passed "An act for enrolling and calling out the national forces," which provided elaborate details for the accomplishment of the object in view, leaving their execution exclusively in the hands of the Federal authorities.

Under the law referred to, the national force was declared to consist, with certain specified exceptions, of "all able-bodied male citizens of the United States and persons of foreign birth who shall have declared on oath their intention to become citizens under and in pursuance of the laws thereof, between the ages of twenty and forty-five years;" and this force was divided into two classes, the first to comprise "all persons subject to do military duty between the ages of twenty and thirty-five years, and all unmarried persons subject to do military duty above the age of thirty-five and under the age of forty-five," the second to comprise "all other persons subject to do military duty;" and it was provided that the latter class "shall not, in any district, be called into the service of the United States until those of the first-class shall have been called." Each Congressional district was formed into an enrollment district, a provost marshal and board of enrollment provided for each, and these districts were again divided into sub-districts, consisting of wards and townships.

Lieut. Col. Bennett H. Hill, 5th U. S. artillery, was appointed by the War Department Acting Assistant Provost Marshal General of the State. Col. Hill proved to be an officer of great executive ability, truly loyal and patriotic. He superintended the enrollment and drafting in Michigan during the war. He was a graduate of the Military Academy at West Point and a native of the District of Columbia.

The following named gentlemen served as provost marshals:

First District—John S. Newberry, of Detroit, who was succeeded by Mark Flanigan, of the same place; headquarters at Detroit.

Second District—Rollin C. Dennison, of Kalamazoo; headquarters at that place.

Third District—Robert J. Barry, of Ann Arbor; headquarters at Jackson.

Fourth District—Norman Bailey, of Hastings; headquarters at Grand Rapids.

Fifth District—Charles M. Walker, of Lapeer, now of Adrian, who was succeeded by William M. McConnell, of Pontiac; headquarters at that point.

Sixth District—Randolph Strickland, of St. John's; headquarters at Flint.

The rendezvous for the reception of drafted men was established at Grand Rapids, and was placed in charge of Gen. S. G. Champlin, formerly of 3d Michigan, and remained under his command until disability caused by wounds rendered his continuance on duty impossible. He was relieved by Col. Norman J. Hall, of the 7th Michigan, who was in turn relieved by Col. Charles H. Town, 1st Michigan cavalry.

The rendezvous was continued at Grand Rapids until March 4th, 1864, when it was changed to Jackson on account of its central location. Col. G. S. Wormer had charge of it until authorized to raise the 30th infantry, when he was relieved on the 20th of November following by Gen. L. Cutler, of Wisconsin, who continued in command until recruiting for the armies ended.

Through these agencies a general enrollment was made during the summer; the following exhibit, is derived from the returns made to Colonel Hill, showing the total numbers so enrolled in the State:

First Congressional District.

Name.	First Class.			Second Class.		
	White	Col.	Total.	Wh.	Col.	Total.
Wayne,	6825	155	6980	4067	76	4143
Monroe,	1870	10	1880	1056	2	1058
Lenawee,	3739	52	3791	1973	9	1982
Hillsdale,	2468	13	2481	1413	2	1415
Total,	14902	230	15132	8509	89	8598

Second Congressional District.

Name.	White	Col.	Total.	Wh.	Col.	Total.
Kalamazoo,	2720	63	2783	1233	18	1251
St. Joseph,	2302	20	2322	1156	5	1161
Branch,	2048	13	2061	1131	2	1133
Allegan,	1794	20	1814	1006	9	1015
Berrien,	2209	78	2287	1244	18	1262
Cass,	1597	164	1761	848	73	921
Van Buren,	1596	62	1658	909	19	928
Total,	14266	420	14686	7527	144	7671

Third Congressional District.

Name.	First Class.			Second Class.		
	White	Col.	Total.	Wh.	Col.	Total.
Eaton,	1498	2	1500	868	—	868
Ingham,	1579	4	1583	986	—	986
Calhoun,	3045	49	3093	1543	20	1563
Washtenaw,	3822	75	3897	1597	30	1627
Jackson,	2996	28	3024	1241	4	1245
Total,	12940	158	13098	6235	54	6289

Fifth Congressional District.

Name.	White	Col.	Total.	Wh.	Col.	Total.
Oakland,	3798	52	3850	1665	7	1672
Livingston,	1814	8	1822	782	2	784
Lapeer,	1486	12	1498	776	...	776
Sanilac,	909	3	912	395	...	395
St. Clair,	2347	9	2356	1343	4	1347
Macomb,	2068	11	2079	1183	...	1183
Total,	12422	95	12517	6144	13	6157

Fourth Congressional District.						
Kent,	2788	7	2795	1804	7	1811
Ionia,	1772	6	1778	904	1	905
Ottawa,	1363	20	1383	862	3	865
Barry,	1320	8	1328	812	3	815
Montcalm,	622	3	625	261	1	262
Muskegon,	925	3	928	271	...	271
Oceana,	229	3	232	92	1	93
Newaygo,	342	...	342	174	1	175
Mecosta,	222	2	224	78	...	78
Mason,	100	...	100	31	...	31
Manitou,	100	...	100	48	...	48
Manistee,	188	...	188	51	...	51
Grand Traverse,	203	...	203	91	...	91
Sheboygan,	36	...	36	24	...	24
Mackinac,	184	...	184	53	...	53
Delta,	139	1	140	25	...	25
Leelanaw,	143	...	143	50	...	50
Benzie,	85	...	85	46	1	47
Muskegon,	51	...	51	19	...	19
Emmett,	27	...	27	15	...	15
Antrim,	55	...	55	15	...	15
Total,	10894	53	10947	5726	18	5744

Sixth Congressional District.						
Clinton,	1366	1	1367	731	...	731
Shiawassee,	1313	2	1315	730	...	730
Genesee,	2375	5	2380	1162	...	1162
Gratiot,	566	5	571	306	...	306
Tuscola,	650	...	650	394	...	394
Huron,	590	...	590	192	...	192
Isabella,	153	...	153	61	...	61
Alpena,	124	...	124	45	...	45
Iosco,	58	...	58	14	...	14
Midland,	189	1	190	44	...	44
Bay,	934	6	940	324	...	324
Saginaw,	2344	4	2348	1047	...	1047
Chippewa,	134	1	135	35	...	35
Marquette, Schoolcraft,	523	2	525	86	...	86
Houghton,	642	...	642	120	...	120
Keweenaw,	903	2	905	253	...	253
Ontonagon,	641	1	642	200	...	200
Menominee,	123	...	123	23	...	23
Total,	13628	30	13658	5767	...	5767

Recapitulation by Districts.

Districts.	First class.			Second class.		
	White.	Colored.	Total.	White.	Colored.	Total.
First Congressional District	14,902	230	15,132	8,509	89	8,598
Second Congressional District.....	14,266	420	14,686	7,527	144	7,671
Third Congressional District.......	12,940	158	13,098	6,235	54	6,289
Fourth Congressional District.....	10,894	53	10,947	5,726	18	5,744
Fifth Congressional District	12,422	95	12,517	6,144	13	6,157
Sixth Congressional District........	13,628	30	13,658	5,767	...	5,767
Total.........................	79,052	986	80,038	39,908	318	40,226

On the completion of the enrollment in each of the several States, a draft was ordered to be made of one-fifth of the first class so enrolled therein; this number, however, to be subject to such modifications as might be produced by an adjustment of the surplus or deficiency existing in the accounts of each State under previous calls. In other words, a State which had furnished more than had been asked for under previous calls of the General Government was to be credited with the excess. In making the computations necessary to this adjustment, the term of service and number of men furnished were alike taken into account, and the advantages to the people of the State of the policy which had prevailed of encouraging three years' enlistments, at periods when other States were placing nine months' or two years' men in the field, became strikingly manifest. A statement sent to the Adjutant-General's office from the War Department gave, on the 26th of May, a surplus to be applied on the impending draft of 4,403 men. It had been the practice, in the absence of official data from Washington, to estimate the quota of Michigan under the calls of 1861 at 19,500, that being about the result of calculations based upon the census returns of population. It appeared by this statement, however, that the Federal authorities had assumed 21,357 as the apportionment of the State under the call referred to. Notwithstanding the diminution occasioned by this discovery, the surplus credited to us still appeared to be considerably less than was due the

State according to its own records, and after correspondence and examination the legitimate credit of the State was estimated on the 19th of September at a total, reduced to a three years' standard, of 9,518, including such as had been enlisted since the statement of May 26th.

The extent of our territory, and the difficulty of communication in some portions of it, with other causes perhaps, delayed the completion of the enrollment until the fall. On the 27th of October, a draft began in the second, third, fourth, fifth, and sixth Congressional districts, and on the 5th of November in the first—the number of enlistments which had been made down to those dates having been previously added to the credits of the several sub-districts. The upper peninsula was not included in the draft.

In making a draft under the existing law, it was provided that fifty per cent. be added to the number required to cover exemptions, &c.—the quota actually called for to be taken in the order of numerical precedence from the whole number drawn. The total number drafted in the State was 6,383. Of these, 261 were delivered at the general rendezvous at Grand Rapids, 643 furnished acceptable substitutes, (43 of whom deserted before reaching rendezvous,) 1,626 paid each $300 commutation money, 1,596 were exempted for physical disability, 330 as aliens, 204 for unsuitableness of age, and 1,069 failed to report. The subjoined table, giving the result in each Congressional district, is interesting:

	First District.	Second District.	Third District.	Fourth District.	Fifth District.	Sixth District.	Total.
Number drafted	532	1402	1083	1147	1197	1022	6383
Drafts delivered at rendezvous	15	76	46	61	16	47	261
Drafts deserted	......	3	......	......	......	......	3
Substitutes delivered	38	97	53	30	351	31	600
Substitutes deserted	1	5	10	......	25	2	43
Paid commutation	176	387	430	281	58	294	1626
Enlisted in service	......	......	......	128	......	......	128
Exempted for physical disability	156	472	191	304	254	219	1596
Exempted for mental disability	......	2	......	......	......	2	4
Exempted as aliens	12	26	42	58	107	85	330
Exempted as non-residents	2	9	10	9	12	12	54
Exempted, over or under age	18	41	36	30	45	34	204
Exempted, only sons of infirm parents, &c	23	51	37	25	45	29	210
Exempted, fathers of dependent children, not twelve years old	5	20	14	14	10	16	79
Exempted, having two brothers in service	3	15	6	......	5	4	33
Exempted, in service March 3, 1863	13	19	12	......	20	7	79
Exempted for conviction of felony	1	1	1	1	......	......	4
Exempted for all other causes	8	13	23	5	8	3	60
Failed to report	61	165	172	193	241	237	1069

The total amount of money paid to the bounty fund of the General Government by men taken under this draft, as commutation to secure exemption from personal service, was four hundred and eighty-seven thousand eight hundred dollars, ($487,800.)

In October a new system of recruiting was adopted by the War Department, allowing to persons properly authorized as recruiting agents $15 for each recruit. Subsequently this allowance was extended to all citizens alike. For the purpose of encouraging volunteer enlistments, Government bounties to volunteers were also largely increased—$302 to those going into service for the first time, and $402 to veterans re-enlisting, while local bounties of liberal amount were offered in most of the counties.

On the 17th of October, the President of the United States issued a proclamation calling upon "the Governors of the different States to raise and have enlisted into the United States service for the various companies and regiments in the field from their respective States, their quotas of 300,000 men." It was further proclaimed that the large bounties previously ordered should be continued to volunteers, and that if any State or district should fail to fill its quota, a draft would be made on the 5th of January ensuing, for the deficiency. The quotas of the several Congressional districts of the State were assigned by the Provost Marshal-General as follows: first district, 2,137; second district, 2,074; third district, 1,861; fourth district, 1,545; fifth district, 1,768; sixth district, 1,913—total for the State, 11,298.

The Governor, ever ready for action when the necessities of the Government required it, desirous of securing a prompt and effective response to the call of the President, issued a stirring proclamation, of which follows an extract, invoking immediate and energetic action by the people to meet the demand without a draft:

"This call is for *soldiers* to fill the ranks of the regiments in the field—those regiments which by long and gallant service have wasted their numbers in the same proportion that they have made a distinguished name, both for themselves and the State. The people of Michigan will recognize this as a duty already too long delayed. Our young men, I trust, will hasten to stand beside the heroes of Antietam, Gettysburg, Vicksburg, Stone river, and Chicamauga.

"The hopes of the rebellion are steadily perishing. The armies of the Republic are in the midst of their country, and they have not the power to expel them.

"Fill up the ranks once more, and the next blast of the bugle for an advance will sound the knell of revolution and herald in the return of peace.

"Fellow-citizens, let us do it *willingly, gallantly, joyously*. The people of Michigan have heretofore earned the gratitude of the country by their promptness and energy in the support of the Government."

This appeal was received by the people of the State with the same cordial response that had characterized their action on all previous demands of the Government, and they went to work with their usual alacrity and success.

The returns and muster-rolls on file show that from December 23, 1862, down to December 31, 1863, there had been mustered thirteen thousand five hundred and sixty-seven, (13,567,) and an aggregate of fifty-three thousand seven hundred and forty-nine (53,749) since the beginning of the war, leaving out of the account all troops disbanded, estimated, and those paying commutation, and confining the statement to the men actually put in service.

Having in our narrative reached the close of 1863, we include the closing notice of Michigan troops in the field from the report of the Adjutant-General of the State for that year, assigning it to its proper place at this time:

"The war against the rebellion has consumed another year. Loyal States have furnished quota after quota of men to support it. Michigan has speedily and cheerfully responded to every call, and fully complied with every requirement of the Government. Michigan will continue to do so until every rebel in arms against the Republic shall be defeated and sue for peace. Michigan is in earnest in this cause, and seeks no other course but to fight on until a peace is successfully conquered, and until every rebel State is brought into submission to the power of the National Government and is made to acknowledge their allegiance to the Constitution and the laws of the land. Michigan, as evinced by the patriotism of her citizens at home and the bravery of her soldiers in the field, is truly loyal, and nobly gives her influence, her means, and the best blood of her people to put down forever this unjust, unreasonable, and selfish rebellion.

"During the present rebellion there have been many encouraging and promising features developed in the prosecution of the war against it that have indicated its successful and satisfactory termination, but none more forcible, or that will fill a brighter page in its history, or denote more strongly the determination of the people of the Union to bring this rebellion to a desirable and permanent issue and to sustain and perpetuate the national existence, or that exhibits more love for the Republic and free institutions than the patriotic and glorious tribute voluntarily made to their country by the re-enlisted veterans who are now swelling the ranks of the grand armies. They are returning in masses to their native States, receiving the well-deserved blessings and thanks of their country, their families and friends, scattering an influence and a power in behalf of their States and their nation that makes every lover of his native land and his race rejoice in great hopefulness in the future. None can doubt their patriotism. None can question their honesty of purpose. They are a hope and encouragement to the loyal and true, and a blight on those who would wilfully suffer a national disgrace. Michigan, in common with her sister States, is proud of her veteran troops returning to her, as they do, from the hard-fought battles of many fields, scarred, wounded, and weather-beaten—glorious evidences of faithful service, true bravery, and gallant deeds—marks that endear them to their State and entitle them to a page in the history of her heroes. Having again pledged themselves to defend their Government against all its enemies, they are returning to the field, carrying with them the blessings of their friends and the gratitude of their State, again, it may be, to face the leaden storm from rebel ranks, and to add new laurels to those already gathered by them on the sanguinary fields of the South; and while the people praise and bless the living heroes who return to them who have participated in those scenes of national strife, and will cause their names to be handed down to future generations as defenders of the freedom of their nation and their race, they will also have a warm place in their memories for those who return not, but who have passed away amidst those scenes of conflict and bravely given up their lives in the same glorious cause, and long remember them with gratitude and reverence for their devotion and sacrifice, and cause the page of history to record them as amongst the greatest patriots of their day and as martyrs to the freedom of all mankind.

"The troops from Michigan have, in common with those from other States, shared in the hardships and dangers of the campaigns of the past year. They have also shared with them in the glory of their victories, and with them nobly and courageously sustained the prowess of the Union arms in every engagement. Michigan rejoices at the laurels gathered by the troops from other States, in common with her own, while gloriously and bravely battling with hers, as companions in arms on the same fields, and laments them as companions in death, falling side by side in the cause of their common country; and while she cheerfully extends to the Union troops in general her mete of praise and gratitude for their bravery in battle, and their devotion to the cause of freedom and free institutions, it belongs to her in duty to her own troops, to award to them her especial, grateful acknowledgement of her indebtedness to them for the eminent and honorable position which she has acquired among her sister States in the prosecution of this war, in vindication of national freedom; and while she would not, by detraction from the meritorious and gallant services of other troops, exalt her own, still she is proud to say that no regiment of her gallant sons has, in a single instance, disgraced either itself or tarnished her honorable and bright escutcheon; but they have been found manfully fighting in the front rank on every field, and have been trusted and relied upon for efficiency in cases of emergency and great danger, and have been specially distinguished as possessing, in the highest degree, that characteristic so essential to success in war—true courage."

The prominent feature in the war operations of 1863 was the important battle of Gettysburg. That battle, which in effect proclaimed with most terrible force to the monster rebellion: "Thus far hast thou dared to come, but must advance no farther at thy peril; back to thy rebel den; henceforth you can only fight on the defensive, for thy aggressive power is broken, and you must crumble to pieces until thou art dead—thy rebel spirit crushed to atoms, never to rise again."

In the beautiful cemetery, where now quietly rest the dead heroes of that terrible strife, lie the bodies of two hundred and twelve (212) brave Michigan men, being the third largest in numbers from any State. Michigan, therefore, in common with her sister States, claims a general credit for her troops on that occasion, but nothing more; the honor is national, not State.

The operations in the field in Virginia during the year closed with the movement made across the Rapidan by the Army of the Potomac and the assault on the enemy's position at Mine Run, which, after a feeble effort on the part of the Union forces, resulted in failure, and the recrossing of the army to its former position. This, of course, neither strengthened the army nor encouraged the hearts of the Northern people; neither were the former disposed to quail under defeat, nor the latter to despair at disappointment. In the West they ended with the splendid Union victory at Mission Ridge, which so closely followed the terrible assault at Chicamauga, and, in a measure, counteracted the effect of that memorable disaster.

The important event occurring with the commencement of 1864 was the return of the "veterans" previously mentioned, who had re-enlisted for another term of service, and were in turn on furlough and reorganizing within the State.

The men of Michigan entitled to re-enlist had availed themselves of the opportunity with great alacrity, and to an extent, in view of the hardships they had already encountered, that was almost surprising.

Five thousand five hundred and forty-five of them accepted the proposition of the Government, entitling the following organizations to which they belonged to the designation of "veteran:" 1st, 2d, and 3d cavalry; 2d, 3d, 4th, 5th, 7th, 8th, 9th, 10th, 12th, 13th, 14th, 15th, and 16th regiments of infantry; the 6th heavy artillery, formerly 6th infantry, and batteries "B," "C," and "E," 1st light artillery, together with 148 of the engineers and mechanics. There were also many others in regiments of other States, for which credits were given to Michigan, although not all made available, either to the State or the soldiers themselves.

The Legislature, on February 5, 1864, authorized the payment of $50 State bounty, from November 11, 1863, to February 4, 1864, to the re-enlisted veterans, and directed the payment of $100 to all soldiers enlisting or re-enlisting after that date, which was continued until May 14th following. Townships, wards, and cities were at this time also empowered by the Legislature to raise money by tax for the purpose of paying bounties to volunteers, not exceeding two hundred dollars to each soldier.

At the commencement of this year there was pending the call of the President, of October 17th, for Michigan's quota of 300,000 men, assigned at 11,298.

On the 1st of February the following order was issued from Washington:

EXECUTIVE MANSION, February 1, 1864.

Ordered: That a draft for five hundred thousand men, to serve for three years or during the war, be made on the tenth day of March next, for the military service of the United States, crediting or deducting therefrom so many as may have been enlisted or drafted into the service prior to the first day of March, and not heretofore credited.

ABRAHAM LINCOLN.

The practical interpretation of this order by the Provost Marshal-General made this merely an extension of the call of October 17, to the amount of 200,000 men, or, in other words, a new call of that number.

On the 14th of March ensuing, the President made an additional order for two hundred thousand men, designating the 15th day of April as the time up to which the quotas could be raised by voluntary enlistments, and as soon after that date as practicable a draft should be made for the deficit on both calls.

An act, approved July 4th, of this year, authorized the President to accept volunteers for one, two, or three years, at the option of the recruit, and limited the term of men drafted to fill deficiencies under the President's calls, to one year. The commutation system was also abolished, as had previously been the distinction of classes as regards age, which had been made in the first enrollment act.

On the 18th of July the President, under authority of this act, issued a proclamation calling for 500,000 men, and directing that credits be allowed to States in the reduction of their quotas for all the men furnished for the military service in excess of all previous calls, and that volunteers be accepted for one, two, or three years, as they might elect; and further, that immediately after the 5th day of September a draft for troops to serve for one year should be made for deficiencies existing at that date.

The appearance of this call received a prompt response on the part of the Governor, who immediately issued his proclamation calling for early and earnest efforts to meet the Presidential requisition upon the people of this State, and pointing out in explicit terms the readiest and most feasible plans of doing so. The proclamation, which belongs to the history of Michigan, finds a proper place here:

"The President of the United States, in pursuance of a law of Congress, has issued his call for five hundred thousand (500,000) volunteers for the military service, and has directed that immediately after the 5th day of September, 1864, a draft of troops, to serve for one year, shall be held in every town or sub-district, to fill the quota which shall be assigned to it, which shall remain unfilled on the said 5th day of September, 1864.

"I believe this call to have been eminently proper and necessary for the public service, and being such, to demand the patriotic, earnest, and hearty response of the people. That it will be met in the same spirit that has put Michigan thus far largely in excess of all previous calls, there can be no doubt. The rebellion, as it approaches its final overthrow, grows steadily more desperate, wicked, and hateful. Covered with the blood of patriots, cursed with the dying breath of starved prisoners, and abhorred by all good men for its barbarous butcheries of the unarmed who have ceased to fight, it must perish utterly. The people of this State, remembering their past sacrifices only as an additional motive to greater exertions in the future, will, I know, enter upon this present duty with the activity and energy which does not admit of failure.

"The quota assigned to the State is eighteen thousand two hundred and eighty-two, (18,282,) of which only a little over twelve thousand (12,000) remain to be recruited, or drafted if the recruiting fails. For the purpose of filling the quota, only two resources are available, viz: 1st. Recruiting in the States declared to be in rebellion, under the act of July 4th, except the States of Arkansas, Tennessee, and Louisiana; and 2d. Recruiting among our own people. The first of these, I believe, will be found of no substantial value to us at present, for obvious reasons. The points at which this recruiting is to be carried on are so remote that the period of fifty days will not be sufficient to enable agents to accomplish very much during that time, and they would meet the active competition of the older States, paying much larger bounties than our laws enable us to do. I shall not, therefore, appoint any such agents to be paid by the State, but will, under proper regulations, appoint such agents for the benefit of any counties, towns, or sub-districts which may request it, paying the expenses of the agencies for themselves. They will, of course, also be entitled to the credits. This course is also justified by the fact that the State has no funds appropriated by law for this purpose.

"Substantially, then, our only resource will be that which has always heretofore been found sufficient, the patriotism of our own people.

"Recruits will be allowed to enlist for one, two, or three years, as they may prefer, and as far as practicable each recruit may select the regiment in which he will enlist. This will always be allowed in the regiments in the field, so long as such regiments are below the maximum number. As an inducement to enlist, the Government of the United States will pay a bounty of one hundred dollars to recruits enlisting for one year, two hundred dollars for those enlisting for two years, and three hundred for those enlisting for three years. Such local bounties will be paid as the people of the several towns, wards, and sub-districts may authorize in pursuance of law. No State bounty can be paid, for the reason that the appropriation made for that purpose is exhausted. For the purpose of aiding the recruiting service and giving direction to the public efforts, six new regiments will be authorized, one of them being located in each Congressional district, and I will receive all the new companies that may be offered during the fifty days of recruiting. All the recruits offered for the new regiments and companies, however, must be enlisted for three years or during the war. Those who enlist for a shorter term than three years will go into the regiments now in the field.

"I earnestly recommend to all those who enlist under this call, whether in the new organizations or the old ones, to do so for the war. This State has thus far raised no troops for a less term than three years. Both for the Government and the soldier the longest term is the best. Let us continue to adhere to this policy, which has given us a most honorable position in the service, and the reputation of the Michigan soldiery, which is now unsurpassed, will continue to grow.

"The work of filling up the quota of the State is for the people. The close of the war visibly approaches, and the sure triumph of the Union cause grows manifest.

"Our troops are now led by tried and victorious generals, leaving nothing to be desired in that direction. Conquering Union armies are in the very midst of the Confederacy, progressing steadily towards the final victory. Let the people of the country stand firmly by the lawful Government, and they can safely meet what is to come."

Immediately following this proclamation orders were promulgated from the Adjutant-General's office authorizing the recruitment of six regiments, one in each Congressional district, permission therefor having been received from the War Department.

On the 26th of July, Col. J. W. Hall was authorized to reorganize the 4th infantry, the term of service of which had expired and the regiment mustered out of service. The rendezvous of the regiment was located at Adrian, where the old 4th was organized, and Col. Hall was made commandant of the camp, with the first district for his operations.

On the 29th of the same month, orders were issued to reorganize the 3d infantry, whose term had also expired. Col. M. B. Houghton, who was connected with the old organization, was entrusted with the charge of raising the new regiment, and its camp was placed at Grand Rapids, with the fourth district for the field of its recruiting.

On the same day the sixth district was provided for by the appointment of Hon. John F. Driggs to take charge of the organization of a new regiment therein, to be called the 31st infantry, with its headquarters at Saginaw.

A regiment for the third district, to be called the 29th infantry, was, on the 9th of August, authorized to be raised at Marshall, with Hon. S. S. Lacey for commandant of camp.

In the second district, Hon. W. B. Williams, of Allegan, was, on the 15th of August, entrusted with the organization of the 28th infantry, with the camp at Kalamazoo.

On the 24th of August, Major John Atkenson, of the 22d infantry, was authorized to raise and organize the 30th infantry, its rendezvous to be at Pontiac.

The exigencies of the services did not permit the complete organization of these regiments before the enforcement of the impending draft.

Seven companies, which had been raised for the 30th at Pontiac, were distributed between the 3d and 4th, four companies going to the former and three to the latter, and the organization of the 30th was abandoned.

The 3d, thus reinforced, completed its organization at once, and being mustered in with 879 officers and men, left camp for Nashville, October 20.

The 4th also was, by the same means, enabled to take the field, (where a number of men belonging to the old organization, whose terms were unexpired, yet remained,) and left the State with 726 officers and men on the 22d of the same month, also for Nashville.

The 28th and 29th were consolidated into one regiment, designated as the 28th, which, after completing its organization at Kalamazoo, took its route thence for Nashville, October 26, with 886 officers and men.

The Sixth District regiment completed its organization from its own territory, and was the first of the new regiments to leave the State, having broken camp at Saginaw and taken its departure for Nashville on the 6th of October, with 854 officers and men. The regiments originally known as the 30th and 29th, having been consolidated with others, as mentioned above, this regiment was numbered the 29th.

Recruiting having been prosecuted with more or less vigor throughout the State, a draft took place on the 10th of June to fill deficiencies under all former calls, including that of October 17, 1863, and those of February 1 and March 14, 1864, which was followed by supplementary drafts in sub-districts which the principal draft failed to fill. And again, on the 20th of September, there was another draft to supply deficiencies under the call of July 18 and those which remained under the calls preceding it.

The results of the efforts made during the first ten months of the year in the several counties of this State to fill the armies of the United States, both by enlistment and by draft, are as follows: The number of volunteers enlisted in the army, 20,041; the number of men drafted, 1,956; the number of veterans re-enlisted, 5,445; the number of men enlisted in the navy, 430; the total credits in numbers, 27,972; the numbers credited on each term of service from the 1st of January to the 31st of October, 1864—one year, 5,002; two years, 39; three years, 22,931.

The men who paid commutation, as provided by laws in force previous to July 4th, are included among the drafted men to the number of 356.

It is shown in this exhibit that the total number of men raised in the State between the 1st of January and 31st of October, 1864, including drafted men commuting, was 27,972; deduct men commuting, 356; total number of men actually raised during the ten months mentioned, 27,616.

The report of the Adjutant-General's department for 1863 showed that the actual number of men furnished by the State from the beginning of the war to December 31, 1863, was 53,749; the number furnished during the first ten months of 1864, as shown above, is 27,616; making a total to November 1, 1864, of 81,365. The true credit of the State, as represented at the War Department, up to the last date mentioned, is obtained by adding the number of men commuting, viz: 1,982; showing the total credit of the State to be, 83,347.

The striking fact is exhibited by these figures that during ten months only of 1864 the State of Michigan had furnished more than half as many men for the service as were sent from the State during the whole of the first three years of the war, and of this large number of men actually furnished only 1,600 were drafted.

The system of preserving records of credits by sub-districts, required by the laws for enrolling and calling out the national forces, did not become practically operative until the 19th of September, 1863. In the books of the War Department enlistments made previous to that date were entered to the credit of the State at large. All that had been made after that were placed directly to the credit of the sub-district furnishing them.

Approximate number of troops furnished by the State prior to November 1st, 1864: Credits from January 1st to October 31st, 1864, 27,972; enlistments prior to January 1, 1864, 49,793; additional enlistments not included in above from January 1, 1864, 2,026; aggregate October 31, 1864, 79,791. This statement does not include the three month's infantry, Michigan companies in regiments of other States, and some 2,000 additional soldiers whose residence could not be ascertained.

The above aggregate is somewhat smaller than the aggregate shown in previous statements to have been furnished, and the difference is caused by the number enlisting in the earlier stages of the war whose residence was not reported or could not be obtained. The entire three months' regiment enlisting in 1861 is for this cause omitted from the figures of the statement.

The term of service of the 11th infantry having expired during the month of September, 1864, a desire was manifested by some of the officers of that regiment to renew its organization. Orders were issued accordingly, on the 3d of that month, and authority given to Col. Wm. L. Stoughton to command the camp of rendezvous at Sturgis.

On the 3d of November, Major-General Hooker, commanding the Department, being here on a personal inspection, recommended to the Secretary of War, that in view of the exposed condition of the frontier, then threatened by outlaws and their sympathizers in Canada, and the limited number of troops posted for its defence, a regiment of volunteers for twelve months be raised in the State for duty along the Detroit and St. Clair rivers. Despatches investing the Governor with authority for this purpose were the next day received from Washington, and on the 7th orders were issued to organize the 30th Infantry, with its rendezvous at Jackson. In acting upon applications for authority to raise companies and parts of companies for this regiment, preference was given to those who had seen service. On the 22d, Lieut. Col. G. S. Wormer, of the 8th cavalry, was appointed colonel of the 30th, and commandant of camp. Its rendezvous and headquarters were, on the 10th December, removed to Detroit.

The approach of the winter caused no abatement of the activity of the Union armies nor checked the increasing magnitude of their operations. To meet the necessities of the gigantic campaigns then going forward under the direction of the Lieutenant-General, the President on the 19th of December issued a call for 300,000 men to supply a deficiency on the call of the 18th of July, and directing that should the quotas assigned not be filled before the fifteenth day of February following, a draft should be made for the deficiency then existing.

The enrollment of the State was carefully corrected and adjusted by the Boards in the several sub-districts, and the quotas assigned to each.

The enrollment of the counties, with their respective quotas under the call, are exhibited in the following table:

Counties.	Enrollment, Dec. 31, '64.	Quota, call of Dec 19, '64.	Counties.	Enrollment, Dec 31, '64.	Quota, call of Dec 19, '64.
Allegan	1,472	206	Gr. Traverse	181	38
Alpena	89	5	Genesee	1,954	86
Antrim	49	10	Gratiot	375	60
Branch	2,220	250	Hillsdale	2,728	218
Berrien	2,439	317	Houghton	780	271
Barry	1,146	165	Huron	213	61
Bay	528	25	Ingham	1,708	279
Benzie	120	26	Ionia	1,813	218
Chippewa	59	66	Isabella	123	15
Cass	1,467	174	Iosco	30	7
Calhoun	3,174	472	Jackson	3,135	420
Clinton	1,347	57	Kalamazoo	2,905	327
Delta	35	....	Keweenaw	1,158	589
Eaton	1,527	234	Kent	2,661	295
Emmet	21	2	Leelanaw	87	18
			Carried forw'd	35,444	4,911

Counties.	Enrollment, Dec 31, '64.	Quota, call of Dec 19, '64.	Counties.	Enrollment Dec 31, '64.	Quota, call of Dec 19, '64.
Br't forw'd..	35,444	4,911	Macomb	2,018	225
Lenawee	4,787	439	Newago	299	57
Livingston	1,619	206	Ottawa	1,436	189
Lapeer	1,300	134	Oceana	212	31
Monroe	1,613	198	Ontonagon	476	316
Montcalm	527	80	Oakland	3,644	471
Muskegon......	407	63	St. Clair	1,895	222
Mecosta	102	15	Sheboygan	35	4
Mason	49	13	St. Joseph	2,209	323
Manitou	28	7	Saginaw........	2,160	130
Manistee........	122	5	Sanilac	573	71
Mackinaw	87	19	Shiawassee ...	1,161	63
Midland	149	5	Tuscola	552	20
Menominee	69	32	Van Buren. ...	1,540	205
Marquette and			Washtenaw ...	3,687	503
Sch'lcraft ...	225	182	Wayne	9,574	871
			Total	77,999	10,010

The end of operations in 1864 found the army of the Potomac in the trenches before Petersburg holding Lee as in a trap, Sherman's army in possession of Savannah, and Thomas successful in Tennessee.

This memorable year was fraught with great results to the nation, effected by the unparalleled fighting of hosts of men, wading deep in human blood through carnage dense.

The day and night advances of Grant's army on Richmond were to the Northern people movements producing intense anxiety, strong hope, fervent prayers for success, and sorrow and sadness for the patriots passing away.

The desperate advance of Hood on Nashville had been most successfully met by General Thomas, his army completely defeated, routed, and driven in hot haste southward in a most demoralized condition.

General Sherman had gallantly driven the enemy from beyond Chattanooga and onwards, had battered down his strong works at Atlanta, then bidding farewell to his friends, and placing both flanks of his noble army in air, swung off for the sea, leaving the nation in great ignorance and intense uneasiness as to his movements and safety, and is first heard from in the dispatch of General Howard, of his army, saying: "We have had perfect success, and the army in fine spirits;" and then by General Sherman himself, sending to Abraham Lincoln a telegram covering the capture of Savannah as a Christmas present.

The State of Michigan commenced 1865 with that determination to crush out the rebellion which had characterized her soldiers and people so far during the war, as expressed through the Legislature in the following resolution, included among the joint resolutions on the state of the Union, approved March 21, 1865:

Resolved by the Senate and House of Representatives of the State of Michigan, That in the name, and in behalf of the people of the State of Michigan, we hereby re-affirm the devotion of this Commonwealth to the Constitution and Government of the United States, and the earnest determination of its people to do everything in their power to support and sustain the National Administration, in all measures for the vigorous prosecution of the existing war, the utter overthrow of armed rebellion, and the punishment of traitors, until a permanent peace shall be secured, based upon the submission of the rebels, the supremacy of the Government, and the establishment of the Federal Union in all its integrity, one and inseparable, throughout the entire land.

The troops from Michigan, while absent from their homes, honoring their State in the field in these important campaigns, were never forgotten by the Executive, nor by the people. Governor Blair, in his message delivered to the Legislature, January 4, 1865, greets them most affectionately from the Capitol of the State, on vacating the chair which he had so well filled, and highly honored with distinguished ability and efficiency during the years of the war that had passed. Who, in the administration of his executive duties, had been so devoted to the best interests of his State, and so true and loyal to his country, so fair and clear in all his public acts, so untiring in the discharge of his arduous and perplexing duties, so eminently pure in his private life, and so thoughtful at all times of the soldier in the field, that his official career had been deservedly marked with great popularity among the troops, as well as with the entire people. The Governor alluded to them in the following beautiful and kindly language:

"GENTLEMEN: Again and for the last time, I commend the Michigan troops to your continued care and support. They have never failed in their duty to the country or to the State. Upon every great battle-field of the war their shouts have been heard and their sturdy blows have been delivered for the Union and victory. Their hard-earned fame is the treasure of every household in the State, and the red blood of their veins has been poured out in large measure to redeem the rebellious South from its great sin and curse. At this hour they stand under the flag of their country, far away from home, in every quarter where the enemy is to be met—along the banks of the father of waters, in the great city at its mouths, on the Arkansas, in the captured forts of the Gulf, by the waters of the Cumberland, the Tennessee, and of the Savannah, in the chief city of the Empire State of the South, among the conquering columns in the Valley of the Shenandoah, and in the trenches under the eye of the Lieutenant-General in the great leaguer of Petersburg and Richmond. Alas, that they are also perishing of cold and hunger, and disease, in the filthy rebel prisons and pestilential camps of the South. In every situation their bravery has won the approval of their commanders, and their heroic endurance of hardships has added lustre to their name. It is my sole regret at quitting office that I part with them. My earnest efforts for their good shall follow them while I live, and now from this place I bid them hail, and farewell!"

During that session of the Legislature the following concurrent resolutions were passed:

Whereas the Hon. Austin Blair, whose valedictory message was delivered to this Legislature on the fifth of January, eighteen hundred and sixty-five, has retired to private life;

And whereas the four years of his administration have been the most laborious, as well as the most perilous in the history both of the State and of the nation, with eleven of the most Southern States banded together in the most unjustifiable rebellion that the world has ever known;

And whereas Governor Blair's administration has been marked by eminent ability, rare integrity, and unsurpassed success, as shown by the enlistments and organization into companies, regiments, and batteries, in the most perfect military order, of over eighty thousand men, as brave, true, and patriotic as ever bared their breasts to any foe; therefore

Resolved, (the Senate concurring,) That the thanks of the people of

Michigan, through this Legislature, are hereby cordially tendered to ex-Governor Blair, for the able and satisfactory manner in which he has, during his administration of the last four years, been able to conduct the affairs of the government of the State.

Following Governor Blair, Henry H. Crapo took the executive chair, bringing to the service of the State and the nation strong and inherent patriotism, great ability, scrupulous honesty of purpose, and a most remarkable and pre-eminent degree of physical and mental energy, with almost continuous application, giving his administration great efficiency and much popularity. The Governor, in his inaugural message delivered to the Legislature, referring to the Michigan troops in the field, for whom he always entertained the most profound respect and the highest appreciation of their valuable services, says, with much eloquence and feeling, while alluding to the great loss of life among them and of the cause in which they were then still engaged:

"This is indeed a fearful sacrifice to be made even in the cause of liberty, justice, and humanity, and fearful is the penalty and terrible is the suffering which the authors and leaders of treason and rebellion deserve and must endure as a just consequence of this enormous crime. These brave men—the Michigan troops—are worthy of all praise. I commend them to your warmest sympathies, to your highest regards, to your active support. They have done heroic deeds on every battle-field; they have won a name for undaunted courage in every conflict with a deadly and persistent foe; they have endured hardships and privations without a murmur, and their loyalty and patriotism have never yet been tarnished. Those who have fallen upon the battle-field or on the march, or have died in hospitals—who now sleep in death, martyrs to the cause of human freedom—our gratitude, our sympathies can never reach. But of those who suffer through loss of them, and of those brave veterans who yet survive, we should ever be mindful. A nation's gratitude should ever be theirs; and justice, at least, should be their reward. * * * *

"Although the rebellion, involving a civil war of unparalleled magnitude, which was inaugurated at the close of the administration of James Buchanan by conspirators and traitors for the overthrow of our Government, still aims its blows at the dismemberment of the Union, causing the devastation of portions of our fair land, depleting the National Treasury, and destroying many of our best, most loyal, and patriotic men, the efforts for its suppression continue to be prosecuted with undiminished vigor and with unfaltering purpose; and the events of the past year have served but to increase our confidence in the permanency and power of our republican institutions. The nation, it is true, has been sorely tried, yet it has exhibited strength and resources far beyond the most sanguine hopes of its friends; while its enemies, both at home and abroad, have been compelled to confess their disappointment." * * * *

Nor were they forgotten by the Legislature of the State; for on the 22d of February, 1865, that body passed the following concurrent resolution:

Resolved by the House of Representatives, (the Senate concurring,) That on this anniversary of the birthday of the Father of his Country the thanks of this Legislature, and through us of the people of the State, are hereby tendered to the soldiers of Michigan who promptly responded to the call of their country in its time of peril; and who by their fortitude and soldierly bearing under the privations and hardships of a soldier's life, "in camp and field, through march and siege," and by their indomitable bravery and heroism on scores of battle-fields, have won exalted honor to themselves and crowned with unfading glory the name and fame of Michigan.

With the great increase of Government, State, and local bounties in 1864 commenced the decrease of patriotism among the masses outside of the armies in the field, and which continued to lessen and lessen, and at the commencement of 1865 was not held out as any part of the inducements to enter the service, enlistments had become a matter of bargain and sale, dollars and cents entirely ruling the action.

On January 1st, 1865, the 11th regiment of infantry was in process of recruitment, and the organization of the 30th, designed for duty on the Michigan frontier, was completed on the 9th and mustered into service with the maximum number, and at once assigned to duty along the Detroit and St. Clair rivers, with headquarters at Detroit. Little progress, however, had been made in filling up the 11th until February, when vigorous measures toward that end were adopted, and on the 4th of March four companies left camp at Jackson for Nashville, Tennessee. On the 18th of the same month the remaining six companies had completed their organization, and on that day also took the route to Nashville, in command of Col. P. H. Keegan, the muster-in rolls of the regiment showing a strength of 898 officers and men.

On February 4th, 1865, the Legislature authorized the payment of $150 State bounty, which continued to be paid until the 14th of May following. Townships were empowered at the same time to pay a bounty of $100, which was paid until recruiting ceased in the State.

The successful operations of the United States armies having brought the war to a close by the utter overthrow of the rebel forces early in the spring of 1865, orders were at once issued to abandon all pending measures for the re-enforcement of the national arms, and recruiting, as well as operations under the draft, ceased on the 14th of April. Previous to that date and subsequent to the 1st of November, 1864, there had been raised in this State 9,382 recruits, of whom 7,547 voluntarily enlisted in the army and 53 in the navy, and 1,782 were drafted, as will appear in the records:

The following is a general summary of results, showing aggregate numbers of the credits allowed to each county in the State from the beginning to the close of the war, 1865: Allegan, 2,175; Antrim, 28; Alpena, 58; Barry, 1,625; Benzie, 70; Bay, 511; Branch, 2,776; Berrien, 3,179; Cass, 1,832; Calhoun 3,878; Clinton, 1,606; Chippewa, 21; Delta, 24; Emmet, 39; Eaton, 1,741; Genesee, 2,518; Gratiot, 646; Grand Traverse, 171; Hillsdale, 2,928; Houghton, 460; Huron, 342; Ingham, 2,097; Ionia, 2,464; Isabella, 137; Iosco, 27; Jackson, 3,232; Keweenaw, 119; Kent, 4,214; Kalamazoo, 3,221; Livingston, 1,887; Lenawee, 4,437; Leelanaw, 98; Lapeer, 1,776; Monroe, 2,270; Montcalm, 640; Macomb, 2,360; Menominee, 19; Marquette and Schoolcraft, 265; Muskegon, 736; Mecosta, 159; Mason 59; Manitou, 10; Manistee, 88; Mackinac, 47; Midland, 129; Newaygo, 412; Ontonagon, 254; Oakland, 3,718; Oceana, 223; Ottawa, 1,547; Shiawassee, 1,753; Cheboygan, 31; St. Joseph, 2,836; Sanilac, 781; St. Clair, 2,581; Saginaw, 2,039; Tuscola, 664; Van Buren, 1,884; Washtenaw, 4,084; Wayne, 9,213; total, 89,173.

The sum paid into the Treasury Department of the United States by drafted citizens of Michigan as commutation money was $594,600.00.

The product of soldiers and credits yielded by the several counties is in its aggregate, as previously intimated, below the total number known to have been furnished by the State, and the difference is caused by the number enlisting in the earlier regiments whose residence could not be ascertained.

The reports of the Adjutant-General's Department at the close of 1864 showed that the actual number of men furnished by Michigan from the beginning of the war to November 1, 1864, was.......................... 81,365
Add the number of men commuting.. 1,982

And the total credits to that time were................. 83,347
The number of men credited by enlistment and draft from November 1, 1864, to the close of the war was................. 9,382

Making the total *credits* of the State, from April, 1861, to April, 1865, the entire period of the war, as shown by the records of this office 92,729
Deducting from this aggregate the number of men commuting...... 1,982

There is left a total of numbers actually furnished in men of........ 90,747

These figures do not include men enlisted in regiments of other States, and are believed to be substantially correct. There is a discrepancy, however, between them and the tables of the War Department, as will be seen by the subjoined letter from the Provost Marshal-General:

WAR DEPARTMENT,
PROVOST MARSHAL-GENERAL'S OFFICE,
WASHINGTON, D. C., Sept. 2, 1865.

His Excellency H. H. Crapo, Governor of Michigan, Lansing:

SIR: I have the honor to inform you that the number of men furnished by the State of Michigan, from April 17, 1861, to April 30, 1865, is ninety thousand and forty-eight, (90,048,) without reference to periods of service, which varied from three months to three years.

I have the honor to be, sir,
Very respectfully,
Your obedient servant,
JAMES B. FRY,
Provost Marshal-General.

The most popular and effective mode of raising men for the national armies throughout the war proved in Michigan to be the system of recruiting volunteers. This system gave to the Union armies their main support. Drafting or conscripting in Michigan did not produce satisfactory results in any respect, while volunteering was popular and successful.

The drafted man, without reason, looks at his position as stripping him of individuality and patriotism, and as making him a mere machine in the hands of the law. This is wrong and unreasonable in him. The nation recognizes no difference between the faithful services rendered the country by the drafted from that of the volunteer soldier, and there should be none; neither should there be any difference in his condition or standing in the army, and there really is none, except that created in the mind of the conscript himself. The faithful services rendered in defence of his country by the drafted man are equally acceptable and profitable to the nation and as creditable and praiseworthy to himself as those rendered by the volunteer. But it seems impossible to divest the mind of the conscript that in allowing himself to be drafted he has not robbed himself of his patriotism, and that he is considered, both at home and in the service, as an unwilling defender of his nation.

Conscripts, as well as the people, should recognize the truth that every nation must possess the power under its laws to compel its citizens to fight in its defence and to protect and secure its national existence against all its enemies either at home or abroad; and this power must be carried into effect, when necessary, by draft or conscription, and if properly and fairly exercised under existing laws, should not be considered by them as an odious or unjust measure, but should be sustained and carried fully into effect when the necessities of the country demand it; but such is not the case.

The conscription, as a general thing, is evaded, when possible, by the loyal as well as by the disloyal to a certain extent, as every man coming within its reach seems to object to it. The rich man puts it at defiance under the law with his money, and the poor man evades it, when he can, with his infirmities. Communities, while truly loyal, will make voluntary subscriptions to raise money to supply commutation to secure their citizens against the operations of the draft, even if the exigencies of the service should be ever so urgent, and almost at the same time, with exemplary loyalty and patriotism, will in like manner make similar contributions to procure volunteers to fill deficiencies caused by this action of theirs. The influence, energy, and means of the people, and the arguments and admonition of the press, have been used to raise men to avoid it as if it were a public calamity to be dreaded and avoided if possible, and hence its unpopularity.

With the surrender of the rebel army, under General Lee, on the 9th of April, 1865, and the subsequent surrender of General Johnston's army, in the same month, the war which had been waged against the Union ended, and soon after the troops belonging to the various States began to leave the field.

The Michigan troops being among the first to receive orders, the 20th regiment arrived in the State June 4, 1865, and others followed in succession, down to June 10, 1866, when the 3d and 4th regiments of infantry reached the State, being the last belonging to the State to leave the field.

On the 14th of June, 1865, Governor Crapo issued the following proclamation of thanks to the returning Michigan troops, which properly belongs to the military history of the State:

"MICHIGAN SOLDIERS—OFFICERS AND MEN: In the hour of national danger and peril, when the safety—when the very existence—of your country was imperilled, you left your firesides, your homes, and your families, to defend the Government and the Union. But the danger is now averted, the struggle is ended, and victory—absolute and complete victory—has perched upon your banners. You have conquered a glorious peace, and are thereby permitted to return to your homes and to the pursuits of tranquil industry, to which I now welcome you! And, not only for myself, but for the people of the State, do I tender you a most cordial greeting.

Citizen soldiers! Recognized by the institutions of the land as freemen—as American citizens, that proudest of all political distinctions—and possessing, in common with every citizen, the elective franchise, which confers the right to an exercise of the sovereign power, you had become so identified and engrossed with the national enterprise and prosperity derived from the untrammeled privileges of republican freedom, that the enemies of those institutions, in their ignorance of the principles upon which they are founded, madly and foolishly believed that you were destitute of manhood. They supposed you had become so debased by continued toil as to be devoid of every noble impulse. They imagined that you were cowards and cravens, and that by the threatenings alone of a despotic and tyrannical oligarchy you could not only be subdued, but robbed of your inheritance of freedom—of your birthright of liberty—those glorious and priceless legacies from your patriotic sires. Through the vilest treachery and the foulest robbery, these wicked and perjured men, whom their country had not only greatly benefitted and favored, but highly honored, believed that by despoiling your country of its reputation, of its treasures, of its means of protection and defence, they had ensured your degradation and defeat.

Fatal mistake! and terrible its consequences to those wicked and forsworn men, as well as to their deluded and blinded votaries!

Soldiers: You have taught a lesson, not only to the enemies of your country, but to the world, which will never be forgotten. With your brave comrades from every loyal State in this great and redeemed Union, you have met these vaunting and perjured traitors and rebels face to face, upon the field of battle, in the front of strongly fortified intrenchments, and before almost impregnable ramparts; and by your skill and valor—your persistent efforts and untiring devotion to the sacred cause of freedom, of civilization, and of mankind—you have proved to those arch criminals and their sympathizers that it is not necessary for men to be serfs and slaves in order to be soldiers, but that in the hands of free and enlightened citizens, enjoying the advantages and blessings conferred by free institutions, the temple of Liberty will ever be safe, and its escutcheon forever unsullied.

Fellow-citizens of Michigan—patriotic citizen soldiers—although you return to us bearing honorable marks of years of toil, of hardship, of privation, and of suffering—many of you with bodies mutilated, maimed, and scarred—mourning the loss of brave comrades ruthlessly slain on the field of battle, tortured to death by inches, or foully murdered in cold blood, not with the weapon of a soldier, but by the lingering pangs of starvation and exposure—yet you will in the future enjoy the proud satisfaction of having aided in achieving for your country her second independence—in vindicating the national honor and dignity—in overthrowing that despotic and unholy power which has dared to raise its hideous head on this continent for the purpose of trampling upon and destroying that inalienable right to life, liberty, and the pursuit of happiness, which is the birthright of all—and finally, in placing the Union, established by the blood of our fathers, upon an imperishable foundation. You will also possess the rich inheritance of meriting the continued plaudits, and of enjoying the constant gratitude of a free people, whose greatness *you* have preserved in its hour of most imminent peril.

In the name of the people of Michigan, I thank you for the honor you have done us by your valor, your soldierly bearing, your invincible courage everywhere displayed, whether upon the field of battle, in the perilous assault, or in the deadly breach; for your patience under the fatigues and privations and sufferings incident to war, and for your discipline and ready obedience to the orders of your superiors. We are proud in believing that when the history of this rebellion shall have been written, where all have done well, none will stand higher on the roll of fame than the officers and soldiers sent to the field from the loyal and patriotic State of Michigan."

Governor Crapo served as Executive of the State until January 1st, 1869, when he was succeeded by Henry P. Baldwin, of Detroit, a gentleman who, although occupying the position of a private citizen throughout the war, rendered valuable service in the cause of the Union, being prominent in the State among its strongest supporters, both in counsel and in pecuniary aid, ready when occasion offered to stand by his country and uphold her glorious flag.

Table showing nativities of Michigan volunteers.

New England States		2,847	
New York, New Jersey, and Pennsylvania		31,137	
Ohio and Indiana		9,506	
Michigan		4,517	
Illinois and Wisconsin		300	
Kentucky and Tennessee		166	
Free States west of Mississippi river		69	
Slave States west of Mississippi river		73	
Southern States not above enumerated		544	
Indiana		145	
Free States, colored		217	
Slave States, colored		956	
Total United States		67,468	
British America, exclusive of Canada	169		
Canada	8,276		
Canada, colored	441		
		8,886	
Total American		....	76,354
England		3,761	
Ireland		3,929	
Scotland		763	
Germany		4,872	
France and French dominions		380	
Spain and Spanish America		22	
Denmark, Sweden, and Norway		381	
Miscellaneous		238	
Miscellaneous, colored		47	
Total foreign		....	14,393
			90,747

Total white	88,941
Total colored	1,661
Total Indians	145
	90,747

We subjoin a list showing the total number of officers and men who served in Michigan regiments and companies, respectively:

1st engineers and mechanics, 3,081; 1st light artillery, 3,333; 13th battery, 255; 14th battery, 222; 1st cavalry, 3,244; 2d cavalry, 2,425; 3d cavalry, 2,560; 4th cavalry, 2,085; 5th cavalry, 1,998—of this number 388 were transferred to 1st cavalry; 6th cavalry, 1,624—of this number 428 were transferred to 1st cavalry; 7th cavalry, 1,779—of this number 312 were transferred to 1st cavalry; 8th cavalry, 3,025; 9th cavalry, 2,057—

of this number 52 were transferred to 11th battery; 10th cavalry, 2,050; 11th cavalry, 1,579—of this number 513 were transferred to 8th cavalry; Merrill Horse, 513; Lancers, 852; Chandler Horse Guards, 204; 1st infantry, (3 months,) 798; 1st infantry, 1,346; 2d infantry, 2,151; 3d infantry, 1,000—of this number 371 were transferred to 5th infantry; 3d infantry, (reorganized,) 1,109; 4th infantry, 1,325—of this number 96 were transferred to 4th infantry; 4th infantry, (reorganized,) 1,300; 5th infantry, 1,950; 6th infantry, 1,957; 7th infantry, 1,393; 8th infantry, 1,792; 9th infantry, 2,272; 10th infantry, 1,788; 11th infantry, 1,329; 11th infantry, (reorganized,) 1,140; 12th infantry, 2,335; 13th infantry, 2,084; 14th infantry, 1,806; 15th infantry, 2,371; 16th infantry, 2,318; 17th infantry, 1,079—of this number 135 were transferred to 2d infantry; 18th infantry, 1,374—of this number 97 were transferred to 9th infantry; 19th infantry, 1,238—of this number 108 were transferred to 10th infantry; 20th infantry, 1,157—of this number 37 were transferred to 2d infantry; 21st infantry, 1,477—of this number 144 were transferred to 14th infantry, 22d infantry, 1,586—of this number 222 were transferred to 29th infantry; 23d infantry, 1,417—of this number 143 were transferred to 28th infantry, and 12 to 29th infantry; 24th infantry, 2,054; 25th infantry, 988—of this number 51 were transferred to 28th infantry; 26th infantry, 1,210; 27th infantry, 2,029; 28th infantry, 1,245; 29th infantry, 1,470; 30th infantry, 975; 1st sharpshooters, 1,364; 1st colored infantry, (102 U. S. C. T,) 1,446; 1st U. S. sharpshooters, 415—of this number 71 were transferred to 5th infantry; 2d U. S. sharpshooters, 163—of this number 48 were transferred to 5th infantry.

The number of men from Michigan who served in organizations of other States and in the regular army, so far as reported, will be found quite inconsiderable, when compared with the aggregate of troops, and is as follows:

Stanton Guard, 103; Provost Guard 130; 23d Illinois, Company A, 281; 33d Illinois, Company B, 2; 37th Illinois, Company D, 63; 42d Illinois, 214; 44th Illinois, 192; 66th Illinois, Co. D, 180; 29th Indiana, 1; 127th Indiana, 1; 20th Indiana battery, 1; 1st Iowa cavalry 1; 7th Iowa infantry 1; 9th Iowa infantry, 1; 9th Kansas cavalry, 1; 1st Missouri engineers, 13; 1st Missouri light artillery, 1; 1st New York cavalry, 98; 70th New York infantry, Co. C, 129; 47th Ohio infantry, 32; 10th Pennsylvania infantry, 1; 11th Pennsylvania cavalry, 1; 4th Tennessee cavalry 2; 12th Tennessee cavalry, 3; 13th Wisconsin infantry, 1; 19th Wisconsin infantry, 1; Mississippi mounted rifles, (colored,) 4; Powell's colored infantry, 4; Mississippi Marine Brigade, 1; band 3d division, 9th army corps, 12; band, 4th division, 13th army corps, 17; band, cavalry corps, 8; veteran volunteer engineers, 10; veteran reserve corps, 389; Hancock's 1st A. C., 153; U. S. Navy, 430; 2d U. S. infantry, 104; 11th U. S. infantry, 242; 12th U. S. infantry, 1; 15th U. S. infantry, 2; 16th U. S. infantry, 20; 19th U. S. infantry, 884; General Service U. S. 186; 5th U. S. colored artillery, 14; 9th U. S. colored artillery, 3; 13th U. S. colored artillery, 21; 3d U. S. colored cavalry, 16; 12th U. S. colored infantry, 1; 31st U. S. colored infantry, 1; 38th U. S. colored infantry. 10; 49th U. S. colored infantry, 1; 53d U. S. colored infantry, 1; 54th U. S. colored infantry, 1; 55th U. S. colored infantry, 1; 61st U. S. colored infantry, 2.

When it is remembered that the population of Michigan in 1864 was 805,379, and that 90,747 able-bodied men took up arms in defence of the Union, the State may well be proud of its record on the score of sincere patriotism.

The following table shows the casualties by wounds and disease in Michigan organizations during the war:

	Enlisted men.		Commiss'ed officers.			Enlisted men.		Commiss'ed officers.	
	Died in action or of wounds.	Died of Disease	Died in action or of wounds.	Died of Disease		Died in action or of wounds.	Died of Disease	Died in action or of wounds.	Died of Disease
Engineers & Mech'cs	8	245	—	—	12th Infantry,	49	372	1	3
1st Light Artillery,	39	313	4	3	13th "	74	266	4	2
13th Battery,	—	4	—	1	14th "	50	173	1	3
14th do.	—	9	—	—	15th "	72	129	3	3
1st Cavalry,	145	195	13	6	16th "	213	135	12	—
2d "	64	270	2	1	17th "	125	146	6	—
3d "	26	314	3	4	18th "	14	295	—	—
4th "	39	296	3	1	19th "	91	135	7	—
5th "	118	172	6	3	20th "	106	165	18	3
6th "	113	228	7	2	21st "	75	271	3	3
7th "	66	265	4	1	22d "	79	282	2	5
8th "	24	287	—	2	23d "	58	218	3	4
9th "	30	134	1	2	24th "	158	114	12	3
10th "	28	224	2	—	25th "	35	123	1	2
11th "	22	105	4	—	26th "	105	145	3	3
Merrill Horse,	10	58	—	—	27th "	211	179	10	4
1st Infantry, 3 mos.	4	4	3	—	28th "	4	118	1	—
1st Infantry,	142	92	15	1	29th "	3	62	1	1
2d "	192	128	11	3	30th "	—	17	—	1
3d "	137	78	4	1	1st Sharpshooters,	114	128	6	—
3d " reorganiz'd	—	113	—	1	1st Mich. (102 U. S)				
4th "	168	105	12	1	Col. Infantry,	9	122	2	—
4th " reorganiz'd	—	190	—	—	1st U. S. Sharpsh'rs	34	28	3	—
5th "	220	151	16	2	2d U. S. "	12	19	1	—
6th "	63	451	2	5	Provost Guard,	—	2	—	—
7th "	170	150	11	4	Co. A 23d Ill. Vol.	3	1	—	—
8th "	191	192	11	4	Co. D 66th Ill. Vol.	13	16	—	—
9th "	17	247	2	4	Co. C 70th N. Y.	17	7	1	—
10th "	80	199	7	3					
11th Infantry,	88	185	5	2					
11th " reorganiz'd	—	89	—	—		3926	9133	249	97

Commissioned officers died in action or of wounds,	249	
" " died of disease,	97	
		346
Enlisted men died in action or of wounds,	3926	
" " died of disease,	9133	
		13059
		13405

It has been found impracticable to obtain a statement of the casualties occurring in all the Michigan companies and among the men serving during the war with troops of other States, hence they are not included in the above table.

Table *giving the dates and places of muster of Michigan Regiments, Batteries, and Companies, the dates at which they left the State, together with the dates and places of muster out, and the dates at which they returned to the State.*

Regiments.	Mustered in.		Left the State.	Mustered out.		Returned to State.	
	Date.	Place.		Date.	Place.	Date.	Place.
1st Eng. & Mech.,	Oct. 29, 1861,	Marshall,	Dec. 17, 1861,	Sept. 22, 1865.	Nashville, Tenn.,	Sept. 26, 1865,	Jackson, Mich.
1st cavalry	Sept. 13, 1861,	Detroit,	Sept. 29, 1861,	March 10, '66,	Salt Lake City, Utah,	Paid & disb'd,	at Salt L. City.
2d "	Oct. 2, 1861,	Grand Rapids,	Nov. 14, '61,	Aug. 17, '65,	Macon, Ga.,	Aug. 26, '65,	Jackson, Mich.
3d "	Nov. 1, 1861,	"	Nov. 28, '61,	Feb. 12, '66,	San Antonio, Texas,	March 10, '66,	" "
4th "	Aug. 29, 1862,	Detroit,	Sept. 26, '62,	July 1, '65,	Nashville, Tenn.,	July 10, '65,	Detroit, "
5th "	Aug. 30, 1862,	"	Dec. 4, '62,	June 22, '65,	Ft. Leavenworth, Ka.,	July 1, '65,	" "
6th "	Oct. 13, 1862,	Grand Rapids,	Dec. 10, '62,	Nov. 24, '65,	" " "	Nov. 30, '65,	Jackson, Mich.
7th "	Jan. 16, 1863,	"	Feb. 20, '63,	Dec. 15, '65,	" " "	Dec. 20, '65,	" "
8th "	May 2, 1863,	Mt. Clemens,	May, '63,	Sept. 22, '65,	Nashville, Tenn.,	Sept. 22, '65,	" "
9th "	May 19, 1863,	Coldwater,	May 20, '63,	July 21, '64,	Lexington, N. C.,	July 30, '65,	Detroit, "
10th "	Nov. 18, 1863,	Grand Rapids,	Dec. 1, '63,	Nov. 11, '65,	Memphis, Tenn.,	Nov. 15, '65,	Jackson, "
11th "	Dec. 10, 1863,	Kalamazoo,	Dec. 17, '63,	June 16, '65,	Knoxville, Tenn.,	Sept. 28, '65,	" "
1st light art'y, A,	May 28, 1861,	Coldwater,	June 1, '61,	July 28, '65,	Jackson, Mich.,	July 12, '65,	" "
" " B,	Nov. 26, 1861,	Grand Rapids,	Dec. 17, '61,	June 14, '65,	Detroit, Mich.,	June 6, '65,	Detroit, "
" " C,	Nov. 28, 1861,	"	Dec. 17, '61,	June 22, '65,	" "	June 13, '65,	" "
" " D,	Sept. 17, 1861,	White Pigeon,	Dec. 9, '61,	Aug. 3, '65,	Jackson, Mich.,	July 22, '65,	Jackson, "
" " E,	Dec. 6, 1861,	Marshall,	Dec. 17, '61,	July 30, '65,	" "	July 16, '65,	" "
" " F,	Jan. 9, 1862,	Coldwater,	March 3, '62,	July 1, '65,	" "	June 24, '65,	" "
" " G,	Jan. 17, 1862,	Kalamazoo,	Feb. 12, '62,	Aug. 6, '65,	" "	Aug. 2, '65.	" "
" " H,	March 6, 1862,	Monroe,	March 13, '62,	July 22, '65,	" "	July 4, '65,	" "
" " I,	Aug. 29, 1862,	Detroit,	Dec. 4, '62,	July 14, '65,	Detroit, "	July 6, '65,	Detroit, "
" " K,	Feb. 20, 1863,	Grand Rapids,	Feb., '63,	July 22, '65,	" "	July 12, '65,	" "
" " L,	April 16, 1863,	Coldwater,	May, '63,	Aug. 22, '65,	Jackson, "	Aug. 19, '65,	Jackson, "
" " M,	June 30, 1863,	Mt. Clemens,	July, '63,	Aug. 1, '65,	" "	July 12, '65,	" "
13th battery,	Jan. 28, 1864,	Grand Rapids,	Feb. 3, '64,	July 1, '65,	" "	June 22, '65,	" "
14th "	Jan. 5, 1864,	Kalamazoo,	Feb. 1, '64,	July 1, '65,	" "	June 21, '65,	" "
Merrill Horse, H,	Sept. 6, 1861,	Fayette, Mo.,	Sept. 3, '61,	Sept. 21, '65,	Nashville, Tenn.,	Paid & disb'd,	at Nashville.
" I,	Sept. 6, 1861,	" "	Sept. 3, '61,	Sept. 21, '65,	" "	" "	"
" L,	Jan. 1, 1863,	———	———	Sept. 21, '65.	" "	" "	"
1st U S S S Co C,	Aug. 26, 1861,	Detroit,	———	———	———	" "	in the field.
" " I,	March 4, 1862,	"	———	———	———	" "	" "
" " K,	March 20, 1862,	"	March 27, 1862,	———	———	" "	" "

M

Regiments.	Mustered in—Date and Place.		Left the State.	Mustered out—Date and Place.		Returned to State—Date & Place	
2d U. S. S. S. co. B,	October 4, 1861,	Detroit,	—	—	—	—	In the field.
1st inf., 3 months,	May 1, 1861,	“	May 13, 1861,	Aug. 7, 1861,	Detroit, Mich.	Aug. 6, 1861,	Detroit, Mich.
“ 3 years,	Sept. 16, 1861,	Ann Arbor,	Sept. 16, 1861,	July 9, 1865,	Jeffersonville, Ind.	July 12, 1865,	Jackson, “
2d infantry,	May 25, 1861,	Detroit,	June 5, 1861,	July 28, 1865,	Delaney House, D. C.	Aug. 1, 1865,	Detroit, “
3d “	June 10, 1861,	Grand Rapids,	June 13, 1861,	June 20, 1864,	Detroit, Mich.	June 20, 1864,	“ “
3d inf., reorganiz'd	Oct. 15, 1864,	“ “	Oct. 20, 1864,	May 25, 1866,	Victoria, Texas,	June 10, 1866,	“ “
4th infantry,	June 10, 1861,	Adrian,	June 25, 1861,	June 28, 1864,	Detroit, Mich.	June 26, 1864,	“ “
4th inf, reorganiz'd	Oct. 14, 1864,	“	Oct. 22, 1864,	May 26, 1866,	Houston, Texas,	June 10, 1866,	“ “
5th infantry,	August 28, 1861,	Detroit,	Sept. 11, 1861,	July 5, 1865,	Jeffersonville, Ind.	July 8, 1865,	“ “
6th H. A.	August 20, 1861,	Kalamazoo,	Aug. 30, 1861,	Aug. 20, 1865,	New Orleans, La.	Aug. 30, 1865,	Jackson, “
7th infantry,	August 22, 1861,	Monroe,	Sept. 5, 1861.	July 5, 1865,	Jeffersonville, Ind.	July 7, 1865,	“ “
8th “	Sept. 23, 1861,	Detroit,	Sept. 27, 1861,	July 30, 1865,	Delaney House, D. C.	Aug. 3, 1865,	Detroit, “
9th “	Oct. 15, 1861,	“	Oct. 25, 1861,	Sept. 15, 1865,	Nashville, Tenn.	Sept. 19, 1865,	Jackson, “
10th “	Feb. 6, 1862,	Flint,	April 22, 1862,	July 19, 1865,	Louisville, Ky.	July 22, 1865,	“ “
11th “	Sept. 24, 1861,	White Pigeon,	Dec. 9, 1861,	Sept. 30, 1864,	Sturgis, Mich.	Sept. 25, 1864,	Sturgis, “
11th inf. reorgan'd	March 16, 1865,	Jackson,	March 18, 1865,	Sept. 16, 1865,	Nashville, Tenn.	Sept. 23, 1865,	Jackson, “
12th infantry,	March 5, 1862,	Niles,	March 18, 1862,	Feb. 15, 1866,	Camden, Ark.	Feb. 27, 1866,	“ “
13th “	January 17, 1862,	Kalamazoo,	Feb. 12, 1862,	July 25, 1865,	Louisville, Ky.	July 27, 1865,	“ “
14th “	Febr'y 13, 1862,	Ypsilanti,	April 17, 1862,	July 18, 1865,	“ “	July 21, 1865,	Detroit, “
15th “	March 20, 1862,	Monroe,	March 27, 1862,	Aug. 13, 1865,	Little Rock, Ark.	Sept. 1, 1865,	“ “
16th “	Sept. 8, 1861,	Detroit,	Sept. 16, 1861,	July 8, 1865,	Jeffersonville, Ind.	July 12, 1865,	“ “
17th “	August 21, 1862,	“	Aug. 27, 1862,	June 3, 1865,	Delaney House, D. C.	June 7, 1865,	“ “
18th “	August 26, 1862,	Hillsdale,	Sept. 4, 1862,	June 26, 1865,	Nashville, Tenn.	July 2, 1865,	Jackson, “
19th “	Sept. 25, 1862,	Dowagiac,	Sept. 14, 1862,	June 10, 1865,	Washington, D. C.	June 13, 1865,	Detroit, “
20th “	August 19, 1862,	Jackson,	Sept. 1, 1862,	May 30, 1865,	Delaney House, D. C.	June 4, 1865,	Jackson, “
21st “	Sept. 4, 1862,	Ionia,	Sept. 12, 1862,	June 8, 1862,	Washington, D. C.	June 13, 1865,	Detroit, “
22d “	August 29, 1862,	Pontiac,	Sept. 4, 1862,	June 26, 1862,	Nashville, Tenn.	June 30, 1865,	“ “
23d “	Sept. 13, 1862,	E. Saginaw,	Sept. 18, 1862,	June 28, 1862	Salisbury, N. C.	July 7, 1865,	“ “
24th “	August 15, 1862,	Detroit,	Aug. 29, 1862,	June 30, 1865,	Detroit, Mich.	June 20, 1865,	“ “
25th “	Sept. 22, 1862,	Kalamazoo,	Sept. 29, 1862,	June 24, 1865,	Salisbury, N. C.	July 2, 1865,	Jackson, “
26th “	Dec. 12, 1862,	Jackson,	Dec. 13, 1862,	June 4, 1865,	Alexandria, Va.	June 7, 1865,	“ “
27th “	April 10, 1863,	Ypsilanti,	April 12, 1863,	July 26, 1865,	Delaney House, D. C.	July 29, 1865,	Detroit, “
28th “	Nov. 10, 1864,	Kalamazoo,	Oct. 26, 1864,	June 5, 1865,	Raleigh, N. C.	June 8, 1866,	“ “
29th “	Oct. 3, 1864,	Saginaw,	Oct. 6, 1864,	Sept. 6, 1865,	Murfreesboro, Tenn.	Sept. 12, 1865,	“ “
30th “	January 9, 1865,	Detroit,	Did not leave.	June 30, 1865,	Detroit, Mich.	Paid and disba	nded at Detroit.
1st S. S.	July 7, 1863,	Dearborn,	July, 1863,	July 28, 1865,	Delaney House, D. C.	July 31, 1865,	Jackson, Mich.
102d U. S. C. T.	Feb'y 17, 1864,	Detroit,	Mar. 28, 1864,	Sept. 30, 1865,	Charleston, S. C.	Oct. 17, 1865,	Detroit, “

FINANCIAL STATISTICS.

Thus far has been given a brief narrative of the most momentous period in our State history, embracing the home work of Michigan in the war, and, although it should be considered small and insignificant when compared with the extent and value of the work accomplished by her troops in the field, and the sacrifice of life there made by them, it was still one of stupendous proportions. Aside from the incessant labor of the people in raising troops, there was much perplexing anxiety, many petty annoyances, great self-sacrifice, and much personal suffering, together with enormous expenditures of money by the State, counties, and townships, and also by individuals—all combined, rendering the burdens and cares of the people at times so heavy as to be almost unbearable. Yet the astonishing statements revealed below, covering over sixteen millions of dollars, expended by the people of Michigan for war purposes, although couched in silent figures, speak eloquently and earnestly of great sacrifice and unbounded patriotism.

During the war the State Legislature passed laws authorizing the payment of State bounties to soldiers, as follows:

Men enlisting from March 6, 1863, to November 10, 1863, (both inclusive,) in any Michigan regiment, company, or battery, except the 10th and 11th cavalry, 13th and 14th batteries, and 1st colored infantry, entitled to $50 State bounty. Men re-enlisting in their own regiments, (after service of two years,) from Novmber 11, 1863, to February 4, 1864, (both inclusive,) entitled to $50 State bounty. Men enlisting or re-enlisting from February 5, 1864, to May 14, 1864, (both inclusive,) in any regiment, company, or battery, if applied on 200,000 call, and properly credited to the sub-district in which they resided at time of enlistment, entitled to $100 State bounty. Men enlisting from February 4, 1865, to April 14, 1865, (both inclusive,) properly credited to sub-districts, entitled to $150 State bounty.

In accordance with these laws, the Quartermaster-General of the State paid in 1863, $134,250; 1864, 867,959; 1865, $383,076; 1866, $438,500; 1867, $11,700; 1868, $18,623; 1869, $28,850; 1870, $26,400, up to and including 31st July; amounting in the aggregate to $1,909,408, leaving still a considerable amount unapplied for.

He also disbursed $60,000 as premiums for the procuration of recruits.

Aside from these amounts, this department expended for war purposes $815,000—making the aggregate disbursements up to July 31, 1870, $2,784,408.

The amounts paid by each county, respectively, during the war for bounty to volunteers prior to December 19, 1863, and liabilities; also, liabilities incurred under the law of 1865, and also liabilities for other objects:

Allegan, ——; Alpena, $3,080; Antrim, $1,200; Berrien, $135,400; Branch, $76,859.91; Barry, $11,400; Bay, $40,913; Calhoun, $49,468; Clinton, $3,768: Cass, $39,909; Chippewa, ——; Cheboygan, $4,524; Delta, $5,326; Eaton, $33,881.85; Emmett, $500; Genesee, $115,820.12; Gratiot, $1,800; Grand Traverse, $350; Hillsdale, $55,919; Houghton, ——; Huron, ——; Ionia, $41,718; Ingham, $58,383.69; Isabella, $6,300; Iosco, $1,089.60; Jackson, ——; Kent, $113,900; Kalamazoo, $400; Keweenaw, ——; Livingston, ——; Lapeer, $51,863.87; Lewanee, $89,485.30; Leelenaw, $330; Midland, $26,458.65; Montcalm, $5,550; Muskegon, $29,950; Macomb, $51,763.75; Menominee, $5,057.85; Mecosta, $3,662.50; Monroe, ——; Manistee, $2,700; Mackinaw, ——; Mason, $2,535.97; Marquette, $13,779.34; Newaygo, $13,727.72; Ottawa, $101,350; Oakland, $237,533;

Oceana, $6,084; St. Clair, $36,350; St. Joseph, $21,700; Saginaw, $49,572; Shiawassee, $4,000; Sanilac, $55,500; Schoolcraft, ——; Tuscola, $600; Van Buren, $14,675.29; Wayne, $369,428.88; Washtenaw, ——. Total, $2,015,588.09.

The following are the aggregate expenditures and liabilities of the various townships, cities and wards of the counties in the State for war purposes, made up from statements of the proper officers, rendered in 1866:

Allegan, $188,898.49; Alpena, $9,781.98; Antrim, $4,638; Berrien, $257,416.97; Branch, $230,086.65; Barry, $180,641; Bay, $61,267; Calhoun, $354,432.32; Clinton, $135,936; Cass, $196,239.86; Chippewa, ——; Cheboygan, $1,525; Delta, $1,200; Eaton, $175,363.58; Emmett, $50; Genesee, $150,488.75; Gratiot, $23,527; Grand Traverse, $12,990.54; Hillsdale, $282,449.21; Houghton, $39,152.71; Huron, $17,230; Ionia, $182,888; Ingham, $203,985; Isabella, $5,775; Iosco, $4,900; Jackson, $439,325.10; Kent, $167,550.50; Kalamazoo, $383,416.61; Keweenaw, $1,000; Livingston, $144,379.22; Lapeer, $129,674.89; Lenawee, $544,557.75; Leelenaw, $4,845.52; Midland, $12,598; Montcalm, $44,861.20; Muskegon, $43,604; Macomb, $289,029.69; Mecosta, $3,340; Monroe, $135,180.69; Manistee, $15,476; Manitou, ——; Mackinaw, $6,727.50; Mason, $807; Marquette and Schoolcraft, $3,000; Newaygo, $12,004; Ottawa, $148,523; Oakland, $586,556.98; Oceana, $14,692.93; St. Clair, $233,291.90; St. Joseph, $557,958; Saginaw, $158,099.59; Shiawasse, $167,203; Sanilac, $95,794.29; Tuscola, $67,631.96; Van Buren, $115,637.90; Wayne, $660,554.88; Washtenaw, $458,563.54; total, $8,157,748.70.

Statement showing amount expended by each county of the State, from 1861 to 1867, for the relief of soldiers' families under the provisions of the Soldiers' Relief Law, approved May 10, 1861:

Alpena, $8.80; Allegan, $80,985.72; Antrim, $666.11; Bay, $21,991.54; Barry, $86,598.15; Berrien, $131,924.45; Branch, $69,121.20; Calhoun, $200,193.66; Cass, $80,883.46; Clinton, $67,443.75; Cheboygan, $368.92; Chippewa, $1,032; Delta, ——; Eaton, $62,103.69; Emmett, $1,948.40; Genesee, $89,087.12; Gratiot, $8,875; Grand Traverse, $10,636.81; Hillsdale, $90,155.96; Houghton, $8,419; Huron, $23,033.50; Ingham, $110,547.09; Isabella, $4,680.45; Ionia, $31,500; Iosco, $1,000; Jackson, $129,401.25; Kalamazoo, $119,984.79; Kent, $76,311; Keweenaw, $3,620; Lapeer, $75,000; Livingston, $34,500; Lenawee, $145,226.20; Leelenaw, $6,487.89; Macomb, $110,339.26; Mecosta, $9,280.09; Mackinaw, ——; Midland, $6,550; Manitou, ——; Mason, $3,200; Manistee, $9,620; Muskegon, $20,000; Marquette, $7,989.16; Menominee, $390; Monroe, $143,762; Montcalm, $40,000; Newaygo, $14,516.72; Ottawa, $56,616.08; Oceana, $18,368; Ontonagon, $4,747.02; Oakland, $127,993.38; Sanilac, $73,111.33; Shiawasse, $50,645; Saginaw, $81,000; St. Clair, $89,427.99; St. Joseph, $96,214; Tuscola, $51,987.22; Van Buren, $99,511.81; Washtenaw, $155,043.15; and Wayne, $547,200. Total, $3,591,248.12.

At the session of 1867 the Legislature most humanely and opportunely appropriated twenty thousand dollars to maintain for two years a temporary "Soldiers' Home" at the Harper Hospital in Detroit. At the session of 1869 an additional sum was appropriated for its support for two years more. This home was established for the maintenance of infirm, maimed, and destitute Michigan soldiers and sailors of the late war. Its management to be under the direction of the State Military Board, at present consisting of Col. D. H. Jerome, of Saginaw, President; Col. Jerome Croul, of Detroit; Col. Alvin T. Crossman, of Flint; Col. Henry L. Hall, of Hillsdale; and Col. S. M. Cutcheon, of Ypsilanti.

The management of the "Home" has been judicious and liberal, affording to the disabled soldier the fullest benefit contemplated under the law, proving of great service to many who have found it necessary to seek its shelter and care. And while it has been liberally conducted, care has been exercised in guarding the State against unnecessary expense and the imposition of the undeserving.

Except for a very short time in the early part of the rebellion, when Capt. E. G. Owen was U. S. Quartermaster at Detroit, Colonel George W. Lee, a well-known and prominent citizen of Michigan, served as Chief United States Quartermaster of the State throughout the war, filling a most important and very responsible position with eminent energy and efficiency and at the same time with most persistent and scrupulous fidelity to the General Government.

In connection with the discharge of his duties, Colonel Lee disbursed in Michigan for the General Government $7,144,812, as follows; 33,050 horses, $3,667,252; transportation of troops and supplies, $1,363,812; forage, $331,697; equipping troops, erection of barracks and hospitals, apprehension of deserters, and other incidental expenses, $1,782,051.

In addition to this large disbursement by the Quartermaster Department, there was a very great expenditure made in the State by the United States mustering and disbursing officer for the subsistence and supplies of troops, but it has been found impossible to reach information as to the exact amount or even to form an approximate estimate.

SANITARY OPERATIONS.

The great beneficent effort of the American masses in the war, the sanitary measure, was very early adopted by Michigan people. The "Michigan Soldiers' Relief Association," of Washington, D. C., is claimed to have been the first of the kind put into the field on the Atlantic slope, and the last to leave it. It was organized in Washington in the autumn of 1861, continued in successful operation until September 19, 1866, and was a source of infinite good to Michigan soldiers, scattering among them friendship, brotherly care, and many comforts and necessaries of life when most needed. The association was composed of the few Michigan citizens then in and around Washington, including the delegation in Congress. The Hon. James M. Edmunds was president, Dr. H. J. Alvord secretary, who was succeeded by C. Clark, and Z. Moses treasurer, all of whom served gratuitously, and with a devotion, energy, and efficiency unsurpassed.

The means to sustain the measure at first were assessed upon the members of the association, but after a short time were derived from contributions made by the people of the State, and amounted to $24,909.24, in the aggregate.

In connection with the enterprise was established at City Point, immediately following Grant's great battles, the famous "Michigan Soup House," so well known throughout the army, which afforded so much relief to the suffering soldier.

Judge Edmunds, in his report, kindly mentions the faithful and patriotic ladies connected with the association during its several years of great usefulness, whose generous and noble natures led them to render such services in the field for Michigan men as have made their names household words at almost every hearthstone in the State, and never to be forgotten by thousands upon thousands of brave men who were recipients of their kindness and motherly care.

The record of Michigan in the great sanitary movement would be incomplete without the following extract from the final report of Judge Edmunds, president of the association:

"The Michigan Soldiers' Relief Association of the District of Columbia was organized in the autumn of 1861. It was the product of necessity, and was composed of the few Michigan men then resident at the National Capital. Soon after the first arrival of troops under the call for 75,000 volunteers, the first Michigan regiment (three months' men) appeared here. It contained many who were personally known to the citizens of Michigan then residents of Washington, and this, with the noble cause in which they were enlisted, soon aroused a deep feeling of friendship between the members of the regiment and all those hailing from the same State. This friendship was manifested by various and numerous acts of kindness and appreciation. Among them, special solicitude for all in the service whose failing health made demands upon this feeling for those attentions which were impossible in the then inexperienced and unprepared state of the hospital service.

"For the first few months the efforts made to relieve and comfort those of our friends in the service were unorganized, and though throwing great labor upon the few engaged, hardly kept pace with the growing demands incident to the rapid increase of the army. The battle of Bull Run, in which our friends suffered severely, aroused afresh the sympathy of all whose hearts beat honestly for the country, and demonstrated the utter inadequacy of the Government preparation for any such sudden emergency. It seemed impossible for the public authorities at this time to appreciate the necessity of ample preparations for the wounded and sick. Their attentions seemed constantly directed to the increase of the army by new enlistments. The importance of providing for its health was but slowly admitted, and hardly admitted at all until it became evident that the ranks could only be kept up by such provisions. To reach this point and this degree of preparation, required the experience of an entire campaign. The consequence was, that there was all the time an urgent call, we might almost say an imperative demand, for volunteer aid. Such aid was cordially given, but yet fell short of what was absolutely essential. It became apparent that we could no longer meet the demand upon us by individual and unorganized effort. We must have system, and assignment of duties. We must have contributions far beyond the means of the small number of Michigan citizens then here. These urgent demands so pressed upon us, that the citizens of Michigan then in the District assembled for consultation, and the result was the organization of the Michigan Soldiers' Relief Association, then composed of a set of officers and an executive committee. It claimed as its members all citizens of the State, residents of the District, and the Michigan delegation in Congress. The association commenced by levying a tax upon its members, which was frequently repeated during the first few months of its existence, and has been resorted to for emergencies from that time to the present.

"This organization was the first of the kind in the field upon the Atlantic slope, and the last to leave it. Its history, so far as it has not been written, will be briefly alluded to in the following pages.

"The association having been thus organized, it was called into full activity in May, 1862, after the Army of the Potomac had made a commencement of its peninsula campaign.

"The battle of Williamsburg, in which several of our regiments participated, filled the hospitals of Baltimore and Fortress Monroe with wounded men; and from this time forward to the close of the war, the whole energies of the association have been taxed to their utmost limits.

"By referring to the reports of our operations for 1862, '63, and '64, it will be seen that our means were limited; but as the services of the individual members of the association have in all cases been gratuitous, and always cheerfully rendered, the money we had was used in such a way as secured the greatest amount of relief.

"In the year 1862, the first in fact of our activity, the whole amount of money received from all sources was........ ....$2,166 13
Expended.. .... 1,945 84
In 1863.. 2,350 39
Expended.. 2,037 61
In 1864.. 6,779 71
Expended.. .... 5,488 48

"This is, of course, exclusive of specific contributions of clothing and hospital stores always liberally furnished by the soldiers' aid societies through the State, and which we endeavored to apply faithfully to the purposes intended.

"In the summer and fall of 1862, after the dreadful closing battles of the peninsula and the disastrous campaign of General Pope, the whole city of Washington became a vast hospital.

"The public buildings, the churches, and many private residences were made receptacles of wounded and sick soldiers.

"Scattered all through these our own brave men lay and languished, and many died. But we are assured that the kind offices of the members of this association assuaged their pains and carried relief to all within their reach: and doubtless many owe their recovery to those special attentions impossible to be secured from the assistants detailed for the care of sick and wounded men in hospital. During the fall of 1862 something like system was inaugurated by the Medical Department of the Government commensurate with the magnitude of the exigency. Columbia College was made a permanent hospital. Carver, Finley, Mount Pleasant, Emery, and subsequently Douglas, Stanton, Campbell, Harewood, and Lincoln, were provided with ample accommodations for twenty thousand patients; and in 1863, with the hospitals in Alexandria, Baltimore, Philadelphia, New York, Annapolis, Frederick, and other places North, the whole operations of the Medical Department assumed something like order, efficiency, and permanency, and it became necessary for us to employ agents who could give their whole time to the work.

"Mrs. Brainard was early engaged, and perhaps the first among our regular workers—she certainly was the last to leave. Her services were invaluable, and have never been fully appreciated and acknowledged. The services of Miss Wheelock, Miss Bateman, Mrs. Mahan, Mrs. Gridley, Mrs. Plum, Mrs. Johnson, Mrs. Hall, the Misses Bull, and others, who have labored in the field and hospitals under the auspices of this association, have all richly earned the thanks of the people of Michigan, and especially of the thousands of soldiers who received their kind ministrations. Their reports are necessarily excluded for want of space. In the summer of 1863 the battles around Fredericksburg, and those of the campaign of Gen. Meade's army in Maryland and Pennsylvania, and the crowning carnage at Gettysburg absorbed our entire energies.

"Our agents were early at their work, and remained as long as there was suffering to be relieved.

"In 1864 the bloody struggles of the Wilderness and Spottsylvania, and the daily conflicts during those forty days of Grant's persistent advance to Richmond, again filled the hospitals around Washington, and gave ample employment to our agents and the members of the association, and drew upon our means so that we were well nigh exhausted.

"It is due to ourselves to acknowledge the generous co-operation of the Christian and Sanitary Commissions during this summer. To the former we have ever been indebted for the most generous consideration and liberality; and to the latter for extraordinary kindness in furnishing our agents, Mrs. Brainard and Mrs. Mahan, with valuable and much-needed supplies, to the amount of more than two thousand dollars in three months, and at a time when our own were exhausted.

"On the 1st of January, 1865, the report of the treasurer shows $1,291.30 available funds on hand. This amount was soon after increased by the most liberal contributions from several associations and individuals in Michigan, and especially from the noble-hearted people of the Lake Superior region, till our whole receipts for the year 1865, including the sum on hand, amounted to $14,914.24.

"With the prospect of a campaign of unexampled activity on the south side of Richmond by the combined armies of Generals Grant and Butler, and the reasonable anticipation of a stout and protracted resistance on the part of the rebels, we early made preparations for meeting promptly the demands that would most likely be made upon our association. We established a magazine of supplies at City Point, and sent thither an effective force to receive and provide for such as should, in the coming struggle, be sent back disabled. We also established in Washington a 'Home,' where our men in passing could find shelter for a night without being thrown into the bad associations of the city.

"It had long been felt that such an asylum was needed, and we had been prevented from establishing one chiefly from scarcity of means. This objection no longer existed, and the association rented and furnished a house, with comfortable and cheap furniture, engaged a competent matron, and from April 1st to September 1st, 1865, were able to provide for the wounded and sick a comfortable resting place. The whole expenditure in this enterprise, as shown by the treasurer's report, was $2,675.38, diminished by the sum of $507.30 received for furniture, &c., on breaking up the house—making the whole expense $2,168.08.

"The sudden and unexpected collapse of the rebellion, and the recall of the Army of the Potomac, and the arrival of Sherman's grand columns in Washington, worn and fatigued by the longest and most remarkable march yet recorded, imposed new work upon us.

"Our returned regiments were visited by our agents, and supplied with much-needed vegetables, pickles, tobacco, bread, &c., to the amount of $4,000. Our force was withdrawn from City Point, and furnished ample employment here till the armies were disbanded and sent home.

"At the 'Home,' during the month of June, all were received who came. Colonel Pritchard's detail for Jeff. Davis' body guard was lodged and feasted. The records, imperfect though they are, have the names of about 8,000 who took one or more meals under the roof and at the tables of the 'Home,' faithfully and ably conducted by the Matron, Mrs. Van Boskerck, whose executive ability, industry, and fidelity cannot be too highly commended.

"The accounts of the 'Home' show that as many as 725 meals were served in a day, and the bread consumed averaged from 300 to 425 loaves a day for many days. Above all the labor and care bestowed upon this house, the matron had especial care of ten or fifteen patients at Douglas and Stanton hospitals, near the house, for two months, visiting them daily, and furnishing them with delicacies.

"The Executive Committee desire here to acknowledge their obligation to all the agents who have been employed, for devotion to their duties, and to all members of the association for cheerful co-operation in the work in which we have been engaged during the bloody struggle now passed.

"All the services rendered by the association have been entirely gratuitous, and the agents have labored for little more than actual expenses. The motives of all, it is believed, were patriotic and humane; and the only reward sought or desired was the consciousness of having discharged well the duties imposed by the exigency. We have at least endeavored well.

"To the individuals and associations at home who have so nobly supported us with contributions of money and material, and surely not least, with their encouraging words of commendation and counsel, we desire to say, that your noble efforts in behalf of the brave and self-sacrificing young men who have given their services, suffered toils, hunger, and thirst, encountered dangers and disease, and death, for the perpetuation of the Government, in defence of liberty, and in the cause of humanity, have no parallel in the annals of the world.

"If there can be any compensations in such a war as we have just emerged from, the chief must be sought in the grand outpouring of generous humanities all over the entire loyal portion of the country, in endeavoring to ameliorate the condition of the soldier, and assuage his sufferings.

"Happily, the war is ended. The grand armies that fought its battles have returned to their families and to peaceful pursuits. Too many, alas, have found their last resting-place far from kindred and from home. They found bloody graves in a hostile land. Their memories live in the hearts of a grateful people, saved by their devotion and valor.

"All honor to the dead hero; his wife and children demand our care, and must not be forgotten or neglected."

In September, 1866, the association discontinued its operations, and among its last acts of kind consideration of the soldier, transmitted to the trustees of Harper Hospital, at Detroit, $1,000, to be by them used in the care and maintenance of such disabled Michigan soldiers as should from time to time become its inmates.

In addition to the Washington Association, the people in the State took hold of the matter and were busy in the noble work. In April, 1862, the "Michigan Soldiers' Relief Association" was formed, with Hon. John Owen as president, Benjamin Vernon, Esq., secretary, and William A. Butler, Esq., treasurer. It continued in successful operation during the entire war, doing much good, collecting from various localities in the State a large amount of useful and necessary supplies and sending them to the front; a portion of the packages forwarded were 331 boxes, 203 barrels, containing almost every conceivable comfort for the use of the soldier, sick or well, viz: Shirts, drawers, socks, handkerchiefs, canned and dried fruits, wines, jellies, pickles of all kinds, spices, books, papers, pins, needles, thread, sheets, quilts, pillow-cases, bed sacks, bandages, pads, lint, in fact everything useful and that were thought necessary.

It also received and expended in 1864 $3,600, which was made use of as stated in Mr. Vernon's report in furnishing relief to sick and destitute soldiers in sums of from one to ten dollars as their necessities required; in sending agents to different points to look after the wants of soldiers; in providing refreshments and meals for returned veterans; in paying rent for "Soldiers' Home" in Detroit, and in burying the dead.

Another most active and useful association, accomplishing much good throughout the war was the "Michigan Soldier's Aid Society," a branch of the "United States Sanitary Commission." It was organized November 6, 1861, and kept its office open until January 1st, 1866, and after that date continued to supply destitute soldiers and soldiers' families, and intended to do so until the fund on hand was expended.

The first officers of the society were: Dr. Z. Pitcher, counsellor; Mrs. Geo. Duffield, president; Mrs. Theodore Romeyn, vice president; Mrs. D. P. Bushnell, treasurer; Miss Sarah T. Bingham, recording secretary; Miss Valeria Campbell, corresponding secretary.

At the close of 1864 the society was reorganized, and the following officers selected:

John Owen, president, associate member U. S. S. Commission; Benjamin Vernor, James V. Campbell, B. E. Demill, vice presidents, associate members U. S. S. Commission; Mrs. S. A. Sibley, president; Mrs. H. L. Chipman, Mrs. A. Adams, vice presidents; William A. Butler, treasurer; Mrs. George Andrews, assistant treasurer; Mrs. W. A. Butler, auditor; Miss Lizzie Woodhams, recording secretary; Miss Valeria Campbell, corresponding secretary.

The association received from various sources throughout the State and sent forward from November 1, 1861, to June, 1863, 3,593 packages; distributed at home during the same time, 2,724 packages; total, 6,317. Most of these were large packages, and consisted chiefly of articles contributed in kind, of what value has not been estimated.

Cash expended from November 6, 1861, to June 1, 1866, $19,633.18; from June 1st, 1866, to April 7th, 1868, $8,496.23; total, $28,129.41.

Of this amount, $11,422.36 was expended on account of "Soldiers' Home," and the balance in purchases and other expenses. The association had on hand April 7th, 1868, $187.01.

From May to November, 1861, between thirty and forty large packages were received from different parts of the State by Mrs. Morse Stewart and Mrs. George Duffield and sent forward, besides an unrecorded amount distributed to regiments in Michigan.

Chaplain Samuel Day, 8th Illinois infantry, Military Agent for U. S. Sanitary Supplies, a most efficient and industrious officer, and now a resident of Ann Arbor, collected in this State in 1863, and forwarded through the U. S. Sanitary Commission at Chicago for distribution in the field, 2,337 barrels of vegetables, (mostly potatoes and green apples;) 167 barrels of onions; 29 barrels of best stock ale. Add to this three thousand one hundred and thirty-seven dollars and fifty-five cents remitted to Sanitary Commission at Chicago for the purchase of vegetables, reducing the same to barrels, would give 5,673 barrels vegetables and 29 barrels ale, giving an aggregate of 5,702 barrels.

Aside from the aid furnished by the associations referred to, there were large amounts both of money and supplies sent by private agents, ministers of the gospel, and many other noble and kind-hearted people who visited the army and hospitals from time to time on errands of mercy and benevolence, largely contributing towards a great cause, which was bountifully sustained without a parallel in the history of nations.

These associations were most opportunely and very substantially assisted in 1864 by the "Ladies' Soldiers' Aid Society of Kalamazoo," under whose auspices a "State Sanitary Fair" was held in September of that year, in connection with the "State Agricultural Fair." It was a complete success, and netted $9,618.78 over expenses.

The following is the report of the Execu ive Committee, made to the Adjutant-General of the State:

JOHN ROBERTSON, *Adjutant-General State of Michigan:*

SIR: Herewith the undersigned submit a report, embracing an account of receipts and disbursements of the "Michigan State Sanitary Fair," held at the village of Kalamazoo, on the "State Agricultural Fair Grounds," on the 20th, 21st, 22d, and 23d days of September, A. D. 1864. The following correspondence exhibits the origin of the "Fair:"

To Mrs. John Potter and Miss Eliza Fisher, of the Ladies' Soldiers' Aid Society, of Kalamazoo, Michigan:

The undersigned, citizens of Kalamazoo county, knowing that you have been active, and have accomplished much—ever since the rebellion commenced—in every good work for the relief of the sick and wounded Union soldiers, would most respectfully suggest that thousands of the patriotic and generous people of Michigan will be glad, in connection with the annual fair of the Michigan State Agricultural Society, to be held on the 20th, 21st, 22d, and 23d days of September, at Kalamazoo, to contribute of their abundance, in money and articles, for the purpose of aiding the wounded and sick of that army which fought in defence of our national flag and the Union, against the traitorous designs of those who hate liberty and love despotism. We would suggest that a fair be held on the grounds to be occupied by the Agricultural Society, for the purpose above mentioned, and we earnestly solicit that you—calling to your aid suitable persons—may devise such plan for the consummation of the foregoing purpose as may be deemed proper.

Signed:—H. G. Wells, Joseph Sill, Allen Potter, John Baker, Daniel Cahill, J. M. Edwards, J. P. Woodbury, N. A. Balch, J. W. Breese, L. H. Trask, George Lewis, Henry Montague, F. W. Curtenius, O. N. Giddings, David S. Walbridge, Marsh Giddings, J. M. Neasmith, B. M. Austin, George A. Fitch, J. W. Mansur, Henry Hoyt, Hiram Arnold, Henry Bishop, Henry Dreese, Samuel W. Walker, J. J. Perrin, Isaiah W. Pursel, Frank Henderson, J. A. B. Stone, James A. Walter, G. H. Gale, Henry Wood, David Fisher, A. Cameron, S. S. Cobb, J. W. Lay, William A. Wood, John C. Bassett, Trowbridge & Bassett, John M'Kibben, Charles Bell, Alfred Thomas, George Colt, W. B. Clark, F. Chase, M. B. Miller, E. A. Carder, G. D. Penfield, J. K. Wagner, E. O. Humphrey, Charles S. May, C. D. Handscomb, Thomas Brownell, James Turner, William A. Hurst, A. C. Wortley, Thomas Browning, S. K. Selkrig, A. H. Geisse, James P. Clapham, Pickering & Wormley, Austin George, A. D. Robinson, W. H. Snow, Z. S. Clark, F. U. Clark, P. L. Haines, H. S. Parker & Co., John Bennett, I. C. Bennett, A. E. Bartlett, Frank Little, D. Putnam, C. S. Cobb, R. S. Babcock, C. W. Hall, H. F. Cock, P. C. Davis, H. C. Briggs.

KALAMAZOO, *August 23d, A. D.* 1864.

TO THE PEOPLE OF THE STATE OF MICHIGAN: The undersigned, of the "Soldiers' Aid Society," of Kalamazoo, pursuant to the foregoing request, after having obtained the kind aid of many ladies and gentlemen of this county, and other parts of the State, have made arrangements for holding a "Michigan State Sanitary Fair," at Kalamazoo, on the 20th, 21st, 22d, and 23d of September, A. D. 1864, at which we hope to avail ourselves of patriotic addresses from his Excellency Austin Blair and other distinguished persons.

It is proposed to devote the entire proceeds of this "Sanitary Fair" to the sick and wounded soldiers, who have gone forth in defence of that flag which is the symbol of Union, and whose brave hearts nerve them to meet suffering and death rather than permit one star to be stricken from its azure field.

One-third of the proceeds of this fair will be distributed through the "Michigan Soldiers' Relief Committee," at Detroit, consisting of C. H. Buhl, B. Vernor, Adjutant-General John Robertson, W. A. Butler, and Anthony Dudgeon; one-third through the "United States Christian Commission," to be distributed by David Preston, E. C. Walker, Caleb Ives, Francis Raymond, J. S. Vernor, and Charles F. Clark, of Detroit, and one-third through the "Ladies' Soldiers' Aid Society," at Kalamazoo.

We ask the people of Michigan, men and women, old and young, to bring or send to us money, or such articles of value as can be spared, for this, a great national purpose.

May we not, especially, appeal to the young men who still remain at home, and who are preserved from the accidents of the battle-field, the long suffering and the weary night watches of the hospital? If home duties and family ties, or impaired health, compel you to resist the inclination to aid your country in this its hour of peril, by active service in the field, we implore you to give of your means, that health may possibly be restored, and comfort administered to the sick and wounded soldiers.

Of the women of Michigan we ask efficient, active aid in this our effort to accomplish a great good; to them, we believe, we shall not appeal in vain.

God's own blessing, we trust, will rest on all men, women, and little children of Michigan who may be thus inclined to strengthen the hearts and hands, and encourage the valor and patriotism of the fathers and husbands, and brothers and sons, who have manfully resisted the overthrow of that Government which good men of the olden time established, and which we humbly pray a righteous God may ever preserve.

RUTH L. POTTER,
ELIZA W. FISHER,
Of the Ladies' Soldiers' Aid Society, Kalamazoo.

It will be noticed that a very brief period elapsed between the time that the idea of holding the "Fair" was first entertained and its occurrence, but the foregoing address was as widely circulated among the people of Michigan as circumstances would permit. The ladies of Kalamazoo county relied mainly upon the various Soldiers' Aid Societies of the State for active co-operation, and in view of all the surroundings, they were not disappointed. The general outline for the "Fair" having been arranged, the work of preparation commenced. Buildings were to be erected, a hall in which articles were to be exhibited and sold to the assembled thousands, and an extensive dining-room for visitors, were to be built, and considering the fact that the lumber was to be brought by teams a distance of twenty-eight miles, the circumstances seemed to be embarrassing. The ladies had determined that all obstacles should be overcome, and their efforts were crowned with success.

Contributions in money, merchandise, produce, animals, implements and works of art, were furnished with a good degree of liberality, from various portions of this State, and in a few instances from beyond the limits of

Michigan. Words of encouragement, with gifts of money or articles for sale, came alike from the rich and the poor. In not a few instances, the widowed mother, whose only son had gone down in the storm of battle, in the Army of the Potomac, or the Army of the West, sent forward her humble contribution, with an invocation that God would bless the soldier who stood ready to yield his life in defence of that Government which had given him protection from infancy to manhood. A little child from an adjoining county, in humble circumstances, furnished her gift, in value the fraction of a dollar, with the simple but earnest request that she might be permitted to give something; she wished to do more, but they were poor; her mother was ill, and her father and only brother were soldiers in the war. This gift, in fact the most liberal of all, was sold and returned by purchasers, again and again, until the amount realized was a handsome addition to the general fund.

On Thursday, the 22d day of September, the "Fair" was duly inaugurated under the direction of the Hon. James B. Crippen of Coldwater, Michigan, who, after appropriate religious services, in a brief address congratulated the assembled thousands upon the liberality which had been evidenced throughout the loyal States in caring for the men of the Union army, and in terms of merited compliment extended to the ladies of the State of Michigan commendation for their zeal and active effort in behalf of the sick and wounded soldier. His Excellency Austin Blair was then introduced, and in an address, able, patriotic, eloquent and replete with interesting incidents of the war, he held the close attention of his audience for an hour. After singing, of rare excellence, by the "Musical Association of Kalamazoo," the vast crowd was dismissed, every man and woman seemingly congratulating themselves that the public exercises had been to them, of great interest, and worthy of the cause for which the "Sanitary Fair" had been planned and arranged.

No objects in the "Fair" seemed to excite so much of interest and fix the attention of the thousands who visited the "Sanitary Hall," as the torn and battle-scarred banners, which had been borne by the regiments of Michigan during the war, and which had been kindly furnished from the Adjutant-General's office. As the multitude gazed on these silent emblems of the brave deeds of the men of Michigan, again and again was heard from mother and father the exclamation, as the flag of some particular regiment was noted, "My son fought under that banner;" and not unfrequently the sad, accompanying remark, "he fell in battle," or "died in hospital."

The "Ladies' Soldiers' Aid Society, of Kalamazoo," desire to express their heartfelt thanks to all who generously contributed to this "Michigan State Sanitary Fair," for the benefit of the sick, wounded, and disabled soldier. To the delegations of ladies and gentlemen from Wayne, St. Clair, Macomb, Lapeer, Lenawee, Hillsdale, Calhoun, Jackson, St. Joseph, Van Buren, Cass, and Allegan counties, who attended during the "Fair," and kindly contributed by active effort to its success, they specially desire to express their great obligation.

It will be perceived by the accompanying account that the net proceeds of the "Fair," already distributed, amounts to $9,300, leaving with the treasurer a small balance to cover any possible outstanding liability, or for future distribution.

MICHIGAN STATE SANITARY FAIR.

1864—*Credit.*

By amount received, admission tickets, for Sanitary Hall......	$1,213 15
By amount received at Presidential ballot-box....................	454 25
By donations in money and sales of articles contributed.........	11,097 40
Total..	$12,764 80

Debit.

To amount paid Kellogg & Co. for lumber for buildings.........	$1,243 91
To labor, printing, and sundry expenses..........................	502 11
To Kalamazoo Horse Association for rent of ground............	276 50
To supplies for dining tables..	1,123 50
To "Kalamazoo Ladies' Soldiers' Aid Society".....................	2,900 00
To "United States Christian Commission," Detroit...............	2,900 00
To "Michigan Soldiers' Relief Committee," Detroit...............	2,900 00
To "Michigan Soldiers' Relief Association," Washington City, per Hon. J. M. Edmunds..	600 00
To cash, balance on hand..	318 78
Total..	$12,764 80

H. G. WELLS,
S. W. WALKER,
JOHN POTTER,
Executive Com. Michigan State Sanitary Fair.

KALAMAZOO, *November* 10, 1864.

Among the various associations instituted during the war for the relief of the sick and wounded soldier, the "Christian Commission" loomed up as a great auxiliary in the great and good work. Possessing an immense strength and energy, with true devotion, it competed most successfully as a sanitary organization, uniting therewith the religious instruction and admonition of good men to the living, and administering kindly consolation to those who were being called away forever.

The following report of the Michigan branch for 1864 finds a proper place at this time:

To JOHN ROBERTSON, *Adjutant-General State of Michigan:*

In accordance with your request, the Michigan branch of the U. S. Christian Commission beg leave to report the nature and extent of its work in behalf of the armies of the Union for the past year.

The commission in this State was first organized on the 15th of June, A. D. 1863, but has practically been in operation but a single year. It had no part in the great work of the Christian Commission at Gettysburg in July, 1863, except that some of our citizens were commissioned at Philadelphia, and acted as delegates on that field. Its first funds of any large amount were received from the thanksgiving collections of last year, which were nearly all poured into our treasury. Since that time the operations of this branch have been steadily enlarging, its resources increasing, and its plan and system of working gaining the favor and approbation of the people.

The plan of the commission is to minister both to the mental and spiritual, as well as the bodily wants of the army. It sends the living preacher, the Bible, and the religious newspapers of all denominations, and all the time it is ministering to the temporal wants of the soldier, and working for the sick, wounded, and dying. It searches for the wounded amid the thickets of the battle-field, and never leaves him till he is discharged from hospital, or a prayer consigns him to a soldier's grave.

All the delegates of the commission are ministers and laymen, selected for their fitness for the work, who labor each six weeks without any compensation, except the consciousness of doing good. All that is given to the commission is dispensed personally by these delegates, and placed by their own hands in the hands of the soldier—not handed over to be dispensed by officials of the Government, or salaried agents of the commission.

This branch of the commission has received from the people down to this time $21,725.20, most of which has been forwarded to the central office at Philadelphia. Stores have been contributed and forwarded to the armies from Michigan amounting in value to about $10,000.

Michigan furnished to us the following delegates, fifty-seven in number, nearly all of whom have spent their full term of six weeks in the work of the commission:

William Harvey, Detroit, Army of the Cumberland.
Rev. Seth Reed, Ypsilanti, Army of the Cumberland.
Rev. J. M. Strong, Clarkston, Army of the Potomac.
Rev. James Walker, Eckford, Army of the Mississippi.
Rev. L. Slater, Kalamazoo, Army of the Cumberland.
James E. Carson, Centreville, Army of the Cumberland.
Rev. E. H. Pilcher, Ann Arbor, Army of the Cumberland.
Rev. B. Franklin, Saline, Army of the Cumberland.
Rev. A. F. Bournes, Dexter, Army of the Mississippi.
Rev. F. R. Gallaher, Hillsdale, Army of the Cumberland.
Rev. W. P. Wastell, Holly, Army of the Potomac.
Prof. A. Ten Brook, Ann Arbor, Army of the Mississippi.
Rev. George H. Hickox, Saline, Army of the Cumberland.
Rev. D. H. Evans, Palmyra, Army of the Cumberland.
Rev. J. J. Gridley, Pinckney, Army of the Mississippi.
Prof. Joseph Eastabrook, Ypsilanti, Army of the Potomac.
Alanson Sheley, Detroit, Army of the Potomac.
Rev. O. C. Thompson, Detroit, Army of the Potomac.
Rev. Wm. Hogarth, D.D., Detroit, Army of the Potomac.
E. C. Walker, Detroit, Army of the Potomac.
Rev. George Duffield, Jr., Adrian, Army of the Potomac.
Samuel W. Duffield, Adrian, Army of the Potomac.
Samuel E. Hart, Adrian, Army of the Potomac.
W. F. King, Adrian, Army of the Potomac.
A. S. Berry, Adrian, Army of the Potomac.
Rev. Daniel E. Brown, Flint, Army of the Cumberland.
Prof. J. C. Plumb, Ypsilanti, Army of the Potomac.
Wm. Patterson, Ypsilanti, Army of the Potomac.
Robert H. Tripp, Hillsdale, Army of the Cumberland.
Rev. H. N. Bissell, Mount Clemens, Army of the Cumberland.
F. S. Walker, Bass Lake, Army of the Cumberland.
Rev. S. E. Wishard, Tecumseh, Army of the Potomac.
Rev. J. W. Allen, Franklin, Army of the Potomac.
Rev. R. R. Salter, D.D., LaSalle, Army of the Mississippi.
Rev. James F. Taylor, Chelsea, Army of the Cumberland.
C. K. Adams, Ann Arbor, Army of the Potomac.
O. C. Thompson, Jr., Detroit, Army of the Potomac.

Rev. John Pierson, Milford, Army of the Potomac.
Rev. J. R. Cordon, Oak Grove, Army of the Potomac.
Rev. Robert H. Conklin, Detroit, Army of the Potomac.
George Andrews, Detroit, Army of the Potomac.
Rev. S. L. Ramsdell, Northville, Army of the Potomac.
Rev. James S. Sutton, Brighton, Army of the Potomac.
Rev. Wm. Harrington, North Adams, Army of the Potomac.
H. B. Denman, Dowagiac, Army of the Potomac.
O. F. Shannon, Fairwater, Wisconsin, Army of the Potomac.
J. P. Garvin, M.D., Kendalville, Indiana, Army of the Potomac.
Rev. O. H. Spoor, Vermontville, Army of the Potomac.
Daniel W. Church, Vermontville, Army of the Potomac.
Rev. E. H. Day, Otsego, Army of the Mississippi.
Rev. Thomas Lowrie, Stratford, C. W., Potomac.
Rev. E. J. Howes, Sylvanus, Mississippi.
Rev. J. A. Ranney, Sturgis, Cumberland.
Prof. O. M. Currier, Olivet, Cumberland.
Prof. H. E. Whipple, Hillsdale, Potomac.
Rev. Mr. Taylor, Tecumseh, Potomac.
All of which is respectfully submitted.

E. C. WALKER, *Chairman.*
CHARLES F. CLARK, *Secretary.*
HENRY P. BALDWIN, *Treasurer.*
DAVID PRESTON,
CALEB IVES,
FRANCIS RAYMOND,
J. S. VERNOR,
Army Com. of the U. S. Christian Com. for Michigan.

VOLUNTEER SURGEONS.

There were times during the war when battles came thick and fast; when rebel bullets felled men like grain in harvest; when the Medical Department of the Government, with all its accustomed foresight and immense resources, with vast preparations to meet coming emergencies, failed in supplying the demand for surgeons in the field, and when the wounded were threatened with extreme suffering; but this deficiency was readily and cheerfully supplied by the medical men of the land. The surgeons of Michigan, without fee or proffer of reward, and at much sacrifice, never failed in promptly and substantially responding on these occasions.

The following extract from a report made in 1864 by Dr. Joseph Tunnicliff, of Jackson, then State agent at Washington, to the Adjutant-General, sets forth their readiness for this service:

"The Potomac Army, under command of Lieutenant-General Grant, crossed the Rapidan May 5, 1864, and from that day onward to about the 10th day of June, there occurred a nearly continuous succession of battles, so frequent that it is a common remark of the soldiers returned from that campaign that it seemed to them like *one continuous battle.*

"Certain it is that the entire region, from the Rapidan to Cold Harbor, was a continuous battle-ground. Three hundred thousand men, in daily and nightly conflict for thirty-five days, produced of necessity a host of wounded, who demanded from not only the Government but the people every possible assistance.

"Not only the Government ambulances and wagons but every other possible means of transportation which could be devised were resorted to by the sick and wounded to reach Fredericksburg, the newly-established base and depot of supplies.

"On the 12th day of May I received from you, General, on behalf of the Governor, the following telegram:

"'To J. Tunnicliff, Jr., *Michigan State Agent:*

"'The Governor directs that you make every exertion to take care of the Michigan wounded soldiers. Employ sufficient assistance to do so, and use what money may be necessary. Should you need any number of assistants from the State, inform by telegraph, and acknowledge the receipt of this dispatch by telegraph.'

"Upon receipt of the above, and after consultation with General Joseph K. Barnes, Surgeon-General—who, permit me to add, is precisely the right man in the right place—I dispatched the following reply:

"'General Robertson—*Sir:* Your telegram is received. Large provision has already been made by the Surgeon-General and the various sanitary commissions to meet the requirements. I have forwarded Mrs. Brainard and Miss Wheelock, with three assistants and twenty boxes of sanitary stores, to Fredericksburg, on the 10th instant. The Surgeon-General directs me to say that he will accept the services of ten (10) experienced surgeons, fully equipped for ten (10) days' service in the field. Direct them to report at this office. I have made provision to have them forwarded.'

"It is with no ordinary pride that I record the fact, that in response to this invitation, thirty-three surgeons, with their assistants, left their business and the comforts of home to volunteer their services, without compensation, to aid their suffering countrymen at this trying period, and among them are many of the most eminent surgeons of our State. I deem it but just that I should append their names:

"Drs. Alonzo B. Palmer, Ann Arbor; D. L. Davenport, E. M. Clark, Detroit; Edward Cox, Z. L. Slater, Battle Creek; C. F. Ashley, W. G. Cox, A. F. Kinney, Ypsilanti; W. B. Smith, Ann Arbor; Gordon Chittock, F. M. Reasnor, Jackson; R. B. Gates, George Barnes, Chelsea; S. C. Willie, East Saginaw; M. F. Baldwin, Flint; Stephen Griggs, E. W. Goodwin, Detroit; E. Church, Marshall; R. H. Davis, Mason; James C. Willson, Flint; H. C. Farrand, East Saginaw; J. E. Smith, Portland; John Smith, Pontiac; J. E. Wilson, Rochester; F. B. Galbraith, C. C. Jerome, Port Huron; O. F. Burroughs, Galesburg; J. P. Nash, Marshall; W. L. Stillwell, Kalamazoo; S. Lathrop, Pine Burr; H. C. Fairbank, Grand Blanc; E. R. Ellis, and L. DePuy, Grand Rapids.

"Thousands of the soldiers of our army—for their labors were not restricted to the soldiers of our State—will remember so long as the pulses of life flow, with grateful hearts, the unselfish devotion and skill with which this body of volunteer surgeons labored to relieve them.

"They were not all assigned to duty at Fredericksburg; for, as the army advanced, some of them were sent to the White House, and many of them to City Point. Most of them remained so long as their services were needed, and I regret to add that a number of them returned in a greatly impaired state of health.

"The following young gentlemen, students of medicine and surgery, forwarded by the citizens of Ann Arbor, reported as volunteer dressers, June 1st, were accepted by the Surgeon-General, and sent to duty in hospitals at City Point: Messrs. O. Marshall, M. O. Bently, P. Martin, J. K. Johnson, and D. V. Dean. They all did *well*—indeed, most of them were so well liked by the medical officers in charge that they were soon employed as assistant surgeons, and placed in charge of surgical wards. It may be well to add here that these young men had nearly completed their course of study preparatory to graduation. The people of Ann Arbor may well feel proud of their contribution. It was what money could not purchase."

SOLDIERS' VOTE IN THE FIELD.

In accordance with an act of the Legislature, approved February 5th, 1864, to enable the qualified electors of this State in the military service to vote at certain elections, the same were held amongst the Michigan troops in the service of the United States on the 7th day of November, 1864. They took place under the supervision of the commissioners appointed in the following letter of the Executive, and were conducted in compliance with the instructions therein contained:

STATE OF MICHIGAN, EXECUTIVE OFFICE,
LANSING, *October* 14, 1864.

The several commissioners appointed and commissioned under the act entitled "An act to enable the qualified electors of the State in the military service to vote at certain elections, and to amend sections 45 and 61 of chapter 6 of the compiled laws," are directed immediately to make and file with the Secretary of State the oath of office required by law, and on or before the 25th day of October instant to report at the office of the Adjutant-General in Detroit, where the necessary poll-books, blank forms, certificates, and instructions, together with copies of the law, will be furnished them. Having been so furnished, the commissioners will immediately proceed to the places where the work assigned them is to be performed. In the performance of their duties they will take the oath of office as the guide, and will do their duty "impartially, fully, and without reference to political preferences or results." It will be proper for them to carry printed ballots with them for the use of the electors of whatever party; but the act forbids them to attempt in any manner to influence or control the vote of any soldier.

Such printed ballots may also be left at the office of the Adjutant-General in Detroit, to be delivered to the commissioners, or they may be delivered directly to the commissioners themselves. In the apportionment of the work it has been found very difficult to make it equal or even to cover the whole ground. The commissioners are therefore required, if necessary, to assist each other, and wherever small bodies of Michigan troops are found with whom no commissioner is present to act as such. The work is apportioned among the commissioners as follows:

ARMY OF THE POTOMAC.

David B. Harrison, Mason, 26th infantry, 1st division, 2d army corps, near Petersburg, Va.

M. D. Hamilton, Monroe, 7th infantry, 2d division, 2d army corps, and company B, 2d U. S. S. S., 1st division, 3d army corps, near Petersburg, Va.

Edwin C. Hinsdale, Detroit, 5th infantry, 3d division, 2d army corps, and companies C, I, and K, 1st U. S. S. S., in the same division, near Petersburg, Va.

John S. Estabrook, East Saginaw, 1st and 16th infantry, 1st division, 5th army corps, near Petersburg, Va.

William W. Wright, Livonia, 24th infantry, 3d division, 5th army corps, near Petersburg, Va.

William Winegar, Grass Lake, 2d, 8th, and 17th infantry, 1st division, 9th army corps, near Petersburg, Va.

Joseph Warren, Detroit, 20th and 27th infantry and 1st sharpshooters, 1st division, 9th army corps, near Petersburg, Va.

Jacob Kanouse, Cohoctah, 1st and 5th cavalry, 1st division, cavalry corps, in the Shenandoah Valley.

Martin Gray, Saline, 6th and 7th cavalry, 1st division, cavalry corps, in the Shenandoah Valley.

Andrew Robinson, Sharon, one company 1st cavalry, and one company 26th infantry, and U. S. hospitals, at Alexandria, Va.

Charles Betts, Burr Oak, 13th and 14th batteries, Fort Foot, Maryland, and hospitals in Washington.

ARMY OF THE CUMBERLAND.

Asher E. Mather, Pontiac, 9th and 22d infantry, General Thomas' Headquarters, near Atlanta, Ga.

William A. Robinson, Grand Rapids, 10th and 14th infantry, 2d division, 14th army corps, near Atlanta, Ga.

Henry L. Hall, Hillsdale, 18th infantry, 4th division, 20th army corps, near Decatur, Ala.

John C. Laird, Mendon, 19th infantry and battery I, 3d division, 20th army corps, near Atlanta, Ga.

L. M. S. Smith, Grand Haven, 13th and 21st infantry, engineer brigade, Lookout Mountain, Tenn.

David Horton, Adrian, 4th cavalry, 2d division, cavalry corps, near Atlanta, Ga.

John McNeil, Port Huron, 2d cavalry, 1st division, cavalry corps, near Franklin, Tenn.

Albert Miller, Bay City, batteries E and D, battery E at Nashville, Tenn., battery D at Murfreesborough, Tenn., and the hospitals at Nashville.

E. D. W. Burtch, Lansing, 1st engineers and mechanics, Cartersville, Ga.

Asa Bunnell, Lyons, company D, 66th Illinois volunteers, and companies B and H, 44th Illinois volunteers, near Atlanta, Ga.

John H. Richardson, Tuscola, 29th infantry, Nashville, Tenn.

ARMY OF THE TENNESSEE.

William Sinclair, Jonesville, 15th infantry, 2d division, 15th army corps, near Atlanta, Ga.

Thaddeus G. Smith, Fentonville, batteries B and C, 16th army corps, battery B, at Rome, Ga., and battery C, at East Point, Ga.

Sylvester Higgins, Charlotte, batteries H and K, 17th army corps, near Atlanta, Ga.

James J. Hogaboom, Hudson, 23d and 25th infantry, and battery F, 2d division, 23d army corps, near Decatur, Ga.

William Hulsart, Romeo, 8th cavalry, Nicholasville, Ky., and batteries L and M, 23d army corps, Cumberland Gap, Tenn.

M. S. Bowen, Coldwater, 9th cavalry, cavalry division, 23d army corps, near Atlanta, Ga.

Henry H. Holt, Muskegon, 10th cavalry, cavalry division, 23d army corps, Strawberry Plain, Tenn.

William A. House, Kalamazoo, cavalry division, 23d army corps, Louisa, Ky.

ARMY OF THE GULF.

Warren S. Crippen, Schoolcraft, 6th heavy artillery, near Mobile, and battery G, New Orleans.

Levi Sparks, Niles, 12th infantry, 2d division, 7th army corps, Duvall's Bluff, Ark.

Nathan H. Bitely, Lawton, 3d cavalry, at Duvall's Bluff, Ark.

William F. Neil, Battle Creek, Merrill Horse, at Duvall's Bluff.

S. O. Kingsbury, Grand Rapids, 3d infantry, Nashville.

W. Y. Rumney, Detroit, 4th infantry, Nashville.

William B. Williams, Allegan, 28th infantry, Nashville.

Josiah Turner, Owosso, hospitals at Annapolis, Baltimore, Philadelphia, and York, Penn.

Weston Flint, hospitals at St. Louis, Mo.

Caleb Clark, hospitals at Washington, and Frederick, Md.

D. O. Farrand, hospitals at Detroit.

AUSTIN BLAIR.

The result of the vote for Presidential electors was as follows:

REPUBLICAN.		DEMOCRATIC.	
Robert R. Beecher	9,402	Samuel T. Douglas	2,959
Thomas D. Gilbert	9,402	Rix Robinson	2,959
Frederick Waldorf	9,402	Henry Hart	2,959
Marsh Giddings	9,402	Royal T. Twombly	2,920
Christian Eberbach	9,402	D. Darwin Hughes	2,959
Perry Hannah	9,402	John Lewis	2,959
Omar D. Conger	9,402	Michael E. Crofoot	2,942
George W. Peck	9,402	Richard Edwards	2,935

The number of imperfect votes was 47.

The vote for Governor was—Henry H. Crapo, Republican, 9,612, and William M. Fenton, Democrat, 2,992.

The infantry regiments which did not vote were the 10th, 11th, 13th, 14th, and 21st; of the cavalry, the 1st, 4th, 6th, and 9th, and of the light artillery, battery G.

RECEPTION OF TROOPS.

Early in June, 1865, and prior to the return to the State of the first troops from the field, a meeting was held in the city of Detroit for the purpose of taking measures to provide for the returning Michigan regiments such refreshments and attention as they might stand in need of on their arrival in the city, and the following committees were appointed:

Committee of Reception.—Ladies—Mrs. Brent, T. K. Adams, Silas Holmes, Walter Ingersoll, John Palmer, J. S. Farrand, L. B. Willard, Jabez Holmes, L. S. Trowbridge, Slocum, and A. C. McGraw. Gentlemen—Rev. George Taylor, Messrs. J. W. Farrell, Ed. Wetmore, W. S. Penfield, F. Wetmore, T. K. Adams, George W. Hudson, Jabez Holmes, E. C. Walker, George Sheley, and H. M. Wright.

Committee of Finance.—Messrs. E. B. Ward, David Preston, C. H. Buhl, John Owen, C. C. Trowbridge, R. N. Rice, Mark Flanigan, W. K. Muir, Edmund Trowbridge, and Ira Davis.

Mr. H. R. Johnson was selected as purveyor and superintendent of tables, and proved the right man in the right place, performing much service and to the satisfaction of all concerned.

By the gratuitous and attentive services of these committees, involving much labor, both early and late, aided by a number of ladies and gentlemen, and sustained by the liberal contributions of the citizens, so generously made, the object was most successfully accomplished, and from June 4th, 1865, down to June 10th, 1866, 14,510 Michigan and 3,506 Wisconsin troops had been received and entertained.

R. N. Rice, Esq., Superintendent of the Michigan Central Railroad, with his accustomed liberality and kindness, permitted the committees to use the upper story of the freight house of the Michigan Central Railroad, which was properly fitted up as a dining hall and appropriately decorated.

During the whole period in which regiments arrived in Detroit, the Rev. George Taylor, of the Methodist Episcopal Church, and formerly chaplain in the 8th Michigan infantry, an agent of the Christian Commission, was permitted by that association to devote his time to the returning troops. He was most attentive, seldom failing to be present on their arrival, taking the management of their reception, and rendering efficient services. Ever ready with a warm and enthusiastic welcome, which our Michigan men as well as those of Wisconsin will long remember.

At Jackson, a rendezvous for returned troops, similar arrangements were generously and liberally made by the citizens, and during the time specified above 10,659 Michigan troops had been received and entertained in a like manner as at Detroit.

Most of these troops arriving in Detroit came via the splendid Detroit and Cleveland line of steamers, then consisting of the Morning Star, (since lost,) Captain E. R. Viger, and the City of Cleveland, Captain William McKay. The kindness extended to so many regiments of Michigan and Wisconsin troops, and especially to returning sick and disabled soldiers, on every occasion by their officers and owners, have most positively identified these steamers with the history of Michigan and Wisconsin troops. Many thousands of them will look back with grateful memory to the time when, weary, dusty, and longing for home and friends, their eyes first caught a glimpse of them and the blue, cooling waters of Lake Erie.

PRESENTATION OF COLORS.

The presentation of the colors of Michigan regiments to the State, which took place in Detroit on the 4th of July, 1866, was an occasion of no ordinary interest to the inhabitants of that city and the people of the State generally. In the Adjutant-General's report for that year is found the following notices of these ragged but interesting standards:

"Next of interest to the return to the State of the men themselves who have so nobly established and sustained its reputation in the field, and so conspicuously aided in the salvation of the nation, is the return of the colors under which their services were so bravely and faithfully performed and so successfully consummated.

"These tattered but honored banners are the cherished and venerated emblems of great public services rendered by the soldiers of the State to the Republic, and are universally acknowledged as the symbols of regimental bravery, individual courage, loyalty, and patriotism; and are recognized as tokens of fraternal associations, formed and cemented in trying times and under most extraordinary circumstances, enduring while life lasts.

"They are, aside from that, indelibly stamped on the hearts of the people, the most forcible mementos of the gallant regiments that so heroically upheld and so persistently stood by them and the country, even in the darkest days of the war.

"They were as little specs in the long lines of the great American armies, yet they were often watched in the advancing columns with intense anxiety, but with strong confidence and hope by the greatest generals of the land.

"To bear them aloft was a signal for rebel bullets, often bringing swift and certain death, but they were never trailed in the dust nor lacked a gallant bearer. On them many a noble son of Michigan has looked his last and bade farewell to life."

On the 19th of May preceding an order was issued from the State Military Department, by direction of the Governor, determining the 4th of July for the presentation of these colors, and extending a cordial invitation to the officers and soldiers of all the regiments to be present. Following is an extract from that order, which finds a fitting place here:

"The appropriateness of setting apart the national birthday for that purpose will be fully recognized and appreciated. Its hallowed memories will remind the patriots present of the gallant struggle of their patriotic forefathers in establishing the Government in the defence and maintenance of which they have been so successfully instrumental.

"The State will be highly honored in receiving on that great national day the cherished evidences of the manhood, courage, and patriotism of its soldiers, and of their eminently gallant and meritorious services to the Republic in its great and successful battle for national existence, and it will proudly accept and faithfully retain and preserve them as sacred mementos thereof and of the loyalty and patriotism of its people.

"The congregated emblems of National and State prowess, and of regimental bravery and fraternal associations there presented, will revive in the mind of every soldier recollections of great and gallant deeds, of days and nights fraught with anxiety, doubt, danger, and death, of sacrifices to patriotism, of hairbreadth escapes, of attacks, of repulses, of sad defeats, of glorious victories, of long and weary marches, of hunger, thirst, and cold, and of sorrow and sadness for fallen comrades; but all will look upon them with reverential pride, and recognize them as having been their guiding star in many brilliant but sanguinary conflicts, having followed them in the victorious charge of the assaulting column, having from them received silent directions when all orders were lost in the din and confusion of contending armies, and having under their tattered but glorious stars and stripes battled long and bravely for the right."

On the 19th of June, in accordance with instructions from the War Department, Major John H. Knight, chief mustering officer, addressed the following letter to the Adjutant-General of the State, at which time the flags were officially delivered at the military headquarters of the State:

OFFICE CHIEF MUSTERING OFFICER,
DETROIT, MICH., *June* 19, 1866.

BRIG. GEN. JOHN ROBERTSON,
Adjutant General State of Michigan, Detroit, Michigan:

GENERAL:—All the regiments sent from the State of Michigan to put down the rebellion of the Southern States having now been mustered out of service, paid off, and disbanded, the time has arrived when I should, in compliance with orders from the War Department, deliver to the Governor of the State the flags turned over to me by the officers of the disbanded regiments.

I have the honor, this day, to deliver to you (you being at the head of the State Military Bureau and its chief officer) all of them in my possession.

Please find a list of the flags inclosed. In turning them over to you I am sensibly reminded that they are the flags under which so many brave and successful deeds have been performed—so many valuable lives given up in the cause of the Union and republican liberty, and such beneficial results obtained.

In the history of the world we are unable to find where mankind was engaged in a better or more glorious cause, or where the results have been more important to the cause of humanity and good government; and if the sons of Michigan have been called upon to give up their lives, and part with the dearest earthly objects, those whose immediate loss has been great thereby have a sweet consolation in the fact that their blood is the seed from which will grow up fruits dear to succeeding millions of freemen, and who will not fail to render that devout homage to their memory whenever they shall gather around the Altars of Liberty to offer up thanks to Him who is great over all, for the glorious heritage which those gallant defenders have so permanently secured. They will, therefore, live in their deeds, whilst a single pillar of the Republic stands. Those who under these flags survived the terrible battles which have been fought during the late rebellion, in the cause of our great and powerful Government, will see and enjoy the rich fruits of their heroic deeds, and with full hearts will join their fellow-countrymen in rendering tribute to the memory of their comrades who fell in the bloody strife. And when all who have participated in the war for the Union have passed away, succeeding generations will catch up the songs of praise now being sung over the glories achieved, and will chant them with renewed and grateful strains through all time to come.

It was very proper that orders were made to deposit these flags with the State authorities. Torn and tattered into mere strips though they be, yet each piece will be most sacredly preserved by each succeeding State administration, and upon all great national occasions when they are brought forth, they will call together not only those who, under their folds battled for the preservation of the Republic, but lovers of liberty from all parts of the State; and they will continually remind the people of the priceless heritage which has been *secured* to themselves and to coming generations. Only those who carried them through the frightful scenes of suffering and death can fully realize the terrible ordeals through which our great nation has been preserved, yet all will be reminded how great is the boon of constitutional freedom; and the warning they will exhibit to treason will be sufficient to stay its hand and compel obedience when inclination would direct acts of rebellion.

By depositing these flags with the State authorities in each State, the authorities of the Government have placed therein a monument in memory of its glories which will be most cherished, and whenever beheld by the people will far surpass, in the feelings of veneration which they will call forth, all the pillars of marble or granite which human genius could build. It will be remembered that they have passed through the scenes of strife, and that they have been carried by the hands of the brave men themselves, who fought and died for our national liberties. It will be seen that on them is inscribed the names of the battles passed through, where the fate of liberty was staked and decided; and with what feelings of reverence will these strips of bunting be looked upon by the father, mother, brother, or sister, whose son or brother marched to victory or glorious death under their folds. Whilst all patriots on viewing these battle-flags will remember and mourn the loss of life and regret the vast expenditures which have been made to preserve our liberties, yet all will rejoice over the glorious results which have been achieved.

Permit me to congratulate, through you, the people of Michigan, for the brilliant and conspicuous part performed by Michigan regiments in the late war for the Union. I believe there is no blot upon their record, but all is bright, conspicuous and glorious, whilst an extraordinary number of personal distinctions shine upon the pages.

Expressing my sensibility of the fortunate honor in being the instrument of the Government for delivering to the State these sacred colors,

I remain your most obedient servant,

JOHN H. KNIGHT,
Brevet Major U. S. Army,
Chief Mustering Officer, Michigan.

The invitation extended by the Governor to the soldiers of Michigan to be present, was responded to in keeping with the great love which they have always borne for the old flag, under all circumstances, and they rallied in great numbers under the war-worn folds of their old banner as in times gone by.

On the day set apart for the purpose, the colors referred to were formally presented by the respective regiments, through his Excellency, to the State.

"I saw the soldiers come to-day
From battle-fields afar;
No conqueror rode before their way,
On his triumphal car;
But Captains, like themselves, on foot,
And banners sadly torn,
All grandly eloquent, though mute,
In pride and glory borne.

"Those banners soiled with dust and smoke,
And rent by shot and shell,
That through the serried phalanx broke,
What terrors could they tell!
What tales of sudden pain and death—
In every cannon's boom—
When e'en the bravest held his breath,
And waited for his doom."

The Hon. M. I. Mills, Mayor of Detroit, presided on the occasion, and, in a most happy speech, welcomed the troops present.

The ceremonies were commenced with prayer, by the Rt. Rev. Bishop McCoskry. The flags were presented on behalf of the troops by General O. B. Wilcox, in a happily conceived and stirring speech, and were received in an eloquent and appropriate address by Governor Crapo, and the ceremonies were closed by the Rev. Dr. Duffield, with an impressive benediction.

It is proper and just to mention that the action of the State authorities was cheerfully aided and most liberally sustained by the citizens of Detroit, and after the presentation, the returned troops partook of a substantial repast, prepared for them by the people, and were waited upon at the tables by over three hundred ladies and a large number of gentlemen.

The affair was graced and honored by the largest and most magnificent celebration ever had in Michigan, and was participated in by the most numerous assemblage of people, from all parts of the State, ever congregated within its borders.

One hundred and twenty-three of these flags were presented, belonging to the various regiments, and are now deposited in the archives of Michigan, there to be sacredly kept and carefully preserved. Around them cluster hallowed memories of companions in arms, of regimental bravery, and State pride, of national grandeur and prowess, of individual heroism, of fallen comrades and family bereavements, and of a nation saved.

THE HARPER HOSPITAL.

In 1863 representations were made to the Government by Colonel Charles S. Tripler, surgeon United States Army, then United States Medical Director in the State, that the erection of a general hospital at Detroit, for the reception and care of sick and wounded Michigan soldiers, was an absolute necessity. Accompanying these representations was an urgent request for immediate action in the matter. Colonel Tripler was ably aided in this effort by Colonel George W. Lee, chief quartermaster, and Dr. D. O. Farrand, assistant surgeon, United States army. The object had also the influence and recommendation of the Governor and military authorities of the State.

After much laborious correspondence and provoking delays, the authority was finally obtained, under an order from the Secretary of War, and the work on Harper Hospital was commenced early in 1864, under the superintendence of Colonel Lee.

Instead of constructing the building with three stories or more, as had usually been the custom, the hospital was made up of eleven one-story buildings, with the offices and dispensary in the centre, and the whole range connected with each other by a covered aisle in the rear, rendering ingress and egress easy and comfortable.

It cost about sixty thousand dollars, aside from the grounds, the use of which was given gratis by the trustees of the Harper Hospital Association. It had a capacity of about eight hundred patients. Particular attention having been given in its construction to ventilation and drainage, with superior water arrangements, coupled with exceedingly capable management, it was known as one of the most complete, comfortable, and best-regulated general hospitals in the West.

When completed, Dr. Farrand was placed in charge, assisted by Dr. W. A. Chandler, Dr. William C. Catlin, Dr. E. W. Jenks, and Dr. G. W. Fitzpatrick.

Early in the spring of 1865 Dr. Farrand was relieved by Dr. Byron Stanton, a surgeon of volunteers, who remained in charge only a few weeks, when he resigned to accept a position in an insane asylum in Ohio.

Dr. Farrand was again placed in charge, and continued on duty until in June or July, when he was, at his own request, transferred to Fort Wayne, near Detroit, to take charge of the hospital at that post.

Dr. Wynkoop, a surgeon of volunteers, from Philadelphia, succeeded Dr. Farrand, and remained in charge until the close of the hospital, in December, 1865. It was, soon after, given by the Government to the trustees of the Harper Hospital, a corporate body, having in view the establishment of a hospital by that name, for charitable purposes, on condition that sufficient accommodation should be at all times furnished as a "Soldiers' Home," for the invalid and destitute Michigan soldiers and sailors, and it is now being in part used for that purpose.

The erection of this hospital, at that time affording so much comfort and aid to the sick and wounded who needed it so much, should be accepted by the people of Michigan as a most favorable and generous recognition of the great claims of the State and her soldiers upon the Government, and the efforts made to secure it by the gentlemen named, should entitle them to the grateful remembrance and thanks of every soldier, and to the kindest consideration of their friends.

THE SOLDIERS AND SAILORS' MONUMENT.

The people of Michigan, gratefully appreciating the services and sacrifices of her sons who gave up the dearest boon to man, life, and of those who risked it in the same glorious cause, early in the war determined to perpetuate their memories and great deeds by erecting a monument chisseled from the white marble or the beautiful granite of America, magnificently and appropriately ornamented with figures of bronze or marble.

This measure was inaugurated at a public meeting held by citizens of Detroit on July 20th, 1861, when it was resolved to erect a monument to the noble dead who had fallen in the war. Judge B. F. H. Witherell, Col. E. Backus, U. S. A., Messrs. Charles C. Trowbridge, J. W. Tillman, and Col. H. A. Morrow were appointed a committee to carry out the resolution. This committee met on the 6th day of August following, and organized by the appointment of Judge Witherell chairman, J. W. Tillman treasurer, and T. W. Palmer secretary.

After several meetings and consultations with friends of the measure it was deemed best to postpone immediate action and await the termination of the war and the crushing out of the rebellion. This desirable result having been reached, a meeting was held in Detroit on July 20th, 1865, when it was resolved to refer the whole matter to a committee of seven, with instructions to prepare and report at a subsequent meeting a full and complete plan of organization, and also to present the names of suitable persons to fill the positions or offices they might recommend. Messrs. J. W. Tillman, C. C. Trowbridge, John Owen, J. F. Conover, T. W. Palmer, B. F. H. Witherell, and John Robertson were appointed such committee, with power to call the next meeting.

A meeting was held on the 11th of August following, when the committee in their report recommended that $50,000 be raised by subscription, and submitted a plan of organization and labor, naming as a board of directors for the management of the business of the association—

Hon. B. F. H. Witherell, Detroit.
Hon. C. C. Trowbridge, Detroit.
J. W. Tillman, Esq., Detroit.
Gen. H. A Morrow, Detroit.
T. W. Palmer, Esq., Detroit.
Hon. H. P. Baldwin, Detroit.
Hon. John Owen, Detroit.
Hon. Henry N. Walker, Detroit.
W. A. Butler, Esq., Detroit.
B. Vernor, Esq., Detroit.
C. F. Clark, Esq., Detroit.
Hon. W. A. Howard, Detroit.
Gen. John Robertson, Detroit.
Hon. J. F. Joy, Detroit.
Major Gen. E. O. C. Ord, Detroit.
Major Gen. O. B. Wilcox, Detroit.
Major Gen. A. S. Williams, Detroit.
His Excellency Gov. H. H. Crapo, Flint.
Hon. E. H. Thompson, Flint.
Ex-Gov. Austin Blair, Jackson.
Hon. James Birney, Bay City.
Hon. E. J. Penniman, Plymouth.
James Burtenshaw, Esq., Ontonagon.
S. F. Page, Esq., Ionia.
Hon. Giles Hubbard, Mount Clemens.
John A. Kerr, Esq., Lansing.
Dr. Potter, East Saginaw.
Hon. Peter White, Marquette.
Hon. T. D. Gilbert, Grand Rapids.
Hon. Hezekiah G. Wells, Kalamazoo.
Hon. R. C. Paine, Niles.
Hon. W. S. Maynard, Ann Arbor.
Talcott E. Wing, Esq., Monroe.
Hon. R. R. Beecher, Adrian.

W. C. McConnell, Esq., Pontiac.
Witter J. Baxter, Esq., Jonesville.
Hon. Charles T. Gorham, Marshall.
Hon. John R. Kellogg, Allegan.
Hon. T. W. Ferry, Grand Haven.
Hon. Edwin Moore, Three Rivers.
Hon. A. H. Morrison, St. Joseph.
Hon. W. L. Bancroft, St. Clair county.
Hon. George Redfield, Cass county.
Morgan Bates, Esq., Grand Traverse.
R. Shelton, Esq., Houghton.
Wm. H. Maltby, Esq., Sheboygan.
Wm. McPherson, Esq., Livingston county.
Hon. Chauncey Davis, Muskegon.
Hon. G. T. Wendell, Mackinac.
Hon. Alex. Campbell, Marquette.
Hon. H. A. Waldron, Hillsdale county.
Hon. H. A. Divine, Montcalm county.
Major A. B. Watson, Newaygo county.
D. Bethune Duffield, Esq., Detroit.
J. F. Conover, Esq., Detroit.
A. Marxhausen, Esq., Detroit.
M. Kramer, Esq., Detroit.
Theodore Romeyn, Esq., Detroit.
C. I. Walker, Esq., Detroit.
Gen. W. A. Throop, Detroit.
Hon. G. V. N. Lothrop, Detroit.
Hon. Wilson Green, Oceana county.
T. W. Flanners, Esq., Ontonagon county.
John Moore, Esq., Saginaw county.
Hon. G. W. Pack, Huron county.
Hon. Luther Smith, Gratiot county.
T. C. Owen, Esq., St. Clair county.
Hon. J. K. Boies, Lenawee county.
Hon. Hugh McCurdy, Shiawassee county.
Col. W. L. Stoughton, St. Joseph county.
Milton Bradley, Esq., Isabella county.
Capt. Roe, steamer Michigan.
Hon. C. A. Stacey, Lenawee county.
Hon. W. G. Beckwith, Cass county.
Hon. S. M. Cutcheon, Washtenaw county.
J. B. Crippen, Esq., Branch county.
Hon. James Armitage, Monroe county.
Hon. N. G. Isbell, Wayne county.
Hon. Jas. B. Walker, Grand Traverse co.
Hon. M. E. Crofoot, Oakland county.
Hon. James A. Sweezey, Barry county.
J. E. Fisher, Esq., Leelenaw county.
Hon. Delos Filer, Manistee county.
Hon. Perry Hannah, Grand Traverse co.
Hon. P. B. Barbeau, Chippewa county.
Hon. Townsend North, Tuscola county.
Hon. Edwin H. Lothrop, St. Joseph county.
J. S. Farrand, Esq., Detroit.
Hon. V. P. Collier, Calhoun county.
Jesse Crowell, Esq., Calhoun county.
Hon. Charles Mears, Mason county.
John Larken, Esq., Midland county.
John L. Woods, Esq., Salinac county.
Major Gen. Pierce, Kent county.
S. W. Hill, Esq., Keewenaw county.
E. S. Ingalls, Esq., Menominee county.
John Roost, Esq., Ottawa county.
Hon. H A. Shaw, Eaton county.
Hon. George Luther, Ottawa county.
Niel Gray, Esq., Macomb county.
Col. J. R. White, Lapeer county.
Hon. P. Hayden, Van Buren county.
Charles Kipp, Esq., Clinton county.
S. M. Seely, Branch county.

From this body the committee designated as the officers of the association Hon. B. F. H. Witherell, president; Gen. H. A. Morrow, vice president; J. W. Tillman, Esq., treasurer; Hon. John Owen, auditor; T. W. Palmer, Esq., secretary, and J. W. Romeyn, Esq., associate secretary.

The committee also named as the executive committee Hon. C. C. Trowbridge, Hon. John Owen, Hon. H. P. Baldwin, Hon. H. N. Walker, J. F. Conover, Esq., and C. J. Walker, Esq., all of Detroit; Ex-Governor Blair, of Jackson; Hon. E. H. Thompson, of Flint, and Hon. S. M. Cutcheon, of Ypsilanti, with the president, treasurer, and secretary *ex officio*.

On June 26, 1867, a meeting was held with Judge Witherell (president) in the chair, when Mr. Trowbridge submitted a report, which he had been selected to prepare, on the relative merits of the various designs sent in by different competing artists.

On the morning of the 27th Judge Witherell died, and the association was called upon to deplore the loss of its original founder, an officer peculiarly interested in its patriotic work, and who gave to it the last hour of his life.

On the 28th of June the various designs, plans, and estimates were examined by the Board of Directors, and their relative merits fully and fairly discussed. On coming together in the afternoon of that day a ballot was had to determine the choice of the directors, when it was found that decided preference was given to the design by Randolph Rogers, the eminent American sculptor, a native of Michigan, and a citizen of Ann Arbor when a young man, who is also the contractor for the entire work.

The monument, when finished, is to stand about forty-six feet, to be crowned by a colossal statue of Michigan ten feet high, a semi-civilized Indian Queen, with a sword in her right hand and a shield in her left; the figure in motion as if rushing forward in defence of her country. Beneath the plinth on which she stands are stars and wreaths. On the next section in front is the dedication, "Erected by the people of Michigan in honor of the martyrs who fell and the heroes who fought in defence of Liberty and Union." On the left are the arms of the State; on the right are the arms of the United States. On the projecting butments below are four allegorical figures seated. These figures, if standing, would be six and a half feet high, and they represent Victory, Union, Emancipation, and History. On the next section below, standing upon projecting butments are the defenders of Liberty and Union, the representations of the army and navy, four statues, seven feet high, soldiers of infantry, artillery, and cavalry, with a sailor of the navy. Between these statues it is proposed to place *bassi relievi*, provided sufficient funds are obtained to defray the cost. In the meantime the panels may be left vacant without injury to the general effect. In the single panel the artist has sketched Mr. Lincoln holding in one hand the emancipation proclamation, and in the other a pen. On either side of the *bassi relievi* are tablets where may be registered the names of battles or other inscriptions. On the outer pedestals are four eagles. All these figures are to be of the finest bronze.

Mr. Rogers presented an estimate for the work in detail, each part being separately stated, the gross sum being $50,000, aside from the architectural part of granite or marble, which he estimated at $10,000, and a contract was entered into accordingly.

The four allegorical figures embraced in his design are not included in this estimate, and if placed on the structure will increase the cost the amount of their value.

The association was incorporated in 1868 by the Legislature, and its affairs are now managed by a Board of Trustees, composed of John Owen, H. P. Baldwin, Theodore Romeyn, Wm. A. Butler, R. A. Alger, George F. Bagley, James W. Romeyn, Henry N. Walker, Thomas W. Palmer, David Preston, J. F. Conover, C. C. Trowbridge, and G. V. N. Lothrop, of Detroit; Austin Blair, of Jackson, and S. M. Cutcheon, of Ypsilanti.

The officers of the association at present are Charles C. Trowbridge, president; John Owen, vice president; Wm. A. Butler, treasurer; James W. Romeyn, and Thomas W. Palmer, secretaries. Committee on Finance, Henry P. Baldwin, George V. N. Lothrop, and George F. Bagley, of Detroit.

In February, 1866, the Rev. George Taylor was employed as the general soliciting and collecting agent, rendering valuable and faithful service.

In March, 1866, General B. M. Cutcheon, of Manistee, volunteered his services in aid of the measure, giving manly energy and successful effort to the cause.

Nearly sufficient funds are on hand to meet the obligations of the association, and they expect to raise an additional sum, adequate to placing the allegorical figures on the monument, and thus complete the full design of the sculptor.

The ornamental figures are being cast at Munich, and the association expect the monument will be completed by the 4th of July, 1871.

The corner-stone was laid in the city of Detroit on July 4, 1867, by Grand Master S. G. Coffinbury, of the Masonic fraternity, in presence of Grand Commanderies and Grand Lodge of that order, and the Grand

Lodge of the order of Odd Fellows, together with a great many lodges of both orders, several lodges of Good Templars, the United States troops from Forts Wayne and Gratiot, with the State troops of the city, and an immense gathering of people from all parts of the State, while the interest of the occasion was very acceptably increased by the eloquent and appropriate oration of Governor Blair.

CEMETERIES AT GETTYSBURG, SHARPSBURG, AND ANDERSONVILLE.

The State of Michigan has always been ready and prompt to respond to calls made for means to improve cemeteries for the heroic dead of the nation, and to raise permanent works of art and beauty in their honor and to perpetuate their memories.

By an act of the Legislature, approved February 3, 1864, the sum of $3,500 of the war fund was appropriated "for the purpose of paying the proportion of this State of the estimated expense of preparing the ground furnishing the Soldiers' National Cemetery, at Gettysburg, in the State of Pennsylvania, and of making improvements upon that portion thereof which is set apart to this State;" which sum the Governor was authorized to disburse for said purposes.

The Governor was also authorized to appoint a commissioner, whenever and for such time as he might deem necessary, to superintend the disbursement of said appropriation, and to take charge of and represent the interest of this State in said cemetery, under his direction and subject to his control. In accordance with this provision, the Hon. T. W. Ferry was appointed.

By an act of the Legislature, approved March 8th, 1865, the further sum of $2,500 of said war fund was appropriated for the purpose of paying the proportion of the expense of this State in completing and keeping in repair said cemetery.

The cemetery contains 3,559 bodies, of which 979 are in the "unknown" lots, and 2,580 identified, are lying in the State lots. Numerically, Michigan stands *third* in the number slain; and proportionably to population she ranks *first* in this sacrifice to be made memorable forever by a nation's gratitude.

Mr. Ferry closes his final and very able report, made to the Governor in 1864, covering his entire duties, with the following eloquent remarks:

"It will, however, matter little *who* were immediately instrumental in devising and developing the sacred memorial which is to hand down to future generations the lustrous records of patriots who prized country above life.

"*They* will be forgotten, while shaft, and speech, and song shall tell of battle and heroism to ages yet unborn. The decisive contest—the turning strife of the war, from which victory, leaping from field to field, eventuated in peace, national liberty, and reunion—*this*, this alone, will be the enduring, emblazoning chaplet which time shall weave for the gallant heroes who sleep beneath the shadow of the nation's mausoleum at Gettysburg."

The State also appropriated at the session of the Legislature, in 1867, her proportion ($3,344.88) for the purchase, preparation, and care of the Antietam National Cemetery at Sharpsburg, Md. The Governor appointed John I. Bagley, Esq., as trustee to represent the State in the corporation formed for the purpose named.

In this resting place Michigan numbers 137 of the heroic dead.

Most favorable locations for the dead of Michigan have been secured by these gentlemen in both cemeteries, and every duty confided to them has been most faithfully executed.

Since the termination of the war, the General Government, through the Quartermaster's Department, has been making most praiseworthy and very successful efforts to gather together the bodies of the soldiers who fell in battle, and who died in hospital, in rebel prison, or by the wayside, into the "national cemeteries" designated by the War Department. With much care and great labor the graves have been prepared and marked with tablets, giving name, company, and regiment. These cemeteries have been enclosed, the grounds laid out and beautified, and persons appointed to protect them from desecration. Proper records, as far as practicable, have been made of those buried in each, and they have been made up in printed volumes, copies of which have been furnished to the various States.

Andersonville, Georgia, a rebel prison pen, associated as it is with the intentional perpetration of the most inhuman barbarities ever committed by a savage or civilized people, is the most noted of the national cemeteries, containing nearly thirteen thousand graves of Union soldiers. Among this number are those of six hundred and twenty-three brave Michigan men, who, sooner than accept the standing proposition to enter the rebel ranks and disown their State and their country, suffered death by starvation, exposure, and every conceivable manner of brutal cruelty inflicted by rebel officers, and with the full knowledge of the Confederate authorities at Richmond.

"Rest on, embalmed and sainted dead,
  Dear as the blood ye gave;
No impious footsteps here shall tread
  The herbage of your grave;
Nor shall your glory be forgot
  While Fame her record keeps,
Or Honor points the hallow'd spot
  Where valor proudly sleeps."

REBEL RAID FROM CANADA.

The State of Michigan, being on the Canadian border, was much harrassed by threatenings of invasion, and at times much exposed to raids of rebel refugees and marauders, who had found a cheerful welcome and congenial companions, with a safe asylum in the provinces, and who were aided in these raids by the Confederate Government at Richmond, and led by its commissioned emissaries, receiving at the same time a hearty encouragement from a very large proportion of the Canadian people, who were in a most unnatural but strong sympathy with the rebellion, and who were ever ready to incite and assist when rebels found it advisable to make incursions into the adjacent States to pillage and destroy.

In the Adjutant-General's report for 1864 is found the following account of a raid made in September of that year, and which is illustrative of the condition of affairs in this respect on the frontier about that time:

"In November, 1863, the War Department was officially notified by the British Minister, Lord Lyons, that from a telegraphic despatch received by him from the Governor-General of Canada there was reason to believe that a plot was on foot, by persons hostile to the United States, who had found an asylum in Canada, to invade the States on that frontier; that they proposed to take possession of some of the steamers on Lake Erie, to surprise Johnson's Island, near Sandusky, and set free the rebel prisoners of war confined there, and proceed with them to attack Buffalo. This information was communicated by the War Department to the Governors of the States bordering on Canada and to the military and civil authorities thereof, and urging them to employ all the means in their power to suppress any attempt to carry the plot into effect. That there was such a scheme on foot, and that it was concocted and put in operation in Canada by the Rebel Government, there can be no doubt, as circumstances have transpired and documentary evidence received during the past year fully confirming it, and that its execution was only prevented at that time by the prompt measures taken by the military authorities in the States referred to, and although their plans were frustrated their determination was still to carry them into effect, and their execution was only deferred until a more favorable opportunity. During the present year the United States military officers, and also the civil and military authorities of the State, have been almost daily in the receipt of rumors and reports from various sources of contemplated raids to be made on American frontier cities and on the shipping of the lakes to burn and destroy, many of which could not be traced to any reliable origin, yet they served to keep up a continual state of excitement and alarm in the cities and villages on the border of the State, and to require the vigilant attention of the authorities, and all the preparations within their power to successfully meet any attempted invasion of the State were made, which were considered at the time ample to repel any force that might be expected of that description. Yet, notwithstanding, there was a distrust and a nervous foreboding of coming mischief amongst the people of the frontier cities and villages. This distrust also prevailed among the railroad agencies and those engaged in the shipping on the lakes, which led to the arming of the community generally as individuals, and of railroad trains and lake and river steamers, and to the establishing of safeguards about private dwellings, public places of business, and railroad depots. This condition of affairs continued; no overt act having been committed, and no visible combination of force having been traced to any locality until the 19th day of September, 1864, when they concluded to make the attempt by seizing the steamer Philo Parsons, belonging to Detroit and running as a passenger boat from that point to Sandusky, in the State of Ohio. On the morning of the day above referred to, four of the raiders, including Bennet G. Burley, one of their apparent leaders, took passage on the said boat at Detroit. On her way down the Detroit river, on her passage to Sandusky, she landed at the Canadian ports of Sandwich and Amherstburg, where the balance of the raiders got on board, the whole, as has since been ascertained, numbering about thirty. The following condensed depositions of W. O. Ashley and D. C. Nichols, belonging to the steamer, taken as evidence on the extradition trial of Burley at Toronto, in Canada, gave a full account of the occurrences on board the Philo Parsons during the time the raiders held possession of her:

"These depositions showed that the steamboat 'Philo Parsons' was owned by the informant Ashley, and other citizens of the United States; that this vessel was a licensed passenger and freight boat, and was plying between the city of Detroit, in the State of Michigan, and the city of Sandusky, in the State of Ohio, and was accustomed to touch in this route at the Canadian port of Amherstburg, and occasionally at Sandwich, and sometimes at Windsor, Canada. Ashley was clerk on board the steamer. On Sunday evening, the 18th of September, 1864, she was lying at the city of Detroit, and the prisoner came on board and said to Ashley that he intended to go down in the morning, and that three of his friends were going with him, and requested the boat might stop at Sandwich to take them. Ashley told the prisoner that if he took the boat at Detroit, and his party were ready, the boat would call for them at Sandwich. The prisoner came on board the next morning, and reminded Ashley of his promise. The boat was stopped at Sandwich, and three persons came on board, without baggage or freight. They were well dressed, in the 'Canadian style.' The prisoner said his friends were taking a pleasure trip, and would probably stop at Kelly's Island. At Amherstburg twenty men or more came on board, roughly dressed, and paid their fare to Sandusky. The only baggage taken on board at Amherstburg was a large old trunk, tied with a cord. In the ordinary course the steamer should have reached Sandusky about five P. M. Neither the prisoner nor his three friends apparently recognized the men who came on board at Amherstburg. The boat reached Kelly's Island about four P. M., and proceeded south from the island toward Sandusky, Kelly's Island being in the State of Ohio, and about five miles from the main shore of the United States. After proceeding about two miles, three men came up to Ashley, drawing revolvers, saying he was a dead man if he offered resistance. Two of them, as Ashley thought, came on board at Sandwich. At this time the prisoner came forward with a revolver in his hand, followed by from twenty-eight to thirty-five men, and leveled the revolver at Ashley, ordering him into the ladies' cabin, where Ashley immediately went, and from which he saw these parties arm themselves from the trunk brought on board at Amherstburg, most of them having two revolvers, and some having hatchets. The prisoner ordered a sulky and some pig iron, which was on deck, to be thrown overboard, which was partly done. Two men guarded Ashley, and they told him they intended to capture the United States steamer 'Michigan,' a war vessel. The prisoner acted as one having authority. His commands were obeyed. Another steamer, called the 'Island Queen,' was seized by the same party, at Middle Bass Island, and the passengers were brought as prisoners on board the 'Philo Parsons.' A person named Captain Bell was of the prisoner's party, and gave some orders. He told Ashley he wanted him in the office. Ashley went there with him and the prisoner. Ashley requested permission to take off the boat's books. They refused. Ashley then said he had some private promissory notes, amounting to about two thousand dollars. The prisoner took them, looked at them, and said he could not collect them, and returned them to Ashley. Bell then said to Ashley: "We want your money." He and the prisoners then had revolvers in their hands. Ashley swore he was in bodily fear, but did not consider his life in danger, if he did their bidding. He opened the money drawer. There was very little money there. The prisoner then said: "You have got more money; let us have it." Ashley took a roll of bills from his vest pocket, and laid it on the desk. Bell took part and the prisoner took part, and they took the money in the drawer (about $10) between them. In the roll of bills taken by them there was a twenty-dollar note of the United States, commonly called greenbacks, issued by the Secretary of the Treasury. It was in use as lawful current money of the United States at the time. It was legal tender for twenty dollars, and was the property of the owners of the boat. The prisoner took this money, as Ashley swore, against his (Ashley's) will. He was put in bodily fear and danger of his life at the time. Directly after the money was taken Ashley was put on shore at Middle Bass Island, by the prisoner and Bell, and the boat steered for Sandusky, with the Island Queen alongside, which last boat was cast adrift in about half an hour. Some of the party said they intended to release the prisoners on Johnson's Island, which is in the State of Ohio, about two miles from Sandusky. The 'Michigan' was lying off Johnson's Island, supposed to guard it. There were about three thousand prisoners of war there, soldiers of the Confederate States. Ashley stated there was a rebellion going on by the Southern States. He could not tell how many States. Captain Bell appeared to be in command of the party on board of the 'Philo Parsons.' He did not say in Ashley's hearing he was in any service, nor for what purpose he took the boat. There were about twenty-five United States soldiers on board the Island Queen, who were captured. The passengers were not prevented from taking their baggage. Nichols confirmed Ashley's testimony in most of the material particulars. He said that Bell came to him in the pilot house, and said he was a Confederate officer, and seized the boat, and took him (Nichols) a prisoner. But he also said the prisoner seemed to be the leader of them. He did not see the money taken. He heard the prisoner say, when the Island Queen was set adrift, that they had cut her pipes so that she would sink. They had taken every person from on board of her. Afterwards the 'Philo Parsons' was steered back towards Detroit. Before this, however, it seems that some of the passengers who were made prisoners were put on shore on the American territory. When, on the return, they had reached the mouth of the Detroit river, some of the party asked Nichols where they were, and he told them 'in Canadian waters,' and some of them said it was well for some of the vessels near them, or they would board them; and they inquired if a certain banker did not live at Grosse Isle, in the Detroit river; and being told by Nichols that one Ives lived there, they replied if it had not been so late they would go and rob him. A short distance above Amherstburg two men landed in a boat on the Canadian side. At Fighting Island Nichols and others, part of the crews of the 'Philo Parsons' and 'Island Queen' were put on shore, and the boat proceeded to Sandwich. Nichols followed her, and in two hours got to Sandwich, and found her there deserted by the whole party, and a piano-forte, a mirror, and some other articles of furniture belonging to the boat had been landed. Some of Nichols' clothing was also taken away. One of the party wore Nichols' India-rubber coat. The male passengers who were taken were, before they were landed, sworn to keep silent as to the transaction for twenty-four hours. The females were asked to promise to do so, but it was not said in Nichols' hearing why this was done. When the 'Island Queen' was cast adrift they were about fourteen miles from Johnson's Island, as the boat would have gone. When coming up the Detroit river, some of the party said they had not made much by coming down. They had intended to take the 'Michigan' if they could. They had a Confederate flag, and compelled Nichols to assist in raising it on the 'Philo Parsons,' when the boat was on Lake Erie, returning towards the Detroit river. It was put about half-way up the flag-staff."

The complicity of the rebel Government, with its agents, sympathizers, and refugees in Canada, in November, 1863, in concocting a raid on the territory of the United States, is apparent from the date of the following appointment, given by Jefferson Davis to Burley, on the 11th day of September of that year, he undoubtedly being one of the naval officers mentioned in the report of the rebel Secretary of War as having been sent into the British provinces with a large number of commissioned and petty officers, to organize an expedition against "Johnson's Island," during the fall of the year referred to.

That the expedition on board the "Philo Parsons," in September, 1864, was ordered by the rebel Government, there can be no doubt, if credence is given to the following "manifesto" of Jefferson Davis, produced on the extradition trial of Burley before the Canadian court at Toronto, as proof that the acts of said Burley, in connection with that expedition, were performed in obedience to the instructions of the rebel Government, and that he should be treated as a belligerent, and not as a pirate and robber:

"CONFEDERATE STATES OF AMERICA,
"NAVY DEPARTMENT, RICHMOND, *September* 11, 1863.

"SIR:—You are hereby informed that the President has appointed you an acting master in the navy of the Confederate States. You are requested to signify your acceptance or non-acceptance of this appointment; and should you accept, you are to sign, before a magistrate, the oath of office herewith forwarded, and forward the same, with your letter of acceptance, to this Department. Registered No. ——. The lowest number takes rank.

"(Signed,) "S. R. MALLORY,
"*Secretary of Navy.*

"Acting Master BENNET G. BURLEY,
"*C. S. Navy, Richmond, Va.*"

On this there was the following endorsement:

"CONFEDERATE STATES OF AMERICA,
"*Richmond, 22d December*, 1864.

"I certify that the reverse of this page presents a true copy of the warrant granted to Bennet G. Burley, as acting master in the navy of the Confederate States, from the records of this Department. In testimony whereof I have hereunto set my hand and affixed the seal of this Department, on the day and year above written.

"(Signed,) "S. R. MALLORY,
"*Secretary of Navy.*" [L. S.]

[MANIFESTO.]

CONFEDERATE STATES OF AMERICA.

"Whereas it has been made known to me that Bennet G. Burley, an acting master in the navy of the Confederate States, is now under arrest in one of the British North American provinces, on an application made by the Government of the United States for the delivery to that Government of the said Bennet G. Burley, under the treaty known as the Extradition Treaty, now in force between the United States and Great Britain; and

"Whereas it has been represented to me that the demand for the extradition of the said Bennet G. Burley is based on the charge that the said Burley is a fugitive from justice, charged with having committed the crimes of robbery and piracy in the jurisdiction of the United States; and

"Whereas it has further been made known to me that the accusations and charges made against the said Bennet G. Burley are based solely on the acts and conduct of the said Burley, in an enterprise or expedition made or attempted in the month of September last, (1864,) for the capture of the steamer 'Michigan,' an armed vessel of the United States, navigating the lakes on the boundary between the United States and the British North American provinces, and for the release of numerous citizens of the Confederate States, held as prisoners of war by the United States at a certain island called Johnson's Island; and

"Whereas the said enterprise or expedition for the capture of the said armed steamer Michigan, and for the release of the said prisoners on Johnson's Island, was a proper and legitimate belligerent operation, undertaken during the pending public war between the two Confederacies, known respectively as the Confederate States of America and the United States of America, which operation was ordered and sanctioned by the authority of the Government of the Confederate States, and confided to its commissioned officers for execution, among which officers is the said Bennet G. Burley;

"Now, therefore, I, Jefferson Davis, President of the Confederate States of America, do hereby declare and make known to all whom it may concern, that the expedition aforesaid, undertaken in the month of September last, for the capture of the armed steamer Michigan, a vessel of war of the United States, and for the release of the prisoners of war, citizens of the Confederate States of America, held captive by the United States of America, at Johnson's Island, was a belligerent expedition, ordered and undertaken under the authority of the Confederate States of America, against the United States of America, and that the Government of the Confederate States of America assumes the responsibility of answering for the acts and conduct of any of its officers engaged in said expedition, and especially of the said Bennet G. Burley, an acting master in the navy of the Confederate States.

"And I do further make known to all whom it may concern, that in the orders and instructions given to the officers engaged in said expedition, they were especially directed and enjoined to 'abstain from violating any of the laws and regulations of the Canadian or British authorities in relation to neutrality,' and that the combination necessary to effect the purpose of said expedition must be made by Confederate soldiers and such assistance as they might (you may) draw from the enemy's country.

"In testimony whereof, I have signed this manifesto, and directed the same to be sealed with the seal of the Department of State of the Confederate States of America, and to be made public.

"Done at the city of Richmond, on this 24th day of December, 1864.

"(Signed,) "JEFFERSON DAVIS.

"By the President:

"J. P. BENJAMIN, *Secretary of State.*"

The following correspondence will show that the military authorities of this State were fully aware of the movements and intentions of the raiders to attempt an attack on Johnson's Island, and that the commander of the steamer Michigan received early information in relation thereto. The military officers at Sandusky were also put on the alert, and a reinforcement, consisting of artillery and infantry, had been promptly ordered there from Cincinnati, which ensured the security of the rebel prisoners against any possibility of rescue:

(1) [TELEGRAM.]

DETROIT, *September* 17, 1864.

TO CAPTAIN JOHN H. CARTER,
Commanding U. S. Steamer Michigan, Sandusky, Ohio:

It is reported to me that some of the officers and men of your steamer have been tampered with, and that a party of rebel refugees leave Windsor to-morrow, with the expectation of getting possession of your steamer.

(Signed,) B. H. HILL,
Lieut. Col. U. S. A., Military Commander.

(2) [TELEGRAM.]

DETROIT, MICH., *September* 19, 1864.

TO CAPTAIN J. C. CARTER,
U. S. Navy, U. S. Steamer Michigan, Sandusky, Ohio:

It is said the parties will embark to-day, at Malden, on board the "Philo Parsons," and will seize either that steamer or another running from Kelly's Islands. Since my last dispatch, am again assured that officers and men have been bought by a man named Cole. A few men to be introduced on board under guise of friends of officers.

An officer named Eddy to be drugged. Both Commander Gardner and myself look upon the matter as serious.

(Signed,) B. H. HILL,
Lieut. Col. U. S. A., A. A. P. M. General.

(3) [TELEGRAM.]

U. S. STEAMER MICHIGAN, OFF JOHNSON'S ISLAND, O.,
September 18, 1864, *via Sandusky.*

TO LIEUT. COL. B. H. HILL,
U. S. A., Military Commander, Detroit, Mich.:

Thanks for your dispatch. All ready. Cannot be true in relation to the officers or men.

(Signed,) JOHN C. CARTER, *Commander, U. S. N.*

(4) [TELEGRAM.]

SANDUSKY, O., *September* 19, 1864.

COL. B. H. HILL, *Detroit:*

Your dispatch of 19th received. I have Cole, and a fair prospect of bagging the party.

(Signed,) J. C. CARTER, *Commander, U. S. N.*

OFFICE MILITARY COMMANDER, DISTRICT OF MICHIGAN,
DETROIT, *September* 21*st*, 1864.

Major C. H. POTTER,
A. Adj. General, Columbus, Ohio:

SIR:—I have the honor to inform you that on Saturday night last, 17th instant, a person called upon me at my hotel, and introduced himself to me as having been for some years a rebel soldier, and recently a refugee in Canada.

He informed me that some of the officers and men of the U. S. steamer Michigan had been tampered with, and that it was the intention of the Rebel Agent in Windsor, Jacob Thompson, late Secretary of the Interior, under President Buchanan's administration, to send a party from Windsor, who, with the assistance of the officers and men, would endeavor to get possession of the steamer. He said that he had been approached to form one of the party, and had consented to do so, and that he would receive more particular information on the next morning, when the party would leave for Malden. He said that with the possession of the steamer Michigan, they would have control of the Lakes for a couple of months, and would lay contribution on all the Lake cities, and had offered very large inducements to the officers and men of the steamer. He stated that after obtaining full information on Sunday morning, he would fail to join the party, and would see me again on Sunday evening.

The statement of the man and his earnestness made some impression on me, and I telegraphed to Captain J. C. Carter, commanding officer of the steamer Michigan, that night, and I enclose a copy marked "1," and his reply marked "2."

On Sunday evening, 18th instant, my informant again crossed the river and saw me. He reported that he had agreed to join the party, and had obtained all the information he could, but at the last moment he had failed them. He said that the party were to take passage on board the steamer "Philo Parsons," at Malden, and would get possession of her before reaching Sandusky; that certain officers and men of the steamer Michigan had been tampered with by a man named Cole, and that an officer of the steamer, named Eddy, could not be bought, and that the intention was to drug him and others.

My informant thought that the captain of the steamer Philo Parsons had also been bought, and if he received any hint on the subject he would give information, and he himself would be compromised.

I went down to the steamer Philo Parsons the next morning at 6 A. M. and saw her. She was too small to be of any danger if taken by the persons, and after mature consideration I came to the conclusion that it would be better to let the steamer go, and place Captain Carter on his guard in a way that it would make an impression on him, so that the whole party could be taken.

See my telegram marked "3," and his reply marked "4."

These plots are being constantly made here. We had the information about this one, and the question was whether it would not be better to let the steamer go and adopt measures to secure her capture, and make an example in this case.

On Tuesday last the Philo Parsons arrived at Sandwich in the possession of some eighteen men, who had taken passage in her at Malden the day before. It seems that after taking possession of her the piratical party seized and sunk a small steamer named the Island Queen, both occurrences taking place in the waters of the State of Ohio. They then proceeded to within four miles of Sandusky, and not probably seeing signals that had been agreed upon, or receiving any assistance that was probably expected from Sandusky, returned to Detroit river and proceeded to Sandwich, C. W., where they plundered the steamer and cut her pipes to sink her and abandoned her. The steamer was, however, recovered by her owners in a damaged condition, half full of water, and brought to this side of the river.

It seems that my telegrams to Capt. Carter led to the arrest of Cole, who made some disclosures that caused the arrest of other parties in Sandusky, the particulars of which will be doubtless communicated to the commanding officer there.

It was unfortunate that Capt. Carter did not proceed to meet the Philo Parsons, as the whole party could have been captured; but there have been so many rumors and reports here of rebel plots that it is hard to discriminate between those having some reality and those purely fabrications. In this case had I placed soldiers on board, whom I could not spare at this time, or defend in any way the departure of the steamer, suspicions of the conspirators would have been aroused, and the matter deferred to a time when we would have had no intimation of it. As the case now stands, the rebel agent in Canada, residing in Sandwich, Colonel Jacob Thompson, has organized an expedition in Canada to seize American steamers. The steamers Philo Parsons and Island Queen were seized, and the latter sunk in American waters; the Philo Parsons plundered while lying in British waters, off the town of Sandwich, an attempt made to sink her, and the persons employed in these acts now residing in Canada under the protection of the British Government.

The United States attorney has addressed a communication to our consul at Windsor to call upon the authorities to arrest the persons committing these outrages, in anticipation of such a demand being made for their delivery, and affidavits will be sent by him to the Secretary of State, and I had an interview this morning both with him and Senator Howard, and everything is being adopted to place the matter in proper legal shape before the Government and the British authorities.

Very respectfully, your obedient servant,

B. H. HILL,

Lieut. Col. U. S. Artillery, Commanding District, Michigan.

OFFICE MILITARY COMMANDER, DISTRICT OF MICHIGAN,
DETROIT, *September* 22, 1864.

Brigadier-General JAMES B. FRY,
Provost Marshal-General, Washington, D. C.:

GENERAL:—I have the honor to transmit herewith a copy of a report, with accompanying papers, made to the Assistant Adjutant-General of the Northern Department, in relation to the proposed attempt to capture the U. S. steamer Michigan and the late piratical acts of the rebel refugees in Canada. The information I communicated to Captain Carter, commanding U. S. steamer Michigan, doubtless led to the arrest of Cole and others and exploded the plot.

The person who gave me the information writes me this morning from Windsor, and states that he has seen several of the parties connected in the raid, and among others Dr. Smith, who told him all connected with the affair. He learns that the person who was to have met them at Kelly Island failed to be there.

This party was to have given the latest information and instructions. The steamer Philo Parsons went within two miles of the steamer Michigan, and it was seen with their night glasses that the Michigan had changed her position to one that commanded the whole island. My informant also writes me that he thinks Col. Jacob Thompson and the entire party engaged in seizing the Philo Parsons have left Windsor.

The person who gave me the information states that he has been some years in the rebel army; that he has been wounded three times, but that owing to injustice done him by Mr. Benjamin, Acting Secretary of War, in not advancing him, he had left the South, and now entertains the most bitter hostility to the Southern cause. He gave me what he stated as his real name, and informed me that he had been a prominent politician in Arkansas and Kentucky, and had twice run for Congress. * * *

I am, very respectfully, your obedient servant,

B. H. HILL,

Lieut. Col. U. S. A., A. A. P. M. General.

The force in the State during the time of these threatened raids on which reliance was placed to defend its borders against any hostile demonstration consisted of six companies of the 2d regiment veteran reserve corps, three companies of State troops, the "Scott Guard," "Detroit Light Guard," and "Lyon Guard," with a section of light artillery, fully equipped and supplied with suitable ammunition; and in addition there were five hundred stand of arms in the State Armory at Detroit, with complete equipments, and abundance of ammunition at all times in readiness for distribution to citizens, with whom there was an understanding and an arrangement to assist in repelling any attack that might be made upon the city or along the river in the vicinity. There was also a small force guarding the arsenal at Dearborn, in which was stored about thirty-five thousand stand of arms. To guard against any attack or landing being made by steamers or vessels from the Canadian side with a hostile intention, several armed steam tugs were employed by the Government in patrolling the river at various points.

THE MICHIGAN CONTINGENT.

The Michigan "Contingent" in the war was largely made up of men who enlisted for three years, and were mainly from the more respectable and industrious of the community. Leaving the peaceful avocations of civil life, these men were disciplined into soldiers and converted into heroes, sometimes even during the operations and emergencies of a single campaign. Patient and obedient under the most rigid discipline, persistent and enduring on the long and tedious march, cheerful and untiring in the trenches, apt in experiment, and most ingenious in construction, they added to all these qualifications and merits true courage in the field, while almost every important action has illustrated their heroism, and almost every battle-field is consecrated with their blood. Their services were eagerly sought for by all the best generals—whether to construct a defence, lead a "forlorn hope," or charge a battery.

The armies of no other nation, even after many years of the training which war brings with it, have evinced so marvellous a developement of soldierly qualities as characterized the American troops during their comparatively short term of service. The annals of the times will rear an imperishable monument to the patriotism of all the States which in the nation's peril gave their sons in the conflict, and the honor of one will be among the precious possessions of the others; but it will be for Michigan to cherish with peculiar pride and tenderness the remembrance and the fame of the gallant band of patriots who, in the fiercest struggles of modern warfare, and among comrades of equal worth and bravery, while preserving the national life and integrity, have reflected undying lustre upon her own escutcheon.

Scarcely had the rebel gauntlet been tossed in defiance, scarcely had the echo of the first rebel gun passed away, scarcely had the electric messenger done its momentous errand—proclaiming the fact of civil war, and that the flag of America had been insulted and struck from its proud perch on Sumter's walls, ere the men of Michigan were in arms, eager and ready to defend and maintain the National Union, and protect its flag, to uphold the honor of their State, and save their glorious birth-right of freemen. They vowed to God and their native land, and pledged their arms and their lives, that the beloved flag of their country should again wave triumphantly on the walls of Sumter, and over every State and inch of ground in the Union, and that the Republic should be saved and forever preserved.

The call of Abraham Lincoln received a ready and substantial response from the people of Michigan. With remarkable dispatch her gallant regiments armed, clothed, equipped, and fully appointed, left the State to meet the enemies of American liberty.

Michigan troops, prompt and prominent at the outset of the rebellion, were also in at its death. They were among those who, under Wilcox, first crossed the Long Bridge into Virginia, and participated in the capture of

Alexandria. They were in the command of the brave and lamented Richardson, who first opened fire upon the rebels at Blackburn's Ford, on July 18, 1861, in the vicinity of Bull Run.

They were with General McClellan in West Virginia, in the first year of the war, and were in South Carolina and Georgia in 1862, and during that year served with the Army of the Potomac on the Peninsula and in Maryland, with General Banks in the Shenandoah Valley, in Virginia under General Burnside, in Louisiana under General Butler, and in Missouri with General Pope and Colonel Mulligan.

In 1863 they bore a conspicuous and gallant part in the ever memorable campaigns under General Hooker, in Virginia, and General Meade, in Pennsylvania, at the defence of Knoxville by General Burnside, at the capture of Vicksburg by General Grant, and on the celebrated Kilpatrick raid against Richmond. They were also engaged in the campaign of General Rosecrans against Chattanooga, and were actively employed in the field at various points in Tennessee, Mississippi, Kentucky, and Louisiana, under other generals.

In 1864–5 they were with General Grant on his great march against Richmond, and bravely participated in most of the hard fought battles of that eventful campaign. They were also with General Sherman on his remarkable march from Chattanooga to the sea, and were prominently engaged in most of his memorable and successful battles, and with General Sheridan in his matchless encounters with the enemy in the valley of the Shenandoah, where, in command of Custer, their sabres flashed in every battle. They took part in the gallant defence of Nashville by General Thomas, and were with Generals Stoneman and Wilson on their raids into North Carolina and Georgia. They were also at the capture of Mobile, and served in Texas and Utah Territory during a part of 1865–6.

Michigan was well represented in the Union armies at the surrender of Lee and Johnston, and a Michigan regiment captured the President of the so-called Confederacy—Jefferson Davis—in his inglorious flight to escape deserved punishment for his infamous treason and rebellion.

Michigan troops, in all the campaigns and battles in which they participated, were most reliable, conspicuously brave and gallant. In every position in which they were placed they were true, self-sacrificing, patient under hardship, murmuring not, meeting death by exposure, starvation, and cruel treatment in rebel prisons, and many more by rebel bullets in sanguinary strife.

From the beginning of the war until its end, the motto of Michigan soldiers was, fight on until every rebel shall be conquered and made to yield obedience, or if needs be utterly destroyed. That motto they most successfully maintained; meeting the enemy on his last field, they, in common with their comrades of the Union army, compelled him to lay down his rebellious arms, to beg not only for quarter but for peace, and submit unconditionally to the terms of their dictation. Having accomplished that, they returned to their homes the preservers of their nation, receiving the plaudits and gratitude of their fellow countrymen, and of every friend of freedom and humanity throughout the civilized world.

To have included in this volume the entire campaigns of these regiments, would have been a most desirable and pleasant labor, but would have engrossed its whole space, and therefore has been abandoned, leaving a subject rich in record of faithful and gallant service and brave deeds for future publication, and giving only a few of the leading achievements of each.

It would also have been very satisfactory to have referred to the special services and achievements of the many companies and men of Michigan, that were connected with regiments of other States, but not having any data from which to sketch them, the matter has been reluctantly deferred. Undoubtedly, they maintain the reputation of Michigan troops, which was always pre-eminently high.

REGIMENT OF ENGINEERS AND MECHANICS.

The celebrated regiment of Michigan engineers and mechanics was raised and organized under the supervision of Colonel William P. Innes, of Grand Rapids, and went to the field in Kentucky December 17th, 1861, in command of that officer. It is but justice to this regiment to state a fact generally conceded by the whole Western army that a more useful regiment, or one performing more valuable service, was not found in that great army, as during its entire service, ending with the surrender of Lee and Johnston, including the great Sherman campaign, scarcely a bridge was built or a road opened for the use of the Western army that was not either wholly accomplished or aided by this regiment. While it was at all times ready and expeditious in the performance of the legitimate duties of an engineer regiment it never failed as a gallant fighting force when opportunity offered. First meeting the enemy at Mill Springs, in Kentucky, January 19th, 1862, then in Mississippi at Farmington May 9th, at Corinth the 10th, and at Perryville, Kentucky, same year, where its reputation as a fighting regiment was fully established; but at Lavergne, Tennessee, January 1st, 1863, it was most signally distinguished, and its gallant conduct in that battle gives it a most enviable page in the history of the war.

While General Rosecrans was fighting the important battle of Stone river, the regiment, then in command of Col. Innes, on the 31st December, 1862, was specially ordered by the commanding general to take a position in the rear of his army at Lavergne, on the main road from Nashville to Murfreesboro, to protect the baggage trains. On the next morning, for greater safety, Colonel Innes formed his wagon train in the form of a half circle and made some hastily-constructed breastworks of logs and such loose material as could be found at hand. This precaution seems to have been taken none too soon, as at 2 P. M. the command was attacked by an overwhelming rebel force of from three to four thousand cavalry, with one section of light artillery, the whole commanded by the rebel Major-General Wheeler. Their object, as afterwards ascertained, was to burn and plunder the heavily-laden trains passing on the pike between Nashville and Rosecrans' army. Col. Innes and his small but gallant regiment, numbering not over 315, fought this superior force until dark, when it was withdrawn with heavy loss, having vainly endeavored to compel a surrender. During this five hours' engagement the enemy made seven separate and distinct charges, sometimes forcing their horses on to the very breastworks, which were as often most gallantly repelled; at the same time their artillery was kept constantly in play, with considerable effect, damaging the wagons, killing some thirty or forty horses and mules attached to wagons both inside and outside the circle. Three times Gen. Wheeler sent a flag of truce to Colonel Innes demanding a surrender, and claiming an increase of his force, to which the colonel replied in a most characteristic manner "that he could not see it;" so long as his ammunition held out he could not see the force of his argument.

A correspondent at the time says: "The scene was at times thrilling beyond description. The rebel horde, exasperated at the successful resistance of the little force, dashed their horses against the circular brush fence, which was only breast high, with infuriated shouts and curses. But the Michigan troops were cool and determined; they loaded fast and aimed well, and, as the troopers rushed on upon all sides, they were met with staggering volleys almost at the muzzle of the muskets. Horses and riders recoiled again and again until they despaired, and soon swept away through the dense forests, leaving over fifty of their dead upon the field, which were buried by our forces. The ground all around that small circle of brush was strewn with dead horses of the rebel troopers, and with their clothing, guns, &c. Truly this was one of the most gallant affairs of the campaign."

Mr. Greeley, in his excellent work, "The American Conflict," notices Col. Innes' extraordinary defence at Lavergne, and says:

"On the whole, the enemy's operations in the rear of our army during this memorable conflict, (battle of Stone river,) reflect no credit on the intelligence and energy with which they were resisted. 'The silver lining to this cloud' is a most gallant defence made on the 1st January by Col. Innes' 1st Michigan engineers and mechanics, only 391 strong, who had taken post on high ground near Lavergne, and formed such a barricade of cedars, &c. as they hurriedly might. Here they were attacked, at 2 P. M., by Wharton's cavalry, whom they successfully resisted and beat off. Wharton's official report is their best eulogium. He was in command of six or eight regiments. 'Wharton.' 'A regiment of infantry, under Colonel Dennis, (Innes,) also was stationed in a cedar brake and fortifications near this point. I caused the battery under Lieut. Pike, who acted with great gallantry, to open on it. The fire, at a range of not more than 400 yards, was kept up for more than an hour, and must have resulted in great damage to the enemy. I caused the enemy to be charged on three sides at the same time by Colonels Cox and Smith and Lieut. Col. Malone, and the charge was repeated four times; but the enemy was so strongly posted that it was found impossible to dislodge him.'"

The regiment lost only two killed and twelve wounded, while the rebel loss, as estimated at the time, was something over a hundred in killed and wounded.

General Rosecrans, in his official report, gave the regiment credit for having successfully repulsed ten times its own number on that occasion.

During the residue of the year the regiment was actively employed in its ordinary duties, building bridges, repairing railroads, &c., with its headquarters in the neighborhood of Elk River Bridge. In the early part of 1864 the regiment, in command of Col. John Yates, was with the advance of Sherman's army on Atlanta, and on the 30th of September had its headquarters there. On the 16th of November it marched from Atlanta as a part of the engineer force of General Sherman's army, performing with remarkable promptness its arduous and important duties on that great march. It is estimated that during that campaign, besides making and repairing a great distance of corduroy road, the regiment destroyed and twisted the rails of thirty miles of railroad tract and built eight or ten important bridges and crossings. At Edisto it constructed a bridge under a severe fire from the enemy's sharpshooters; continuing its faithful and important services throughout the rest of the campaign and until the arrival of Sherman's army at Washington. Early in June it was ordered to Louisville, Kentucky, and thence to Nashville, where it was mustered out of service on the 22d of September.

THE CAVALRY BRIGADE,

CONSISTING OF THE 1ST, 5TH, 6TH, AND 7TH REGIMENTS.

The 1st regiment of cavalry was organized during the summer of 1861, by Col. T. F. Brodhead, and left its rendezvous in Detroit on the 29th of September for Washington, in command of that officer. It lay in camp at Frederick, Md., a considerable portion of the winter, and its principal service was on the upper Potomac, in the Shenandoah Valley, and near the eastern slopes of the Blue Ridge. It was in action at Winchester, March 23, 1862; at Middletown, March 25th; at Strasburg, March 27th; at Harrisonburg, April 22d; at Winchester again, May 24th; at Orange Court-House, July 16th; at Cedar Mountain, August 9th; and at Bull Run, August 30th. At the latter action its commanding officer, Colonel Brodhead,* was mortally wounded, and died September 2d, and its casualties in that engagement showed 7 killed, 13 wounded, 7 prisoners, and 106 missing.

During November and December following, and the early part of 1863, the regiment, in command of Colonel Charles H. Town, was engaged on grand guard duty in front of the defences of Washington, on a line extending from Edward's Ferry to the mouth of the Occoquan.

During the raid about the Union lines, made by the rebel Gen. Stuart, in February, 1863, a detachment of fifty-six men of this regiment were sent out to watch his movements. Near Occoquan the enemy came in range of the carbines of this party, and fell back in confusion at the first fire. Discovering the weakness of the force opposed to them, the rebel cavalry recovered and charged vigorously with a large force, before which the detachment retired, fighting from behind bushes, &c., during a pursuit of several miles, with a resulting loss to Stuart's troopers of fifteen in killed and wounded, and to themselves of none. On the 27th of June, the regiment took up its line of march northward in the Gettysburg campaign.

The 5th cavalry was organized under the authority given by the War Department and the Governor to Colonel J. T. Copeland, then in the 1st cavalry. Its organization began in July, 1862, and it was mustered into service as a regiment on the 30th of August, at its rendezvous in Detroit. The regiment was subjected to a long delay in procuring its arms and equipments, and left the State only partly armed, but fully equipped, mounted, and clothed, on the 4th of December following, for Washington. A number of men were lost by desertion previous to its departure, and its rolls show that down to that period it had carried the names of 1,305 officers and men. A battery of light artillery was raised in connection with this regiment, which was classed as the 9th Michigan battery, and originally known as Daniel's. This battery was afterwards designated as Battery "I," 1st Michigan light artillery.

On November 29, 1862, Colonel Copeland was appointed a brigadier-general of volunteers, being succeeded in the command of the regiment by Colonel Freeman Norvell, who was promoted from lieutenant-colonel on the 31st of December. He served in command of the regiment in the field until the 27th of February following, when he resigned. Major R. A. Alger,

---

*Report of Major Charles H. Town, commanding 1st Michigan: * * "Col. Thornton F. Brodhead, mo tally wounded at Bull Run, Va., August 30, 1862, while gallantly leading his men to the charge." * * * * *

While on his death-bed in the field, almost the last words to his attending surgeon were, "The Old Flag will triumph yet."

In his letter to his wife, he writes: "I fought manfully and now die fearlessly."

of the 2d cavalry, was commissioned as colonel on the 28th of the same month, and served in that capacity down to September 20, 1864, when, on account of ill health, he was compelled to resign.

The 6th regiment of cavalry was organized at Grand Rapids, under authority granted to Hon. F. W. Kellogg by the War Department, sanctioned by the Governor. It was rapidly filled, and mustered into service on the 13th of October, 1862, its rolls carrying the names of 1,229 officers and men. It left its rendezvous on the 10th of December following, in command of Col. George Gray, taking the route to Washington, fully mounted and equipped, but not armed.

The 7th regiment of cavalry was also raised at Grand Rapids, under the same authority. Two battalions of this regiment left the State for Washington on the 20th of February, 1863, and the remaining companies joined them in May following. The regiment entered the field in command of Col. W. D. Mann.

These regiments served to the end of the war, bearing so important a part in the great struggle for union and freedom as to become eminently famous throughout the length and breadth of the land, as the "Michigan Cavalry Brigade."

The 1st cavalry, while in command of Colonel Brodhead, served in the command of General Alpheus S. Williams, of Michigan, in 1862, and covered the retreat of General Banks' army from the Shenandoah Valley, serving with much distinction, and rendering very important service in that affair, being continuously under fire.

Following the surrender of Lee and Johnston, and consequent collapse of the Southern Confederacy, this brigade, which had served during the war with the Army of the Potomac, was sent West to St. Louis, Mo., thence to Fort Leavenworth, where the 5th cavalry were mustered out of service, except the men having two years or more to serve, and these were transferred to the 1st and 7th. The regiments then crossed the Plains to the Rocky Mountains, for the purpose of aiding in suppressing the war which was then being waged by several Indian tribes on citizens of the United States in the Territories of the far West. These orders caused much justifiable dissatisfaction in the brigade, indicating as they did the commencement of another arduous campaign, which, in consideration of past long and faithful services, they thought might have been spared them, especially as the campaign was for an object foreign to their contract of service. But remembering their noble record, and adhering to their uniform high degree of discipline and subordination, and having in view the honor of a State whose troops had never disgraced it, obeyed the orders and crossed the plains.

After reaching the Rocky Mountains, the men of these regiments, with certain exceptions, were, in violation of the orders of the War Department, consolidated into one regiment, designated as the 1st regiment Michigan veteran cavalry, four companies of which were stationed at Fort Bridger and eight companies were sent forward to Camp Douglas, at Salt Lake City. The regiment garrisoned these two stations until March 10, 1866, when it was mustered out of service, paid off, and disbanded.

Owing to gross injustice done these troops by the officers of the Government in Utah, in the settlement of their transportation account, the War Department was asked by the State authorities to make certain additional allowance, which was refused, when an appeal was made to Congress. The claim having been promptly and properly presented, it was supported and insisted upon by the Michigan representatives of both Houses of Congress, then composed of Chandler and Howard in the Senate, and in the House, Beaman, Driggs, Ferry, Longyear, Trowbridge, and Upson, who, ever true to the interest of the soldier, determined that this claim should be secured and justice done, and therefore united their influence and effort for that purpose, and with commendable zeal and great ability, together with close attention and much tact, procured an enactment for their relief.

While these Michigan troops were engaged in this service, Captain Osmer F. Cole, of the 6th cavalry, was killed in action with Indians at Tongue river, M. T., August 30, 1865.

At the request of the Governor of the State, a special report was made by the Adjutant-General, covering the unlawful and unauthorized consolidation of the Michigan cavalry brigade, consisting of the 1st, 6th, and 7th regiments, into an organization to be known as the 1st regiment of Michigan cavalry, detailing the ill-treatment and injustice attending the detention in service and muster-out and payment of that regiment. On this report a claim was made to the War Department for an additional allowance of transportation. The claim was rejected on the ground that the parties for whom the allowance was asked had already received from the Government all that existing law provided for in such cases. It therefore became necessary to apply to Congress for special relief. Accordingly, the matter was referred to Senator Chandler for presentation to Congress, and which received at his hands the fullest attention, aided by Senator Howard and our members of Congress—Beaman, Ferry, Upson, Driggs, Trowbridge, and Longyear. These gentlemen, as before stated, properly concerned for, and true to the interest of the Michigan soldiers, by their concerted action in Congress, ultimately succeeded in securing the passage of the following enactment, rendering the justice so essentially due to those who had never faltered in the soldier's line of duty:

"*And be it further enacted*, That there is hereby appropriated for the payment of the travelling expenses of the members of the 1st regiment of Michigan cavalry from the place in Utah Territory where they were mustered out of service, in the year 1866, to the place of their enrollment, a sum sufficient to allow to each member $325, deducting therefrom the amount paid to each for commutation of travel, pay and subsistence, by the Government, when thus mustered out, and that the accounts be settled and paid under the direction of the Secretary of War."

The selection of special engagements in which these regiments most distinguished themselves respectively, has been abandoned, because of their services in the field being so united in the operations of the Michigan cavalry brigade. It has, therefore, been deemed best to take official reports of General Custer, covering certain movements, as illustrating more fully than any others on file the brilliant and important achievements of these gallant regiments during the rebellion. To these have been added extracts from reports of other officers, while in command of the brigade and of regiments respectively.

Following is General Custer's report, made August 22, 1863, covering the operations of his cavalry during a portion of the battle of Gettysburg:

"In compliance with instructions received from the headquarters of the 3d division, I have the honor to submit the following report of the part taken by my command in the engagements near Gettysburg, July 3, 1863:

"At an early hour on the morning of the 3d, I received an order through a staff-officer of the brigadier-general commanding the division, to move at once my command, and follow the first brigade on the road leading from 'Two Taverns' to Gettysburg.

"Agreeably to the above instructions, my column was formed and moved out on the road designated, when a staff-officer of Brigadier-General Gregg, commanding 2d division, ordered me to take my command and place it in position on the pike leading from York to Gettysburg, which position formed the extreme right of our line of battle on that day. Upon arriving at the point designated, I immediately placed my command in position, facing towards Gettysburg. At the same time I caused reconnoisances to be made on my front, right, and rear, but failed to discover any considerable force of the enemy. Everything remained quiet till 10 A. M., when the enemy appeared on my right flank, and opened upon me with a battery of six guns. Leaving two guns and a regiment to hold my first position and cover the road leading to Gettysburg, I shifted the remaining portion of my command, forming a new line of battle at right angles to my former line. The enemy had obtained correct range of my new position, and were pouring solid shot and shell into my command with great accuracy. Placing two sections of battery M, 2d regular artillery, in position, I ordered them to silence the enemy's battery, which order, notwithstanding the superiority of the enemy's position, was successfully accomplished in a very short space of time. My line, as it then existed, was shaped like the letter L, the shorter branch formed one section of battery M, supported by four squadrons of the 6th Michigan cavalry, faced toward Gettysburg, covering the Gettysburg pike; the long branch, composed of the remaining two sections of battery M, 2d artillery, supported by a portion of the 6th Michigan cavalry on the left and the 1st Michigan cavalry on the right, with the 7th Michigan cavalry still further to the right and in advance, was held in readiness to repel any attack the enemy might make coming on the Oxford road. The 5th Michigan cavalry was dismounted and ordered to take position in front of my centre and left. The 1st Michigan cavalry was held in a column of squadrons, to observe the movements of the enemy. I ordered fifty men to be sent one mile and a half on the Oxford road, while a detachment of equal size was sent one mile and a half on the road leading from Gettysburg to York, both the detachments being under the command of the gallant Major Webber, who, from time to time, kept me so well informed of the movements of the enemy that I was enabled to make my dispositions with complete success. At 12 o'clock an order was transmitted to me from the brigadier-general commanding the division, by one of his aids, directing me, upon being relieved by a brigade from the 2d division, to move with my command and form a junction with the 1st brigade on the extreme left. On the arrival of the brigade of the 2d division, commanded by Col. McIntosh, I prepared to execute the order. Before I had left my position Brigadier-General Gregg, commanding the 2d division, arrived with his entire command. Learning the true condition of affairs in my front, and rightly conjecturing that the enemy was making his dispositions for vigorously attacking our position, Brigadier-General Gregg ordered me to remain in the position I then occupied.

"The enemy was soon after reported to be advancing on my front. The detachment of fifty men sent on the Oxford road were driven in, and at the same time the enemy's line of skirmishers, consisting of dismounted cavalry, appeared on the crest of the ridge of hills on my front. The line extended beyond my left. To repel their advance, I ordered the 5th Michigan cavalry to a more advanced position, with instructions to maintain their ground at all hazards. Colonel Alger, commanding the 5th, assisted by Majors Trowbridge and Ferry, of the same regiment, made such admirable disposition of their men behind fences and other defences as enabled them to successfully repel the repeated advance of a greatly superior force. I attributed their success in a great measure to the fact that this regiment is armed with the Spencer repeating rifle, which in the hands of brave, determined men, like those composing the 5th Michigan cavalry, is, in my estimation, the most effective fire-arm that our cavalry can adopt. Colonel Alger held his ground until his men had exhausted their ammunition, when he was compelled to fall back on the main body. The beginning of this movement was the signal for the enemy to charge, which they did with two regiments, mounted and dismounted. I at once ordered the 7th Michigan cavalry, Colonel Mann, to charge the advancing column of the enemy. The ground over which we had to pass was very unfavorable for the manœuvering of cavalry, but, despite all obstacles, this regiment advanced boldly to the assault, which was executed in splendid style, the enemy being driven from field to field until our advance reached a high and unbroken fence, behind which the enemy were strongly posted. Nothing daunted, Colonel Mann, followed by the main body of his regiment, bravely rode up to the fence and discharged their revolvers in the very face of the foe. No troops could have maintained this position; the 7th was, therefore, compelled to retire, followed by twice the number of the enemy. By this time Colonel Alger, of the 5th Michigan cavalry, had succeeded in mounting a considerable portion of his regiment, and gallantly advanced to the assistance of the 7th, whose further pursuit by the enemy he checked. At the same time an entire brigade of the enemy's cavalry, consisting of four regiments, appeared just over the crest in our front. They were formed in column of regiments. To meet this overwhelming force I had but one available regiment—the 1st Michigan cavalry, and the fire of battery M, 2d regular artillery. I at once ordered the 1st to charge, but learned at the same moment that similar orders had been given by Brigadier-General Gregg. As before stated, the 1st was formed in column of battalions. Upon receiving the order to charge, Colonel Town, placing himself at the head of his command, ordered the 'trot' and sabres to be drawn. In this manner this gallant body of men advanced to the attack of a force outnumbering them five to one. In addition to this numerical superiority, the enemy had the advantage of position and were exultant over the repulse of the 7th Michigan cavalry. All these facts considered, would seem to render success on the part of the 1st impossible. Not so, however. Arriving within a few yards of the enemy's column the charge was ordered, and with a yell that spread terror before them, the 1st Michigan cavalry, led by Colonel Town, rode upon the front rank of the enemy, sabering all who came within reach. For a moment, but only a moment, that long, heavy column stood its ground; then, unable to withstand the impetuosity of our attack, it gave way into a disorderly rout, leaving vast numbers of their dead and wounded in our possession, while the 1st, being masters of the field, had the proud satisfaction of seeing the much-vaunted 'chivalry,' led by their favorite commander, seek safety in headlong flight. I cannot find language to express my high appreciation of the gallantry and daring displayed by the officers and men of the 1st Michigan cavalry. They advanced to the charge of a vastly superior force with as much order and precision as if going upon parade; and I challenge the annals of warfare to produce a more brilliant or successful charge of cavalry than the one just recounted. Nor must I forget to acknowledge the individual assistance rendered by battery M, 2d regiment of artillery, in this charge. Our success in driving the enemy from the field is due, in a great measure, to the highly efficient manner in which the battery was handled by Lieutenant A. C. M. Pennington, assisted by Lieutenants Clark, Woodruff, and Hamilton. The enemy made but slight demonstration against us during the remainder of the day, except in one instance he attempted to turn my left flank, which attempt was most gallantly met and successfully frustrated by Second Lieutenant J. H. Kellogg, with company H, 6th Michigan cavalry. We held possession of the field until dark, during which time we collected our dead and wounded. At dark I returned with my command to Two Taverns, where I encamped for the night.

"In this engagement my command lost as follows: Nine officers and sixty-nine men killed, twenty-five officers and two hundred and seven men wounded, seven officers and two hundred and twenty-five men missing; making a total of five hundred and forty-two. Among the killed I record the name of Major N. H. Ferry, of the 5th Michigan cavalry, who fell while heroically cheering on his men. It would be impossible for me to particularize in those instances deserving special mention; all, both men and officers, did their duty. There were many cases of personal heroism, but a list of their names would make my report too extended. To Colonel Town, commanding the 1st Michigan cavalry, and to the officers and men of his regiment for the gallant manner in which they drove the enemy from the field, great praise is due. Colonel Mann, of the 7th Michigan cavalry, and Colonel Alger, of the 5th Michigan cavalry, as well as the officers and men of their commands, are entitled to much credit for their united efforts in repelling the advance of the enemy. The 6th Michigan cavalry rendered very good service by guarding both my right and left flank; also by supporting battery M under a very hot fire from the enemy's battery. Colonel Gray, commanding the regiment, was constantly seen wherever his presence was most needed, and is deserving of special mention. I desire to commend to your favorable notice Lieutenants Pennington, Clark, Woodruff, and Hamilton, of battery M, 2d artillery, for the zeal and ability displayed by each on this occasion. My thanks are personally due to the following named members of my staff, who, on many occasions, exhibited remarkable gallantry in transmitting and executing my orders on the field:

"Captain G. A. Drew, 6th Michigan cavalry, Assistant Inspector General.

"First Lieut. R. Baylis, 5th Michigan cavalry, Acting Assistant Adjutant General.

"First Lieut. Wm. H. Wheeler, 1st Michigan cavalry, A. D. C.

"First Lieut. Wm. Colerick, 1st Michigan cavalry, A. D. C.

"I desire also to mention two of my buglers, Joseph Fought, company D, 5th U. S. cavalry, and Peter Boehn, company B, 5th U. S. cavalry; also Orderlies Norvall Churchill, company L, 1st Michigan cavalry, George L. Foster, company C, 1st Michigan cavalry, and Benjamin H. Butler, company M, 1st Michigan cavalry."

Following the battle of Gettysburg, these regiments were engaged with the enemy in Maryland during July at the following points: Monterey 4th; Cavetown 5th; Smithtown, Boonsboro', Hagerstown, and Williamsport 6th; Boonsboro' 8th; Hagerstown and Williamsport 10th; Falling Waters 14th; and Snicker's Gap, Va., on the 19th.

They were also engaged in Virginia at Kelly's Ford September 13th, at Culpepper Court-house September 14th, at Raccoon Ford September 16th, at White's Ford September 21st, and at Jack's Shop September 26th.

At the second battle of Hagerstown, July 10th, 1863, the rebels becoming panic-stricken, abandoned their wagons, ammunition, arms, tents, and even provisions. Hundreds of them, fearing Kilpatrick's men, fled to the right and left to avoid their terrific charges, and subsequently surrendered themselves. One strapping fellow surrendered to a little bugler who was attached to General Custer's brigade. As he passed down the line, escorting his prisoner, a Colt's revolver in hand, he called out: "I say, boys, what do you think of this fellow?"

Report of Colonel C. H. Town, commanding 1st Michigan, covering a portion of the operations of his regiment around Gettysburg:

* * * "We moved early on the morning of the 4th of July to Emmetsburg, thence to Monterey. Before reaching the latter place the enemy was discovered in force upon the hills to the right of the road. The regiment, being in advance of the column, was sent on a road leading to Fairfield Gap. The enemy having possession of the gap, a charge was made by one squadron, which, with the remainder of the regiment deployed as skirmishers, was successful in driving the enemy from the gap. The regiment held the position until the entire column had passed, though the enemy made desperate efforts, with superior numbers, to drive us out. Our loss here was heavy. Captain William R. Elliott, while bravely leading his company, was mortally wounded, and died the next morning, and Lieutenant James S. McElhenny, commanding company G, was killed instantly.

"I must embrace the present opportunity to pay a parting tribute to the memory of the noble men whose names I have above mentioned. Elliott and McElhenny were, indeed, true types of the American soldier. They devoted their whole time to their duties, ever ready and faithful in their discharge. They died as the Union soldier loves to die—leading in the charge.

"On the 6th of July the regiment was in support of a battery at Hagerstown, fortunately without loss. * * * * *

"Permit me here to speak of the late Captain Charles I. Snyder, of this regiment, who was mortally wounded while gallantly leading a squadron of the 18th Pennsylvania cavalry, in the streets of Hagerstown. He had been detailed for some days as an aid to General Kilpatrick, and was ordered by that officer to assist in the charge. Fearlessly he entered upon his duty, and nobly did he discharge it. Meeting six sturdy Confederates, he engaged them single-handed, cutting three of them out of the saddle and putting the rest to flight, though he received the pistol shot which caused his death, and a sabre cut on the head as well, early in the melee. The memory of this brave and noble-hearted man will ever be cherished with brotherly fondness by the officers and men of the 1st Michigan cavalry." * * * * * * *

Captain Snyder died of his wounds at Hagerstown, on July 1st, following.

The 1st cavalry lost at Gettysburg 80 men and 11 officers killed, wounded, and missing, out of 300. The 7th cavalry had 16 killed, 41 wounded, 12 missing, and 12 prisoners. Casualties of 5th and 6th are not reported.

General Kilpatrick, in his report, referring to the engagement at Falling Waters, July 14, 1863, says:

* * * "The enemy was, when first seen, in two lines of battle, with arms stacked, within less than one thousand yards of the large force. A portion of the 6th Michigan cavalry, seeing only that part of the enemy behind the earthworks, charged. This charge was led by Major Webber, and was the most gallant ever made. At a trot they passed up the hill, received the fire from the whole line, and the next moment rode through and over the earthworks, sabering the rebels along the entire line, and returned with a loss of thirty killed, wounded, and missing, including the gallant Major Webber, killed." * * * * *

Captain David G. Royce and Lieutenant Charles E. Bolza, 6th Michigan, were killed in this action, Lieutenant Bolza in the charge, and Captain Royce in action succeeding it.

Report of Colonel R. A. Alger, commanding 5th Michigan, in which he refers to the services of his regiment at Gettysburg, says:

* * * "The 5th has won an enviable reputation. Every moment brings a sad gloom over all our hearts for the noble Ferry. He was instantly shot through the head, while leading his battalion at Gettysburg. He was a brave officer. I cannot supply his place."

NOTE.—A correspondent says of the cavalry on the Gettysburg campaign: "In sixteen days, one division of our cavalry has had fifteen battles, with infantry, in nearly all to contend against, captured and destroyed nearly or quite one thousand loaded wagons and between three and four thousand horses and mules; taken between four and five thousand rebel prisoners, destroyed one-half of the rebel General Stuart's cavalry force, and so demoralized the balance, that when a green (or blue) militia regiment, (the Philadelphia Blues,) with a regiment of Green Mountain Boys, attacked them while posted behind earth-works at Hagerstown, the whole command fled panic-stricken—or at Williamsport, where Custer's brigade of Michiganders, with Pennington's battery, captured more than man for man, from an enemy whose force consisted of four times their numbers, and strongly located behind earth-works. This is cavalry fighting, the superior of which the world never saw. The cavalry also contributed largely to the success of our arms at Gettysburg."

The same correspondent in noticing the engagement at Falling Waters, which immediately followed Gettysburg, says: "Hearing that a force had marched towards Falling Waters, General Kilpatrick ordered an advance to that place. Through some mistake, only one brigade, that of General Custer's, obeyed the order. When within less than a mile of Falling Waters, four brigades were found in line of battle, in a very strong position, and behind half a dozen Eleventh-Corps or crescent-shaped earth-walls. The 6th Michigan cavalry was in advance. They did not wait for orders, but a squadron, companies D and C, under Captain Royce (who was killed,) and Captain Armstrong, were deployed as skirmishers, while companies B and F, led by Major Webber, (who was killed,) made the charge. The line of skirmishers was forced back several times, but the men rallied promptly, and finally drove the enemy behind the works. A charge was then made, the squadron passing between the earth-works. So sudden and spirited was the dash, and so demoralized were the enemy, that the first brigade surrendered without firing a shot. The charging squadron moved directly on, and engaged the second brigade, when the brigade that had surrendered seized their guns, and then commenced a fearful struggle. Of the one hundred who made the charge, only thirty escaped uninjured; seven of their horses lay dead within the enemy's works."

A correspondent says of the cavalry on the right of our army at Gettysburg, and who noticed a charge of the 7th cavalry: "But little has been said of the part taken by the cavalry on the right at Gettysburg, Friday, July 3d. General Gregg's division, assisted by General Custer's brigade, of General Kilpatrick's division, rendered an important service here. The enemy seemed determined to capture our batteries and turn the flank. The movement was only prevented through the stubborn bravery of the troops. The 7th Michigan, a new regiment, charged up to a stone wall under a front and flank fire from a concealed enemy, charging in column by company, closed *en masse*. When the first company reached the wall, and was brought to a sudden stand, the balance of the column, being in a very exposed position, was thrown into some confusion. The regiment was recalled, when the 1st Michigan, Colonel Town, made a more successful charge."

In a report of Col. Alger commanding 5th cavalry, is found the following: "At 3 A. M. on the 1st of September, 1863, we moved towards Port Conway, arriving there at 2 P. M. The enemy's pickets and skirmishers were driven across the river, and the regiment advanced to the bank, exposed to a severe fire from the enemy's artillery, which was in position on the south side of the Rappahannock. Two gunboats and some supplies were destroyed and we moved back, returning to camp on the following day; Lieut. P. S. Leggett, a gallant young officer, was killed. He was serving on the staff of Gen. Kilpatrick, and is mentioned in the official report of that officer, as 'a young man of great daring, perseverance and energy,' and was on several occasions sent by the General inside of the enemy's lines, and succeeded in gaining much information in regard to their strength, position, &c."

Under date of October 24, 1863, covering operations of his cavalry during that month, General Custer in his report says:

"In compliance with instructions received from the general commanding the division, I have the honor to submit the following report of the operations of my command from October 9th to October 23d, 1863:

"On the night of October 9th, my picket line, which extended along the north bank of Robertson river in the vicinity of James city, was attacked, and a portion of the line forced back upon the reserves; at the same time my scouts informed me that the enemy was moving in heavy column toward my right; this report was confirmed by deserters. In anticipation of an attack by the enemy at daybreak, I ordered my entire command to be saddled at 3 A. M., on the 10th. At daylight the enemy began by cautiously feeling my line; but seeing his inability to surprise us, he contented himself with obtaining possession of Cedar Mountain, which point he afterwards used as a signal station. At 1 P. M. I received orders from the general commanding the division to report with my command at James City. The head of my column arrived in the vicinity of that point at 3 P. M. The enemy had already obtained possession of the town, and had brought several guns to bear upon the position I was ordered to take. Battery M, 2d U. S. artillery, under command of Lieutenant Pennington, was unlimbered, and succeeded in shelling the enemy out of the woods on the right of the town. At the same time, Colonel Alger, of the 5th Michigan cavalry, who held the extreme left of my line, moved forward with one battalion of his regiment, under the gallant Major Clark, and charged the battery. The charge, although daring in the extreme, failed for want of sufficient support. It was successful so far, however, as to compel the enemy to shift the position of his battery to a more retired point. Night setting in prevented us from improving the advantage we had gained. Most of my command rested on their arms during the night. Early in the morning I retired on the road leading to Culpepper, which point I reached without molestation from the enemy. It was not until the rear of my column was leaving the town that the enemy made his appearance, and attempted unsuccessfully to harass my rear guard. On the hills north of the town I placed my command in position to receive an attack. The enemy not feeling disposed to accept the invitation, I retired on the road leading to Rappahannock Station. My column had scarcely begun to march before the officer commanding the rear guard, Colonel Mann, of the 7th Michigan cavalry, reported the enemy to be pressing him closely. At the same time a strong column was seen on my outer flank, evidently attempting to intercept our line of march to the river. The vigorous attacks now being made upon my rear guard compelled me to place my battery at the head of the column, and to employ my entire force to keep the enemy from my guns. My advance had reached the vicinity of Brandy Station, when a courier hastened back with the information that a brigade of the enemy's cavalry was in position directly in my front, thus cutting us completely off from the river. Upon examination, I learned the correctness of the report. The heavy masses of the rebel cavalry could be seen covering the heights in front of my advance. When it is remembered that my rear guard was hotly engaged with a superior force, a heavy column enveloping each flank, and my advance confronted by more than double my own number, the perils of my situation can be estimated. Lieutenant Pennington at once placed his battery in position, and opened a brisk fire, which was responded to by the guns of the enemy. The major-general commanding the cavalry corps at this moment rode to the advance. To him I proposed, with my command, to cut through the force on my front, and thus open a way for the entire command to the river.

"My proposition was approved, and I received orders to take my available force and push forward, leaving the 6th and 7th Michigan cavalry to hold the force in rear in check. I formed the 5th Michigan cavalry on my right, in column of battalions; on my left I formed the 1st Michigan in column of squadrons. After ordering them to draw their sabres, I informed them that we were surrounded, and all we had to do was to open a way with our sabres. They showed their determination and purpose by giving three hearty cheers. At this moment the band struck up the inspiring air 'Yankee Doodle,' which excited the enthusiasm of the entire command to the highest pitch, and made each individual member feel as if he was a host in himself. Simultaneously both regiments moved forward to the attack. It required but a glance at the countenances of the men to enable me to read the settled determination with which they undertook the work before them. The enemy, without waiting to receive the onset, broke in disorder and fled. After a series of brilliant charges, during which the enemy suffered heavily, we succeeded in reaching the river, which we crossed in good order. From the 11th to the 15th instant my command was employed in picketing and guarding the flank and rear of the army. On the afternoon of the 15th, the brigade being posted on Bull Run battle ground, I detailed Major Kidd with his regiment, the 6th Michigan cavalry, to reconnoitre the position and strength of the enemy in the vicinity of Gainesville. The reconnoisance was entirely satisfactory, and showed the enemy to be in considerable force at that point. Sunday, the 18th instant, at three P. M., the entire division was ordered to move on the pike leading from Groveton to Warrenton. The 1st brigade moved on the pike, the 2d moved on a road to the left of, and parallel to the pike, but soon encountered the enemy, and drove him as far as Gainesville, where the entire command bivouacked during the night. The 1st Vermont cavalry, under Colonel Sawyer, deserves great credit for the rapidity with which they forced the enemy to retire. At daybreak on the morning of the 19th my brigade took the advance, and skirmished with the enemy's cavalry from Gainesville to Buckland; at the latter point I found him strongly posted upon the south bank of Broad Run. The position for his artillery was well chosen. After a fruitless attempt to effect a crossing in his front, I succeeded in turning his left flank so completely as to force him from his position. Having driven him more than a mile from the stream, I threw out my pickets and ordered my men to prepare their dinner. From the inhabitants of Buckland I learned that the forces of the enemy with whom we had been engaged were commanded by General J. E. B. Stuart in person, who, at the time of our arrival at that point, was seated at the dinner-table eating, but, owing to my successful advance, he was compelled to leave his dinner untouched—a circumstance not regretted by that portion of my command into whose hands it fell. The 1st brigade took the advance. At this point I was preparing to follow, when information reached me that the enemy was advancing on my left from the direction of Greenwich. I had scarcely time to place my command in position to resist an attack from that direction before the enemy's skirmishers appeared. Pennington's battery opened upon them, while the 6th Michigan cavalry, under Major Kidd, was thrown forward and deployed as skirmishers. One gun of Pennington's battery, supported by the 1st Vermont cavalry, was placed on my extreme left. The 1st Michigan cavalry, under Major Brewer, acted as a reserve, and as a support for the remaining five guns of the battery. The 7th Michigan cavalry, under Colonel Mann, were engaged in the woods on my right. At first I was under the impression that the skirmishers were composed of dismounted cavalry, but later developments convinced me that it was a very superior force of infantry that now confronted me. After completing his disposition for attack, the enemy advanced upon me. In doing so he exposed a line of infantry of more than a mile in extent. At the same time he opened a heavy fire upon me from his artillery. Pennington's battery, aided by the 6th Michigan cavalry, poured a destructive fire upon the enemy as he advanced, but failed to force him back. A desperate effort was made to capture my battery. Pennington continued to fire until the enemy was within twenty yards of his guns. He was then compelled to limber up and retire to the north bank of Broad Run. The other portions of the command followed. The 1st Michigan cavalry was intrusted with the duty of covering the movement—a task which was gallantly performed. My command being very exhausted, I retired to the vicinity of Gainesville, where I encamped for the night. Major Clark, 5th Michigan cavalry, was detached with his regiment with one battalion. When the command retired to the north bank of Broad Run, he, with a small portion of his battalion, became separated from the rest of the command, and were captured by the enemy. Computing my losses from the 9th instant, I find them to be as follows: Nine men killed, two officers and forty-one men wounded, eight officers and one hundred and fifty-four men missing.

"Before closing my report, I desire to make honorable mention of the highly creditable manner in which both officers and men of my command have discharged their duty during the long and arduous marches as well as the hard-fought engagements of the past few days. Too much praise cannot be given to the officers and men of battery M, 2d artillery, for the gallantry displayed on more than one occasion. For the untiring zeal and energy, added to the unflinching bravery displayed in transmitting and executing my orders upon the field, my acknowledgments are due to the following members of my staff: Captain R. F. Judson, A. D. C.; Lieut. R. Bayless, A. A. D. C.; Lieut. William Colerick, A. D. C.; and to Lieutenant E. G. Granger, A. A. A. G. Lieut. Granger, while leading a charge at Brandy Station, had his horse shot in two places. Surgeon Wooster, of my staff, in addition to his professional duties, rendered me valuable assistance by aiding in transmitting my orders."

Lieut. George W. Robinson, 1st cavalry, was killed in action October 21st, 1864.

After the severe engagement at Buckland's Mills on November 19th, the regiments met the enemy on the 26th at Morton's Ford.

On the 28th of February, 1864, the brigade broke camp at Stevensburg, Virginia, and started on the cavalry raid to Richmond under General Kilpatrick.

Following is an extract from a report of the officer in command of the 5th Michigan regarding the part taken by his regiment in that affair:

"Taking part in the raid made by the cavalry under Gen. Kilpatrick to the outer defences of Richmond, the main body of the regiment crossed the Rapidan, and moving via Spotsylvania and Beaver Dam Station to Hungary Station, and thence down the Brook Turnpike to within five miles of the city of Richmond. Being here attacked, March 2d, by a large body of the enemy's forces the Union cavalry were obliged to retire. The main body of the regiment joined Gen. Butler's forces at New Kent C. H. A detachment of the regiment had accompanied the force under Colonel Ulri

Dahlgren, marching via Frederick's Hall Station to Dover's Mill, twelve miles above Richmond, on the James river, where it arrived on the 2d of March. The command then moved down to within five miles of Richmond, the detachment being in the advance and charging the enemy's lines near the city drove them from their first line of fortifications. Following up the movement, the command drove the enemy from one line to another until a point was reached within two miles of the city, when it was found impossible to advance further with so small a force. Retreating from in front of the city the command endeavored to force its way to the Union forces beyond the Chickahominy. The detachment of the 5th, with another portion of the command became separated in the night, which was cold, rainy, and very dark, from the main body under Dahlgren. Although attacked by the rebels, who were posted in strong force near Old Church, they succeeded in cutting their way through and in joining the regiment near White House Landing on the following day. At Yorktown, on the 11th, the regiment embarked on transports for Alexandria, whence it moved to Stevensburg, where it arrived April 18th."

The commanding officer of the 6th Michigan says of his regiment in the same affair:

"On the 28th of February, leaving camp at Stevensburg, it started on the cavalry raid to Richmond under General Kilpatrick. Its division being attacked near Mechanicsville on the night of the 2d of March it was obliged to retire, a portion of the 6th cavalry forming a part of the rear guard. Having succeeded in joining the forces at New Kent Court-house, the regiment moved down the Peninsula, and, embarking on transports, proceeded to Alexandria, whence it returned to its former camp at Stevensburg."

In the report of the 7th cavalry is found the following:

"This regiment, on the 7th of November, 1863, joined the advance of the Army of the Potomac toward the Rappahannock. On the morning of the 26th it crossed the enemy's rifle-pits near Morton's Ford, and moving forward captured prisoners from the rear of the rebel column. It was employed on picket duty until the 28th of February, when it started on the 'Kilpatrick raid.' On the afternoon of the 29th it arrived at Beaver Dam Station, on the Virginia Central Railroad, after a twenty hours' march, and assisted in burning the station and destroying the track. Resuming the march, it arrived before Richmond on the afternoon of the next day, and while on picket during the night was attacked by a superior force. After a desperate fight, being unsupported, it was obliged to retire, with a loss in missing of forty-four, among whom was its commanding officer, Lieut. Col. A. C. Litchfield, who was taken prisoner. Having reached Yorktown, the command moved from thence to Alexandria by transports, and marched to its former camp near Stevensburg."

Entering the campaign of 1864, the brigade crossed the Rapidan on the 5th of May with the Army of the Potomac.

The 1st cavalry, being absent from the field in Michigan on veteran furlough, did not participate in the "Kilpatrick raid," but returned in time to enter on the great campaign of 1864 under General Grant.

General Custer, in a report dated July 4, 1864, covering the operations of his command in that campaign, says:

"In obedience to the instructions of the general commanding the division, I have the honor to submit the following report of the operations of this brigade from May 4th to June 30th. On the 4th of May this brigade left camp near Culpepper and marched to Stony Mountain, where it encamped during the night, picketing from the Mountain to the Rapidan.

At 3 o'clock on the following morning the march was resumed in the direction of Germania Ford; the point of crossing was afterwards changed to Ely's Ford, from which point we moved to Chancellorsville, and encamped about one mile beyond on the Fredericksburg plank road. At 2 o'clock on the morning of the 6th, we moved by the Furnace road to its intersection with the Brock pike, taking a position to hold the intersection. Communication was also opened with General Gregg's division, which was then at Todd's Tavern. While in position at the cross-roads, an order was received from the division commander, directing me to take the 1st and 2d brigades and move out on the Brock pike for the purpose of harassing Longstreet's corps, which was reported to be moving on Hancock's left flank. Before the order could be executed, my pickets on the Brock pike, under Captain Maxwell, 1st Michigan, were driven in, and a large force of the enemy's cavalry appeared on my front. Most of my command were concealed by the woods, only the pickets and reserve being visible to the enemy. This fact induced the enemy to charge; but the 1st Michigan, under Lieutenant-Colonel Stagg, charged the enemy's advancing column and repulsed him handsomely, killing and wounding a large number of the enemy. My entire line was then thrown forward and advantageously posted in a ravine fronting an extended open country. The enemy made repeated and desperate efforts to drive me from this position, but was defeated each time with heavy loss. Failing to dislodge me by attacking my front, he moved a heavy force of dismounted men through the woods on my right, intending to turn my right flank and gain possession of the Furnace road in my rear. Discovering this movement, I sent the 5th Michigan cavalry, Colonel Alger commanding, and the 6th Michigan cavalry, Major Kidd commanding, to check the advance of the enemy, and if possible drive him to the open country beyond. About this time, Colonel Devin reported to me with the 2d brigade. A section of artillery, sent to me by General Gregg, also arrived. Eight guns were placed in a favorable position for silencing the guns of the enemy. I directed Colonel Devin to support the battery placed in position with one of his regiments. The 17th Pennsylvania was sent, dismounted, into the woods on my right, to reinforce the 5th and 6th Michigan cavalry, which at this time were hard pressed by the enemy. With the remaining portion of his command, Colonel Devin was instructed to protect and to hold the left flank. When these dispositions were completed, I ordered the battery of eight guns to fire as rapidly as they could be loaded and aimed, while the three regiments dismounted on my right were ordered to advance. Captain Maxwell, 1st Michigan, with one squadron, charged the enemy in front. The enemy, after contesting the ground obstinately, were driven from the field in great disorder, leaving his dead and many of his wounded upon the ground. We also captured a considerable number of prisoners, who informed us that we had been engaged with Fitz Hugh Lee's division of cavalry. Orders having been received not to pursue the enemy beyond this point, we remained on the field until near night, establishing communication in the meanwhile with the left of the 2d corps. Just before dark, I received orders to withdraw my command and encamp near the Furnace. On the morning of the 7th, we reoccupied the ground we held the day before. Upon arriving at the intersection of the Furnace road and Brock pike, the 1st Michigan was thrown forward to hold the road leading to Todd's Tavern. The enemy were encountered in heavy force about three-fourths of a mile beyond the cross-roads. A portion of the 1st Michigan was dismounted, and advanced through the woods on both sides of the road, while the remainder of the regiment, under Captain Brevoort, moved up the road mounted. After a short but severe engagement, the enemy was driven back towards Todd's Tavern, which point was soon after occupied by our forces under General Gregg, whose right flank connected with my left. But little fighting occurred on my front during the remainder of that day. On the 8th, we moved from Todd's Tavern to 'Silver,' a point on the Fredericksburg plank road, where the entire corps was massed. At daylight, on the morning of the 9th, the corps started on the 'Richmond raid,' this brigade being in the advance. After a short halt at Childsbury, where the division was massed, we moved on the road leading to Beaver Dam Station, on the Virginia Central railroad. Just before reaching the North Anna river, the advance guard reported a train of the enemy's ambulances to be in sight. Major Brewer, of the 1st Michigan cavalry, with one battalion of his regiment, was ordered to push forward and capture them; after which he was to move rapidly on Beaver Dam Station, the remainder of the brigade to follow closely in support. Before reaching the station, the advance encountered a considerable force of the enemy, conducting upwards of four hundred Union prisoners to Richmond. Major Brewer gallantly charged the enemy, and succeeded in recapturing all our men and quite a number of their captors. Among the recaptured men of our army was one colonel, two lieutenant-colonels, and a considerable number of captains and lieutenants, all belonging to infantry regiments, and having been captured during the battles of the Wilderness. Pressing on, we obtained possession of Beaver Dam Station, where we captured three trains and two first-class locomotives. The trains were heavily laden with supplies for the army. In addition, we captured an immense amount of army supplies, consisting of bacon, flour, meal, sugar, molasses, liquors, and medical stores; also several hundred stand of arms, and a large number of hospital tents, the whole amounting to several millions of dollars.

After supplying my command with all the rations they could transport, I caused the remainder to be burned. I also caused the railroad track to be destroyed for a considerable distance. The enemy made frequent attempts during the night to drive me from the station, but were unsuccessful. On the following day this command moved with the corps to the south bank of the South Anna, crossing at Ground Squirrel Bridge. On the 11th the enemy's cavalry, under Major-General J. E. B. Stuart, was met at Yellow Tavern, near the intersection of the telegraph road and Brock Pike. The 2d and reserve brigades were first engaged; afterwards the brigade was thrown in on the left of the reserve brigade, connecting on my left with the right of the 3d division. The enemy was strongly posted on a bluff in rear of a thin skirt of woods, his battery being concealed from our view by the woods, while they had obtained a perfect range of my position. The edge of the woods nearest to my front was held by the enemy's dismounted men, who poured a heavy fire into my lines. The 5th and 6th Michigan were ordered to dismount and drive the enemy from his position, which they did in the most gallant manner, led by Colonel Alger, of the 5th, and Major Kidd, of the 6th. Upon reaching the woods I directed Colonel Alger to establish the 5th and 6th upon a line near the skirts of the woods, and hold his position until further orders. From a personal examination of the ground, I discovered that a successful charge might be made upon the battery of the enemy by keeping well to the right. With this intention I formed the 1st Michigan cavalry in column of squadrons under cover of the woods. At the same time I directed Colonel Alger and Major Kidd to move the 5th and 6th Michigan cavalry forward and occupy the attention of the enemy on the left, Heaton's battery to engage them in front, while the 1st charged the battery on the flank. The bugle sounded the advance, and the three regiments moved forward. As soon as the 1st Michigan moved from the cover of the woods the enemy divined our intention, and opened a brisk fire from his artillery with shell and canister. Before the battery of the enemy could be reached there were five fences to be opened and a bridge to cross over, which it was impossible to pass more than three at one time, the intervening ground being within close range of the enemy's battery. Yet notwithstanding these obstacles, the 1st Michigan, Lieutenant-Colonel Stagg commanding, advanced boldly to the charge, and when within two hundred yards of the battery, charged it with a yell which spread terror before them. Two pieces of cannon, two limbers filled with ammunition, and a large number of prisoners were among the results of this charge. While it is impossible to mention all the names of the officers of the 1st Michigan who distinguished themselves by their gallantry in this charge, I cannot forbear from referring specially to the conduct of Major Howrigan, of this regiment, whose bravery on this occasion rendered him conspicuous. He was the first to reach the rebel battery, and in doing so received a wound in the arm. Lieutenant-Colonel Stagg, who commanded the 1st Michigan in the charge, with the officers and men of his command, deserve great credit for the daring manner in which the rebel battery was taken. The assistance of the 5th and 6th Michigan cavalry, by engaging the enemy in front, was also most important. After the enemy was driven across a deep ravine, about a quarter of a mile beyond the position held by his battery, he rallied and reformed his forces, and resisted successfully the further advance of the 1st Michigan. The 7th Michigan, commanded by Major Granger, was ordered forward at a trot, and when near the enemy's position, was ordered to charge with drawn sabres. Major Granger, like a true soldier, placed himself at the head of his men, and led them up to the very muzzles of the enemy's guns; but, notwithstanding the heroic efforts of this gallant officer, the enemy held their position, and the 7th Michigan was compelled to retire; but not until the chivalric Granger had fallen, pierced through the head and heart by the bullets of the enemy. He fell, as the

---

NOTE.—The regiment had charged through and driven the enemy out of the first line of woods near "Yellow Tavern," and had reached an open space, when the command was given to cease firing; just at that instant a rebel officer, who afterwards proved to be General J. E. B. Stuart, rode up with his staff to within about eighty rods of our line, when a shot was fired by a man of the 5th. John A. Huff of company E, remarked to him: "Tom, you shot too low, and to the left;" then turning round to Col. Alger who was near, he said: "Colonel, I can fetch that man." The Colonel replied, "Try him." He took deliberate aim across a fence and fired—the officer fell. Huff turned round to the Colonel and coolly said: "There's a spread eagle for you."

Huff had won the first prize for shooting while serving in Berdan's Sharpshooters, and was a most remarkable shot. He was from Macomb county, Mich., and died June 23d, 1864, of wounds received in action at Cold Harbor on the first of that month.

Pollard, in his "Lost Cause," says of the death of General J. E. B. Stuart: "An expedition of Federal cavalry, commanded by General Sheridan, was directed to make a bold dash around Lee's flank towards Richmond. It passed around the right flank of the Confederates to the North Anna river; committed some damage at Beaver Dam; moved thence to the South Anna and Ashland Station, where the railroad was destroyed; and finally found its way to the James river, where it joined the forces of Butler. On the 10th May, a portion of Sheridan's command under Custer and Merrill, were encountered by a body of Stuart's cavalry near Ashland, at a place called Yellow Tavern, on the road to Richmond. An engagement took place here. In a desperate charge, at the head of a column, Gen. Stuart fell, terribly wounded. He was immediately taken to Richmond, and every effort made to save his valuable life, but in vain; he died the next day."

warrior loves to fall, with his face to the foe. The united efforts of the 1st, 5th, 6th, and 7th, assisted by Keaton's battery, and the 1st Vermont, under the gallant Colonel Preston, proved sufficient, after a short contest, to rout the enemy and drive him from his position. His defeat was complete. He fled, leaving a large number of dead and wounded in our hands. Among the dead was the body of the notorious Colonel Henry Clay Pate. From facts obtained on the battle-field, and from information derived since, I have reason to believe that the rebel General J. E. B. Stuart received his death wound from the hand of private John A. Huff, of company E, 5th Michigan cavalry, who has since died from a wound received at Hawes's Shop. After the enemy had been driven across the upper Chickahominy, this command remained upon the battle-ground until after midnight, when it moved in rear of other portions of the command, towards Meadow Bridge, by way of the Brook Turnpike. On arriving near the bridge, this brigade was ordered by the Major-General commanding the corps to take the advance and open the way across the Chickahominy at this point. The enemy, after destroying the bridge, had taken a very strong position upon the opposite side, from which they commanded the bridge and its approaches by artillery, infantry, and dismounted cavalry. The 5th Michigan, under Colonel Alger, was dismounted and crossed the river on the railroad bridge, a short distance below. The 6th Michigan, under Major Kidd, also crossed the same bridge, dismounted. These two regiments advanced far enough to protect the pioneers while building the bridge. This being done, the 7th Michigan, two regiments from Colonel Devin's brigade, and two regiments from General Merritt's brigade, crossed the bridge to the support of the 5th and 6th Michigan. The enemy had improved the natural strength of their position by heavy breastworks. After a hard contest, from which we suffered severely, the enemy was driven from his position, leaving his dead and wounded in our hands. His retreat was so rapid that pursuit by dismounted men was impossible, and the 1st Michigan, supported by the regiments of the reserve brigade, commanded by Colonel Gibbs, was sent forward and drove the enemy for two miles, returning with many prisoners.

"In this engagement the enemy lost heavily in officers; among others, General Gordon, mortally wounded. From this point the entire command moved to Gaines' Mills, this brigade being in advance, when the entire command encamped for the night. The following morning, May 13th, we marched to Bottom's Bridge and encamped. May 14th we arrived at Malvern Hill, and opened communication with General Butler's forces. May 17th, about dark, started on our return to the army. May 18th crossed the Chickahominy at Jones's Bridge, and about two P. M. reached Baltimore Cross-roads, when we encamped until the 20th. This brigade was then detached from the corps for the purpose of destroying the Richmond, Fredericksburg, and Virginia Central Railroads at their crossing of the South Anna. On the morning of the same day reached Hanover Court-house, where we burned two trestle bridges over Hanover creek, and destroyed about one mile of railroad at that place, capturing some commissary stores at the station. Not deeming it advisable to encamp at that point, we marched back to Hanover town. The next morning returned to Hanover Court-house, when we ascertained that a brigade of rebel cavalry had occupied the town that night, and had retired in the direction of Hanover Junction. A heavy force of the enemy, consisting of infantry, cavalry, and artillery, was also reported at the railroad bridge on the South Anna. Leaving the 6th and 7th Michigan to hold the cross-roads at Hanover Court-house, the 1st and 5th Michigan were ordered to move in the direction of the South Anna, and ascertain the strength and position of the enemy. They had not proceeded beyond two miles when the enemy were discovered in strong force in front, while a heavy column of his was reported to be moving on our left flank. Not desiring to bring on an engagement at this point, and having accomplished the main object of the expedition, the command was withdrawn and rejoined the division the following day at the White House, where we crossed the Pamunkey about dark, and encamped about one mile from the river. May 23d, marched to Herring Creek, and encamped about two miles from Dunkirk. The following day marched to near Milford Station. May 25th, we rejoined the Army of the Potomac. May 26th, we broke camp and marched until midnight, reaching Darney's Ferry, on the Pamunkey. The ferry was held by a portion of Butler's brigade, of the enemy's cavalry. The 1st Michigan, under command of Lieut. Col. Stagg, were ordered to drive the enemy from the banks, and cover the laying of the pontoon bridge. After a brisk engagement we obtained possession of the opposite bank of the river, capturing a number of prisoners. After the bridge was completed the whole command crossed, this brigade being in the advance. At Hanover Town this brigade was divided, the 1st and 6th Michigan moving up the direct road to Hanover Courthouse, the 5th and 7th taking a road to the left, leading to Hawes's Shop. The 1st and 6th had proceeded but a short distance from Hanover Town, when they encountered a superior force of the enemy's cavalry, dismounted and holding the woods on each side of the road. The enemy, by his superiority in numbers and his advantage in position, successfully checked the further advance of the 1st and 6th Michigan until, ascertaining the fact, I ordered the 5th and 7th to move by a road leading from Hawes's Shop to the rear of the enemy's position. A considerable force of the enemy was found holding this road; but the advance of the 5th Michigan, under Capt. Hastings, supported by the main body of the regiment under Capt. Magoffin, charged and drove them in great disorder. Upon arriving near Crump Creek, the enemy took up a new position and attempted to prevent our further advance. The 5th Michigan was dismounted and deployed on the right, while the 7th Michigan charged with the sabre on the left. The enemy, not waiting to receive our charge, fled in confusion across Crump Creek, followed by the 7th Michigan, which charged them three miles, returning with a large number of prisoners. The position now held by the 5th Michigan was almost in rear of that portion of the enemy confronting the 1st and 6th Michigan. My diminished numbers, and the exhaustion of both men and horses, prevented me from making an attack upon the enemy's rear. I contented myself by making a diversion in favor of the 1st and 6th Michigan, the effect of which was to relieve them from the presence of the enemy in their front, who, estimating the force in their rear to be a vastly superior one, gave way in a disorderly rout. The 1st and 6th Michigan were moved forward, and united with the 5th and 7th Michigan, when we took up a position on Crump Creek. We encamped on Crump Creek until the following morning, when the 2d division, being attacked by the whole force of cavalry of the enemy, we were ordered to Gen. Gregg's assistance. After marching to Hawes's Shop, we moved down the Richmond Road near the vicinity of Eanon Church. Owing to the thick woods and dense underbrush (in front of the enemy's position) it was impossible to manœuvre the command mounted. The entire brigade was therefore dismounted and formed in line, crossing the road at right angles; the 1st and 6th Michigan being formed on the right of the road, the 5th and 7th Michigan on the left of the road, the left of the 6th connecting with the right of the 7th. In this manner the brigade moved forward until near General Gregg's line of battle, when a gap was opened in his line for our occupation. By this time the engagement had become general throughout the entire line and the firing very heavy.

"Severe losses had been inflicted on both sides without decided advantage to either. As soon as all necessary disposition had been made, this brigade moved forward and engaged the enemy. The 5th and 7th Michigan, in their advance, were exposed to a well-directed cross-fire from the enemy, as well as to a heavy fire in their front. More than once were they compelled to give ground before the destructive storm of bullets which was showered upon them, but only to advance again with courage and determination. Seeing that it was within the power of the 1st and 6th Michigan to advance and dislodge that portion of the enemy which had poured such a destructive cross-fire into the ranks of the 5th and 7th Michigan, I gave the order for the two former regiments to advance their line, which order was obeyed with promptness, the men moving forward with a cheer, driving the enemy from his position in great confusion, and compelling him to leave the ground strewn with his dead and wounded. At the same time, the 5th and 7th on the left of the road advanced, and were successful in dislodging the enemy from their front, inflicting upon him a terrible loss. The pursuit was kept up until the enemy had placed himself beyond the range of our guns. From an examination of the ground after the engagement, it was ascertained that the loss of the enemy was far heavier than during any previous engagement of the same extent and duration. The havoc was particularly great in Butler's brigade of mounted infantry, composed of seven large regiments, principally from South Carolina. Our loss in this engagement was greater than in any other of the campaign. Captain Maxwell, of the 1st Michigan, Captain Oliphant, Lieutenants Brewer, Osborn, and Muthersell, of the 5th Michigan, were severely wounded, and Captain Dodge, of the 5th Michigan, slightly wounded. Lieutenant James Christiancy, one of my personal aids, while gallantly cheering on the men in the thickest of the fight, and at the moment when the tide of battle was being turned in our favor, received two wounds, one of which carried away the end of his thumb, the other inflicting a very dangerous and painful wound through the thigh; at the same time his horse was shot under him. Lieutenant Nims, of my staff, also had his horse shot under him. We held our position here until after dark, when we were relieved by the infantry. We marched back and encamped on the Pamunkey, about one mile from the Tolopotomoy creek. The following day we crossed the creek, and encamped about one mile from New Castle ferry, where we remained until 3 P. M. on the 30th, when we marched to Old Church. Here we found the reserve brigade engaged with the enemy, who had taken up a position on the Matedequin creek. Being ordered to the support of General Merritt, I ordered the 5th Michigan on the right of the road, dismounted, the 1st and 7th Michigan on the left, also dismounted. As soon as I had formed my line, I ordered it to advance. The men went forward with a yell, and in a very short time we had driven the enemy from his position. The 5th Michigan, on the right of the road, moved forward much faster than the regiments on the left, those on the left having met a larger force, who opposed them with great determination. I then ordered the 6th Michigan, (then in reserve,) mounted, to charge them; but before I could get that regiment up, the enemy had been driven from the field, leaving his dead and wounded in our hands. In this fight we captured a large number of prisoners. Lieutenant E. G. Granger, of my staff, was struck on the left shoulder by a spent ball. We encamped at Parsely's Mills, on the Matedequin.

"*May* 31.—About 3 P. M. the brigade moved toward Cold Harbor; the 6th Michigan moved by a country road, with orders if possible to connect with the right of Colonel Devin's brigade. Arriving near that place, we found the reserve brigade hotly engaged with a superior force of cavalry, infantry, and artillery. The rebels had a strong barricade on the crest of the hill on which Cold Harbor is situated, which was well defended. All our efforts to dislodge the enemy for a time were unsuccessful, until the 5th Michigan and a portion of the reserve brigade were ordered to move on one of the enemy's flanks. The enemy, finding their position turned, began to abandon their works. At this moment one battalion of the 1st Michigan, under Major Brewer, was ordered to charge the enemy with drawn sabres. This charge produced the desired effect. The enemy, without waiting to receive it, threw down their arms and fled, leaving their dead and wounded on the field.

"This position being an important one, and having received orders to hold it at any cost, measures were taken to put it in as defensible condition as possible.

"We remained on the ground that night, the troops sleeping on their arms. Soon after daybreak the next morning, a portion of the line held by the 1st Michigan was attacked by a large force of the enemy. Heavy firing was kept up for a long time, but the enemy, finding our position too strong, withdrew. It was here that Captain Brevoort, of the 1st Michigan, one of the most gallant officers in the corps, was killed; also Captain Haslet, of the same regiment, was wounded. We were then relieved by a portion of the 6th corps, after which we moved back to within a few miles of Parsely's Mills and encamped. June 2d, we moved toward the Chickahominy, and encamped at Bottom's Bridge. We remained here till the 4th, when we moved to the Old Church Tavern; 5th, encamped at Shedley's, near Hawes' Shop; 6th, encamped at Newcastle Ferry; 7th, crossed the Pamunkey, marched about a mile beyond Aylett's, and remained there till the next morning, when we moved to Hening Creek and encamped; June 9th, encamped at Young's Bridge; June 10th, encamped within three miles of Louisa Court-house. About daylight of the 11th, the 7th Michigan, who were on picket on the road leading to the court-house, was attacked by Wickham's rebel cavalry. As soon as I received notice of this attack, I ordered the 1st Michigan to move to the support of the 7th. The enemy did not follow up his attack. We then moved toward Travillian Station. The other brigades of the division had already moved by another road, and I was ordered to connect with them at the station. The force by which we had been attacked followed us up, but did not press my rear very close. My advance had arrived within a short distance of the station, when I received word from Captain Hastings, commanding the advance, that there was a wagon train in sight. I immediately ordered the 5th Michigan (Col. Alger) to charge them. This regiment charged down past the station, capturing a large number of wagons, ambulances, caissons, and about eight hundred led horses. These being the horses of the force engaging General Merritt and Colonel Devin. I then sent the 6th Michigan forward to the support of the 5th. They had gone but a short distance, when the rebels charged them in the rear. I then dismounted a portion of my command, and very soon had driven the enemy from my front. I moved down to the station, and discovered a large force of the enemy with a battery in position on the right of the road. I ordered Major Brewer with the 7th Michigan down the road mounted, with orders as soon as my battery opened to charge them with drawn sabres. I had then one section of Captain Pennington's battery in position near the station-house, and had sent orders for the 1st Michigan, which was in the rear, to move forward as rapidly as possible to charge the enemy on his left flank at the moment the 7th Michigan charged him in front. But this regiment was fully employed in holding the enemy, who were making a vigorous assault on our rear; consequently, before those dispositions could be made, the enemy had gained possession of the woods on our right, and poured such a destructive fire on the cannoneers that they were compelled to change the position of the section. Colonel Alger, acting under the impulse of a pardonable zeal, did not halt at the station as the order required, but advanced more than a mile beyond, hoping to increase his captures. The enemy, taking advantage of this, interposed his force between Colonel Alger's rear and the advance of the 6th Michigan, reoccupying the station and cutting Colonel Alger off from support.

"Disappointed in not meeting the other brigades of the division, with which I expected to form a junction at this point, and the enemy having shown himself in heavy force on all sides, I was compelled to take up a position near the Station, from which I could resist the attacks of the enemy, which were now being made on my front, right, left, and rear. As firing could now be heard in the direction from which the reserve and 2d brigades were expected, I determined to hold my position until reinforcements could arrive. The enemy made repeated and desperate efforts to break our lines at different points, and in doing so compelled us to change the position of our batteries. The smallness of my force compelled me to adopt very contracted lines. From the nature of the ground and character of the attacks that were made upon me, our line resembled very nearly a circle. The space over which we fought was so limited there was actually no place which could be called under cover, or in other words, the entire ground was within range of the enemy's fires. This fact induced the officer who had charge of the pack-trains, caissons, headquarters wagons, and all the property we had captured, to seek without orders a place of safety. In doing so he conducted them into the lines of the enemy, when they were re-captured. In causing this mishap he acted on his own responsibility, impelled by fear alone, and I might add that for his conduct on this occasion the President of the United States has dismissed him from the service for cowardice and treachery.

"About this time the enemy charged one of my guns, but before he could get it from the field the 7th Michigan, led by Major Brewer and Walker, charged them, killing and wounding quite a number. Twice the enemy charged this gun, but were unsuccessful in its capture. In this charge Major Brewer was severely wounded. After the enemy had been driven from this point, I started with the 7th Michigan after the trains. We came upon the rear of them, and recaptured two caissons, three ambulances, and several wagons. The enemy's force being so much greater than mine, I did not deem it advisable to follow. I then ordered this regiment back to its position on the line. At this time we had connected with the other brigades of the division. In this fight Majors Kidd and Deane, of the 6th Michigan were captured, but were shortly afterwards retaken by a portion of their own regiment, led by Captain Birger. Also in this fight Lieutenant Richard Baylis, of my staff, received a severe and painful wound through the shoulder while bravely leading a successful charge against a superior force of the enemy. He continued to fight and encourage the men until compelled to leave the field from loss of blood. Captain Jacob L. Greene, my A. A. G., was here taken prisoner. With unfeigned sorrow I am called upon to record the death of one of the 'bravest of the brave,' Sergeant Mitchell Belvir, of the 1st Michigan cavalry. He has been my color-bearer since the organization of this brigade. He received his death wound while nobly discharging his duty to his flag and to his country. He was killed in the advance, while gallantly cheering the men forward to victory.

"The men remained on the line all that night. The next day, about 4 P. M., we moved out on the road to Gordonsville, this brigade being in the advance. We had marched but a few miles when we found the enemy in very strong position. I immediately dismounted the 6th and 7th Michigan, sending the 6th in on the left of the railroad, the 7th on the right, holding the 1st and 5th in reserve. Soon these regiments became hotly engaged. A portion of the reserve brigade was then sent to connect with the right of my line. I also ordered the 1st and 5th to move out and reinforce the 6th and 7th. At this time the engagement became general. We had been fighting in this manner for some time, gaining no advantage, when I received orders from the General commanding the division to advance my line, and, if possible, dislodge the enemy; but the position proving too formidable, I deemed it best to withdraw my command to the position previously held at the forks of the road. We held this position until midnight, when we withdrew. Our loss of officers in this engagement was very heavy. Captain Carr, Lieutenants Pulver and Warren, killed; Captain Duggan and Lieutenant Bullock, wounded—all of the 1st Michigan. Captains Hastings and Dodge, of the 5th Michigan, wounded; also, Captain Lovell and Lieutenant Ranouse, of the 6th Michigan, wounded. We marched all night, and in the morning recrossed the north branch of the North Anna, near which we encamped. On the 14th encamped at Shady Grove Church; 15th, encamped near Guinea Station; 16th, eight miles beyond Newtown; 17th, near Walkerton; 18th, near King and Queen Court-house; 19th, moved to Dunkirk; 20th, crossed the Mattapony river, and that night encamped near the Pamunkey; 21st, crossed the Pamunkey near White House; 22d, crossed the Chickahominy at Jones' Bridge, and encamped near the river; from this point we moved on the morning of the 24th to Charles City Court-house, where we encamped for the night; 25th, moved to a point near the James river; 28th of June, crossed the James river; 29th, moved to Prince George Court-house; 30th, encamped near Reams' Station. During these operations this brigade has captured 14 commissioned officers, 318 enlisted men, two pieces of artillery, with limbers filled with ammunition, and has mortally wounded Major-General J. E. B. Stuart and Brigadier-General Gordon, of the rebel cavalry. It would be unjust to the brave officers and men who compose my command, did I close this report without uttering one word in recognition of their bravery, daring, and endurance, as exhibited during the late campaign. Where so many instances of individual heroism occurred, it is impossible to particularize. The desire to discharge all duties in a faithful and patriotic manner seemed universal throughout the command. I can only return my thanks to the regimental commanders, and to the officers and men under them, for the promptness and energy with which they carried out my orders. My thanks are also due to Captain Pennington and Lieutenants Woodruff and Egan, for the skillful and dashing manner in which their guns were handled. Words cannot express my gratitude to the members of my staff, who, on all occasions, rendered me the most hearty support, and to whose able assistance I was frequently indebted for the success of our arms. Captain Charles Walker, who served as volunteer aid on my staff throughout the entire campaign, participating in every engagement with great credit and distinction to himself, is deserving of the highest praise for his courageous and patriotic example. Below I append a recapitulation of our losses during the whole campaign:

"My staff officers, 3 wounded and 2 missing."

	Killed.	Wounded.	Missing.	Total.
1st Michigan, officers......	3	5	1	9
Enlisted men................	37	133	64	234
5th Michigan, officers.....	....	8	1	9
Enlisted men................	12	52	135	199
6th Michigan, officers.....	1	2	1	4
Enlisted men................	28	58	63	149
7th Michigan, officers.....	1	1	1	3
Enlisted men................	12	98	13	123
Total...................	....	....	....	733

On the 31st of July the brigade was ordered to proceed to Washington, and thence to the Shenandoah Valley, where the regiments engaged the enemy at the following points: Winchester, August 11; Front Royal, August 16; Leetown, August 25; Shepherdstown, August 25; Smithfield, August 29; Berryville, September 3; Summit, September 4.

Extract from the report of Col. R. A. Alger, commanding 5th regiment:

* * * "Moved to Yellow Tavern, on Brook Turnpike, where we met Stuart's cavalry in force, May 10th and 11th, 1864. The regiment was dismounted here and ordered to the left of the road, to drive the enemy from a piece of woods which they occupied on the opposite side of a large open field. Charging across the field under a heavy fire, the enemy was driven from his position across a ravine. Reforming the line, an order was received from the general commanding to charge the enemy in our front and right, as he was going to charge a battery on the right of the road. This order executed, and arriving at a point commanding a hill in rear of a rebel battery, an officer, accompanied by a large staff and escort and carrying a large flag, was seen coming on to the hill from the rear. This officer was shot by Private John A. Huff, company E, 5th Michigan cavalry, formerly of Berdan's sharpshooters. He was immediately carried to the rear by his staff. About thirty minutes later the hill was gained, and a woman and negro stated that General Stuart had been shot on the hill above-mentioned, and first brought to her house and afterwards carried away in an ambulance. Rebel accounts agree with the statement of this woman, also what was seen by us. In this engagement the brave Capt. Benj. F. Axtell was mortally wounded and left at a citizen's house on the battle-field." * * *

Capt. Benj. F. Axtell was wounded and taken prisoner at Yellow Tavern May 11, 1864. Died of his wounds in Libby Prison.

Extract from the report of Colonel James H. Kidd, commanding 6th regiment:

"May 12th, 1864, we reached Meadow's Bridge, on the Chickahominy; found the bridge gone and the crossing disputed by the enemy's dismounted men and infantry, with strong breastworks and artillery. From the swampy nature of the ground it was impossible to bring artillery to bear upon them. 'The stream must be crossed at all hazards' was ordered, and the 5th and 6th Michigan were assigned the duty. Dismounting, the two regiments crossed on the ties of a railroad bridge, one man at a time, in the face of a galling fire of musketry and artillery, succeeded in gaining a foothold on the opposite bank, and subsequently charging the enemy, driving him in confusion, killing and capturing a large number. This is one of the most desperate fights in which the regiment was ever engaged, and attended with but few casualties. Lieut. Thomas A. Eddie, one of our bravest and most efficient officers, was instantly killed by a shot through the head."

Extract from the report of Colonel R. A. Alger, commanding the 5th Michigan:

* * * "On the 28th of May, 1864, we were ordered with the brigade to support Gen. Gregg's division, which had already become engaged with the enemy near Hawes' Shop. The brigade dismounted, formed in line, and moving forward became hotly engaged immediately. The ground over which this regiment passed was covered with pine shrubs, affording no shelter from the fire of the enemy, who was strongly posted in heavy timber, on high ground, and behind formidable breastworks of logs. Charging into the woods, the enemy, after an obstinate resistance, fighting our men hand to hand, was driven with great loss, leaving the ground strewn with his dead and wounded. Of eleven officers and one hundred and forty men of this regiment engaged, five officers and fifty men were killed or wounded. Capt. David Oliphant, a gallant officer, was mortally wounded while cheering on his men in the thickest of the fight." * * *

Captain Oliphant died of his wounds on June 4th following.

On the "Sheridan raid," commencing May 10th, 1864, the battle of "Hawes' Shop" was fought on the 28th of the same month. In that severe engagement the Michigan cavalry brigade took a most prominent part. Colonel James H. Kidd, then in command of the 6th Michigan cavalry, in a report says of the part taken by his regiment and the brigade on that occasion:

"On the 28th May fought the battle of 'Hawes' Shop.' Gregg's men were falling back. Gen. Custer was ordered to support him. The brigade was dismounted. The 6th had the right of the road, its left resting thereon; the enemy was in the woods; we formed in the open fields. Gen. Custer ordered three cheers and a charge; the cheers were given and the order to charge obeyed. In a minute the fight was hand to hand. The rebels fought with desperation, but were routed. They left their dead and wounded in our hands and many prisoners. In ten minutes, out of 140 men I had engaged 33 were killed or wounded; 12 were killed instantly, 4 died before morning. The ground where the regiment fought was covered with rebel dead and wounded. The trees were riddled. Infantry officers who saw the fight spoke of it as one of the most desperate they ever witnessed. It is not boasting to say that the gallantry displayed by the men of the Michigan brigade in this fight was extraordinary, unexampled."

General Sheridan, referring to the action at Trevillian Station, June 11th and 12th, 1864, says:

"The cavalry engagement of the 12th was by far the most brilliant one of the present campaign. The enemy's loss was very heavy. My loss in captured will not exceed 160. They were principally from the 5th Michigan cavalry. This regiment gallantly charged down the Gordonsville road, capturing 1,500 horses and about 800 men, but were finally surrounded and had to give them up."

Extract from a report of Colonel James H. Kidd, 6th Michigan:

"On the morning of the 11th of August, 1864, we marched at daylight, and took up position beyond Opequan creek, toward Winchester. A section of Ransom's battery was charged upon by the enemy. Capt. Mather, with a battalion of the 6th Michigan, happening to be at hand, repulsed the charge and saved the battery, at the sacrifice, however, of his own life. He was instantly killed while urging his men forward." * * *

In a report of Major George G. Briggs, 7th cavalry, mention is made of the action at Front Royal, or "Crooked Run," August 16th, 1864, as follows:

* * * "On the 16th August the regiment took an active part in the action at Front Royal, where we charged a whole brigade of rebel cavalry, completely routing them, capturing 100 prisoners, a large number of horses and arms. Lieut. Lucius Carver was killed in this charge." * * *

Extract from report of Col. R. A. Alger, commanding 5th Michigan:

"Early in the afternoon of August 16, 1864, the enemy attacked the pickets in our front, near Front Royal. The regiment was immediately saddled and moved out, afterwards dismounted and advanced over the brow of a hill. Here the enemy was found just forming in line preparatory to a charge. The regiment charged and drove the enemy into the river, capturing sixty-five prisoners, and killing and wounding a large number. In this engagement Lieutenant E. G. Granger, who was serving on the staff of General Custer, was killed." * * * *

Extract from a report of Colonel Peter Stagg, commanding 1st Michigan, covering the action at Shepherdstown, Va., August 25, 1864:

* * * "Arriving near Kearneysville, August 25, 1864, we came upon the enemy's cavalry and drove him about a mile. Again moving forward, we discovered long columns of rebel infantry marching up on our flanks, when we were ordered back. At Shepherdstown we halted for a short time, and the enemy's cavalry soon appeared in our front and flank. This force we charged with the brigade and drove back to their supports, but in doing so became cut off from our main force and surrounded by rebel infantry. The brigade, after desperate fighting, almost hand to hand, succeeded in crossing the Potomac near Sharpsburg, Md. Captain Fred. A. Buhl was mortally wounded while bravely doing his duty." * * *

Captain Buhl died of his wounds at Annapolis, Md., 15th September following.

Of the engagement with the enemy near Winchester, on the 19th of September, 1864, General Custer, in his report of 28th of that month, says:

"I have the honor to submit the following report of the part taken by my brigade in the engagement of the 18th instant, near Winchester, Va.

"In compliance with instructions from division headquarters, my command was in readiness to move from its encampment near Summit Point at 2 o'clock on the morning of the 19th. It being the intention to reach the Opequan, some five miles distant, before daylight, the march was begun soon after 2 A. M., and conducted by the most direct route across the country, independent of roads. My brigade moved in advance of the division, and reached the vicinity of the Opequan before daylight, and unobserved by the enemy, whose pickets were posted along the opposite bank. Massing my command in rear of a belt of woods and opposite a ford, situated about three miles from the point at which the railroad crosses the stream, I waited the arrival of the division commander and the remainder of the division. At daylight I received orders to move to a ford one mile and a half up the stream, and there attempt a crossing. This movement was also made beyond the view of the enemy, and my command was massed opposite the point designated, in rear of a range of hills overlooking the Opequan. Owing to a reconnoissance made at this point by our forces a few days previous, the enemy were found on the alert, thereby destroying all hopes of securing possession of the ford by a surprise. Two regiments, the 25th New York and 7th Michigan, both under command of that reliable soldier, Lieutenant-Colonel Brewer, of the 7th Michigan, were selected to charge the ford and obtain possession of the rifle-pits upon the opposite bank. By request of the senior officer of the 25th New York cavalry, that regiment was placed in advance, and both regiments moved, under cover of a hill, as near to the ford as possible without being exposed to the fire of the enemy. At the same time, the 6th Michigan cavalry, Colonel Kidd commanding, advanced, dismounted, to the crest overlooking the ford, and engaged the enemy on the opposite bank. Everything promised success, and the order was given for the column of Colonel Brewer to charge.

"Accordingly, both regiments moved rapidly towards the ford. The advance of the 25th New York reached the water, when the enemy, from a well-covered rifle-pit opposite the crossing, opened a heavy fire upon our advance, and succeeded in repulsing the head of the column, whose conduct induced this entire portion of the command to give way in considerable confusion. No responsibility for this repulse could be attached to Lieutenant-Colonel Brewer, who had left nothing undone to insure success. Giving him orders to reform his command under the cover of the ridge of hills before mentioned, and directing Colonel Kidd to engage the attention of the enemy as closely as possible, while such a disposition of sharpshooters was made as to quiet that portion of the enemy lodged in the rifle-pits covering the ford. The 1st Michigan cavalry, Colonel Stagg commanding, which had been held in reserve, was ordered to accomplish what two regiments had unsuccessfully attempted. No time was lost, but aided by the experience of the command which preceded it, the 1st cavalry secured a good position near the ford.

"Colonel Stagg, detaching two squadrons as an advance guard, under Lieutenant-Colonel Maxwell, one of the most dashing and intrepid officers of the service, ordered the charge, and under cover of the heavy fire poured in by the 6th Michigan, gained a footing upon the opposite bank, capturing the rifle-pits and a considerable number of prisoners. The enemy retired about one mile from the ford in the direction of Winchester, and took a position behind a heavy line of earthworks, protected in addition by a formidable *chevaux de frise.* My entire command was moved to the south bank of the stream, and placed in position along the ridge just vacated by the enemy. About this time, a battery of horse artillery, under command of Lieutenant Taylor, reported to me, and was immediately ordered into position within range of the enemy's works. Prisoners captured at the ford represented themselves as belonging to Breckinridge's Corps, and stated that their corps, with Breckinridge in command, was posted behind the works confronting us. Deeming this information reliable, as the results of the day proved it to be, I contented myself with annoying the enemy with artillery and skirmishers, until the other brigade of the division, having effected a crossing at a ford lower down, established connection with my left. Acting in conjunction with a portion of Colonel Lowell's brigade, an advance of the 1st and 7th Michigan and 25th New York was ordered to test the numbers and strength of the enemy. This movement called forth from the enemy a heavy fire from his batteries. It failed, however, to inflict serious damage. Lieutenant-Colonel Maxwell, who headed the charging column, as was his custom, succeeded in piercing the enemy's line of infantry and reaching to within a few feet of their artillery. Overwhelming numbers alone forced him to relinquish the intent of their capture, and he retired, after inflicting a severe loss upon the enemy. This advance, while clearly developing the position and strength of the enemy, was not without loss on our part.

"Among those whose gallantry on this occasion was conspicuous was Lieut. Jackson, of the 1st Michigan cavalry, who, while among the foremost in the charge, received a wound which carried away his arm and afterwards proved mortal. He was a young officer of great promise, and one whose loss was severely felt. At this time the engagement along the centre and left of our line was being contested with the utmost energy upon both sides, as could be determined by the heavy firing both of artillery and small arms. While it was known to be impossible to carry the position in my front with the force at my disposal, it was deemed important to detain as large a force of the enemy in our front as possible, and thus prevent reinforcements of other parts of their line. With this object in view, as great a display of our forces was kept up as the circumstances would allow. At the same time skirmishing was continued with little or no loss to either side. From the configuration of the ground the enemy was enabled to move or mass troops in rear of his position unseen by my command. Either divining our intentions of delaying him, or receiving orders to this effect, he abandoned the position in our front and withdrew towards our left. In the absence of instructions I ordered a general advance, intending, if not opposed, to move beyond the enemy's left flank and strike him in reverse. I directed my advance towards Stevenson's Depot, and met with no enemy until within two miles of that point, when I encountered Lomax's division of cavalry, which at that time was engaged with Averill's division, advancing on my right on the Martinsburg pike. Our appearance was unexpected, and produced such confusion upon the part of the enemy that though charged repeatedly by inferior numbers they at no time waited for us to approach within pistol range, but broke and fled. Soon after a junction was formed with General Averill on my right, which, with the connection on my left, made our line unbroken. At this time five brigades of cavalry were moving on parallel lines. Most, if not all, of the brigades moved by brigade front, regiments being in parallel columns of squadrons. One continuous and heavy line of skirmishers covered the advance, using only the carbine, while the line of brigades, as they advanced across the open country, the bands playing the national airs, presented, in the sunlight, one moving mass of glistening sabres. This, combined with the various and bright-colored banners and battle-flags, intermingled here and there with the plain blue uniforms of the troops, furnished one of the most inspiring as well as imposing scenes of martial grandeur ever witnessed upon a battle-field. No encouragement was required to inspirit either men or horses. On the contrary, it was necessary to check the ardor of both until the time for action should arrive. The enemy had effected a junction of his entire cavalry force, composed of the divisions of Lomax and Fitz Hugh Lee. They were formed across the Martinsburg and Winchester pike, about three miles from the latter place. Concealed by an open pine forest, they awaited our approach. No obstacles to the successful manœuvering of large bodies of cavalry were encountered. Even the forests were so open as to offer little or no hindrance to a charging column. Upon our left, and in plain view, could be seen the struggle now raging between the infantry lines of each army, while at various points the small columns of light-colored smoke showed that the artillery of neither side was idle. At that moment it seemed as if no perceptible advantage could be claimed by either, but the fortunes of the day might be decided by one of those incidents or accidents of the battle-field which, though insignificant in themselves, often go far towards deciding the fate of nations. Such must have been the impression of the officers and men composing the five brigades now advancing to the attack. The enemy wisely chose not to receive our attack at a halt, but advanced from the woods and charged our line of skirmishers. The cavalry were here so closely connected that a separate account of the operations of a single brigade or regiment is almost impossible. Our skirmishers were forced back, and a portion of my brigade was pushed forward to their support. The enemy relied wholly upon the carbine and pistol; my men preferred the sabre. A short but closely contested struggle ensued, which resulted in the repulse of the enemy. Many prisoners were taken and quite a number of both sides left on the field. Driving the enemy through the woods, in his rear the pursuit was taken up with vigor. The enemy dividing his column, from necessity our forces did likewise. The division of Gen. Averill moved on the right of the pike, and gave its attention to a small force of the enemy which was directing its retreat towards the commanding heights west of the town.

"My command, by agreement with General Averill, took charge of all forces of the enemy on the pike, and those in the immediate vicinity of the ground to its left. Other portions of the 1st division made a detour still farther to my left, so that that which had lately been one unbroken line was now formed into several columns of pursuit, each with a special and select object in view. Within three-fourths of a mile from the point where the enemy had made his last stand, he rallied a portion of his force. His line was formed beyond a small ditch, which he no doubt supposed would break, if not wholly oppose, an attacking column. Under most circumstances such might have been the case, but with men inspired with a foretaste of victory, greater obstacles must be interposed. Without designating any particular regiments, the charge was sounded, and portions of all the regiments composing my brigade joined in the attack. The volleys delivered by the enemy were not enough to check the attacking column, and again was the enemy driven before us, this time seeking safety in rear of his line of infantry. Here he reformed for his last attempt to check our advance. The batteries of the enemy were now enabled to reach us, an advantage they were not slow to improve. At this time a battery of the enemy, with apparently little support, was being withdrawn. My command, owing to the repeated charges, had become badly broken, rendering it impossible for me to avail myself of the services of a single organized regiment. With detachments of each regiment, a charge was ordered upon the battery, which, but for the extreme smallness of our numbers, would have proved successful. Lieutenant Louensbery, 5th Michigan cavalry, with great daring, advanced with a handful of men to within a few paces of the battery, and was only prevented from capturing it by an infantry support, hitherto concealed, and outnumbering him. Sergeant Barber, 5th Michigan cavalry, clerk at headquarters, distinguished himself in this charge as my color-bearer. He carried the colors in advance of the charging column, and was conspicuous throughout the engagement until severely wounded in the latter part of the day. It being necessary to reform my regiments before attempting a further advance, advantage was taken of a slight ridge of ground within one thousand yards of the enemy's line of battle. Behind this ridge, and protected from the enemy's fire, I formed as many of my men as could be hastily collected. Two guns, which had been annoying us on our right, were now charged and taken by the 1st and 5th regular cavalry. This gave us possession of a portion of the main line of the enemy's fortifications. At the same time our infantry on the centre and left had, after our successes on the right, been enabled to drive the enemy, and were now forcing him towards the town. Still determined to contest our further advance, the enemy now contracted his lines. This gave me an opportunity to move my brigade to a small crest, within five hundred yards of the enemy's position. This movement was entirely unobserved by him, his attention being drawn towards the heavy lines of our infantry, now advancing in open view far to our left. At this moment I received an order from the division commander to charge the enemy with my entire brigade. Having personally examined the situation, and knowing that a heavy force of the enemy was lying down behind these works, facts of which I knew the division commander was ignorant, I respectfully requested that I might be allowed to select my own time for making the charge. My reasons for this course were, that I was convinced the advance of our infantry on the centre and left would compel the force in my front to shift its position to the rear, and the most favorable moment to strike it would be after this movement had commenced, not while they were awaiting us in rear of their works. My opinions were verified. Watching the enemy until his force had arisen from behind their works and commenced their retrograde movement, I gave the command to charge. The order was obeyed with zeal and alacrity upon the part of all. The 1st, 5th, 6th, and 7th Michigan, with a portion of the 25th New York, advanced in one line, most of the command using the sabre alone. Officers and men seemed to vie with each other as to who should lead. Among those in advance, my personal attention was attracted to Colonel Stagg, commanding 1st Michigan, Lieutenant-Colonel Brewer, commanding 7th Michigan; also Captain Warner, of the same regiment; to Colonel Kidd, commanding 6th Michigan cavalry, and to Colonel Hastings, commanding 5th Michigan cavalry. Each of these officers led his regiment with most commendable valor. The enemy, upon our approach, turned and delivered a well-directed volley of musketry, but before a second discharge could be given, my command was in their midst, sabering right and left, and capturing prisoners more rapidly than they could be disposed of. Further resistance upon the part of those immediately opposed to us was suspended. A few batteries posted on the heights near the town continued to fire into our midst, fortunately, killing more of their own men than of ours. Their fire was silenced, however, as we advanced towards them. Nothing more remained but to collect the prisoners and other trophies of the victory. No further resistance was offered; the charge just made had decided the day, and the entire body of the enemy, not killed or captured, was in full retreat up the valley. Many of the prisoners cut off by my command fell into the hands of the infantry, whose advance soon reached the ground. My command, however, which entered the last charge about five hundred strong, including but thirty-six officers, captured over seven hundred prisoners, including fifty-two officers; also seven battle-flags, two caissons, and a large number of small arms. It is confidently believed, that, considering the relative numbers engaged, and the comparative advantages held on each side, the charge just described stands unequaled, valued according to its daring and success, in the history of this war. Night put an end to the pursuit, and this brigade bivouacked on the left of the valley pike, three miles from the battle-field. Our loss was by no means trifling. A numerical list of casualties has already been forwarded. Among the gallant dead who fell on that day is Captain North, of the 5th Michigan cavalry, whose bravery has rendered him conspicuous on scores of battle-fields. It is with the deepest regret that I record the fall of Lieutenant-Colonel Brewer, of the 7th Michigan cavalry, who fell at the moment of victory while leading his regiment in the final charge. I believe I am correct in stating that he fell farthest in advance of those who on that day surrendered their lives in their country's cause. Possessed of ability qualifying him for much higher positions than those he filled, he was invariably selected to command expeditions involving danger, and requiring experience, daring, and sagacity, and invariably did he perform the duty assigned to him with credit to himself and to the satisfaction of his commanding officers. Known and respected by all his brother officers, his memory will always be cherished by every member of this command; and of him all will say he was a soldier *sans peur et sans reproche*. Instances of personal daring and gallantry during the engagement were numerous, and deserving of particular mention, but it is impracticable to include this list in a report of this character. A few have been referred to, having impressed themselves upon my personal notice at the time. I will only add in this connection that both officers and men did their duty, and not a single case of misbehavior occurred throughout the entire engagement. The assistance derived from the zealous and persevering efforts of the members of my staff deserves to be recorded. My orders were transmitted with accuracy and celerity, frequently delivered under a heavy fire. Of the numerous charges made by my command, there were none that were not participated in by one or more of my staff. They were particularly energetic in rallying and reforming regiments broken or repulsed in the charge.

"The following-named staff officers particularly distinguished themselves: Major G. A. Drew, 6th Michigan cavalry, A. I. G.; Captain L. H. Barnhart, 6th Michigan cavalry, A. A. A. G.; Lieutenant E. F. Norvell, 1st Michigan cavalry, A. D. C.; Captain E. F. Decker, 1st Michigan cavalry, A. A. D. C.; Lieutenant G. S. White, 5th Michigan cavalry, A. A. D. C.

"Surgeon Wooster, 1st Michigan cavalry, was extremely attentive to the wants of the wounded, and discharged his duties with marked success."

Three of the battle-flags taken in the engagement of September 19th, at Opequan, near Winchester, were captured by men of the Michigan regiments; two of them by members of the 5th cavalry, Sergeant Henry M. Fox, of company M, (commissioned afterwards as 2d lieutenant,) who enlisted at Coldwater, August 12, 1862; Corporal Gabriel Cole, of company I, who enlisted at Allegan, August 19, 1862; and Sergeant John Winter, company and place of enlistment unknown. One of them was taken by Private Ulrick L. Crocker, of company M, 6th cavalry, who enlisted at Vergenes, Kent county, September 29, 1862.

These men are all reported in the Official Army Register of the volunteer force, as having been awarded medals of honor by the Secretary of War; and it is officially reported that they were given as rewards for acts of bravery in the capture of the flags referred to.

Lieutenant Albert F. Jackson, 1st cavalry, wounded at Winchester September 19, 1864, died of his wounds on November 12th following.

At Winchester the 1st cavalry had seven killed, twenty-five wounded, and one missing. The 7th cavalry lost four killed and nineteen wounded. Losses of 5th and 6th not reported, but are supposed to be equally heavy.

After the important engagement at Winchester the regiments were engaged at Luray, September 24th; at Port Republic, September 26th, 27th, and 28th; at Mount Crawford, October 2d; at Woodstock, October 19th; at Cedar Creek, October 19th; at Newton, November 12th, and at Madison Court-house on December 24th.

On the 27th of February, 1865, the brigade formed part of the force with which General Sheridan made his movement against General Early's army, and on the rebel communications in the direction of Gordonsville and Richmond, and at that date moved with the cavalry corps towards Staunton, and on the 8th of March participated in an engagement with a part of the rebel cavalry, under General Rosser, near Louisa Court-house, and assisted in routing it and capturing the town, in which a large amount of property was destroyed, including the railroad depot, with rolling stock and telegraph office. It also participated in taking up the track and destroying the railroad property on the line of the Lynchburg and Gordonsville railroad, and in the destruction of the locks, aqueducts, and mills on the line of the James river canal. The command having reached White House Landing, March 19th, in time to take part in the final battles of the Army of the Potomac, soon after, with the cavalry corps, took position on the left of the line of that army, and on the 30th the regiment became engaged with the rebel cavalry and assisted in driving them within their works at Five Forks. It was also engaged with the enemy at the same point on the 31st and on April 1st; and on the 2d at the South Side railroad; and on the 4th at Duck Pond Mills; on the 6th at the battle of the Ridges, or Sailor's Creek, and on the 8th and 9th at Appomattox Court-house.

Colonel James H. Kidd, 6th Michigan, commanding brigade, in his report of the engagement at Cedar Creek, October 19, 1864, says:

* * * "The picket line of the 7th Michigan cavalry having been driven in early in the morning, the entire brigade moved out to its support. Found the enemy strongly posted, with artillery in position. We were ordered back, and took possession on the right, and afterwards on the extreme left of the army, repulsing several charges, and driving the enemy until overcome by superior numbers. That the Michigan brigade was engaged the casualties bear witness. One stand of colors and many prisoners were captured. Darkness intervened to prevent perfect success. Kershaw's division, which confronted us, was utterly broken and scattered. All the regiments of this brigade deserve special mention. They never behaved with more consummate gallantry. I regret to report the loss of Captain Shier, 1st Michigan cavalry, who was mortally wounded while leading a charge. A gallant officer, a polished scholar, an accomplished gentleman, his loss is keenly felt by all who knew him."

Captain Shier died of his wounds, October 31st following.

In the report of Colonel Stagg, 1st cavalry, commanding brigade, the following reference is made to the battle of Five Forks, April 1, 1865:

* * * "The next morning we moved forward, passing over the ground from which we had been driven the day before. Our brigade being in advance, we soon came upon the enemy, strongly posted behind a large swamp, through which it was impossible to penetrate. Moving to the right, the enemy's cavalry appeared in our front and was driven to his main line of works, occupied by Kershaw's division. In the afternoon the regiment participated in the final charge and capture of these works, taking many prisoners and pursuing the flying enemy until long after dark. In this engagement Lieutenant Orwin M. Bartlett was killed; also, Lieutenant George C. Whitney."

Colonel Kidd, 6th Michigan, says of his regiment, in an engagement near Five Forks: "On the 4th of April the regiment charged the enemy's line of battle, near Beaver Mills, Va., losing in the charge Lieut. S. H. Finney, a gallant officer."

NOTE.—"On the morning of the 30th of March, 1865, the 7th regiment of Michigan cavalry is found with the gallant Phil. Sheridan on the right flank of the rebel army near Five Forks, Va. For thirty days previous the regiment had, with the balance of Sheridan's cavalry, been constantly on the march, being of the command with which he moved from the Shenandoah Valley on the 27th of February, and undertook his celebrated raid to the James river, and which was attended with such important and brilliant results. Little time had been allowed for recuperating from the effects attending a service so arduous as that through which they had just passed, when, on the morning of March 30th, the 7th Michigan numbering less than three hundred men, and after marching all night in rain and over heavy roads, Colonel Geo. G. Briggs, then commanding the regiment, received orders to move with promptness to the support of the 6th Pennsylvania cavalry and the 2d U. S. cavalry regulars, holding a position on the extreme right of the Union lines, and which was being strongly pressed by a strong force of the enemy's cavalry. Upon reaching the point and reporting to the officer in command, the regiment was immediately placed in position to support a charge which was ordered to be made upon the enemy's line by the two regiments named, and which, although made with spirit and in splendid style, was not only met with firmness by the enemy, but they were forced to retire in some confusion. The enemy seeing his advantage immediately charged down upon the retreating force confident of success. The 7th regiment being formed in columns of squadrons, sabres drawn, moved gallantly forward for a counter charge. The task before it was a difficult one. Steady was the command as they rapidly passed forward through the lines of retreating men to meet the on-coming and confident foe. A moment, and the charge is sounded, and with shouts of 'Sheridan' and 'Victory,' they dash into the fire of death. Not a man faltered. The veterans of 'Gettysburg,' the 'Wilderness,' and 'Winchester,' with the names of FIFTY battles on their banners, were on their mission, and victory or death must follow. A moment, and the shock of contending arms and shouts of contestants filled the air. A moment, and the rebel line wavered, then broke and fled the field in a confused rout, leaving in the hands of the 7th the commanding officer of their brigade and a large number of prisoners—the remainder fled for safety behind the fortifications of the infantry, three miles to the rear, closely followed by the '7th.' For the part the regiment took in this action, it received the compliments of the commanding General."

The Michigan Cavalry Brigade had fought throughout the rebellion and was in at its death, being gallantly engaged at Sailor's Creek April 6th, 1865, the last great day's fighting of the war. Mr. Greeley says of that day: "Crook now holding Sheridan's left (facing eastward) advanced to Deatonsville, where Lee's whole army was moving rapidly westward. He immediately charged, as directed by Sheridan; well knowing the inferiority of his force, but determined to detain the enemy, at whatever cost, until supports on our side could arrive. The result justified the daring, Crook was repulsed; but meantime Custer, with his division of horse, struck again farther on, gaining the road to Sailor's Creek, a petty tributary of Appomattox, where Crook and Devin, coming promptly to his support, he pierced the rebel line of march, destroying 400 wagons and taking 16 guns with many prisoners. Ewell's corps following the train, was thus cut off from Lee. Its advance was now gallantly charged by Colonel Stagg's Brigade, (Mich.;) and thus time was gained for the arrival of the leading division of the 6th corps pursuing the Confederate rear, when Ewell recalled, fighting stoutly till Wharton's division also came up, and a part of our infantry advancing, were momentarily repelled by a deadly fire. But the odds were too great. Ewell's veterans, inclosed between our cavalry and the 6th corps, and sternly charged by the latter, without a chance of escape, threw down their arms and surrendered. Ewell himself and four other Generals were among the prisoners, of whom over 6000 were taken this day."

THE SECOND CAVALRY.

On November 14, 1861, the 2d cavalry, raised by Col. F. W. Kellogg, moved from their rendezvous at Grand Rapids, destined for St. Louis, Mo., and on their arrival there, Captain Gordon Granger, U. S. A., assumed command as colonel. The regiment was stationed during the winter at Benton Barracks, near that city. Early in March, 1862, it left that point to take part with the forces of General Pope in the operations against Island No. 10, a strongly fortified position near New Madrid. The 2d first encountered the enemy near Point Pleasant, Mo., March 9th, and was soon afterwards engaged in the siege of the island, which continued from March 14th until April 7th, when it was surrendered. After the reduction of that stronghold, the regiment moved with General Pope's command, and joined the army under General Halleck in front of Corinth, where it was actively engaged in operating on the flanks of the rebel army, until the evacuation of that place by the rebels.

Colonel Granger, having been promoted to the rank of brigadier-general, March 26, 1862, Captain P. H. Sheridan, of the regular army, was commissioned by Governor Blair as colonel of the regiment on the 25th of May following.

Throughout the long and arduous services of this gallant regiment in the field, which terminated with the rebellion, it was the terror of rebels whenever it came in contact with them. Being always superbly armed and equipped, and the men being brave, and all of them most excellent shots, it seldom attacked without defeating and routing them, and never without severely punishing them, even when compelled to retire before immense odds.

Perhaps none of its many engagements will awaken in the minds of the members of the regiment more vivid recollections than those of Boonville, July 1, 1862, and Dandridge, December 24, 1863, where on both occasions it most signally distinguished itself.

During the last week of June, 1862, Colonel Sheridan, while his regiment was stationed at Corinth, was ordered with his brigade, consisting of the 2d Michigan, (his own regiment,) the 2d Iowa cavalry, Colonel Hatch, and two pieces of artillery, supported by two companies of infantry, to relieve a brigade stationed at Boonville, Miss., some twenty miles south of Corinth on the Mobile and Ohio railroad, being at that time the extreme outpost of the army in that direction. The movement was duly accomplished so far as the cavalry were concerned, but the artillery and its support did not arrive at their destination until in the evening of the 1st of July. The rebel General Chalmers, then in that vicinity, gaining information from citizens regarding the strength of the command at Boonville, and expecting to make an easy conquest, attacked Sheridan's pickets at 8 A. M., on July 1st, with (as was afterwards ascertained) 7,000 mounted men. At that hour there was but one company on picket, company K, 2d Michigan cavalry, commanded by Captain A. P. Campbell. Taking advantage of the cover of the woods, he checked the enemy long enough to receive a reinforcement of three companies, numbering only from thirty to fifty men each. The ground, although presenting advantages for defence in woods and small hills, yet had one disadvantage, in having numerous roads centering on Boonville, by which the enemy could approach in almost any direction. The 2d Michigan cavalry was armed at that time with Colt's revolving rifle and pistol, making twelve shots to a man, either of them very destructive at from twenty-five to eighty rods. The men of the regiment had been drilled by Colonels Granger and Sheridan to fight mounted and dismounted, either as cavalry or sharp-shooters, as the nature of the engagement might demand. When, therefore, they were attacked by Chalmers, and his fire returned with so much power and effect from troops on foot, he thought he had been misinformed as to the strength of the force at Boonville. He advanced with double lines dismounted, and double columns on either flank, mounted, with lines extended far enough to swing round on either flank, rendering the position of Captain Campbell in great danger of being surrounded and his force captured, while a solid column charged in the centre on the road. Their charge was met gallantly, by comparatively a mere handful of men, with such effect that they staggered back, and many fell almost at the muzzle of the rifles. Taking advantage of their momentary wavering, a new position was chosen a few rods to the rear, and Campbell was again in readiness to meet them. Inch by inch the ground was contested by the desperate fighting of the 2d Michigan, nobly protected on the flank by the 2d Iowa. Every man seemed to know his strength, and to take pride in using it to the fullest extent. When a charge was made by the enemy, instead of taking to their horses, which were kept under cover a few rods in the rear, they emptied their rifles of six shots at long range, then drew their revolvers, and before they had given them six more, the enemy never failed to turn to the rear in confusion.

This continued until about 2 P. M., the command having fallen back about a mile and a half, and to within half a mile of the camp, when Col. Sheridan, finding the enemy most determined, and affairs becoming critical, viewing at a glance the situation, ordered one battalion by a circuitous route to charge the enemy in the rear—200 men to charge 7,000!—yet they did it gallantly. At the same time, a supply train arriving from Corinth, Sheridan ordered the engineer to give a lively and cheering blast with his whistle, and the reserve to yell with a will, thus leading the enemy to believe that reinforcements were arriving, he withdrew his force to Tupelo, and left Sheridan and his handful of brave men masters of the field.

Next day 125 of the enemy's killed were buried, and numbers of his wounded were left at houses in the neighborhood, and he carried off full loads of wounded in his ambulances. The 2d Michigan lost forty-one in killed and wounded.

After the affair at Boonville the regiment was engaged in skirmishes with the enemy at various points in Mississippi, Kentucky, and Tennessee in 1862.

Colonel Sheridan having been commissioned as brigadier-general of volunteers July 1st, he was succeeded in command of the regiment by Lieut. Colonel Archibald Campbell, who was promoted to the colonelcy. During February and March, 1863, it was stationed at Murfreesboro' and Franklin. It made many important reconnoissances on the roads leading out of these places, and had numerous skirmishes with the rebels. In February it was engaged on the 18th near Milton, on the 19th at Cainsville, and on the 27th near Spring Hill. On the 4th and 5th of March it had a severe skirmish with the enemy under Generals Van Dorn and Forrest on the Columbia Pike, the regiment losing one killed, four wounded, and one captured. From the 8th to the 12th it participated in an important reconnoissance, during which the enemy were driven across Duck river. March 25th it had a sharp encounter with a large force of rebels under Stearns and Forrest, killing and wounding a large number of the enemy, and capturing fifty-two prisoners and a number of wagons loaded with arms, ammunition, and baggage, with a loss to the regiment of one died of wounds, six wounded, and two missing. On the 4th of June, while returning to Franklin from Triune, it had a brisk skirmish, with a loss of two killed and three wounded. Marching to Triune on the 6th, it remained at that point until the advance of the army from Murfreesboro', when it moved forward with the cavalry division to which it was attached. On the 23d it was engaged at Rover. On the 24th it drove the enemy through Middletown, and on the 27th charged the rebels into Shelbyville. On the 2d of July it aided in driving the enemy from Elk River Ford, and on the 3d from Cowan. In the early part of September the regiment was actively engaged in scouting among the mountains near Chattanooga and in northern Georgia. On the 18th, 19th, and 20th it was in the great battle of Chicamauga. Leaving Rankin's

Ferry, on the Tennessee, October 3d, the regiment participated in the chase after the rebel cavalry under General Wheeler, who were then engaged in making a raid on the communications of the army. During the pursuit of Wheeler the regiment crossed the Cumberland Mountains, marching on the 3d, 4th, and 5th of October one hundred and three miles, and on the 6th, 7th, and 8th eighty-two miles, the greater portion of the distance over rough and mountainous roads. October 31st the regiment was encamped at Winchester, East Tennessee.

Capt. James Hawley, of this regiment, was killed in action at Chicamauga September 20th, while serving on Gen. Stanley's staff.

Near Dandridge, East Tennessee, December 24, 1863, Col. A. B. Campbell, in command of a brigade of cavalry, composed of the 2d Michigan, 9th Pennsylvania, and 1st Tennessee, attacked and drove a portion of the enemy's cavalry through that place, and then halted north of the town with no enemy in sight. At 2 P. M., same day, the rebels, under cover of the hills and by a curve in the road, rapidly pushed in, in rear of the command with two brigades of cavalry, cutting Colonel Campbell off from his only source of retreat. The enemy, at the first dash, captured two pieces of artillery, but they were immediately recaptured and pushed to the rear. Colonel Campbell at once determined to cut his way out by the left flank, which, by a bold and gallant dash, was accomplished. The command then fell steadily back before this superior force, fighting desperately on foot, and so closely followed by the enemy that for four hours it was found impossible to bring the artillery into position. Just at dark the guns were brought to bear and opened with much vigor, checking the enemy, thereby giving the brigade an opportunity to form in good shape, when it mounted and unpursued thereafter by the enemy reached its camp at New Market, with a loss of twenty in killed, wounded, and missing.

This stubborn and close fighting exhibits the strength of men when drilled to rely upon themselves and their superior arms instead of being entirely dependent upon officers, who may not always be able to communicate orders to every part of the field in a running fight. In this affair all knew the dangers incidental to a retreat before a superior force, and fought steadily and with true courage. Mounted men with sabres could do nothing dismounted at such a time, and of course were compelled to keep out of the way; so that during the hottest of the fight only a portion of the 2d Michigan cavalry were engaged out of the whole brigade, and not to exceed four hundred men. The engagement will be recognized by all who were in the regiment at that time as one of the hardest fights in which it had participated and one calculated to excite panic and disaster.

Pressed strongly by an overwhelming force through broken woods in a strange country, hardly knowing which direction to take, many of the officers and men not having received a command from headquarters during the entire fight, yet preserving almost a perfect line, together with the persistent fighting throughout the affair, reflects credit upon every man engaged.

On the 25th the regiment encamped at Mossy Creek. It remained at and near this place until the 14th of January, 1864, having on the 29th of December a skirmish with the rebels, in which its casualties were 1 killed, 1 wounded, and 2 taken prisoners. On the 14th of January the regiment marched to Dandridge, and on the 17th skirmished with the enemy, who were advancing on Knoxville, under General Longstreet. On the 19th the regiment fell back to Knoxville, and again crossing the Holston river, it bivouacked on the 23d on Flat creek, and on the 26th on Pigeon river. Marching at midnight on the 26th, it participated in an attack the next day on a brigade of rebel cavalry, from whom it captured 3 pieces of artillery and 75 prisoners, the loss of the regiment being 11 wounded and 2 missing.

Following the 2d through its services that followed, it is found engaging the enemy at numerous points in 1864. At Dug Gap, Ga., May 13th and 14th; at Ettoway river on the 26th, 27th, and 28th, losing at these points 16 in killed and wounded. On the 7th of October following, the regiment, in command of Colonel Thomas Johnson, engaged the enemy on Cypress river, with a loss of 6 in killed and wounded. Among the killed was Lieutenant Russell T. Darrow. November 1st it marched from Blue Waters towards Shoal creek, Alabama, and was attacked by the enemy at that point on the 5th, and, after a gallant defence, was forced back to Four Mile creek, sustaining a heavy loss. From the 9th to the 14th it was in camp, doing ordinary scouting and picket duty. On the 15th it broke camp and made a reconnoissance to the right of its position, and encamped at Taylor's Springs, and remained there until the 20th, when it marched to Lexington, Tenn., and on the 21st to Lawrenceburg, where it was attacked by the enemy on the afternoon of that day, and fell back towards Campbellsville and near Columbia, skirmishing at both these points. The 25th it crossed Duck river, and the 28th was in line of battle near the Lewisburg pike. On the 29th it retired to Spring Hill, and was engaged in skirmishing during the day at that place and at Bethesda Church. On the 30th it was engaged at Franklin, fighting all day, sustaining a loss of 1 killed, 17 wounded, and 3 missing. The regiment marched from near Franklin, December 1st, to within a few miles of Nashville, and was in line of battle during the night. On the 2d passed through that city, crossing the Cumberland river, went into camp at Edgefield, and remained there until the 12th, when it recrossed the Cumberland, passing through Nashville, and encamped on the Charlotte pike. On the 15th it advanced about two miles, dismounted and skirmished during that day and next; at sunset mounted and proceeded in the direction of the Harpeth river, swimming that stream, and thence marching to Spring Hill. Crossing Duck river on the 23d, and passing through Columbia on the 24th, it met the enemy at Richland creek, and fought him all day, charging and driving him sixteen miles, losing 1 killed and 6 wounded; skirmishing at Pulaski on the 25th, and at Sugar creek on the 26th, passing Taylor's Springs on the 28th, reaching Waterloo on the 31st.

On the 17th of January, 1865, it broke camp, crossing the Tennessee river, and passing through Eastport, Iuka, and Burnsville, Miss., taking six prisoners; thence proceeded to Corinth and Farmington on the 19th, and returning via Iuka, taking five prisoners, and thence, via Eastport, crossing the Tennessee river, reached Waterloo on 21st, and remained there until March the 11th, when, breaking camp, it recrossed the Tennessee river, marched to Chickasaw, Ala., and was there in camp until the 22d, when it again broke camp, passing through Frankfort and Russellville on the 24th, crossed Big Ford creek on the 25th, reaching Eldridge on the 26th, passed Jasper and crossed the Mulberry river on the 28th, and Black Warrior river on the 29th, and the 30th reached Elytown. Crossed Black Warrior again on April 1st, at Johnston's Ferry, swimming the horses. Skirmished with the enemy on the 2d at Trion, and on the 3d arrived at Tuscaloosa, surprising and taking prisoners the pickets, capturing the city, three cannon, and taking a large number of prisoners. After destroying a large number of buildings containing rebel stores, and burning the bridge, the regiment marched to Bridgeville, where it was attacked on the 6th, and, after a brisk engagement, with a loss of three wounded, repulsed the enemy. Continuing the march towards Northport, passed it and Windham's Springs. On the 13th crossed Wolf creek; on the 14th, Lost creek and Black Water; on the 19th, Black Warrior and the Coosa, at Luff's Ferry; on the 22d, reaching Talladaga. Skirmished with General Hill's brigade on the 23d, losing two killed and taking one piece of artillery.

THE THIRD CAVALRY.

The 3d cavalry, also raised under the direction of Col. Kellogg, soon followed to the field the 2d cavalry. Moving from Grand Rapids in command of Lieut. Col. R. H. G. Minty November 28, 1861, for Benton Barracks, Missouri, where Col. J. K. Mizner assumed command of the regiment. Its first engagement with the rebels was at New Madrid, Missouri, March 13th, 1862, where it commenced a most creditable career, giving traitors a lively idea what Michigan cavalry were and what they might expect in the future, and this the regiment made them understand and realize to the fullest extent during the entire war. The 3d, after the surrender of Island No. 10 to the Union forces under General Pope, joined the army in front of Corinth, and served there until its evacuation by the rebels. The regiment then entered on the campaign of General Grant in Mississippi and served under General Rosecrans, encountering the enemy with much success in numerous engagements and skirmishes. At Iuka on September 19th, 1862, while in command of Captain L. G. Wilcox, Col. Mizner, being chief of cavalry, it became conspicuously distinguished; having the advance of the forces under General Hamilton, moving eastward on the Tuscumbia road, it engaged the enemy in a most vigorous and dashing manner. Capt. Wilcox, in his report of the affair, says:

* * * "At a late hour on the 18th instant, while encamped at Davenport's Mills, near Jacinto, I directed company A, Captain Dyckman, to examine the Iuka road, running northeast from the Mills and midway between the Tuscumbia and Burnsville roads, in order to determine the practicability of moving wagon or artillery trains on the road, and whether any portion of the road was occupied by the enemy.

"The reconnoissance was properly and promptly made, and the road found to be impracticable for moving trains, but passable for infantry and cavalry. The road was occupied by pickets, who fired upon the reconnoitering party.

"At 4 o'clock on the following morning, pursuant to instructions from Col. Mizner, I took eight companies of my command, leaving four in camp, and proceeded in light marching order along the Tuscumbia road east to its intersection with the Russellville road, about six miles east of Jacinto, where my command took the advance of General Hamilton's division and moved in the direction of Barnett's Corners. I had moved about two miles further when I found indications of the presence of rebel cavalry; the indications were more marked as we proceeded, and as we arrived at the brow of the hill, about one half mile west of Barnett's, a volley was fired into the head of the column. The rebel force seemed well supported, and I immediately dismounted twenty men and sent them, in command of Capt. Latimer, into the woods to the right. Twenty more were sent into a corn-field to the left in command of Lieut. Mix, and companies A and F, under Capt. Dyckman, were sent forward on the road. After a sharp skirmish of about fifteen minutes the rebels were driven from the woods, leaving one man killed and one horse; also, one man, horse, and equipments were taken by Capt. Latimer. From this point (Barnett's) a running fight was kept up, the rebels falling back to a branch of the Cripple Deer creek, distant about four miles. On arriving at the branch we found that the rebel cavalry had rallied at a house situated on an elevation four hundred yards distant and commanding the road. The advance, under Sergeant H. D. Cutting, company K, charged up the road at full gallop and drove them from their position into the woods; but the enemy rallied, two squadrons strong, and forced the advance to retire. Sergeant Cutting's horse was shot, which was the only casualty occurring to my command in this instance. A number of shots were fired into the head of the column, killing a lieutenant on Gen. Hamilton's staff. I at once wheeled the cavalry into line on the road side and uncovered a column of infantry, which moved to the front and deployed on either side of the road, and drove the enemy from the cover of some buildings behind which they were sheltered.

"A column of infantry then moved in advance, and position having been taken at a point about one and a half mile from Iuka, pursuant to orders received from Col. Mizner, I immediately moved with four companies, viz: Company K, Capt. Newell; company E, Capt. Latimer; company F, Capt. Kiese; and company A, Capt. Dyckman, to the front, and moved out to the right of Constable's Ohio battery; Lieut. Adams commanding the advance guard.

"After proceeding about one half mile, Lieut. Adams, perceiving a body of cavalry on a hill directly east of the battle-field, attacked and drove them away with considerable loss. I then formed my men behind the brow of the hill, dismounted a portion, and poured an irregular fire into the enemy's left flank and upon those who showed themselves in our front with considerable effect, twenty-two dead having been afterwards found, who must have fallen by our hands. During the time that we were in this position the enemy occasionally gave us a heavy volume, but the nature of the ground was such that no casualties had occurred until near sundown, when the enemy seemed to manifest a disposition to gain our position. I immediately dismounted all the men that could be spared, sending the horses into the woods in our rear, and opened a destructive fire upon them. They immediately fell back, and made no further attempt to advance upon us. We took a first lieutenant, bearing the stand of colors belonging to the 3d Louisiana infantry. Capt. Latimer was wounded in the shoulder, also two privates slightly. Six horses were lost. After dark I moved my command to the left of the road, in rear of the infantry, where I was joined by the other four companies of my command, which had been employed in reconnoitering on either flank during the afternoon."

General Rosecrans, ever ready to acknowledge the merits of the soldier as well as the officer, says in his report of this important battle:

"During the action, five privates of the 3d Michigan cavalry, beyond our extreme right, opened fire, captured a rebel stand of colors, a captain and lieutenant, sent in the colors that night, alone held their prisoners during the night, and brought them in next morning."

The battle of Iuka was sanguine, the firing heavy and rapid, and the ground was being hotly contested, when, night coming on, became masters of the field, and closed the scene of carnage. Morning revealed the fact that during the darkness of the night the enemy had left the field and was rapidly moving southward, while the Union troops made a vigorous pursuit for many miles, becoming several times hotly engaged, and causing him repeatedly to form line of battle to check the Union advance.

The 3d was actively occupied with the enemy after the affair of Iuka. Being in engagements at Corinth October 3d and 4th; at Hatchie October

6th; Hudsonville November 14th; Holly Springs November 19th; Lumkin's Mills November 30th; Oxford December 2d; Coffeeville December 5th; Brownsville January 14th, 1863; Clifton February 20th; Panola July 20th; Grenada August 14th; Byhalia October 12th; and Wyatt's Ford, Tallahatchie river, October 13th. In addition to these principal engagements, the regiment has participated in a large number of skirmishes of minor importance. In the affair at Grenada the 3d was in the advance. It gained possession of the town after a sharp engagement, and immediately commenced the destruction of the enemy's machinery and rolling stock accumulated at this point. Over sixty locomotives and more than four hundred cars were destroyed. At Byhalia and Wyatt's Ford the regiment was warmly engaged. In these actions the enemy were completely routed with large loss. The 3d cavalry aided largely in driving the notorious rebels, Richardson, Dawson, and Cushman, from West Tennessee, together with numerous bands of guerrillas that infested that section, and who were destroyed or dispersed by it.

During November and December, 1863, this regiment was almost constantly engaged in scouting and in various expeditions through Northern Mississippi and Western Tennessee, visiting most of the important places in that section. It had frequent encounters with the enemy's forces under Generals Forrest and Chalmers. Engagements and skirmishes in which the regiment participated occurred at Ripley, Mississippi, November 29th; Orizaba, Mississippi, November 30th; Ellistown, Mississippi, December 3d; Purdy, Tennessee, December 22d; and Jack's Creek, Tennessee, December 24th.

During the months of November, 1864, and February, 1865, this regiment constituted the garrison of the post at Brownsville Station, on the Memphis and Little Rock railroad, and was also occupied in scouting along the line of that road, making several expeditions as far south as Arkansas Post, on the Arkansas river, collecting large droves of cattle, and thereby furnishing nearly all the beef required for the supply of the entire army then serving in the Department of Arkansas. At Brownsville Station the regiment erected a complete set of winter quarters and stables, so neatly and tastefully arranged as to present the appearance of an important town, which attracted so much attention as to result in a change of its name from "Brownsville Station" to "Michigan City." The very active duty of the regiment at that time was so conducive to the health of the men that 1,008 were daily reported present for duty, and less than three per cent. were on the sick list. Early in February the regiment was selected to constitute part of a division then being organized for active and important service in early spring, and was assigned to the 1st brigade, 1st division, 7th army corps, and moved to Brownsville. On the 14th of March the brigade was transferred from the Department of Arkansas to the Military Division of West Mississippi, to join the troops under Major-General Canby, designed to operate against Mobile, and the regiment proceeded by steamer to New Orleans, arriving at Carrolton, La., March 23d, and embarked for Mobile early in April. After the fall of Mobile, it was employed on outpost duty until the surrender of the Confederate forces east of the Mississippi river, when the regiment was selected as the escort of Major-General Canby on the occasion of his receiving the formal surrender of the rebel General Taylor and his army. It left Mobile May 8, and marched across the country to Baton Rouge, La., reaching there on the 22d. When Major-General Sheridan assumed the command of the Military Division of the Southwest, the regiment was selected and ordered to report to him for duty, and was immediately prepared to join the expedition to Texas, and left Baton Rouge for Shreeveport, June 10th, and commenced its march into Texas from the latter place July 10th, traversing two-thirds the breadth of that State, arriving on the 2d of August at San Antonio. At that point the regiment was stationed, performing garrison duty and employed in the necessary scouting for the protection of the frontier as far as the Rio Grande, on the Mexican border, and in furnishing escorts for supply trains. The regiment comprised a part of the 1st brigade, 1st cavalry division, Military Division of the Gulf, and had its headquarters at San Antonio until February 15, 1866, when it was dismounted and mustered out of service.

THE FOURTH CAVALRY.

The Western rebel troops in the war were made to know the 4th Michigan cavalry, and undoubtedly most of them that are alive now have not forgotten them. The regiment was raised and organized by Col. R. H. G. Minty, previously Lieutenant-Colonel 3d Michigan cavalry. Under his command it left the State for the field in Kentucky, September 26, 1862. It fought its first battle at Stanford, in that State, on the 14th of October following, and was thus early initiated into the realities of the great rebellion.

The 4th was in the advance in the attack on Morgan and his guerillas at Stanford, and joined in pursuit as far as Crab Orchard. It also led the attack on Lebanon, Ky., November 9, driving in Morgan's pickets at a gallop, and entered the town, 543 strong, two miles in advance of the infantry, driving out Morgan with 759 men and two pieces of artillery, and capturing a large amount of commissary stores and clothing.

It was engaged at Rural Hill on the 15th, Baird's Mills on the 30th, Hollow Gap, December 4th, and at Wilson's Creek on the 11th.

On the 13th of December the 4th marched from Nashville, where it had been stationed since the 28th of November, 1862, to Franklin, captured the rebel pickets, drove out the enemy, 1,300 strong, killed, wounded, and captured a number of them, with their colors, and destroyed an immense quantity of stores. On the 15th a detail of 40 men belonging to the regiment were captured on the Murfreesboro pike while, it was claimed, they were under the protection of a flag of truce. Breaking camp on the 26th, the regiment moved in the extreme advance of the army from Nashville, and commenced the fighting at Lavergne. December 31st it had a sharp skirmish with a large force of the enemy's cavalry, which it repulsed and drove back, the 4th losing 3 killed and 7 wounded. The 4th was the first regiment to enter Murfreesboro, January 5, 1863. May 22d following, the regiment, with detachments of the 1st and 2d brigades (the 4th and two companies of U. S. cavalry being in the advance,) charged into the camp of the 1st Alabama, 8th Confederate, and 2d Georgia cavalry, and, after a severe engagement, routed them, taking 55 prisoners, and destroying their camp equipage, stores, etc. The colors of the 1st Alabama (since presented to the State of Michigan) were captured by Sergeant-Major Clark and Privates Wilcox and Parker, of the 4th Michigan.

During its whole term of service it proved a most reliable and gallant regiment, deservedly proud of its fighting reputation, accomplishing an uncommon amount of duty. The fighting of this regiment seems to have been so uniformly brave and effective that the colonel has found some difficulty in selecting the engagements in which he considers it was most distinguished, as will appear from a special report to the Adjutant-General of the State, dated January 4, 1867, in which he states:

"I find it rather a difficult matter to satisfactorily give you the information called for in your letter of the 20th ultimo.

"The 4th Michigan cavalry has so often distinguished itself, both by the brilliancy of its charges and the stubbornness of its fighting, that I doubt if you will find two men agree on the two engagements in which it was most distinguished.

"Some would claim Stone River where it charged three times, each time driving a brigade of rebel cavalry from the field; others, some of the many 'raids' around Murfreesboro', where the sabre charges of the 4th Michigan and 7th Pennsylvania were the admiration of the entire Army of the Cumberland; others, the fight with Dibrell's brigade at Sparta and Sperry's Mill, on the 9th and 17th of August, 1863, or the hard day's fighting at Reed's Bridge, near Chicamauga, on the 18th of September, where the 4th Michigan, 7th Pennsylvania, and 4th regular cavalry (973 of all ranks) fought the entire of Hood's corps from 7 o'clock in the morning until 5 o'clock in the evening, leaving 102 rebel dead within one hundred yards of the eastern end of the bridge, and preventing the carrying out of Bragg's order of battle of that date, the first part of which reads:—'1. Johnson's column (Hood's) on crossing at or near Reed's Bridge will turn to the left by the most practicable route, and sweep up the Chicamauga towards Lee & Gordon's mills.'

"Some again would claim Lovejoy's Station, Ga., on the 20th of August, 1864, where the same little brigade, then numbering under 800 men, scattered Ross's Texan brigade, sabering over 500 of them.

"After considering the subject fully, I selected Shelbyville, Tenn., on the 27th of June, 1863, and Latimer's Mill, Ga., on June 20, 1864. At both these places the success of my brigade was mainly attributable to the brilliancy and tenacity of the fighting of the 4th Michigan cavalry, then under command of Major F. W. Mix.

"At Shelbyville I found myself with a force of 1500 men in front of formidable breastworks, with an abatis of over one-fourth of a mile in width in front of them, behind which Generals Wheeler and Martin had an opposing force of 4,000 men, and three pieces of artillery. I detached the 4th Michigan, in command of Major Mix, well to the right, with orders to force their way through the abatis, and assault the works, and if successful to turn to the right and sweep up the entrenchments, promising that so soon as I heard their rifles speaking, I would make the direct assault on the Murfreesboro' and Shelbyville pike. They did their work so well that as I entered the works on the main road they joined me from the right, having carried the works and taken prisoners from six different regiments. The fruits of that day's work were the whole of the enemy's artillery and 599 prisoners, while over 200 dead bodies were afterwards taken out of Duck creek, into which I had driven Wheeler and his entire command."

The loss of the regiment was only seven wounded and nine prisoners.

The important part taken by the 4th cavalry in the great battle of Chicamauga, while in command of Major Mix, warrants it in being placed among the many engagements in which that regiment distinguished itself.

In Col. Minty's report of the part taken by his command from the 13th to the 24th September, 1863, including the battle of Chicamauga, he says:

"September 13th.—With the 4th U. S. cavalry, 4th Michigan cavalry, 7th Pennsylvania cavalry, and one section of the Chicago Board of Trade battery, I marched from Chattanooga, and reported to Major-Gen. Crittenden, commanding 21st army corps, at Gordon's Mill.

"September 14th.—Under orders from Major-Gen. Crittenden, I crossed Missionary Ridge into Lookout Valley.

"September 15th.—Marched back to Gordon's Mill, where Gen. Crittenden ordered me to proceed to Pea Vine Valley, and encamped near Leet's Cross-roads. I crossed the Chicamauga at Reed's Bridge, and shortly before dark encamped on Pea Vine creek, near Peeler's Mill, and sent out scouts towards Grayville, Ringold, Leet's, and Rock Springs. Same night I reported to Major-General Crittenden the information brought by these parties, and in answer received a letter from Capt. Oldershaw, A. A. G., 21st army corps, of which the following is an extract: 'The major-general commanding directs me to acknowledge the receipt of your letter of this date, informing him that Forrest is at Ringold, Longstreet at Dalton, Pegram at Leet's, and Buckner at Rock Springs; all this would indicate infantry, which the major-general cannot believe.'

"September 16th.—Strong scouting parties advanced towards me from Ringold and Leet's; they were promptly met, driven, and followed. At the same time my pickets on the Lafayette and Harrison road, which lies between Pea Vine Ridge and the Chicamauga, were attacked from towards Lafayette, thus threatening my communications via Reed's Bridge. I immediately fell back to that road, thus securing the bridge, but at the same time I kept possession of the roads in Pea Vine Valley by picketing strongly. My scouts towards Leet's ran into the rebel infantry and lost one man shot through the head. This was promptly reported to Major-General Crittenden, whose answer was the same as yesterday, viz: 'Nothing but dismounted cavalry.'

"September 17th.—Slight skirmishing between my scouts and those of the enemy. The scout from Grayville reported that General Steadman's brigade of the reserve corps had passed through that place on a reconnoissance towards Ringold. On the return of my courier from Gordon's Mill he reported Col. Wilder's brigade of mounted infantry was encamped on the west side of the Chicamauga creek, at Alexander's Bridge, about two miles above me.

"September 18th.—At 6 A. M. I sent one hundred of the 4th U. S. cavalry towards Leet's, and one hundred from the 4th Michigan and 7th Pennsylvania towards Ringold. At about 7 A. M. couriers arrived from both scouts, with information that the enemy was advancing in force. I immediately strengthened my pickets on the Lafayette road, and moved forward with the 4th Michigan and one battalion of the 4th regulars and the section of artillery and took up a position on the eastern slope of Pea Vine Ridge, and despatched couriers to Major-General Granger at Rossville, Colonel Wilder at Alexander's Bridge, General Wood at Gordon's Mill, and Gen. Crittenden at Crawfish Springs. On this day the 4th Michigan lost eleven in killed and wounded and three as prisoners. The enemy, infantry in force with about 200 cavalry, advanced steadily, driving my skirmish line back to my position on the side of the ridge. The head of a column getting into good range I opened on them with the artillery, when they immediately deployed and advanced a strong skirmish line. At this moment I observed a heavy column of dust moving from the direction of Graysville towards Dyer's Ford; I sent a courier to Col. Wilder asking him to send a force to hold the ford and cover my left, and sent my train across the creek. As the force from Grayville advanced I fell back until I arrived on the ground I had occupied in the morning. Here Col. Miller, with two regiments and two mountain howitzers, reported to me from Col. Wilder's brigade. I directed Col. Miller to take possession of the ford, and again advanced and drove the rebel skirmish line over the ridge and back on their line of battle in the valley, where a force was in position, which I estimated at 7,000 men. Thirteen sets of regimental colors were visible.

"The rebel line advanced, and I was steadily driven back across the ridge. My only means of crossing the creek was Reed's Bridge, a narrow, frail structure, which was covered with loose boards and fence rails, and a bad ford about three hundred yards higher up. I masked my artillery behind some shrubs near the ford, leaving one battalion of the 4th regulars to support it, and ordering the remainder of that regiment to cross the bridge, holding the 4th Michigan and 7th Pennsylvania in line to cover the movement. Before the first squadron had time to cross the head of a rebel column carrying their arms at 'right shoulder shift,' and moving at the double quick, as steadily as if at drill, came through the gap not five hundred yards from the bridge. The artillery opening on them from an unexpected quarter evidently took them by surprise, and immediately checked their advance, again causing them to deploy. The 4th Michigan followed the 4th regulars, and the 7th Pennsylvania the 4th Michigan. One squadron of the 4th regulars, under Lieut. Davis, most gallantly covering the crossing of the 7th Pennsylvania. One squadron of the 4th Michigan, under Lieut. Simpson, on picket on the Harrison road, was cut off by the rapid advance of the enemy; they made a gallant resistance, and eventually swam the creek without the loss of a man. The artillery crossed the ford in safety, and I placed it in position to dispute the crossing of the bridge, from which Lieut. Davis's men had thrown most of the loose planking. Here I was soon hotly engaged and was holding the rebels in check, when I received a note from the officer in charge of my wagon train (which I had sent back to Gordon's Mill) stating 'Col. Wilder has fallen back from Alexander's Bridge; he is retreating towards Gordon's Mills, and the enemy is crossing the river in force at all points.' I sent an order to Col. Miller to join me without delay; and on his arrival I fell back to Gordon's Mill, skirmishing with the enemy, who followed me closely. With less than 1,000 men, the old 'first brigade' had disputed the advance of 7,000 from 7 o'clock in the morning until 5 o'clock in the evening, and during that time fell back only five miles. On arriving at Gordon's Mill my men were dismounted, and, with Col. Wilder's brigade and a brigade from Gen. Van Cleve's division, repulsed a heavy attack about 8 o'clock P. M. We lay in position all night within hearing of the enemy and were without fires, although the night was bitterly cold. At break of day General Palmer's division relieved us. I then moved to the rear and procured forage for our horses and rations for the men, who had been entirely without since the previous morning.

"September 19th.—Moved along the rear to the left to protect the trains moving into Chattanooga. Camped near Rossville.

"September 20th.—Under orders from Major-General Granger, I marched to the ford at Missionary Mills, and sent strong patrols to Chicamauga Station and Graysville without meeting the enemy. Towards the afternoon I received orders from General Granger to take possession of the position then occupied by him on the Ringold and Rossville road. On arriving on the ground I found that General Granger had already marched to the assistance of General Thomas. Being anxious to know what was in front of me, I pushed forward towards Red House Bridge, and found Scott's brigade of cavalry and mounted infantry, about 1,500 strong, moving into position on our side of the creek. I immediately attacked them, and after a spirited skirmish of about an hour's duration drove them across the creek, with considerable loss.

"September 21st.—During the night General Thomas fell back to the heights of Missionary Ridge at Rossville, and this morning I found myself about two miles directly in front of his line of battle. The rebels advanced in three columns from the direction of Missionary Mills, Red House Bridge, and Dyer's Ford. I skirmished with their advance for a couple of hours, and then fell back to Rossville, with a loss of one officer and seven men killed and one officer and thirteen men wounded. I was then ordered to the left to watch the movements of the enemy.

"September 22d.—Under orders from Major-General Thomas, the 4th regulars moved during the night to Rossville and took possession of the gap vacated by our retiring infantry, At 6 A. M. I heard firing in the direction of Rossville; leaving strong pickets in the passes over the ridge I moved forward with the 7th Pennsylvania and 4th Michigan to support the 4th regulars, but found that Capt. McIntire had judiciously fallen back, the enemy having turned his flank by advancing on the road from Gordon's Mills. I retired to Chattanooga, skirmishing sharply.

"September 23d.—With the 3d Pennsylvania and 4th Michigan I worked in the trenches all night, and at 4 A. M. crossed the Tennessee river and encamped at Oposum creek, from whence I picketed the river from Washington to Sandy Shoals.

"The loss in my brigade from the day I was detached from the division until I crossed the Tennessee river on the 24th was under 100 men, of whom only 15 were missing, and of those 15, 9 are known to be either killed or wounded; while during that time, in prisoners alone, I took from the enemy 439 men."

Colonel Minty, in calling the attention of the commanding General to the gallant conduct in the battle of Chicamauga of certain officers of his brigade whom he considered entitled to special mention, says of Lieutenant Simpson, 4th Michigan cavalry:

"Lieutenant J. H. Simpson, 4th Michigan cavalry, commanded the squadron of his regiment on picket on the Harrison Road, on the 18th, which was cut off by the rapid advance of the enemy. After fighting as long as he possibly could, he swam the Chicamauga and brought in his squadron, with no casualties but one man and one horse slightly wounded."

On the 30th, the regiment, in command of Major Horace Gray, having been ordered to Cotton's Ferry, on the Tennessee river, to support a battalion of U. S. cavalry, it was attacked and driven back by a large body of Wheeler's rebel cavalry, who had crossed the river. Here Lieutenant Edward Tucker was mortally wounded, and died at Chattanooga on the 7th of October following.

On the 1st of October it again had a skirmish with Wheeler's cavalry, who was engaged in making a raid on the communication of the army. The 4th participated in the pursuit of Wheeler, and on the 3d skirmished with his rear-guard.

On the 28th or March, 1864, excepting a detachment of 128 mounted men, the 4th proceeded, via Chattanooga and Stevenson, to Nashville, where it arrived on the 31st. It here received new horses and equipments and was armed with the Spencer carbine. On the 14th of April the regiment marched to Columbia, Tenn., where it joined the 2d cavalry division. Marching from this place with 878 men present, on the 30th, the regiment proceeded through Shelbyville and Tullahoma, and over the Cumberland mountains to Bridgeport, Ala., thence crossed the Raccoon, Lookout, and

Pigeon mountains to Lafayette, and thence across Taylor's Ridge, to Villanon, Ga., where it arrived May 10th. On the 15th the command attacked the enemy's cavalry at Tanner's Bridge, nine miles from Rome, routing and pursuing them seven miles, when meeting a superior force with artillery, it retired, the regiment having lost in the affair 6 wounded and 4 missing, and captured a number of prisoners. From Woodland, on the 18th, seven companies were sent towards Kingston on a reconnoissance. Meeting rebel cavalry, the detachment drove them for some miles, and until it encountered a force of rebel infantry in front. The enemy's cavalry then threw themselves on its flanks and rear, and nearly enveloped the detachment, but it finally succeeded in cutting its way through with the loss of 24 in killed, wounded and missing. Among the wounded was Lieutenant Randolph, mortally, who died on the 30th of that month.

Colonel Minty, in his report to the Adjutant-General of the State already referred to, says, regarding the operations of his command at Lattimer's Mill, on Noonday creek:

"To give you some idea of the magnitude of the fight at Lattimer's Mill, I hand you herewith a copy of a supplementary report of the battle, made by me as brigade commander, on the 7th July, 1864, to Captain R. P. Kennedy, Assistant Adjutant-General, and which is as follows:

"I beg to hand you the following extracts from a letter published at Atlanta, Ga., in the afternoon edition of the *Memphis Appeal* of the 25th June, 1864, as a supplementary report of the fight at Lattimer's Mill, on the 20th June:

"'On the 20th instant, two divisions—Kelly's and Martin's—and one brigade—Williams'—of our cavalry, went round to the left flank and rear of Sherman's army, it was said, to capture a brigade of Yankee cavalry, stationed at McAfee's. We succeeded in getting to the right place, where the enemy—Minty's brigade—was vigorously attacked by Williams and a portion of Anderson's brigade. After a sharp conflict the enemy were driven from the field, Hannon's brigade having come up and attacked them on the flank. The Yankees fought desperately and fell back slowly, with what loss we are unable to ascertain, as they carried off their wounded and most of their dead. To one who was an eye-witness, but not an adept in the 'art of war,' it seemed very strange that the whole Yankee force was not surrounded and captured. Dibrell's brigade was drawn up a few hundred yards from and in full view of the battle-field, with Martin's whole division immediately in the rear. This is one of the best fighting brigades the Yankees have, and to have captured or routed it would have added a bright feather to the plume of the successful hero accomplishing the feat. After he (Minty) had been driven from his first position, Martin's whole division was brought up, and lost several men of Allen's brigade. Brigadier-General Allen had his horse shot. The 8th Confederate and 5th Georgia, of Anderson's brigade, lost several killed and wounded. Williams' Kentucky brigade lost several good soldiers.'"

Colonel Minty adds in his report: "According to the above, there was the following rebel force in the field: Kelly's and Martin's divisions, consisting of the brigades of Anderson, (six regiments,) Hannon's, (five regiments,) Allen's, (five regiments,) and Johnson's, (five regiments,) and the independent brigades of Williams and Dibrell, composed of five regiments each, say in all twelve regiments, with an average of 300—3,600; the 5th Georgia numbered over 800. The entire force I had engaged was 7th Pennsylvania, 170 men, and 4th Michigan, 283—in all 453. These few men held their ground against the repeated assaults of the enemy for over two hours, and when I ordered them to fall back, they retired slowly, in good order. I beg to call the attention of the General commanding to the heavy loss sustained by this small force. In a loss of over twelve per cent. the very small proportion reported missing shows how steadily and stubbornly they fought."

General Minty adds in a note to this report: "My loss in this engagement was 2 officers and 65 men. The Marietta (Ga.) papers acknowledge a loss of 94 killed and 351 wounded. Two battalions 4th Michigan repulsed three sabre charges, made by the 8th Confederate and 5th Georgia, numbering over 1,000 men, and one battalion, led by Captain Hathaway, repulsed a charge made by Williams' Kentucky Brigade, by a counter charge."

The 4th Michigan lost 37 killed and wounded and 3 missing, including among the killed Lieutenant T. W. Sutton.

Having crossed the Chattahoochie river, the regiment, in command of Major Mix, on the 18th of July, 1864, participated in a raid on the Atlanta and Augusta railroad, and destroyed the track for several miles. From the 22d to the 24th it was engaged in a raid on Covington, on the same railroad, and in destroying the bridges and track. On the 27th the command marched through Decatur, covering the "Stoneman raid." Encamping at Flat Shoals, it was there surrounded by the rebel cavalry, but on the 28th succeeded in cutting its way through, and fell back to Lithonia, on the Augusta railroad. From the 1st to the 14th of August the 4th was employed as infantry, occupying a portion of the trenches in front of Atlanta that had been vacated by the 23d corps.

The 4th, still in command of Major Mix, composed a part of General Kilpatrick's force while on his celebrated raid around the rebel army then defending Atlanta. This force consisted of the 3d division of cavalry, about 2,500 strong, commanded in person by General Kilpatrick, Minty's and Long's brigades of the 2d cavalry division, numbering about 2,554, with two sections of the Chicago Board of Trade battery, in command of Lieut. Robinson. Kilpatrick made a complete circuit, occupying four days, fighting almost the entire time superior numbers, and whipping them with half their force. General Garrard, of the 2d division did not accompany the expedition, consequently, Col. Minty, of the 4th Michigan, then the ranking colonel, took command of the brigades of that division.

At 1 o'clock, on the morning of the 18th of August, Minty's command broke camp and left our lines for the rendezvous of the expedition at Sandtown, arriving there at 6 A. M. The movement was commenced under cover of darkness, to prevent, if possible, any information being obtained by the enemy; yet, a rebel letter, captured on the 20th, dated at Atlanta on the 18th, gave the number of Minty's command, and the destination of the raiders. On the morning of the 19th, Minty reported to General Kilpatrick at Sandtown, and received his orders, and that night the command moved off on their bold undertaking, the 3d division in the advance, skirmishing all the way, until the West Point railroad was reached near Fairbern, where the first rebel assault was made. The enemy struck the column on the left flank, with artillery and dismounted cavalry, with so much force as to cut the 7th Pennsylvania, in command of Major Jennings, in two, but were immediately reinforced by the 4th Michigan, commanded by Major Mix, when a vigorous and irresistible attack was made on the enemy driving him from the ground in great disorder. Pursuing the rebel force to Flint river, it was found that the bridge had been destroyed, the stream deep, and bottom bad for crossing, while Ross and Furgerson's brigades of cavalry presented a bold front on the east bank, and with artillery disputed the passage. The artillery was promptly in position, and soon silenced the rebel batteries; instantly the 1st, 3d, and 4th Ohio and 4th Michigan cavalry dismounted, formed in line, and under cover of a destructive fire of grape and canister directed on the rebel rifle pits, and with a yell, dashed forward on the double-quick to the bank of the river, where a deadly fire was poured into the rebels at short range, dislodging their sharp-shooters, when the column crossed the river on the stringers of the burned bridge, leaving the 7th Pennsylvania, one section of artillery, and the led horses on the west bank. Minty, with his command dismounted, then advanced on Jonesboro, the 4th Michigan being deployed as skirmishers, 1st Ohio, 4th U. S., in line, with one section of artillery in the centre, and the 3d and 4th Ohio following in column, driving Ross and Ferguson into town where they took shelter in the houses, and opened a sharp fire. While Minty was getting his artillery in position to riddle the buildings, the rebels mounted their horses and vacated in disorder. The 3d division was then quickly brought up, and the destruction of the town commenced, two-thirds of it being destroyed by fire.

While this was being done, Ferguson and Ross were reinforced by a brigade of infantry, and took a position near Kilpatrick's forces, entrenching themselves by felling timber, &c. Kilpatrick's main object being to destroy the railway, and not whipping the enemy, except when necessary in the execution of his purpose, that same night left Jonesboro. Striking east about five miles, he then marched direct for Lovejoy's Station, on the Macon road. At daybreak the next morning his flight from Jonesboro was discovered by the enemy, who started in pursuit with his cavalry. At one and a half miles from Lovejoy's Station, the 2d division in the advance, Minty's brigade leading, followed by Long's, the 4th Michigan was detached, with orders to gain possession of and destroy the railroad; and was engaged in tearing up the track, when the column moving down the direct road to the station encountered the enemy's mounted pickets, who were driven in by the 7th Pennsylvania in fine style; but skirmishing was continued until within a quarter of a mile of the station, where the force was dismounted. In the meantime the 4th U. S. cavalry had been sent to reinforce the 7th Pennsylvania, but before their line was fairly formed a whole rebel infantry brigade, which was lying in ambush without skirmishers out, poured into the ranks a terrific volley, and with yells rushed over the small party, killing, wounding, and taking prisoners nearly the entire party, who fought bravely until their arms were wrested from them. Long's brigade was immediately formed, artillery placed in position, and the rebels were quickly repulsed, with severe loss. Scarcely had this been accomplished when a whole division of rebel cavalry, (Jackson's,) 5,000 strong, composed of Armstrong's, Ferguson's, and Ross's brigades, were seen coming down on the left and rear on the keen run, accompanied by ten pieces of artillery. Cleburn's division of cavalry, 10,000 strong, was advancing rapidly on the right and front, while Reynolds, with seven regiments of infantry, was coming in quickly on the left and front. Before Kilpatrick had time to learn what was coming, a spirited attack was made on the rear, but he soon comprehended the situation. Minty's brigade was instantly withdrawn and hastily formed in line in column of regiments. The 7th Pennsylvania, Major Jennings, on the right; 4th Michigan, Major Mix, in the centre, and the 4th U. S., Captain McIntire, on the left; Long's brigade was formed in rear, and the 3d division was formed on the left of the road. The advancing enemy was immediately most gallantly attacked by a charge of Minty's brigade, which is described by a correspondent of the Cincinnati *Commercial* as follows:

"While the various regiments were being manœuvred into position to meet the onslaught of the rebels, who were sweeping down upon them, the men had time to comprehend the danger that surrounded them—rebels to the right of them, rebels to the left of them, rebels in rear of them, rebels in front of them—surrounded; there was no salvation but to cut their way out. Visions of Libby Prison and starvation flitted through their imagination, and they saw that the deadly conflict could not be avoided. Placing himself at the head of his brigade, the gallant and fearless Minty drew his sabre, and his voice rung out clear and loud: 'Attention, column! forward, trot; regulate by the centre regiment; march, gallop, march!' and away the brigade went with a yell that echoed away across the valleys.

"The ground from which the start was made, and over which they charged, was a plantation of about two square miles, thickly strewn with patches of woods, deep water cuts, fences, ditches, and morasses. At the word away went the bold dragoons, at the height of their speed. Fences were jumped and ditches were no impediment. The rattle of the sabres mingled with that of the mess kettles and frying-pans that jingled at the side of the pack mule brigade, which were madly pushed forward by the frightened darkies who straddled them. Charging for their lives and yelling like devils, Minty and his troopers encountered the rebels behind a hastily constructed barricade of rails. Pressing their rowels deep into their horses flanks, and raising their sabres aloft, on, on, on, nearer and nearer to the rebels they plunged. The terror-stricken enemy could not withstand the thunderous wave of men and horse that threatened to engulf them. They broke and ran just as Minty and his troopers were urging their horses for the decisive blow. In an instant all was confusion. The yells of the horsemen were drowned in the clashing of steel and the groans of the dying. On pressed Minty in pursuit, his men's sabres striking right and left, and cutting down everything in their path. The rebel horsemen were seen to reel and pitch headlong to the earth, while their frightened steeds rushed pell-mell over their bodies. Many of the rebels defended themselves with almost superhuman strength; yet it was all in vain. The charge of Federal steel was irresistible. The heads and limbs of some of the rebels were actually severed from their bodies, the head of the rider falling on one side of the horse, the lifeless trunk upon the other.

"The individual instances of heroism were many. Hardly a man flinched, and when the brigade came out more than half the sabres were stained with human blood.

"It was, all admit, one of the finest charges of the war. Fully one hundred men fell under the keen sabres of Minty's brigade. The praises of Minty and his command are upon every tongue. The 4th U. S., 4th Michigan, 1st, 3d, and 4th Ohio regiments charged over a rebel battery of three guns on the left of the road; but no sooner had our men passed than the rebels again seized the cannon, and reversing them, poured grape and canister into the charging columns. General Kilpatrick, seeing this, with his staff and others, about thirty in all, moved forward to capture the guns; but found a high staked-and-ridered fence between him and the battery. Seeing the predicament in which the general was, Private William Bailey, a young Tennessean belonging to company I, 4th Michigan, an orderly to Colonel Minty, coolly rode up to the fence, dismounted in face of a severe fire, tore down the fence, remounted, rode up to the battery, shot the captain, took possession of the horse and arms, and rode out. He was immediately followed by a party of men who captured the battery and spiked the guns. In the charge Minty's brigade captured three stand of colors. The 4th U. S. taking two and the 4th Michigan one."

The position of General Kilpatrick's force, and the overpowering numbers opposing him, rendered his condition most critical, leaving him to choose between surrender or almost certain annihilation in the effort to extricate himself. He chose the latter, and was relieved from his dilemma by the gallant fighting of Minty's brigade, and thus enabled to accomplish successfully the object of the expedition.

The casualties in the brigade and the Chicago Board of Trade battery on this raid were 1 officer and 32 men killed, 6 officers and 92 men wounded, 3 officers and 20 men missing, (wounded,) and 4 officers and 48 men missing.

The casualties in Minty's brigade during the campaign, ending in the occupation of Atlanta, were 2 officers and 44 men killed, 6 officers and 106 men wounded, and 7 officers and 83 men missing.

The regiment arrived at Lithonia on the 21st, having made a circuit around Atlanta, and been in the saddle and almost constantly engaged since its departure from Sandtown on the 18th, the marches having been made over roads that had become very rough from heavy rains. From Lithonia the regiment returned to Sandtown. Marching thence through Atlanta, it crossed the Chattahoochie river on the 19th, and encamped near Roswell. Less than 150 mounted men were present at this time for duty. A detail of 50 men, sent out as guard for a foraging train from Roswell, were attacked by a force estimated at over four times their number; but, after a sharp conflict, the detachment repulsed the enemy, its loss being only one wounded and two missing. On the 1st of October the regiment again returned to Sandtown, and on the 2d and 3d engaged the enemy for several hours on each day, on Sweetwater creek, but with slight loss. On the 4th the regiment arrived at Marietta, where it joined the 2d cavalry division, and moved with it in pursuit of the rebel army, then engaged in its northward movement to the Tennessee river. The command skirmished with the enemy for several hours on the 5th, and on the following day the rebels having vacated their position, the command attacked their rear guard and captured a brigadier general and colonel, with other prisoners. The enemy having moved to Dallas and occupied their old works at that place, were attacked by the command and driven out. On the 10th the command was engaged near Rome, and on the 12th crossed the Ostewaula river and attacked the rebel force, but after driving them several miles the latter opened with artillery, and the command retired. On the 13th the enemy were again attacked and two pieces of artillery and a large number of prisoners taken from them. Recrossing the Ostewaula river, the regiment marched through Rome, Kingston, and Adairsville, to Resaca, thence via Summersville and Galesville, Ala., to Little river, where, on the 20th, it engaged General Wheeler's cavalry, forcing them to retire. The dismounted men had from time to time been sent to the rear, and with the exception of 217 sent to Chattanooga, were employed in garrisoning the block-houses on the railroad between Nashville and Huntsville. On the 17th of September, Corporal Charles M. Bickford and 17 men of the regiment, in a block-house, were attacked by the rebel cavalry under General Wheeler, numbering over 8,000, with artillery. Although the enemy shelled the block-house for over five hours, they could not force a surrender, and finally retired with a loss of 8 killed and 60 wounded. The corporal was promoted to be a commissioned officer, and the names of the men were honorably mentioned in general orders.

The regiment, in command of Lieut. Col. B. F. Pritchard, was at Gravelly Springs, Ala., during the month of February and part of March, 1865. During the early part of March preparations had been made for active service, and on the 12th the command broke camp at 12 P. M. and reached Waterloo on the 13th, crossing the Tennessee river to Eastport, Miss. It remained there until the 22d, and then commenced its march southward, over mountains, crossing rivers and creeks and through swamps, building miles of corduroy road, reaching the Black Warrior river on the 29th, and which was that day crossed by swimming the horses, losing one man and between thirty and forty horses. During the night the Locust was crossed in the same manner. On the 31st the command crossed Shades creek and the Cahawba river, passing the battery over the railroad bridge after it had been laid with ties, losing five or six mules and horses by their tumbling over the narrow bridge and falling nearly a hundred feet, killing them instantly. The brigade to which the regiment was attached being in the rear of its division, the 2d, the 4th division having the advance, became engaged with Forrest's command, and had a sharp fight on the 1st of April near Mulberry creek, capturing three pieces of artillery. On the same day the regiment, with its brigade, crossed the Big Mulberry and about midnight encamped at Plantersville. On the 2d the brigade, being in the advance, started at 4 o'clock A. M. on the direct road to Selma, distant about twenty miles, reaching the fortifications in front of that place at 2 P. M. on the same day. They were found to be stronger and more perfect than those at Atlanta, consisting of an inner line of redans and redoubts, mounted with 12-pounder howitzers and 20-pounder Parrots. The main and outer line, which extended entirely around the city from river to river, consisted of twenty-five redoubts or bastions connected by curtains, the parapet being about twelve feet high and surrounded by a ditch and well-built palisade, in front of which was swampy ground partially covered with abattis. These works were defended by General Forrest, with a force estimated at nine thousand. The 2d division, in which was the 4th Michigan, was ordered to assault the works on the Summerville road and the 4th division those on the Plantersville road. About the time the assault was to take place the rear of the 2d division was attacked by Chalmer's division of rebel cavalry. The 3d Ohio and 72d Indiana, with a portion of the 98th Illinois, were immediately detached to hold them in check, leaving in the 2d division only about 1,483 men to make the assault. It, however, moved forward under a terrific fire, going at the work with a cheer, and had possession of the main line in twenty minutes, losing in that brief space of time 324 in killed and wounded. General Long, commanding the division, had been shot in the head shortly after the division moved to the assault, Colonel Minty, of the 4th Michigan, assuming command, leading the division in the assault, and is reported to have been the first man to get inside the works alive; Corporal Booth, company A, 4th Ohio cavalry, being killed as he entered the works just ahead of Col. Minty. The rebels were soon swept from the main line of works, and then the inner line of redans was carried in detail by assault, and possession had been gained of the entire inner line when the 4th division reached the outer works. The result of this gallant affair was the capture of the city, with twenty-five pieces of artillery in position, besides seventy-five pieces in the navy-yard, with a large amount of ammunition and stores, together with other property, and twenty-eight hundred prisoners.

On the 7th of May Lieut. Col. Pritchard was directed by Col. Minty to proceed with the regiment as rapidly as possible to Spaulding, in Irwin county, and picket the Ocmulgee river from Hawkinsville to the mouth of the Oconee river, for the purpose of preventing the escape of Jefferson Davis, who was then supposed to be making his way to the Atlantic coast, and if he got on his track to follow him wherever he went, and to capture or kill him without fail. At Abbyville he became satisfied that Davis had already crossed the Ocmulgee, and ascertained that the 1st Wisconsin cavalry was following him closely in the direction of Irwinsville. With one hundred and fifty-three of the best mounted men of the regiment he followed the line of the Ocmulgee for some miles, and then took a bridle path or blind road through the woods towards Irwinsville, and arrived at that place about 2 o'clock A. M. on the 10th, and found that Davis had not yet passed. Pretending to be a part of his escort, Col. Pritchard gained information from a rebel citizen that Davis was encamped in the woods about three-fourths of a mile north of the town. The camp was at once surrounded, and at about 3 o'clock A. M. the force closed in and captured him and his party. Davis attempted to escape, disguised in his wife's travelling cloak, with a shawl thrown over his head, but private Adrian Bee, of company L, and Corporal Munger, of company C, espied his military boots beneath his feminine attire and commanded him to halt. The following morning, while *en route* for Macon with the captives, information was received of the proffered reward of $100,000 for his capture. On arriving at Macon Col. Pritchard, Capt. Hudson, Lieut. Stauber, and Lieut. Purinton, with twenty-two men, were detailed to escort Davis to Washington, D. C. The regiment remained at Macon until the 21st, when it was started *en route* for home, feeling that in the capture of Jeff. Davis it had finished its work.

NOTE.—In the account given in the annals of the Army of the Cumberland of the capture of Franklin, on Dec. 13, 1863, is found the following notice of the 4th Michigan cavalry: "Company I of the 4th Michigan cavalry, dismounting, took position near the bridge and opened fire on the mill; the remainder of the 4th Michigan dismounted under cover of the rising ground on which the 7th Pennsylvania were formed, and advanced at the double-quick, passed the position of the 7th Pennsylvania, waded across the river and drove the rebels from the town. Colonel Minty was the first man across the river, and as he scrambled up the south bank, he took a rebel officer. The 4th Michigan had passed through the town and were following the enemy out on the Columbia and Carter's Creek pikes on foot, before any of the mounted men had crossed the river. The enemy left one captain and four privates dead in the town and ten severely wounded, and fifteen or twenty prisoners were captured."

Col. Minty, in his report of the operations of the brigade commanded by him in the battle of Stone river, says: "Captain Mix of the 4th Michigan, with about fifty men, not only drove two hundred of the enemy for over two miles, but held his position against a full regiment of rebel cavalry. Lieut. Eldredge with eighteen dismounted men attacked the enemy, routed him, and re-captured a wagon loaded with ammunition."

Col. Minty, in his report covering the service of his brigade at the battle of Shelbyville, specially mentions officers for gallant conduct, as follows: "Lieut. and Adjutant Hudson, 4th Michigan cavalry, acted with great gallantry throughout the entire action; he was severely wounded by a musket ball through the shoulder."

Regimental commanders make honorable mention of the following: "In 4th Michigan cavalry, Captains Pritchard, Hathaway, Robbins and Grant; Corporal Hoffmaster of company L, (most gallant conduct,) and Private Mason Brown of company I."

The regimental commanders (including Major Mix, 4th Michigan) are named by Colonel Minty as deserving of special mention for their promptness and the manner in which they handled their respective commands.

Following is Bragg's circular to his army directing the movements of the 18th, which indicates the important position held by the 4th Michigan cavalry:

HEADQUARTERS ARMY OF TENNESSEE,
IN THE FIELD, LEET'S TANYARD, *Sept.* 18, 1863.

[Circular.] I. Johnson's column (Hood's) on crossing at or near Reed's bridge will turn to the left by the most practicable route, and sweep up the Chicamauga towards Lee and Gordon's mills.

II. Walker, on crossing at Alexander's bridge, will unite in this move and push vigorously on the enemy's flank and rear in the same direction.

III. Buckner, crossing at Tedford's ford, will join in the movement to the left and press the enemy up the stream from Polk's front at Lee and Gordon's mills.

IV. Polk will press his forces to the front of Lee and Gordon's mills. * *

By command of General Bragg, G. W. BRENTT, A. A. G."

Says an officer writing to Col. Minty, and who had the opportunity of knowing: "It will I think be seen that you held on that day (Sept. 18th) the key of the position, (the left of the army,) and so successfully that the rebel plan was frustrated. It cost General Thomas thousands of men to maintain it, persistently fought for on the two subsequent days. Had the rebels succeeded, early in the morning of the first day of the battle, in taking Reed's bridge, not only Col. Wilder but the whole army would have been seriously compromised. I am sure had General Rosecrans known all the facts he would have added the 18th to the number of days 'the army could not have dispensed' with the services of the cavalry.

"The more I consider the facts concerning the situation of the army, and learn of the rebels, the prouder I become of our little brigade. 'Preston's division effected an unobstructed passage at Huntsford,' (says 'Ord,' the correspondent of the *Mobile Tribune*, Rebel.) Not so with Johnson and Walker at Reed's and Alexander's bridges Without them there was no 'sweeping up the Chicamauga and vigorously pressing the enemy's flank and rear;' and when the passage was effected, your persistent presence and line of retreat made the rebels fear to 'turn to the left' and expose to you their flank and rear. It was not cavalry you were fighting, as Bragg's order proves. Forrest was on the rebel right, but the bulk of the rebel cavalry was watching at Catlett's Gap. On the whole, Colonel, while you have earned many laurels, at no time can I find you doing such valuable service to the Army of the Cumberland, as on the 18th of September, 1863."

In 1864, while the block-houses on the Chattanooga & Nashville Railroad were being guarded by detachments of the 4th Michigan cavalry, one of them was garrisoned by twenty-three men of that regiment, only seventeen of whom were armed; they were under the command of Corporal Chanclor M. Bickford of Algansee, Branch co., Mich. On September 17th they were attacked by General Wheeler's whole command, eight thousand men, with three pieces of artillery. A summons of surrender was sent twice, but steadily refused. At half-past 12 o'clock M. the rebels opened with their artillery, and for two hours and a half continued to shell the block-house, at one time being not more than ten or fifteen rods distant. Seven times the rebels were made to change the position of their artillery, and were finally forced to retreat at about six o'clock in the evening with a loss of eight men killed and sixty wounded. The block house was struck during the engagement twenty-five times by artillery. Corporal Bickford was promoted to a Second Lieutenancy, and the names of the gallant men who were under his command were honorably mentioned in orders.

Col. Minty, in his report of the operations of his command at the capture of Selma, Ala, in mentioning officers deserving special notice for gallant conduct, says of Major Burns, 4th Michigan: "Major Burns, 4th Michigan cavalry, my A. A. A. G., was amongst the first to enter the works, and acted in the most gallant manner throughout the entire action."

Copy of the original letter written with a pencil by Col. Pritchard, announcing the capture of Jefferson Davis:

HEADQUARTERS 4TH MICHIGAN CAVALRY,
ABBEVILLE, GA., *May* 11*th*, 1865.

CAPT. SCOTT, A. A. A. G., 2d Division, C. C. M. D. M.

Sir:—I have the honor to report that at daylight yesterday at Irwinsville, I surprised and captured Jeff Davis and family, together with his wife's sister and brother, his Postmaster-General (Ragan) his private Secretary (Colonel Harrison,) Col. Johnson, A. D. C. on Jeff's staff, Col. Morris, Col. Lubbock, Lieut. Hathaway, also several unimportant names, and a train of five wagons and three ambulances, making a most perfect success, had not a most painful mistake occurred by which the 4th Michigan and 1st Wisconsin collided which cost us two men killed and Lieut. Boutelle wounded through the arm, in the 4th Michigan, and three men wounded in the 1st Wisconsin. This occurred just at daylight after we had captured the camp, by the advance of the 1st Wisconsin, not properly answering our challenge, by which they were mistaken for the enemy. I returned to this point last night and shall move right on to Macon without awaiting orders from you as directed feeling that the whole objects of the expedition are accomplished. It will take at least three days to reach Macon as we are 75 miles out and our stock is much wearied. I hope to reach Hawkinsville to-night.

I have the honor, Sir, to be, very respectfully, your ob'dt servt,

D. B. PRITCHARD, Lieut. Col. 4th Michigan.

The following are the names of the officers and men of the regiment who were present at the capture of Jefferson Davis and party, on the morning of the 10th of May, 1865:

Lieut. Colonel Benjamin D. Pritchard, commanding. Julian G. Dickinson, Adjutant. Perry J. Davis, Quartermaster. Charles T. Hudson, Captain Co. E. Henry S. Boutelle, 1st Lieut. Co. C. Silas J. Stauber, 1st Lieut. Co. G. Alfred B. Purington, 2d Lieut. Co. I. John Bennett, 2d Lieut. Co. B.

Company A—Sergeants Thomas Davis, Thomas Riley, George A. Simmons, Rezin Wright. Corporals Darwin Dunning, Robert L. Reynolds, Lyman J. Russell. Privates William Balon, Daniel C. Blinn, Gilbert Coata, James Fullerton, Casper Knable, Philo Morse, Charles W. Nichols, Henry Provost, George Rinke.

Company B—Sergeants A. A. Braley, E. A. Ford. Corporals B. B. Bennett, William Crow, C. F. Parker, J. F. Sherburne, U. B. Tuttle. Privates Augustus Armstrong, J. J. Bontel, Frank Crim, John Nichols, A. F. Shepherd, W. P. Steadman, William V. Wood, L. H. Wilcox.

Company C—Corporals David J. Curry, George M. Munger, Reuben Palmerton, Abram Sebring. Privates James F. Bullard, David Dillon, Frank C. Leach, James H. Lynch, (Stephen B. Munson, killed,) Ranseler Riggs, John Rupert, Harmon Stevens, William J. Smith.

Company D—Corporal James H. Place. Privates John Brown, Thomas Hunter, Burt Judson, Horace C. Jenney, William H. J. Martin, Jacob E. Munn, William Parker, Francis E. Thompson, Z. H. Wilcox.

Company E—Sergeants George A. Bullard, David B. Green. Corporals Dewitt C. Carr, William H. Crittenden, (John Hines, killed,) Charles W. Tyler. Privates Silas Bullard, George F. Delmage, William F. Driesman, Henry Johnson, Robert G. Tripp, John G. Stevens, Peter Seqany, Oscar E. Tefft.

Company F—Sergeant John Correnton. Corporals DeWitt C. Cobb, William F. True. Privates Joseph Bellinger, Henry Bradock, Dennis Drescoe, Henry Frickey, John F. Grossman, Ira Harrington, Jr., Homer Hazelton, B. Franklin Nichols, James Patterson, George Raab, William Wright.

Company G—Sergeants John Cavanaugh, Jeremiah F. Craig, Jacob N. Frash, James F. O'Brien, William H. Palmeteer. Corporals John Ballou, George Myers, Leander B. Shaw, George W. Van Sickle. Privates Daniel Graham, David Cunningham, Joshua Parks, Cary Reed, John A. Skinner, Joseph Odrin.

Company I—Sergeants Lester P. Bates, Elias F. Pierce. Corporals Preston W. Brown, Jerome B. Heath. Privates George W. Rodwell, Martin L. Brown, George M. Dutcher, William Dill, Charles Flugger, Daniel E. Krumm, Patrick McKennedy, Charles W. Middaugh, Hiram McCollough, Martin R. Pettit, Luke M. Thayer.

Company K—Sergeant Ansel Adams. Corporal Alonzo Moe. Privates Thomas Folley, Decatur Jaycox, John H. Kelch, Edwin Mabie, Smith B. Mills, James R. Norton, Jacob D. Newith, John Nelson, Enoch L. Rhodes, Nathaniel Root.

Company L—Sergeants Benjamin K. Colf, Joseph Hoffmaster. Corporals Charles C. Marsh, William Oliver. Privates Andrew Bee, Benjamin F. Carpenter, Daniel Edwards, E. Lane, J. W. Linsley, William Munn, William Newkirk, George Noggle, Perry Phelps, Jesse J. Penfield, Joseph Stewart.

Company M—1st Sergeant Wesley D. Pond. Corporals Simeon Huff, Henry Shanahan. Privates Andrew Anderson, Robert Arnold, Emanuel Beazan, John Vautyle.

A commission was appointed by the War Department which decided that the 4th Michigan cavalry were entitled to the reward for the capture of Jeff Davis, and directed how it should be distributed. But when the appropriation came before Congress, a claim was set up by the 1st Wisconsin cavalry, which deferred the passage of the bill from time to time until the close of the session, July, 1868, when the bill authorizing the expenditure was finally passed. The claim of the 4th Michigan was ably advocated by the Michigan Delegation, but the matter was so managed by Congress that the award of the Commission so far as the money in question was concerned, was set aside, and the amount distributed as follows: General Wilson, commanding U. S. cavalry in that region of country, $3000; Lieut. Colonel Pritchard, 4th Michigan, $3000; Colonel Harnden, 1st Wisconsin cavalry, $3000; Captain Joseph A. O. Yoeman, 1st Ohio cavalry, $3000. The remainer of the $100,000 was distributed equally to the members of these organizations then with the expedition.

THE EIGHTH CAVALRY.

The rebel General Morgan, on his memorable raid through Kentucky, Indiana, and Ohio in 1863, found some Michigan troops after him, as they were generally after rebels on almost every other occasion during the rebellion, and they troubled them somewhat on this occasion. Among them were the 8th Michigan cavalry, then in command of Lieut. Col. G. S. Wormer, who pursued Morgan for sixteen successive days and nights, and on overtaking him at Buffington's Island, in the Ohio river, on July 19th, the regiment, together with other troops, vigorously attacked his forces; and, after a brisk fight, routed him, driving his command in great confusion, taking five hundred and seventy-three prisoners, four hundred and eighty-seven horses and mules, with a large quantity of arms.

A detachment of the regiment, in charge of Lieut. Boynton, afterwards led a force commanded by Major Rue, 9th Kentucky cavalry, which pursued and captured Morgan near New Lisbon, Ohio, on the 26th of July, 1863. This detachment was on the right of the command at the time of his surrender, and under its standard the final terms were consummated.

This regiment left the State in May, 1863, and down to the fight at Buffington's Island had been engaged with the enemy at Triplet's Bridge, Lebanon, Lawrenceburg, and Salvica, Kentucky, becoming thus early, after it reached the field, prominently and actively at work battling the rebellion and nobly maintaining the high standard of Michigan troops. The regiment was raised and organized by Col. John Stockton, who commanded it until health failed him, and proved a brave and efficient body of men, accomplishing much hard service and passing through many desperate encounters with the Western rebel troops, and always acquitting itself gloriously, whether in partial defeat or in complete and substantial victory. While the record of the regiment is bright and dazzling, and numbers many successful and brilliant battles, none of them perhaps appear to more advantage than the severe fights at Athens and Calhoun, East Tennessee, September 26th and 27th, 1863, in which its brigade, being the 1st of the 4th division, 4th army corps, became engaged with Forrest's and Wheeler's cavalry, estimated at 15,000, and where the regiment, in command of Colonel Wormer, occupied a prominent position, fought stubbornly, and lost forty-three men in killed, wounded, and missing. On October 28th following, while on a reconnoissance from Loudon, it became engaged in a severe action, losing nine wounded.

Conspicuous also are its gallant achievements while checking the advance of Longstreet's army on Knoxville, when the regiment, in command of Major Edgerly, participated in covering the retreat of the Union forces, then falling back before the rebel army from Lenoir Station on Knoxville. On that occasion the regiment was engaged with the enemy constantly from the 12th until the 19th November, and afterwards took part in the glorious and successful defence of Knoxville until the raising of the siege on the 5th of December, when it joined in pursuit of the rebel army, skirmishing with their rear guard and driving them at every point until Bean's Station was reached, where it became heavily engaged on the 14th December, but succeeded in pushing them with loss from every position. For its decided bravery, determined fighting, and the valuable service rendered the army, the regiment was complimented in special orders by General Burnside. The regiment, commanded by Lieut. Col. Mix, formed a portion of Stoneman's cavalry, which covered Sherman's right on his advance upon Atlanta, and on July 4th, 1864, became conspicuously distinguished at the Chattahooche river, where, after a hard fight with Armstrong's brigade of rebel cavalry with an artillery support, the regiment charged and drove the brigade across the river. For this gallant conduct it received at the time the cheers of General Stoneman and his staff. It also took part in the fruitless raid of Stoneman on Macon in July, and even in that fearfully disastrous undertaking won glorious distinction as a fighting regiment. When Stoneman became entirely surrounded, and surrender was evident, the 8th Michigan, then in command of Col. Mix, unwilling to lay down their arms to the rebels, and bearing in mind the honor of their State as well as their own, obtained permission from the commanding general to cut their way out, and, dashing forward, commenced their desperate undertaking, surrounded entirely by the enemy, engaging him hand to hand. Colonel Mix being captured, owing to the loss of his horse, Major Buck assumed command, and succeeding in forcing through the enemy by persistent and stubborn fighting, he undertook to reach the Union lines near Atlanta, but failed. After a hard march, much fatigue and exposure, having been seven days and eight nights in the saddle, pursued and harassed, he was overtaken, and, after a severe engagement, a large number were made prisoners; yet a portion of the regiment reached the Union lines.

This regiment was serving in Tennessee on November 1st, 1864, and brigaded with the 14th and 16th Illinois cavalry, and at that date, with its brigade, was on the march from Nashville to Pulaski for the purpose of watching the movements of Hood, who was then on his northern expedition from Atlanta. Having reached Pulaski, the regiment, on the 6th, moved on a scout to Lawrenceburg and returned, and again on the 12th to Waynesboro'. Returning from that point, it marched to Mount Pleasant on the 14th and 15th, and remained there in camp on the 16th, on the 17th and 18th was on the march to Waynesboro', company C having a skirmish with the enemy. Having reached Waynesboro', on the 18th, 19th, and 20th nearly the whole regiment was engaged day and night in scouting by detachments, one being sent to Lawrenceburg to form a junction with General Hatch, who was then falling back from the Tennessee river, near Florence; one to Clifton, another towards Savannah, all returning and joining the command on the 20th. On the 21st, information having been received that Forrest was advancing towards Lawrenceburg, the command fell back to within eleven miles of Mount Pleasant and went into camp. In the meantime communication had been opened with General Hatch, and on the 23d a detachment of one officer and twenty-five men of the regiment was sent back towards Waynesboro', which met the enemy about seven miles out and near Henryville, where it kept a whole regiment in check until company B was sent forward as a re-enforcement, but before it reached there it was attacked and driven back and the detachment cut off. It was then ascertained that the enemy had succeeded in getting a position between General Hatch and the command. A battalion of this regiment was ordered to hold the road in front, while the brigade fell back three miles to the junction of the Mount Pleasant and Lawrenceburg roads, and there threw up a barricade and made a stand for the purpose of checking the enemy should he succeed in driving the battalion. During that time the battalion was holding him in check, although vigorously attacked and closely pressed; and, after a stubborn and gallant resistance, the enemy succeeded in throwing a heavy force on its left flank and driving it back to within a short distance of the barricade, where it made a determined stand, but was attacked by a superior force, and, before it could fall back on the command, the enemy had gained its rear. The attacking force was discovered by the brigade, but, owing to the darkness, it was supposed to be the battalion falling back, and therefore no effort was made to check it. At that time the balance of the 8th Michigan was ordered to a position behind the barricade; but before it could be properly posted the enemy made a desperate charge on the whole line, and so unexpected was the attack that it threw the two other regiments of the brigade into confusion, producing a perfect stampede, when the 8th Michigan, with great coolness maintaining its position, poured a volley into his ranks, checking his advance, then gave him a second volley, when he retired. In the meantime the battalion of the 8th Michigan that had been left in front to hold him in check, and which had now been cut off from the main command, cut its way through the enemy under a heavy fire and rejoined the brigade, having lost several killed and wounded.

About daylight on the morning of the 24th the pickets were again attacked, the brigade falling back about two miles, closely followed by the enemy, when he threw a heavy column on both its flanks, compelling it to retreat in double-quick to Columbia, the enemy pursuing closely. On reaching that point, a division of infantry, from the 23d army corps, which had just arrived there, succeeded in driving him back, and prevented the whole of General Forrest's command from dashing into the town and capturing it. On the 25th a detachment of fifty men of the regiment was sent to Hardison's Mills, on Duck river, for the purpose of crossing, to ascertain if the enemy was moving in that direction, and next day the brigade was ordered to that point, and picketed the different fords along the river for six or eight miles. On the morning of the 28th the advance of Hood's army was discovered moving towards the fords, and about noon he had driven in the advance pickets, and at 2 P. M. he opened fire at almost every ford, but he was kept in check until the communication with General Johnson was cut off by the enemy crossing at one of the fords east of Columbia, and also on the left of the command, when the detachments at the fords were ordered back; then the brigade became completely surrounded, when one regiment (7th Ohio) succeeded in cutting its way through the enemy, in its rear, still leaving the remaining portion of the command (in which was the 8th Michigan) completely and closely surrounded. The regiment, together with the 14th and 16th Illinois, being armed with Springfield muskets, dismounted, and with bayonets fixed, charged through the enemy in gallant style, driving over 100 rebels into the river. A detachment of 40 men of the regiment had been cut off at one of the lower fords, but succeeded in extricating itself with but little loss. Next morning the command fell back six miles on General Hatch's division, which had been drawn up in line of battle, to check any further advance of the enemy. On the following morning the whole cavalry force fell back to near Franklin, the infantry having already evacuated Columbia and taken position at Franklin. On the 30th the enemy made several attempts to drive the cavalry in, but failed. Towards evening he massed a strong force, and made a desperate attack, but was repulsed with heavy loss. Next morning, December 1st, before daylight, the whole command had commenced falling back towards Nashville, and when within six miles of that place the cavalry made a stand, but the enemy did not come up. During the night the whole cavalry force moved inside the lines at Nashville.

THE NINTH CAVALRY.

The capture of the notorious rebel General Morgan and the rout of his forces while on his raid of robbery and plunder in Indiana and Ohio, in

1863, should to a very great extent be attributed to the 9th Michigan cavalry, then commanded by Colonel James I. David, by whom it had been raised and organized.

After the regiment, while in command of Lieutenant-Colonel George S. Acker, had participated in the attack on Morgan's troops, at Buffington's Island, on July 19th, acquitting itself with much distinction, a detachment of the regiment, in command of Major W. B. Way, with a section of battery L, 1st Michigan light artillery, on July 24th, joined in pursuit of Morgan's fleeing cavalry. Proceeding by cars to Mingo Junction, on the Ohio river, thence marched to La Grange and Stuebenville, overtaking Morgan near Stuebenville, July 25th. The command skirmished with his forces, driving him during the night, and on the following morning succeeded in pressing him into an engagement near Salineville, which resulted, after a severe fight, in the complete defeat and rout of his command, with a loss of 23 killed, 44 wounded, and 305 prisoners. Morgan, flying with a remnant of his troops, was then chased until, meeting the forces under General Shackleford, he surrendered.

At the beginning of November, 1863, the regiment was at Henderson Station, East Tennessee, and seems to have performed a considerable amount of scouting during the month in that portion of the State. Its December return notes its march towards Knoxville on the 6th, and a skirmish with the enemy on Clinch Mountains on the 7th, during a march of 30 miles. On the 10th, while on reconnoissance, it met the enemy two miles from Moorestown, and successfully engaged them. The 12th was occupied, with its brigade, in a sharp action near Russelville. The position of the regiment at Bean's Station was attacked on the 14th, and the command fell back toward Rutledge. The next two days the regiment, in command of Major S. Brockway, (Colonel Acker being wounded at Bean's Station,) while acting as rear-guard, was engaged in constant skirmishing near Rutledge. Later in the month it was in skirmishes at Dandredge and Mossy creek. On the 16th of January following, the regiment—then in command of Major M. F. Gallagher—moved from Dandredge in the direction of Bull's Gap, and encountered the enemy's infantry in large force at Kinsboro's Cross Roads. After a severe fight of about half an hour the regiment fell back on Dandredge, having lost 32 in killed, wounded, and missing.

In June, 1864, this regiment was again found fighting with the notorious Morgan, near Cynthiana, Ky. It appears that on June 9th, the regiment, then in command of Col. George S. Acker, was in camp at Nicholasville, and ordered to scout as far as Bayley's Cross-roads, a distance of fourteen miles, with orders that if the enemy was found to engage him. Not finding him Col. Acker returned. On June 10th he marched to Lexington, where a battalion of the regiment, in command of Major McBride, met with a portion of Morgan's command, had a brisk skirmish, and retired. On June 11th the regiment marched to Paris and bivouacked for two hours; after dark started for Cynthiana, leading the horses the most of the way, so as to make as little noise as possible. Just at daylight on the 12th the enemy was found behind rail barricades; the 11th Michigan cavalry and 12th Ohio cavalry were in line of battle on foot for the purpose of driving him from the barricades, while the 9th Michigan charged the enemy on his left flank in most splendid style, taking 300 prisoners, about 500 horses, and a large quantity of small arms, also a number of beef cattle. This charge was a brilliant affair, completely routing him and driving great numbers of his troops into the Licking river in much confusion, and thoroughly demoralized.

On the 27th of November the regiment moved in the direction of Waynesboro', and on the 28th was engaged, while covering the rear of the division, losing two men killed and one wounded. Near Louisville, on the 29th, the regiment drove two brigades of the enemy from a mill, after a slight engagement. Proceeding towards Waynesboro' on the 1st, 2d, and 3d of December, skirmishing during the night of the 2d; encamped on the night of the 3d; attacking Wheeler's cavalry on the 4th, driving them through Waynesboro' in great confusion, the regiment charging with their sabres, taking four hundred prisoners, and losing two killed and five wounded, and one officer taken prisoner. For its conduct in that gallant charge, the regiment received special notice in the report of the commanding general to the War Department. During the 5th and 6th the march was continued, the enemy attacking the regiment vigorously; on the 7th a charge was made by the 2d battalion, in command of Major McBride, at Cypress Swamp, and after a severe fight, in which it lost two killed, two wounded, and five missing, he was compelled to retire. In this charge fell the gallant Captain Frederick S. Ladd.

The 9th was the only Michigan cavalry regiment having the honor of marching with General Sherman's army to the ocean, and composed the escort of General Kilpatrick when he opened communication between that army and the Atlantic coast, and at the time when that important and interesting dispatch from General Howard, of Sherman's army, dated December 9, 1864, to the American fleet in St. Catherine's Sound on the coast of Georgia, reaching it on the 13th of that month, saying, "We have had perfect success, and army in fine spirits."

On that great campaign of General Sherman from Atlanta to the sea, the regiment, in command of Col. Acker, served with the cavalry of Gen. Kilpatrick. On the morning of the battle of Waynesboro', Kilpatrick had broke camp at 4 A. M., and when within about two miles of Waynesboro' struck the rebel General Wheeler's command. The 9th Michigan was the third regiment in column, the 92d Illinois were acting as skirmishers, and the 10th Ohio cavalry in line mounted. On reaching within about a mile of the town, the enemy made a stand, when the 10th Ohio charged, but were driven back in confusion. The 9th Michigan was then ordered to charge, and had to form while on the run from column of fours to that of battalions, driving the enemy from the field, taking 100 prisoners and a large amount of small arms, and losing only one man killed, three wounded, and five horses shot. The charge was spoken of with favorable comment by General Kilpatrick, and the brigade commander, General S. Atkins, in their official reports.

In the Cleveland *Herald*, of July 27, 1863, is found a detailed account of the capture of Morgan, from which the following extract is taken:

"At this time the utmost alarm existed among the people of Salineville. The houses were closed, doors and windows locked and barred, and women and children stampeding into the country with whatever portable property could be carried along. The men, who had weapons and courage, turned out to resist the progress of the dreaded rebel, while all the others fled with the women and children.

"In a short time the expected rebels made their appearance, coming around a bend in the road. On catching sight of the infantry they halted, and turned their horses heads in another direction. Before they could get out of the trap they found themselves in, Major Way, with 250 men of the 9th Michigan cavalry, dashed among them and commenced cutting right and left. The rebels made but a brief resistance; a few shots were fired by them, and then the whole party broke in utter confusion. The scene that followed was almost ludicrous, and could only be matched by the previous stampede at Buffington Island. Men dismounted, threw down their arms, and begged for quarter, whilst others galloped round wildly in search of a place of escape, and were 'brought to time' by a pistol shot or sabre stroke.

"Morgan himself was riding in a carriage drawn by two white horses. Major Way saw him, and galloping up, reached for him. Morgan jumped out at the other side of the carriage, leaped over a fence, seized a horse, and galloped off as fast as horse-flesh, spurred by frightened heels, could carry him. About two hundred of his men succeeded in breaking away, and following their fugitive leader. In the buggy thus hastily 'evacuated' by Morgan were found his 'rations,' consisting of a loaf of bread, some hard-boiled eggs, and a bottle of whiskey.

"A few of our cavalry were wounded, two or three seriously. Lieutenant Fisk was shot through the breast; his wound is dangerous, and he has telegraphed for his wife to come from Michigan."

THE TENTH CAVALRY.

The 10th cavalry was organized at Grand Rapids, under the supervision of Col. F. W. Kellogg, and went to the field in Kentucky in December, 1863, in command of Colonel Thaddeus Foote, first encountering the rebels at House Mountain, Tenn., in January, 1864, subsequently at Bean's Gap, March 26th, and at Rheatown, April 24th following, and next day a more important engagement followed at Carter's Station, near Jonesboro, Tenn., when the regiment, in command of Lieutenant-Colonel L. S. Trowbridge, together with the 3d Indiana cavalry, were sent to destroy the large railroad bridge over the Watauga river. Colonel Trowbridge was to be supported, if necessary, by Manson's brigade, of Cox's division, 13th corps, which marched up as far as Jonesboro, twelve miles from Carter's Station. The bridge was defended by the rebel General A. E. Jackson, called "Mudwall Jackson," with a strong force, occupying a strong redoubt, with extensive and well-constructed rifle-pits. The Union force had one mountain howitzer, commanded by Lieutenant E. J. Brooks, but owing to a very limited amount of ammunition, he was unable to accomplish much, yet made some remarkably telling shots. It was soon ascertained that there was no possible way of reaching the bridge without first dislodging the enemy from their strong position, and this had to be accomplished at much risk by passing over perfectly open ground for a distance of two hundred yards, swept by a very sharp and hot cross-fire from the opposite side of the river. Yet, being the first heavy undertaking of the regiment, Colonel Trowbridge felt unwilling to retire without accomplishing something, as it would produce an unfavorable effect upon his command. He therefore decided to make an attempt, dismounting about one-third of his men. With this small force he ordered an advance upon the enemy's position at double-quick, when they gave way in great disorder, leaving their works and taking shelter in a large mill near at hand, Major Israel C. Smith being the first man to enter the redoubt and Captain Benjamin K. Weatherwax the second. As soon as the redoubt was gained, an attempt was made to drive the enemy out of the mill, but the charging force was met with such a terrible and destructive volley that it was abandoned. In this daring and gallant attempt Captain Weatherwax lost his life, being shot through the heart. Colonel Trowbridge, in a special report of the affair, says of him:

"Thus was lost to us one of the most gallant and worthy officers whom I have ever met. Full of noble and generous sympathy, the loftiest patriotism, with that courage which knows no fear, his loss was most deeply felt by the entire regiment." The fight was a brilliant success, though obtained at a loss of seventeen killed and wounded, and must be recognized as an uncommon victory, considering it was gained by dismounted cavalry, new and undisciplined, over a much superior force of well-trained infantry, holding strong defensive works, and having, in addition, to meet a most galling cross-fire of the enemy, thus rendering the success uncommon at that stage of the rebellion, and should be classed among the most gallant minor victories of the war.

This regiment was stationed at Strawberry Plains, in East Tennessee, November 1, 1864, engaged in fortifying that point and in the usual routine of camp duty and occasional scouting. On the 16th General Breckinridge, with a large rebel force, made his appearance in front of the garrison, and on the 17th commenced a vigorous attack with artillery from the opposite side of the Holston river, and at the same time threatening it in the rear with a heavy cavalry force. Constant skirmishing and occasional artillery firing was kept up for four days, the enemy being repulsed on the 24th, when he withdrew. During the remaining portion of the month, and up to December 6th, the regiment was employed in constructing fortifications at that point, when, on the receipt of orders, it marched to Knoxville, and soon after made an expedition to Saltville, Va., and destroyed the salt works at that point, being engaged with the enemy at Kingsport, December 12th; at Bristol, December 14th, and at Saltville, December 20th. Returning to Knoxville, it had a skirmish at Chucky Bend, January 10, 1865. Remaining at Knoxville until March 21st, the brigade to which it was attached marched to Upper East Tennessee, under command of Brevet Brigadier-General Palmer. Joining the expedition under General Stoneman, in his raid into North Carolina, the regiment was engaged with the enemy at Brabson's Mills on the 25th, and at Boonville, N. C., on the 27th. Proceeding, via Wilkesboro, and thence down to Yadkin river, in the direction of Salisbury, reaching the Tennessee and Virginia railroad at Christiansburg, April 5th, it assisted in destroying over one hundred miles of that railroad, together with the bridges. This accomplished, the regiment made a rapid march of ninety-five miles to Henry Court-house, making the distance in twenty-two hours. At that point it became engaged with a superior force of the enemy's cavalry and infantry on the 8th, which, after a brisk fight, retired, the regiment losing in the affair Lieutenant Kenyon and three men killed, and one officer and three men severely wounded, the loss of the enemy not being ascertained.

The regiment, in command of Colonel Trowbridge, had been detached at Salem, on the 10th, and sent to destroy the bridge over Abbott's creek, and then, if not opposed, to join General Stoneman at Salisbury. The 10th marched all night; one battalion, in command of Captain James H. Cummins, was sent to High Point to attract the enemy in that direction, and succeeded in destroying over $300,000 worth of rebel stores without loss. Meanwhile, the other two battalions, not numbering more than 250 men, were marching in an opposite direction. It was important to destroy the bridge before daylight, and on being informed that there was no enemy near, the colonel sent forward two companies in command of Capt. Roberts for that purpose. While the remaining force was moving leisurely along, and as daylight was breaking, it suddenly came upon the pickets of the enemy, when it was ascertained that Ferguson's brigade of Wheeler's cavalry, numbering 1200 men, were about a mile ahead. The horses of the command were much worn out and jaded, and the force only about one-sixth that of the enemy, and twenty miles from any support, rendering a contest extremely hazardous and almost without hope of success; and as General Stoneman was then expected to be at work at Salisbury, and needed assistance, it was important to draw off the force for that purpose if possible, and it was therefore determined to fall back as soon as the two detached companies of Captain Roberts had returned. In order to await for them the command was put in position for defence. Colonel Trowbridge determined in case of attack to make the best fight possible. Soon Captain Roberts returned, and reported that he had slipped past the enemy, and had destroyed the bridge as directed. The chief object of the movement having been accomplished, the command commenced to retire by alternate squadrons, leaving Captain Dunn, with his plucky company, to hold the rebels in check until the command could get properly started. As soon as the movement was discovered, the enemy attacked with great vigor, not only with a superior force of cavalry, but with a large body of infantry, sending a column upon each flank, making an attempt to surround this little band, and rendering it necessary to fall back by squadrons as rapidly as practicable. Each squadron, after holding a position as long as possible, wheeled into column and trotted back, and took up another position, fighting most gallantly in defence of each. This fight lasted for six miles, when the enemy, despairing of closing in upon this handful of brave men, and disheartened by their losses, which had been considerable, stopped their pursuit, and Colonel Trowbridge, with his plucky comrades were permitted to retire and rejoin the main command.

Strange as it may appear, after such hard and disadvantageous fighting, his loss was only two taken prisoners, while that of the enemy, judging from reports in rebel newspapers, and from other sources, especially from the statements of Colonel Wheeler of General Wheeler's corps, must have been from 50 to 75 in killed, besides a large number wounded.

This was a most remarkable fight, and shows what can be done with brave men commanded by cool and gallant officers.

Another instance, among the many, showing the stubborn fighting of this gallant and patriotic regiment, occurred August 24, 1864, at Strawberry Plains, East Tennessee, where Major Standish, with 125 men of his regiment, and Colvin's Illinois battery, repulsed in most splendid style an attack of Wheeler's cavalry corps, six thousand strong, with nine pieces of artillery.

During this attack, seven of Standish's men by hard fighting held McMillan's Ford, on the Holston river, for three and a half hours against a brigade of rebel cavalry, killing forty or fifty of them, but were finally surrounded and captured.

Colonel Trowbridge furnishes the following incident connected with the repulse of Wheeler at Strawberry Plains, on August 24, 1864:

"Eight men were sent to guard McMillan's Ford, on the Holston; one of them went off on his own hook, so that seven were left. One of them was a large, powerful fellow, the farrier of company B, by the name of Alexander H. Griggs, supposed to belong to Greenfield, Wayne county. These seven men actually kept back a rebel brigade from crossing that ford for three and a half hours by desperate fighting, killing forty or fifty. During the fight this big farrier was badly wounded in the shoulder, and the rebels, by swimming the river above and below the ford, succeeded in capturing the whole party.

"General Wheeler was much astonished at the valor of these men, and at once paroled a man to stay and take care of this wounded man. Approaching the wounded farrier, the following dialogue is said to have taken place:

"*General Wheeler.* Well, my man, how many men had you at the ford?

"*Griggs.* Seven, sir.

"*Wheeler.* My poor fellow, don't you know that you are badly wounded? You might as well tell me the truth; you may not live long.

"*Griggs,* (indignantly.) I am telling the truth, sir. We had only seven men.

"*Wheeler,* (laughing.) Well, what did you expect to do?

"*Griggs.* To keep you from crossing, sir.

"*Wheeler,* (greatly amused, and laughing.) Well, why didn't you do it?

"*Griggs.* Why, you see, we did until you hit me, *and that weakened our forces so much that you were too much for us.*

"Wheeler was greatly amused, and inquired of another prisoner, (who happened to be a horse farrier too,) 'Are all the 10th Michigan like you fellows?' 'Oh, no!' said the man, 'we are the poorest of the lot. We are mostly horse farriers and blacksmiths, and not much accustomed to fighting.' 'Well,' said Wheeler, 'if I had 300 such men as you I could march straight through h—l.'"

Col. Trowbridge, in a recent report, says of the engagement at Strawberry Plains, November 16, 1864:

"In November, 1864, I had a sharp fight at Strawberry Plains, East Tennessee, with Breckinridge. I had 700 men, some of them indifferently armed, and many of them very indifferent soldiers, made up of stragglers from a dozen different commands. Breckinridge had 5,000 men, among them John B. Palmer, formerly of Detroit, who commanded the artillery and infantry, and ranked as a brigadier-general in the rebel army. I had a section of Wood's Illinois battery, and Breckinridge had nine or ten pieces of artillery. We had a brisk fight, and by good fighting and a show of boldness Breckinridge was repulsed. I think some credit was due the men under my command for the manner in which they acquitted themselves, as well as to myself as their commanding officer; but, strange to say, next day the telegraph announced to the country that General Ammen had repulsed Breckinridge at Strawberry Plains after a hard fight. General Ammen was then the district and division commander, and was then at his headquarters in Knoxville. I had never communicated with him on the subject, and he could have known no more about the fight than a man at the time in Sitka."

The following is furnished by Col. Trowbridge:

"When General Stoneman went to capture Salisbury, N. C., in 1865, he met the enemy at a little stream a few miles from town. The stream had very high and precipitous banks and could not be forded. The only way to cross it was by a narrow bridge, which was effectually commanded by the enemy's artillery. After trying for some time to get them out of their position with his artillery without success, Stoneman called to him Major Smith, of the 10th, and said: 'Major, I want you to take twenty men, armed with the Spencer carbines, and cross this creek and flank those fellows out there.' Smith took his twenty men, and, crossing the creek on a log out of sight of the enemy, steadily approached and fired a volley into their flank, when the whole force broke in the greatest confusion. Stacy, with his Tennessee cavalry, was on them in an instant, and the fight was over. Results: 19 pieces of artillery, 1,100 prisoners, and supplies enough for an army of 100,000 men. This exploit of Major Smith and his gallant little band was as daring as it proved successful.

"One of the most gallant things of the war occurred in East Tennessee at the time when Wheeler made his raid through there in August, 1864. Major Smith, of the 10th, was sent out from Knoxville with seventy-two men, all the mounted force that could be mustered, to scout in the direction of Strawberry Plains and ascertain the position of the enemy. With the true spirit of a cavalry man, he ordered his advance guard to charge the first party of rebels they should see. They discovered the enemy two and a half miles from Flat Creek Bridge, and, according to orders, charged them in gallant style. Smith followed up with his command. The enemy proved to be the 8th Texas cavalry, 400 strong. Smith routed them completely, captured their commanding officer, a lieutenant colonel, and thirty or forty prisoners, and was hotly pursuing them at a full gallop when he came to Flat Creek Bridge—a long, high, and narrow bridge. Over this Smith charged, to find himself confronted by Humes' division of rebel cavalry, 2,000 strong, drawn up in line of battle, scarcely three hundred yards from the bridge. Of course he had to get away, which he succeeded in doing without any very great loss, though the enemy charged him for seven miles. The boldness of the thing annoyed the rebels not a little, and they ever after entertained a wholesome fear of the 10th Michigan cavalry.

"In the summer of 1864 I was ordered to go up near the Virginia line to capture a large number of horses that were said to be in pasture. It was not expected that I would meet the enemy before I reached Kingsport, but unfortunately for the success of my enterprise I met them at Bean's Station. I at once ordered Capt. Roberts, with two companies, to charge them. One of the companies was commanded by Lieut. afterwards Captain Brooks. Brooks was smarting under some ill treatment from a superior officer, and immediately dashed forward with his company. After routing the rebels handsomely and charging them for a couple of miles, Capt. Roberts wisely ordered a halt. But Brooks had gone ahead with a few men, and actually kept up that charge with three men with him for a distance of ten miles and a half. Captain Brooks was afterwards rewarded for his gallantry by the brevets of major and lieutenant colonel."

THE ELEVENTH CAVALRY.

On the 10th of December, 1863, the 11th cavalry, which Colonel F. W. Kellogg had been authorized to raise, left Michigan for Kentucky, in command of Colonel S. B. Brown, of St. Clair, who had recruited and organized the regiment. After its arrival in Kentucky it was employed in protecting the eastern district of that State from incursions of parties of thieving rebels from Virginia, performing a vast amount of service, and first met the enemy at Pound Gap on May 17th, 1864. Out of the many battles and skirmishes in which this regiment participated with much credit, none, it is deemed, appear to have proved the sterling bravery and efficiency of this pattern cavalry regiment than the important battles of Saltville, Va., October 2d, 1864, and Marion, Va., December 17th of the same year, as they will undoubtedly be considered by the regiment and those familiar with its history as among its principal engagements.

In August of that year the regiment was at Camp Burnside, on the Cumberland river. On the 17th of September following it was ordered to Mount Sterling, Ky., and thence engaged with its division, in command of Gen. Burbridge, in a raid to Saltville, Va. Encountering the enemy at McCormick's Farm, Ky., on the 23d, and then at Laurel Mountain, Va., on the 29th, and at Bowen's Farm on the 30th and October 1st. Having experienced a long and hazardous march, through a rocky, barren country, and being in the advance, skirmished daily with the enemy, who contested every foot of the ground with much vigor and persistence, the command of Gen. Burbridge, on the morning of the 2d, came upon the enemy's works at Saltville, defended by the troops of Breckinridge, Echols, and Williams, numbering about 22,000, including 7,000 militia. The whole of Burbridge's command, numbering less than 4,000 effective men, were ordered to move on the enemy's works; a different point of attack being assigned to each brigade. The nature of the ground and the fact that the enemy greatly outnumbered the Union troops, and being behind strong embankments defended with twenty pieces of artillery, rendered the undertaking a very hazardous and desperate one. The brigade commanded and led by Col. Brown, and to which the 11th cavalry, then in command of Lieut. Colonel Mason, were attached, carried the main work in most brilliant style, and were the only troops that effected a lodgment within the defences. The fact that the 11th cavalry alone lost eighty-six in killed, wounded, and missing, more men than were lost by any other brigade of the command, proved conclusively that the success of the troops under Brown was not the result of lack of courage or of determined and desperate fighting on the part of their opponents, but was a result of their own gallant and persistent fighting. The rebel position proving too strong to be held, the command, after most stubborn fighting, was withdrawn, but not until all its ammunition had been expended. On the retreat the 11th constituted the rear guard, and next day skirmished with the enemy's advance, and the day following the battle was renewed near Sandy Mountain, where the regiment became cut off from the division and surrounded by a body of cavalry numbering about 4,000, under "Cerro Gordo" Williams. After a very sanguinary conflict of over an hour, the enemy closing in upon the regiment, Col. Mason determined on fight before surrender, gallantly led the regiment to the charge, and succeeded, after a bloody hand-to-hand encounter, in cutting through the rebel lines, punishing the enemy so severely that he abandoned any pursuit. This brilliant affair was not accomplished without loss, which included the gallant Mason, a noble soldier; he was mortally wounded in the charge and died next day.

Long and numerous marches and almost continuous battles and skirmishes followed the engagements at Saltville and Sandy Mountain, the regiment acquitting itself creditably on all occasions.

On December 4, 1864, it was at Bean Station, East Tennessee, and on the 11th, in command of Lieutenant-Colonel Charles E. Smith, moved with the force of General Stoneman on his raid into North Carolina, and after a long march and much fighting at various points, the command reached Marion, Va., on the 17th, when a detachment of the 11th, then forming a part of the brigade of Colonel Brown, coming upon the enemy under Breckinridge, charged his cavalry and opened the engagement, which continued with much vigorous fighting for thirty-six hours, during which repeated and daring charges were made by both sides, and the enemy, after the most determined fighting, fell back in disorder across the mountains into North Carolina. A detachment of the 11th Michigan, numbering one hundred and twenty officers and men, under the command of Captain E. C. Miles, held a bridge during the whole engagement which was of much importance, being the key to the position held by the Union troops. Captain George B. Mason, while gallantly attempting to reinforce Captain

Miles with a squadron of the regiment, was mortally wounded. The bridge was stubbornly held under a severe fire from a heavy force on the opposite side of the river, and, in addition to the loss of Captain Mason, Lieutenant Davis and five enlisted men nobly fell in its defence. For this important service, the detachment of Captain Miles received the highest praise from General Stoneman, and the regiment was thanked in the general orders of the department commander for its meritorious and valuable services in the battle of Marion.

On the 19th of January, 1865, the regiment being stationed at Lexington, Ky., moved to Mount Sterling, and was engaged in scouting the eastern portion of Kentucky. On February 23d it started to join General Stoneman's command at Knoxville, reaching there, via Louisville, Ky., and Nashville, Tenn., March 15th, when it was assigned to 2d brigade, and formed part of the force on Stoneman's expedition through East Tennessee, North and South Carolina, and Georgia. The command left Knoxville, March 17th, and passed through Boon, N. C., on the 27th, crossed the Yadkin river on the 30th, passing through Mount Airy on the 31st, Hillsdale, April 1st, and arrived at Christiansburg April 3d, where it destroyed a portion of the East Tennessee railroad, and passing through Danbury, April 9th, Germantown, April 10th, and arriving at Salisbury, April 12th, it engaged a superior force of the enemy, and captured 1,800 prisoners, 22 pieces of artillery, and destroyed a large amount of property, and also the railroads and telegraph lines leading from that point. In this engagement Captain John Edwards was killed. From Salisbury the command marched via Taylorsville on the 14th, passing Lenoir Station on the 15th, and was engaged at Morgantown on the 17th. On the 19th it proceeded to Swananoa Gap, and passing through Rutherfordton on the 20th, Hendersonville on the 23d, arriving at Ashville on the 26th, taking at that point two hundred prisoners, and capturing a large amount of property, including artillery. Passing again through Hendersonville on the 27th, the command entered South Carolina, via Saluda Gap and Cæsar's Head, arriving at Anderson Court-house May 1st. It destroyed the remnant of the rebel treasury, then moved to Carnesville, Ga., on the 3d, and to Athens on the 4th, and on the 11th captured the cavalry escort of Jefferson Davis near Washington, moving to Hartwell on the 13th, the command guarding the crossing points of the Tugaloo and Savannah rivers. On the 22d, crossing the Savannah river, reached Maxwell's Farm, S. C.; on the 23d, Greenville, and on the 25th, Ashville, N. C., and Greenville, Tenn., on the 27th; Strawberry Plains on the 29th, Knoxville on June 3d, and arrived at Lenoir Station June 4th, and encamped until the 24th, when the regiment moved by rail to Pulaski, and on the 20th of July it was consolidated with the 8th Michigan cavalry.

THE "MERRILL HORSE" CAVALRY.

In September, 1861, two companies of cavalry were raised respectively by Captain James B. Mason and Captain Jabez H. Rogers, at Battle Creek, and in January, 1863, another company was recruited by Captain Almon E. Preston, of the same place. These companies were designated as companies H, I, and L of the regiment known as the "Merrill Horse," a Missouri organization, and served during the whole term of the service with the Western armies. It is known to have been actively engaged, and to have seen much service in the field during the period covered by this report, but the returns of these companies are very meagre in the details of their operations, consequently it has been impossible to give a full and satisfactory sketch of their movements and services.

It has been ascertained that they were in engagements and skirmishes as follows: Memphis, Mo., July 18, 1862; Moor's Mill, Mo., July 28, 1862; Kirsville, Mo., August 6, 1862; Brownsville, Ark., August 25, 1863; Bayou Mecoe, Ark., August 27, 1865; Ashley's Bayou, Ark., September 7, 1863; Little Rock, Ark., September 10, 1863; Benton, Ark., September 11, 1863; Princeton, Ark., December 8, 1863; Little Missouri River, Ark., April 3, 4, 1864; Prairie Dehan, Ark., April 12, 13, 14, 1864; Camden, Ark., April 15, 1864; Jenkins' Ferry, Ark., April 29, 30, 1864; Franklin, Mo., October 1, 1864; Otterville, Mo., October 10, 1864; Independence, Mo., October 22, 1864; Big Blue, Mo., October 23, 1864; Trenton Gap, Ga., March 22, 1865; Alpine, Ga., March 24, 1865; Summerville, Ga., March 25, 1865.

On May 1, 1865, they were at Resaca. On the 9th left for Kingston, arriving there same day, and on the 20th started with the regiment for Atlanta as an escort to a supply train, arriving at that point on the 23d, and were then ordered to return with the train loaded with cotton to Chattanooga. On September 21st following they were mustered out of service at Nashville, and soon thereafter paid off and disbanded. They were known as Michigan companies, and their officers were commissioned by the Governor of the State.

THE LIGHT ARTILLERY.

The regiment of Michigan light artillery was composed of twelve six-gun batteries. It was commanded by Colonel C. O. Loomis; but, from the character of that arm of the service, the batteries were never brought together as a regiment.

Battery A, originally designated Loomis's, left the State under command of Colonel Loomis, on July 1, 1861, for the field in Western Virginia; and at Rich Mountain, in July following, while serving with General McClellan, first engaged the enemy, and thus early in the war gave the rebels a taste of its pluck.

Passing through the Western Virginia campaign, it was transferred to Kentucky, and was in advance in the route of the rebels from Bowling Green.

At the battle of Perryville it played an important part, saving by its gallant and effective service the right wing of the Union army from being flanked.

Fighting through many other battles, where its vigorous action, stubborn pluck, and brilliant dash gave it an enviable reputation throughout the whole army, it is found hotly engaged during the memorable days and nights of hard and desperate fighting in the bloody battle of Stone River, where it lost heavily, but achieved a most noted distinction, second to no battery in the service, and the history of the times will bear witness to its noted fame in the ages that shall follow.

From the annals of the Army of the Cumberland, we take the following extract:

"During the battle of Friday, at Stone River, General Rousseau rode up to Loomis's battery, and saw there a youth of the battery holding horses, and in the midst of a very tempest of shot and shell. He was so unconscious of fear, and so elated and excited, that, being debarred from better occupation than holding horses, his high spirits found vent in shouting out songs and dancing to the music. The General was so well pleased with his whole deportment, that he rode up to him and said: 'Well done, my brave boy; let me shake hands with you.' A few days after the fight, General Rousseau visited the camp of the battery, and mentioning the circumstance to the commanding officer, expressed a desire to see the youth again. 'Step out, McIntire,' said the officer. The youth came forward, blushing deeply. The General again commended his conduct, and said: 'I shook hands with you on the battle-field, and now I wish to do it again in the presence of your brother soldiers. May you carry the same brave spirit through the war, and come out safely at last, as you are sure to come out honorably.' The General again shook his hand warmly in the presence of his officers and of his companions."

The gallant services of this battery and Guenther's, fighting by its side, were conspicuous, demanding the attention of the general officers, while General Rousseau, specially noticing them in his report, says:

"As the enemy emerged from the woods in great force, shouting and cheering, the batteries of Loomis and Guenther, double-shotted with canister, opened upon them. They moved straight ahead for a while; but were finally driven back with immense loss. In a little while they rallied again, and, as it seemed, with fresh troops again assailed our position, and were again, after a fierce struggle, driven back."

This high compliment to their fighting qualities is strongly endorsed in the "Rebellion Record," by Mr. Greeley, who says:

"After debouching from cedars, Loomis and Guenther could find no good position for their batteries, and the whole line fell back under severe fighting, the left wing flat upon the ground, the right covered by a crest. The two batteries now swiftly wheeled into favorable positions and poured double-shotted canister into the enemy. The 23d Arkansas was literally swept away by their devouring fire. Loomis and Guenther were wild with delight at their success. The baffled enemy came no farther. The field was red with the blood of their slain."

At Chicamauga, September 19th and 20th, the record is nobly maintained and gloriously almost ended. There, sooner than abandon its position, it suffered nearly annihilation; making one of the most determined defences on record; dealing to the rebel hosts, pressing up in masses to the muzzle of the guns, utter destruction within its entire range; but finally had to surrender the guns so dearly prized, Lieut. Van Pelt, its commander, fighting most heroically for their preservation, and dying by their side. Mr. Greeley, in noticing this great struggle on the 19th, says:

"It was now 9 A. M., and while Baird and Brannan were making the required movements, Palmer's division, of Crittenden's corps, came up and took position on Baird's right. By 10 A. M. Croxton's brigade, of Brannan's division, had become engaged, driving back Forrest's cavalry, when Ector's and Wilson's infantry brigades were sent in by Walker to Forrest's support. Croxton, of course, was brought to a dead halt; but now Thomas sent up Baird's division, and the rebel brigades were hurled back badly cut up. Hereupon, Walker in turn sent up Liddell's division, making the odds against us two to one, when Baird was in turn driven; the rebels charging through the lines of the 14th, 16th, and 18th U. S. regulars, taking two batteries.

"One of the batteries here lost was the 1st Michigan, formerly Loomis's, regarded by the whole army with pride, and by those who served in it with an affection little short of idolatry. It had done yeoman service on many a hard-fought field, and was fondly regarded as well nigh invincible. But now abandoned by its supports, who recoiled before a rebel charge in overwhelming force, with all its horses shot, and most of its men killed and wounded, it could not be drawn off, and was doomed to be lost. Its commander, Lieut. Van Pelt, refused to leave it, and died, sword in hand, fighting—one against a thousand—by the side of his guns."

Battery B went to the field from Grand Rapids about the latter part of 1861, in command of Capt. W. S. Bliss, and was in the desperate fight at Pittsburg Landing, and while heavily engaged became cut off from its infantry supports by the enemy's cavalry, losing four of its guns and having sixty of its officers and men taken as prisoners. The battery was reorganized after the exchange of officers and men taken at Pittsburg Landing, and passed through much hard and useful service and many severe engagements, including the defence of Corinth by Gen. Rosecrans in 1862. It was with the army while advancing on Atlanta in 1864, and engaged the enemy at Resaca on the 14th, 15th, and 16th of May, where Lieut. Wright was severely wounded. It was also engaged at Lay's Ferry, Calhoun Ferry, Rome Cross-roads, and Cave Springs, Georgia, and at Turkey Ridge, Alabama.

On November 13th it commenced the memorable march with General Sherman's army from Atlanta, and on the 22d following engaged the enemy at Griswold, near Macon, doing excellent service, distinguishing itself by steady, rapid, and precise firing, doing much execution. In this engagement the brigade to which it was attached, numbering only about 1,500, defeated the enemy in very superior force, killing, wounding, and taking prisoners from 1,500 to 2,000, the brigade losing only about eighty. The loss of the battery was seven wounded, including its commander, Capt. A. F. R. Arndt; two of the enlisted men losing each a leg and one an arm. In this engagement the battery behaved most gallantly, and fought until the last round of ammunition was expended, all the horses of one gun killed, and only saved the piece by drawing it from the field by the prolong.

Lieut. Bliss, of this battery, was taken prisoner at the battle of Shiloh, Tennessee, April 6, 1862, and was sent to Montgomery, Ala., where he was murdered by a rebel sentinel May 1st, 1862, under the following circumstances: Lieut. Bliss had permission to go to a house near the prison and purchase milk for the convalescent officers in the prison; on one of these errands, accompanied by a sentinel and while waiting for the canteens to be filled by the woman of the house, he was ordered by the rebel sentinel to "Hurry up." Bliss replied, "Yes, as soon as I can get my canteens." The sentinel cocked his musket and placed the muzzle against Lieut. Bliss's breast. Bliss said, "I hope you will not shoot me." The sentinel replied, "Yes, I will, you damned Yankee;" and at the same moment fired. Bliss fell to the ground and never spoke again; he lived about three-quarters of an hour after being shot. So far as is known no action was taken by the rebel authorities in the matter.

This statement regarding his death was given by the woman of the house where it occurred and who was an eye-witness of the murder. The woman was obliged soon after to flee North to save her own life, she having shown many acts of kindness to the Union troops who were prisoners of war at that place.

Battery C first met the rebels at the siege of Corinth, Mississippi, in May, 1862. On September 16th following the battery, in command of Capt. A. W. Dees, was sent from Burnsville on a reconnoissance towards Iuka, Miss., made by the 2d brigade, 2d division, Army of the Mississippi. About six miles from that place the command was met by the enemy's pickets, which were driven in, and the force advanced. The line of battle was formed on a hill commanding the country for about a mile. Two of the guns of the battery (10-pounder Parrott and 10-pounder howitzer) were placed on the brow of the hill, throwing shot and shell. The other two guns of the battery were soon after into position, and the firing continued for about fifteen minutes. The force advanced through an open field below the hill, and, reaching the wood on the other side, turned to the right, when the infantry and cavalry advanced and opened fire on the enemy. The firing was brisk on both sides for a short time, when a retreat was ordered, the battery covering. On falling back to the hill before-mentioned a halt was made, the battery reopened fire, and shelled in several directions. On the advance of the skirmishers toward a wood about a mile distant the enemy opened a brisk fire from the edge of the wood, when the battery again opened fire from a 10-pounder Parrott, shelling the enemy with such good effect that he very soon left the wood. Soon night came on and the firing ceased.

On the morning of the 3d October, 1862, the battery, in command of Lieut. George Robinson, with a section of the 8th Wisconsin battery, all being under the command of Lieut. C. A. Lamberg, of battery C, marched from a point on the Kossuth road, four miles from Corinth, with the 1st brigade, 2d division, Army of Mississippi, towards Corinth, and took a position southwest of the town. On the morning of the 4th, the battery was stationed on the north of the Memphis and Charleston Railroad Depot. About 4 A. M. the enemy commenced shelling the town, throwing several shells into the battery, but without effect. The battery was placed in position a short distance to the right, and afterwards in rear of General Rosecrans' headquarters, with an Ohio battery on its right; seeing the enemy's skirmishers in front, firing was commenced on them about 8 A. M., when they disappeared. Later in the day a large force of the enemy appeared, advancing on the right and front of the battery, when it again opened fire, driving them back into the woods. They soon advanced in greater force, when the guns were double-shotted with canister, and a rapid fire was opened with good effect for about an hour, but the enemy continued to advance. The infantry on the right of the Ohio battery broke, when it limbered up and retired, leaving the right flank of the Michigan battery exposed and without support. The enemy being within twenty yards of the guns, and unable to maintain the position, it limbered to the rear and moved to the south side of the Memphis and Charleston railroad, and from there to the rear of General Rosecrans' headquarters, when the firing ceased; the enemy being driven back at all points in a very demoralized condition. During the engagement the battery lost eleven in wounded and missing, and had six horses killed and eight wounded.

On this occasion it acquired a high reputation for efficiency and bravery and as a serviceable and reliable battery.

The battery, in command of Capt. George Robinson, served on the Atlanta campaign with much enviable reputation, and participated in the siege of that stronghold. After its fall it followed Sherman to the sea, and among other battles on that great campaign was hotly engaged at the South Edisto, S. C., on February 9th, 1865, acquiring much distinction and losing several killed and wounded.

Battery D, on leaving the State in 1861, proceeded to Kentucky, and first encountered the rebels, damaging them much at Hoover's Gap, Tennessee, on the 26th of June, 1862, when Rosecrans was advancing on Tullahoma and Chattanooga.

It seems from the record of this battery that its most prominent fight was at the great battle of Chicamauga on the 19th and 20th September, 1863, where, in command of Capt. J. W. Church, it became closely and hotly engaged, behaving in splendid style, but losing heavily, having nine wounded and three missing; among the wounded was its commander.

It was also in the assault on Mission Ridge November 25th following. On the preceding day the battery aided in covering Hooker's advance up Lookout Mountain. On both of these occasions it proved a serviceable battery, and its splendid firing and valuable services attracted much attention.

Battery E, raised and organized, in connection with the regiment of engineers and mechanics, by Captain John J. Dennis, left the State in 1861, going into the field with the Western army, was attached to General Crittenden's command at the battle of Pittsburg Landing, and there first met the rebels. In 1864 it accompanied General Rousseau on a raid into Alabama and Georgia, and was engaged at the battles of Coosa and Cheraw, Alabama.

The battery participated with much credit in the gallant defence of Nashville by General Thomas, in December, 1864, gaining an enviable reputation in that important affair.

The first station of battery F in the field was at West Point, Ky., where, under command of Captain John S. Andrews, who raised and organized the battery, it garrisoned that post for several months in the spring of 1862. Its first engagement with the enemy was at Henderson, Ky., in that year. After undergoing much hard service, with a great amount of marching in 1863 and in the early part of 1864, it is found in May of that year with General Sherman's army, on the Atlanta campaign, and attached to the 2d division, 23d corps. It passed through numerous engagements on that campaign, maintaining a high reputation for promptness and efficiency. Among its principal encounters with the enemy may be classed its severe fight at Utoy creek, Ga., on August 4, where, in command of Lieutenant Miller, it vigorously engaged the enemy with some loss, and had the equipments and wheels of two guns literally shot to pieces, but bravely holding its position and finally silencing two rebel batteries. In this affair the battery attracted much attention and favorable comment on account of its stubborn and effective fighting.

The battery was transferred with General Scofield's command to the North Carolina coast early in 1865. Being stationed at Newbern on March 3d, it left that point, in command of Captain Paddock, with the 1st division, 23d corps, and became engaged with the enemy at Wise's Forks, March 10th, with some loss in killed and wounded. In this engagement the battery maintained its previous high reputation for gallant service and daring pluck.

The next battery that left the State for the field was G, raised and organized in 1862 by Captain C. H. Lamphere, in connection with the 13th infantry, at Kalamazoo, and was stationed at West Point, Ky., in February following, whence it proceeded to Cumberland Gap, East Tennessee, in May, and first engaged the enemy at Tasewell.

In November following it was ordered to Memphis, and from thence to the Yazoo river, Miss., and, in command of Captain Lamphere, took an active part in the battle of Chickasaw Bayou, December 28th and 29th, and was heavily engaged, losing ten wounded, two mortally, with eight horses killed or disabled. The loss of the battery at this point indicates its gallant and valuable service.

It participated in the Vicksburg campaign, and served with the 2d brigade, belonging to the 9th division, 13th corps. The battery was engaged in the fight near Port Gibson, on May 1, 1863, where it acquired much distinction, and was mentioned in the report of General McClernand as follows: "The splendid practice of Lamphere's and Foster's batteries disabled two of the enemy's guns, and contributed largely to this success."

The rendezvous of battery H was in Monroe in connection with the 15th infantry, and left that place, under command of Captain Samuel De Gobyer, on the 13th of March, 1862, to report to General Halleck at St. Louis; thence it was ordered to New Madrid, Mo. Served afterwards in Kentucky, West Tennessee, and Northern Mississippi, and took an active part in the Mississippi campaign preceding the siege of Vicksburg.

At Thompson's Hills, Miss., May 1, 1863, it first encountered the rebels, and then at Raymond, May 12th following, where it received much favorable comment on its rapid and effective fire. Greeley, in his "American Conflict," on noticing the battle of Raymond, makes the following mention of the gallant and valuable services rendered by the battery in that affair:

"The fight here was a short one. The rebels opened with great fury, attempting to charge and capture De Gobyer's battery, which was in position in our front, but being repulsed by a terrific fire of grape and canister, they broke and fled precipitately."

The following extract from the "Rebellion Record" still further credits the battery for excellent and gallant service on the occasion referred to:

"Shortly after the opening of the fight, Captain De Gobyer's battery (8th Michigan) was ordered to the front, and took a commanding position for the purpose of dislodging the enemy from the woods, the infantry having proven itself inadequate to the task. The James rifled guns of De Gobyer's battery opened, and commenced pouring a heavy fire of shell into the rebel columns. The enemy now, for the first time, opened artillery upon us. His aim was good, succeeding in making our infantry change position. But his purpose was to silence the 8th Michigan battery, and he failed in that. Finding it impossible to silence the guns with artillery, the rebels attempted a charge upon the battery. A regiment of men essayed the hazardous undertaking. While they were removing a fence, preparatory to making the decisive dash, the battery opened on them. Our men fired two shells into their midst, both of which burst among them, killing and wounding a large number, and causing the entire column to fall back in disorder. At their inglorious withdrawal our infantry sent up a few rousing cheers, which had the effect of accelerating the speed of the fugitives, and inspiring our whole command with a new zeal and determination to press forward to a victory of which they felt certain, even when the fortunes of the day seemed to turn against them.

"The rebels, defeated in their attempt to capture our battery, found themselves compelled to fall back to a position immediately in the rear of Farnden's creek."

The battery participated in the fight at "Champion Hills," with loss, and then was actively engaged in the siege of Vicksburg until its surrender, where, on the 28th of May, its gallant commander, Captain De Gobyer, received a wound, which caused his death on the 8th of August following.

Battery I, raised and organized in Detroit by Captain J. J. Daniels, left the State with the 5th cavalry on December 4, 1862, for Washington, D. C. On April 27, 1863, Captain Daniels, with his battery, encountered the rebels at Aldie, Va.; then at Gettysburg, during that great battle, where on July 3d it became heavily engaged, losing one killed and four wounded, and acquiring much credit for vigorous and brave fighting. On October 27th following it was ordered to the Department of the Cumberland, arriving at

Nashville on the 12th of November. In April, 1864, it was attached to the 3d division, 20th corps, and afterwards participated in the Georgia campaign, and was in the various engagements of that great undertaking, including the memorable siege of Atlanta.

On the 27th and 28th of June, when under command of Captain L. R. Smith, it fought the enemy at New Hope Church with loss; on the 17th at Lost Mountain, losing some; and at Marietta, on July 13th, again became engaged and lost lightly.

These are some of the most noted fights of this battery, in all of which it behaved with determined courage and perseverance, securing final success in these as well as in all others in which it was engaged.

The next battery (K) went from Grand Rapids, under command of Captain John C. Schultz, arriving at Washington, D. C., March 1, 1863, and served on duty at various forts in that vicinity, until October 28th, when it left Washington for Nashville, Tenn., and was again assigned to garrison duty and service on gunboats and transports on the Cumberland river. A portion of the battery assisted with much spirit and vigor in repelling an attack of the rebel General Wheeler's force on Dalton, Ga., in 1864.

Battery L had its rendezvous at Coldwater, being organized by Captain Charles J. Thompson, in connection with the 9th cavalry, and went to Kentucky in May, 1863. First fought the rebels at Triplett's Bridge, Ky., on June 15th following. A portion of the battery was the first artillery to open on Morgan's forces at Buffington's Island, on July 19th, and gained much notoriety by its rapid and effective fire on that occasion.

The last battery of the regiment (M) left Dearborn, its rendezvous, under command of Captain Edward G. Hillier, and went to Indianapolis in July, 1863, thence in the pursuit of Morgan, then on his raid through Indiana and Ohio. In the latter part of 1863 and in 1864 it served in East Tennessee, and was engaged with the enemy at Blue Springs, October 10th; at Walker's Ford, December 2, 1863; and at Tazewell on January 21, 1864, behaving on every occasion with uniform efficiency.

The 13th battery, commanded by Captain C. H. O'Riordan, left Grand Rapids, where it was recruited, and arrived in Washington on the 7th of February, 1864. During its service it was mostly stationed in the forts around that city, and for a short time was mounted as cavalry for scouting purposes. On the 11th and 12th of July, 1864, under command of Captain Charles Dupont, it assisted in the defence of Fort Stevens against an attack of Early's forces then threatening Washington. On that occasion it proved a serviceable and reliable battery, its fire being used with good effect on the enemy.

On February 1, 1864, the 14th battery moved from Kalamazoo for Washington, under the command of Captain Charles Heine, and garrisoned forts in that vicinity during its entire service. While General Early was seeking to attack Washington it took a creditable and conspicuous part in the action near Forts Stevens and Slocum on the 11th, 12th, and 13th of July, 1864.

THE SHARP-SHOOTERS.

The regiment of Michigan sharp-shooters, organized and commanded by Colonel C. V. De Land, commenced its services in Indiana in 1863, in pursuit of the notorious rebel Morgan, while he was raiding through that State and Ohio, having an encounter with his rear-guard. The regiment was afterwards stationed at Chicago, guarding rebel prisoners, and subsequently joined the 9th army corps at Annapolis, Md., in March, 1864, and with much distinction and gallantry participated in the important battles of that celebrated corps which followed.

In May, 1864, the sharp-shooters belonged to Colonel Christ's 2d brigade, of the 2d division, commanded by General O. B. Wilcox, and commenced their first important engagements with the enemy in the memorable battles of the Wilderness, sustaining a loss of twenty-five in killed, wounded, and missing.

On these occasions they performed commendable service for a new and inexperienced regiment, and in the second day's battle bore an active and distinguished part with their veteran associates; and soon following these battles came that of Spottsylvania, in which it became signally celebrated. On May 9th the 9th corps moved forward in the direction of Spottsylvania, the 3d division in the advance, and before noon encountered the enemy, when the lines were formed, the sharp-shooters, in command of Colonel C. V. De Land, on the left. Immediately the division experienced severe fighting; for a time the line wavered, but advanced quickly, gaining ground all day, and on the 10th, with the corps, crossed the Po river, and went into position on the heights southwest of the river, where its artillery commanded the junction of the two great wagon roads which the rebels had to hold in order to cover Richmond. Heavy skirmishing continued on the 11th, and the height of the fighting was reached on the next day, said to have been acknowledged by the Generals of both armies as one of the bloodiest of the campaign. The rain having continued for two days, the roads had become totally impassable, and it was only by the most persistent and overtasking exertions that the 9th and 2d corps were joined and put in a defensive position. The rebel General, moving on plank and macadamized roads, took quick advantage of this state of affairs to make a tremendous onslaught upon the 9th corps while thus isolated and unsupported, with a swollen and almost impassable river in its rear. General Burnside, not waiting to be attacked, initiated the action, and the fighting commenced at 4 o'clock A. M., the 1st division (Crittenden's) in front, assisted by the 2d division (Potter's) maintained the action until noon, when the 3d division (Wilcox's) was put in, when a most determined and vigorous attack was made by the 1st brigade, under General Hartranft, which drove the rebels into their works and gave the Union troops a most decided advantage, and the division was instantly formed and ordered to assault the main line of works, while, at the same time, as was afterwards ascertained, Anderson's corps of the rebel army had been preparing to charge to dislodge the Union troops.

The Federal line swiftly advanced, with a cheer, to the desperate contest. Answering back came the shrill yell of the rebel hosts, as if in confident defiance. Midway the space between the two lines of battle the two charging columns met, amid the thick smoke of battle, in a dense thicket of pines; the bloody struggle commenced, and almost in an instant after the first shock they became mixed in inextricable confusion, and the charge became a series of furious and unrelenting hand-to-hand encounters. At length the superior numbers of the rebels began to force the Union lines to retire; regiment after regiment fell slowly and sullenly back, and the whole left was in retreat. The terrible sacrifice of the troops attest their valor and the magnitude of the struggle.

On a little knoll, among the thick spindling pine, where their rifles commanded the country for their full range, rallied two Michigan regiments—the 1st sharp-shooters, Colonel De Land, and the 27th, Major Moody, while a little back, in a ravine, was the 14th New York battery, supported by the 2d Michigan infantry. The combat, slowly, sullenly, disastrously rolling down from the left, was bursting upon them, when Colonel Humphrey, of the 2d Michigan, commanding brigade, cool as an iceberg and resolute as fate, said: "Boys, this must be stopped." The leaden hail pattered and whistled with terrific furor, but the little band stood firm. More than once the bold rebels laid their hands on the guns of the battery only to be driven back by well-directed volleys. A cheer arose, the rebels were checked, broken, but not defeated; in incredible short time they had reformed, and again the fearful struggle was renewed. On the right stood the 27th, fighting with unequalled coolness and bravery; everything on the left of the sharp-shooters had been swept away, and the attack on their front and flank, with both infantry and artillery pouring in shot and shell, was terrific; but they gallantly held their ground. On the left of the sharp-shooters were a company of civilized Indians, in command of the gallant and lamented young Graveraet, an educated half-breed—as brave a band of warriors as ever struck a war-path; they suffered dreadfully, but never faltered nor moved, sounding the war-whoop with every volley, and their unerring aim quickly taught the rebels they were standing on dangerous ground. The fighting continued on. Near night a rumor runs along the lines that ammunition is gone, and the cry of give them the steel is received with a cheer. The attack has again been repulsed, and the storm lulls; the fight is losing its horrid fury, and with a fearful burst of artillery it sinks into a scattered skirmish, but not until the darkness came did the battle cease. During this fearful and bloody day Col. De Land was twice struck and prostrated by the flying missiles, but badly injured as he was remained faithful to his command. The regiment lost 34 killed, 117 wounded, and 4 missing. Among the killed was Major John Piper, a brave and lamented officer, who, after several years of hard and faithful service, fell by a shot through the brain.

Passing through Grant's great campaign on Richmond with much credit and crossing the James river, it arrived with its division in front of Petersburg June 16, 1864, and on the next day, while in command of Major Levant C. Rhines, became so heavily engaged and so specially distinguished in charging and holding the enemy's works and repelling his repeated assaults to retake them that this bloody battle becomes one of the most prominent events in the history of the regiment.

The position of the regiment being on the extreme left of the corps, and the 5th corps failing to connect the line after the capture of the rebel works, a large gap was left through which the rebels poured their troops, and most severe fighting occurred, the regiment most gallantly repulsing the enemy in two successive and vigorous charges, taking two officers and eighty-six men prisoners, and the colors of the 35th North Carolina, which were captured by Corporal Benj. F. Young, of company I, who was promoted for distinguished gallantry on the occasion. During the engagement the left of the regiment became completely enveloped, and was placed in a position compelling it either to surrender or cut its way through the rebel lines; the last-named resort was determined on, and having first destroyed the national color of the regiment to prevent its falling into the hands of the enemy, then commenced fighting its way out, and finally succeeded in getting through the rebel lines. The gallant Major Rhines fell in this desperate struggle, together with 31 killed and died of wounds, 46 wounded, and 84 missing.

Capt. Thomas H. Gaffney died at Washington, D. C., June 20th, 1864, of wounds received in action before Petersburg June 17th, 1864.

Lieut. Garrett A. Graveraet died at Washington, D. C., July 10, 1864, of wounds received in action before Petersburg June 17, 1864.

Capt. George C. Knight and Lieut. Martin Wager killed before Petersburg; the former in action June 17th, and the latter in the trenches June 23d, 1864.

On the 30th of July the regiment led its brigade in the charge on the rebel works contiguous to the fort which was blown up by the "mine," and aided in carrying the works, taking about fifty prisoners. The rebels having finally succeeded in retaking the works it was obliged to retire, with a loss of three killed, twelve wounded, and thirty-three missing. The regiment remained in front of Petersburg until the 19th of August, when it was ordered to move to the Weldon railroad. Soon after its arrival it assisted in retaking a line of works from which our forces had been driven. Its loss in this affair was one killed and two wounded. Until the 28th of September the regiment was here engaged in the erection of fortifications. On the 30th of September it participated in the battle near Peebles' House, with a loss of three wounded and sixteen missing. The casualties of the regiment while in the trenches in front of Petersburg were twenty-seven killed and died of wounds and six wounded. On the 27th of October the regiment took part in the movement toward the South-Side Railroad, and was engaged during the day in skirmishing with the enemy, losing five men wounded.

On April 2d, 1865, the regiment, while in command of Lieut. Col. W. A. Nichols and in the brigade of Col. Ralph Ely, again most signally acquired a very enviable notoriety and great credit for a most daring and brilliant achievement while making a demonstration in front of Petersburg, on the left of the enemy's works, for the purpose of drawing troops from his right while our forces were attacking him at other points. After making two efforts, under a very severe fire of musketry and artillery, the regiment succeeded in getting hold on his works to the extent of its regimental front, which it held for an hour under a terrific fire. The object of the attack having been attained it was ordered back to its former position, having suffered a heavy loss. On the next day, about 4 A. M., it was again ordered to advance, under the supposition that the enemy was withdrawing. On moving forward and finding that he had evacuated his works, it pushed on and was the first regiment to enter Petersburg, and, while Col. Ely was receiving the surrender of the city, raised the first national flag on the court-house of that rebel stronghold.

The capture of Petersburg was long and anxiously looked for, as leading to the immediate possession of Richmond by the Union forces. It was finally accomplished, the rebel army fled, and Richmond fell. Michigan troops were prominently instrumental in bringing about the result. Colonel Ely's brigade of Michigan regiments, belonging to Wilcox's division, (1st,) 9th corps, were, as previously stated, the first to enter the city and place their colors on the public buildings, raising one flag on the court-house and another on the custom-house; Colonel Ely himself receiving the surrender of the city from the authorities.

Gen. Wilcox, in the following report of the operations of his division in that affair, says:

"I have the honor to report the operations of this division in the field from the 29th of March to the 9th of April, 1865, inclusive.

"On the night of the 29th of March, at half-past 10 o'clock, the enemy opened on my lines, stretching from above Fort Morton to the Appomattox, with all their artillery of every description and some musketry from their main line. At about 11 o'clock the artillery lulled. I expected an advance of the enemy's troops and was ready to receive them, but no attack was made, and a desultory firing of artillery only continued through the night.

"It afterwards appeared from the official reports of the enemy that they thought that we had made an attack; in fact, Major-General Gordon reported such to be the case, and that they had handsomely repulsed us; but although we were under orders from corps headquarters to be ready to attack, and I had caused to be distributed axes for cutting the enemy's abatis, yet no sort of attack was actually ordered or made on our front.

"The sensitiveness of the enemy seemed to encourage our men. Preparations were made on the 31st as well as on April 1st for a night attack opposite Forts Steadman and Haskell, 3d brigade, and at a point in front of Ely's brigade, nearer the Appomattox. Through the night of the 2d various demonstrations were made along the line, and the enemy's picket-pits captured at various points, in pursuance of orders from corps headquarters, made in aid of operations being carried on on the left of the army.

"At about 1 o'clock, on the morning of the 2d April, orders were received from corps headquarters to mass one brigade (except garrisons) by 4 o'clock on the same morning near Fort Sedgwick, on the 2d division front, where Gen. Hartranft was to make a real attack with his division and a brigade from each of the other divisions, while, by the same order, I was directed to make a vigorous demonstration along my whole division line with the rest of my troops at the same hour.

"Col. Harriman was accordingly detached, with staff officers who knew the road, tools, ammunition, and every possible aid, to report to Hartranft; and this brigade was in position and formed at the moment required.

"The demonstration along the line began precisely at 4 by the 2d brigade, Brevet Col. Ralph Ely; 3d brigade, Brevet Col. G. P. Robinson, and Col. Wm. J. Bolton, commanding 51st Pennsylvania, left on the 1st brigade line of entrenchments. Some of the enemy's picket-pits were captured near the "Old Crater" by Col. Bolton. The pickets of the 3d and 2d brigades, strongly reinforced, advanced handsomely, the artillery opened vigorously, and large portions of the enemy were down to oppose what they considered a real attack in force.

"On the extreme right, near the Appomattox, a portion of Ely's brigade actually carried some two hundred yards of the enemy's works; but our lines, two miles in length, were too much attenuated to hold the ground. Some seventy-five prisoners were secured and brought in. Three regiments were withdrawn from other points and double-quicked to the point, but before it could be reinforced the enemy had recovered it.

"The effect of the movement, however, on the grand result was most happy, inasmuch as it contributed to weaken the enemy's line in front of Fort Sedgwick, where the real attack was completely successful.

"For the handsome part performed by Harriman's brigade of this division at the latter point I respectfully refer you to his own report and that of Brevet Major-Gen. Hartranft, commanding at that part of the line.

"Through the day offensive demonstrations were kept up, and the batteries playing in aid of the more serious work of the day going on further to the left.

"In the afternoon and evening the enemy strengthened their line opposite me; but about midnight of the 2d reports came up from Colonel Ely, commanding 2d brigade, and Col. James Bentliff, now commanding 3d brigade, by virtue of his rank, that there were signs of the enemy's withdrawing from our front, leaving only their picket line. I gave orders to the 2d brigade commanders to press through as soon as possible.

"At about 2 A. M. on the 3d some of our parties broke through.

"Bentliff's brigade advanced upon Cemetery Hill and Ely's more directly into town, with a section of Stone's battery. I gave Col. Ely orders to take measures to at once secure order in the city.

"At 4.28 one of Ely's flags, that of the 1st Michigan sharp-shooters, was raised on the court-house, and that of the 2d Michigan on the custom-house a few minutes later, and guards were posted about the town."

The 2d and 20th Michigan infantry and 1st Michigan sharp-shooters were in the 2d brigade, commanded by Col. Ralph Ely, of the 8th Michigan.

The 8th and 27th Michigan were in the 1st brigade.

The 17th Michigan were acting as an engineer regiment at division headquarters.

THE FIRST INFANTRY.

The 1st Michigan—the regiment which, under Colonel Wilcox, led the advance of Michigan troops to the front—although hurriedly organized and hastily equipped, left the State a pattern regiment in every respect, none better having preceded it to the National Capital from any State; arriving there at a critical time, when that place was in great and immediate danger of being attacked and captured by the rebels, whose troops then picketed the Potomac. Its presence aided much in establishing confidence among those in authority, that the Capital was safe, and its appearance in Pennsylvania avenue was hailed with the cheers of loyal thousands. As it passed in review before the lamented Lincoln it received his highest praise, and through them he thanked the State for their prompt appearance in Washington.

The regiment was assigned to Heintzelman's division, and under Colonel Wilcox led the advance of the Union army across the Long Bridge into Virginia, on the 24th of May, driving in the rebel pickets, and entering Alexandria via the road, simultaneously with the regiment of Ellsworth's Zouaves that entered it by steamer.

The 1st Michigan took possession of the railroad depot, capturing near there a troop of rebel cavalry, numbering one hundred, with their horses and equipments.

At the battle of Bull Run the regiment belonged to the brigade commanded by Colonel Wilcox, and was in the hottest of the fight, eagerly pressing forward on the enemy, losing heavily, but fighting stubbornly and gallantly.

The Fire Zouaves, after charging bravely, but in vain, upon one of the heaviest of the rebel batteries, fell back, when the Michigan 1st, then commanded by Major Bidwell, which had been constantly associated with the Zouaves ever since Ellsworth fell at Alexandria, moved promptly and rapidly forward and took their places. They charged in double-quick upon the battery once and again in splendid style, and yet it was not taken. They pushed forward to the attempt a third time, and were again driven back before the deadly fire of the enemy. But the attack was not abandoned; the brave fellows rallied for a fourth time to the deadly work; but it was all in vain, the battery could not be taken.

On that disastrous field the 1st established the highest standard for Michigan troops, so uniformly and so remarkably maintained throughout the entire war. Its dead were found nearest the enemy's works.

In the engagement the loss of the regiment was heavy. Among the number were Captain Butterworth, Lieutenants Mauch and Casey wounded and taken prisoners, and who afterwards died of their wounds in rebel custody. Colonel Wilcox was wounded, and, falling into the hands of the enemy, was held as a prisoner at Richmond for about fifteen months.

The regiment, on the expiration of its three months' term of service, returned to the State, and was mustered out August 7, 1861. It was soon after reorganized as a three years' regiment, and left for the Army of the Potomac August 16, 1861, commanded by Colonel John C. Robinson, then captain in the U. S. A., who continued to command it until April 28, 1862, when he was appointed a brigadier-general of volunteers, and was succeeded in command by Colonel H. S. Roberts, promoted from lieutenant-colonel. It went to the Peninsula with McClellan, and was in the engagements at Mechanicsville, June 26th; at Gaines' Mills, June 27th; at Malvern Hill, July 1st; and at Gainsville, August 29th. The losses of the regiment in these engagements were not reported, excepting Captain O. C. Comstock who was killed at Gaines' Mills.

It rendered most gallant and valuable service in many hard-fought battles during the war, and suffered severe losses in killed and wounded.

Among its numerous engagements none perhaps will be more vividly remembered by the regiment than the disastrous charges so bravely made, but with such fearful loss, upon the rebel position along the Warrenton and Centreville turnpike on August 30, 1862, during that disastrous series of engagements near Manassas, now known as the Second Battle of Bull Run.

The regiment, under command of Colonel Roberts, was in General Fitz John Porter's corps, and had during the day been posted in the woods fronting the enemy's lines, and near one of his most important batteries. At 4 P. M. the order was given to advance and dislodge the rebels. The 1st Michigan, with the 18th Massachusetts and the 13th New York regiments of infantry, deployed column, and with cheers charged—

"Forward, the Light Brigade!
Was there a man dismay'd?
Not tho' the soldier knew
Some one had blundered;
Theirs not to make reply,
Theirs not to reason why,
Theirs but to do or die—
Into the Valley of Death
Rode the six hundred.

"Cannon to right of them,
Cannon to left of them,
Cannon in front of them,
Volleyed and thunder'd;
Storm'd at with shot and shell,
Boldly they rode, and well,
Into the jaws of Death,
Into the very mouth of hell,
Rode the six hundred."

They instantly found themselves the target of a terrific fire from ambushed infantry of the enemy, and from five batteries, four of which had been masked, and hitherto unseen. The charge was a murderous one, and within a few moments fell eight officers and fifty per cent. of the regiment. The men stood their ground bravely and with veteran coolness, under these trying circumstances, and when the impossibility of success became a certainty, and the order to retreat was given, fell back in good order to the woods, and reformed their division. Had victory been possible, their courage and persistency would have won it. Their demeanor amid disaster and defeat affords one of the greatest examples of true courage.

Chaplain Arthur Edwards, then with the regiment, and who rendered most valuable and very acceptable service during the entire engagement, and throughout his whole term in the army was an exemplary chaplain, wrote at the time as follows:

"The regiment deployed column and with cheers advanced towards the enemy, our right resting near the railroad embankment, the centre and left near a stone wall and railroad cut, in each of which places was posted a rebel battery. On our right and front was a force of the enemy's infantry, and as we advanced the regiment was subjected to a murderous fire from infantry and a cross-fire from five rebel batteries. The regiment suffered severely in crossing the open space. Colonel Roberts fell at an early moment after it deployed out of the woods. Four captains and three lieutenants—Captains Charles E. Wendell, Russell H. Alcott, Eben T. Whittelsey, Edward Pomeroy, and Lieutenants H. Clay Arnold, J. L. Garrison, and W. Bloodgood—met their death, and more than fifty per cent. of the regiment were either killed or wounded.

"Colonel Roberts was an active, efficient, brave, beloved, and is now a sincerely lamented leader. Captains Wendell, Alcott, Whittelsey, Pomeroy, and Lieutenants Arnold, Garrison, and Bloodgood were excellent officers, whose loss will be felt by the regiment, and mourned by their personal acquaintances.

"The regiment went into battle with twenty officers and two hundred and twenty-seven men. Of the former but four are in camp unhurt, and of the latter hardly one hundred and fifty. In the action the 1st was placed in the centre. In front was a rebel battery, and so destructive was its fire and so commanding its position, that General Porter ordered our brigade (Martindale's, of Morrell's division) forward to capture it. The service was so desperate, and so very sure were our officers of the death that awaited them, that they shook hands with each other in farewell. Like heroes they pressed on to the charge, until, coming within range, the enemy opened four additional batteries, hitherto masked, and poured in a deadly fire. Thus were they exposed to a cross-fire from five batteries at short range, throwing grape and canister, and to a flank fire of infantry. The result may be easily seen. Men fell like grain in harvest. Colonel Roberts was shot in the breast by a Minie ball, and lived about ten minutes. His words were: 'I am killed; tell Captain ——— to take command of the regiment.' He seemed to feel that he was about to fall, for previous to his going to his place in line, he called me aside, and, after leaving some private messages, said: 'I trust that Michigan will believe that I tried to do my duty.'"

After the death of Colonel Roberts, Lieutenant-Colonel Franklin W. Whittelsey was promoted to the colonelcy of the regiment, but was absent from the field on account of injuries received on the Peninsula campaign.

The regiment was engaged at Antietam, September 17th, at Shepherdstown Ford, September 20th, and at Fredericksburg, December 13th and 14th. At Fredericksburg it was commanded by Lieutenant-Colonel Ira C. Abbott, and was heavily engaged, and lost one officer (Captain J. B. Kennedy) and seven men killed, together with seven officers and thirty-three men wounded.

After this engagement the regiment lay in camp near Falmouth until the 27th of April following, when it moved with its corps and division in the direction of Chancellorsville. Crossing the Rappahannock and Rapidan, it reached that battle-ground on the 30th, after four days of forced and heavy marching, and entered into action there with twenty-three officers and two hundred and forty muskets. Between the 1st and 5th of May its losses in the various engagements in that vicinity were three men killed and seventeen wounded. Again resuming its camping ground near Falmouth, it lay there until the 28th of May, when the division to which it was attached moved to Morrisville, a two day's march, and on the 9th of June crossed the river as support to a cavalry force which advanced to Brandy Station, fighting all day, and returning to camp on the 10th. On the 14th it broke camp at Morrisville, and on the 19th and 21st was in brisk skirmishes with the enemy's cavalry at Aldie. On the 26th the regiment crossed the Potomac into Maryland at Edward's Ferry, and after laborious and exhausting marches, under a broiling sun, it reached Gettysburg, Penna., at 1:30 A. M., of the 2d of July. It entered into battle the same day with a force of twenty officers and one hundred and twenty-five men, sustaining a loss during the engagement of Captain Amos Ladd and four men killed, with six officers and twenty-five men wounded. Among the wounded was Colonel Abbott, disabled early in the action, who was succeeded in command by Lieutenant-Colonel W. A. Throop. It joined in the pursuit of the enemy on the 5th, and on the 18th recrossed the Potomac into Virginia, aided in driving the rebels through Manassas Gap, and went into camp at Warrenton on the 27th, and at Beverley Ford on the 8th of August.

In the battle of the Wilderness, commencing May 5, 1864, this regiment, in command of W. A. Throop, especially distinguished itself. It was in Bartlett's (3d) brigade, of Griffin's (1st) division, 5th corps, in the van of Grant's celebrated movement on Richmond, which ultimately culminated in the fall of the rebel capital and the surrender of Lee's army.

Near Robertson's Tavern, on the morning of the 5th, its picket line first discovered the advance of the Southern forces upon its division, in the thickest of the Wilderness. It fired the first musket of that glorious campaign, and its brigade checked the rebel advance on the road leading to Orange Court-house, and opened thus the last act of the great drama. In the opening engagements of the campaign it especially distinguished itself, and so constantly was it under fire, and so perilous were the duties to which it was assigned, that on the evening of the 8th, after a brilliant and successful charge at Alsop's Farm, its gallant commander was only able to muster twenty-three men fit for active service. Colonel Throop, in his report of the engagement on the 5th, states: "The regiment was detailed on the morning of the 4th of May to picket in front of the brigade, covering the road leading to Orange Court-house, and connecting on the left with the pickets of the 2d brigade. There was at this time no enemy in our front, and during the night I received orders that the troops would move at 5 A. M. of the 5th. At 5:30 A. M. I received written orders to withdraw my pickets and rejoin the brigade on the road to the Old Wilderness Tavern. Fifteen minutes before receiving the order to withdraw, the enemy was discovered coming down the road towards us, with a strong force of infantry, preceded by cavalry. I therefore retained my picket line in position, disposing my reserves to cover my right flank and hold the road. The cavalry of the enemy approached to within four hundred yards of my picket line on the road, and his infantry deployed to the right and left of the road in line of battle. The disposition of his forces was immediately reported by me, and the 18th Massachusetts and 20th Maine regiments were sent out to my support, and moved up to the rear of my picket line, and formed in line of battle. The enemy had thrown out a very heavy line of skirmishers in my immediate front, and pushed them boldly forward into the edge of the wood against my lines, but without firing. Our lines having been formed, and everything in readiness, an attack was ordered, and I pushed my skirmish line forward at double-quick over an open field of a quarter of a mile, driving the enemy's picket line into the woods and on to their line of battle. I was followed up by my brigade in two lines of battle, and the fight became general. Part of my skirmish line fought that of the enemy in the woods hand-to-hand, using the bayonet. Captain Bradish, a most gallant officer was killed, and Captain Stanway and Lieutenant Raymond were wounded, the former severely in the arm, while almost at the very muzzle of a rebel gun."

During the following eight days it was almost continuously engaged in battle or in skirmishing, sustaining large losses, especially at the battle of Alsop's Farm, on the 8th, where the regiment came out of the engagement with only twenty-three men. Pressing forward with the army, it participated in the battles of Spottsylvania, thence moved to the North Anna, and on the 23d took part in the engagement at Jericho Mills. Crossing the Pamunkey river, it advanced to near Cold Harbor and participated in the engagements near that place.

Proceeding to James river with the army, it crossed that stream on the 16th of June, and on the 17th arrived in front of Petersburg and became engaged in the ordinary duties in the trenches. On the 30th of September following the regiment participated in the movement of that date on the right of the enemy's line, near Poplar Grove Church, and participated in the desperate fighting that ensued. Unaided it stormed and carried two strong fortifications and a portion of one line of works. During this action the officer commanding the regiment, Capt. James H. Wheaton, was killed.

On the 6th of December, the regiment, in command of Major George Lockley, started on a raid along the Weldon railroad. After crossing the Nottaway river the regiment assisted in destroying several miles of that railroad. Proceeding as far as Hicksford it returned, arriving at its former encampment on the 12th. Remaining there until February 5th, 1865, it broke camp and moved to the left of the line and participated in the engagement on the 6th at Hatcher's Run, losing three killed and three taken by the enemy. It remained in camp near that place until the 29th of March. On the 25th of March the regiment was engaged in an attack on the enemy's right at Hatcher's Run, having several wounded. On the morning of the 29th it broke camp and engaged the enemy the same day on the White Oak road, and also on April 1st at Five Forks, at Amelia Court-house on the 5th, at High Bridge on the 6th, and at Appomattox Court-house on the 9th.

Captain Lewis C. Randell was killed in action at Laurel Hill, May 10th, 1864.

Lieut. Wm. S. Woodruff died June 28th, 1864, of wounds received in action on the 27th of that month.

Following is the report of Gen. Wilcox, dated at Detroit September 3d, 1862, and addressed to the Adjutant-General of the army at Washington:

"My brigade, the 2d of Heintzelman's division, marching in rear of Franklin's brigade, arrived at the Sudley Ford at about half-past 12 P. M. July 21, 1862. The brigade now consisted of the 1st Michigan, 11th New

York, (Fire Zouaves,) 38th New York, and Arnold's battery. The 4th Michigan had been left at Fairfax Station and Fairfax Court-house by the order of Gen. McDowell. Halting for rest and water, I obeyed the general's orders to post Arnold's battery on a hill commanding the ford, with the 1st Michigan for support, and at 1 o'clock pushed forward with my two remaining regiments up the Sudley and Brentville road. We marched about two miles and came up on the right of what I suppose to have been Franklin's line, near the junction of the Warrenton and Sudley roads. The troops on our left were engaged in a desultory fire with the enemy, posted in the thicket and ravine across the Warrenton road, not far from the Henry House. The 28th New York was quickly formed in order of battle, and the Zouaves were hastening into line, when I received an order to detach a regiment for the support of Ricketts' battery, (of Franklin's brigade,) posted on a hill a quarter of a mile to our right and front, near Dogan House. I led up the Zouaves for this important service, leaving the 38th under its gallant and experienced Col. Hobart Ward. Ricketts was soon ordered to take a new position near the Henry House. The Zouaves followed in support, and finally formed line on the right flank of the battery, with two companies in reserve.

"Up to this time the enemy had fallen back, but now he formed the remains of his brigades engaged with Hunter in the morning, viz: Bee's, Bartow's, and Evans', in a new line, appuyed upon Jackson's brigade of fresh troops, making altogether 6,500 infantry, 13 pieces of artillery, and Stuart's cavalry, according to Gen. Beauregard's report. This force was posted in the belt of woods which skirted the plateau southwardly and lying in the angle formed in that direction between the Warrenton and Sudley roads, about a mile from the Warrenton road, and with its left resting on the Brentsville and Sudley roads. Ricketts' battery had crossed the Sudley road from its post near Dogan's House, and was within musket range of the woods which stretched from that road around from his right towards his front, and forming a pocket which almost enveloped the battery with its support.

"The enemy were first discovered by Col. Heintzelman lining the woods in our front. He ordered up the Zouaves, commanded by Col. Farnham. The ground was slightly rising before us, and the enemy opened a heavy but not destructive fire as we reached the crest. The Zouaves returned the fire, but immediately fell back, bewildered and broken. Stuart's cavalry charged upon them from the woods on the right, but were scattered by a fire from the two reserve companies, with a loss (as ascertained from the Southern papers) of twenty-nine killed and wounded.

"Meantime Ricketts' cannoneers were being picked off. With Colonel Heintzelman's approval and a promise of reinforcements, I collected some one hundred Zouaves, and, with Capt. Douney and others of their officers, made a dash into the woods on our right and killed, wounded, and captured about thirty of the enemy. Returning in a few minutes, I found the field cleared of both friend and foe except the killed and wounded.

"The horses, men, and two officers of Ricketts' battery lay stretched upon the ground, but the enemy had not yet seized it.

"Recrossing the Sudley road, I met the 1st Michigan, Major Bidwell commanding, and marching back with this regiment we found the enemy now drawn up in a thin line across the field and in possession of the battery; advancing to the fence on the roadside the 1st Michigan opened fire, the right wing fell back to reload, owing to a blundering order, but the left stood firm, expelled the enemy and retook the battery. The troops here opposed to us I believe to have been the 7th Georgia.

"Colonel Heintzelman now came up and ordered us promptly forward, and with the promise of another regiment it was my design to turn the enemy's left. The left wing of the 1st Michigan recrossed the field, struck into the woods beyond the Zouaves, succeeded in destroying and capturing a small number of the enemy and pushing back his extreme left out of that part or point of the woods adjacent to the Sudley road.

"Meantime the right wing of the 1st Michigan reformed and advanced in good order. I met it and we pushed on toward the next point of woods. From this point I found the enemy's left discovered us by our fire and we became engaged with their rear rank, their front being occupied by the advancing troops of Franklin's or Sherman's brigade. The officers and men of the 1st Michigan stood up bravely at this critical moment, holding on anxiously for reinforcements. But from all I can learn, the 38th, which was ordered up to me, were directed to the left of the Henry House, (instead of to the right and along the Sudley road,) came in contact with the enemy's centre and never reached me.

"It was now nearly four o'clock. General Beauregard had been gathering new reinforcements; General Kirby Smith had joined him with a portion of Johnston's army. Our scattered troops were contending in fractions against the enemy's army in position and massed on the plateau, with his artillery sweeping every approach. Gen. Johnston was bringing fresh troops to turn our right. The 28th Virginia attacked my own handful from the rear in the woods, and I had the ill fortune to be wounded and a few moments afterward captured. But I was spared witnessing the disaster which further pursued our arms.

"In this report I have only endeavored to supply partly the information that was not known or found in any other report in consequence of my capture. Permit me to add further, that the 38th New York was distinguished for its steadiness in ranks, and for gallantly repelling a charge made upon it by the 'New Orleans Tigers.' The Zouaves, though broken as a regiment, did good service under my own eyes in the woods, and detachments of them joined various other regiments in the fight. The 1st Michigan deserves the credit of advancing farther into the enemy's lines than any other of our troops, as their dead bodies proved after the battle. I only regret that from the fact of my separation from Arnold's battery, I cannot add any testimony of my own to the well known gallantry with which he and his command conducted themselves."

THE SECOND INFANTRY.

The 2d infantry, under command of Col. J. B. Richardson, by whom it had been organized, with much promptness followed the 1st regiment to the war in Virginia, and was in time to be present in the first engagement, being in the brigade of Richardson, which opened fire upon the rebels at Blackburn's Ford, on the 18th of July, 1861, and which covered the retreat of the army from Bull Run on the 21st following.

The regiment, under command of Col. O. M. Poe, participated in all of the engagements on the Peninsula, first meeting the enemy on that campaign at Williamsburg, on May 5, 1862, where it lost 17 killed, 38 wounded, and 4 missing; at Fair Oaks, on the 27th; at Charles City Cross-roads, on June 30th, and at Malvern Hill July 1st. At Fair Oaks it lost 10 killed and 47 wounded, while its bravery was so marked as to receive the following notice in the published history of the time:

"Meantime, Heintzelman had sent forward Kearney to recover Casey's lost ground, and a desperate fight was going on at the extreme left. The enemy had been successfully held in front of Couch's old entrenched camp, until Kearney's division arrived, when he staid the torrent of battle. One after another his gallant regiments pushed forward, and pressed back the fiery rebels with more daring than their own. Here the 55th New York won new laurels, and Poe's 2d Michigan was bathed in blood. Five hundred of them charged across the open field against ten times their number, and stopped them in mid career, losing 17 brave fellows in that one desperate essay."

Immediately following the battles on the Peninsula it entered on the campaign of General Pope, and was engaged with the enemy at Bull Run August 28th, 29th, and 30th, and at Chantilly on the 1st of September.

On the 12th of December following, the regiment, then commanded by Lieutenant-Colonel Louis Dillman, participated in the engagement at Fredericksburg with slight loss.

The 2d was transferred early in 1863 to another field of operations with the 9th corps, and served with distinction on the Grant campaign in Mississippi, terminating with the fall of Vicksburg and the defeat and route of Johnston at Jackson. It was also in the campaign of Burnside in East Tennessee, and was actively engaged in the defence of Knoxville against the attacks of Longstreet, and in the various battles with his forces in that vicinity. Although the survivors of this noble regiment can look back upon their campaigns in Virginia and recount with much justifiable pride their numerous battles, yet, Jackson and Knoxville will ever hold prominent places in their memories, as engagements in which the regiment specially distinguished itself and sustained heavy loss.

Immediately following the surrender of Vicksburg, General Sherman with his army, a part of which was the 9th corps, moved in pursuit of General Johnston, who was then in the vicinity of Jackson, and reached there on the 10th of July. The 2d regiment belonged to the 2d brigade, 1st division, and on the 11th of July became engaged with the enemy, making one of the most daring and gallant charges of the war. Col. Humphrey, commanding the regiment, in his report thus details its movements on that occasion:

"At 5 A. M. I was ordered by Col. Leasure, commanding the brigade, to deploy my regiment as skirmishers on the left of the skirmish line of the 1st brigade—to keep my connection with it perfect—to be guided in the movements of my line strictly by those of the regiment on my right, and to advance until I drew the fire of the enemy's artillery.

"I at once deployed my regiment as directed, and moved forward, meeting with only slight opposition from the enemy, until about 6 o'clock, when he opened a brisk fire along my whole line. We had come up to the enemy strongly posted in front of my right on a deep water course, and of my left in a heavy woods. For an hour a brisk skirmish was kept up. The enemy made a determined resistance, but was gradually forced back toward his support.

"At 7 A. M. the order came down the line from the right to 'forward! double-quick!' The men at once advanced with a cheer, drove in the enemy's skirmishers through their camps, and intc their reserves, strongly posted in a deep ravine, charged and broke the reserve, and drove it up out of the ravine into its main support, drawn up in line of battle on the top of the south bank of the ravine, charged under a hot fire of musketry and artillery up the steep bank against the main body, *broke this line*, and drove the enemy within his works.

"We waited now for our support to come up, but on sending for it were surprised to find *we had none.* The regiment on my right, for some reason unknown to me, advanced but a short distance, then fell back to the line left by it a few moments before. By some mistake the three companies (C, F, and H) on the left did not advance with the rest of the regiment in this charge, which was made with about one hundred and seventy men. Fifty of these, almost one-third, had fallen. The enemy was being reinforced, and we were entirely without support, with no connection on the right and no troops on our left. Thus situated, to hold for any length of time the ground we had so dearly won would be impossible. I therefore put my men under cover of the bank of the ravine, through which we had advanced, within twenty yards of the enemy's works, and held the position until the wounded were carried to the rear, and then *following* the movement of the regiment on my right, fell back to the line from which we had advanced an hour before."

In this charge the regiment had 9 killed, 39 wounded, among whom were Lieutenants Sheldon, Stevenson, and Montague, and 8 taken as prisoners.

The 2d was also specially distinguished on several occasions during the siege of Knoxville by Longstreet in 1863, and particularly so on the 24th of November, when under command of Major Cornelius Byington (Colonel Humphrey being in command of the brigade) it so gallantly charged a strong force of rebels protected by entrenchments and a house which they occupied, driving them from their position and leveling the house and works to the ground. In the charge the regiment lost in killed and wounded, out of 161 officers and men engaged, 86. Among the killed were Lieutenants William Noble (adjutant) and Charles R. Galpin, and Major Byington and Lieutenant Frank Zoellener mortally wounded. This charge is handed down in the history of the day as among the most brilliant of the war.

Returning with its corps to the Army of the Potomac, on the 5th of May, 1864, it crossed the Rapidan, taking part with that army in the great campaign which had just commenced, sharing in its sufferings, its privations, and its glory. On May 6th, in command of Colonel W. Humphrey, it participated in the battle of the Wilderness, losing 6 killed and 32 wounded and missing. On the 10th, 11th, and 12th it was in the battle at Spottsylvania Court-house, where it lost 2 killed and 9 wounded; among the killed was Captain James Farrand; and on the 3d of June, at the battle of Bethesda Church, where its loss was 2 killed and 36 wounded. From Bethesda Church the regiment marched to Cold Harbor. June 12th it crossed the Chicahominy river, and on the morning of the 14th, and during the night of the 15th, crossed to the south side of the James river. It participated in the engagement before Petersburg on the 17th and 18th of June, losing on the 17th 8 killed, including Captain James Bradley, 74 wounded, and 4 missing; on the 18th, 14 killed, 69 wounded, and 2 missing. During the attack which followed the springing of the mine on the 30th of July, the regiment lost 6 killed, 14 wounded, and 37 missing, Captain John S. Young and Lieutenant John G. Busch being among the killed. Withdrawing from in front of Petersburg, it marched with its corps to the Weldon railroad, and in the action of the 19th of August on this road the regiment lost 1 killed, 2 wounded, and 2 missing. Participating in the movement on the right flank of the rebel army, on the 30th of September, in the engagement near Poplar Spring Church, it lost 7 in wounded and 12 missing. The regiment remained in camp from the 30th of September to October 27th, near "Peeble's House." On the latter date, in the advance on the "Boydton Plank Road," it lost 7 wounded and 7 missing. On the 28th it returned to its camping ground near Peeble's House, where it remained on the 31st of October following. On the 25th of March, 1865, the regiment participated in the affair at Fort Steadman, sustaining a heavy loss, and on the 3d of April was engaged in the capture of Petersburg.

The correspondent of the *New York Tribune,* in writing regarding the stampede from Bull Run, says:

"I was told that a few regiments, beside the three faithful ones of Blenker's brigade, had come in in fair order; and that they were the 2d and 3d Michigan and the Massachusetts 1st, of Richardson's brigade. I should be glad if it were so."

It is to be hoped that the correspondent lived long enough to be made glad, on being fully satisfied of the fact that he had been correctly informed of that well-established truth regarding the conduct of Richardson's brigade referred to, and which was so well understood and made so generally known immediately following the battle, by the issue of a general order by McDowell, in which it was stated that Richardson's brigade were the last troops to leave the field.

The following is the official order relative to the part taken at Williamsburg by Berry's brigade, composed of the 2d, 3d, and 5th Michigan:

HEADQUARTERS 3D BRIGADE, KEARNEY'S DIVISION,
ON WILLIAMSBURG BATTLE-FIELD, May 8, 1862.

Special Orders:

The commander of the brigade takes great pleasure in making this official communication to his command: That they, by *heroic fortitude,* on Monday last, by making a forced march through mud and rain, each vying with the other to see who could most cheerfully stand the hardships the time called for, making thereby a march that others shrank from, coming into a fight at double-quick, made doubtful to our side by the overwhelming mass of the enemy poured upon our centre; by a rapid deploy and quick formation, and by coolness, precision, and energy, beat back the enemy, recapturing our lost position and artillery, and also by a heroic charge, took a stronghold of the enemy, and thereby dislodged him and drove him on the plain below his well-chosen position, have done themselves great honor, have honored the States of Michigan and New York, and have won a name in history that the most ambitious might be proud of.

Our loss of brave comrades has indeed been large. We mourn the departed. "Green be the turf above them." They have a place in our heart's memory, and in the history of our common country.

Soldiers! you have won by your bravery the hearts of all your commanders—brigade, division, corps, and even those higher in command.

Soldiers, I thank you; my superiors thank you; your country thanks you, and will remember you in history.

Our labors are not yet over; the insolent rebels that have endeavored to destroy, and have laid to ruin and waste portions of the best Government and the finest land of earth, are still in force, and to be conquered in our fights. I have pledged you, men of the 3d brigade, in all future trials. I know my men; they are not pledged in vain.

Commanders of regiments will have this order read at the head of their respective regiments this afternoon.

R. G. BERRY,
Brigadier-General, Commanding 3d Brigade.

Official: EDWIN M. SMITH, A. A. A. G.

Extracts from correspondence of *New York Tribune* in relation to the battle of Williamsburg:

"The 2d Michigan took into action only sixty men, the rest being left behind, exhausted with the quick march through the mud and rain. Yet they lost one out of every five engaged. The regiment was in the hottest of the fight. By the confessions of prisoners, 800 of Berry's men (mostly Michigan) drove back at the point of the bayonet 1,600 rebels.

"There were four companies of the 2d Michigan heavily engaged at Williamsburg, two in command of Captain William Humphrey and two commanded by Captain W. J. Handy. The other companies of the regiment were partially engaged. The regiment lost in the action 17 killed, 38 wounded, and 4 missing.

"In the rifle-pits in front of the 5th Michigan, sixty-three dead rebels were found, *every one of them killed by the bayonet.*

"On June 30th the enemy had advanced about noon. The Union troops had fallen back about two miles and taken a position near Charles City Cross-roads or White Oak Swamp. The battle commenced about 1 o'clock. The 2d, in command of Major Dillman, was engaged from half-past 4 P. M. until an hour after dark, being under a continuous fire of musketry during the whole of that time, but having the cover of the woods and of a temporary breastwork of logs, rails, and sods hastily thrown together, the loss of the regiment was comparatively light. The enemy charged three times in heavy columns on the position held by the division to which the 2d belonged. They advanced under a heavy fire from a long line of infantry and six pieces of artillery, and were most gallantly repulsed each time, being compelled to retire, under a heavy and murderous fire, under cover of the woods on the opposite side of the field, leaving the open space between the two lines literally piled with the dead and wounded.

"Down to the time our troops fell back in the night the enemy were busy, close up to our line, carrying away the dead and wounded. The wounded were continually calling out the number of their regiments and the States from whence they came, in order that they might be found by their friends. In this way it was ascertained that at least twenty-one regiments had been engaged with Kearney's division during the afternoon.

"On July 1st, at 2 A. M., the pickets were ordered in, and the retreat again commenced. At 5 A. M. the regiment reached Maxwell's Landing, on the James river, and was soon after marched, with its brigade, to the right and front of the line then being formed to meet a threatened attack of the enemy. On reaching the position indicated the brigade was placed in position to support our batteries, then playing with terrible effect on the enemy's advancing columns or replying to the fierce fire kept up from his batteries. The 2d remained in this position until 12 M., when it was drawn back under shelter of Malvern Hill. During the whole of that time the shot and shell from the enemy's guns came sweeping through the Union ranks dealing out death in every direction. At midnight the regiment again commenced the march down the river, and reached the encampment near Harrison's Landing next morning at about 9 A. M.

"On the retreat to Harrison's Landing, and in the various engagements occurring on the march, the gallant conduct of Sergeants Sheldon, company C, Tulloch, company H, McGee, company I, Higgins and Delano, company E; Corporals Sannard, company F, Fuller, company D, and Thurlby, company B; Privates Henry H. Harrington, company B, and Philander Walworth, company D, are specially noticed in the report of the commanding officer of the regiment. In the battles of Charles City Cross-roads and

Malvern Hill Philander Walworth, of company D, who had been wounded on a scout on the 19th June, with his leg swollen and stiff, refused to leave the ranks, and was constantly in his place gallantly doing his duty."

The regiment is mentioned in connection with the operations at Knoxville on November 24th, 1863, in the "Rebellion Record" as follows:

"November 24th.—Skirmishing commenced early and briskly on our left front this morning. The rebels had gained a hill and thrown up rifle-pits near the round house during the night. The 48th Pennsylvania and 21st Massachusetts, during the morning, charged the pits and driving the rebels out at the point of the bayonet, covered the trenches, and returned to their own with a loss of two killed and four wounded. On our left, for some hours, the fire of the sharpshooters was quite hot from a house above and the rebel trenches. The 2d Michigan charged there also in the most gallant manner and drove the rebels back, a fierce and bloody engagement ensued with great loss on both sides, our boys remaining in possession of the works, which they obliterated and fell back."

The regiment also lost heavily at the charge following the springing of the mine July 30th. It belonged to Wilcox's division. In the Annual Cyclopædia is the following notice of its division and corps:

* * * "At length the 9th corps was reformed after a fatal delay, and with Gen. Potter's division on the right, Ledlie's in the centre, and Wilcox's on the left, under cover of the fire of two guns, began the charge. At every step the fire of the enemy in front and on each flank concentrated with greater fury upon them, and ploughed their ranks with slaughter. The charge was checked on the side of the crest, there was a halt, and finally, the whole line wavering under terrible odds, recoiled to the fort."

Lieut. Edward A. Sherman was wounded before Petersburg June 18th, 1864, and died of his wounds August 18th following.

Lieut. Nelson Fletcher was killed in action near Ox Ford, North Anna river, May 24th, 1864.

Lieut. George S. Williams, wounded at Cold Harbor June 3d, 1864, died of his wounds June 15th following.

In General Wilcox's report of the attack made by the rebels upon Fort Steadman on our line of works before Petersburg, March 25th, he says of that affair, and regarding the defence of Battery No. 9, also in the line of the Union works, and near the fort mentioned:

"At a quarter past 4 o'clock, on the morning of the 25th March, 1865, the enemy attacked the entrenchments held by the 3d brigade of this division, (1st and 9th corps.) The brigade picket officer, Captain Burch, 3d Maryland, reports that he visited the picket line at 4 o'clock of that morning, and saw that the men were on the alert. After visiting the line he returned to his headquarters in front of Fort Steadman and Battery No. 11. He states that in a few minutes after his return a man on the lookout gave notice that the enemy were approaching; at the same time the men on the post fired their pieces. One column moved towards the right of Battery No. 10; a small column moved towards a point between Fort Steadman and Battery No. 11; a third column moved direct towards Steadman. These columns were preceded by a strong storming party, which broke through the pickets, clubbing their muskets, and made openings in the abatis. The trench guards made sufficient resistance to arouse the garrison of the enclosed works in the immediate neighborhood; but the column which struck to the right of Battery No. 10 quickly succeeded in breaking through and effecting an entrance to that battery, which is entirely open in the rear. This success gave them at once a great advantage over Fort Steadman, as the ground just in rear of Battery No. 10 is on a level with the parapet of the fort.

"The fort had also a comparatively small line of infantry parapet, particularly was this the case in front, which was cut up with embrasures for artillery. The garrison of the fort consisted of a detachment of the 14th New York heavy artillery, under Major Randall, and made quite a spirited resistance; but were finally overpowered, and most of them captured.

"The commanding officer of the brigade, Brevet Brigadier-General A. B. McLaughlin, had reached Battery No. 11 from his headquarters before this, and given some directions about the disposition of the troops on the left flank.

"The guns and even the mortars in both Steadman and Battery No. 11 were used against the enemy. Detachments of the 1st Connecticut heavy artillery at the mortars behaved very handsomely. General McLaughlin was captured near the gorge of the fort, but whether after the enemy had got in, or while they were attacking is unknown. Captain Swords, ordnance officer on my staff and division staff-officer of the day, also reached Fort Steadman from these headquarters before it was fully in the enemy's possession, and was captured at the fort.

"The right column, with the aid of troops from Steadman, now succeeded in gaining Battery No. 11. Their left column turned down the works to their left towards Battery No. 9, taking the 57th Massachusetts in the trenches in flank and rear, capturing a part of them. The remainder retired to the rear, reassembled, and afterwards did good work as skirmishers with General Hartranft's troops. The 2d Michigan fought the enemy on this flank, from their bomb-proofs and traverses, in the most spirited manner, until they were drawn in by order of their brigade commander (Brevet Colonel Ralph Ely) to Battery No. 9, which, though small, is an enclosed work.

"In pursuance of my orders, Colonel Ely deployed perpendicular to and to the rear of his entrenchments, a portion of the 1st Michigan sharp-shooters as skirmishers promptly taking them from the right of our line for this purpose. I also directed him to press the enemy on his left as much as possible. Finding themselves opposed in this direction, the enemy halted for more of their troops to come up.

"The enemy's skirmishers now came down the hill directly to the rear of Steadman, and moved towards my headquarters, the Friend House, the Dunn House battery, and in the direction of Meade's Station, and this for a time rendered my communication with the 3d brigade long and circuitous. Meantime, I had ordered out the 17th Michigan, acting as an engineer regiment attached to my headquarters, and sent word to the commanding officers of the 200th and 209th Pennsylvania, encamped between Meade's Station and Dunn House battery, to move respectively, one to the Friend House, and the other in front of the Dunn House battery. These regiments promptly appeared. Brigadier-General Hartranft, commanding the 3d division, now came up in person, and I requested him to move his available force direct upon the fort. He promptly and gallantly took command of the two regiments already out, without waiting for the rest of his command. I ordered the 17th Michigan to deploy as skirmishers on his right. This regiment, with only one hundred men in its ranks, under command of Major Mathews, moved forward at the same time with General Hartranft's line, capturing most of the enemy's skirmishers in their front, about twenty-five in number, and inclining to the right, connected with the skirmishers of Ely's brigade. While Hartranft was operating in rear of Steadman the enemy's force, which had moved towards Battery No. 9 and halted, was reinforced by Ransom's brigade, and opened an attack upon that battery. This attack was handsomely repulsed by my skirmishers and troops of the 2d brigade in Battery No. 9, assisted by artillery, particularly one piece of Romer's battery, under Major Romer himself. The enemy attempted to retreat back to their own entrenchments when they were charged by detachments of the 2d Michigan, who captured some prisoners. Troops of the 20th and 2d Michigan also threw themselves into the picket line of the 2d brigade, and poured such a fire on the flank of the enemy that over 300 threw down their arms and surrendered themselves on the spot."

After several other sharp engagements the enemy were repulsed on both flanks by troops of Wilcox's division, and much demoralized by the artillery fire, broke in small detachments from Steadman back to their own lines, pursued by the Union troops. The 17th Michigan, on the extreme right of the division, dashed forward and gained the trenches held by the enemy, taking many prisoners.

The 2d brigade was commanded by Col. Ralph Ely, 8th Michigan, in which were the 1st Michigan sharp-shooters, 2d and 20th Michigan infantry.

The 17th Michigan was on detail at division headquarters as engineer regiment.

THE THIRD INFANTRY.

The 3d infantry, raised at Grand Rapids, was patriotic and prompt, and in command of Colonel Daniel McConnell, who had organized the regiment, took the field soon after the 2d regiment, in time to participate with the brigade (Richardson's) in the engagement with the rebels at Blackburn's Ford. It afterwards belonged to Berry's celebrated brigade, of Kearney's division, and passed through the battles of the disastrous Peninsula campaign. It fought at Williamsburg, May 5th; at Fair Oaks, May 30th; at Glendalale, or Charles City Cross-roads, June 30th; at Malvern Hill, July 1st; being particularly distinguished at Fair Oaks, while in command of Colonel S. G. Champlin, where its losses were 40 killed, 124 wounded, and 15 missing. Among the wounded was Colonel Champlin, and among the killed Captain Samuel A. Judd.

Lieutenant-Colonel A. A. Stevens, commanding the regiment after Colonel Champlin was wounded, makes mention in his report of the part taken by the 3d in this engagement as follows:

"At about 2 o'clock P. M., an order was received to take our position in rear of the redoubt on our right, which was immediately complied with. We remained in this position but a short time, when we took up the line of march across the fields and parallel with the Williamsburg road, hastening as rapidly as possible towards the front, where our troops had for some time previously been actively engaged. The distance being about one mile and a half from the redoubt to the scene of action, was soon passed over, when Colonel Champlin received orders to lead his regiment at once into action, deploying at the same time in line of battle upon the left of the road, our right resting upon an abatis, while the left was thrown forward at a double-quick into a thicket of pines.

"The engagement now became general, and it was with the greatest difficulty that our corps of sharp-shooters, under command of Captain Judd, could penetrate this mass of fallen timber and dislodge the enemy from their strong position; but the steady and cool behavior of our men, and with the telling effect of the deadly aim of their rifles, soon compelled them to fall back, while our regiment pressed forward, charging through the fallen timber and driving the enemy beyond the fence in rear of the camp of General Palmer's brigade, some eighty rods distant, when they again formed and made another stand. It was at this time that the brave Colonel Champlin received a severe wound, which prevented him from taking further part in the action.

"I also beg leave to call your attention to the gallant Captain Judd, who fell while bravely leading our sharp-shooters in the early part of the action. He was one of the 'bravest of the brave,' and his loss will be deeply regretted by the regiment and all who knew him."

Prince De Joinville, having watched the determined and persistent fighting of the Michigan troops at Fair Oaks, says in his able report of the operations of McClellan's army on the Peninsula of Berry's brigade:

"Meanwhile Heintzelman rushes to the rescue with his two divisions. As at Williamsburg, Kearney arrives in good time to re-establish the fight. Berry's brigade of this division, composed of Michigan regiments, (2d, 3d, and 5th infantry,) and an Irish battalion, advanced firm as a wall into the midst of the disordered mass which wanders over the battle-field, and does more by its example than the most powerful reinforcements. About a mile of ground has been lost, fifteen pieces of cannon, the camp of the division of the advanced guard, that of Gen. Casey, but now we hold our own."

The 3d was in the engagement at Groveton (or Bull Run) August 29th, losing twenty killed and a large number missing, and at Chantilly on September 1st.

This regiment, in command of Col. Byron M. Pierce, on the 1st of November, left Edward's Ferry, Maryland, and, marching by Warrenton, encamped at Falmouth November 23d. Crossing the Rappahannock on the 13th of December, it was under fire three days at the first battle of Fredericksburg, sustaining a loss of nine in wounded.

The regiment was also specially engaged at Chancellorsville, being in the 3d brigade, 1st division, (Birney's,) 3d corps, (Sickles',) one of the divisions which formed part of the troops composing the reconnoissance in force made by Gen. Sickles to ascertain the position of Stonewall Jackson, who was threatening an attack on the extreme right of our army. In this movement Gen. Sickles became cut off from his communications, which were afterwards regained by a desperate night attack. Colonel B. R. Pierce, then commanding the regiment, in his report mentions the affair as follows:

"April 28, 1863, we broke camp and once more moved towards the Rappahannock, crossed it at United States Ford May 1st, and moved up near the Chancellorsville House and went into position, supporting the first line of battle. On the 2d we were moved to the front and drove the enemy four miles, but soon found that he had turned the right flank of the 11th corps and that we were nearly cut off, but fell back to near our position of the morning before, and there charged the woods at 10 P. M. and opened communication with the main army. At daylight of the 3d we were fired into by the enemy, and after a long and severe struggle were forced back one mile to a new position, which we held until the morning of the 6th, when we recrossed the river and occupied our old camps, our whole loss in this movement was sixty-three killed, wounded, and missing."

The attack on the morning of the 3d was most desperate; the infantry of the enemy were advanced in overwhelming numbers for the purpose of crushing the Federal line, but were checked by the forces of Sickles and Slocum. The 3d lost in this hard-fought battle sixty-three in killed, wounded, and missing. Among the killed was Capt. Joseph Mason.

The regiment was engaged at Gettysburg July 2d, 3d, and 4th, and sustained its share of the desperate rebel attack upon the 3d corps near "Round Top." Its losses in the three days were forty-one killed, wounded, and missing.

On the 7th of November, 1863, the 3d, in command of Lieut. Col. M. B. Houghton and then serving in the 2d brigade, 3d division, 2d corps, moved forward with the Army of the Potomac to Kelly's Ford, on the Rappahannock, and thence marched to Brandy Station, on the Orange and Alexandria railroad, where it went into camp. On the 26th the regiment took part in the Mine Run campaign, engaging the enemy on the 27th at Locust Grove and on the 30th at Mine Run. Having fallen back with the army, it again arrived at its camp at Brandy Station on the 2d of December, having lost during the movement thirty-one killed, wounded, and missing. On the 23d of December one hundred and eighty of the regiment re-enlisted as veteran volunteers. Returning to this State, these veterans were given the usual furlough of thirty days, at the expiration of which they returned to the regiment. Crossing the Rapidan at Ely's Ford on the morning of the 4th of May, 1864, the regiment advanced and encamped at Chancellorsville. On the three following days the regiment participated in the battles of the Wilderness, sustaining a heavy loss, including Capts. Andrew Nickerson and Milton Leonard, killed on the 6th. It was also engaged at Todd's Tavern on the 8th. On the 12th, at Spottsylvania, it participated in the successful charge of the 2d corps, capturing a number of prisoners and two rebel battle flags. Prior to this engagement the 3d was consolidated temporarily with the 5th infantry. The regiment also took part in the engagement on the North Anna river; thence it marched to the Pamunkey, which it crossed on the 27th and advanced toward Cold Harbor, and took part in the fight at that place on June 7th. In addition to the engagements mentioned, the 3d also participated in a number of minor actions and skirmishes. Its loss during the month of May was 31 killed, 119 wounded, and 29 missing. On the 9th of June, at Cold Harbor, Va., the regiment, with the exception of the re-enlisted men and such as had joined since the date of original organization and certain designated officers, were ordered to proceed to this State for the purpose of being discharged. The remaining officers and men were formed into a battalion of four companies and attached to the 5th Michigan infantry. The order consolidating these regiments was confirmed by special orders of the War Department issued on the 13th of June, 1864. On the 20th day of June the organization, which had been one of the first in the field, was formally mustered out of the United States service.

The career of this regiment was brilliant throughout the war, and, while it maintained its reputation for bravery and effective service in all other engagements, Fair Oaks, Chancellorsville, and Gettysburg stand out prominently in its glorious record.

The regiment having been mustered out of service on the 20th of June, orders were issued from the Adjutant-General's office of the State to reorganize the regiment. Col. M. B. Houghton, of the old regiment, was authorized to proceed with this duty, and the camp was fixed at Grand Rapids. The regiment left for the field in Tennessee on the 20th October following, proceeding to Nashville, and from thence to Decatur, Alabama. On the 23d of November, while stationed there, its advance picket on the Moulton and Courtland road was driven in, when five companies moved out and encountered a small force of the enemy, driving it back without loss. On the 25th the regiment moved towards Murfreesboro', Tennessee, arriving there on the 27th, and was ordered to duty at Fort Rosecrans. While Gen.

Milroy was engaged at the Cedars, with the principal part of Forrest's command, Faulkner's brigade of mounted infantry, on the 7th of December, made a dash on the picket line at Murfreesboro', driving in the pickets, and gaining possession of the town, when four companies of the regiment, together with four companies of the 181st Ohio, with a section of artillery, after a spirited engagement of an hour, repulsed the enemy, re-establishing the picket line, drove him for nearly two miles, when the command was withdrawn and returned to the fort. On the 9th, while the regiment was on a foraging expedition, it came up with the rear guard of the enemy, consisting of the 7th and 12th Kentucky mounted infantry, taking five prisoners. On the 15th it marched to the relief of a supply train which had been attacked on the way from Stevenson, Ala., and on approaching the point a skirmish took place, when the force retired, leaving their dead and wounded on the ground.

Although going into service late in the war, with but little opportunity offered to make its record, this regiment fully demonstrated its reliable fighting qualities and acquitted itself with credit, maintaining to the fullest extent, when occasion offered, the gallant reputation of the old 3d.

THE FOURTH INFANTRY.

The 4th infantry went to the field with great dispatch, in command of the lamented Colonel Woodbury, who had recruited and organized it at Adrian. The regiment was in the first Bull Run engagement, and retired from that field in good order, covering the retreat of the Union army from that disastrous affair. It went to the Peninsula with General McClellan, and was the first regiment to open fire upon the rebels at New Bridge, May 24, 1862—the commencement of what are known as the seven days' battles, when five companies of the regiment crossed the Chicahominy a short distance above New Bridge, wading the stream under a heavy fire. The gallantry of the regiment was made at the time the subject of a dispatch to the War Department from General McClellan, which mentioned the affair as follows: "Three skirmishes to-day. We drove the rebels from Mechanicsville seven miles from New Bridge. The 4th Michigan about finished the Louisiana Tigers. Fifty prisoners and fifty killed and wounded." The 4th, in common with the other Michigan regiments, maintained the honor of our State, and nobly acquitted itself in all the engagements of the Peninsula campaign, but probably in none more so than in the sanguinary conflict at Malvern Hill, where it became conspicuously and specially noticeable in resisting the numerous and desperate charges of the rebels on its lines, the men fighting until all their cartridges were expended, then using those taken from the boxes of their fallen comrades. On that field fell its brave commander, Colonel Woodbury, while at the head of his regiment. His military career had been as bright as the record of his regiment, and had he been spared, his services would have placed him high in rank and fame, as he was gifted with all the requisites to render success certain. It also lost two other meritorious officers, Captains Du Puy and Rose, while Captain Spalding and Lieutenants Gordon and Earle were wounded, and from June 26th to July 1st, both inclusive, the aggregate loss in the regiment was 53 killed, 144 wounded, and 49 missing. In a report made by Captain John F. Randolph immediately following the engagement, he says:

"The enemy commenced the attack about 2 P. M., and at 4 o'clock the action became general. The regiment held its ground against fearful odds until its ammunition was expended, when it fell back, contesting every foot of the ground until relieved by the 2d New Jersey. At evening the action closed, and we again held our first line. Our loss was heavy in both officers and men. It was here Captain Richard Du Puy fell, while gallantly leading his men.

"On the following morning our position was again changed, and about 3 P. M. the enemy appeared in our front in heavy force. We were ordered to advance, and in a few moments came within range of the enemy, when we opened a destructive fire. Colonel Woodbury was everywhere present, and by his example and courage inspired every one with renewed vigor. About half an hour after the action commenced he was mortally wounded, the ball penetrating the head just above the right eye. While being borne from the field his last words were: 'Good-bye, boys.' Captain A. M. Rose was also killed about the same time."

At Shepherdstown Ford, September 21, it forded the Potomac in face of a battery, killed and drove off the enemy, and captured the guns. The regiment was also in the battles at Fredericksburg, December 13th and 14th, where its casualties were 9 killed, 41 wounded, and 1 missing.

On the 30th and 31st of December the regiment was engaged in a reconnoissance to Morrisville, making a march of thirty-three miles on the latter day. It was engaged in a movement of the 20th of January, 1863, but, marching only a few miles, returned to camp near Falmouth, where it remained until May 1st. May 4th it participated in the battle of Chancellorsville, with a loss in killed, wounded, and missing of 30.

Following the regiment to Gettysburg, we find it prominently engaged on that important and bloody battle-field, bearing a part of the brunt with the 5th corps, and sustaining a loss of 26 killed, 66 wounded, and 79 missing. Among the killed was its noble commander, Colonel H. H. Jeffords, a gallant and patriotic officer, who was killed by a rebel bayonet while rescuing the colors of his regiment from traitorous hands, and among the wounded were Captains French, Robinson, and McLean, and Lieutenants Brown, Vreeland, Barrett, Westfall, and Seage.

After the death of Colonel Jeffords, Lieutenant-Colonel Lombard assumed command of the regiment.

In the battle of the Wilderness, the 4th being in the 2d brigade, 1st division, (Griffin's,) of the 5th corps, became heavily engaged with loss. Greeley says:

"At noon General Griffin, whose advance had been driven in, was ordered to push forward the 1st division of the 5th corps to the right and left of the turnpike and feel the enemy. An advance of less than a mile, stretching across the turnpike, brought them in contact with the enemy, under Lieutenant-General Ewell, posted on a wooded declivity. A sharp engagement ensued for an hour, when the pressure of the enemy could no longer be resisted. General Griffin's division was driven back, leaving two pieces of artillery in the hands of the enemy."

In this engagement fell Colonel Lombard and Captain W. H. Loveland, the former while gallantly leading his regiment, and the latter while bravely doing his duty. The Colonel died next day, and Captain Loveland on the 31st of the same month, both efficient and courageous officers.

Malvern Hill, Gettysburg, and the Wilderness will never be forgotten by the survivors of the 4th Michigan.

On the night of the 7th the command moved towards Spottsylvania, arriving at Laurel Hill on the morning of the 8th. It here became engaged with the enemy, and again on the 9th. On the 10th it assisted in a charge upon and capture of the enemy's rifle pits, losing 20 killed and wounded.

On the 11th and 12th the regiment was in the advanced lines of the corps, and on the 13th and 14th was engaged as skirmishers. On the evening of the latter date the command moved to the left of the army near Spottsylvania Court-house, and remaining there until the 19th, it then took part in the movement to the North Anna river, which it crossed on the 24th near Jericho Mills, the regiment participating in the engagement at this place. On the night of the 26th the regiment recrossed the North Anna river and marched to Hanovertown, crossing the Pamunkey river on the 28th. On the 29th, 30th, and 31st of May, and 1st of June, it was engaged as skirmishers, and on the 3d it participated in the capture of the enemy's line of works near Bethesda Church. On the 5th the regiment marched to Bottom's Bridge, and on the 14th crossed the James river at Wilcox's Landing, whence it proceeded to the lines in front of Petersburg, where it arrived on the 16th. On the next day the regiment was engaged as skirmishers, and on the 19th participated in the engagement of that date, losing eight killed and wounded.

The term of the regiment having expired on the 19th of June, 1864, it returned to the State on the 26th, and on the 28th the companies were mustered out of service. A portion of the regiment remained in service on duty with the 1st infantry, and served with it until the close of the war, when they joined the new organization.

The regiment was reorganized under orders of July 26, 1864, Col. J. W. Hall, late lieutenant-colonel of the regiment, taking command of its camp at Adrian. On the 22d of October following it left Adrian, and arrived at Decatur, Ala., on the 28th, in time to participate in the defence of that town, which had been attacked by the rebel army under Hood. In this engagement it lost five in killed and wounded, establishing a reputation in the field worthy of the brave old regiment.

General Meade at Chancellorsville directed General Griffin to send two regiments to hold an important point. The General reported to him that he had sent them. General Meade asked, "Can they hold it?" Griffin replied, "General, they are Michigan men." Meade insisting on being assured, said emphatically, "Can they hold it?" Griffin quickly and emphatically answered, "General, they can hold it against hell!" They were the 4th and 16th Michigan.

THE FIFTH INFANTRY.

The 5th infantry, usually designated the "Fighting Fifth," left Detroit for Virginia on the 11th of September, 1861, commanded by Colonel Henry D. Terry, and first commenced to battle for the Union and freedom at Williamsburg, on May 5th following, while serving in Berry's brigade of Kearney's division. In this engagement the regiment behaved with great gallantry, and was eminently efficient; but sustaining a loss, in a force of 500, of 34 killed and 119 wounded, including among the killed Lieut. James Gunning, and among the wounded Lieutenant-Colonel S. E. Beach. On May 31st it went into the action at Fair Oaks with a force of about 300, losing 30 killed, 116 wounded, and 5 missing, Captain L. B. Quackenbush and Lieutenant Charles H. Hutchins being among the killed, and Lieut. Charles S. Traverse mortally wounded, and died on the 22d July following. It was again engaged on the Chicahominy June 25th, at Peach Orchard on the 29th, and at Charles City Cross-roads on the 30th, where it lost 51 in killed, wounded, and missing. Among the killed was Lieutenant W. T. Johnson, and among the wounded Major John D. Fairbanks, commanding the regiment, who died of his wound in Washington on the 5th of July following, regarded as a brave and exemplary officer. It had also a part in the action at Malvern Hill with slight loss; and was employed at Manassas August 28th, 29th, and 30th, and at Chantilly on September 1st. It was engaged heavily at Fredericksburg on the 13th of December following, with a strength of only 330, where it lost 10 killed and 73 wounded; among the former being its commanding officer, Lieutenant-Colonel John Gilluly, a most gallant and worthy officer. On the 15th it recrossed the Rappahannock and encamped near Falmouth. On the 20th of January, 1863, the regiment took part in the movement of that date, marching to Bank's Ford, but without crossing the river, returned to its old camp and went into winter quarters.

The 5th under command of Lieutenant-Colonel E. T. Sherlock, was engaged at the Cedars, May 2, 1863, and at Chancellor's on the 3d, where it formed a part of the division of the 3d corps, which attacked and cut off the rear of Stonewall Jackson's forces in his movement threatening the destruction of the right flank of the Union army. It also participated in the desperate and dashing midnight charge, which stands without a parallel in the war, made for the purpose of opening the communication with the Union army which had been lost in the movement. In this charge Stonewall Jackson fell.

Next morning the 5th together with the 3d Michigan charged and drove a brigade of rebels, taking a number of prisoners, and holding the enemy in check until the division formed on a second line. Lieutenant Colonel Sherlock fell in the engagement of the 3d, a brave and meritorious officer, and the aggregate loss of the regiment in both battles was 7 killed, 43 wounded, and 31 missing. Major Pulford and Lieutenants Colton and Hanlon were among the wounded.

At Gettysburg, on July 2d, the regiment, then commanded by Col. Pulford, after marching ten miles in three hours during the day, at 4 P. M. became heavily engaged with the enemy in defending Sickles' advanced position, the men using the cartridges of their fallen comrades. Its casualties were great, losing in one hour 105. Among the killed were Captain Generous and Lieutenant Phelan, two valuable officers. In the list of wounded were Colonel Pulford, Major Mathews, and Lieutenants Colville, Pierce, Rouse, Braden, Hurlbut, and Stevens.

On the 3d of July it assisted in repelling the final charge on Cemetery Hill. During both days its losses were 19 killed, 86 wounded, and 4 missing.

The 5th was encamped, on the 1st of November, 1863, near Bealton Station, on the Orange and Alexandria railroad. On the 7th it crossed the Rappahannock at Kelly's Ford, and bivouacked near Brandy Station on the 12th, occupying winter quarters which the rebel forces had abandoned. Participating in the movement of the army to Mine Run, the regiment crossed the Rapidan on the 26th, and on the 27th was actively engaged at Locust Grove, losing a number in killed and wounded, Lieut. Daniel B. Wyker being among the killed. On the 29th the regiment arrived in front of the enemy's position at Mine Run, and on the 30th supported a battery for 36 hours. Falling back with the army, the regiment reached its former camp, near Brandy Station, on the 30th of December.

On the 3d of May, 1864, the regiment, in command of Colonel Pulford, entered upon the great campaign of the war. It crossed the Rapidan at an early hour on the 4th, and at 4 P. M. reached the old battle-field at Chancellorsville, having accomplished a distance of thirty-four miles in seventeen hours, the men each carrying the weight of five days' rations and sixty rounds of cartridges. On the 5th the enemy were met on the road leading to Orange Court-house. The regiment participated in the desperate struggle which ensued, sustaining, in this and the following day, a severe loss in killed and wounded. Captain George W. Rose was here mortally wounded, and died of his wounds on the 20th. On the 6th, in command of Captains Walkenshaw and Shook, each commanding a wing, Colonel Pulford and Major Mathews being wounded on the day previous, it shared in a successful charge on the enemy's works, Sergeant Joseph Kemp capturing a stand of rebel colors. In this charge Captain Wilberforce Hurlburt, while leading his company, was shot through the head and instantly killed.

On the 17th, the enemy having retreated, the regiment followed in pursuit, overtaking them at noon on the 8th. A portion of the regiment was deployed as skirmishers, and the whole command was under a heavy artillery fire during the remainder of the day and until noon of the 10th. On the 11th the regiment was again engaged, suffering severely from the fire of the enemy's musketry and artillery. On the 12th, the 5th (with which the remnant of the 3d Michigan infantry had been temporarily consolidated,) participated in the charge made on the enemy's works on the right, at Spottsylvania Court-house. The command captured in this charge two stand of rebel colors, one taken by William Renwick, company D, and the other by Corporal Benjamin Morse, of company E. Both were members of the 3d infantry.

After various forced marches the regiment arrived in front of the enemy's position, on the North Anna river, on the 23d, and assisted in taking their works on the north bank of that stream, capturing a number of prisoners, and driving the rebel forces into and across the river. It engaged on the 24th in stregthening the works erected, the command holding their position under a heavy fire. During the afternoon the regiment crossed the river in the face of a very heavy fire of shot and shell, and again compelled the enemy to retire before them. Here Lieutenant Samuel Pearce was killed. At an early hour on the 27th it recrossed the North Anna, forming part of the force that effectually covered the movements of its corps, and at 11 A. M. marched toward the Pamunkey river, which it crossed at 4 P. M. of the same day, having marched fifteen miles in five hours. On the 29th, 30th, and 31st, strong breastworks were thrown up, the men working day and night, although living on scanty rations and almost worn out with the rapid marching and fatigues of the campaign. On the latter date the regiment took part in a charge upon and capture of a strong line of rebel works. It reached the position at Cold Harbor on the 5th, and immediately commenced the construction of breastworks. The 3d Michigan infantry was at this point on the 10th, permanently consolidated with the 5th.

Leaving Cold Harbor on the 12th, and crossing the Chicahominy at Long Bridge, the command reached Charles City Court-house on the 13th, and on the 14th crossed the James river, arriving in front of Petersburg at 10 P. M. of the 15th. On the 16th it threw up intrenchments during the day, and at evening (again in command of Colonel Pulford) was heavily engaged with the enemy, assisting in taking one of their lines of works. On the 18th the regiment again participated in a successful charge on the enemy's lines, holding their position on the 19th and 20th under a heavy fire. Crossing the Suffolk railroad on the 21st, the regiment moved on the enemy's right and engaged as skirmishers. The rebels flanking its position, it was obliged to retire with some loss. It, however, advanced later in the day and retook its position.

October 27th it marched to the Boydton plank road, and participated in the attack made on the enemy's right, sustaining a small loss in officers and men, including among the killed Adjutant J. F. McGinly and Lieutenant S. A. Boyd. The regiment captured a large number of prisoners in this battle. Having returned to its old position in front of Petersburg, on the 31st of October it received orders to garrison Fort Davis, on the Jerusalem plank road. The casualties in the engagements in which the regiment participated during the year were: At Kelly's Ford, 1 wounded; Locust Grove 1 killed, 15 wounded, 2 missing—total, 18; Mine Run, 3 wounded; Wilderness, 38 killed, 167 wounded, 16 missing—total 221; Spottsylvania Court-house, 6 killed, 60 wounded, 9 missing—total, 75; North Anna river, 1 killed, 9 wounded, 1 missing—total, 11; Tolopotamy Creek, 2 killed, 4 wounded, 11 missing—total, 17; before Petersburg, 15 killed, 52 wounded, 19 missing—total, 86; Deep Bottom, 12 wounded; Boydton Plank Road, 9 killed, 52 wounded, 43 missing—total, 105; being an aggregate of 73 killed, 365 wounded, and 101 missing, and a total of 549.

On the 25th of March, 1865, the regiment participated in the attack on the enemy's works near Hatcher's Run, where it assisted in driving him from his first line of works, after a heavy engagement of four hours. Remaining at that point until the 29th, it moved about six miles to the left, and on the morning of the 30th the regiment was deployed as skirmishers and became engaged with the enemy's pickets, and after driving them within their main line of works, near Fort Harney, fire was opened on the regiment from three batteries, but it succeeded in holding its ground until the 5th corps got into position, when the line was maintained. On the 2d the regiment, with the 1st Massachusetts heavy artillery, made a demonstration on the enemy's works for the purpose of developing his position and strength. This being accomplished with but small loss, the command held its position during the night, and the next morning the regiment, with its corps, participated in the general assault on the enemy's fortifications, which resulted in carrying his entire line of works and the capture of Petersburg, and is reported to have been the first regiment to raise its colors on the works. In following up the retreat of that part of the enemy which took the line of the South Side railroad, the regiment was deployed as skirmishers, and on the 4th and 5th pressing his rear guard closely. On the 6th he made a stand at Sailor's creek to protect the crossing of his baggage, when the brigade made a charge, capturing 173 wagons, the regiment taking a stand of colors and 145 prisoners. The enemy being followed up closely by the brigade, on the 7th and 8th, the regiment acting as flankers and skirmishers, became engaged at New Store, and on the 9th was in the front in line of battle at Glover Hill at the surrender of Lee.

This regiment was continually "pitching in" whenever opportunity offered, and had space permitted it would have been interesting to have traced its entire career in the war of the rebellion, as its fighting record from Williamsburg to Appomattox Court-house is most glorious and brilliant.

The following letter of Gen. Berry, on Michigan troops and Michigan, was written to a friend in Washington:

"To all my sick and wounded in hospital you chance to visit give my warmest regards for their welfare. May they speedily recover. So gallant a set of men should not suffer for want of anything. I trust they will be amply provided for, as you intimate they are. A nobler set of men never lived. Any man can win fights with such material. I have received ten times more credit than I am entitled to for the part performed by my poor self in the late bloody battle. Such troops as I lead are bound to conquer, no matter who leads them.

"Please give my compliments to all those Michigan men in Washington who take such interest in this brigade. Say to them that they are fortunate to hail from such a State that has such gallant sons. God bless the State and people of Michigan for the part it and they have taken to crush out this most unholy of all rebellions.

"Truly, your sincere friend,

"H. G. BERRY,

"*Brigadier-General in command of Brigade.*"

The brigade referred to was composed of the 2d, 3d, and 5th Michigan infantry and the 1st and 37th New York infantry, and this letter was written immediately following the last battle on the Peninsula.

The following letter is from Gen. Phillip Kearney:

HEADQUARTERS THIRD DIVISION,
HEINTZELMAN'S CORPS, *May* 10, 1862.

His Excellency AUSTIN BLAIR, *Governor of Michigan:*

SIR:—It gives me great pleasure to address you in order to bring to your immediate notice the noble and brave manner with which the troops of your State in my division conducted themselves in the engagement before Williamsburg on the 5th instant. The 2d, under Col. Poe, and the 5th, under Col. Terry, behaved in the most handsome manner. I have the honor to transmit herewith the reports of the colonels of these regiments, together with that of their general, Gen. Berry, commanding brigade, and also a copy of one sent in by myself to headquarters. I also send you a copy of the killed and wounded. Col. Poe served more immediately under my own command, and the gallantry and soldierly qualities he displayed rendered him particularly conspicuous. Col. Terry's regiment (5th) took a rifle-pit of much strength after a severe contest and held possession until the close of the action.

Very respectfully, PHILLIP KEARNEY.

The following is a copy of the last letter written by Col. Sherlock, and was completed when the movement commenced which terminated in the battle of Chancellorsville, and in which he fell gallantly leading his regiment:

WEDNESDAY MORNING, *April* 29, 1863.
On the march.

MY DEAR PARENTS:—We left our old camp yesterday afternoon at 4 o'clock in a rain storm. Last night, about 10 o'clock, we halted in a pine grove below Fredericksburg, and about a mile from the river. It appears that Hooker is going to attack the enemy in his strongholds and on his right and left flanks. There appears to be no disposition to attack the enemy's centre, which is in the city. There is great surmising in the army as to the probabilities of Hooker's success; a great many shake their heads; but there is one conclusion we have all come to, and that is, that Hooker will fight and the loss of life will be awful, for Hooker has to make a reputation. This morning is very foggy. Got to stop; order to move. You can see Mary's letter. God bless you all.

EDWARD.

THE SIXTH INFANTRY.

The peculiar regiment of Michigan was the 6th infantry, afterwards organized as heavy artillery. This splendid and gallant regiment was peculiar by reason of its entire isolation, almost amounting to exile, from the rest of the Michigan troops during the whole term of its faithful service. It left the State in August, 1861, commanded by Col. F. W. Curtenius, under whose direction it was raised and organized, to join the army in the field, but was detained at Baltimore, where it remained on duty most of the following winter; thence sailed to Ship Island, Mississippi, and in April, 1862, left that place for New Orleans, constituting a part of Gen. Butler's force, and was one of the first regiments to occupy the city on its surrender. Serving during its whole term in the extreme South, it suffered much from the complaints incident to that climate, losing more men by disease than any other regiment from this State.

The regiment was engaged at Sewell's Point, Virginia, March 5th; at Port Jackson, Louisiana, April 25th; at Vicksburg, Mississippi, May 20th; at Grand Gulf, Mississippi, May 27th; and at Amite river, Mississippi, on the 20th of June following.

The battles of Baton Rouge and Port Hudson, prominent in the history of the rebellion, are among the most conspicuous in which the 6th was engaged, and were important in their results, being most decided victories, securing to the Union arms strong positions on the line of the Mississippi river, and which were held during the war. At Baton Rouge, August 5th, 1862, while that place was being heavily attacked by the rebel forces in very superior numbers under Breckinridge, the regiment, then in command of Capt. Charles E. Clark, received and repulsed the principal attack made on that day by the troops led by General Clark, of Mississippi, against the right wing of the Union forces, which, if successful, would have caused the loss of a large part of our artillery and given the enemy a most advantageous position, and might have led to very damaging results.

The Union forces were commanded by General Thomas Williams, U. S. A., a native of Detroit, and was killed during the engagement, immediately after saying to the 21st Indiana, "Boys, your field officers are all gone. I will lead you." His force consisted of seven regiments of infantry, viz: 6th Michigan, 30th Massachusetts, 7th Vermont, 14th Maine, 21st Indiana, 4th Wisconsin, and 9th Connecticut; Nims 2d Massachusetts battery, Everett's 6th Massachusetts battery, Manning's 4th Massachusetts battery, and a section of a battery taken by the 21st Indiana, and attached to that regiment, under command of Lieut. Brown.

The enemy's force consisted of the 4th and 30th Louisiana, two Mississippi regiments, the 3d, 4th, 5th, 6th, 7th, and 8th Kentucky, two Tennessee regiments, and one Alabama regiment, with thirteen pieces of artillery, and a large guerilla force. Their attacking force numbered fully 6,000 while the Union force engaged was not over 2,000.

In this engagement the regiment fought by detachments, one commanded by Captain John Cordon, one on picket, under Captain Garret J. Spitzer, and the other commanded by Captain Harrison Soule.

The importance of the repulse was acknowledged by General Butler in a congratulatory order issued soon after the affair, in which the regiment was highly complimented for its gallant and valuable services, conspicuous bravery, and most determined fighting.

Following the battle of Baton Rouge the regiment was engaged at Bayou Teche, January 14th, and at Ponchetoola, La., May 16, 1863.

The regiment, commanded by Col. Thomas S. Clark, formed part of the force of General Banks which invested Fort Hudson, and which compelled its surrender. Col. Clark, in a report, thus mentions the part taken by his regiment on that occasion:

"On the 23d of May, 1863, arriving before that stronghold, the regiment was placed in the most advanced position, and maintained it until the surrender, on the 9th of July. During the siege of this formidable place, it participated in three desperate assaults upon its works. In the assault of the 27th of May the regiment, commanded by Col. Clark, led the division of General T. W. Sherman, and lost more than one-third of the men it had engaged, including Lieut. Fred. T. Clark, who fell while gallantly leading company D to the charge. In this affair Captain Montgomery led a forlorn hope of 200 volunteers belonging to the regiment. An assault was made on the 14th of June, when the 6th, then commanded by Lieutenant-Colonel Bacon, advanced by detachments. The leading detachment, commanded by Captain John Cordon, one by Captain Stark following, with the balance of the regiment bringing up the rear. On the 29th of June, the regiment, then commanded by Captain Cordon, again advanced to the assault, when thirty-five of the regiment, composing a forlorn hope, assailed the enemy's works at the point known as the Citadel. The party succeeded in gaining the ditch, but were overpowered and driven back, with a loss of 8 killed and 9 wounded. Among the killed was Sergeant Madison O. Walker, who led the detachment."

In this desperate undertaking, Private Charles Dustin, company F, from Dundee, Mich., got over the ditch and into the enemy's works, bringing out a rebel captain at the point of the bayonet, whom he delivered up to the commanding officer of the regiment.

The conduct of the 6th was so gallant and efficient during the siege that it received the thanks of General Banks; and on the 10th of July it was transferred to the artillery arm of the service on account of its faithful and valuable service.

This regiment was stationed at Port Hudson, La., until the 11th of March, 1864, when the requisite number having been mustered in as Veteran Volunteers to preserve the organization, it started for Michigan. The regiment arrived at Kalamazoo, where it was furloughed for thirty days. Having again assembled at Kalamazoo, it returned to Port Hudson, where it arrived on the 11th of May, with a very large number of recruits, enlisted while in Michigan. On the 6th of June the regiment was ordered to Morganzia, to serve as infantry, where it remained until the 24th of June. From Morganzia it proceeded to Vicksburg, Miss., where it served with the engineer brigade. Leaving Vicksburg, July 23d, it moved to the mouth of the White River, and thence to St. Charles, Ark., where it was attached to a regiment of infantry. A detachment of the regiment, while on a transport *en route* from Vicksburg to the White River, was attacked by a rebel battery, losing two killed and a number wounded. Remaining but a short time at St. Charles, the regiment again returned to Morganzia, where for a time it was employed as engineers, but soon after its arrival it was ordered to report to the chief of artillery, and again returned to duty as heavy artillery. The regiment was present at the bombardment and surrender of Fort Morgan, Ala., but arrived too late to participate.

Almost the entire service of this regiment during the war was rendered in the extreme Southern States, and on the 1st of November, 1864, it was stationed in Alabama, and garrisoned, with its headquarters and companies A, B, D, G, and K, at Fort Morgan, and Fort Gaines, Dauphine

Island, Mobile Bay, with companies C, E, F, H, and I. Companies B, C, E, F, and H were detached on the 23d of December, and joined an expedition under Major-General Gordon Granger, to operate from Pensacola against Mobile, and were temporarily attached, as infantry, to the brigade of General Bertram, which led the advance, and so remained until the campaign was advanced from Mobile Point and Pensacola, on the 27th of January, 1865, when Bertram's command made a heavy demonstration on Mobile, the whole command being recalled at night and hurriedly transferred to the advancing force from the East, the detached companies of this regiment being ordered to their former stations in Forts Morgan and Gaines. On the 31st of March companies A and K were detached from the command at Fort Morgan, and ordered to the front, to report to Gen. Granger, and were each equipped with a battery of 10-inch mortars, and on their arrival at the front were ordered into position under the guns of Spanish Fort; there they did very fine execution at a range of 1,400 yards. After the fort was taken, these companies were ordered to man and turn the heavy captured guns, consisting of 7-inch Brooks' rifled and 100-pound Parrotts, on the rebel Forts Huger and Tracy, and with them performed good service until all the enemy's works within range were reduced, and Mobile surrendered.

On the 9th of July following the regiment took steamers for New Orleans, and on the 20th of August was mustered out of service.

In General Butler's order is found the following paragraphs:

"The commanding General has carefully revised the official reports of the action of August 5th, at Baton Rouge, to collect the evidence of the gallant deeds and meritorious services of those engaged in that brilliant victory.

"The name of the lamented and gallant General Williams has already passed into history.

"The 6th Michigan fought rather by detachments than as a regiment, but deserves the fullest commendation for the gallant behavior of its officers and men. Companies A, B, and F, under command of Captain Cordon, receive special mention for the coolness and courage with which they supported and retook Brown's battery, routing the 4th Louisiana and capturing their colors, which the regiment has leave to send to its native State.

"Captain Charles E. Clark, acting Lieutenant-Colonel 6th Michigan, prevented the enemy from flanking our right, bringing his command at the critical moment to the support of Nim's battery. Lieutenant Howell, company F, 6th Michigan, and Lieutenant A. T. Ralph, acting adjutant, for intrepedity; Captain Spitzey, 6th Michigan, in command of the company of pickets, who handsomely held in check the enemy's advance; the fearless conduct of Lieutenant Howell, company F, and Sergeant Thayer, company A, 6th Michigan regiment, after they were wounded, in supporting Lieutenant Brown's battery.

"Captain Soule and Lieutenant Fassett, company I, 6th Michigan, as skirmishers, were wounded, and deserve special notice for the steadiness of their command, which lost heavily in killed and wounded."

Lieutenant G. Weitzel, (afterwards Major-General,) then Chief Engineer Department of the Gulf, and present with the troops in the engagement, says in his official report: "Three companies of the 6th Michigan covered themselves with glory in recovering from a large force two guns, posted on the right of the Magnolia Cemetery, which temporarily were left by our forces. These same three companies captured the colors of the 4th Louisiana, but only after they had shot down four successive color-bearers."

NOTE.—Mr. Greeley, in his reliable "American Conflict," says of the operations at Port Hudson, May 27, 1863: "Never was fighting more heroic than that of our army, assailing nearly equal numbers behind strong defences, approached only through almost impassable abatis, swept by rebel shell and grape. If valor could have triumphed over such odds, they would have carried the works; but only abject cowardice or pitiable imbecility could have lost such a position to so small an army; and the rebels also fought well."

In the valuable work, the "American Encyclopedia," is found the following notice of the same affair: "At 2 o'clock A. M. (27th) an assault was commenced on the works on the centre and left of the centre by the divisions under General Augur and Brig. General Sherman, (T. W.) The enemy was driven into his works and the Federal troops moved up to the fortifications, holding the opposite side of the parapet with the enemy."

At the siege of Port Hudson the 6th was under the command of General T. W. Sherman, so prominently engaged on May 28th, and which consisted of the 6th Michigan H. Artillery, 2nd (Duryea's) Zouaves, 128th and 147th regiments N. Y. Infantry, with the 26th Conn. Infantry, and 21st Indiana and 2nd Vermont Batteries.

An officer serving at the time with the rebel army in Port Hudson, in his diary says of that day's work: "About nine o'clock in the morning the attack was made in the woods on Col. Steadman's (rebel) centre, and upon the line of fortifications on General Beall's right. The latter attack, that of Sherman's brigade, was the most imposing in appearance. Emerging from the woods at the distance of about four hundred yards from our breastworks, the Zouave regiment charged in line of battle across an open field. The gay colors of their uniforms contrasted brilliantly with the green and sombre shades of the trees and field, making a fine mark for our fire. As soon as they appeared in sight our artillery opened on them with spherical case, many of them bursting right in their ranks, but the gaps were quickly closed up, and they came on in splendid style. As they lessened the distance, our gunners substituted grape for shrapnel, and when they finally came within one hundred and fifty yards our guns were double-charged with canister, and the infantry receiving the order at the same time to fire, the field was swept with a storm of musket balls and grape-shot.

"The advancing line of Zouaves wavered and then halted, while they were dropping from the ranks, mown down by our deadly fire, which now became an incessant rattle of musketry, intermingled with rapid discharges of canister from the guns.

"The Zouaves, after wavering for a while in indecision, finally broke and scattered, most of the men throwing themselves flat on the ground behind stumps, logs and inequalities of the ground where they now commenced sharp-shooting. * * *

"As soon as the Zouaves broke, Sherman's brigade came out of the woods in column, and played to the right and left in line of battle, as prettily as if they were on drill. Our artillerists again had recourse to shell and shrapnell, and the infantry opened on this advance sooner than before. Their charge was a good one, and had the advantage of the Zouave line of Sharp-shooters, some of whom were within a hundred yards of our works, and whose Minie balls were whistling over our parapet.

"But our men, though opposed by an enemy ten times their number, kept up a withering fire, and after the brigade had approached a little nearer than the Zouaves had done, it finally hesitated and wavered. At this sure precursor to a repulse, our boys sent up a shout of triumph for the victory they now saw certain. The enemy's officers and many of the men ran ahead of the line and urged the others on, but in vain; their confidence in themselves was gone. Some of them, in the hopes of inspiring others, started a cheer, but it died away in a weakly strain, and, the rear rank giving way, the front rank turned also, and the whole force made for the woods to the sound of our ringing cheers. At the woods they rallied, and reforming their line under our artillery fire they again charged. It was useless; we knew that troops we had once driven back so far would not succeed on a second trial under similar circumstances. After coming within fifty or sixty yards of where they first broke, they wavered again and speedily broke and ran thoroughly defeated."

THE SEVENTH INFANTRY.

The 7th Michigan—the gallant forlorn-hope regiment at the battle of Fredericksburg—was recruited and organized under the direction of Colonel Ira R. Grosvenor, at Monroe, and leaving that point for the field on the 5th of September, 1861, first encountered the enemy in the affair at Ball's Bluff, Va., October 21st following, where, in command of that officer, it gained credit even in that disastrous engagement. It afterwards moved with McClellan to the Peninsula, and endured the hardships and disappointments of that barren campaign, participating in common in its victories and defeats, but always with much credit, and had the honor to serve in the rear-guard of the army on the retreat to Harrison's Landing.

It also took part in the Maryland actions. At the battle of Antietam it is reported to have lost more than half its force engaged, including Captain Allen H. Zacharias, who died of his wounds on January 1st following, and among the killed were Captain J. H. Turrill, Lieutenant J. P. Eberhard, and Lieutenant John A. Clark.

But one of the great feats of the war, than which none will appear brighter in history, was reserved for the 7th at Fredericksburg, on December 11, 1862, when Burnside concluded to cross the Rappahannock and attack the rebels in that stronghold. The upper pontoon had been laid part of the way by the engineers during the night of the 10th. Daylight exposed them to the fire of the enemy's sharp-shooters, which drove them off. Volunteers were called for to cross the river and gain a position to protect the laying of the bridge. Immediately the 7th Michigan, under the gallant Baxter, rushed to the boats, crossed the stream in full view of both armies, under a most terrific fire from the enemy's sharp-shooters, losing heavily, but vigorously charging the rebels on the opposite bank, drove them from their rifle-pits, taking a number of prisoners and holding the ground. Colonel Baxter, having fallen severely wounded, recrossed the river, while the regiment, with the 19th and 20th Massachusetts, which had crossed by the second trip of the boats, dashed up the hill into the city, driving the enemy from house to house, and from stronghold to stronghold, capturing nearly as many prisoners as the regiment numbered, and inflicting a severe loss in killed and wounded, while their own loss was also heavy, including among the killed Lieutenant Franklin Emery, of the 7th Michigan. The river thus protected, the laying of the pontoons was speedily accomplished, on which Burnside crossed a portion of his army.

Engaging with the Army of the Potomac in the Pennsylvania campaign, this regiment underwent the laborious and forced marches by which it was marked, rendered more arduous by the intense heat of the weather. On the 27th of June the regiment was detailed as wagon guard at 7.45 A. M., marched by a circuitous route to near Urbana, Md., where it halted at 3 A. M., on the 28th, a distance said by citizens to have been thirty-seven miles; on the 28th it marched six miles to Monocacy. On the 29th it marched at 9 A. M., and reached Uniontown at 9 P. M., thirty-miles in twelve hours; thus, in three days, marching seventy-five miles. The regiment arrived on the field at Gettysburg on the 2d of July and was immediately sent to the front on Cemetery Hill, having fourteen officers and one hundred and fifty-one men. It occupied the same position until the close of the battle on the 3d. The loss of the regiment at Gettysburg was twenty-one killed and forty-four wounded. Among the killed were Lieut. Colonel Amos E. Steele, commanding the regiment, and Lieut. Albert Slafter, both gallant officers.

Entering on the campaign of 1864, it is found in command of Major S. W. Curtis, crossing the Rapidan at Ely's Ford on May 4th and on the 5th becoming engaged at the Wilderness, with small loss. On the 6th it lost eight killed, thirty-eight wounded, and eight missing. On the 8th it moved to the left, near Po river, and on the 9th crossed. On the 10th it was exposed to a severe fire from sharp-shooters, losing four wounded, and on the same day, in an assault on the enemy's works on the right, at Spottsylvania Court-house, it lost five killed and eight wounded. On the 11th it lost three wounded. On the 12th the 7th took part in Hancock's charge on the left of the enemy's line, in which its casualties were eleven wounded. On the 13th it lost three killed and ten wounded. Withdrawing with the army from in front of the enemy's works at Spottsylvania Court-house, the regiment arrived at the North Anna river on the 23d, and was engaged as skirmishers on the 24th at Chesterfield Ford, where the regiment lost one killed and three wounded, including Lieut. Charles Oakley mortally, who died on the next day. On the 26th it was employed in the rear guard of the army, in the flank movement of the latter across the Pamunkey river, arriving at the Tolopotamy creek on the 28th. On the 30th and 31st of May and 1st of June it was engaged as skirmishers, with a loss of six killed and nine wounded. On the 1st the regiment again served as rear guard for the army in the movement to Cold Harbor, and on the 3d, in a charge on the enemy's works, lost two killed and fourteen wounded. From the 3d to the 10th its casualties were one killed and twelve wounded. It crossed the James river with the army and arrived in front of Petersburg on the evening of the 15th. From this date to the 25th of July the regiment was engaged in labor on the fortifications and on picket, losing three killed and twenty wounded. The regiment, like the other Michigan regiments in the Army of the Potomac, had gone gallantly through the forced marches and hardships of the campaign, and now, with equal fortitude, it endured with them the labors in the trenches before Petersburg. On the 27th the 7th, with its corps, crossed the James river at Deep Bottom, but on the 29th returned to its former position before Petersburg, having lost during the movement two men wounded. It remained here employed in fatigue and picket duty until August 12th, when it again moved to Deep Bottom, and on the 14th and 17th was engaged in the battles of Strawberry Plains and Flussier's Mill, losing three killed and eleven wounded; Lieut. Harty S. Felt mortally, who died on the 24th following. On the 20th the regiment returned to near Petersburg. On the 25th it was engaged in the battle of Ream's Station, on the Weldon railroad; its casualties in this action being one killed, four wounded, and eight missing.

Passing through the various campaigns of the Army of the Potomac, acquitting itself nobly in every battle in which it became engaged, the regiment is found on the 26th of October, 1864, in the hottest of the fight at Hatcher's Run, near Burgess' Farm and Boydton Plank Road, where its corps, the 2d, was heavily engaged, and in which the 7th Michigan, then only eighty-five strong took twenty officers and four hundred and eighty men prisoners, while Sergeant Alonzo Smith, (afterwards first lieutenant,) captured the colors of the 26th North Carolina infantry, for which he was presented with a medal of honor by the Secretary of War. Through some misunderstanding the 7th was left on the line after the Union troops were withdrawn, and remained in that condition until the morning of the 28th, when Col. Lapointe, then in command, finding that his regiment had been left alone on the field, formed his men and explained to them their perilous situation, telling them to stand by him and they could find their way out. They commenced at once their dangerous undertaking, marching 12 miles through the country held by the enemy, gallantly fighting their way at almost every step, pursued and harassed constantly by cavalry threatening to cut them off, but they arrived safe within our lines at sundown of the same day. Gen. Hancock, their corps commander, complimented the regiment highly on the occasion, and characterized the undertaking as one of the most praiseworthy and daring of the war.

On April 2d, 1865, the regiment, together with details from the 1st Minnesota and 19th Massachusetts, charged the enemy's works at Cat Tail Creek, capturing two forts and three guns, then sweeping down the line, captured five other forts, well defended by infantry, and during the day taking about five hundred prisoners and several horses. The regiment is reported to have been the first to break the rebel lines in front of the 2d corps. After marching with the division to the rear of Petersburg, the regiment was deployed as skirmishers up the South Side railroad, in advance of the division, taking many prisoners and contrabands, and capturing great numbers of horses and mules. On April 3d it marched ten miles, continuing the march on the 4th and 5th; on the 6th it received orders to report to General Smith, and was put in the advance of the skirmish line of the 3d brigade, taking a number of prisoners during the day, and at 9 P. M. rejoined the division, having marched about thirty miles. On the morning of the 7th it marched with its brigade, until near High Bridge, in the vicinity of Farmville, when, together with the 59th New York, it was deployed as skirmishers to cover the front and flanks of the brigade, and moving on the enemy, it participated in capturing many prisoners, advancing to within half a mile of Farmville, when the enemy, throwing a heavy column of infantry and cavalry on the right and rear of the skirmish line, its connection with the brigade was cut off; but as soon as the advance on its rear was discovered, the skirmish line was faced to the rear, and charged the advancing force; but the enemy being superior in numbers, the line was repulsed, the regiment losing three officers and thirty-four men prisoners, including one officer severely wounded. In the afternoon the regiment was relieved from the front, and rejoined its brigade. On the 8th the march was continued until 12 P. M., and on the 9th marched about five miles, when General Lee's army surrendered.

There was found in the pocket-book of Captain Zacharias a note, dated Fair Oaks, June 28, 1862, and is as follows:

"Allen Howard Zacharias was born May 15, 1833, in Clear Spring, Washington county, Maryland, and removed with his father to Monroe county, Michigan, in 1841. Graduated A.B. from the University of Michigan, June, 1860. Went to Mississippi in September, and became a professor, and in February, 1861, principal of the State Military Institute, at Brandon, in that State. Resigned his position in May, and returned to Michigan, when, from a solemn sense of duty, enlisted as a corporal, and was promoted first lieutenant June 25th, and to a captaincy March 10, 1862; was with the regiment at Yorktown, West Point, and Fair Oaks, May 31st and June 1st."

Upon the other side of the paper was found the following:

"FRIEND: If you find my body lifeless upon the field, bury it decently, mark its resting place, and inform my friends in the regiment and my father. Do this, and you shall be liberally rewarded, and have the gratitude of my friends.

(Signed) A. H. ZACHARIAS,
"Captain, Company K, 7th Michigan."

He did not fall on the retreat to James river, but fell in Maryland, the place of his nativity, and near the spot on which he first saw the light. In his hand, while laying on the bloody field, was found an old envelope, written over as follows:

"*To Peter K. Zacharias, Monroe, Michigan:*

"DEAR PARENT, BROTHERS, AND SISTERS: I am wounded—mortally, I think. The fight rages around me. I have done my duty; this is my consolation. I hope to meet you all again. I left not the line until nearly all had fallen, and colors gone. I am getting weak; my arms are free, but below my chest all is numb. The enemy trotting over me; the numbness up to my heart. Good-bye, all.

"Your son, ALLEN."

He was found and conveyed to a field hospital, and the scrap sent to his friends by a kind-hearted private of the 4th Maine battery. Being so near the place of his nativity, he was soon found by friends—Mr. Joseph B. Loose, of Hagerstown; Rev. Dr. Zacharias, his uncle, from Frederick; Rev. J. S. Loose, of Greencastle, Penna., and conveyed to the house of Mr. Loose, of Hagerstown, where he was joined the next day by his sister Kate, who was visiting in Reading, Penna., and in a short time by his father. But they could not save him. His body was brought home to Michigan for interment, and on the 3d of January was placed by the side of his mother, in the cemetery of the German Reform Church in Ida, Monroe county, Michigan.

Lieutenant John J. Brown died at Alexandria, October 2, 1863, of wounds received on picket, September 18, 1863.

THE EIGHTH INFANTRY.

The 8th infantry, recruited by Col. W. M. Fenton, of Flint, might well be designated as the wandering or itinerant regiment of Michigan, leaving the State on the 27th of September, 1861, commanded by that officer, for the field in Virginia. It embarked at Annapolis, Md., as part of the expedition to Hilton Head, under Gen. T. W. Sherman. Down to November 1, 1862, it had been engaged in nine battles, occurring in four different States, South Carolina, Georgia, Virginia, and Maryland, and afterwards served in the various campaigns of the 9th corps in Tennessee, Mississippi, and, down to the close of the war, in Virginia. This brave and patriotic regiment commenced its battles at Port Royal, S. C., November 7, 1861, and was engaged most creditably in several others from that time to April 16, 1862, when it became specially noted in the spirited engagement on the reconnoisance made from on board the steamer Honduras by Col. Fenton, at Wilmington Island, Ga., on that day, where, after landing from the boats, it encountered the 13th Georgia, about 800 strong, armed with Enfield rifles, and drove them from the field in confusion, with loss, and leaving their dead on the ground. The object of the reconnoisance having been effected, the regiment, about dark, re-embarked on board the steamer. Its loss, out of a force of 300 men, were 10 killed and 35 wounded. Here fell two gallant officers, Adjutant N. Minor Pratt, killed instantly, and Lieutenant Frederick M. Badger, who died of his wounds at Beaufort, S. C., three days after the battle.

On June 16th following it was most signally distinguished in the assault made upon the enemy's works at Secessionville, on James Island, S. C., by a command of General Hunter's forces, under General Benham. The direct attack was made by General Stevens with the brigade led by Col. Fenton, and composed of the 8th Michigan, commanded by Lieutenant-Colonel Frank

Graves, 7th Connecticut, and 28th Massachusetts, and the brigade of Col. Leisure, comprising the 79th New York Highlanders, 46th New York, 100th Pennsylvania, and four detached companies of artillery. At first break of day the entire command was in motion, with strict orders to maintain most perfect silence, and to rely exclusively on the bayonet—to resort to firing only in case of manifest necessity. The force pressed forward, surprising and capturing the enemy's pickets and advanced promptly in line of battle without firing a gun to within one hundred yards of the enemy's works, when it received his fire of grape and canister, in advancing over the narrow strip of dry land, not over two hundred yards wide, between the marshes, being the only route by which the works could be reached, and that obstructed by an almost insuperable abatis, while the works were protected by a ditch seven feet deep, and having a parapet nine feet high.

The 8th Michigan being in the direct advance, immediately supported by the Highlanders, was completely swept by grape and canister at close range from six guns on the works, as well as by their musketry. Under this dreadful and destructive fire, and in defiance of these formidable defences, parties composed of officers and men from the 8th Michigan and 79th New York succeeded in gaining the parapet, but were shot down in the act; and, finally the assaulting force finding it impossible to carry the works had to withdraw. In Col. Fenton's report, covering the part taken by his brigade in the affair, is found the following:

"The order not to fire, but use the bayonet, was obeyed, and the advance companies reached the parapet of the works at the angle on our right and front, engaging the enemy at the point of the bayonet. During our advance the enemy opened upon our lines an exceedingly destructive fire of grape, canister, and musketry, and yet the regiment pushed on as veterans, divided only to the right and left by a sweeping torrent from the enemy's main gun in front. The enemy's fire proved so galling and destructive that our men on the parapet were obliged to retire under its cover. The field was furrowed across with cotton ridges, and many of the men lay there loading and firing as deliberately as though on their hunting grounds at home."

This was one of the most dashing assaults of the war, but made at a distressing sacrifice of life, the 8th Michigan losing 185 in killed, wounded, and missing out of 534, including 12 out of 22 officers. Captains Simeon C. Gould and Benjamin B. Church here fell mortally wounded, while bravely doing their duty; officers possessing great courage and true patriotism.

After the engagement at James Island, the 9th corps joined the Army of the Potomac in the Pope campaign, and the 8th was in the battles at Bull Run, August 29th and 30th, and at Chantilly on September 1st, losing heavily, including Lieut. W. A. Brown among the severely wounded, of the 1st, causing his death during that month.

Immediately following these engagements the 8th, with its corps, entered upon the Maryland campaign, and was conspicuously a participant in these important affairs.

The regiment took a part in the campaigns of the 9th corps in Mississippi and East Tennessee in 1863, and participated in the advance of General Sherman on Jackson, Miss., becoming engaged at that place on the 10th and 16th of June, but without serious loss.

From the 1st to the 14th of November, 1863, the 8th infantry was encamped at Lenoir Station, East Tennessee. The rebels, under General Longstreet, having commenced their advance on Knoxville, the 8th, with other forces, were ordered on the 14th to Hough's Ferry, on the Holston river, but during the night returned to Lenoir Station, and on the 16th commenced the retreat to Knoxville. Being rapidly followed by the enemy, a stand was made at Campbell's Station. A brisk engagement ensued, in which the loss of the regiment was eleven in wounded. The pursuit of the rebels was here checked, but during the night the retreat was continued, the regiment arriving at Knoxville on the morning of the 17th. During the retreat to Knoxville, and the siege of that place, which was immediately commenced by the rebel forces, the regiment endured many hardships and privations, suffering especially from want of sufficient food and proper clothing. The 8th, during the entire siege, occupied the front line of works. On the 29th of November the regiment assisted to repel the assault of the rebels on Fort Sanders, the enemy being driven off with large loss. On the 5th of December the rebels withdrew from in front of Knoxville, and the 8th engaged in the pursuit as far as Rutledge, but on the 16th returned to Blain's Cross-roads, where it encamped.

On the 4th of May the regiment commenced the campaign with the Army of the Potomac in its advance on Richmond, crossing the Rapidan at Germania Ford on the 5th. The 8th was prominently engaged during the advance in the Wilderness, and lost many brave men. On the 6th its casualties were ninety-nine in killed, wounded, and missing, including its commander Colonel Frank Graves, a gallant young officer of much promise, who fell by wounds while commanding his regiment, and was brutally murdered by rebels because he would not submit to indignity and robbery at their hands. On the 8th the regiment, then commanded by Colonel Ralph Ely, marched through Chancellorsville to Spottsylvania Court-house, and on the 12th participated in the heavy assault on the enemy's entrenchments at that point, losing forty-nine officers and men, among the killed being Lieutenant Edgar A. Nye. In the attack on the rebel lines at Bethesda Church, near Cold Harbor on June 3d, it was hotly engaged, and lost an aggregate of fifty-two, including among the killed Major W. E. Lewis. The regiment took part in the attacks on the works before Petersburg on the 17th and 18th of June, losing forty-nine, Lieutenant Thomas Campbell being among the killed of the 17th. These three officers who lost their lives in the battles of their country were highly esteemed in their regiment for their many soldierly qualities and moral worth. On the 30th of July it was in the engagement following the explosion of the mine, losing thirteen in killed and wounded. On the 19th of August it participated in the repulse of the enemy's assault on our lines at the Weldon road, sustaining a loss of thirty killed, wounded, and missing. Here fell the gallant Major Belcher, a brave, honest, and patriotic soldier. On the 30th it crossed the Weldon road, and took a part in the engagement of that date, near Poplar Grove Church, sustaining a loss of eight wounded.

The regiment, while in command of Major R. N. Doyle, also distinguished itself most conspicuously on the 2d of April, 1865, in front of Petersburg, when it engaged in the assault upon the enemy's position at Port Mahon, where it took part in carrying the works at that point, and is claimed to have been one of the first regiments to place its colors on that rebel stronghold, and was among the first troops to enter Petersburg. In this affair it lost Capt. Henry B. Burritt, who was killed during the assault.

The following is the report of Colonel Fenton of the operations of his regiment at Wilmington Island, where it was specially engaged and lost heavily: and in reading it, as well as the various other official reports contained in this volume, the people of Michigan cannot but be proud of the record which was made by their troops upon the battle-fields of the Union:

HEADQUARTERS 8TH REGIMENT MICHIGAN VOLS.,
(ON BOARD STEAMER HONDURAS,)
OFF WILMINGTON ISLAND, GA., 11 O'CLOCK P. M.,
April 16, 1862.

Lieut. W. L. M. BURGER,
Acting Assistant Adjutant General, Tybee Island, Ga.:

SIR:—I have the honor to report for the information of the general commanding—

That in compliance with special orders No. 41 I embarked with seven companies of the 8th Michigan regiment as an escort to Lieut. J. H. Wilson, Topographical Engineer, on a reconnoissance of Wilmington Island.

Two companies, under command of Captain Pratt, were landed at Scrivens' Plantation, with orders from Lieut. Wilson to skirt Turner's creek on the left. The other five companies were landed at Gibson's Plantation. Two of these companies were ordered to skirt Turner's creek, on the right; a third was to take the road to the right, towards the ferry at Caston's Bluff, to protect a boat party up Oatland creek, and the remainder to secure the landing.

After one company of the five was landed Lieut. Wilson proceeded in a boat to Turner's creek.

Owing to the small number of boats and the distance from the steamer, which was grounded, some delay occurred in the disembarcation. I directed Lieut. Col. Graves to follow with the second company and to skirt Turner's creek, but, being misdirected, he took the road to the right towards Carson's Bluff; and on landing with the remaining companies I received information that the enemy were in force at Fleetwood Plantation, and to the left of the road. This rendered the reconnoissance of Oatland creek with boats useless, and I ordered the companies all in; and, stationing the remaining companies to guard against an attack at our landing, sent out strong pickets on both roads.

I believe the advance of the company to the right instead of along Turner's creek saved my command, as it sooner enabled me to post the men to advantage and take a position from which the enemy's approach could be observed. The enemy proved to be the Georgia 13th, about 800 strong, armed with Enfield rifles. As they approached, about 4 o'clock P. M., with a strong body of skirmishers in the skirting of woods below the road, the companies I had stationed to the right and left of the road, in accordance with my instructions, opened fire. I immediately sounded the charge for advance of companies in the rear of the first line. The first line, mistaking the signal, fell back to the next cover. A constant and effective fire was kept up on both sides from cover of trees and bushes for an hour or more. Lieut. Wilson, who had returned with the boat party, here proved of great service to me. He took a party, at my request, to the left, and I ordered a company to the right to flank the enemy. Both operations were successful; and in a few moments the enemy retreated in confusion, leaving several dead on the field, followed by our men with loud cheers.

It being now about sunset I recalled our troops, and giving to Lieut. Wilson the command of pickets stationed to guard against surprise, formed the companies in line as originally posted, sent the dead and wounded in boats to the ship, and gradually and very quietly, under cover of night, withdrawing the men, sent them on board as fast as our limited transportation would allow. At the last trip of the boats I embarked, accompanied by Lieut. Wilson, Lieut. Col. Graves, and the remainder of my command, (at about 10 o'clock P. M.,) and immediately brought on board the two companies left at Scrivens' Plantation.

After the enemy retreated we were unmolested. It is due to the officers and men of the command to say that generally they behaved with cool and intrepid courage.

Adjutant Pratt fell dead near my side gallantly fighting, musket in hand, and cheering on the men. Our loss, I regret to say, was comparatively heavy; ten killed and thirty-five wounded out of a command of three hundred men. Among the wounded is acting Lieut. Badger, of company C, who was in charge of the advance picket, and exhibited undaunted courage. He with one of his men was made prisoner; both escaped and were brought in when the enemy retreated.

The captain of the Honduras is deserving of great credit for his kind attention to the wounded; indeed he afforded us every facility for the comfort of officers and men in his power.

I respectfully refer to Lieut. Wilson's report, (which I have read,) and it contains some facts not embraced in this report; among others in relation to the men detailed in charge of the field-piece on board ship, who were vigilant and attentive.

Herewith is transmitted a list of casualties.

I am, &c.,

WM. M. FENTON,
Colonel 8th Regiment Michigan Volunteers.

In an order issued immediately following the engagement by General Stevens, he says:

"You were ordered not to fire, but to push forward and use the bayonet. You obeyed the order. You formed in line under a terrible fire of grape, canister, and musketry. You pushed to the ditch and abatis of the work from right to left. Parties from the leading regiments of your two brigades, the 8th Michigan and 79th Highlanders, mounted and were shot down on the parapet, officers and men. These two regiments covered themselves with glory, and their fearful casualties show the hot work in which you were engaged."

Mr. Greeley, in his "American Conflict," says:

"Stevens had these in position at 3.30 A. M. at our outer picket line within rifle range of the enemy and advanced at 4—the morning being dark and cloudy—so swiftly and noiselessly that he captured most of the rebel pickets and was within one hundred yards of the main defences not having fired a shot, when Lamar opened on him with grape and canister, ploughing bloody lines through the storming party, and destroying its compactness, if not impairing the momentum of its charge. The 8th Michigan—Col. Fenton's own—was in the direct advance, supported by the Highlanders, with the residue of both brigades ready and eager to do and dare all that men might; and if well directed valor could have carried the enemy's works by direct assault they would have done it."

The gallant conduct of Major Belcher (then a lieutenant) at the battle of South Mountain is noticed by General J. D. Cox, commanding the Kanawha division, in his report of the part taken by his division in that engagement, as follows:

"I cannot close this report without speaking of the meritorious conduct of First Lieut. H. Belcher, of the 8th Michigan, a regiment belonging to another division. His regiment having suffered severely on the right, and being partly thrown into confusion, he rallied about one hundred men and led them up to the front. Being separated from the brigade to which he belonged he reported to me for duty, and asked a position where he might be of use till his proper place could be ascertained. He was assigned a post on the left and subsequently in support of the advanced section of Simmons' battery, in both of which places he and his men performed their duty admirably, and after the repulse of the enemy in the evening he carried his command to their proper brigade."

THE NINTH INFANTRY.

The most prominent events in the history of the 9th infantry, (organized and taken to the field by Colonel W. W. Duffield,) to which its members will refer with justifiable exultation, are its brilliant defence of Murfreesboro, Tenn., on July 13, 1862, and the part borne by it in the great battle of Stone River, 1863. This defence of Murfreesboro was made against a powerful cavalry force, led by the able and notorious General N. B. Forrest, said to have been one of the most capable cavalry commanders in the rebel army.

The Union forces at Murfreesboro at the time referred to were, on the morning of the attack, in the immediate command of Brigadier-General Thomas L. Crittenden. Colonel Duffield, who had been formerly in command, having only returned from a leave of absence the night previous, had not assumed command, but was with his regiment, and was severely wounded early in the engagement. Five companies—A, C, E, G, and K—of the 9th, under command of Lieutenant-Colonel Parkhurst, and numbering two hundred and fifty men, were at the time encamped in Murfreesboro. A Minnesota regiment and a Kentucky battery were encamped on the east bank of Stone river, a distance of more than a mile and a half from the camp of the 9th. These troops comprised all the Union forces in and around Murfreesboro. At 4 o'clock on the morning of the 13th the regiment was aroused by the camp guard, and had barely got into position when it was charged most furiously by over two thousand rebel cavalry. A desperate engagement ensued, at one time assuming the phase of a hand-to-hand fight, but, after a struggle of more than half an hour's duration, the enemy was repulsed, broke, and fled in the wildest confusion, followed in close pursuit by a company of the 9th, acting as skirmishers, under command of Captain C. V. De Land. He soon after rallied, however, and charged a second time, but without success. Perceiving the weakness of the Union troops, and relying upon their superior numbers, they did not abandon the attack, but for more than eight hours kept up irregular skirmishes and assaults that were harassing and exhausting.

Simultaneously with the attack upon the camp, company D of the regiment, in the immediate command of Lieutenant Wright, acting as provost guard in the town of Murfreesboro, was attacked in their quarters, in the Court-house, by a large force of Georgia cavalry. The company defended their position with desperate fighting, and held it for two and a half hours, killing and wounding a large number of the enemy, until the lower part of the building was set on fire and nearly consumed, when they were compelled to surrender.

Meanwhile, Colonel Parkhurst had repeatedly applied to Colonel Lester, in command of the Minnesota regiment, for reinforcements, but without success, that officer (subsequently dismissed for cowardice on the occasion) definitely refusing to aid his comrades in their desperate situation.

It becoming evident that no assistance was possible, and the disparity between the strength of his own and the assailing forces rendering all hope of escape or permanent success in repelling assaults impossible, Colonel Parkhurst surrendered his command, which had been reduced to one hundred and thirty-seven men. The courage and the skill of the resistance they had encountered was acknowledged by the rebels, and their loss in the affair far exceeded that of the gallant defenders of Murfreesboro. This was one of the most brilliant of the minor events of the war, and must be classed amongst those rare manifestations of courage truly Spartan. The loss of the regiment was Lieutenant Alpheus Chase and thirteen killed and seventy-eight wounded.

Colonel Duffield, in his report of the affair at Murfreesboro, says:

"The attack was made at daybreak on the morning of the 13th by Brigadier-General N. B. Forrest, with over three thousand cavalry. A Texan and Georgia regiment, about eight hundred strong, attacked the detachment of the 9th Michigan. So fierce and impetuous was their attack that our men were forced nearly to the centre of their camp, falling back steadily and in order, with their faces to the foe. But upon reaching the centre of our camp, their line was brought to a halt, and after twenty minutes of nearly hand-to-hand fighting, the enemy broke and fled in the wildest confusion."

In the important five days' battle of Stone River the 9th, in command of General Parkhurst, acted as a select guard for Major-General George H. Thomas, and its duties were mainly those of a provost guard. On the second day of the fight, however, it rendered services which were vital to the Army of the Cumberland. The rebel charge upon the right wing, in command of General McCook, of Rosecrans' army, resulted in its utter defeat and rout, followed by demoralization which seriously threatened the safety of the entire line. The defeated troops commenced a most disorderly movement towards Nashville, but at the bridge over Overall's creek Col. Parkhurst stationed the 9th, intercepted the fugitives, rallied and reformed them in line, strengthened his position with artillery and cavalry, and succeeded in checking the rebel pursuit and in driving off their cavalry by a series of skillful and daring charges. The scattered organizations were then reformed, and the damage of the morning partially repaired. Had it not been for this important service the stampede of McCook's command would unquestionably have affected the whole army, and might have disastrously influenced the course of the battle and changed the complexion of the war. As it was it nullified many of the worst results of a serious check and paved the way for the triumphs of the next three days. In all its engagements the 9th never served the "old flag" more faithfully or effectively than on that wintry day when it stemmed the tide of defeat at Overall's creek and despoiled disaster of its worst results. The regiment being still on the same duty at the battle of Chicamauga performed most valuable service. It was also engaged at Mission Ridge on the 25th of November.

On the 3d of May, 1864, the 9th, in command of Lieut. Col. Wm. Wilkinson, marched from Chattanooga with the headquarters of the Army of the Cumberland and participated with that army in the campaign in Georgia, being present at the actions of Rocky Face Ridge, Resaca, Dallas, Kenesaw Mountain, and the other engagements of the campaign preceding and including the siege of Atlanta. It also accompanied the army in the march around Atlanta to Jonesboro', and aided in destroying the railroad from that place and in the performance of other duties. It entered Atlanta on its evacuation by the rebel army, and was engaged in provost duty until that city was evacuated by our forces. The regiment then returned to Chattanooga.

The regiment on November 1st was at Marietta, Georgia, *en route* from Atlanta to Chattanooga, Tennessee, by rail, having left the former place the day previous. On the 6th it reached Chattanooga, where it remained in camp doing guard duty at the headquarters of the Army of the Cumberland, also picket duty for that post until the 27th of March, 1865, when, Gen. Thomas having removed his headquarters to Nashville, it was ordered to that point, and on the 29th arrived there by rail, and was assigned to duty guarding the military prison, and also at General Thomas's headquarters. The regiment continued at Nashville performing the same general service until September 15th, when it was mustered out.

Lieut. Charles F. Fox was killed in action at Mumfordsville, Kentucky, September 2d, 1862.

THE TENTH INFANTRY.

The 10th infantry, organized at Flint by Col. Charles M. Lum, first met the enemy in battle near Corinth, Miss. Among the most marked events in the history of this splendid regiment were the affair at Buzzard's Roost, Georgia, February 25th, 1864; the battle of Jonesboro', September 1st, 1864, and the engagement at Bentonville, March 19th and 20th, 1865.

The regiment having re-enlisted as veterans at Rossville, Georgia, February 6th, the men were anxiously awaiting their veteran furloughs of thirty days to enable them to return to their homes, when, on the 23d of February, the emergencies of the service required a movement of the 14th corps, to which the regiment belonged, in the direction of Dalton; and an order was received by Lieut. Col. Dickerson, then commanding the regiment, from brigade headquarters to prepare for an immediate movement, with sixty rounds of ammunition and three days' rations, and at 8 A. M. on that day commenced moving. After marching as far as Ringold, fourteen miles, the regiment bivouacked and remained until daylight the following morning, and then moved through Hooker's Gap, in White Oak Ridge, coming up with the main force (which had moved out on the 22d) about a mile and a half north of Tunnell Hill, when the brigade to which the 10th belonged formed in line of battle on the extreme left of the army and to the left of the road leading to Tunnell Hill.

The enemy lay encamped in considerable force about one mile south of Tunnell Hill. The brigade moved through the woods on the left of the town in such a direction as to strike the enemy on his right flank, while the main force moved up directly in front and opened with artillery on his intrenched camp. As the brigade came out of the woods in sight of the rebel camp their rear guard was seen moving hurriedly towards Dalton, when a force of cavalry was immediately sent in pursuit, while the 10th formed in column of companies and followed. About 2 P. M. the force came in sight of Buzzard's Roost, where the enemy had taken up a very strong position. The Union force formed in line of battle, when the enemy opened an artillery fire, which was immediately replied to, and a line of skirmishers kept up a brisk fire. This position was held until dark, when the line fell back a short distance and bivouacked for the night.

On the morning of the 25th orders were received by Colonel Dickerson to take a position with his regiment on the left of the 60th Illinois (which was in the same brigade) on the top of one of the spurs of the mountain and conform to the movements of that regiment. After occupying this position for a short time the regiment moved forward and took possession of the top of another spur, from which could be seen the enemy in his fortified position. At this time a brisk fire was being kept up by both skirmish lines. About 3 P. M. the division to which the 10th belonged commenced a forward movement, when the enemy opened a most galling infantry fire from the top of Rocky Face in front, while two or more batteries on the right and front threw shot and shell raking the ravines and sweeping the tops of the spurs. The regiment advanced coolly and steadily over the spurs and through the ravines until its colors were flying defiantly almost in the face of the enemy. Halting just under the crest of one of these spurs the men were directed to lie down and load and fire at will. In consequence of the elevated position of the enemy on the right and left his fire was most galling and murderous, and to which the regiment was very much exposed for nearly thirty minutes. Colonel Dickerson not receiving any orders, and seeing no troops advancing to his support, was compelled to fall back a short distance to a gulley, where the 60th Illinois had already reached. Here a halt was made for a short time and then fell back on the double-quick. In coming out of the ravine Col. Dickerson was knocked down by a mass of earth thrown against him by a shell; partially recovering from the shock, and while moving towards his regiment, he was wounded in the heel by a musket ball, and being unable to travel fast fell into the hands of the enemy. The regiment lost in this affair twenty-two killed and fifty-six wounded.

The loss in this gallant regiment at that time was a very peculiar and most severe hardship and was much regretted, as the regiment had only re-enlisted a few days before, and the friends of those who bravely fell had been fondly hoping to meet them on the return of the regiment to the State.

The 10th, returning from its veteran furlough in Michigan, arrived at Chattanooga May 11, 1864, and on the following day left there to participate in the Georgia campaign. It arrived at Resaca on the 16th. Marching on the 16th for Rome, it arrived in front of that place on the 17th, and on the 18th participated in its capture. On the 28th it took position in front of the rebel lines at Dallas. June 1st the regiment moved to the left toward Lost Mountain, and after several changes of position, reached the base of Kenesaw Mountain on the 19th. On the 27th of June it acted in the reserve of a column that charged the rebel lines. Its casualties during the month of June were two killed and died of wounds, and twelve wounded. On the 3d of July the regiment marched in pursuit of the enemy, who had evacuated the position of Kenesaw Mountain, and on the 17th crossed the Chattahoochie river. On the 19th it advanced to near Durant's Mill, on Peach Tree creek, where it took part in the actions of that date, and of the day following. On the 21st it participated in a reconnoissance toward Atlanta, and on the 22d had position in front of that place on the right of our lines. With the exception of the reconnoissance to Sandtown on the 28th the regiment remained in front of Atlanta during the remainder of July. Its casualties during the month were four killed and eighteen wounded. While on a reconnoissance on the 29th it encountered the enemy and captured a number of guns, horses, etc. Being cut off by the rebels, it was obliged to return by a circuitous route, in which it succeeded without loss.

The movement of General Sherman upon Hood's communications near Atlanta, which culminated in the important battle of Jonesboro', September 1, 1864, and the evacuation of Atlanta by the rebels, in which the 14th corps took a most prominent part, again gave the 10th Michigan a most enviable page in the history of the war. The regiment, under command of Major Burnett, having moved with its corps on Jonesboro', was acting as a support to a charging column, which became broken and demoralized. The six left companies of the 10th moved quickly forward and took their places, bravely carried the enemy's works, took 400 prisoners, and captured a stand of colors. In this daring and gallant advance fell the brave Burnett, with 30 killed and 47 wounded, including Lieut. John Knox killed and Captain H. H. Nimms mortally wounded—a heavy loss—but the regiment aided very materially, and with much distinction in the last battle of the great Atlanta campaign which secured to the Union arms one of the most important points held during the rebellion, and gave the death-blow to the rebel armies in Georgia.

The 10th, commanded by Colonel Lum, was with Sherman on his march to the sea, and at Bentonville, on the 19th and 20th of March, 1865, again added to its already enviable reputation as a fighting regiment. Moving in advance of its corps on the 18th, six companies being deployed as skirmishers, the enemy was reached about noon, and a severe skirmish ensued, when the regiment was ordered to take position at the junction of the Smithfield and Goldsboro' roads. During the night it was attacked, but succeeded in repulsing the enemy, and holding its position until relieved by the 20th corps on the 19th, when it marched rapidly forward and formed on the right of the second line of battle. About 4 P. M. the enemy moved up in heavy masses, driving in the skirmishers, and advancing to within a few rods of the first line, he discharged a terrific fire along his whole front, and immediately charged the works. The first line, in which was the 14th Michigan, replied with a well-directed and effective volley, checking the enemy's advance, and before he could recover from its effects, the 14th Michigan jumped over its works and charged, driving him in confusion from the field, and taking a large number of prisoners. The regiment, with the remainder of the brigade, then moved forward to the first line, and in a few moments, the enemy having broken through the first division, was discovered coming in on the left flank. The line was at once changed to the opposite side of the works, and after pouring a volley into the enemy's ranks, charged and drove him at the point of the bayonet in great confusion from the field, taking many prisoners, and capturing a large amount of arms. On the 20th the regiment skirmished with the enemy during the entire day and night; and thus ended its last battle for Union and freedom.

NOTE.—On the 3d of January, 1863, companies A and D, while guarding a supply train on the Murfreesboro' road, were attacked by a large force of guerrilllas and repulsed them, killing 15 and taking as many prisoners, without loss to themselves. On the 25th of January, a squad of men, guarding a construction train, were captured by 200 rebel cavalry. Twenty-seven men of the 10th, being on duty near, went forward on double-quick, routed the rebels, killing and wounding a large number, captured a lot of guns, horses, etc., and saved the train which had been set on fire. April 10th, a detail of 46 men, guarding a railroad train, were attacked by three or four hundred guerrillas. Overpowered by numbers, they were compelled to give up the train; but, repulsing the enemy's pursuit and falling back a short distance, they were reinforced by 15 men from a neighboring stockade, returned and saved a portion of the train, which had been set on fire. The loss in this affair was 8 killed and 12 wounded, including among the killed Lieutenant Frank M. Vanderburg.

First Lieut. and Adjutant Sylvester D. Cowles was killed while on the skirmish line at Farmington, in front of Corinth, Miss., May 26, 1862.

At Kenesaw Mountain, June 27th, the 10th infantry, was in General Davis's division (2d) of the 14th corps, a notice of which is found in the "Annual Cyclopedia, 1864," as follows: "For the second and more important attack portions of General Newton's division of the 4th corps and of General Davis's division of the 14th corps were selected. At a given signal the troops rushed forward with buoyant courage, charged up the face of the mountain amidst a murderous fire from a powerful battery on the summit, and through two lines of abatis, carried a line of rifle-pits beyond and reached the works. The colors of several of the regiments were planted before the latter, and some of the men succeeded in mounting the ramparts, but the deaths of Generals Wagner and Harker, and the wounding of General McCook, the destructive fire of both musketry and artillery and the difficulty of deploying such long columns under such fire, rendered it necessary to recall the men. General Newton's troops returned to their original line, while General Davis's 2d brigade threw up works between those they had carried and the main line of the enemy, and there remained."

THE ELEVENTH INFANTRY.

The great and important battles of Stone River and Chicamauga will always be referred to by the 11th infantry as among the most desperate in which it was engaged during its gallant career, and in which it was most eminently distinguished, and lost heavily. Few regiments on those fields were harder pressed or defended themselves more heroically, and the members of the regiment refer to their services on these occasions with justifiable pride. At Stone River the regiment, commanded by Col. Wm. L. Stoughton, was hotly engaged during the entire battle, being in Negley's division of Thomas's corps, which, on December 31st, held the ground near the centre of the Union lines, where it received and checked the onset of the rebel forces, which came sweeping on in column of divisions after having driven the corps of McCook from its position; and is acknowledged to have been one of the fiercest assaults of the day, and in which the enemy was dreadfully punished. The 11th Michigan, with the 19th Illinois, charged in advance, and drove back an entire rebel division; and, after the retrograde movement of their own division, these regiments made another dash to the front, driving the enemy. In the engagement the 11th lost 32 killed, 79 wounded, and 29 missing. The noble stand taken by Negley's division, and its persistent fighting on that day, undoubtedly aided much in preventing a most disastrous result.

Colonel Stoughton in his official report of the part taken by his regiment in the engagement, says:

"On the morning of the 31st of December heavy firing was heard to our right and front, and apparently rapidly approaching the position occupied by the 2d brigade. The regiment was immediately formed and marched to the brow of the hill, near brigade headquarters. The skirmishing soon after indicated the approach of the enemy to the right of this position, and my regiment was formed in line of battle, under cover of a ledge of rocks, about one hundred yards in this direction. The skirmishing continued with much spirit for nearly an hour, when a heavy roar of musketry and artillery announced that the principal attack of the enemy was being made on our left and rear. I immediately gave orders to change front on first company, which was promptly executed under a heavy fire, and the regiment advanced in line of battle to the crest of the hill, from which Shoult's battery had just been driven, and poured a well directed and effective fire into the advancing columns of the enemy. The firing continued with spirit and energy until orders came to retire. The fire of the enemy was apparently concentrated upon this point, and was terrific. Men and officers fell on every side. The regiment fell back about eighty yards, was again formed, and delivered its fire upon the enemy as he advanced over the hill, and then retired to the cover of the cedar woods in our rear. Here some confusion was at first manifested. A large number of regiments had fallen back to this place for shelter, and the enemy's infantry and artillery opened upon us from all sides, except to the left, towards the Murfreesboro pike. Order, however, was promptly restored by our division and brigade commanders, and my regiment, with others, moved slowly to the rear, keeping up a steady fire upon the enemy. When nearer the cleared field to the right of the Murfreesboro pike, the regiment was rallied, and held the ground for twenty or thirty minutes; it was then marched about half way across the open field, when orders came to charge back into the cedars. My regiment promptly obeyed my orders, rallied on the colors, and charged back into the woods with great gallantry, checking the enemy by the sudden and impetuous attack. After delivering one volley, orders came to retire, and the regiment fell back in good order to the left of the Murfreesboro pike. Here closed the active operations of the day.

"On the 2d of January we were again called into action. In the afternoon of that day we were posted as a reserve, in an open field in the rear of our batteries on the right of the left wing of our army. Between 3 and 4 o'clock the enemy made a heavy attack with artillery and infantry on our front. My command was kept lying upon the ground, protected by a slight hill, for about half an hour. At the expiration of this time the enemy had driven back our forces on the opposite side of the river, one regiment crossing in great disorder, and rushing through our ranks. As soon as the enemy came within range, my regiment with the others of this brigade, rose up, delivered its fire, and charged across the river. In passing the river my line of battle was necessarily broken, and I led the regiment forward to a fence on a rise of ground, and reformed the line. Here the firing continued for some time until the enemy was driven from his cover and retreated through the woods. My regiment was then promptly advanced to the edge of the woods, and continued to fire upon the enemy as he fled in disorder across the open field in front to his line of entrenchments. At this time the ammunition was nearly exhausted, and my regiment, with the others in advance, formed in line of battle, threw out skirmishers, and held our position until recalled across the river. The 11th was among the first that crossed Stone river and assisted in capturing four pieces of artillery, abandoned by the enemy in his flight. I cannot speak too highly of the conduct of the troops under my command. They fought with the bravery and coolness of veterans, and obeyed my commands, under the hottest fire, with the precision of the parade ground. The officers of my command behaved with great gallantry and firmness. Where all nobly discharged their duty, it would, perhaps, be unjust to discriminate. Lieutenants Wilson and Flynn were killed while gallantly leading their companies. Major Smith and Lieutenants Hall, Briggs, and Howard were wounded, the two former severely, and Lieutenant Hall is a prisoner."

At Chicamauga the regiment, in command of Lieutenant-Colonel Melvin Mudge, was then in the brigade of Colonel Stoughton, being the 2d brigade, 2d division, 14th corps. This brigade constituted part of the command of General Thomas, and on the last day of that sanguinary conflict held one of the most important points on his line of defence against a largely superior force, the regiment fighting most persistently, successfully repelling charge after charge of the enemy, losing seven killed, (including Captain Charles W. Newbern,) seventy-six wounded, and twenty-three missing, and was one of the last regiments to retire from the field in the darkness of that fearful night, when the army fell back. Next morning Colonel Stoughton took up a position in front of Rossville, covering the approach to the battle-field, and held it during that day, and in the night fell back on Chattanooga, covering the rear of the retiring army. In the movement Colonel Stoughton drew off his artillery by hand, to escape the notice of the enemy. He remained on his picket line until past 4 A. M., when, hearing the enemy stirring, he successfully withdrew his pickets and made a forced march to Chattanooga without the loss of a man, thus most successfully accomplishing a very dangerous and important duty, for which he was afterwards complimented personally by General Thomas.

After the battle of Mission Ridge, in November, 1863, where the regiment, under command of Major Benjamin G. Bennett, participated in the decisive charge, losing its gallant commander and thirty-nine in killed and wounded, the regiment, being in the 2d brigade, 1st division, 14th corps, moved forward on the Atlanta campaign, partaking creditably in all the important battles. On July 4th following, it took a part in the successful charge on the enemy's works near Marietta, losing thirteen in killed and wounded, including among the severely wounded Colonel Stoughton, who lost a leg. It was engaged at Peach Tree Creek, on the 20th of that month, with a loss of eleven killed and wounded, and on the 7th of August it was in the charge on the enemy's works in front of Atlanta, losing Lieutenant Edward Catlin and fifteen men killed and wounded.

The period for which the regiment enlisted having expired, it was ordered to Chattanooga on the 27th of August. The rebel General Wheeler being then engaged in making a raid into Tennessee, the regiment, immediately after its arrival at Chattanooga, on the 30th, was ordered to join the column in pursuit, and marched to Murfreesboro, and thence to Huntsville, Ala., but without meeting the enemy. It returned to Chattanooga on the 13th of September. Leaving here two commissioned officers and one hundred and fifty men—veterans and recruits whose term had not expired—the regiment started for Michigan on the 18th, arriving at Sturgis on the 25th. On the 30th of September it was mustered out of service.

THE TWELFTH INFANTRY.

The bloody battle of Shiloh, April 6th and 7th, 1862, first tried the metal of the 12th infantry, and substantially established its reputation as a fighting regiment. Leaving the State, in command of Col. Francis Quinn, on March 18th, it hurriedly reached Pittsburg Landing barely in time to participate in that important engagement. A portion of the regiment was among the troops that first discovered and engaged the enemy in his advance upon the Union lines, and this timely discovery and their persistent opposition to his advance, without doubt, saved their division from entire capture, and must have done much towards saving the whole army from a complete surprise. The 12th was in Col. Peabody's brigade of Prentiss' division, which occupied the position just attacked by the rebel forces. During the night preceding the battle of the 6th, Col. Peabody had been advised by Lieut. Col. Graves, of the 12th Michigan, of the approach of the enemy, and on this information he took the responsibility to order from his brigade two companies of the 12th Michigan, commanded respectively by Captains Graves and Cravath, and two companies of the 25th Missouri as a reconnoissance, the whole under command of Major Powell, 25th Missouri, who, about 3 o'clock on the morning of the 6th, met the advance troops of the enemy and fought them until daylight, gradually falling back until he reached the 12th Michigan and 25th Missouri, which had advanced some distance in front of their color line. These two regiments fought the enemy until overpowered, when they fell back to their color line, reformed again, and defended their line until again overpowered, when they retired to a third position, which was held until the division was completely surrounded and a large portion of it made prisoners. The 12th escaped capture, maintaining its organization, and next day engaged the enemy, losing in both days 266 killed, wounded, and missing, including among the mortally wounded Lieutenant Alex. G. Davis, who died at Cincinnati on the 21st of April following.

It also participated in the affair at Iuka September 19th, and in the battle at Metamora October 5th.

The regiment, in December following, was guarding the Mississippi railroad from Hickory Valley to near Bolivar, Tennessee, with its headquarters at Middleburg. On the 24th of that month the force at Middleburg, consisting of one hundred and fifteen officers and men, in command of Colonel W. H. Graves, were attacked by a large force of Van Dorn's cavalry, consisting of three brigades, in all about three thousand strong, by which they were surrounded and their surrender demanded. About 10 o'clock on the morning of the day of the attack Lieut. Col. Dwight May, of the regiment, left Middleburg for Bolivar, distant some seven miles, and when about two miles from Middleburg he saw horsemen approaching; as he neared them he observed that they wore the blue overcoat of our army, but noticing the peculiar gait of their horses and their suspicious movements, he halted and was adjusting his field glass to scrutinize them more closely, when the advance guard fired at him and put their horses to their utmost speed towards him; they were then only about twenty rods off. He immediately wheeled his horse and started for camp, they in pursuit, discharging their arms at him during the chase, but having the better horse he succeeded in reaching the camp of his regiment and instantly reported the circumstances to Col. Graves, who in his report states:

"The advance of Gen. Van Dorn's command soon made its appearance, and a flag of truce was sent in by a lieutenant colonel of staff, which I met. The officer asked who is in command; I answered 'I am;' whereupon he surveyed me from head to foot (I had been playing ball that morning, pants in boots, having on a jacket without straps) with a disdainful air and said: 'Gen. Van Dorn demands a surrender of you and the whole damned thing immediately; we don't want to bother with you.' It was my intention to have asked if he had artillery, but his important demeanor did not set well as may be imagined, and I upon the spur of the moment replied, give my compliments to the general and say to him, I have no doubt he can whip us, but while he is getting a meal we will try and get a mouthful; he then remarked, 'that is what you say, is it?' To which I made answer, that is what I say, is it; and he wheeled, put spurs to his horse, and I double-quicked to my command, which was located in a depot platform, with planks doubled and port-holes cut, and a block or rather log-house having port-holes. The enemy advanced until I fired a musket, (which was the signal when my men were to fire,) when the enemy broke up in confusion and sought log buildings and ditches, where they fought us for two hours and twenty-five minutes, and finally left us 'monarchs of all we surveyed,' in one sense.

"The whole force of Gen. Van Dorn was between five and six thousand, about one-half of which fought us, the balance holding the horses. They lost (as near as I can recollect) 135 killed, wounded, and prisoners, among the latter three officers wounded, one mortally. There were six of my men wounded through the port-holes, one killed, and thirteen taken prisoners,

W

mostly on picket along the railroad. Over one thousand rounds were fired by the men of the 12th during the action."

For this gallant and successful defence of Middleburg, so remarkable for the disparity in numbers, the regiment (with several others along that line of railroad that had successfully defended their posts) was complimented for bravery by General Grant in general orders, and declared by him to be deserving of the thanks of the army, which was in a measure dependent for its supplies on the road they so nobly defended.

Embarking on transports at Memphis to take part in the campaign against Vicksburg the regiment arrived at Chickasaw Bayou, near the rebel stronghold, on the 3d of June. Disembarking at Sartalia, on the Yazoo river, the regiment marched to Mechanicsburg, skirmishing on the march with the rebel cavalry. From thence it proceeded to Hayne's Bluff by an exhausting march, during which a number of men fell under the oppressive heat. The regiment remained at Hayne's and Snyder's Bluffs until the fall of Vicksburg, July 4th. It embarked on the 28th, in command of Lieut. Col. May, for Helena, Ark., near which it encamped until the 13th of August, when it marched from Helena with the army, and on the 11th of September went into camp near Little Rock. On the 26th and 27th of October the regiment moved to Benton, Ark. The 12th continued on duty in Arkansas, in command of Col. May, until the 15th of February, 1865, when it was mustered out of service.

THE THIRTEENTH INFANTRY.

The daring bravery of the 13th infantry, raised and organized by Col. Charles E. Stuart, of Kalamazoo, is attested by its persistent fighting and splendid achievements on many fields.

This regiment left Kalamazoo on the 12th of February, 1862, under command of Col. Michael Shoemaker. Its route was through Kentucky and Tennessee via Bowling Green and Nashville. It reached the battle-field at Pittsburg Landing, after a forced march, near the close of the second day's fight, and thenceforward, until the evacuation of Corinth, was engaged in picket and fatigue duty with the forces that captured that post. The 13th was the last of General Buell's command to leave northeastern Alabama on the withdrawal of our forces from that region in August, and was among the troops of the same army which fell back upon Louisville.

On the 10th of November, 1862, this regiment marched from Silver Springs, Tenn., and formed part of the forces that drove the enemy from Lebanon. Proceeding to Nashville, it was then engaged in guarding forage trains, and on picket duty, from the 25th of November to the 26th of December, when it marched with the army under General Rosecrans on Murfreesboro'. It was deployed as skirmishers on the 29th in the advance, and suffered some loss. It participated in the bloody engagements at Stone River, on the 30th and 31st of December, and 1st, 2d, and 3d of January, the regiment going into action with 224 muskets, and losing out of this number 25 killed or died of wounds, 62 wounded, and 8 missing. On the 31st of December it recaptured, by a bayonet charge, two guns which had fallen into the hands of the enemy.

The 13th was particularly distinguished at Stone River, under Colonel Shoemaker, and at Chicamauga, under the command of Col. J. B. Culver.

In a recent report, Col. Culver says: "They will always be remembered with pride and sorrow by every member of the 13th. *Pride*, in the acknowledged gallantry of the regiment, and *sorrow*, for our brave comrades who fell there." He says further: "At the battle of Stone River, the 13th supported the 6th Ohio Independent Battery; and early on the morning of the memorable 31st of December, 1862, our brigade was detailed by verbal orders of General Rosecrans, and directed to go to the support of General R. W. Johnson, of McCook's corps, who was on the extreme right of the line, and was being forced back by overwhelming numbers of the enemy. The order was promptly executed, and while getting into position we were attacked by the advancing columns of the rebel General Hanson's division, which we stubbornly resisted for fifteen or twenty minutes, when three of the regiments of the brigade retired in disorder, leaving the 13th to protect the battery. Our position was in a cotton-field, without protection. We fell back about 300 yards to the edge of a cedar thicket, formed on the left of the battery, and delivered such a destructive fire that an entire brigade of the enemy were held in check for over thirty minutes; but we were again compelled to retire, losing *one-third* of the entire regiment dead or wounded, together with two guns from the battery. We reformed again about 150 yards to the rear of the second position, and being opportunely supported by the gallant 51st Illinois infantry, we made a dashing charge with the bayonet, broke and routed the rebel line, recaptured the two guns, took 150 prisoners, and defeated the purposes of the enemy on this part of the field, namely, getting possession of the Murfreesboro' pike. On this field the 13th lost Captain Clement C. Webb.

Colonel Shoemaker, in his report of the part taken by his regiment in that great struggle, says:

"My report of the 5th having been made in great haste, was necessarily very brief, and for the better understanding of the movements of this regiment during the several days of battle, commencing on the 29th and ending on the 3d instant, submit the following:—In the evening of the 29th, when ordered to cross the river, we were on the left, the 51st Indiana in the centre, and the 73d Indiana on the right. My regiment commenced crossing as soon as our skirmishers were fairly on the other side. The skirmishers were company A, commanded by Lieut. Hanarsdale, and company F, commanded by Lieut. James R. Slayton. They drove the enemy rapidly, the regiment following quite close upon them. When in line in the cornfield, after receiving the 3d volley from the enemy, we were ordered to fix bayonets and prepare to receive a charge of cavalry. As my regiment was somewhat in advance of the 51st Indiana, and my right covering their left, I moved my regiment to the left and rear, so as to connect with the 51st Indiana, but still leaving my left somewhat in advance, and in such a position as would have enabled us to enfilade any force which might charge the centre. Our position was now a very strong one, being in the edge of the woods. Here we remained until ordered to recross the river. On the 31st, being in reserve, when our brigade was placed in position on the extreme right of the army, we occupied an open field in the rear of where the 64th and 65th regiments of Ohio volunteers, and 73d regiment of Indiana volunteers, were engaged with the enemy. When the battery retired we were ordered to fall back to the position we held when the enemy advanced upon us. When they opened fire upon us the other regiments of the brigade had passed by on our right to the rear, and we did not see them again until after the close of the engagement. My regiment was in line during the engagement, and delivered their fire with such precision and rapidity that the whole force of the enemy were brought to a stand at the fence in our front, and held there for at least twenty minutes, when their left, which extended considerably beyond our right, having advanced so as to make it apparent that they would soon turn my right flank, I gave the order to retire; but again formed the regiment within twelve or fifteen rods of the first line; but broke and retreated precipitately when charged by me. The 51st Indiana advanced only to within three rods of our first line, and then threw forward skirmishers. My regiment charged past the first line and to the right, down to near the fence, and full thirty rods in advance of our first position, overtaking and capturing the enemy from the place where the guns were recaptured, which was to the right and in front of our first line of battle, to the houses in our front, and into the cornfield on a line with the houses. The artillery ceased firing a short time before we opened upon the enemy, and fell back out of sight, with all but the guns captured. The enemy broke up the guns of the dead on the first line of battle while they occupied it. A lieutenant, whom we captured, informed me that our fire was very destructive, and that their loss in wounded must largely exceed ours. On the 1st inst., my regiment was exposed to a scattering fire all day, but was not actually engaged. At night we were ordered to the extreme front to protect the 6th Ohio battery, and lay on our arms all night. On the 2d inst., while supporting our battery, my regiment was exposed to a terrible fire from the artillery of the enemy, the number of guns playing upon us at one time being, as stated by Capt. Bradley, eighteen. Though necessarily inactive, my regiment steadily maintained its position for over an hour, when one of our batteries commenced playing upon us from the rear. I then withdrew my regiment a few rods to the left to a less exposed situation. In the afternoon we crossed Stone's river with our division, and remained there, doing duty both Friday and Saturday night. On Sunday morning we recrossed the river and bivouacked near the hospitals."

Colonel Harker, commanding the brigade in which the 13th was serving, in his report says of the regiment at Stone river:

"The 13th Michigan, from their position, fired upon the enemy with telling effect, and having caused his ranks to waver, followed up the advantage with a charge, supported by the 51st Illinois, which had come to our relief. They completely routed the enemy. The 13th Michigan retook the two pieces of artillery abandoned by our battery, and captured fifty-eight prisoners. For this act of gallantry Colonel Shoemaker and his gallant regiment are deserving of much praise."

The gallant service of this regiment at Stone River, on December 31st, cannot be over-estimated, as it was pre-eminently prominent among the brave regiments that breasted the fearful current of disaster which was sweeping away the Federal right, fighting desperately in turning the tide of affairs in favor of the Union army, and during the following days of that great conflict never wavered in any position assigned it, and when the roll of the regiment was called at the close of the five days of this sanguinary strife, all answered to their names except the dead and wounded.

In the fearful struggle at Chicamauga this noble regiment, under command of Colonel J. B. Culver, displayed again its brilliant fighting qualities in the efficient service rendered on the 18th of September, while deployed as skirmishers, near Lee and Gordon's Mills, holding a position until 12 M., on the 19th, against a strong line of the enemy's skirmishers, supported by a section of artillery. On the 19th it rejoined its brigade and division some distance to the left of the Mills, executing the movement under a heavy fire of the enemy, on the double-quick, with the thermometer at ninety degrees above. Soon after the regiment charged in a handsome and gallant manner, checking the onset of the rebels, who were forcing back a part of the brigade. In this charge it lost heavily, including among the killed Captains D. B. Hosmer and Clark D. Fox, and Lieutenant Charles D. Hall; all fell while nobly battling with treason and rebellion. In the engagement the regiment went in with 217 officers and men, and lost 14 killed, 68 wounded, (of whom 11 died,) and 25 missing.

This regiment was serving in Georgia on the 1st of November, 1864, and on the 3d was at Tilton, when it received orders to proceed to Romeo, where it remained until the 7th, when it joined the army of General Sherman, at Kingston, and was assigned to 2d brigade, 1st division, 14th corps, and formed a part of the general army that "marched down to the sea." The regiment, with its brigade, reached Savannah on the 16th of December, and was on duty in the trenches before that city until the 21st, when the enemy evacuated the place. On January 17th, 1865, the regiment moved forward with the army on the march through the Carolinas, and was engaged at Catawba River, S. C., February 29th, and at Averysboro, N. C., March 16th, and again at Bentonville on the 19th, where it fought the enemy the entire day, sustaining a loss of 110 killed, wounded, and missing. Amongst the killed was its commanding officer, Colonel W. G. Eaton. Pending the negotiations attending the surrender of Johnston's army, the regiment was stationed on the Cape Fear river, twenty-six miles south of Raleigh, and on the 30th of April it started, with the army, homeward, reaching Richmond on the 7th of May, and Washington on the 19th, and on the 24th participated in the grand review of General Sherman's army at the National Capital.

NOTE.—Greeley, in "The American Conflict," says of the battle of Stone River: "Bradley's 6th Ohio Battery at one time lost two of its guns; but they were subsequently recaptured by the 13th Michigan." There was connected with the recapture of these guns an incident worth recording of Julius Lillie, Orderly Sergeant of Company E. Harker's brigade, except the 13th Michigan, had been driven off the field with heavy loss; Bradley's 6th Ohio Battery, attached to this brigade, retreated with a loss of two guns. The 13th Michigan, left alone, had nobly maintained their position until they had lost over one-third of their number, and were about being surrounded. Col. Shoemaker then ordered them to retire, but, after moving them a few rods through quite a dense undergrowth, he reformed them and ordered them to charge the advancing enemy, which they did, every man shouting and yelling like so many born devils. The rebels, ten times their number, not being able to see their strength for the intervening thicket, and supposing they had fallen into an ambuscade, broke and fled. The 13th pursued them entirely off the ground, over an open space, into a woods full half a mile from the place of the fight. The rebels fired as they retreated, but were so closely pursued they had no opportunity to form, and the 13th took over fifty prisoners, besides recapturing the two guns belonging to Bradley's battery. As the regiment, every man on the full run, approached the guns, several men sprung forward to be the first to reach them, but Sergeant Julius Lillie outstripped all competitors, and as he reached them slapped his hand on one of the guns; at that moment a shot from one of the retreating rebels struck him in the right side, and, probably from the position in which he was standing, passing along without cutting the inner coating of his intestines, came out about eight inches from its entrance, causing of course an ugly wound. This was on the afternoon of Wednesday, the 31st day of December, and although the regiment was under fire every hour of daylight from this time until Saturday night, and slept every night on their arms on the battle field, yet Lillie refused to leave his command and go to the hospital, but remained with his regiment during the whole period and would only allow himself to be relieved from duty after the enemy had evacuated Murfreesboro and victory was assured to our forces.

THE FOURTEENTH INFANTRY.

The 14th regiment moved from Ypsilanti on the 17th of April, 1862, in command of Colonel Robert P. Sinclair, of Grand Rapids, under whose direction it had been recruited, and joined the Western army at Pittsburg Landing, Tenn. It was under Pope in the advance on Corinth, and was engaged in repeated skirmishes with the enemy while in front of that stronghold. In November and December of that year it was stationed at Stone river, in command of Lieutenant-Colonel M. W. Quackenbush. On the 3d of January following it participated in the great battle at that point, having marched from Nashville during the night previous, through mud and rain, a distance of thirty miles.

On the 21st of May, 1864, the regiment was ordered to proceed to Bridgeport, Ala., and thence moved by forced marches to Dallas, Ga., where, joining the army under General Sherman on the 4th of June, the regiment participated in all the active movements of the campaign until the fall of Atlanta. It was engaged at Kenesaw Mountain on the 15th of June, and on the 5th and 6th of July it charged and drove the rebels from their rifle-pits at the Chattahoochie river, capturing a number of prisoners. Its casualties in the latter engagement were 9 killed and 35 wounded. On the 7th of August the regiment assisted in taking two lines of rebel works, and driving the enemy from the field, killing and wounding a number, and taking 92 prisoners, suffering a loss of 8 killed and 27 wounded. In this affair Lieutenant Joseph Kirk was mortally wounded and died next day.

The battle of Jonesboro, Ga., on September 1, 1864—the last of Sherman's great and brilliant operations around Atlanta, when he opened the gate of his great highway to the sea—and the important engagement at Bentonville, N. C., on the 19th and 20th of March, 1865—his last contest with the enemy on that remarkable and unequalled campaign which astonished the world—were the fields on which the 14th infantry gained much of its enviable reputation, by very prominently distinguishing itself in glorious achievements which added much to the success of these important affairs. The regiment was in the 14th corps, so conspicuously engaged at Jonesboro, and during that bloody conflict, while in command of Col. Henry R. Mizner, this gallant Michigan regiment charged the enemy with great enthusiasm, at fixed bayonets, first at quick, and then at double-quick, and without firing a gun or raising a shout carried the rebel works in its front, filled with the enemy, capturing Sweet's rebel battery of four 12-pounder Napoleon guns, shooting and bayoneting the artillerists at their guns, in the act of firing, and taking as prisoner General D. C. Govan, who surrendered his command to Sergeant Patrick Irwin, the first man inside the works. Govan had in his possession the sword of Major Cooledge, 16th U. S. infantry, who fell at Chicamauga. In the command surrendered were Captain Williams, A. A. A. G., Major Weeks, 2d Arkansas infantry, and three hundred enlisted men. During the charge the colors of the 1st Arkansas infantry were captured by Lieutenant Weatherspoon and Sergeant Smith, of company A, who killed one of the color-guard while in the act of firing upon Weatherspoon. Gaining the works, the colors of the regiment were gallantly planted on them by Sergeant Steiner, and were among the first placed on that rebel stronghold. After passing the first line of works, a second four-gun battery was captured, when one of the guns was instantly turned upon the fleeing enemy by Lieutenant Gifford, and a fire delivered with telling effect.

On November 1st the regiment, in command of Lieut.-Colonel George W. Grummond, broke camp at Rome, Ga., and commenced the grand march to Savannah, moving via Kingston and Atlanta, and thence through Milledgeville, destroying many miles of railroad; reaching Savannah on the 16th, it lay in front of that city until the 21st, when the enemy evacuated the place. At that point the regiment remained until January 20th following, when it moved forward with the army, on the march through the Carolinas, reaching Sister's Ferry on the 28th, where it remained ten days, assisting in repairing the roads on the opposite side of the Savannah river, which had become impassable. Having crossed the river on the evening of February 6th, the march through South Carolina was commenced on the 8th. Moving on what is called the Augusta road, and proceeding onward, crossed the Salkehatchie, South and North Edisto, Broad, Catawba, and Big Pedee rivers, arriving at Fayetteville, N. C., March 10th, the regiment having lost on the march down to that time twenty-two men, captured while foraging. Reaching Cape Fear river, it crossed on the 12th, the enemy's rear-guard picketing along a small stream, about one mile distant, over which there was a high bridge, the plank of which had been removed by the enemy. On approaching that point it was found to be held on the opposite side by two regiments of cavalry. The 14th Michigan was ordered to push forward and drive the enemy from his position, and establish his line one mile in advance. The night being very dark, the men were obliged to cross in single file on the timbers. They pushed across very rapidly, however, and engaged the enemy, driving him over two miles, capturing his camp and a large quantity of forage, killing one and taking two prisoners. The regiment established its line, and remained there until the 14th, when it was relieved by the advance of the 1st division. On the morning of the 15th the march was resumed. Skirmishing with the enemy was kept up the entire day, and until 10 o'clock next morning, when he made a decided stand near Averysboro, and a severe battle ensued. The 1st brigade, 2d division, of which the 14th Michigan formed a part, was ordered immediately to the front, and placed on the extreme left of the line, having to cross a deep and wide ravine in getting into position. The brigade was formed in two lines, the 17th New York and 14th Michigan composing the first line, and the 10th Michigan and 60th Illinois the second. The first, advancing under a severe fire, gallantly carried the first line of the enemy's works, taking a number of prisoners, but the enemy, becoming heavily reinforced, and after repeated attempts to carry the position, strongly supported by the second line, the men behaving exceedingly well, it was found impossible to dislodge him, the brigade holding its position until next morning, when the enemy abandoned his work, the regiment losing in the engagement twenty-two killed and wounded, including two officers wounded.

At Bentonville on the 19th and 20th of March, 1865, the regiment, then in command of Lieut. Col. George W. Grummond, was fiercely assaulted in hurriedly constructed works by a largely superior force, which it successfully repulsed, and then most gallantly charging over its own works captured most of the assaulting party; and soon afterwards, on ascertaining that a flanking force of the rebels had taken possession of the works the regiment had but just left, it was instantly faced by the rear rank, charged, and retook the works at the point of the bayonet. During these charges the regiment took 19 officers and 390 enlisted men prisoners, together with the colors of the 54th Virginia and 65th North Carolina regiments. The loss of the 14th in this engagement was 23 in killed and wounded and 4 in prisoners.

The successes of the 14th on these occasions were among the most glorious in the Sherman campaigns, illustrating most forcibly the heroism of the regiment and placing it squarely up to the high standard of Michigan troops.

THE FIFTEENTH INFANTRY.

The 15th, in command of Col. J. M. Oliver, by whom it was organized, first met the rebels at Shiloh on the 6th and 7th of April, 1862. Arriving there only the day before the battle, it next morning became hotly engaged, and was thus early initiated into the sad realities of war, and at a great sacrifice, losing in the engagements of both days two officers and thirty-one men killed and one officer and sixty-three privates wounded and seven missing. Capt. George A. Strong and Lieut. Malvin W. Dresser, two officers of much merit, being among the killed of the 6th. After the affair at Shiloh the regiment composed a part of the force under Gen. Halleck which compelled the rebels to abandon Corinth. The 15th was in General Rosecrans' army when his position at Corinth was assaulted by the rebel forces under Price in October, 1862. At that time the regiment, under command of Lieut. Col. McDermott, held the outpost of that army at Chewalla, on the Memphis and Charleston railroad, and about ten miles from Corinth, where it met and checked the advance of Price, and most signally made its mark as a most reliable and brave regiment. On the morning of the 1st of October the pickets of the 15th were driven in, the regiment holding the enemy in check during the day; in the evening was reinforced by the 14th Wisconsin and a section of a 12-pounder battery, the whole force in command of Colonel J. M. Oliver, of the 15th Michigan. The command fought during the 2d and 3d against overwhelming numbers, contesting every inch of ground, but falling back gradually upon Corinth, several times being completely flanked and obliged to retire on the double-quick, with the enemy on both flanks. It is claimed that the admirable disposition made by Col. Oliver of his force and the steadiness and gallantry of the men engaged delayed an army of 40,000 (or thereabout) at least twenty-four hours in making their main and final attack upon Corinth, thus enabling General Rosecrans to make the disposition of his forces which most successfully secured the repulse of the enemy and compelled him to make a most disastrous retreat.

November 2d, 1862, the 15th was ordered with its division to move from Corinth, where it had been stationed, to Wolf Creek. From that point the regiment proceeded to Grand Junction November 19th, to serve as garrison and provost guard. It was also employed while at Grand Junction in guarding the Memphis and Charleston railroad and in scouting after guerillas. The regiment remained at Grand Junction and at La Grange until June 5th, 1863, when it was ordered to Vicksburg, Miss., with the 1st division, 16th corps, to which it had been attached since January 1st. Arriving at the mouth of the Yazoo, June 11th, the 15th proceeded up the river and disembarked at Hayne's Bluff. Having been attached temporarily to the 9th corps, it participated with it in the advance on Jackson on the 4th of July. The Big Black river was crossed on the 6th (this regiment leading) on rafts and by swimming, and until the arrival of the national forces before Jackson the regiment was engaged in skirmishing with the rebels. It participated in the movements of the 9th corps until the enemy were driven across the Pearl river on the 17th. On the 23d it began its march back to the Big Black. It was here attached to the 2d brigade, 4th division, 15th army corps. The 15th corps having been ordered to reinforce the Army of the Cumberland, the regiment arrived at Memphis, Tenn., October 8th, and at Corinth, Miss., on the 17th. On the following day it proceeded to Iuka, where it remained until October 25th, and on the 1st of November it arrived at Florence, Ala.

On the 4th of May, 1864, the 15th arrived at Chattanooga from Michigan, where it had been on veteran furlough. Being encamped at Rossville, near that point, it moved to participate in the Georgia campaign, taking part in the engagements that occurred during the movement on Resaca. On the 17th the command marched to Dallas via Adairsville. Entrenching it remained in its works, with occasional skirmishing, until the 1st of June, when it moved to near New Hope Church, and on the 5th to Ackworth. On the 10th the regiment marched to Big Shanty, and on the 15th moved to the right of the line, and with its brigade supported a force which attacked and drove the enemy from their works. Marching on the 19th, command moved to the right of the railroad facing Kenesaw Mountain, where it remained un il the 25th. Moving to Marietta on the 3d of July, the regiment marched thence on the 4th, and on the 8th arrived at Nickajack creek and entrenched in view of the enemy's works. Marching via Marietta to Rossville, the regiment crossed to the south side of the Chattahoochie river on the 14th. On the 17th it moved to Cross Keys, and on the 18th marched toward Decatur, going into line of battle, though not becoming engaged. On the 20th it moved forward via Decatur several miles, and on that and the following day engaged in skirmishing with the enemy.

On the 21st the regiment, in command of Lieut. Col. F. S. Hutchinson, became eminently distinguished, rendering most gallant and valuable service. Early on the morning of that day the rebels attacked in flank and rear the 17th corps, which was on the left of the 15th corps, driving it back with much loss. About 1 o'clock the 15th Michigan was ordered to fill a gap on the extreme left of its corps, about one mile distant from the position it then occupied. The regiment moved on the double-quick, and upon coming into line near the position indicated found it in possession of the enemy; it, however, moved gallantly forward in line, striking the enemy upon the flank, driving him from his position, taking 17 officers and 167 men as prisoners and capturing the colors of the 5th Confederate infantry, and also the colors of the 17th and 18th Texas, (consolidated,) and suffering a loss of four killed and six wounded. This was the advance of two rebel divisions which were massed in a wood but a short distance in the rear. The promptitude with which the movement was executed by the 15th deterred the remainder of the rebel force from making a forward movement, and thus prevented the enemy from breaking our lines, and probably averted disaster from that part of the field.

On the 27th following the regiment proceeded to the extreme right of the army. While advancing in line on the 28th the enemy attacked and were driven off with heavy loss, their dead and wounded being left on the field. The casualties in the regiment during the action were 38 wounded.

During the remainder of the month and until the 26th of August the regiment was engaged in the trenches before Atlanta, skirmishing almost daily with the rebel troops. On the 28th it moved on the Atlanta and Montgomery railroad, which, on the following day, it assisted in destroying. On the 30th the regiment marched to the east side of Flint river, near Jonesboro', and entrenched. An assault made by the enemy on the 31st was repelled with heavy loss. On the 1st of September the skirmishers advanced and captured a number of prisoners at Jonesboro'. Moved forward to Lovejoy's Station on the 2d, the regiment entrenched and there remained until the 5th, having continued skirmishing with the enemy. On the 6th the command withdrew to Jonesboro'. On the 8th it proceeded to East Point, where it remained during the month. Leaving East Point on the 4th of October the regiment marched, via Marietta, Altoona, Kingston, Rome,

Calhoun, Resaca, Snake Creek Gap, Lafayette, Summersville, and Galesville, in Georgia, and Little River, King's Hill, Cedar Bluff, and Cave Springs, in Alabama, and participated in the skirmishes and engagements that occurred during the pursuit of the rebel army under Hood in Northern Georgia and Alabama, the regiment marching during this month two hundred miles.

On November 1st, 1864, it left Cave Springs, Ala., in the 3d brigade, 2d division, 15th corps, moving via Marietta and Powder Springs, Georgia, to Atlanta, and soon after commenced the march with Gen. Sherman's army to Savannah and thence to Washington, having been engaged with the enemy at various points on that remarkable march.

Captain Charles H. Barnaby was killed in action before Atlanta August 13, 1865.

THE SIXTEENTH INFANTRY.

The 16th was raised and organized during the summer of 1861 by Col. T. B. W. Stockton, and for sometime was known as "Stockton's Independent Regiment," afterwards as the 16th Michigan infantry, which accounts for its having so high a numerical designation. This regiment commenced its battles with the siege of Yorktown in April, 1862, and ended them at Appomattox Court-house in April, 1865, having passed through the various campaigns of the Army of the Potomac with much credit and a glorious celebrity, serving during the whole war in the 3d brigade, 1st division, 5th corps.

Among its various battles none perhaps appear more prominent in its history than Gaines' Mill and Peeble's Farm. In the former engagement, on the 27th of June, 1862, the 3d brigade was commanded by Col. Stockton, and in the early part of the day the 16th lay in reserve, and was held in that position under a heavy fire from the enemy's works on the Richmond side of the Chicahominy, and the rebel lines in front and left, until about 2 P. M., when the rebels made a desperate advance in several columns deep upon the Federal lines. The 16th was ordered to the front to assist in repelling the attack, and went in gallantly on the double-quick under a very destructive fire from the rebel batteries, driving the enemy in its front back to his former position. The regiment then formed in the brigade line on the extreme left of the corps, holding the position under constant fighting until about 5 P. M., losing heavily. About this time the enemy massed on their right and opposite the front of the brigade, and threw column after column in, causing the troops on the right to break, whereupon the 16th was ordered to fall back to the river; but not thinking of "retreat," faced about and stood its ground until overwhelmed by numbers and compelled to *retreat* to the river. Here the gallant Major N. E. Welch, in command of the regiment, and his brave officers rallied their men, and with stragglers from other regiments, numbering in all about 1,000, again charged over dead and dying comrades, until their line met "Jackson's corps," and where, within short range, the rebels opened upon the whole line with fearful effect, mowing the men down like grass, compelling the brigade to fall back, the 16th losing three officers and forty-six men killed, six officers and one hundred and ten enlisted men wounded, and two officers and fifty-three enlisted men missing. Among the killed were Captain Thomas C. Carr and Lieutenants Byron McGraw and Richard Williams, officers of much promise and courage. The few that were left succeeded in reaching the opposite side of the Chicahominy, leaving Col. Stockton, who from exhaustion and the loss of his horse, which had been shot under him, and Captains Mott and Fisher, together with Surgeon Wixom, prisoners in the hands of the enemy.

The regiment was engaged at Malvern Hill July 1st, with a loss of forty-two in killed, wounded, and missing. In August following it joined Pope's army at Fredericksburg, and fought at Bull Run on the 30th of that month, sustaining a loss of three officers and thirteen men killed, four officers and fifty-nine men wounded, with seventeen missing. Captain R. W. Ransom, Lieutenants Michael Chittick and John Ruby were the officers killed.

Leaving Harper's Ferry on the 1st of November, 1862, this regiment arrived at Falmouth on the 23d. Crossing the Rappahannock on the 12th of December, it participated with the Army of the Potomac in the battle of Fredericksburg, losing three killed, twenty wounded, and eight missing. The regiment crossed the Rappahannock and the Rapidan, and from the 2d to the 5th of May, 1863, was engaged at the battle of Chancellorsville, with a loss of one killed and six wounded. Marching with the army in June, on the 21st it was engaged in the battle of Middleburg, commanded by Col. N. E. Welch, capturing from the enemy a piece of artillery and nineteen officers and men, with a loss on the part of the regiment of nine wounded, including Captain Judd M. Mott (mortally) who died June 28th following.

The 16th, by a series of forced marches, arrived at Gettysburg, Penn., on the 1st of July, and on the 2d, 3d, and 4th, it participated in the battles of that place, sustaining a loss of three officers and twenty-one men killed, two officers and thirty-four men wounded, and two men missing. Lieuts. Brown, Jewett, and Borden were among the killed. July 5th, the regiment engaged in the pursuit of the enemy, arriving at Williamsport, Md., on the 11th. It crossed the Potomac at Berlin on the 17th, and on the 23d was at the battle of Wapping Heights, though not actually engaged. Participating in the movements of the army in October, on the 10th it crossed the Rappahannock, recrossed on the 11th, and as skirmishers advanced to Brandy Heights, but did not become engaged. Falling back with the army, on the 23d it marched to Auburn.

In November the regiment was encamped on the Orange and Alexandria railroad, and on the 7th again moved forward with the army, and during the movement to the Rappahannock it participated in the capture of the enemy's works on the left bank of that stream, losing three in wounded. On the 26th it was in the advance on Mine Run.

Engaging in the campaign of 1864, on the 4th of May the regiment crossed the Rapidan at Germania Ford, in command of Major R. T. Elliott. On the 5th it was detailed to guard the wagon train at Wyckoff Ford. On the 6th and 7th the regiment participated in the battle of the Wilderness, without loss on the 6th, but on the second day losing thirty-five in killed and wounded. On the morning of the 8th the regiment proceeded by a forced march to Spottsylvania Court-house. During the evening of the 8th, while attempting to pass an almost impassable swamp, a portion of the regiment was attacked, the enemy making an attempt to capture that portion engaged, but the rebels were thrown into confusion by its fire, during which a charge was made and a rebel colonel and a large number of men were taken prisoners. The loss to the regiment was small, and was mainly in prisoners, who were subsequently recaptured by our cavalry. The regiment remained in the neighborhood of the Spottsylvania Court-house until the 21st, when it moved with its corps toward the North Anna river. On the morning of the 22d, while acting as advance guard for its corps, the regiment encountered the rear guard of the enemy near Polecat creek. Four companies were deployed as skirmishers, who, advancing, drove the enemy from their position, and captured a large number of prisoners. On the 24th it forded the North Anna river. The enemy having attacked and caused a portion of the line to retire, the 16th, with other forces, was ordered to regain possession of the ground. The movement, although made under a very heavy fire, was successful, the enemy being driven back with great loss. On the 24th the regiment moved to a point on the Virginia Central railroad, and on the 25th to near Little river. Recrossing the North Anna on the 26th and 27th, it proceeded by forced marches toward the Pamunkey river, which it crossed at Hanovertown on the morning of the 28th, and went into line of battle on the South creek, throwing up a line of breastworks. On the following morning the regiment moved to near Tolopotamy creek. On the 30th it again moved forward. During the afternoon, the army having become engaged, the regiment was ordered into position on the left of the line. Though exposed in an open field to a raking fire, the men stood their ground with great pertinacity, protecting themselves by throwing up earthworks with their hands, bayonets, and tin plates. Major Elliott, while leading the regiment, was here killed, when Captain George H. Swan assumed command. The enemy were finally driven back, and the regiment held the ground during the night. On the 1st of June the 16th drove the enemy from the rifle-pits, which it succeeded in holding against all efforts to retake them. On the 2d, 3d, and 4th, the 16th was engaged in the vicinity of Bethesda Church. On the 5th it moved to near Cold Harbor, and on the 6th to Dispatch Station. June 13th, while in command of Captain Guy Fuller, it crossed the Chicahominy at Long Bridge, *en route* for the James river, which it crossed on the 16th, arriving in front of Petersburg on the following day. From this time to the 15th of August, when it was placed in reserve, the regiment was employed in the trenches in front of Petersburg. It participated in the movement, on the 18th of August, on the Weldon railroad, and remained in this vicinity, constructing and occupying a portion of the line of defences, until the 30th of September.

At Peeble's Farm, or Poplar Grove Church, the regiment also became most signally distinguished. At 3 o'clock A. M., September 30, 1864, the 5th corps moved to the left, until it reached near an old church in the woods, where sharp skirmishing began. The 3d brigade was got into line for a charge—the 83d Pennsylvania, temporarily in command of Major B. F. Partridge, of the 16th Michigan; 32d Massachusetts, commanded by Colonel Edmunds, and the 16th Michigan, commanded by the lamented Welch, advancing on the works on Peeble's Farm, the 16th Michigan having the centre, striking the angle of the fort first, climbing the works, and engaging the enemy in a hand to hand fight for some time, while the other regiments came in on the right and left, and thus carried the works, taking all the rebels who defended them, and capturing the guns, but losing in the 16th Michigan ten killed and forty-two wounded, including the commander, Colonel N. E. Welch, who was instantly killed while going over the enemy's works, sword in hand, leading on his regiment in that dashing charge.

Major Partridge received a bullet through his neck and two other wounds while gallantly leading the 83d Pennsylvania to the attack on the works.

During the months of October and November the regiment lay in the trenches near Poplar Grove Church, Va., and in December accompanied its corps on the raid to Bellfield, where it assisted in destroying about sixteen miles of railroad. It was in the trenches before Petersburg during the month of January, 1865, and on February 6th and 7th, in command of Colonel Partridge, was engaged with the enemy at the battle of Dabney's Mills, or Hatcher's Run, where it lost heavily; on March 25th at Hatcher's Run; at White Oak Swamp on the 29th, at Quaker Road on the 31st, and at Five Forks on April 1st, and, following Lee's army until its surrender, on the 5th it was engaged with the enemy at Amelia Court-house, on the 6th at High Bridge, and at Appomattox Court-house on the 9th, thus participating in the last day's fighting of the gallant Army of the Potomac.

NOTE.—At the battle of Fredericksburg in December, 1862, after fighting all day and part of the night, the troops lay down on their arms and were soon asleep. The ammunition wagon of a Michigan regiment coming up, the mules hungry and thirsty, being halted near the sleeping place of the Colonel, gave one or more of their peculiar howls, which suddenly awoke the Colonel, who, much provoked at being thus so unceremoniously disturbed, and in his bewildered condition thinking that the noise was made by the musicians of the regiment, called to his Adjutant to "put these damned buglers under arrest and send them to the rear; they will jeopardize the safety of the whole army."

John Steele, a private in Company K, 16th Michigan, having his right arm shot off at Middleburg, Capt. Hill said to him, a few minutes after: "John, you cannot carry a musket any more." John replied, with tears in his eyes: "No, Captain, but I can carry the colors, can't I?"

While the 16th Michigan was engaged at Cold Harbor, a Maryland regiment broke while under fire, and when falling back was checked and held by the 16th. The Colonel of the regiment struggled to rally it, but without success, when he hurriedly advanced to Col. Partridge, and, with tears streaming down his manly face, exclaimed: "Colonel, would to God that I commanded a Michigan regiment!" He had hardly said these words when a rifle bullet passed through his body killing him instantly.

THE SEVENTEENTH INFANTRY.

The 17th Michigan, the gallant and celebrated "Stonewall" regiment of Wilcox's division, 9th corps, was organized, drilled, and disciplined at Detroit Barracks by General James E. Pittman, late Inspector General of Michigan. A short time before it left the State Colonel W. H. Withington was commissioned as its colonel, and it went to the field under his command August 27th, 1862, going immediately into the Maryland campaign under McClellan. In a little more than two weeks after leaving the State Col. Withington and his regiment met the enemy in the sanguinary and important action of South Mountain. On the evening of the 13th of September the regiment marched from Frederick City, where it had bivouacked the night before, with the rest of the 9th corps. It marched out on the National Turnpike in the direction of South Mountain, and about midnight rested for a few hours not many miles from Middletown. Before daybreak on the morning of the 14th Middletown was passed, and the base of the mountain reached about 9 A. M. The enemy was found in force on each side of a gap, holding each crest of the mountain, and strongly posted behind the stone fences and other available shelter, with their batteries in commanding positions enfilading the main road. The regiment was ordered to move off the main road and advance up the Sharpsburg road. This movement was executed by the regiment in common with the rest of Wilcox's division, which had proceeded far up the road toward the crest of the mountain, and moving to the support of a section of Cooke's battery, which had been sent up the mountain to open on the enemy's guns on the right of the gap, was about to deploy, when the rebels suddenly opened at two hundred yards with a battery throwing shot and shell, killing several in the regiment and driving back the battery, the cannoneers, with their horses and limbers, rushing through the dense ranks, causing a temporary panic among some of the troops that might have resulted in the loss of the guns had the enemy taken advantage of it. The 17th promptly changed front under a heavy fire of shot and shell and moved out with the 79th New York to protect the battery, and lay in line of battle until nearly 4 o'clock P. M. exposed to a severe fire from Drayton's brigade of South Carolina infantry in the immediate front, without being able to reply to it, and having grown impatient of delay and anxious to advance, the order to charge upon the enemy was received with enthusiastic cheers. The regiment, being on the extreme right of Wilcox's division, moved rapidly forward through an open field upon the enemy's position under a storm of lead from the stone fences in front and from the batteries on the right, with cheer after cheer sent up in defiant answer to the rebel "yell," the 17th most daringly advanced to within easy musket range without firing a shot, when it opened a murderous fire upon the enemy, which was kept up for a short time, steadily advancing, the extreme right of the regiment swinging round and getting an enfilading fire upon the rebels entrenched behind the stone walls. Unable to stand this destructive fire they broke in confusion, the left of the regiment gallantly charging over the walls with shouts of triumph, pursuing the fleeing remnants of Drayton's brigade over the crest and far down the slope of the mountain, gaining and holding the key-point of the battle. The splendid conduct and extraordinary services of the 17th in this action gave the regiment at the time much celebrity, and has since been given in history as among the most brilliant achievements of the war. The 17th suffered severely, losing Lieut. George Galligan and 26 men killed and 114 wounded.

In a recent account given by Col. F. W. Swift, then a captain, of the part taken by his regiment in that battle, he says:

"Our men having been so long exposed to the fire of the enemy, without being able to reply, had grown impatient at the delay, and the order to move forward and charge upon the enemy was received with shouts of enthusiasm. We moved out from our sheltered position through an open field and upon the enemy's position, exposed to a storm of lead from behind the stone fences in front and from the enemy's batteries on the right. Our regiment was on the right of the division, which was composed mostly of old troops, and our men moved upon the enemy as if jealous of the laurels their veteran coadjutors might win. With cheer after cheer, sent up in defiant answer to the rebel 'yell,' they advanced to within easy musket shot, when they opened a murderous fire upon the enemy, which was kept up for some time, the regiment steadily advancing, and the extreme right of the regiment swinging around and getting an enfilading fire upon the rebels entrenched behind the two stone walls on the left of the road. Unable to stand this murderous fire the enemy broke in dismay, the left of the regiment charging with shouts of triumph over the walls and pursuing the remnant of Drayton's brigade over the crest and far down the slope of the mountain, thus gaining and holding the key-point of the battle."

Three days afterwards, at Antietam, it was again in battle, sustaining a further loss of eighteen killed and eighty-seven wounded. The next day it was in the front skirmishing with the retreating enemy, and had one man killed.

On the 19th of March, 1863, the 9th corps, then stationed in Kentucky, was ordered to reinforce General Grant in Mississippi, and the regiment, in command of Col. C. Luce, left with it to engage in that campaign, and participated in the advance on Jackson by Gen. Sherman, engaging the enemy on the 11th of June with light loss.

After the campaign in Mississippi the corps returned to Kentucky and engaged in the movements of the Army of the Ohio in East Tennessee in September and October following.

With its division it moved from Knoxville to Blue Springs, but did not participate in the engagement at that place. Returning to Knoxville on the 14th of October, it marched from thence on the 20th, and proceeded via Loudon to Lenoir. The regiment remained at that point until November 14th, 1863, when it marched to the Tennessee river, below Loudon, to oppose the advance of the rebels under Longstreet, then moving on Knoxville. It lay under arms during the night, and on the following morning commenced falling back, closely followed by the rebel forces. It continued to retreat on the 16th with its corps, its brigade moving in the rear of the army and the regiment acting as the rear guard. While crossing Turkey creek, near Campbell's Station, the enemy attacked in force, and a severe engagement ensued. In this action the loss of the regiment was seven killed, nineteen wounded, and ten missing. During the night of the 16th the regiment moved with the army to Knoxville, assisting actively in the defence of that town while besieged by the enemy. On the 20th of November the regiment charged the enemy's line and destroyed several houses that were occupied by rebel sharp-shooters. Lieut. Josiah Billingsly and one man were killed by the enemy's shells while the regiment was returning to the trenches. On the 24th Lieut. Col. Loren L. Comstock, then in command of the regiment, was killed. On the night of the 28th the skirmish line of the regiment was driven in and sixteen men were captured by the rebels.

Returning to Virginia and with its corps joining the Army of the Potomac and engaging in the great campaign of 1864, it crossed the Rapidan at Germania Ford on the 5th of May, and on the 6th encountered the enemy at the Wilderness, losing seven killed and thirty-nine wounded. On the 8th the regiment moved via Chancellorsville towards Spottsylvania. On the morning of the 9th the division of General Wilcox, to which the regiment belonged, moved upon the enemy in the vicinity of Spottsylvania Court-house and found him in force, occupying a commanding position on the Ny river. The 2d brigade was ordered to cross the river and feel for the enemy. Romer's New York battery being brought into position opened fire; the 17th, commanded by Col. C. Luce, was temporarily detached from the 1st brigade to support it. Meanwhile the 1st and 2d brigades, having become engaged, found the enemy in superior force, and two regiments had been repulsed with considerable loss from a very important and commanding position, leaving many of their wounded on the field. The 2d brigade, which was on the extreme right of the division, being left in great danger of being flanked and cut off, its commander sent back to division headquarters for reinforcements, the 17th was ordered to advance for that purpose; the order was promptly obeyed, and the regiment bravely crossed the stream on double-quick, and advanced rapidly up the road to the position held by the 2d brigade and formed on its left.

It was soon ascertained that the enemy, who it seems had retired from the crest of the hill from which they had repulsed our troops, were again advancing in force for the double purpose of gaining the crest and flanking the division; and it became necessary for the brigade to check the advance instantly, and a movement was immediately commenced for that purpose. The 17th, commanded by Col. F. W. Swift, making a half wheel, advanced at double-quick up the hill and occupied the crest just as a brigade of rebel troops were advancing up the other slope. The regiment promptly opened a well-directed volley upon them, doing great execution, and in spite of the frantic efforts of their officers they broke and fled in great disorder, leaving many of their dead and wounded, thus securing by this well-timed and rapid movement a very important position, which the regiment held and fortified, thereby saving the dead and wounded of our troops, which had been repulsed in the first attack, from falling into the hands of the enemy, and at the same time relieving the 2d brigade from its perilous position, and which was handsomely acknowledged by Col. Christ commanding.

In the engagement, out of 225 the regiment lost 23 killed, 73 wounded, and 93 as prisoners. Among the killed were Captain John S. Vreeland and Lieutenant Alfred E. Canfield.

During the attack of the rebels on Fort Steadman in the line of works before Petersburg, on March 25, 1865, the regiment was advanced as skirmishers, and succeeded in repelling those of the enemy, taking sixty-five prisoners, the regiment losing one killed and two wounded.

General Wilcox, in his report of the part taken by the 1st division, 9th corps, at South Mountain, says of the 17th Michigan in that engagement:

"I planted a section of Cook's battery near the turn of the road (Sharpsburg) and opened fire on the enemy's battery across the main pike. After a few good shots the enemy unmasked a battery on his left, over Shiver's Gap, from a small field enveloped by woods. He threw canister and shell, and drove Cook's cannoneers and drivers down the road with their limbers; Cook gallantly remained with his guns. [Cook here lost one man killed, four wounded, and two horses killed.] The attack was so sudden, the whole division being under fire—a flank fire—that a temporary panic ensued until I caused the 79th New York, Lieutenant Colonel Morrison, and 17th Michigan, Colonel Withington, on the extreme left, to draw across the road facing the enemy, who were so close that we expected a charge, to take Cook's battery. The 79th and 17th here deserve credit for their coolness and firmness in rallying and changing front under a heavy fire.

"I received orders from Generals Reno and McClellan to silence the enemy's batteries at all hazards. Sent picket report to Reno, and was making disposition to charge—moving 17th Michigan so as to cross the hollow and flank the enemy's guns—when the enemy charged out of the woods on their side, directly upon our front, in a long heavy line, extending beyond our left to Cox's right. I instantly gave the command, 'Forward!' and we met them near the foot of the hill, the 45th Pennsylvania in front. The 17th Michigan rushed down into the hollow, faced to the left, leaped over a stone fence, and took them in flank. Some of the supporting regiments, over the slope of the hill, fired over the heads of those in front, and after a severe contest of some minutes, the enemy were repulsed, followed by our troops to the opposite slope and woods, forming their own position.

"The 17th Michigan, Col. Withington, performed a feat that may vie with any recorded in the annals of war, and set an example to the oldest troops.

"This regiment had not been organized a single month, and was composed of raw levies."

In General McClellan's report the regiment is spoken of as follows:

"General Wilcox praises very highly the conduct of the 17th Michigan in this advance, a regiment which had been organized scarcely a month, but which charged the enemy's flank in a manner worthy of veteran troops."

The New York press at the time made the following comment on the part taken by the 17th at South Mountain:

"The enemy, as usual, sought every advantage, particularly that of numerous stone fences, behind which they assailed our men fiercely. But the impetuous charges of some of our regiments, particularly that of the 17th Michigan, but two weeks from home, carried everything before it, and the dead bodies of the enemy on that mountain crest lay thick enough for stepping-stones. The greatest slaughter at *this* point was among General Drayton's brigade, composed mainly of South Carolinians and some Georgians. Nearly the whole of this brigade was either killed, wounded, or captured."

Extract from the report of Captain F. W. Swift, covering operations of his regiment on November 16th, 20th, and 25th, 1863:

"On the 16th we marched for Knoxville. Our regiment being detached as rear guard, was attacked by the enemy's advance guard about half-past 9 A. M., near Campbell's Station, and after severe fighting through the day, we retired during the night to Knoxville. Lieut. A. P. Stevens was mortally wounded, and died at Knoxville December 11th following.

"On the night of the 20th the regiment was ordered to burn a house occupied by the enemy's sharpshooters. This was done successfully; but while returning to camp, Lieut. Josiah Billingsly was killed by a shell from one of the enemy's guns.

"On the 25th a musket ball from the enemy's skirmish line struck Lieutenant-Colonel Comstock, wounding him so severely that he died the same evening."

THE EIGHTEENTH INFANTRY.

In the summer of 1864 the 18th Michigan, a regiment composed of as fine and intelligent a body of men as went to the field during the entire war, was known wherever it served as one of the best disciplined, as well as one of the most reliable in the service.

Its rendezvous was at Hillsdale, and for the purpose of organization the camp was placed in charge of Hon. Henry Waldron. On the 4th of September the regiment left Hillsdale, in command of Colonel Charles C. Doolittle, under orders to report at Cincinnati.

On the 1st of November, 1862, this regiment was stationed at Lexington, Ky., and remained at that point until February 21, 1863, when it marched toward Danville, arriving on the 22d. On the 24th, with the forces under General Carter, it retreated from Danville to the Kentucky river, skirmishing with the rebels under General Pegram during the retreat. On the 28th the regiment joined in the pursuit of Pegram, following the rebels as far as Buck Creek, making a long and rapid march, partly over a rough, mountainous road. On April 2d it returned to Stanford. On the 7th it was ordered to Lebanon, and thence proceeded by railroad to Nashville, arriving at Nashville April 14th.

The regiment was stationed at this point, doing provost guard duty, until the 11th of June, 1864. On the 12th it arrived at Decatur, Ala., where it formed part of the garrison. On the 28th it made part of a force which surprised the camp of Paterson's brigade of rebel cavalry, at Pond Springs, Ala., capturing all their camp equipage, wagons, ambulances, and commissary stores, with some prisoners. On the 25th of July the regiment assisted in routing the same rebel brigade at Cortland, Ala. In both of these expeditions the regiment was in the advance, and was the only infantry engaged. On the 1st of September it left Decatur to reinforce the garrison at Athens, Ala., against a threatened attack by General Wheeler, then engaged in a raid through Tennessee. It arrived in Athens just in time to prevent the command of the rebel General Roddy from entering and pillaging the town. The regiment remained at Athens until the 8th, when it joined Colonel Streight's brigade, of General Steadman's command, then in pursuit of Wheeler, and marched to Shoal Creek, within seven miles of Florence, Ala. Being in the advance, it here overtook and skirmished with Wheeler's rear guard. The pursuit being abandoned, the regiment returned to camp at Decatur, September 11th.

On the 24th of September following a detachment of the regiment, consisting of two hundred and thirty-one officers and men, under Captain Weatherhead, of the 18th, with a detail of one hundred and fifty men from the 102d Ohio, the whole commanded by Colonel Elliott, of that regiment, left Decatur to reinforce the garrison of Athens against an attack from the forces under the rebel General Forrest. When within two miles of that place, they were met by a force of the enemy, since ascertained to be about four thousand strong. They fought their way through in the most gallant manner, and, after five hours of hard fighting, during which they had expended all their ammunition, and having got within sight of the fort, found it in possession of the enemy, it having been surrendered but a short time before, and being overwhelmed by the superior force of the enemy, they were compelled to give up the contest. Only one officer and seventeen men escaped; the others were either killed, wounded, or captured. The determined fighting and gallant conduct of these detachments is acknowledged not to have been excelled by any troops during the war.

At the time of the advance of General Hood's army upon Nashville in 1864, the regiment formed a part of the garrison of Decatur, the whole force of the post being in command of Colonel Doolittle, and on the 26th, 27th, 28th, and 29th of October, the 18th in command of Lieutenant-Colonel Hulbard, participated in the defence of that post against the rebel army of Tennessee, estimated variously at thirty or forty thousand, under General Hood. The place was ably and gallantly defended and the assault most bravely repelled by Colonel Doolittle, with his small force, having on the first day only fifteen hundred men, on the second twenty-five hundred, and five thousand on the last day. During the attack, Captain Moore, of the 18th, with about fifty men, was sent out to dislodge a line of the enemy's sharp-shooters, who had established themselves in the rifle-pits, within three hundred yards of our works. This movement was executed in fine style, under a galling fire from the enemy's main line, which was not over five hundred yards distant, Captain Moore driving them from their cover and bringing in five officers and one hundred and fifteen men as prisoners. This brilliant exploit of Captain Moore and his men has probably not been surpassed for daring bravery throughout the war. On these occasions the 18th was most signally distinguished, and while faithfully illustrating the reliable and superior fighting qualities of the regiment, they will also be recognized as prominent affairs in its history.

On the 1st of November, 1864, this regiment was in garrison at Decatur, Ala., where it remained until the 25th, when the evacuation of the line of the Memphis and Charleston railroad, from Decatur to Stevenson, was commenced. Then it left Decatur, marching along the line of that railroad to Stevenson, a distance of eighty miles, reaching that point December 2d, where it was employed building fortifications until the 19th.

when it was ordered back to Decatur, via the Tennessee river. On the 23d the regiment was landed at Whitesboro, and marched to Huntsville, to aid in repelling a threatened attack by Forrest, and on the 24th returned to Whitesboro and re-embarked for Decatur, arriving there on the 28th. It remained at that point, doing garrison duty, until the 11th of January, 1865, when it proceeded by rail to Huntsville, and was there engaged on post duty. On June 20th the regiment was ordered to Nashville for muster out.

THE NINETEENTH INFANTRY.

The 19th was raised in the counties of Branch, St. Joseph, Cass, Berrien, Kalamazoo, Van Buren, and Allegan. Its camp was at Dowagiac, and was commanded by Colonel Henry C. Gilbert, who went into the field as colonel of the regiment, and nobly met his death for his country while leading his regiment upon a rebel battery at Resaca.

It broke camp at Dowagiac on the 14th of September, 1862, and took its route to Cincinnati, and thence to Nicholasville, Ky.

On the 1st of January, 1863, this regiment was stationed at Danville, and belonged to the Army of Kentucky. This army, having been transferred to the Department of the Cumberland as a "reserve corps," the 19th moved with its brigade to Nashville, where it arrived February 7th, proceeding thence to Franklin. On the 4th of March, with 600 cavalry and 200 additional infantry, it took part with its brigade in a reconnoissance in force. After a march of four miles, skirmishing commenced with the enemy's scouts and advanced pickets, but the rebels retiring, the brigade encamped, the 19th having lost in the skirmish one wounded. The march having been resumed on the following day, the enemy were met in force at Spring Hill, near Thompson's Station. It was then serving in Colonel Coburn's brigade, of General Baird's division, Army of Kentucky.

On March 4th the brigade, composed of the 33d and 85th Indiana, 22d Wisconsin, and 19th Michigan, numbering in all about 1,587 men, strengthened by 200 of the 124th Ohio, with detachments of three regiments of cavalry, about 600 strong, and one battery of six guns, left Franklin to make a reconnoissance in force on the Columbia pike. About four miles out, the scouts and advance pickets of the enemy were met, when sharp skirmishing commenced, in which the 19th participated with slight loss. In the skirmish the enemy was driven back, with a loss of fifteen killed and wounded. Moving forward, he was again encountered at a short distance, but night coming on, the force went into camp.

Early on the morning of the 5th the march was resumed, leaving the 124th Ohio in charge of the wagon train. After marching about two miles the cavalry met the enemy's pickets, and a heavy skirmish was continued until the command came in sight of Thompson's Station, the enemy falling back. Advancing a short distance, and where the railroad joins the pike, the enemy opened fire with a heavy battery. Colonel Coburn immediately formed his line, and ordered a section of the battery to occupy a hill on the left of the pike, sending the 19th Michigan and 22d Wisconsin to support it. The 33d and 85th Indiana, with the other guns of the battery, took position on a hill on the right. The enemy had two batteries on a range of hills three-quarters of a mile in front, and south of the position occupied by the Union troops. The 33d and 85th Indiana made a demonstration on the left of the enemy to draw him out, or charge his batteries, according to circumstances. This was commenced and continued under a most galling fire from the enemy's batteries. Upon reaching the station, the skirmishers unmasked two whole brigades of dismounted rebel cavalry posted behind stone walls and other defences. It being impossible to advance farther under the incessant and severe fire, the regiments were ordered to retire to their former position on the hill, supported by two companies of cavalry; but for some reason or other the cavalry did not accompany them. No sooner had the two regiments commenced to fall back than they were pursued by two rebel regiments, one from Arkansas and the other a Texan, both firing rapid volleys into the retiring ranks, and at the same time were under fire from the rebel batteries. As soon as they reached the hill they faced about and drove the enemy in turn in double-quick, killing Colonel Earle, of Arkansas. The rebels again rallied, and charged desperately, but were driven. It then became evident that Colonel Coburn had encountered the entire cavalry of Bragg's army, commanded by General Van Dorn, about 18,000 strong, in six brigades, under the command of Generals Forrest, Wheeler, French, Armstrong, Jackson, Martin, and Crosby.

The rebels then advanced upon the left, where were posted the 19th Michigan and 22d Wisconsin. These regiments opened fire upon the enemy and held him in check for some twenty minutes. At the time the left was first attacked, that portion of the battery there stationed, hurriedly left that part of the field without orders, leaving the two regiments without artillery to assist them in repelling the enemy, then charging desperately. At the same time Lieut. Col. Bloodgood, of the 22d Wisconsin, with three companies of that regiment, left the field without orders, moving off by the left flank, and joining the retreating cavalry and artillery. Forrest checked in his advance, made a circuit with his whole force, beyond the ground occupied by Coburn, to the east, with the intention to turn his left flank. The 19th and 22d was then moved on the west side of the pike, leaving the 33d and 85th to protect the hill on its south face. The four regiments had scarcely formed line, lying down behind the crest of the hill, when Armstrong's brigade charged from the east and the Texans from the south, when a severe contest ensued, and the fighting became terrific. Three times the rebels gallantly charged up the hill from the east, and thrice were they forced back. In one of their charges the 19th Michigan captured the colors of the 4th Mississippi and four prisoners. The fighting was close and desperate. The enemy having gained possession of the hill on the east of the road, were hurling grape and canister into the ranks like hail, and the battle raged furiously. But it was a hopeless struggle; defeat was only a question of time. The ammunition was getting short, and Forrest getting between them and Franklin was advancing from the north. A new line was formed by Coburn's force, facing north, to meet the new line of advance. Forrest was met and held in check until the last round of ammunition was fired. The gallant and brave little band then fixed bayonets to charge and break the enemy's lines, and escape; but just as they were about to charge it was discovered that the enemy had still another line in reserve, and a battery began to open and form a new position. Escape was hopeless, and to avoid useless loss of life, the command surrendered, having lost 113 in killed and wounded out of 512 who went into action.

Colonel Gilbert had his horse shot under him in the early part of the engagement, and behaved most gallantly. When he offered his sword to the Confederate commander, he declined to receive it, saying, that "an officer who was so brave in battle, and commanded so gallant a regiment, deserved to retain his arms."

During Sherman's advance upon Atlanta the 19th was in the 1st brigade,

4th division, 20th corps, and at Resaca, May 15th, 1864, became conspicuously and desperately engaged, when, with the brigade, it gallantly charged a four-gun battery, captured the artillery, and held the position. In this charge Colonel Gilbert, commanding the regiment, was mortally wounded while leading and urging on his men, and died at Chattanooga on the 24th of that month. In the same engagement Capt. C. H. Calmer was killed at the muzzle of a gun while leading his company in the charge; while the loss in the regiment was 14 killed and 66 wounded. On the 19th the regiment, in command of Major E. A. Griffin, charged into Cassville and assisted in driving out the enemy, losing one in killed, four wounded, and capturing four guns. It again engaged at New Hope Church on the 25th of May, where it sustained a loss of five in killed and forty-seven wounded, including among the killed Lieut. Charles Mandeville and among the wounded Capt. Charles W. Bigelow, who died on the 29th of his wounds. On the 15th of June it was again engaged at Golgotha, losing four killed and nine wounded, and at Culp's Farm June 22d, where its casualties were thirteen wounded. Among the severely wounded was Major Griffin, who died of his wounds next day. Following up the rebel army after its evacuation of the position at Kenesaw Mountain and crossing the Chattahoochie, the regiment, under the command of Major John J. Baker, participated in the repulse of the fierce attack of the enemy on our lines at Peach Tree Creek on the 20th July. The loss of the regiment in this battle was four killed, with Major Baker, and thirty-five wounded.

During the siege of Atlanta, from July 22d to August 25th, the regiment, in command of Capt. David Anderson, constructed several strong lines of works, but, although under the fire of artillery and sharp-shooters, did not participate in any of the engagements that took place. Its loss during the siege was two killed and six wounded. The regiment did not take part in the flank movement to the south of Atlanta, but falling back with its corps, took position at Tanner's Ferry, on the Chattahoochie river, where it remained until the 2d of September. At this date the greater portion of the regiment, with a force under Col. Coburn, of its brigade, made a reconnoissance toward Atlanta. This force advanced to the city limits, and finding it evacuated by the enemy, excepting by a few cavalry, took possession. On the following day the remainder of the regiment entered the city with its corps.

The 19th formed part of Sherman's army on that remarkable march from Atlanta to the sea, participating in the numerous engagements of its corps with credit and distinction.

At the battle of Averysboro', N. C., on March 16, 1865, the regiment bore a brilliant part, acquitting itself with its usual bravery and vigor. Colonel David Anderson, then in command of the 19th, in a recent report, says:

"On the 16th of March the enemy was met near Averysboro', and a battle ensued, in which the regiment, then in the 2d brigade, 3d division, 20th corps, took an active and important part. The brigade to which the regiment was attached being ordered to assault the enemy's works, the order was gallantly and promptly obeyed, resulting in the taking of the works, the regiment capturing two pieces of artillery and many prisoners. In this assault we lost two brave officers, Captain Leonard Gibbon and Lieutenant Charles G. Purcell, and four men killed and fifteen wounded, several severely."

Although the 19th may have acquired celebrity in other engagements, yet those named will undoubtedly be remembered as prominent events in its history, illustrating its brilliant conduct in battle, and must be indelibly stamped on the memories of the survivors of this gallant regiment.

NOTE.—Company D of this regiment, numbering 50 men, being stationed at a stockade on the Nashville and Chattanooga Railroad, at Stone River, were attacked on the 5th of October, by a large force of rebel cavalry and artillery under Maj. Gen. Wheeler, and after a short but hopeless resistance, having lost six in wounded, the company surrendered; but, after having been plundered, were released. Lieut. Baldwin reports in relation to this affair, that, having expected an attack, he had early on the morning of October 5th put his command in good condition to meet it. About half-past 7 A. M. on that day a body of mounted troops numbering about 150, dressed in Federal uniform, came within 300 yards of the stockade, and on account of their uniform were taken for U. S. troops and not molested. They fell back behind a small grove and for the two hours following troops were coming to the front and taking position, completely surrounding the stockade, when a flag of truce was sent in by the rebel commander, and a demand made in the name of Major-General Wheeler of unconditional surrender. Not feeling inclined to comply with the request without a struggle, Lieut. Baldwin declined the proposition and sent back a reply "that he would have to fight before he got me." On the receipt of this reply fire was opened from a battery which was promptly responded to by musketry. The fire was kept up for an hour and a half, throwing nearly forty charges of grape, canister, solid shot and shell. Of these, ten shot passed through the stockade, knocking the logs to pieces, causing more injury from the splinters than from shot. Lieut. Baldwin, deeming it useless to attempt to hold his position any longer against such odds, and expecting no assistance, surrendered his command, losing six wounded, while the loss of the enemy was ascertained to be two killed and eight wounded. The rebel force consisted of two divisions of cavalry with twelve pieces of artillery. Lieut. Baldwin's men were disarmed, stripped of their overcoats, and marched out on the Shelbyville Pike, nearly to Guy's Gap, where they were searched, money and all articles of value taken from them, and then the company was unconditionally released, when under a pass from General Wheeler, it returned to its encampment at the stockade, and next morning marched from Murfreesboro.

THE TWENTIETH INFANTRY.

The 20th regiment was recruited from the counties of Washtenaw, Jackson, Calhoun, Eaton, and Ingham. Its camp was at Jackson, with Tidus Livermore, Esq., as commandant. It left Jackson for Washington September 1st, 1862, in command of Colonel A. W. Williams, and was soon after attached to the 1st brigade, 1st division, 9th corps, of the Army of the Potomac.

Early in 1863 the regiment left the Army of the Potomac with the corps, and soon commenced the campaign in Kentucky, Mississippi, and Tennessee.

While the corps lay in Kentucky the 20th Michigan occupied Monticello for a few days, and on May 6th fell back to the Cumberland river, near Jamestown, where the river makes a grand curve known as "Horse-shoe Bend." On Friday, May 8th, a hundred picked men of the regiment, in command of Capt. D. W. Wiltsie, had pursued and driven off the band of the notorious "Champ Ferguson," while three companies, under Captain Barnes, had been placed on picket at the "Narrows," about two miles from the ferry, on the south side of the Cumberland; in the meantime the regiment, with the exception of the detachments named, had crossed to the north side by the evening of the 9th, and this movement had just been accomplished when a courier reached the headquarters of the regiment with intelligence that Capt. Wiltsie's command, attacked by a heavy force, had been driven back, while the pickets under Capt. Barnes were being attacked above. Lieut. Col. W. Huntington Smith, in command of the regiment, (Col. Williams being sick,) directed Major Cutcheon to proceed to the front and make a reconnoissance; and who, upon ascertaining the condition of affairs and convinced that the most advantageous position to fight the advancing enemy was at the "Narrows," rallied the scattered detachments of Wiltsie and Barnes, and, leading them back to the "Narrows," posted them just in time to meet and bravely repulse a sharp attack of the enemy, ascertained to be the advance guard of General John Morgan. During the early part of the night of the 9th Col. Smith had come up with the remainder of the regiment, increasing the force to a little upwards of three hundred. On the morning of the 10th the attack was resumed; the front required to make a proper defence against such a superior force was necessarily very extended, the command being distributed to the best advantage possible for that purpose; the left wing of the regiment was commanded by Col. Smith and the right wing by Major Cutcheon. The enemy pushed forward with much confidence a brigade, driving in the pickets, assaulting in front and flank the main line, itself scarcely more than an ordinary skirmish line, but he was promptly and decisively repulsed, with much loss, after this sharp but desultory fight. During the afternoon the command was reinforced by a hundred dismounted men of the 11th Kentucky cavalry, with one piece of the 13th Indiana battery. At 4 P. M. it was resolved to take the offensive. Across a road, about two hundred yards in front, lay the enemy in line; under cover of a rapid fire from the gun the force advanced in double-quick to the charge with the bayonet, routing him in gallant style and driving him to the woods. In a very short time he threw forward his reserve brigade, making the odds in his favor ten to one, forcing back the command to its first position with severe loss, part of the fighting being hand-to-hand and most desperate. In defending this position the contest was maintained for nearly three-fourths of an hour, when the enemy succeeded in turning their left, forcing them back to a new position. General Morgan then demanded a surrender, stating that he had an entire division, and that further resistance was useless. He was invited to "come and take them;" but declined the invitation. Another reinforcement of a hundred men was received, which covered the withdrawal of the force to the river, when it recrossed in the presence of a vastly superior force without further loss.

This affair must be considered as one of the most notable minor engagements of the war. A handful of men, comparatively, without supports, with retreat cut off by a stream one hundred and fifty yards wide, deep and rapid, without entrenchments, repulse the charge of a large brigade, and then in turn drive them with the bayonet; then maintain a desperate fight with an entire division of nearly four thousand men, and finally withdrawing from the field in good order, saving the piece of artillery, bringing off the wounded, and recrossing the river in face of the enemy. In this battle the loss of the 20th was forty-four killed, wounded, and missing, including among the killed Lieutenant William M. Green, a valuable officer, while the rebels acknowledged a loss of one hundred and seventy-five in killed. For its gallant conduct on this occasion the regiment received the highest commendation from General Burnside and his hearty thanks.

The 20th infantry was, on the 1st of November, 1863, at Lenoir Station, East Tennessee, where it remained until the 14th. The enemy making at this time their advance toward Knoxville, the regiment was ordered to Hough's Ferry, with other forces, to check their advance, but on the 15th fell back to Lenoir Station, the regiment covering the retreat, and holding the Loudon road during the night. On the 16th the army continuing the retreat to Knoxville, the 20th, with the 2d and 17th Michigan infantry, were constituted the rear guard. The enemy followed them up with great vigor, and at times pressed them very heavily. At Turkey Creek, near Campbell's Station, the rear was attacked by the enemy in force, but successfully sustained the attack for over two hours, when they were reinforced. The loss of the 20th during this action was thirty-three in killed and wounded. Among the former was its commanding officer, Lieutenant-Colonel W. Huntington Smith, who was among the first to fall. He was a brave and efficient officer, and his loss was deeply felt by the regiment.

On the morning of the 17th the regiment, in command of Major Byron M. Cutcheon, arrived at Knoxville, having marched all night over bad roads, it being the third night that it had been without rest. The enemy made their appearance before Knoxville on the 17th, and commenced the siege, which continued until the 5th of December. The 20th occupied an exposed position on the line of defences, losing heavily, including Captain W. D. Wiltzie, an officer of great ability and courage, who was wounded on the 25th, and died on the 27th of November.

In March, 1864, the 9th corps was transferred to the Army of the Potomac, and on the 21st of that month the regiment proceeded on its march to Virginia. Having joined the Army of the Potomac, the 20th, then in command of Colonel Cutcheon, and serving in the 2d brigade, 3d division, crossed the Rappahannock on the 4th of May, and the Rapidan, at Germania Ford, on the 5th. It participated in the battle of the Wilderness on the 6th, losing eight killed, wounded, and missing. On the 8th the regiment formed part of the rear guard in the movement of its corps to Chancellorsville. On the 9th it took part in the engagement on the banks of the Ny river, and on the 12th, in command of Major George C. Barnes, Colonel Cutcheon being wounded, it participated in the attack on the enemy's works at Spottsylvania Court-house, sustaining a loss in the action of thirty killed, eighty-two wounded, and thirty-one missing. Among the killed were Captains R. P. Carpenter and Walter McCollum, Lieutenants David E. Ainsworth, and James B. Gould.

Crossing the James river, the regiment arrived in front of Petersburg on the 16th, and on the next day was engaged as support to the force attacking the enemy's lines, suffering but slight loss. On the 18th the regiment charged over an open field, and through a cut in the Suffolk railroad, to a point near the enemy's lines, where it constructed rifle-pits. During this attack it suffered severely from a galling cross-fire, and lost more than one-half of the number engaged, including Major Barnes, commanding regiment, mortally wounded, and Captain W. A. Dewey and Lieutenant George P. Hicks, killed.

While this regiment, during its term of service, displayed persistent firmness and true courage on all occasions, perhaps there was no position in which it was placed that exhibited the bravery and endurance of the men to more advantage than in the charge made at the "crater," or springing of the mine, July 30, 1864. That affair, although resulting in a needless and miserable failure, was one of the most daring and desperate undertakings of the war, involving the advance of nearly a whole corps, closely massed, over open ground, and exposed to a murderous and withering fire, driving large portions of the force into the mine, which soon became a perfect slaughter pen, and from which there was no escape except through the leaden storm which led to certain death.

The assaulting force was the 9th corps with the 18th in support, the 2d in reserve on the right, and the 5th on the left, the whole closely massed, with Ledlie's division in advance, Wilcox's and Potter's next in support, and the colored division (General Ferrero) in the rear. The fuse was to be lighted at 3½ o'clock A. M., but owing to some unavoidable delay the explosion did not occur until twenty minutes of five, after sunrise. A heaving and trembling of the earth was followed by huge clouds of earth, and all the contents of the fort, guns, caissons, limbers, and the soldiers which manned them, being thrown into the air.

The 20th was commanded by Col. B. M. Cutcheon, and belonged in the brigade commanded by Col. William Humphrey, 2d Michigan, and was serving in Wilcox's division, in which were five other Michigan regiments, the 2d, 8th, 17th, 27th and 1st sharp-shooters. When the mine was sprung the 20th advanced at double-quick and formed in the brigade column in rear of the works, the regiment being the third battalion in the column. At 8:30 A. M., it formed in the trenches for the charge, the 2d Michigan on its right and the 46th New York on its left, and was ordered to follow and be guided by the movements of the regiment on the right. It moved by the right flank on double-quick toward the enemy's works. Colonel Cutcheon, seeing great numbers of the troops crowding behind the fort in much confusion, moved by the left flank, throwing his regiment upon the enemy's rifle-pits to the left of the fort, capturing between thirty and forty of the enemy, including two commissioned officers. When the first counter charge was made the regiment moved rapidly over the rifle-pits, and into the left of the fort, and when the stampede of troops occurred it stood firm, actively and persistently participating in repelling the rebel charges, both in the forenoon and afternoon, displaying much courage and coolness. At about 2:30 P. M., the last charge was made by the rebels, when nearly all the Union troops fell back, by order of General Griffin, to their main line. A part of the 20th was still in the fort, and at 3 P. M., the colors of the regiment were still flying on the works, defended by about thirty of the men. Of these about ten made their escape, and the others were made prisoners, among whom were Alexander Bush and Frank Phillips, color-bearers, who previous to their capture cut up the colors and staff of the regiment in small pieces, and buried them in the sand to prevent their falling into the hands of the enemy.

The regiment took part in the action of the 30th September following, near Poplar Spring Church, losing Captain Oliver Blood and Adjutant J. E. Seibert, killed, and a number in prisoners.

In November of that year the 20th, commanded by Colonel C. B. Grant, was encamped at Peeble's Farm in front of Petersburg, engaged on picket duty. On the 28th of that month it moved with its division to the extreme right of the line east of Petersburg, and during that night took position in the trenches, the regiment occupying Battery No. 9, near the Appomattox river, and relieving a portion of the 2d corps. The enemy having been apprised of the movement, had posted sharp-shooters in convenient positions, who kept up a continuous fire through the night, killing and wounding several men of the regiment.

During the winter the regiment continued in position, within range of the enemy's fire from mortar batteries in front, and also on the right flank from batteries across the river, mounted with Whitworth and sixty-four-pounder rifle guns. From these points he usually opened fire at intervals of three or four days, driving every man to the shelter of the works. The picket trenches being only about two hundred yards apart at that point from those of the enemy; consequently, much annoyance and danger were experienced from the fire of his pickets; and on February 15, 1865, while Captain H. F. Robinson was riding along the lines, he was killed by a rebel sharp-shooter. Owing to the insufficiency of shelter and scarcity of fuel, the men in the trenches suffered much hardship, while at the same time their duties were arduous, being engaged on picket or fatigue duty every other day. About March 1st, the enemy was observed strengthening his works in front, as if he expected an assault. On the 13th the regiment was under arms, anticipating an attack; and on the 15th it received orders to be ready to move at a moment's notice. All the sick were sent to City Point, and the men required to sleep on their arms every night. On the morning of the 25th, about 4 o'clock A. M., the command was aroused by sentinel's cry of "A charge!" and the men were immediately ordered to the works. It was still dark, and no one seemed to comprehend the nature or extent of the attack. There was an irregular firing heard a short distance on the left, and it was soon ascertained that the enemy had captured Fort Steadman, and that he was swinging around to the right in rear, with the intention of capturing all on the right of the captured fort; and nothing but the vigilance and bravery of this regiment and the 2d Michigan, which occupied the line between Battery No. 9 and Fort Steadman, prevented the success of his movement. The 2d Michigan was forced back into Battery No. 9, with considerable loss in prisoners. All the rebel batteries in front of the position were opened on that portion of the line occupied by the 20th and 2d Michigan, also the guns of the captured fort, while the enemy was pouring in at the breach, and at the same time preparing for a charge in front. The 17th Michigan, advancing from division headquarters, charged rapidly on the advance in front, but was driven back by a superior force. Reforming, it again charged, the 20th and 2d Michigan charging gallantly on the right, covered by the guns of Fort McGilvery. The enemy, seeing that success was impossible, became utterly demoralized, and retreated hastily in great disorder to his works. The regiment was then deployed along the picket-line, and succeeded in capturing about 350 of the retreating enemy, who were delivered inside our lines. During the attack the regiment lost nine wounded, three mortally.

On the 26th, anticipating another attack, the regiment was constantly under arms. On the 29th the enemy opened a furious fire, wounding four men, and on the 30th the regiment was ordered out through the covered way to the picket trench, receiving orders, together with the 2d Michigan, and 1st Michigan sharp-shooters, to make a dash on the rebel works. It was decided that the 2d Michigan should make the charge, supported by the 1st sharp-shooters on the left, and the 20th on the right. The 2d started on the charge, preceded by fifty axmen to cut away the *chevaux de frise*, but the furious fire of the enemy indicated that he was fully prepared, and the attack at that point was abandoned. Fort Mahon, about two miles to the left of the position held by this regiment, was captured by our troops on April 1st, while at the same time a heavy demonstration was made on the right by the 1st Michigan sharp-shooters, which captured and for a short time held a portion of the enemy's works; and the 20th, together with the whole brigade, was kept in constant readiness for a charge, should not our forces succeed in holding Fort Mahon; and a heavy artillery fire was kept up during the whole day and night by all our batteries, and during the 2d, the regiment was held in readiness for a charge; and at 3 o'clock A. M., on the 3d, it was ordered towards the right to support the 1st Michigan sharp-shooters in a charge on the enemy's works, as it was supposed that he was evacuating. On arriving at the point indicated, the sharp-shooters, followed by the 2d and 20th Michigan, charged into the city, capturing a number of prisoners, guns, and small arms, and at 4:10 A. M., the flag of the 1st Michigan sharp-shooters was raised on the Court-house of Petersburg, that being the 1st regiment which entered the city, and the 20th was immediately detailed on provost duty.

While the historic page of this reliable and gallant regiment is bright and dazzling—exhibiting a long list of brilliant and important battles—there are none of them which set forth in stronger light its daring achievements and faithful service than these important engagements, in which its fighting qualities were so severely tested and so nobly maintained.

THE TWENTY-FIRST INFANTRY.

The 21st had its rendezvous at Ionia, and was recruited from the Fourth District, comprising the counties of Barry, Ionia, Montcalm, Kent, Ottawa, Muskegon, Oceana, Newaygo, Mecosta, Mason, Manistee, Grand Traverse, Leelenaw, Manitou, Oceola, Emmet, Mackinac, Delta, and Cheboygan. J. B. Welch, Esq., was appointed commandant of camp. The regiment left its quarters on the 12th of September, 1862, with orders to report at Cincinnati. It was immediately pushed into Kentucky.

At Perryville, October 8th,.a little less than a month after it left the State, the 21st regiment, commanded by Colonel Ambrose A. Stevens, received its first baptism in the blood of the rebellion. It belonged to Colonel Nick Greusel's brigade, and was led to its position in the fight by General Phil. Sheridan in person, and although losing heavily, it, at the same time, established a glorious reputation as a fighting regiment, which was eminently maintained at Stone River, Chicamauga, and Bentonville.

At Stone River the 21st, then commanded by Lieutenant-Colonel William B. McCreery, was in Sill's brigade, of Sheridan's division, and became hotly engaged, fighting desperately and continuously against immense odds, losing 17 killed, 85 wounded, and 37 missing, including among the mortally wounded Captain Leonard O. Fitzgerald, a gallant officer, who died of his wounds a few days after the battle.

General Sheridan, in a portion of his report covering the operations of his division in that important engagement, says:

"The enemy appeared to be in strong force in a heavy cedar woods across an open valley in my front, and parallel to it—the cedar extending the whole length of the valley—varying from two hundred to four hundred yards.

"At two o'clock on the morning of the 31st General Sill, who commanded my right brigade, reported great activity on the part of the enemy immediately in his front. This being the narrowest point in the valley, I was fearful that an attack might be made, and therefore directed two regiments from the reserve to report to General Sill, who placed them in position in very short supporting distance of his lines. At four o'clock the division was assembled under arms, and the cannoneers at their pieces. About fifteen minutes after seven o'clock the enemy advanced to the attack across the cotton field on Sill's front. This column was opened upon by Bush's battery, of Sill's brigade, which had a direct fire on its front, and by Hescock's and Houghtaling's batteries, which had an oblique fire on its front from a commanding position, near the centre of my line; the effect of this fire upon the advancing column was terrible. The enemy, however, continued to move forward until he had reached nearly the edge of the timber, when he was opened upon by Sill's infantry, at a range of not over fifty yards. As this attacking force was massed several regiments deep, the destruction to it was great. For a short time it withstood the fire, then wavered, broke, and ran. Sill directed his troops to charge, which was gallantly responded to, and the enemy was driven back across the valley and behind his entrenchments. The brigade then fell back in good order and resumed its original lines. In this charge I had the misfortune to lose General Sill, who was killed."

The enemy soon rallied and advanced to the attack. General Sheridan, after making several movements with brigades of his division and with his artillery, intending to meet successfully the advancing enemy, and gallantly attacking at several points against immense odds without success, finally took a position on Negley's right, and placed his batteries in position. "In this position," says Sheridan, "I was immediately attacked, when one of the bitterest and most sanguinary contests of the whole day occurred. General Cheatham's division advanced on Roberts' brigade, while heavy masses of the enemy, with three batteries of artillery over the open ground which I had occupied in the previous part of the engagement, and at the same time opened fire from the intrenchments in the direction of Murfreesboro. The contest then became terrible. The enemy made three attacks, and was three times repulsed, the artillery range of the respective batteries being not over two hundred yards. In these attacks Roberts' brigade lost their gallant commander, who was killed. There was no sign of faltering with my men, the only cry being for more ammunition, which, unfortunately, could not be supplied, on account of the discomfiture of the troops on the right of our wing, which allowed the enemy to come in and capture the ammunition train."

General Sheridan, in specially mentioning by name various brigade, regimental, and battery commanders of his division—one of whom was Lieut.-Colonel W. B. McCreery, 21st Michigan—says:

"I refer with pride to the splendid conduct, bravery, and efficiency of the following regimental commanders and the officers and men of their respective commands."

At Chicamauga the regiment, in command of Col. McCreery, belonged to the same brigade as at Stone River, and then commanded by Gen. Lytle, was serving in Sheridan's division of the 4th corps. On September 20th, while the division was advancing to the support of General Thomas, it became heavily engaged, and captured prisoners from four different rebel divisions. The 21st was in the hottest of the fight, behaved with great courage, never yielding except when overcome by immense odds, but after a brave but fruitless effort against a perfect torrent of the enemy was compelled to give way.

In General Sheridan's report is found the following extracts:

"On the morning of the 20th September I rearranged my lines, and formed myself in a strong position on the extreme right, to which I had been assigned, but which was disconnected from the troops on my left.

"At about 9 o'clock the engagement again opened by a heavy assault upon the left of the army, while everything was quiet in my front. To resist the assault that was being made on the left the interior divisions were again moved. * * *

"Immediately afterwards I received orders to support General Thomas with two brigades, and had just abandoned my position and was moving at double-quick to carry out the order when the enemy made a furious assault, with overwhelming numbers, on Davis' front, and coming up through the unoccupied space between Davis and myself, even covering the front of the position I had just abandoned, Davis was driven from his lines, and Laiboldt, whose brigade was in column of regiments, was ordered by Major-General McCook to charge, deploying in front. The impetuosity of the enemy's charge, together with the inability of Laiboldt's command to fire in consequence of the ground in his front being covered with the men of Davis's division, who were rushing through his ranks, caused this brigade also to break and fall to the rear. In the meantime I had received the most urgent orders to throw in my other two brigades. This I did at a double-quick, forming the brigade of General Lytle—composed of the 36th and 88th Illinois, 24th Wisconsin, and 21st Michigan—and Col. Bradley's brigade, now commanded by Col. W. H. Walworth, to the front, under a terrible fire of musketry from the enemy. Many of the men were shot down before facing to the front. After a stubborn resistance the enemy drove me back nearly to the Lafayette road, a distance of about three hundred yards. At this point the men again rallied, drove the enemy back with terrible slaughter, and regained the line of the ridge on which Col. Laiboldt had originally been posted. In this charge we took a number of prisoners, and the 51st Illinois captured the colors of the 24th Alabama.

"Here, unfortunately, the enemy had strong supports, while I had none to relieve my exhausted men, and my troops were again driven back to the Lafayette road after a gallant resistance. In this engagement I had the misfortune to lose Gen. Lytle, commanding my first brigade, and many of the best and bravest officers of my command."

Among the names of the officers mentioned by Gen. Sheridan as specially distinguished are Col. W. B. McCreery (wounded and taken prisoner) and Lieut. Col. Morris B. Wells, (killed,) 21st Michigan.

In this sanguinary engagement the 21st lost most heavily, having 11 killed, 48 wounded, and 35 taken prisoners. Among the wounded was Captain Edgar Smith mortally, who died near Chattanooga on the 11th of October following.

On November 1st, 1864, the 21st, then in command of Lieut. Col. L. K. Bishop, was at Dalton, Georgia, where it received orders to march to Kingston and join the 14th army corps; and on arriving there was assigned to the 2d brigade, 1st division, when it started for Atlanta, and on the march assisted in tearing up the railroad track and destroying everything in its rear, reaching that point on the 15th, and on the following day after the destruction of that place moved with Gen. Sherman's army towards Milledgeville, arriving there on the 22d, and then took up a line of march in the direction of Augusta; and on reaching within about forty miles of that point turned directly south towards Savannah, and arrived at the works in front of that place on the 10th of December, and there relieved a part of the 20th army corps, which held a portion of the works on the south side of the canal, being the most exposed position on the whole line. There the men, being obliged to lay in the trenches, without tents and lightly clad, few of them having blankets, suffered extremely from cold and also from hunger, as their rations were short.

On the 20th of January following the regiment commenced the campaign through the Carolinas. Crossing Cape Fear river on the 13th of March and moving forward met the enemy at Averysboro' on the 16th, and, after a severe engagement, he was compelled to retreat during the night. Continuing the march, again encountering the enemy at Bentonville on the 19th, when the 21st, in command of Capt. Arthur C. Prince, again gained much celebrity for gallant and daring service, encountering the enemy and becoming heavily engaged; it lost in killed and wounded six officers and eighty-six enlisted men out of two hundred and thirty.

While the 21st has on every occasion been much distinguished and always recognized as a fighting regiment, Stone River, Chicamauga, and Bentonville will stand out as among its principal engagements.

THE TWENTY-SECOND INFANTRY.

The 22d regiment, so distinguished at Chicamauga for one of the most dashing and desperate bayonet charges of the war, was raised in the counties of Oakland, Livingston, Macomb, St. Clair, and Sanilac by the talented and much lamented Governor Wisner, who went to the field in command of the regiment. Leaving the State for Kentucky on September 4th, 1862, he served faithfully and with much distinction until attacked with typhoid fever, of which he died at Lexington, Ky., January 4, 1863. Col. Wisner was much devoted to his regiment and the cause of his country, which he most warmly espoused; his honorable adherence to both, and his high sense of duty, induced him to remain in the field until disease had fastened upon his system, prostrating him beyond a chance of recovery. Had health not failed him and life been spared his great ability, nobleness of character, firmness, and courage, would have rapidly advanced him to a high rank, and placed him prominently in the history of his country which he loved so well.

The regiment, in command of Col. Heber Le Favour, first met the enemy, under Gen. Pegram, at Danville, Ky., March 24th, 1863, and was subsequently engaged at Hickman's Bridge, Ky., Pea-vine Creek, and McAffee's Church, Tenn.; then followed Chicamauga, the great and disastrous conflict of the "River of Death." In that battle, on Saturday morning, September 19th, Gen. Whitaker was reinforced by Mitchell's and McCook's brigades and by the 22d Michigan and 89th Ohio, under Colonel Le Favour. The command of Col. Le Favour was attached to Col. Whitaker's own brigade, and that day and night were placed in line of battle.

Sunday, at 9 A. M., the deadly strife commenced on General Thomas' line, which was shattered and compelled to fall back. General Whitaker was ordered to move to the right and reinforce Thomas at a point some four miles distant. Moving rapidly, he soon found the rebel cavalry in position to check him, but quickly drove them off, and succeeded in establishing himself near the right of Thomas' line. General Steadman, commanding 1st division, reserve corps, received instructions from Thomas that the enemy must be driven from the hill on his right. General Whitaker was ordered to the work, and advanced in two lines—the first, composed of the 96th Illinois, on the right, 115th Illinois in the centre, and the 22d Michigan, in command of Lieutenant-Colonel Sanborn, of that regiment, on the left; the second line—40th Ohio on the right, 84th Indiana in the centre, and 89th Ohio on the left, and in rear of the 22d Michigan, both lines under command of Colonel Le Favour. Charging in gallant style on the enemy's lines, they drove them from the hill full half a mile. Here the rebels rallied, and Longstreet's forces came rushing down in masses eight lines deep. The gallant brigade received and repulsed them with terrible loss. Colonel Sanborn was severely wounded while in front of his regiment. The color-sergeant, Philo J. Durkee, and Corporal Stansell were killed in turn, and Corporal Vincent severely wounded, while bravely bearing the colors of the 22d to the front. The rebels drove the brigade to the foot of the hill at the second onslaught, where it again formed, and again gallantly retook the crest. Colonel Le Favour informed General

Whitaker that ammunition was exhausted. "You must use your steel," was the reply. The enemy again furiously advanced. The sun had gone down; in the twilight it was difficult to distinguish friend from foe. The 22d rushed forward, led by Colonel Le Favour in person, with fixed bayonets and empty muskets, under a most terrific fire of grape and musketry, met the charge of the enemy, and repulsed and drove him at every point. General Steadman sent an order to fall back, but it was too late; before it arrived the regiment was closed in upon at both flanks and cut off. This brave and most desperate charge, General Steadman declared, saved that immediate portion of the army.

A correspondent says: "Whitaker said he would take the ridge, and he did it. This is the way it was done: The six regiments of the 1st brigade were formed in two lines; the first, comprising the 96th Illinois, Colonel Thomas E. Champion, on the right; 115th Illinois, Colonel J. H. Moore, in the centre; and the 22d Michigan, Colonel Le Favour, on the left. Then came the order to advance. With a yell, the first line bounded forward on the double-quick. Up and down the little hills and through the narrow valleys which intervened they pressed hastily forward, until they came within short range of the rebel musketry, which opened upon them furiously, while the grape and canister from the battery on the ridge swept cruelly through the ranks. Almost exhausted with their hurried march and their long-continued double-quick, the troops recoiled for a moment under that withering fire; but ere the most timid could think of retreating, Colonel Champion promptly gave the command to halt, lie down, and fire, which was obeyed on the instant. There the line lay for five minutes, responding resolutely to the fire of the enemy. That five minutes was a terrible ordeal for our soldiers, for during that short period their ranks were more than decimated. Then came the order to fix bayonets and charge upon the enemy. The ardor of the men overcame their fatigue, and, tired as they were, they resumed the double-quick march as they advanced up the ridge, right in the face of a galling fire. If a man fell—and many did—he was left to enrich the soil of Georgia with his life's blood; or, if able, to creep, alone and unassisted, to the rear, for none who were able to march left the ranks, which were kept well closed up, and the line was firmly maintained."

The same correspondent, in giving the names of many who distinguished themselves, says of Colonel Le Favour:

"And Colonel Le Favour, who led his 22d Michigan on a bayonet charge, after they had expended all their ammunition, should not be forgotten when the roll of honor is made out."

On this day the 22d lost in killed, wounded, and missing 372 out of 584, including among the mortally wounded Captains W. A. Smith and Elijah Snell, brave and meritorious officers. Most of the missing were taken prisoners in the charge, among whom was the commanding officer—Colonel Le Favour.

In this charge the regiment was almost annihilated, but gained an imperishable page in history.

NOTE.—The following extract from the report of General Whitaker, shows the nature of the conflict in which the 22d was engaged at Chicamauga: "My command was then moved by the flank in two lines, at double-quick time up the valley for nearly a mile under a heavy fire of shell from a rebel battery. Several were killed and wounded in this charge. Arriving at the point occupied by Gen. Thomas, we found him sorely pressed and yielding stubbornly to superior numbers. I was directed to drive the enemy from a ridge on which he had concentrated his forces in great numbers, supported strongly by artillery, and was imminently threatening destruction of the right by a flank movement. Forming my command in two lines, 96th Illinois on the right, 115th Illinois in the centre, and 22d Michigan on the left of the first line. Both lines then advanced at double-quick against the enemy. The conflict was terrific, the enemy was driven nearly half a mile; rallying, they drove my command a short distance, when they in turn were driven again with great loss. Both lines had been thrown into the conflict on the second charge, and the whole line kept up a deadly and well directed fire upon the enemy who fought with great determination and vigor. The 22d Michigan after fighting for nearly three hours, having exhausted its ammunition, boldly charged into the midst of overwhelming numbers with the bayonet, driving them until overcome by superior numbers."

In Company C of this regiment served the infant, but heroic soldier "Johnny Clem." This boy is a native of Newark, Ohio. In the spring of 1863, having scarcely seen 12 summers, he followed an Ohio regiment to Nashville, at that time the seat of war in the West. On the 4th of July following, he enlisted in the 22d Michigan regiment, and took part in all its campaigns down to the bloody engagement at Chicamauga. His heroism in the last-mentioned battle brought him to the notice of General Rosecrans, who, with other deserved honors, promoted him to the rank of sergeant. A complete outfit for the infantile "orderly" was forwarded to General Thomas's headquarters by some citizens of Cincinnati, and its presentation was the occasion of the following pleasant sketch by a correspondent from that city: "Of course you remember the story of little Johnny Clem, the motherless atom of a drummer boy, 'aged 10,' who strayed away from Newark, Ohio; and the first we knew of him, though small enough to live in a drum, he was beating the long roll for the 22d Michigan. At Chicamauga he filled the office of 'marker,' carrying the guidon whereby they form the lines; a duty having a counterpart in the surveyor's more peaceful calling, in the flagmen who flutters the red signal along the metes and bounds. On Sunday of the battle, the little fellow's occupation gone, he picked up a gun that had fallen from some dying hand, provided himself with ammunition, and began putting in the periods quite on his own account, blazing away close to the ground like a fire-fly in the grass. Late in the waning of the day, the waif left almost alone in the whirl of the battle, a rebel Colonel dashed up, and looking down ordered him to surrender. 'Surrender,' he shouted, 'you little d—d son of a ——.' The words were hardly out of his mouth, when Johnny brought his piece to 'order arms,' and as his hand slipped down to the hammer, he pressed it back, swung up the gun to the position of 'charge bayonet,' and as the officer raised his sabre to strike the piece aside, the glancing barrel lifted into range, and the proud Colonel tumbled from his horse, his lips fresh-stained with the syllable of vile reproach he had flung on a mother's grave in the hearing of her child." While the prisoners of his regiment, taken in that fearful charge, were being marched to the rear, they were fired upon by a rebel force. Clem dropped as if shot, and after laying for some time and until the rebels had moved off, he travelled to Chattanooga during the night, a distance of about ten miles. He was mustered out of service by order of the Secretary of War, at Atlanta, Ga., September 8th, 1864. After his discharge, Clem went to school at Indianapolis, at the expense of the late General Thomas, who took a special and fraternal interest in his welfare. The letters from the great general to the little hero of Chicamauga, as might be expected, were models of simplicity. He closes one with these words: "Remember that modesty and self-denial are among the best of the virtues." Johnny now holds an appointment at West Point. He is no longer "an atom of a drummer boy," but a promising student, five feet one-eighth of an inch in height, active and very intelligent, bidding fair to graduate high.

THE TWENTY-THIRD INFANTRY.

The 23d, raised and rendezvoused at East Saginaw, under the direction of Colonel David Jerome, commandant of camp, left the State for the field in Kentucky, September 18, 1862, under command of Colonel M. W. Chapin; and after much hard service on long and tedious marches, performing a great amount of duty in garrison, and guarding railroad trains, acquiring an enviable reputation as a reliable and serviceable regiment, first met the rebels at Paris, Ky., on July 19, 1863, where a brief but spirited skirmish occurred, resulting in the route of the enemy.

Later in the same year, in the harassing engagements around Knoxville, immediately preceding the investment of that place by Longstreet, the regiment, under command of Colonel Chapin, took a most active part, participating at Campbell's Station; losing in the various battles and skirmishes 8 killed, 23 wounded, and 8 missing. It was also prominently engaged in the gallant and successful defence of that place by General Burnside.

Colonel Chapin commanded the regiment with much ability and conspicuous courage in the field, until April 15, 1864, when his health failed him, compelling him to resign, and Lieut. Col. O. S. Spaulding was promoted to the colonelcy.

Although this reliable and model regiment acquitted itself with much celebrity in every encounter with the enemy in which it was engaged, Campbell's Station, Resaca, Franklin, and Nashville will always be recognized as prominent among its many hard-fought battles; and the memories of those fields, on which so much patriotism and daring courage were evinced, will last while a soldier of that noble regiment lives.

In November, 1863, while General Burnside occupied East Tennessee, and while his troops were falling back from Loudon on Knoxville, the 23d Michigan, then commanded by Major W. W. Wheeler, the 111th Ohio, the 107th Illinois, and the 13th Kentucky, all under command of Col. Chapin, composed the 2d brigade of General White's 2d division, of the 23d corps.

The brigade had been engaged with its division in a severe encounter with the advancing forces of Longstreet at Huff's Ferry, on November 12, when Colonel Chapin moved forward with his brigade to the attack on the double-quick, and after a severe fight against immense odds, drove the enemy back for over three miles, when he took a strong position on a hill, which he thought impregnable, defended as it was by three regiments of Longstreet's celebrated corps; but a charge was made by the 2d brigade, and in fifteen minutes the hill was cleared and the rebels routed, with heavy loss.

Next morning at daylight the troops took up the line of march to Lenoir's, the 2d brigade covering the retreat, and skirmishing with the enemy during the day. Lenoir's was reached about 4 P. M., when it was discovered that the main rebel force had taken a position to give battle. Necessary preparations were immediately made to meet their attack; but no demonstration was made by the enemy that evening. At daylight next morning the retreat was continued. Marching in the direction of Knoxville, the retreating troops were overtaken by the enemy near Campbell's Station at midday, on the 16th, when a severe engagement immediately ensued, which is described by a correspondent of the Louisville *Journal* as follows:

"One brigade of the 9th corps was in advance, the 2d brigade of the 23d corps in the centre, and one brigade of the 9th corps as rear guard. The skirmishing was begun by the 9th corps, forming in rear of General White's command, which formed in line to protect the stock, etc., as it passed to the rear, and to cover the retreat of the 9th corps, which was the rear guard, and was to file past it. Again was the 2d brigade in position where it must receive the shock of battle, and must sustain more or less the honors already won. The arrangements for battle had hardly been completed before the cavalry came in from the front, followed by the infantry of the 9th corps, and two heavy lines of the enemy emerged from the woods three-quarters of a mile in front. Each line consisted of a division, and were dressed almost wholly in the United States uniform, which at first deceived us. Their first line advanced to within eight hundred yards of General White's front before that officer gave the order to fire. Henshaw's and the 24th Indiana batteries then opened on them with shell, but they moved steadily forward, closing up as their lines would be broken by this terrible fire, until within three hundred and fifty yards of our main line, when the batteries mentioned opened on them with canister, and four batteries in the rear and right and left of General White, opened on their rear line with shell. This was more than they could stand. Their front line broke and ran back some distance, where they reformed and deployed right and left, and engaged the 13th Kentucky and 23d Michigan on the right, and the 111th Ohio and 107th Illinois on the left, which were supported by General Ferrero's command, of the 9th corps. This unequal contest went on for an hour and a half. The only advantage over them so far was in artillery—they not having any in position yet. It seemed to be their object to crush the inferior force opposing them with their heavy force of infantry. The men were too stubborn; they would not yield an inch, but frequently drove the rebels from their position, and held their ground. Finding they could not move them with the force already employed, the rebels moved forward another line of infantry, heavy as either of the first two, and placed in position three batteries. Their guns were heavier and of longer range than those of the 2d brigade, and were situated to command General White's position, while his guns could not answer their fire. They got the range of these guns at once, and killed and wounded several gunners, and disabled several horses, when General White ordered them back to the position occupied by those in the rear, the infantry holding the position covered by the artillery on the hill. An artillery fight then began, which continued nearly two hours, till it was growing dark, and the order was given for our troops to fall back to resume the march to Knoxville.

"Of Col. Chapin, commanding the 2d brigade, I need not add to what I have said. His excellent management of the troops upon three fields, and his personal bravery, have attached him to his men as few commanders are attached. His staff, Captains Gallup and Sheldon, and Lieut. Pearson, are worthy followers of their brave leader."

This correspondent, in mentioning the names of the several regimental commanders in the brigade as behaving nobly, includes the name of Major Wheeler.

The regiment arrived at Knoxville at 4 A. M., on the 17th, after a march through mud and rain of twenty-eight miles, having lost in the several movements 8 killed, 23 wounded, and 8 missing.

At Resaca, on May 14, 1864, the 23d, commanded by Col. Spaulding, still in the 2d brigade, then commanded by General Hascall, and belonging to General Judah's division (2d) of the 23d corps, with its brigade, engaged the enemy, and took a most gallant part in assaulting his strong position at that point, losing heavily.

Colonel Spaulding, then in command, in his report makes the following mention of the services of his regiment in that affair:

"An assault on the enemy's works was ordered. The assaulting column was formed in three lines, this regiment being in the second line, advancing over an open field within easy rifle-shot of the enemy's position, under a terrible fire of musketry and artillery. The regiment in advance of the 23d broke, and was driven back, and the one in our rear followed them. We pushed forward until we reached a deep creek, which it was impossible to cross, and held our position until ordered back. In this advance the regiment lost 62 killed or wounded. Lieutenant William C. Stewart was among the killed."

In the *American Cyclopædia*, for 1864, is found the following:

"A division (Judah's) of the 23d corps, and Newton's, of the 4th corps, moving over comparatively level ground, succeeded, after a desperate struggle, in forcing the enemy to abandon an important position on the outer line. Although the Federal troops were unable to hold this, they succeeded in advancing their line and getting their artillery into a position to prevent the enemy from reoccupying the works."

At Franklin the regiment, in command of Col. Spaulding, was serving with the 2d division of the 23d corps, Major-General Scofield, and in the 2d brigade, commanded by Col. O. H. Moore, of the 25th Michigan. On November 4th, 1864, it left Johnsonville by rail for Columbus, Tennessee, and there joined the army, opposing the advance of Hood on his Northern campaign. Arriving at Columbia on the 25th, while a heavy skirmish was in progress, two companies of the regiment were engaged on the skirmish line, and at midnight the forces were ordered to withdraw to the south side of Duck river, where works were thrown up. On the 28th the regiment crossed to the north bank, skirmishing with the enemy across the river, and on the 29th fell back towards Franklin, arriving there on the morning of the 30th, where the army was immediately put in position, throwing up slight works.

At 4 P. M. the enemy, in great force and with much vigor, attacked in four lines, and, after a most desperate assault, was repulsed with great loss; but the attack was again renewed and continued at intervals until 10 P. M., when he made a most determined effort, advancing as with a death struggle, planting his colors on the works in front of the 23d Michigan, but was handsomely repulsed by the regiment in a hand-to-hand fight with the bayonet. This deadly encounter and most determined successful defence by Col. Spaulding and his gallant regiment was seldom if ever equalled during the war.

In the engagement Capt. David M. Averill fell mortally wounded.

At Nashville, on the morning of December 15th, 1864, while that place was being assaulted by Hood's rebels, the regiment, as a part of the army of General Thomas, moved on the enemy, and served with conspicuous bravery and marked efficiency in the engagements of that eventful day and the next, which, after most desperate fighting, resulted in driving Hood's forces in a demoralized condition from all their positions, giving to the Union arms one of the most substantial and important victories of the rebellion.

On the 15th Col. Spaulding, with his regiment, then in the brigade of Col. Moore, made a most daring and dashing charge on a position occupied by a portion of the enemy's infantry posted behind a heavy stone wall on the crest of a hill, which it carried in most brilliant style, capturing more prisoners than there were men in the line of the regiment. The flag-staff was shot in two and the color sergeant severely wounded, but before the colors fell to the ground they were grasped by Corporal Freeman, of the color guard, and bravely carried forward.

The regiment afterwards served with much credit and distinction with its corps in North Carolina until the close of the war.

The 23d corps having received orders to proceed to Washington, D. C., the regiment left Columbia, Tenn., on January 1st following, and marched for Clifton, a point on the Tennessee river, distant 250 miles, where it arrived on the 8th, and on the 16th embarked on steamers for Cincinnati, Ohio; reaching there on the 22d, immediately took rail for Washington, D. C., and, arriving there on the 29th, moved to Camp Stoneman and continued at that point until February 9th, when it went to Alexandria, where, on the 11th, it embarked with its corps on transports for Smithville, N. C., at the mouth of Cape Fear river, reaching that point on the 15th. On the

17th the movement was commenced against Fort Anderson, and on the 18th our troops were advanced to within a few yards of the fort and intrenched under a heavy fire of musketry and artillery, and on the morning of the 19th occupied the fort, the 23d Michigan being the first to enter. Engaging again the enemy at Town Creek on the 20th, capturing two pieces of artillery and taking 350 prisoners, a movement was immediately made up the south bank of the river above Wilmington, and on the night of the 22d the troops moved back ten miles to cross the river for the purpose of rejoining General Terry. The crossing was made on boats from the fleet on the morning of the 23d, when it was found that Wilmington had been evacuated during the previous night. The advance was resumed on March 6th. Proceeding up the coast, reached Kingston just at the close of the action at that point, having marched 125 miles in six days, and for the last twenty-four hours without halting, except long enough to draw rations and issue thirty additional rounds of ammunition to the men. On the 20th left Kingston and occupied Goldsboro' on the 22d, the enemy retiring on the approach of our forces. Gen. Sherman's army arriving at Goldsboro' on the 23d, the regiment was sent back ten miles, to Mosely Hall, to guard the railroad at that place while the army was being supplied, and on April 9th moved with the grand army on Raleigh, which was reached and occupied on the 13th. The regiment remained there until the surrender of Johnston's army on the 21st, when, on the 3d of May, it marched for Greensboro', distant ninety miles, reaching there on the 7th. On the 9th went by rail to Salisbury, remaining there until June 28th, when it was mustered out of service.

THE TWENTY-FOURTH INFANTRY.

The celebrated 1st brigade of the 1st division, 1st corps, known as the "Iron Brigade," was the 24th Michigan, organized and commanded by Col. Henry A. Morrow, and which was so distinguished at Gettysburg in 1863. On Wednesday morning, July 1st, the commencement of that most important and sanguinary battle, which in the war was second to none in glory to the Union arms, fraught with mighty consequences and great with victory, culminating in results vital to the Republic. Major-General Reynolds, in command of the 1st corps, advanced on the Emmetsburg road from Marsh creek to Gettysburg, where he arrived about 10 o'clock A. M. and marched directly through the town. General Hill's corps was ascertained to be posted but a short distance in front, and a body of Heth's division of that corps was discovered holding a position on the Chambersburg road, and were driven from it by the cavalry under Buford. The rebel division coming up Buford was compelled to retire, when the 1st corps made its appearance, Gen. Wadsworth, commanding the 1st division, having the advance. The division of Gen. Doubleday following formed on the left, and that of Gen. Robinson on the right. Gen. Reynolds advanced his line hastily, almost before his troops were well formed, and soon encountered a heavy force of the enemy's infantry, which were charged by the 1st division and driven from the valley in front and over the ridge at the farther side, although with a heavy loss by the destructive fire of the enemy. In this charge the "Iron Brigade" gallantly dashed up and over the hill and down into the ravine through which flows Willoughby's Run, where the 24th took a large number of prisoners, being a part of General Archer's brigade. After advancing to the crest of the hill beyond the run the regiment halted and threw out skirmishers to the front and also to the left; here General Reynolds, upon going out to the front to reconnoitre, was killed by a shot from the enemy. Orders were then given to withdraw to the east bank of the stream, and the brigade marched into what are known as McPherson's woods and formed in line of battle, the 24th in the centre, the 7th Wisconsin on the right, and the 19th Indiana on the left. In this movement Lieut. Col. Flanigan was severely wounded and compelled to leave the field. Skirmishers were immediately deployed in front of the brigade and became at once engaged with the enemy.

Colonel Morrow, considering the position held by his regiment untenable, suggested to the commanding general a change, but he was ordered to hold the ground at all hazards. The enemy advanced in two lines of battle, his right extending beyond and overlapping the left of the brigade. The fire of the 24th was held until the enemy came within easy range, when a well directed volley was poured into his ranks, but from the nature of the ground in front, little injury was inflicted, and his advance not being checked, he came pressing rapidly on in heavy masses, his men yelling like demons. The 19th Indiana, on the left of the 24th, fought most nobly, but was overpowered by immense odds, and, after severe loss, was forced back, exposing the 24th to an enfilading and cross fire. Orders were then given to swing back, so as to face the enemy now on the flank. While the movement was being executed, the enemy advanced in such numbers as compelled the 24th to retire to a new position. In the meantime, the regiment had lost most heavily in officers and men. The second line being promptly formed, a most desperate and determined resistance was made, but the enemy accumulating in overwhelming force in front, the brigade was driven to a third position, the regiment again losing severely and almost decimated. Major E. B. Wight, acting lieutenant-colonel, being wounded, left the field, and scarcely a fourth of the men taken into the engagement could be rallied. Corporal Andrew Wagner, of company F, one of the color guard, having the colors, was ordered by Colonel Morrow to plant them at a point to which he designed to rally the regiment, and while doing this he was shot in the breast and greatly injured. Colonel Morrow snatched the flag from the hand of the wounded soldier, and was rallying the remnant of the regiment, when Private William Kelly, of company E, rushed to the front and grasped the colors, shouting triumphantly, "The Colonel of the 24th shall never carry the flag while I am alive," and the gallant fellow was instantly killed by a bullet from the enemy. The colors were then seized by Private Silburne Spaulding, and carried by him for some time, when Colonel Morrow again took them, and continued to rally his men until he was wounded and left the field; he afterwards fell into the hands of the enemy, but ingeniously made his escape. The command then devolved on Captain Albert M. Edwards, who, with much energy and conspicuous bravery, rallied all that was left of the noble regiment, under a most galling and murderous fire, and fell back to Culp's Hill, which it assisted in holding against the determined assaults of the enemy for the two succeeding days. The colors of the 24th were found after Colonel Morrow was wounded in the paralyzed hands of a wounded soldier, whose name is unknown, and who probably lies with the gallant dead of Gettysburg. The field over which the 24th fought, from its first line of battle in McPherson's woods to the barricades near the Seminary, was strewn with killed and wounded, its loss being extremely large, exceeding, perhaps, that of any other regiment of equal strength in that great and important engagement—losing 316 in killed and wounded out of 496, and in addition, 80 of the enlisted men and 3 officers were reported as missing in action, many of whom have never been heard from, and were undoubtedly killed. This engagement will always be considered as prominent among the many hard fights in which the regiment took a part. Colonel Morrow, in his report, says:

"At an early hour in the morning, July 1st, we marched in the direction of Gettysburg, seven miles distant. The report of artillery was soon heard in this direction, indicating that our cavalry had become engaged, and our pace was considerably quickened. About 9 A. M. we arrived near the town, when we filed off to the left, and moved forward into line of battle at double-quick. The cavalry immediately in our front was hotly engaged. We were ordered to advance at once, no time being allowed for loading the guns; the regiment was halted for that purpose, but was ordered to move forward without loading, which was done. Charging up and over a hill and down a ravine, we captured a large number of prisoners. The enemy advanced in two lines of battle, their right extending beyond and overlapping our left. The men were directed to withhold their fire until the enemy should arrive within easy range. This was done, but the nature of the ground was such that we inflicted but little injury on the enemy at this time. Their advance was not checked, and they came on rapidly, yelling like demons. We were forced back to a new position, where a line was promptly formed; but, after a desperate struggle, we were again forced to retire to a third position, beyond a slight ravine. Our loss was very large, exceeding, perhaps, the losses sustained by any one regiment of equal size. Out of twenty-eight officers, twenty-two were killed or wounded, and of 468 men, 316 were killed or wounded. During the engagement the flag was carried by nine different persons, four of the number having been killed and three wounded. All of the color guard were killed or wounded. The officers killed were Captains William J. Speed, Malachi J. O'Donnell, Lieutenants Walter H. Wallace, W. S. Safford, Newell Grace, R. H. Humphreville, Gilbert A. Dickey, and Lucius D. Shattuck.

"Of these nothing less can be said than that their conduct in this memorable battle was brave and daring, and was creditable alike to themselves and the service. It will not be disparaging to his brave comrades who fell on this terrible but glorious day, and who sleep with him in honored graves, to say that the death of Captain Speed was a severe loss to the service, and an almost irreparable one to the regiment. He was amiable, intelligent, honorable, and brave, and was universally respected and esteemed by all who knew him.

"Captain O'Donnell was a young officer who had given strong proofs of courage and capacity, and whose death was deeply deplored by the regiment.

"Lieut. Wallace served in the Peninsula campaign, and lost an eye at the battle of Fair Oaks. He was a brave officer and honorable man, and a good disciplinarian.

"Lieut. Dickey joined the regiment in the capacity of commissary sergeant, and for his integrity, capacity, and attention to duties, was promoted to sergeant-major, and afterwards 2d lieutenant. He had given great promise of future usefulness and distinction.

"Lieuts. Grace, Humphreville, Safford, and Shattuck were distinguished in the regiment for their attention to every duty, for the amiability of their manners, and for unflinching courage in battle."

There were no battles in which this fine regiment was a participant that it did not acquit itself nobly; and were it necessary to cite more examples than that of Gettysburg to establish the twenty-fourth as one of the best fighting regiments, selections might be made from almost any of its battles, commencing with Fredericksburg, December 12, 1862, where it lost Lieut. David Birrell, a most promising young officer, and seven men killed, sixteen wounded, and eighty missing, and ending with Dabney's Mills, February 17, 1865, where, under command of Lieut. Col. A. M. Edwards, it was heavily engaged, losing twenty in killed and wounded. Especially might reference be made to Fitzhugh's Crossing, April 29, 1863, in the advance on Chancellorsville, when, supported by the 6th Wisconsin, the regiment, commanded by Col. Morrow, crossed the Rappahannock, driving the rebels from their rifle-pits, and taking 103 prisoners—a daring achievement, commanding at the time the notice of the entire army for gallant and successful service. In this affair the 24th lost 25 in killed and wounded.

Were it necessary to cite more occasions on which the 24th distinguished itself, to establish a fighting reputation, the principal engagements of the Army of the Potomac in the campaign of 1864 might be introduced.

With the opening of that campaign the 24th, under command of Colonel Morrow, and then serving in the 1st brigade, 4th division, 5th corps, broke camp on the evening of the 3d of May, crossed the Rapidan at Germania Ford on the 4th, and on the evening of the 5th encountered the enemy in the Wilderness. During this engagement the regiment captured a number of prisoners and a stand of colors from the 48th Virginia rebel infantry. Its loss during the battles of the Wilderness, between the 5th and 7th, were 18 killed, 46 wounded, and 42 prisoners and missing. Among the killed were Captain George Hutton and Lieut. William B. Hutchinson, and among the severely wounded was Colonel Morrow. On the night of the 7th of May, Lieut. Col. A. M. Edwards in command, the regiment withdrew from the Wilderness, and marched rapidly towards Spottsylvania Court-house. At the latter place it was under fire almost every day until the 21st, sustaining a loss of 11 killed, 39 wounded, and 1 missing. The regiment crossed the North Anna river May 23d. The enemy almost immediately attacked, but were repulsed with large loss. The loss of the 24th was 3 killed, 8 wounded, and 5 missing. On the 28th the regiment crossed the Pamunkey river near Hanovertown. It participated in the fighting attending the advance to Cold Harbor, and in the battles and skirmishes near that point, sustaining a loss of 3 killed and 15 wounded. June 16th it crossed the James river at Wilcox's Landing, and marched toward Petersburg. On the 18th it participated in the unsuccessful assault on the enemy's works surrounding that city, going into action with 120 men, and of this number, losing nearly one-third in killed and wounded, including among the killed Lieutenant and Adjutant Sevill Chilson. From this date until the movement on the Weldon railroad, on the 18th of August, the regiment was actively employed in duties attending the siege of Petersburg. Its loss in the various actions and skirmishes, and from the fire of the enemy's artillery and sharp-shooters, to which it was exposed, was 8 killed, 36 wounded, and 5 missing. August 18th it participated in an engagement on the Weldon railroad, having one man wounded. On the 19th the enemy massed a heavy force on their front, and attacked their position. The regiment succeeded in holding its ground for a short time, and thus saved a large portion of its brigade from capture. The casualties of the regiment during this action were twenty-five in the aggregate. The regiment also participated in the battle of the 21st of August, in which the rebel attack on our lines was repulsed with large loss, the 24th capturing during the battle eleven rebel officers, one stand of colors, a large number of arms, and sixty men, while its loss was very slight. The regiment participated in the battle of Hatcher's Run on the 27th of October. The division captured a large number of prisoners during the night of the 27th; and on the morning of the 28th the regiment was sent on picket, and covered the retreat of the army back to their old works in front of Petersburg.

NOTE.—A special of the N. Y. *Tribune* says of the "Iron Brigade" at Gettysburg: "Reynolds has ridden into the angle of wood a bowshot from this Seminary, and that he cheers the Iron Brigade of Meredith as they wheel on the flank of the oak trees for a charge. Like a great flail of steel they swing into the shadows with an huzza that is as terrible as a volley; low crouching, dismounted, by his horse's head, the General peeps into the depths of the grove: 'Boom!' from the oaken recesses breaks a hailstorm of lead, and Reynolds, with the word of command upon his tongue, falls forward bloodily. The light of pride in his eye grows dull as blindness; the bronze flush on his face is veined with blue; two men bear away a dripping stretcher to the edge of the town; the architect of the battle has fallen dead across its portal. Grief, terror, have no space to live in. Across the brook and up the ridge, with a yell that is shot through and through with their own volleys, two jagged arcs of gray leap into sight, wheeling, the one for the wood, the other pushing through the gorge of the old railway. Huzza! From the skirts of the oaks the great double doors of the Iron Brigade shut together, with a slam as of colliding mountains, folding between them fifteen hundred rebel prisoners of war. Patrick Maloney, a brawny Irishman in blue, seizes General Archer by the throat: 'Right about face, Gineral! March!' Ere you can think, the disarmed column is over the Seminary ridge, and the grinning Celt has said to Wadsworth, looking on from the Seminary shadows: 'Gineral Wadsworth, I make you acquainted with Gineral Archer.'" Patrick Maloney, referred to, belonged to the 24th Michigan.

Following is an extract from a letter of General S. Meredith, written to Colonel Morrow in the same month in which the battle of Gettysburg was fought: "Although still confined to my bed by severe injuries received in the late battle of Gettysburg, I cannot longer delay tendering to you, and to the brave men under your command, my heartfelt thanks for the gallant bearing of yourself and regiment in the battle of the 1st inst. No troops ever fought more bravely than did those of the 24th on that occasion. The 'old Iron Brigade' being among the first on the field, it had to meet the first shock of a desperate attack of a far superior force, and nobly did it do its duty."

THE TWENTY-FIFTH INFANTRY.

The 25th recruited under the superintendence of the Hon. H. G. Wells, commandant of camp, a splendid and well-disciplined regiment, commanded by Col. O. H. Moore, then a captain in the 6th U. S. infantry, left Kalamazoo for the field in Kentucky, September 29, 1862, and on December 27th following, first tested the realities of war by engaging the enemy under the rebel General Pegram, at Mumfordsville, Ky., thus early commencing a career of fighting for the Union, which it nobly and forcibly maintained during its whole term of service, ending with the war. The regiment was specially distinguished on July 4, 1863, at Tebbs', near Green River Bridge, Kentucky, where it most gallantly repulsed an overwhelming rebel force, with heavy loss. About July 1st Colonel Moore was stationed, with five companies of his regiment, on the north side of Green river, ten miles north of Columbia, on the main road running from Columbia to Lebanon, Ky., and on the 2d of July was advised of the fact that the rebel General John H. Morgan was about crossing the Cumberland river to invade the State, with a cavalry force of from three to four thousand men. Being left to exercise his own discretion independently, and there being no Union troops nearer than at a post thirty miles distant, he felt that it was his duty to retard the progress of the great rebel raider, if but for a few hours, as they might prove precious hours to the country. He might have retreated with entire success, but from patriotic motives he chose to fight, when he could scarcely entertain the hope that he and many others would ever live to tell the story of that terrible battle.

After surveying the surrounding country, he selected a strong position for a battle-field, on the south side of Green river, about two miles from the encampment, in a horse-shoe bend of the river, through which the road ran, on which the rebel forces were advancing. This chosen battle-ground, which was at the narrows entering the bend of the river, afforded high bluff banks, which protected the flanks of the command, and also compelled the rebels to fight him upon his own front. The Colonel instructed his command that there were no rebel troops organized that could whip them upon their own front, with the flanks protected, and with this judgment he was ready to engage ten times his own number of the enemy, feeling confident that his finely disciplined troops would do ten times better fighting than that of the rebels.

On the evening of the 3d of July, General Morgan encamped with his entire command, about five miles south of Green river, and Colonel Moore, after dark, advanced with his command of five companies, numbering less than three hundred men, about two miles toward the enemy, leaving the river in his rear, and occupied the ground which he had previously selected, and prepared for the battle. The defence, which had been completed that night, consisted of some felled trees on the battle-line, which was in the rear of an open field, and was intended more particularly as an obstruction to the advance of cavalry, while to the front, about one hundred yards in the open field, was thrown up a temporary earth-work, which was intended to check the advance of the enemy, and more especially to command a position where the enemy would evidently plant their battery. This work was not intended to be held against charges of a superior force, on account of the flanks not being strong, and was occupied by only about seventy-five men, who were instructed that when it became necessary to abandon the work, it should be done by flanking to the right and left from the centre, so as to unmask the reserve force on the battle line and expose the enemy to their fire. This work was located, in anticipation of its capture by the rebels, a little down the slope of the field, so that when it was in possession of the enemy it would be useless, and leave him exposed to a deadly fire.

At the gray of morning the fire of the rebels upon the pickets resounded through the woods, and the entire rebel division, under General Morgan, was pressing upon the front. The fire was returned with spirit as the pickets retired to the breast-work, where they joined about seventy-five of their comrades, already in the advance work, and there, with their united fire as sharp-shooters, held the enemy in check, without exhibiting their numbers and the real object of the work.

The rebel artillery, of four pieces, had gained the anticipated position, and at once opened fire with some effect, when General Morgan suspended firing, and under flag of truce, sent forward the following dispatch:

HEADQUARTERS MORGAN'S DIVISION, IN THE FIELD,
IN FRONT OF GREEN RIVER STOCKADE, July 4, 1863.

To the Officer Commanding Federal Forces at Stockade near Green River Bridge:

SIR: In the name of the Confederate States Government, I demand an immediate and unconditional surrender of the entire force under your command, together with the stockade.

I am, very respectfully,

JNO. H. MORGAN,
Commanding Division Cavalry, C. S. A.

Colonel Moore rode forward between the lines, where he met the delegation of rebel officers, who appealed to him with marked courtesy and diplomacy, urging the surrender of his command, and promising kind treatment, as their only interest was to move forward on their course. Colonel Moore replied: "Present my compliments to General Morgan, and say to him that, this being the 4th of July, I cannot entertain the proposition to surrender."

Col. Allston, Morgan's chief of staff, said: I hope you will not consider me as dictatorial on this occasion; I will be frank; you see the breach we have made upon your work with our battery; you cannot expect to repulse General Morgan's whole division with your little command; you have resisted us gallantly and deserve credit for it, and now I hope you will save useless bloodshed by reconsidering the message to General Morgan. To this the Colonel replied: Sir, when you assume to know my strength you assume too much; I have a duty to perform to my country, and therefore cannot reconsider my reply to General Morgan. The rebel officer seemed moved by these remarks, extended his hand, and, with a moist eye, said: "Good-bye, Col. Moore; God only knows which of us may fall first." They turned their horses and galloped in opposite directions, and at once renewed the conflict. No sooner had the rebel battery re-opened fire than Col. Moore commanded the force to "rise up and pick those gunners at the battery." No sooner was the command given than a deliberate and deadly fire by rank was delivered, which silenced the battery. Col. Johnson's brigade then charged the work, and the little command abandoned it, as previously instructed; and when the rebels reached it they found that it availed them nothing against the deadly fire which was poured into them from the main force on the battle line in the timber.

The rebel foe, with a hideous yell, charged across the open field a number of times in the face of a terrific fire, which repulsed them on each occasion, with severe loss. The conflict was almost a hand-to-hand struggle with nothing but a line of felled trees separating the combatants. At the same time the rebels were engaged in cutting out a gorge leading through the precipitory bluff into the river bottom, which had been obstructed with felled timber. The entrance was finally effected, and a regiment, commanded by Col. Chenault, opened fire upon the right flank of the line of Union troops. This was a most critical and trying moment; the rebels had gained an important point; to defeat it was of the utmost importance; a company had been held in reserve for any emergency which might arise during the battle; it was now brought forward, deployed as skirmishers across the river bottom, with the right flank extending beyond the rebel line, and presented the appearance of being the advance line of reinforcements.

The strength of Col. Moore's command was a matter of doubt with the rebels, rendered more so by his having instructed his men to keep quiet and pour in as rapid and deadly a fire as possible. As cheering was suppressed nothing but the efficacy of the firing afforded ground for estimating their strength, and when Col. Moore brought forward and manœuvered the reserve company with the shrill notes of his bugle, it had the desired effect of impressing the rebels with the idea that reinforcements of cavalry or artillery were advancing, and by the bold front and deliberate firing of the line of skirmishers the rebel command in the river bottom was routed, the rebel colonel commanding killed, and they were promptly driven back through the gorge through which they entered, disheartened and defeated. New courage inspired the heroic little band who had sustained eight determined charges upon their front when the attack upon their right flank was defeated. The enemy, having met with a heavy loss after a battle of four hours' duration, retreated, leaving a number of killed and wounded upon the field greater than the entire number of the patriotic little band that opposed them. Among the number of killed and wounded were twenty-two commissioned officers.

The rebel command effected a crossing six miles down the river and proceeded on their march. It was his intention, as General Morgan declared, to capture the city of Louisville, but this unexpected and terrible repulse cost him more than twelve hours delay, and caused him, which fact he stated, to change his plans and to abandon his attack upon Louisville. By this brilliantly fought battle the city of Louisville was saved from sack and pillage and the Government from the loss of an immense amount of property, consisting of munitions of war and army supplies amounting to the value of several millions of dollars. This splendid victory was acknowledged by Major-General Hartsuff in the following order:

HEADQUARTERS 23D ARMY CORPS,
LEXINGTON, KY., *July* 17, 1863.

General Order, No. 12.

The general commanding the corps extends his thanks to the two hundred officers and soldiers of the 25th Michigan regiment, under Col. O. H. Moore, who so successfully resisted by their gallant and heroic bravery the attacks of a vastly superior force of the enemy under the rebel Gen. John Morgan, at Tebbs' Bend, on Green river, on the 4th of July, 1863, in which they killed one-fourth as many of the enemy as their own little band amounted to and wounded a number equal to their own.

By command of Major-General Hartsuff:

GEO. B. DRAKE, *A. A. G.*

The Legislature of Kentucky also acknowledged the services of Colonel Moore and his command on that occasion in complimentary resolutions.

Rev. John S. C. Abbott, the historian, has written a beautiful description of this battle in the August number of Harper's Magazine, 1865.

The rebel General John Morgan admired Col. Moore's generalship so much in conducting this battle that he sent him complimentary messages and declared that he was worthy of promotion, and accordingly announced that he promoted him to the rank of brigadier-general.

Col. Allston, the chief of Morgan's staff, was captured a few days after the battle, and with him his private journal, which was published, and in speaking of this battle of the 4th of July, he says:

"Gen. Morgan sent in a flag of truce and demanded the surrender, but the colonel quietly remarked, 'if it was any other day he might consider the demand, but the 4th of July was a bad day to talk about surrender, and he must therefore decline.' The colonel is a gallant man, and the entire arrangement of his defence entitles him to the highest credit for military skill. We would mark such a man in our army for promotion."

The movements of the regiment during the summer campaign of 1864, in Georgia, were identified with those of the Army of the Ohio, which formed a part of the army under command of General Sherman. During this campaign the regiment participated in the various engagements at Rocky Face Ridge, May 19th; Resaca, May 14th; Altoona, May 26th to May 29th; Pine Mountain, June 15th; Culp's Farm, June 22d, and Nickajack Creek, July 1st. On the 9th of July the regiment crossed the Chattahoochie river, and on the 22d appeared in front of Atlanta. It took an active part in the siege of that place. On the 6th of August it charged and assisted in carrying the enemy's works near East Point. The regiment also participated in the flank movement west and south of Atlanta, to Jonesboro, which was followed by the evacuation of Atlanta by the rebel army.

The regiment was most conspicuously distinguished at Resaca, where, in command of Lieutenant-Colonel Benjamin F. Orcutt, it participated in the desperate charge made by Judah's division, of the 23d corps, and Newton's, of the 4th corps, driving the enemy from a strong and well fortified position, and, although not held, enabled General Sherman to advance his lines and get his artillery into such a position as to render it impossible for the enemy to again occupy the place. This charge was made under a most murderous fire of musketry and artillery, first across an open field, and then over a stream, with the water near waist deep, and bordered with thick bushes and vines, cut and lopped down in such a manner as to entangle the troops. In the charge the regiment lost about fifty men in a very few minutes. Among the killed was Adjutant E. M. Prutzman.

At Nickajack Creek, near Kenesaw, on the 1st of July following, the 25th, still in command of Lieutenant-Colonel Orcutt, again most signally maintained its fighting qualities as a regiment, while making a flank movement with its division (Hascall's) to the extreme right of General Sherman's army, the regiment advancing seven miles during an intensely hot day, continually under fire of musketry and artillery from early in the forenoon until dark, and being engaged in two brilliant and successful charges during the day, driving the enemy from every position, securing the desired point known as the cross roads, near Nickajack creek. The position thus obtained was held and strongly fortified during the night, and the force increased early on the morning of the 2d by the coming up of the 17th corps. The result of this movement was the evacuation by General Johnston of his strong position on Kenesaw Mountain and abandonment of all his works between that place and the Chattahoochie.

On the 1st of November, 1864, this regiment was near Rome, Ga., serving in the 1st brigade, 2d division, 23d corps, and on the 2d marched to Resaca, then took rail to Johnsonville, Tenn., where it arrived on the 5th, and remained there until the 14th, when, with its brigade, it marched to Centreville to guard several important fords on Duck river. It was engaged at Pine Creek on the 26th and at Franklin on the 30th, and soon after the engagement at the latter place it was ordered with its brigade to Nashville, but owing to the rebel General Hood having invested that place, it was compelled to make a circuitous march of two hundred and fifty miles by way of Clarksville to reach that point, and at one time was within the rebel lines, but under cover of a dark night made its way out and arrived at Nashville December 8th, and on the 15th and 16th took part in the battle before that city, with a loss of one killed and seven wounded. The regiment was afterwards identified with all the movements of the 23d corps in its march to Columbia in pursuit of Hood's army. From Columbia the regiment marched to Clifton, on the Tennessee river, distant two hundred and fifty miles, where it embarked on steamers for Cincinnati, and thence proceeded by rail to Washington, D. C., and soon after took transports for North Carolina, where it participated in the movements of General Schofield's army.

After the surrender of the rebel forces under Johnston, the 25th was sent to Salisbury, where it remained until June 24th, when it was mustered out of service.

THE TWENTY-SIXTH INFANTRY.

The 26th—the celebrated skirmish regiment of the 1st brigade, 1st division, 2d corps—left Jackson for the field in Virginia on December 13, 1862, in command of Colonel Judson S. Farrar, under whose direction it had been recruited. Soon after the arrival of the regiment at Washington, it was ordered on provost duty at Alexandria, Va. It remained thus employed until April 20, 1863, when the regiment proceeded to Suffolk, Va. It participated in the several expeditions subsequently made to the Blackwater. In one of these, May 23d, a portion of the regiment became engaged in a skirmish in the vicinity of Windsor, losing Captain John C. Culver, mortally wounded, who died next day.

The 26th had acquitted itself with much credit in several battles when it entered on the great campaign of 1864 with the Army of the Potomac, bravely fighting through the Wilderness and at Corbin's Bridge and Nye River, and then most signally distinguishing itself at Po River and Spottsylvania. On May 9, 1864, the regiment, in command of Major L. Saviers, marched to Po river, crossed, deployed as skirmishers, and advanced about two miles, captured a few stragglers, halted, and laid in skirmish line all night, in close proximity to the enemy, who was busy throwing up works. On Tuesday morning, the 10th, General Grant's army occupied the same position as on the previous day. His line stretched about six miles on the northerly bank of the Po, and took the general form of a crescent, the wings being thrown forward. The 2d corps, across the Po, now held a line on the right, nearly parallel to the road from Shady Grove Church to the Court-house. The 5th corps held the centre, being on the east side of the Po, and the 6th corps held the left, facing toward the Court-house. Further on the left was the 9th corps, under General Burnside. In front was a dense forest. The enemy held Spottsylvania and the region north of the Court-house; his position was well supported by breastworks, and along the centre was the forest and underbrush, lining a marsh partially drained by a run. The conflict opened in the morning by a terrific fire of artillery, which was incessant all the forenoon. A most vigorous and gallant attack was made by the 5th corps and by Generals Gibbon's and Birney's division of the 2d corps on the centre of General Lee's army. In the meantime the enemy had turned General Barlow's division, (1st,) of the 2d corps, on the right, but it was finally extricated without much loss. In this movement of the enemy the 26th was attacked from the rear, and after a spirited resistance was compelled to move out by the left flank, and took a position to cover the recrossing of the troops, and when accomplished, crossed to the opposite side of the river. On the next day (Wednesday, the 11th) the position of the two armies was nearly the same as on the previous day. During the morning there was brisk skirmishing. The regiment, in command of Major L. Saviers, was sent out to reconnoitre the enemy's position, moved up the north bank of the Po about two miles, crossed, deployed as skirmishers, and advanced down the south bank to find his left and develop his force, attacked and drove in his pickets, charged a strong skirmish line, driving them into their works, gaining and holding a position under a heavy fire for half an hour, within three hundred yards of the enemy's intrenchments. Having accomplished the object of the reconnoissance, the regiment recrossed the river and returned to the picket line, with a loss of three killed and fifteen wounded. It was determined during the day to make an assault early the next morning on the enemy's left, where their batteries were so strongly posted as to annoy General Grant's lines. The 2d corps was selected to make this movement. Soon after midnight, in the darkness and storm, General Hancock changed the position of his corps from the extreme right to the left, filling up the space between Generals Wright and Burnside. It was then near ground well commanded by the enemy, and requiring a quick advance in the morning. At 11 P. M. the 26th, having been relieved from the picket line, commenced the movement to the left of the 6th corps at Spottsylvania, where the division had preceded it, and in the darkness being misled, had marched all night, only reaching the ground where the division, being in the first line, was massed for the assault, just in time for the regiment to form in column without halting, aligning its ranks as it advanced. The regiment moved up in gallant style, and was the first to reach the rebel works, (striking them at an angle,) which were carried after a hand-to-hand fight with the bayonet, capturing two brass guns immediately in rear of the enemy's line, which had been fired only once, and just as the works were entered. The regiment passed on without halting, and soon became mingled with the other regiments coming up in left and in rear, and with these charged along the rebel line at a run, rolling it up for more than a mile, capturing a large number of prisoners, guns, and colors. When about a mile from the angle referred to, another line, running nearly perpendicular to the line being rolled up, was encountered, which sharply contested the advance. Having unavoidably become much broken up, and being opened on by a heavy fire from the woods on the right and left, were obliged to fall back, losing half the ground gained, though the men who thronged their works had been made prisoners and sent to the rear. Several pieces of the captured artillery were left in the hands of the enemy, as they could not be drawn off. The regiment was reformed and moved with the brigade to the woods on the left, where rifle-pits were constructed. The enemy having, by repeated and desperate assaults, retaken the works on the left, near the angle, the regiment was ordered to that; creeping along by the right flank on the outside of the works, until it overlapped the rebel line about half the length of the regiment, its right resting near the point where a large oak tree, twenty-two inches in diameter, standing almost on the first line of rebel works, was literally cut down by musket bullets, partly coming from the 26th.

In the Richmond *Examiner's* account of the battle of Spottsylvania occurs the following:

"A TREE HEWN DOWN BY BULLETS.—Most people have doubted the literal accuracy of the dispatch concerning the battle of Spottsylvania, which alleged that trees were cut down under the concentrated fire of Minie balls. We doubted the literal fact ourselves, and would doubt it still but for the indisputable testimony of Dr. Charles McGill, an eye-witness of the battle. The tree stood near our breastworks at a point upon which at one time the most murderous musketry fire that ever was heard of was directed. The tree fell inside our works, and injured several of our men. After the battle Dr. McGill measured the trunk, and found it twenty-two inches through, and sixty-one inches in circumference, actually hacked through by the awful avalanche of bullets packing against it. The foliage of the tree was trimmed away as effectually as though an army of locusts had swarmed on its branches. A grasshopper could not have lived through the pelting of that leaden storm; and but for the fact that our troops were protected by breastworks they would have been swept away to a man."

The regiment fought for more than one hour over the rebel works, almost musket to musket, losing a large number killed and wounded, when the enemy made signals of surrender by waving handkerchiefs on their rammers. Firing ceased, and the rebels were called to come over, when their whole line for seventy or eighty yards rose up and started to come in; but the moment firing ceased the enemy advanced a fresh line, which came up from their supports to the works with a cheer, when most of those who had started to surrender turned and jumped into the works again. About twenty who were immediately in front of the regiment were taken. The regiment fought this new line for half an hour, when it was relieved and moved to the left, where it joined the brigade and remained during the night. In this memorable affair, which lasted fourteen hours, the regiment lost twenty-seven killed, four commissioned officers and ninety-three men wounded, and fourteen missing, most of whom are now known to have been killed. Major Saviers, commanding the regiment, was struck four times by the enemy's bullets while gallantly doing his duty, and seven out of the nine color-guards were killed or wounded. The regiment was specially complimented by Generals Barlow and Miles for its noble conduct and persistent and vigorous fighting during the day, and had the credit of first planting its colors on the enemy's works.

Leaving its position at Spottsylvania Court-house on the night of the 20th, the regiment marched to the North Anna river, where it arrived on the 23d. On the 24th it crossed the North Anna at Jericho Bridge, under a heavy fire from the enemy's artillery, and after a spirited skirmish the rebels were driven into their works. The casualties of the regiment in the engagement were five killed and nine wounded. It recrossed the North Anna on the night of the 26th, and marched toward the Pamunkey. Crossing that river on the morning of the 28th, it advanced to the vicinity of Hawes' Shop, and threw up breastworks. On the 29th it moved down the Richmond road, drove in the enemy's pickets, and developed their position on the Tolopotamy creek. Three companies were engaged in skirmishing with the enemy on the 30th, losing one killed and three wounded. On the 2d of June the regiment arrived at Cold Harbor; and advancing as skirmishers on the enemy, near Gaines' Hill, succeeded in driving them into their intrenchments. It afterwards charged their works across an open field; but, finding them occupied by the enemy in force, and being under a fire of grape and canister, the regiment was obliged to retire. The casualties sustained in the assault were fifteen wounded and five missing. From the 3d to the 12th the regiment was on the skirmish line and in the intrenchments, and lost three men killed, seven wounded, and one missing. At midnight, on the 14th, it crossed the James river at Wilcox's Landing, and on the morning of the 16th arrived in front of Petersburg. The regiment participated in the assault of the 16th, in which the first line of the enemy's rifle-pits were carried. It lost in the attack its commanding officer, Captain James A. Lothian, who was mortally wounded, and two men killed and nine wounded. On the 17th, the regiment, commanded by Captain A. G. Dailey, participated in the capture of the enemy's line of works, losing in the charge two killed and seven wounded. A detachment was engaged as skirmishers on the 18th, with a loss of one killed and one wounded. On the 22d the regiment assisted in repulsing an assault made on our lines, near the Williams House. Its loss in the attack was two men taken prisoners.

The 26th also attracted much enviable notice by its gallant fighting at Deep Bottom, July 27 and 28, 1864, where the enemy in front of the 2d corps occupied rifle-pits defended by a battery. An advance was made by the corps, during which General Miles' brigade, in which was the 26th, flanked the whole position under a brisk fire, driving the enemy in much confusion, capturing four guns and taking some prisoners, the 26th Michigan constituting a part of the skirmish line which led the assault. On the 28th the regiment made a reconnoissance between New Market and Charles City road to discover the enemy's left, when it attacked and drove in splendid style double its own strength for half a mile, and then pushed them into their earthworks in much confusion. For this gallant and dashing affair, and the operations of the day preceding, the regiment was specially complimented by General Hancock in general orders.

On the 16th of August it encountered the enemy near the White Oak Swamp, losing three killed, fourteen wounded, and seventeen taken prisoners. Among the latter was the officer commanding the regiment, Captain A. G. Dailey. The regiment recrossed the James river on the 20th, and reached the lines in front of Petersburg on the 21st. On the 22d it marched to the Weldon railroad, and until the 24th was employed in the destruction of that road near Ream's Station. On the 25th it was engaged in the battle at the latter point, assisted in repelling the repeated assaults of the enemy, and after the works were taken by the rebels participated in the charge in which they were retaken. Its loss in the action was three wounded and fourteen missing.

On the 25th of March, 1865, immediately following the evening's attack on Forts Steadman and Hancock, in the line of the works in front of the 9th corps, the regiment, in command of Captain S. H. Ives, with the brigade, was ordered to make a charge on the enemy's works in front of its position, and succeeded in capturing a portion of them, taking several prisoners, and continued fighting during the day with slight loss. The brigade occupied that position until the army commenced its flanking movement to the left on March 29th, when it was deployed during the day as skirmishers, in front of the corps, and at night was relieved. On the 30th it again skirmished the entire day, the regiment losing several men, and on the 31st it marched in column until about noon, when it again took the skirmish line, and participated in a running fight with the enemy until it was relieved. From the 1st to the 6th of April it was engaged in pursuing the retreating army, fighting every day. On the 6th the regiment took a very active part in the capture of a train of 260 wagons, containing baggage, provisions, and ammunition, and was the first regiment to attack the train. The pursuit of the enemy continued on the 7th, 8th, and 9th, and the regiment was in the skirmish line at the surrender of Lee's army, and through its lines General Grant operated with his flag of truce in arranging the terms of surrender. From March 28th until April 9th the regiment had captured our 400 prisoners, and during that time its losses had been, killed and wounded, about sixty, or more than one-fourth of its number present for duty, and had often been complimented by the brigade and divison commanders as the best skirmish regiment in the corps.

THE TWENTY-SEVENTH INFANTRY.

Although the 27th, organized by Col. D. M. Fox, did not leave the State until April, 1863, it engaged the enemy at Jamestown, Ky., in June following, and before the war ended had passed through four distinct and prominent campaigns with the 9th army corps, to which it belonged: One in Mississippi, the siege of Vicksburg and Jackson; Burnside's campaign in

East Tennessee, including the defence of Knoxville; Grant's campaign of great battles in the spring and summer of 1864 and the siege of Petersburg, including the surrender of Lee's army; took part in thirty general engagements and skirmishes, and by its never-varying firmness, stubborn fighting, and bravery in action well earned the complimentary remarks of the division commander when he said: "I always feel sure that portion of my line occupied by the 27th Michigan is perfectly safe."

The regiment left its rendezvous at Ypsilanti April 12, 1863, and proceeded via Cincinnati to Kentucky, and was stationed at various posts in that State until the 9th corps, to which it was attached, was sent in June to Mississippi. It moved with the army in its advance on Jackson, Miss., in July, and in a skirmish near that place on the 11th of that month lost two killed and five wounded. After the evacuation of Jackson by the rebels it participated in a reconnoissance to Pearl river, and thence returned to Milldale, Miss. During the following month, August, the regiment returned with the 9th corps to Kentucky. On the 10th of September it was ordered to proceed to Cumberland Gap. It arrived at the Gap on the 20th, and from thence marched to Knoxville, Tenn., arriving at that place September 26th.

Breaking camp at Lenoir Station, East Tennessee, on November 14th, 1863, the regiment marched to Hough's Ferry. On the 16th the army commenced the retreat to Knoxville, closely followed by the rebel army under General Longstreet. In order to effect the safe withdrawal of the trains a stand was made at Campbell's station. In the engagement the 27th participated, losing three killed, eight wounded, and ten missing. The retreat was continued to Knoxville, where the regiment actively assisted in the defence of the city during the siege. In the assault made by the rebels on Fort Sanders, November 29th, the loss of the regiment was one killed and nineteen missing. The casualties of the regiment during the month of November were 4 killed, 4 mortally wounded, 17 severely wounded, and 29 missing; total, 54. The regiment marched, on the 7th of December, in pursuit of the retreating enemy, following them to Rutledge, whence, after remaining in camp three days, it fell back to Blain's Cross-roads, where it encamped until the 16th of January, 1864. During the period following the 14th of November the suffering and hardships of the regiment were very severe, particularly during the retreat to Knoxville and the siege of that place, from want of rest and an insufficient supply of food and clothing. At Mossy creek, in March, the regiment was joined by two new companies which had been raised in the State, together with a large number of recruits, numbering in all 362 men. On the 17th it marched, via Knoxville, Hall's Gap, Ky., and Camp Dick Robinson, to Nicholasville, Ky. The march to this place was accomplished in fourteen days, an average of nearly seventeen miles a day. Proceeding thence by cars the regiment arrived at Annapolis, Md., April 5th. Two companies of sharp-shooters joined the regiment at Annapolis. April 23d the regiment moved via Washington and Manassas to Warrenton Junction, Va., where it joined the Army of the Potomac on the 29th. It crossed the Rapidan on the 5th of May, in command of Major Samuel Moody, and on the 6th participated in the battle of the Wilderness, sustaining a loss of eighty-nine in killed and wounded. Among the killed being Lieut. James Plummer and Lieut. Arthur Christian, while among the wounded was Major Moody.

At Spottsylvania, May 12th, the 27th most eminently exhibited that strong, enduring courage, unyielding firmness, which distinguished it when victory was hopeless, and at the assault on Fort Mahon, April 2d, 1865, it manifested gallant and impetuous action when success seemed hopeful. The condition of the troops on the morning of the battle of Spottsylvania was very unfavorable for an important and desperate assault. For the whole previous week the army had been almost constantly fighting, marching, or throwing up earthworks, and the men were much exhausted. It had rained for several days preceding the 12th, and that morning a dense fog prevailed effectually concealing any movements of the enemy. One of his batteries, occupying a position raking the part of the line held by the 27th, firing at random, and chance shots from their sharp-shooters frequently took effect, and the men of the regiment were compelled to lie on their arms without an opportunity of replying; all were circumstances calculated to try them to the utmost, and dispel that spirit and enthusiasm so necessary for a successful attack.

The regiment belonged to the 1st brigade, 3d division, 9th corps; the position held by the brigade was at the foot of a hill covered with a heavy second growth of pine, and held by the enemy's skirmishers strongly supported. A short time before the fog arose the brigade was ordered to dislodge the enemy from the hill and push forward to the extreme edge of the woods and hold the position until the support came up, preparatory to an assault on his works. At the command the brigade moved briskly forward, encountering a strong resistance, but steadily advanced through the timber to an open field; the fog was rising, and the enemy discovered strongly intrenched in well-built earthworks, not more than one hundred and twenty-five yards distant; the intervening space was an open field, carefully cleared, affording no protection to an advancing column. They immediately opened with a terrific fire of artillery and musketry, and soon after a strong force of the enemy came rushing in on the left flank of the brigade then still advancing, and, although strongly and persistently resisted, swept steadily up the line, checking the movement, taking several hundred prisoners, including one regiment almost entire, and driving back a great portion of the command in disorder, leaving nothing on the left of the regiment except the Michigan sharp-shooters. The 27th, then commanded by the brave Major Moody, who afterwards died of wounds received at Cold Harbor, held its position, and swinging back the left of his regiment Major Moody opposed a strong front to the enemy, checked his advance, and finally forced him from his immediate front and back to his works. The fire of the enemy continuing with much vigor and effect, an angle in his works enabling him to pour in a very destructive cross-fire from the left, Major Moody sent to the corps commander asking permission to fall back a few yards over the brow of the hill and await supports, but he received in reply orders not to fall back an inch. The supports, made up mostly of raw troops, fell back as soon as they reached within range of the heavy fire of the enemy, and the assault was abandoned; in the meantime an aid had withdrawn unobserved the regiment holding the flank on the right of the 27th, the enemy then pressed eagerly and rapidly forward, delivering a heavy enfilading fire on the 27th. The right of the regiment was immediately swung back, and a well-directed fire checked his advance, but a galling fire was kept up by the enemy on the front and both flanks. The enemy hitherto kept closely down behind his works, now poured in volley after volley of musketry with fearful effect, and delivered his artillery fire with increased rapidity and precision. The ammunition of the 27th was gone, the cartridge-boxes of the dead and wounded had been emptied and used, and the regiment was at the mercy of the enemy, but not a man flinched. The brave old Major Moody, then suffering from a wound received in the Wilderness, moved along the line in front of his regiment under a fearful fire encouraging his men to hold their ground until support came, saying, "General Burnside says we mustn't fall back an inch; d——d hard order, but must obey it." The fight continued on, but slackening in force, and was ended by the darkness of night. In this fearful contest the regiment lost 27 killed, 148 wounded, and 12 missing. Lieutenant John Armour being among the mortally wounded and who died next day.

The brigade commander remarked, with regard to the 27th, that "during the engagement not a single man belonging to the regiment attempted to pass to the rear unless wounded."

Marching to the North Anna river, the 27th, then in command of Col. D. M. Fox, lost in the operations of the 24th and 25th of May three killed and eight wounded. Having crossed the Pamunkey and moved forward with the army to Bethesda Church, the regiment participated in the engagement at that point on the 3d of June, with a loss of sixteen killed and sixty wounded; among the former being Lieut. Charles H. Seymour and Lieut. Charles T. Miller, and among the latter was Major Moody mortally, who died on the 20th of the same month. Marching to Cold Harbor, it took part in the operations there, and, crossing the James river with the army, advanced to the front at Petersburg. On the 17th and 18th it took part in the charges made on the enemy's works.

Colonel Fox being wounded on the 17th, the command of the regiment was assumed by Captain E. S. Leadbetter. During the month the loss of the regiment was 21 killed, 149 wounded, and 23 missing. These casualties occurred principally in the battles of the 17th and 18th, and included Lieutenant J. W. Brennan, killed on the 18th.

On the 30th of July following the regiment, with its division, was in the gallant charge upon the enemy's lines following the "explosion of the mine" under the rebel works, in front of Petersburg, and under a heavy and most destructive fire, reached the "crater," with great loss in killed and wounded; among the latter was Colonel William B. Wright, commanding regiment. The casualties during July were 24 killed, 92 wounded, and 27 missing.

The regiment, in command of Captain Charles Wait, occupied a portion of the intrenchments in front of Petersburg until the 19th of August, when it marched to the Weldon railroad. On the 19th and 20th of August it participated in the battles fought near that road. Its losses in these two engagements were 9 killed, 8 wounded, and 39 missing, including among the killed Lieutenant Mason Vosper. During September, until the 29th, the regiment was engaged principally in the construction of fortifications, roads, etc. On the 29th it moved to the west of the Weldon road, and on the 30th took part in the battle near Peeble's Farm, or Poplar Grove Church, with a loss of 10 wounded and 1 missing. Lieutenant Theodore S. Mead here received a wound of which he died at Washington on October 16th following. On the 27th and 28th of October the regiment took part in the movement on the South Side railroad, but did not become engaged. On the 31st it was in camp near what is called the Peebles' Farm House.

On November 1st following the regiment was engaged on picket duty and holding a road, about seven miles west of Petersburg, Va., and on the 29th moved to the right and took a position in the works in front of Petersburg, relieving the troops of the 2d corps. In that position it remained, doing very heavy and arduous picket duty until April 1st following, when it was ordered to make a demonstration on the enemy's line directly in front of Mine Fort, as it was supposed that he was withdrawing from that point.

The demonstration was made, but it was found that he was still in force, and the command fell back to the main line of works again, when a movement was made one mile to the left, where line of battle was formed in rear of Fort Sedgwick, and preparations made to charge at daybreak on the following morning, and at 4 A. M. on the 2d, the regiment charged on the rebel Fort Mahon, capturing its eastern wing. Fort Mahon, prominent among the chain of forts in the line of works before Petersburg, and the key to the position on that part of the line, was a large, strongly built frame and earth-work, protected on the front and both flanks by a deep ditch and two lines of *chevaux de frise*; the front was still farther protected by a strong line of rifle-pits, which extended the whole length of the Petersburg fortifications outside the *chevaux de frise.*

The assaulting column was formed by regiments in mass in front of the works, which at that point were about three hundred yards distant from the fort. The main assault was to be made by a large brigade of new troops, that had never participated in an engagement, and the brigade to which the 27th belonged was to act merely as a support, and for that purpose was drawn up in two lines, the 27th on the right of the rear line.

Just before daybreak the assaulting column was ordered to advance. They moved forward rapidly and silently, but were soon discovered by the enemy's outer line, and a heavy fire was opened. The inner line almost instantly responding to the alarm, opened a deadly fire of artillery and musketry. The new troops wavered for a moment, then dashed gallantly forward, and soon after their hearty cheers announced success, their men coming to the rear with wounded, shouting exultingly to the old brigade, "Now boys, we have taken the fort for you, and, for God's sake, see if you can't hold it." But the firing every moment increasing in vigor, the news from the front began to be doubted, and soon the command was given: "Forward, 1st brigade;" when, with a hearty cheer, they advanced gallantly on the double-quick. Soon the head of the column came up with the new brigade, and found them only in possession of the rifle-pits, and it was found impossible for the 1st brigade to pass them, and the assault was likely to prove a failure, when the quick eye of Wait—the gallant young colonel of the 27th Michigan—took in the situation at a glance—failure and death to halt and await orders; disgrace to fall back; the only alternative to attempt the fort with one hundred and twenty-three men. A moment's delay would have been fatal; he instantly changed the direction of his regiment by the right flank, unmasked his command, charged again to the front, and nobly advanced, at the double-quick, on the fort. The brigade commander, fearing the result, shouted at the top of his voice: "Don't attempt the fort, Colonel; break the lines to the right." The Colonel's strong, clear voice, rising above the deafening uproar, answered back with gallant spirit: "*Fort or nothing!*" Taking up the cry, the whole regiment, with one voice as it were, shouted exultingly: "*Fort or nothing!*" Partaking of the bravery of their Colonel, the men doubled their exertions and rushed onward for the fort. The formidable *chevaux de frise* which they had dreaded for months was soon reached and quickly cleared, and on they rushed. The rebel artillery, heavily charged with grape, soon belched forth in awful salvo, but it passed harmlessly over the regiment, being too near the fort, and, happily, out of range. The ditch was soon cleared, and clambering up the embankment, the colors of the 27th were planted on the parapet. The enemy resisted, but with a rousing cheer, such as victorious troops only can give, the whole regiment in mass poured into the fort. One hundred and fifty-nine—twenty-six more than the regiment numbered—surrendered on the spot. Without a moment's delay, the captured guns (six in number) were turned upon those who escaped, and with good effect. The 27th was thus in possession of this stronghold, and the first break had been made in the works on that side of the city.

Next day, as the brigade returned to their old quarters, after having passed through Petersburg, the 51st Pennsylvania, a large regiment, which had held the brigade line during the charge, crowded to the side of the road, and taking off their hats gave three hearty cheers for the 27th Michigan, a high compliment, and seldom paid by one old regiment to another, showing in the strongest manner possible the merit of the 27th in the assault on Fort Mahon.

Major Moody, in his last communication before his death, made to the Adjutant-General of the State, giving the casualties of the regiment in the battles of the Wilderness and Spottsylvania, says: "In conclusion, the brave and gallant conduct of both officers and men of my command in these engagements, have not only sustained but added new honor to our State and country." He wrote in pencil at the foot of the page: "This statement has been made in our rifle-pits, and this is all the paper I could get." The Major was then suffering from a wound received in the Wilderness May 6th. He died June 20th following, from a wound at Cold Harbor June 3d.

NOTE.—The late Major Moody of the 27th Michigan, formerly a well known Lake Superior as well as sea captain, while in command of his company at Jackson, Miss., and while in line of battle behind some protection, being desirous of saving his men from the fire of the enemy, repeatedly cautioned them against exposing themselves, and failing to do so satisfactorily, losing all patience with them, rushed in front of the company, calling aloud at the top of his voice: "Boys, bear a hand and keep down, or by Jupiter if you don't, I'll send every mother's son of you aft," (meaning the rear,) inferring that he would do their part of the fighting himself. On another occasion, while advancing in line of battle in the Wilderness under a heavy fire, anxious to keep his alignment in the excitement around him forgot his tactics and military phrases, and went back to his native element, the sailor, and was heard all over the line giving his commands: "Luff, boys, luff—steady, steady—luff, luff—there, steady—now give 'em every shot in the locker."

The following is an extract from the report of Captain Charles Wait: "The regiment was engaged at Cold Harbor June 3d, and charged the enemy's works in our front, carrying his first line with heavy loss, but holding the position until about 10 P. M., when it was relieved and withdrawn to the second line. In this engagement, Major Moody received a wound which caused his death. The loss of this gallant officer is deeply mourned in the regiment. Though suffering from illness and a wound received in the Wilderness, he had steadily remained at his post of duty, on all occasions manifesting rare courage and entire devotion to the cause in which he yielded up his life."

THE TWENTY-EIGHTH INFANTRY.

The 28th, raised and rendezvoused at Marshall, under the direction of the Hon. S. S. Lacy as commandant of camp, left the State for the field in Tennessee October 26, 1864, under the command of Lieut. Col. Delos Phillips. It arrived at Louisville, Ky., on the 29th, and on November 10th it was ordered to Camp Nelson, Ky., for the purpose of guarding a wagon train from that point to Nashville, where it arrived on the 5th of December, and was assigned to temporary duty at that post. The advance of Hood on Nashville soon brought the 28th to face the realities of war, and under command of Col. W. W. Wheeler, participated in the defence of that place by General Thomas, from the 12th to the 16th of that month, when it fully established a reputation as a gallant fighting regiment, and at once reached the uniform high standard of Michigan troops.

After the battle of Nashville the regiment was attached to the 23d corps, which was soon after sent to the Atlantic seaboard to constitute a part of the force concentrating in the vicinity of Wilmington intended to co-operate with General Sherman's army on its approach to the coast. The regiment belonged to the 2d brigade, 1st division, (Ruger's,) and arrived at Morehead City February 24, 1865, and on March 2d moved with its division towards Kingston, and joined General Cox. Meeting the enemy at Wise Forks, the 28th, commanded by Col. Wheeler, took an active part in the battles of the 8th, 9th, and 10th, at that point. On the 8th the regiment was engaged in heavy skirmishing during that entire day and the night following. On the 9th the enemy pressed Cox's lines strongly, without making an assault, and at the same time attempted to turn his right, but failed on account of a prompt reinforcement, of which the 28th formed a part. On the morning of the 10th the enemy made a fierce and determined charge upon the left, breaking the lines, but were repulsed. The brigade to which the 28th belonged charged the rebels on the double-quick, driving them back, and taking over three hundred prisoners, among whom were several field officers. About two o'clock the same day they made a heavy and desperate onset on the left and centre of General Cox, but most signally failed, the point having been strongly and promptly reinforced from the right. The 28th, with its brigade, being among the first to arrive, fought the enemy most gallantly for about two hours, when they were most decisively repulsed, leaving their dead and wounded and a large number of prisoners, and during the night they fell back across the Neuse, burning the bridge in their rear.

In this spirited engagement the regiment lost Lieut. Mathew Holmes and six men killed, and thirteen wounded.

Continuing the march, the regiment reached Kingston on the 14th, and Goldsboro' on the 21st, when the brigade was placed on duty guarding the line of the Atlanta and North Carolina railroad. On the 9th of April the regiment marched again to Goldsboro', and on the 13th arrived at Raleigh, and after the cessation of hostilities was engaged on duty at Goldsboro', Raleigh, Charlotte, Lincolntown, Wilmington, and Newbern, until June 5, 1866, when it was mustered out of service.

Lieut. John E. Kenyon died February 2, 1866, of wounds received January 27th previous, while arresting murderers in Pitt county, N. C.

THE TWENTY-NINTH INFANTRY.

When the rebel General Hood was on his Northern campaign in 1864, for the purpose of overrunning Tennessee, getting possession of Nashville and Louisville, and threatening the cities on the Ohio river, the 29th Michigan, (recruited and rendezvoused under the supervision of the Hon. John F. Driggs, M. C.,) under command of Colonel Thomas M. Taylor, was stationed at Nashville, where it had arrived from Michigan October 3d; and on the advance of Hood upon Decatur, Ala., it was sent forward to that point, arriving there on the 26th, just in time to march from the cars to its position in line, to meet the advance of Hood's forces, then attacking that place. Col. Charles C. Doolittle, of the 18th Michigan, was in command of the post of Decatur, and for some days previous to the 26th had been watching the movements of Hood's army, as well as those of Forrest and Roddey, and had scouted the surrounding country as thoroughly as possible. On the morning of the 26th he sent out several detachments on the Sommerville and Courtland roads, one of which met a pretty strong force about three miles out on the Sommerville road, and was obliged to retire. Not expecting the advance of Hood's army, for a day or two at least, Col. Doolittle was of the opinion that it might be a scouting party of Roddey's command; but, at half past one o'clock P. M., on the same day, his videttes reported the enemy advancing on the place. He immediately made preparations for action, and rode to the advance post on the Sommerville road, and on seeing the enemy's columns forming into line with skirmishers out, he ordered the 2d Tennessee cavalry to hold the enemy in check, and then hurried back to headquarters, and made the necessary disposition of his force to meet the coming attack.

Battery A, 1st Tennessee light artillery, supported by the reserve picket of the 18th Michigan that had been ordered up, soon got into position in a small redoubt commanding the Sommerville road and vicinity, and at once opened fire on the enemy's line of battle. The 10th Indiana cavalry had also been ordered up, and was engaged at various points looking after and checking the advance of the enemy. Finding that he could hold the rebels in check, Col. Doolittle, about twenty minutes after the artillery opened fire, ordered the right wing of the 29th Michigan, which had just arrived by rail from Nashville and been placed behind the breastworks on the left flank, to move to the front and occupy the line of rifle-pits on the left of the redoubt. This they accomplished in the most gallant style under a hot fire from the enemy's artillery and musketry, which they withstood with firmness. Soon after the other wing of the regiment was ordered out, and one hundred of the men, in command of the major, was sent to what was known as Fort No. 1. Battery I, 1st Ohio light artillery, had been ordered forward and opened on the enemy, the fight continuing until dark, the rebels being unable to gain any advance, notwithstanding he made several attempts to charge the line. Col. Doolittle then withdrew the advance force inside the main works, leaving one hundred men of the 29th Michigan to strengthen the picket line and hold the line of the rifle-pits. In the engagement of this day the pickets on the Union line, from the redoubt to the river on the right, remained in their position, and when night came the picket line was in tact. It was ascertained that the attack was made by Walthal's division, 5,000 strong, of Stewart's corps, Hood's army, and were fought by Col. Doolittle with less than 500 men and a small amount of artillery. During the night of the 26th the Union forces were receiving reinforcements, and on the 27th nothing more important occurred than the driving back of the enemy's skirmishers on the front and right flank. On the 28th, about 3 A. M., the enemy drove in a portion of the pickets on the right, and established themselves in gopher holes within four hundred yards of the works. An attempt was made early in the morning to dislodge them and re-establish the line, but the enemy were too well protected to be moved. Some time afterwards they were surprised by Capt. W. C. Moore, 18th Michigan, with about fifty men of that regiment and a few clerks and orderlies from district headquarters, who made a most daring and dashing attack on them, driving them from their holes like scared rats, and taking 115 prisoners. During the day the battle became general, the Union troops having been reinforced and numbering about 5,000, had made a most determined defence; and early on the morning of the 29th it was ascertained that the enemy's forces had all been withdrawn except a strong rear guard, and at about 4 P. M. he was driven out of his last line of rifle-pits.

The noble and successful defence of Decatur by Col. Doolittle against such enormous odds was among the most gallant and remarkable of the war, and its importance, in view of its effect upon the great battle of Nashville which soon followed, was second to no minor engagement during the rebellion.

The exemplary conduct, vigorous and splendid fighting of Col. Taylor's regiment and his officers, although less than a month in the field, could scarcely have been excelled by long tried veterans.

On the 31st of October, 1864, this regiment was stationed at Decatur, Ala., garrisoning that place until November 24th, when it marched to Murfreesboro', Tenn.; arriving there on the 27th, it composed a part of the force at that point during the siege of Nashville and Murfreesboro' by the enemy under Hood, and was engaged with the enemy on the 7th of December at Overall creek. On the 13th it was sent out as the escort of a railroad train to procure fuel, when it was attacked by a superior force of infantry and artillery near Winchester Church, when a severe battle ensued, in which the enemy was repulsed with loss, the regiment losing seventeen killed, wounded, and missing. The enemy having taken up the track, the regiment succeeded in relaying it under fire and saved the train, bringing it into Murfreesboro' by hand after the engine had been disabled by a shell. On the 15th and 16th, while guarding a forage train at Alexandria, near Murfreesboro', it became engaged with two brigades of the enemy's cavalry on the Shelbyville Pike with slight loss, and was also engaged at Nolansville on the 17th. In the affair on the 15th Lieut. Frederick Van Vliet was killed. On the 27th it was moved by rail to Anderson, and was assigned to duty guarding the Nashville and Chattanooga railroad; remaining there until July following, it moved to Dechard and thence to Murfreesboro', arriving there on the 19th, and was employed on garrison duty until September 6th, when it was mustered out of service, and on the 8th left for Michigan, arriving on the 12th at Detroit, where it was paid off and discharged.

The 30th regiment was raised under authority from the War Department for special service on the Michigan frontier, its term of service being for one year; and by orders from this Department dated November 7, 1864, its recruitment commenced, under the direction of Col. G. S. Wormer, with rendezvous at Jackson, which was afterwards changed to Detroit, where the organization was completed January 9, 1865. The companies were stationed at different points along the Detroit and St. Clair rivers and in other parts of the State, as follows: A and B at Fort Gratiot, D at St. Clair, E at Wyandotte, K at Jackson, H at Fenton, G in Detroit, and C, F, and I at Detroit Barracks. The regimental headquarters were for some time at Jackson, then at Detroit, and on January 24th were removed to Fort Gratiot. The regiment continued on duty at those points until June 30th, when it was mustered out of service.

THE COLORED REGIMENT.

The only Michigan colored regiment in the war was the 102d U. S., raised by Col. Henry Barns, of Detroit, organized by Lieut. Col. W. T. Bennett, and in March, 1864, took the field in command of Colonel H. L. Chipman, then a captain in the regular army, who had procured a leave of absence for that purpose. The regiment first faced the enemy at Baldwin, Florida, in August following, where it was suddenly attacked by a force of rebel cavalry, which it easily repulsed and scattered, and by its splendid conduct on that occasion fully convinced its officers of the reliable and gallant fighting qualities of their men. But these qualities were more fully manifested at

Honey Hill, S. C., on November 30th following, at Tillifinny December 7th, and at Devereax Neck on the 9th by a detachment of the regiment, consisting of twelve officers and three hundred men, that had been sent from Beaufort to join the forces of General Foster. This detachment was commanded by Capt. Montague, Col. Chipman being in command of a brigade. At the points named the officers and men referred to, most gallantly engaged a superior force of the enemy, sustaining an aggregate loss in these affairs of sixty-five in killed and wounded; Capt. A. E. Lindsey being among the killed and Lieut. H. H. Alvord among the severely wounded.

From the 11th to the 18th April, 1865, the right wing, in command of Col. Chipman, was engaged on a most hazardous and daring expedition from Charleston, S. C., to join General Potter on the Santee river, striking it at Nelson's Ferry, distant about seventy miles. The march was made through the country held by the enemy, the command subjected to great danger of attack from superior force, and of being cut off from all reinforcements and overwhelmed, enduring much hardship and fatigue, and meeting a large body of the enemy's cavalry, which, after a brisk and vigorous fight, were driven off. Encountering the rebels again on the 18th, while on the march in the direction of Camden, a skirmish ensued. On the 19th the command succeeded in rejoining the left wing.

The left wing had marched from Georgetown on the 5th, commanded by Major Clark, with an expedition under command of General Potter. After much hard marching and considerable skirmishing with the enemy on the 8th, 15th, and 17th; and on the 18th, near Manchester, met the enemy in force at Boykins, when, with the 54th Massachusetts colored infantry, it flanked the rebels attacking them with much spirit and gallantry, driving them in great disorder in the direction of Statesburg. Next day the two wings again united, and under command of Col. Chipman, came up with the enemy near Singleton's plantation, when a successful flank movement was made by the regiment, which resulted, after a most gallant brush, in forcing him to abandon a strong position, and in routing him most thoroughly.

The regiment being encamped on the 20th and 21st, having companies A, B, and C (under command of Major Clark) on the picket line, on the morning of the 21st company A was attacked by two hundred of the enemy, which it handsomely repulsed. At 12 M., on the 21st, the enemy sent in a flag of truce, with dispatches from General Beauregard, stating that Generals Sherman and Johnston had cease hostilities, when the column marched back to Georgetown, arriving there on the 25th.

On the 29th the regiment received orders to proceed to Charleston, and next day embarked on transports, arriving at that point the same day, and went into camp on Charleston Neck, where it remained until May 7th, and then broke camp and marched for Summerville, and reaching there on the 8th, encamped until the 18th, then proceeded by rail to Branchville, and thence, on the 25th, to Orangeburg, where it was engaged on provost guard and fatigue duty until July 28th, when it marched for Winnsboro', arriving there on the 3d of August, and during the remainder of that month was engaged on the same duties as at Orangeburg. Sometime in the month following the regiment returned to Charleston, where it was mustered out of service September 30th, and proceeded to Michigan, arriving on October 17th at Detroit, where it was paid off and disbanded.

While the regiment was engaged during its term of service in many other battles and skirmishes, and behaved well in every respect, the actions above referred to will always be recognized as prominent in its creditable history.

THE MILITIA GUARDS.

Throughout the war the entire militia of the State consisted of three companies of the force known as the "State Troops:"—the "Scott Guard," "Detroit Light Guard," and the "Lyon Guard."

The Scott Guard was originally organized at Detroit, October 11, 1861. Having tendered its services in response to the Governor's call for volunteers, of April 17, 1861, the company was accepted as one of the uniformed militia companies, and was assigned as company A in the 2d infantry. Those members of the company who did not accompany the Guard at this time continued the organization under its old name.

The Detroit Light Guard was organized November 16, 1865. This company tendered its services in response to the Governor's proclamation of April 17, 1861, calling for volunteers. It was accepted, and was assigned as company A in the 1st regiment of infantry, (three months' men.) During the noted riot in the city of Detroit, on the 6th of March, 1863, it rendered efficient service in preserving the peace, guarding the jail, and patrolling the district where the disturbance occurred.

The Lyon Guard was organized at Detroit October 3, 1861. On the occasion of the riot in Detroit on the 6th of March, 1863, the company rendered material aid to the public authorities—patrolling the streets and otherwise assisting in preserving the peace.

These companies maintained their organization during the war, and rendered valuable service in guarding against raids by Southern rebel refugees from the borders of the provinces of Canada, threatened to be made from time to time on the city of Detroit and along the line. They were placed on duty as patrols and guards, and were found at all times ready for any service. They aided much in sustaining a feeling of security among the inhabitants during excitement consequent to the threatened raids referred to.

Notwithstanding the great efficiency of Michigan troops in the field during the recent war, her militia has always been extremely deficient, and is now scarcely deserving to be named as such, consisting of only six companies of State troops.

In 1866, the Adjutant General of the State made a special report, under date of November 27th, to the Governor of the State on that subject, in which he says:

"The Legislature of the State passed at its extra session of 1862 an act for the reorganization of the military forces of the State of Michigan, which was approved January 18, 1862.

"Since the passage of the law referred to, and down to this date, only three companies have been mustered into the service of the State as State troops. These companies are in the city of Detroit, and were in existence long before the passage of that law, so in fact none have been organized under its operations, and it is evident that so long as it remains as it is, none are likely to be. I have, therefore, thought it proper at this time to make a special report on that subject.

"The national defence of the Republic, aside from its navy, consists of a small standing army and its militia. The former is acquired by volunteering, and the latter by a general liability, with some exemptions, of all men of proper age and sufficient physical ability to serve, when required.

"The militia, when well organized, equipped and disciplined, offers the most acceptable and safest guarantee for national defence and domestic peace. It does not invite a desire to assume the offensive, yet is ever ready for the defensive. It is the army of the masses, and creates no special military organization. It engenders no distinction between citizen and soldier, no antagonistic interests and aims between the people and the army, no false pride or selfish motive which seeks hostility only to obtain fame and military advancement. It guards alike the life and honor of the Nation, and the independence and liberty of the citizen, and does not exhaust or diminish the industrial resources of the country, nor does it endanger its freedom by placing a great military power in the hands of one man, or a set of men, whose ambition or selfishness might lead them to usurp the Government and abridge or destroy the liberties of the people, and it far more advances the national defence by possessing a greater numerical strength than any standing army which any nation could sustain.

"It is obvious that the maintaining of a large standing army is not in keeping with the spirit of American institutions, nor will it ever receive the sanction of the people. The country will be willing only to support such a permanent military force in time of peace as may be absolutely necessary for protecting its frontier and aiding the civil authority in the enforcement of the law. Therefore the main military strength of the Republic will be in its militia, and, such being the case, the maintaining thereof should be a fixed policy in every State in the Union, and to be effective and reliable should be permanently and systematically organized.

"It has been fully demonstrated during the late civil war that a well organized and equipped militia is of the utmost importance, not only to the General Government, but to a State itself, being relied upon as the main national defence against foreign invasion and civil war, and to defend the State against hostile attacks on its borders, to maintain the enforcement of its laws when necessary, and to guarantee the peace and protect the lives and property of its people. Therefore it is unquestionably the interest of the State of Michigan to be prepared promptly and successfully to meet emergencies of that nature by a complete enrollment and organization of its militia, and by maintaining a small active force of State troops well armed and equipped ready for service on the shortest notice possible.

"On the outbreak of the recent rebellion few States were in a condition to render much service to the Government by their militia, and the greater proportion of them not any. This condition of affairs rose from the defectiveness of their militia system and the little attention that had been given to the proper organization of their State militia or State troops.

"Yet, what little had been done in this respect proved to be of infinite value to the Government, as it is generally conceded that to the organization of State troops the nation was indebted at that time for the safety and preservation of its capital. The non-effective condition of the militia of the various States was, to a certain extent, excused by the country for the reason that there had been but little, if any, indications of a foreign war for a long period of years, and a rebellion against the Government had not been thought of; hence the States had been unthinkingly lulled into a state of security, although unwarranted in history. By the inauguration of the rebellion and during its progress, however, that idea of security has been fully exploded, and a lesson has been taught by experience and at a great cost that it is necessary in peace to prepare for war, and that this maxim should be adhered to at all times. As it is questionable how far States will be held excusable hereafter, in view of the General Government trusting and depending upon them for action and preparation in this matter, if not found ready on all occasions and under all circumstances to respond to the call of the country with their proportion of well organized and equipped militia for the defence of the nation, it behooves them to give their attention to this matter. Undoubtedly many of the States will be prepared, but should any be found deficient in this respect in any future contingency it will place them as States in a very unfavorable position before the country and the world; one in which, it is hoped, Michigan will not be found, as she can ill afford to lose her deservedly high reputation acquired during the past struggle by any failure on her part of this description."

With these remarks, our history of Michigan during the Rebellion, is brought to a conclusion.

THIRD PART.

BIOGRAPHICAL HISTORY OF MICHIGAN.

BIOGRAPHICAL HISTORY OF MICHIGAN.

ABBOTT, JAMES.——His father, bearing the same name, was a native of Ireland, and established himself in the wilds of Michigan as a fur-trader, before the Declaration of Independence; and the son was born in Detroit in 1775. He commenced active life by following the same business of his father; was postmaster of Detroit from 1808 until 1827, excepting when the English were in possession; was for many years Receiver of public moneys for the Land Office in Detroit; served as a quartermaster-general in the war of 1812; as major of militia in 1835; also as a judge for several years of the Court of Common Pleas; and died in Detroit, full of honors, March 12, 1858.

ALLEN, JOHN.——He was born in Rockbridge county, Va., December 30, 1772; went with his father to Kentucky in 1780; was educated at a school kept in Bardstown; and after studying law in Staunton, Va., returned to Kentucky, and began the practice of his profession in Shelbyville. He was following it successfully there at the time the war broke out in 1812, when he raised a regiment of riflemen for service under General Harrison. He was killed, while in the performance of his duty, under trying circumstances, at the massacre of Frenchtown, on the River Raisin, January 22, 1813. His name was given to one of the prominent counties of Kentucky; and the historian, McAfee, when mentioning the fact that he was shot down by an Indian, says:—"The savage had the honor of shooting one of the first and greatest citizens of Kentucky."

ALLOUEZ, CLAUDE.——He was a Jesuit missionary, who visited Lake Superior in 1665. He went as far west as Point Keweenaw, and spent a considerable time in a fruitless search for copper; and then continuing his journey to La Pointe, the ancient residence of the Ojibwas, where he established a mission, and astonished the natives with pictorial representations of Hell and the Judgment Day. He spent about two years in that locality, instructing the different tribes of the Northwest, and collecting information about the country and people west of Lake Superior. In 1667 he returned to Quebec to procure assistance in his field of labor, and to urge the planting of a French colony in that remote region. He was successful, and two days after his arrival, he began his return to La Pointe, accompanied by competent assistants. In 1669 he founded a mission at Green Bay, where he endured many hardships; and whatever his merits may have been, it is certain that he and La Salle were not on good terms, it being asserted that he intrigued against the explorer. In 1671 we find him stationed at the Saute de Ste. Marie, where he delivered a curious speech to the Indians, which will be found translated in Parkman's "Discovery of the Great West." According to one of his published letters, he said that the Indians called Lake Michigan *Machihiganing.* The last that we know of him is, that in 1687 he was at St. Louis, on the Mississippi. While confined to his bed by illness, on hearing that La Salle was approaching that region, he stole away from the mission, and disappeared, as if to shun a meeting with the man he had injured.

Adam, John J.——He was among the earlier emigrants to the Territory of Michigan; a lawyer by profession; and on several occasions was elected to the State Legislature. In 1837 he was appointed a Regent of the University of Michigan, which position he resigned in 1840; in 1842 he was elected State Treasurer; in 1845, and from 1848 until 1850, he was Auditor-General of the State; and from 1844 to 1846, and again from 1848 until 1851, he was Treasurer of the University of Michigan.

Adams, L. B.——She was the daughter of John Bryan, who emigrated to Michigan from New York in 1823, and was born in the latter State in 1818. Her early education was obtained through private tutors. She was married in 1841 to James R. Adams, who was an editor at White Pigeon and Kalamazoo, and died in 1847; in 1848 she went to Kentucky as a teacher, where she remained three years, and then returned to Michigan, and was for several years a regular writer for the press, especially the Detroit *Advertiser* and the *Michigan Farmer*, and also for the New York *Tribune.* Finding that her literary labors were injuring her health, she obtained a position in the Museum of the Agricultural Department in Washington, where she was associated with the Commissioners Isaac Newton and Horace Capron, and Professor Townend Glover, all of whom highly appreciated her services, and she died in Washington city on the 28th of June, 1870, deeply lamented. She was a writer of graceful verse, and many of her poetic productions were associated with her much loved Michigan and the Valley of St. Joseph.

Anderson, John.——He was born in Scotland, but emigrated to Canada when quite a young man, and, after spending some little time in Montreal, settled on the River Raisin, in Michigan, as an Indian trader about the year 1805. During the war of 1812 he was captured by the British and Indians, but made his escape and went with his family to Dayton, Ohio. He was a brave man, a good citizen and patriot, and one whom everybody loved and respected. He filled with credit many local offices of honor and trust; exerted great influence among the early settlers in and about Frenchtown; and as he could speak not less than eleven Indian dialects and thoroughly understood the Indian character, he did much, after the war, to make the tribes of Michigan peaceable and friendly. He was for many years an elder in the Presbyterian Church, and died at Monroe in 1841, leaving one son, Alexander Anderson, who was a lawyer and an accomplished man, and who also died a few years ago. He had a daughter who became the wife of Warner Wing.

AUGUR, CHRISTOPHER COLON.——He was born in New York, but, having taken up his residence in Michigan, he was appointed a cadet at West Point from that State in 1839. His first service was on Lake Ontario, from 1842 to 1845; he was on duty in Texas when the Mexican war broke out, and after participating in the battles of Palo Alto and Resaca de la Palma and serving as a staff officer during the war was made a captain; he was subsequently stationed in Florida, on the Niagara, at Fort Columbus, in California, at Fort Vancouver, in Oregon, and fought against the Indians in Washington Territory. When the rebellion commenced he was on duty as an instructor at West Point; was made brigadier general of volunteers and stationed at Washington; was engaged at Fredericksburg and in the Shennandoah Valley; had command of the Fifth Army Corps at Cedar Mountain and severely wounded; was made brevet colonel in the regular army for gallant and meritorious services; was next on duty in New Orleans and at Port Hudson, and was made major general of volunteers for gallant and meritorious services; in 1863 he was placed in command of the military department of Washington; and in 1867 was assigned to the command of the department of the Platte, where he is serving at the present time.

BACON, DANIEL S.——He was among the earliest emigrants from the Eastern States to the Territory of Michigan, and for well nigh half a century was a resident of Monroe. He was born in Onondaga, New York, in 1798, commenced his career as a school teacher on the River Raisin in 1822; paid considerable attention to farming; subsequently formed a partnership with Levi S. Humphrey in the prosecution of various kinds of business; and then adopted the profession of law, which he practiced with success. He was at one time a member of the Legislative Council of the Territory; judge of probate, which he held for many years; president of the Bank of Monroe, and also a director of the Michigan Southern Railroad Company. He also held a number of other local positions, in all of which he acquitted himself with ability and a dignified bearing, ever maintaining a pure character, which made him one of the most popular men of his time. He died in Monroe May 18, 1866, at an advanced age, and will long be remembered by troops of friends for his great personal and moral worth, and as a true friend of his adopted State. At the time of his death he held the office of judge of probate for the county of Monroe.

BACON, DAVID.——He was the father of the eminent Rev. Dr. Leonard Bacon, of New Haven, and was sent out as a missionary in 1800 by the Connecticut Missionary Society, and commenced his mission in Detroit, where he remained two years. His next field of operations was on the Maumee, from which locality he removed to the island of Mackinaw, and from that place he returned to Detroit. In his first journey to the West he went on foot from Hartford to Buffalo, carrying a pack on his back. After a year's sojourn in Michigan he returned to Hartford, married a wife, and started a second time for the Western wilderness. While pursuing his avocations in Michigan his favorite mode of travelling was by the birch canoe; and it was while he was residing in Detroit that his distinguished son was born. Rev. David Bacon was also the founder of the town of Tallmadge, in Ohio, where, we believe, he closed his life. He was one of those men who are called visionary and enthusiastic by men of more prosaic and plodding temperament. He had not a liberal education, but was a man of eminent intellectual powers and of intensely thoughtful habits, and really coveted the self-denying labors to which he subjected himself for the honor of his Divine Master.

BAGG, JOHN S.——He was born in Lanesborough, Berkshire county, Massachusetts, in 1809; when fifteen years of age he went to Oneida county, New York, where he acquired an academical education; he then studied law, and came to the bar of that State in 1835. In 1836 he removed to Michigan and took up his residence in Detroit; and having at once purchased of Sheldon McKnight the *Free Press* newspaper, entered upon the career of an editor and politician, which he maintained with ability and a high reputation until his death, which occurred in Detroit on the 10th of March, 1870. In 1837 the *Free Press* establishment was destroyed by fire, and he lost all he possessed, but he was a man of rare energy, and soon worked out of all his difficulties, and was subsequently prosperous in all his business pursuits. The *Free Press* has long been considered the leading Democratic journal of the State, and among those who were associated with its leading editor and proprietor at different times may be mentioned Silas Bagg, Henry Barnes, A. Smith Bagg, and John H. Harmon. He was a warm personal friend of President Polk, by whom he was appointed Postmaster of Detroit, which position he held for four years; and by President Buchanan he was appointed Marshal for the District of Michigan and held that office for three years. For several years before his death his health was infirm, and he endured his long-continued sufferings with the fortitude of a Christian, and when he died, was lamented by a large circle of attached friends.

BALDWIN, HENRY P.——He was born in Coventry, Rhode Island, February 22, 1814; was left an orphan when a boy, and after receiving a good education was a mercantile clerk at Pawtucket for eight years before becoming of age, after which he was engaged for several years in business on his own account in Woonsocket. In 1838 he emigrated to Detroit, and, identifying himself with the interests of Michigan, became President of the Second National Bank of Detroit; was for two years a State Senator; and he was elected Governor of Michigan for the term commencing with 1869 and ending with the year 1870, to which position he brought a full store of general information gathered from foreign travel and the study of men and books. It is due to his Excellency, moreover, to state that for much of the information contained in this volume the compiler is indebted to him—for a variety of important documents bearing upon the condition of the State, over which he has presided with acknowledged ability. Re-elected in 1870 for a second term.

BARRY, JOHN S.——He was born in Vermont in 1802; was educated at the public schools of that State; and while a young man went to Georgia and resided for a number of years at Atlanta. He subsequently emigrated to the Territory of Michigan and settled in the town of Constantine, where he resided until his death. Although educated for the legal profession, he turned his attention to mercantile pursuits. His first public service was rendered as a member of the first Constitutional Convention, in which, as the records show, he took a leading part; upon the organization of the State Government he was elected a State Senator, and in 1841 he was chosen Governor of the State and re-elected in 1843, and also in 1849. He was also, on two occasions, a Presidential Elector. In 1840 he took a special interest in the cultivation of the sugar beet, and with a view of obtaining information in regard to its manufacture visited Europe. His last public service was as a member of the Democratic Presidential Convention held in Chicago in 1864. He was Governor of Michigan during the period of her greatest financial troubles, and, although an active politician, he ever maintained a high character for integrity and fidelity to the welfare of the State. He died in Constantine January 15, 1870.

BALDWIN, AUGUSTUS C.——Was born in Salina, New York, December 24, 1817; received a common-school education, and having lost his father when young, became dependent upon his own efforts for support; in 1837 he emigrated to Michigan and settled in Oakland county; studied law, and at the same time taught school, and came to the bar in 1842. In 1844 and 1846 he was elected to the Legislature of Michigan; in 1853 and 1854 was Prosecuting Attorney for his adopted county; was a delegate to the Charleston and Baltimore Conventions of 1860; and in 1862 he was elected a representative from Michigan to the Thirty-eighth Congress, serving on the Committees on Agriculture and Expenditures in the Interior Department. Was a delegate to the Chicago Convention in 1864, and to the Philadelphia "National Union Convention" of 1866.

BATES, ASHER B.——He was one of the early settlers in Detroit after Michigan became a Territory, and a lawyer by profession. After holding the office of Recorder for some years, he was, in 1838, on the resignation of Augustus S. Porter, made Mayor of Detroit. In 1855 he was appointed a commissioner by the General Government to prosecute certain business in the Sandwich Islands, after which he became a subject of the King of those islands, was raised to the dignity of Attorney-General, and has ever since continued to reside in that remote region.

BAYFIELD, HENRY WOLSEY.——Although a native of England, this distinguished man has long been highly esteemed by the people of Michigan, on account of his services as the most successful marine surveyor of the Great Lakes which form the eastern and northern boundaries of the State. He entered the English navy in 1806, shared with Lord Cochrane in the attack on the French fleet in 1809, saw much service in the waters of the West Indies, South America, and Portugal, and in 1814 took command of a gun-boat on the Great Lakes. In 1815 he was assigned to the duty of surveying Lake Ontario; in 1817 was appointed Admiralty Surveyor, and from that year until 1823 he was engaged in surveying Lakes Erie and Huron; and then proceeded to survey Lake Superior, which he accomplished in the schooner *Recovery,* of one hundred and fifty tons, at that time the only vessel on the lake. In 1825 he returned to England and prepared a series of charts of his American work, which have ever since been the leading authorities among all the people of Canada and the Northwest. In 1827 he returned to Canada and completed a survey of the River and Gulf of St. Lawrence, and was the first man to make known the wonders of the river Saguenay. In 1834 he became a Captain, and in 1856 a Rear Admiral, and for many years past has spent much of his time in promoting the cause of science in connection with the learned societies of Canada and England, in which latter country he is believed to be living in the enjoyment of his exalted reputation.

BEAMAN, FERNANDO C.——He was born in Chester, Windsor county, Vermont, June 28, 1814; removed with his father to New York when a boy, and left an orphan at the age of fifteen; received a good English education at the Franklin County Academy; studied law in Rochester; removed to Michigan in 1838, and commenced the practice of his profession; was for six years Prosecuting Attorney for Lenawee county; was Judge of Probate for four years; was a Presidential Elector in 1856; and in 1860 was elected a Representative from Michigan to the Thirty-seventh Congress, serving on the Committee on Roads and Canals. Re-elected to the Thirty-eighth Congress, and served on the same committee, and also on that on Territories. Re-elected to the Thirty-ninth Congress, serving on the Committees on Territories, the Death of President Lincoln, and Frauds on the Revenue, and as chairman of that on Roads and Canals. He was also a delegate to the Philadelphia "Loyalists' Convention" of 1866, and re-elected to the Fortieth Congress, serving on the Committees on Reconstruction and Appropriations; also re-elected to the Forty-first Congress.

BIDDLE, JOHN.——He was born in Philadelphia; was a Major in the war of 1812, acquitting himself with bravery; held the position of Paymaster in the army; also that of Indian Agent; and was a Delegate to Congress from the Territory of Michigan from 1829 to 1831, when he was appointed Register of the Land Office at Detroit, Michigan. For some years before his death he had been travelling in Europe, and died at the White Sulphur Springs, Virginia, August 25, 1859, aged about seventy years. He was a man of literary culture, and wrote many interesting papers bearing upon the history of Detroit as well as the State of Michigan, some of which were published in a small volume, jointly with others, many years ago.

BINGHAM, KINSLEY S.——He was born at Camillus, Onondaga county, New York, December 16, 1808; received a fair academic education; taught school for a time at Bennington, Vermont; spent three years in the office of a lawyer as clerk; emigrated to Michigan in 1833, and settled upon a farm; he was elected to the Michigan Legislature in 1835, and was five years a member of that body; three years elected Speaker; he was a Representative in Congress from Michigan from 1847 to 1851, and served on the Committee on Commerce; and was elected Governor of Michigan in 1854 and 1856. He also held in other years the offices of postmaster, supervisor, prosecuting attorney, judge of probate, and brigadier-general of militia. In 1859 he was elected a Senator in Congress from Michigan for six years. Died at Oak Grove, Livingston county, Michigan, October 5, 1861.

BISHOP, LEVI.——He was born in Russell, Hampden county, Massachusetts, October 15, 1815; received a good common school education; in his fifteenth year, he became an apprentice-clerk in a leather manufactory, where he remained until 1836, when he removed to Michigan, and continued his business for four years in Detroit. In 1839, while in the act of firing a salute, as a member of a volunteer company, he lost his right arm; soon after that accident he began the study of law, and on completing a course of three years was admitted to the bar of Michigan; in 1842 he was elected a justice of the peace; and in 1846 he became a member of the Detroit Board of Education, serving as such twelve years, and much of that time as its president. In 1857 he was elected a Regent of the State University, holding the position for six years; and in 1860 he visited Europe, and enjoyed the advantages of being a good French scholar. Always a hard student, and earnestly devoted to his profession, he occasionally delivered a lecture on literary topics and amused himself by writing poetry; in 1864 he published a poem entitled "*The Dignity of Labor*," and in 1870, in very superior style, a more ambitious work in twenty-eight cantos, entitled "*Teuchsa Grondie*," devoted to the romantic Indian lore of the river Detroit, and surrounding country.

BLACKMAN, DANIEL.——He was born in Newtown, Fairfield county, Connecticut, December 31, 1821; received an academical education, and as his opportunities would permit taught a country school; and, having studied law, was admitted to the bar at Fairfield in 1845. For six years thereafter he practiced his profession in Danbury, and in 1851 he removed to Michigan, and located himself in Cassopolis. On the death of Nathaniel Bacon, of Niles, who died in November, 1869, he was nominated to fill the vacancy as judge of the Circuit Court of the second circuit, on a people's ticket, and, although a Democrat in politics, he was duly elected.

BLAIR, AUSTIN.——Was born in Caroline, Tompkins county, New York, February 8, 1818; graduated at Union College in 1839; studied law, and, removing to Michigan, practiced the profession in that State. After holding the local offices of county clerk of Eaton county, and prosecuting attorney for Jackson county, he was elected to the Legislature, and afterwards to the Senate of the State; was Governor of Michigan from 1861 to 1865, and took an important part in assisting to put down the rebellion; and in 1866 he was elected a Representative from that State to the Fortieth Congress, serving on the Committees on Foreign Affairs, Rules, and Militia.

He was also re-elected to the Forty-first and Forty-second Congresses, serving, during the former, on important committees. He resides in the city of Jackson.

BOISE, JAMES R.——He was for ten years or more professor of Greek in the University of Michigan; after which he removed to Illinois, and held a similar position in the University of Chicago. He is the author of several text-books for colleges, among which is a Greek Prose Composition, adapted to the first book of Xenophon's Anabasis, which was well received by the learned public. Further particulars, the compiler has been unable to procure.

BONAVENTURE, FATHER.——He was a priest of the order of St. Francis; served as a missionary on the Detroit station in the forepart of the eighteenth century; gave the name of St. Anne to the French parish at Detroit, and also to the old French church, which long stood a memorable relic of a former age on the site of the present French church in the same city. Further information respecting his life has been sought for in vain.

BRADLEY, EDWARD.——He was born in East Bloomfield, Ontario county, New York, in April, 1808; spent his boyhood on a farm; when twenty-eight years of age he was appoined Associate Judge of the Common Pleas of that county; in 1839 he removed to Michigan, and engaged in the practice of law; in 1842 he was elected to the Senate of Michigan; and was a Representative from that State to the Thirtieth Congress. He died in New York city, while on a tour for the benefit of his health, August 5, 1847.

BRADY, HUGH.——He was born in Northumberland county, Pennsylvania, in 1768; entered the army as an ensign in 1792; served as a lieutenant under General Wayne in his campaign against the Indians on the Maumee; was made a lieutenant in 1794; a captain in 1799; and as a colonel distinguished himself at the battles of Chippeway and Niagara Falls, in the last of which he was wounded; in 1822 he was promoted to the rank of brigadier general for ten years' faithful service. He also took part in the war with Mexico, and for meritorious conduct he was made a major general in 1848. He was for many years stationed in Detroit, and died in that city April 15, 1851, universally regretted. A township in the State, as well as a fort at the Saute de Ste. Marie, were named after him. The immediate cause of his death was an accident, by which he was injured, while riding his horse, whose feet became entangled in a roll of wire. He left a manuscript journal of his services and adventures while with General Wayne, which has been pronounced of great value.

BROCK, ISAAC.——He was born in the island of Guernsey October 6, 1769; educated at Rotterdam; and in his fifteenth year he became, by purchase, an ensign in the British army. By the year 1799 he had risen to the rank of lieutenant colonel and distinguished himself in Holland, where he was wounded. In 1801 he was on duty in the Baltic, and in 1802 sailed for Canada; in 1806, as colonel, he was placed in command of troops in the two Provinces of Canada; and in 1810 he became a major general. The crowning event of his life, as claimed by Henry J. Morgan, was his visit to Amherstburg with two hundred and fifty militia and the taking of Detroit in 1812, and for which service he was made a Knight of the Bath; but the greatness of this exploit was considerably modified by Sir Allan McNab in 1859, when he confessed that it was on account of the "imposing advance" of Brock on Detroit "that the terrified garrison, the fort, the guns, and munitions of war were all surrendered at Detroit." He was a man of many noble personal qualities, and though unfortunate in losing his life at the battle of Queenstown on the 13th of October, 1812, a monument was erected to his memory on the banks of the St. Lawrence, and he is remembered by the people of Canada with high regard and affection

---

BROOKE, GEORGE MERCER.——He was born in Virginia and entered the army from that State as First Lieutenant in 1808; and from 1842 to 1845 he was on duty in Michigan at the Detroit Barracks, with which city he was closely identified, both officially and socially. He served under General Scott in the war with Great Britain, and was promoted in 1814 to the rank of Brevet Colonel for his gallantry at Fort Erie, where he was wounded; in 1824 he was made a Brigadier General by brevet for ten years' faithful services in the Northwest and in Florida; and in 1848, for important duties performed in connection with the Mexican war, he was promoted to the rank of Brevet Major General. It was while serving on the Northern frontier that he performed an act of rare heroism. The American and English armies were facing each other, and one night it was found that the latter were erecting a battery. Precisely where, none could tell, and then it was that Lieut. Brooke took a lantern under his arm, threw a cloak over his shoulders, and went in pursuit of the battery, leaving directions behind him that when the commanding officer saw his lamp in the top of a tree he might open fire. He succeeded in his plan, and in a moment after he had descended from the tree the iron hail was poured into the British works, and they were abandoned. He was the first man to establish a fort in Florida in 1824, which bore a conspicuous part in the operations against the Seminoles, and was named by the Government to his honor. During the war with Mexico he was stationed at New Orleans, and performed a very important part in forwarding troops and munitions of war. He died at San Antonio, Texas, March 9, 1851; and when General Lorenzo Thomas was arranging the National Cemeteries after the rebellion, he found the grave of his old friend General Brooke in a dilapidated condition, and had the remains removed to a more suitable spot, which is now marked by an appropriate monument. General Brooke was a most accomplished gentleman, and a great lover of angling, and, by way of amusing himself, invented a peculiar kind of fish hook, which has been quite popular with the piscatorial fraternity. During a part of his service at Detroit there was a British regiment stationed on the opposite side of the river, with which his men had crossed bayonets during the war, and he was very popular with the British officers. So much so, indeed, that when the British regiment was ordered home from Canada the officers invited him to a last dinner in Quebec, which he accepted, and then they presented him with a valuable watch in a gold box.

BROWN, CHARLES R.——He was born in Columbia, Lorain county, Ohio, in 1836; educated at the Baldwin University; was for a time Principal of the Freedom Academy, in Portage county; and in 1855 commenced the publication of a paper in Cuyahoga county called *Pure Grit*, which was not successful. He subsequently studied law, and in 1860 he removed to Michigan and settled in St. Joseph, Berrien county. Not long afterwards he was elected a Circuit Court Commissioner; in 1866 he was elected to the Legislature; in 1867 he removed to Kalamazoo; and in April, 1869, he was elected a Judge of the Ninth Judicial Circuit. He is the editor of a monthly periodical entitled "*Reports of Cases, tried and determined at Nisi Prius, in the Circuit Courts of Michigan.*"

BROWN, DANIEL.——He was born in Lexington, Massachusetts, in the year 1775; spent some years in Windsor, Vermont, serving in the Legislature; and afterwards located in the State of New York, where he held many offices of trust and honor. In 1826 he took up his residence in Ann Arbor, Michigan, when the site of the city was almost an unbroken wilderness. To his forethought, energy, and public spirit was the place indebted for the first impulse in its career of prosperity; he was for fifty years a prominent member of the Masonic fraternity; and after a useful and honorable life he died at Ann Arbor in 1857.

BUEL, ALEXANDER W.——Was born in Rutland county, Vermont, in 1813; graduated at Middlebury College in 1830; taught school for several years in Vermont and New York, during which period he prepared himself for the practice of the law. In 1834 he took up his residence in Michigan; in 1836 was attorney for the city of Detroit; in 1837 was elected to the State Legislature; in 1843 and 1844 was prosecuting attorney for Wayne county; in 1847 was again elected to the Legislature, and was Speaker of the Lower House in 1848; and from 1849 to 1851 was a Representative in Congress from Michigan, and was a member of the Committee on Foreign Affairs. Died in Detroit April 17, 1868.

BURT, WILLIAM A.——He was born in Worcester, Massachusetts, June 13, 1792; after receiving a good education in the State of New York, he studied surveying and nautical astronomy, and was for several years employed as an engineer in the county of Erie. In 1824 he removed to Michigan, locating near Detroit, where he was engaged in surveying and mill building, and served several terms in the Council of the Territory, and enjoying the friendship of General Cass. In 1832 he received from Governor Porter the appointment of District Surveyor; was appointed a Deputy Surveyor for the United States, and originated the idea which led to the invention of the solar compass, which became a great success, and was highly appreciated by the scientific world. Between 1840 and 1847 he was employed in surveying the northern peninsula of Michigan, and introduced a variety of important improvements in connection with his invention of the solar compass and the modes of geological surveying; in 1844 and 1845 he was associated with Douglass Houghton in his scientific labors, and his discoveries had an important bearing on the develoņement of the mineral treasures of northern Michigan. In 1851 he visited Europe, and for his compass received from the Industrial Exhibition of London a prize medal. In 1856 he obtained patents in the United States, England, France, and Belgium for an equatorial sextant, but he was not permitted to bring it to perfection before his untimely death, which occurred on the 18th of August, 1858. During his long residence in Michigan he was called upon to fill many positions of trust and honor, among which were Commissioner of Internal Improvement, Judge of the Circuit Court, and member of the State Legislature for several terms; and when he died he left a spotless reputation. He was also one of the prime movers in the erection of the Saute de Ste. Marie Canal.

BUSH, CHARLES P.——He became a citizen of Michigan about the year 1837, locating himself in Livingston county; was a Presidential Elector in 1845; in 1847 he removed to the town of Lansing, of which he was one of the founders; was elected a member of the State Senate, and exercised a prominent influence in procuring the removal of the seat of Government, and by his energy and business capacity acquired a handsome fortune. He was a ready debater, very much of a politician, and was a member of the Constitutional Convention of 1850. He died at Lansing July 4, 1857, in the forty-ninth year of his age.

CADILLAC, ANTOINE DE LA MOTTE.——This man was the founder of Detroit, and the Cass manuscripts, which were edited and published by Mrs. E. M. Sheldon, in 1856, contain a very full account of his operations on the soil of Michigan. Not long after his first arrival in Canada from France he received the title of Lord of Mount Desert, and having revisited Europe, he came out into the wilderness again, and, as the personal friend of Louis XIV., he was made Commandant of Affairs in 1696 of the Lake country, and on the 24th of July, 1701, arrived at Detroit with fifty soldiers and fifty Canadian traders and canoemen and two missionaries, and proceeded at once to build a fort, which he named in honor of Pontchartrain, the French Colonial Minister. Its avowed object was to secure to France the immense fur trade of the Northwest. He was a zealous Roman Catholic, but opposed to the Jesuits, and as that order held the reins of Government in Canada, he and his immediate followers had anything but a peaceful time. He first visited the Lake country in 1696, and was for several years stationed at Mackinaw, and as he remained at Detroit until 1711, he must have spent about fifteen years in the Territory. He was a "bold, ambitious, and enthusiastic man," had a kind heart, but arbitrary manners, and was the possessor of more than ordinary literary abilities. Various letters which he wrote to the Home Government, from Detroit, contain many very interesting particulars respecting the country and the people of that early time. With his commission as Commandant he received a tract of land, fifteen acres square, "wherever on the Detroit the new fort should be established."

CAMPBELL, HENRY MUNROE.—He was born in Stillwater, Saratoga county, New York, September 10, 1783. In 1810 he removed to Buffalo, where he resided until May, 1826, when he removed to Detroit, with which place he was subsequently identified, and where he died in January, 1842. Most of his life was spent in business. During the War of 1812 he served as Lieutenant of a volunteer artillery company, organized in Buffalo. He was instrumental in getting up the parish of St. Paul's Church, Buffalo, and was also constantly warden or vestryman of St. Paul's, Detroit. He was active in organizing the Episcopal Church in Michigan into a diocese in 1833 and 1844, and was one of the first delegates to the General Convention in 1835, and was for many years a member of the standing committee of the diocese. He was a Judge of the Court of Common Pleas at various times, both in New York and Michigan, and, as such, acquired an exalted reputation.

CAMPBELL, JAMES V.——He was born in Buffalo, New York, February 25, 1823, and was the son of Henry Munroe Campbell, with whom he removed to Detroit in 1826. He graduated at St. Paul's College, Long Island, in July, 1841; admitted to the bar in 1844; elected to the (First Independent) Supreme Court of Michigan in March, 1857, (the term beginning January, 1858,) and was re-elected in 1863. In 1859, upon the organization of the Marshall Professorship in the University of Michigan, he was appointed to that position: and the other offices which he has filled have always been connected with his profession or the educational interests of the State.

CARVER, JONATHAN.——He was born in Stillwater, Connecticut, in 1732; after serving as a captain in the old French war, became enamored of a wayward and wandering life; and spent several years travelling through the interior parts of North America, a portion of which time he spent in Detroit and Michilimacinac. In 1778 an account of his travels was published in London, where he died in great poverty in 1780. His life was written by Dr. Lettsom, and it was in consequence of his account of Carver's ill-requited labors for the English Government, that the "Literary Fund" was established. A portion of his interesting book of travels, described with considerable minuteness the country now occupied by the States of Michigan, Illinois, Minnesota, and Wisconsin, and a few years ago, a mutilated edition of his volume was published in New York as a description of Wisconsin.

CASS, LEWIS.——Born in Exeter, New Hampshire, October 9, 1782. Having received a limited education in his native place, at the early age of seventeen he crossed the Alleghany Mountains on foot, to seek a home in the "Great West," then an almost unexplored wilderness. Settled at Marietta, Ohio; he studied law, and was successful. Elected at twenty-five to the Legislature of Ohio, he originated the bill which arrested the proceedings of Aaron Burr, and, as stated by Mr. Jefferson, was the first blow given to what is known as Burr's conspiracy. In 1807 he was appointed by Mr. Jefferson Marshal of the State, and held the office till the latter part of 1811, when he volunteered to repel Indian aggressions on the frontier. He was elected colonel of the 3d regiment of Ohio volunteers, and entered the military service of the United States at the commencement of the war of 1812. Having by a difficult march reached Detroit, he urged the immediate invasion of Canada, and was the author of the proclamation of that event. He was the first to land in arms on the enemy's shore, and, with a small detachment of troops, fought and won the first battle, that of the Tarontoe. At the subsequent capitulation of Detroit he was absent on important service, and regretted that his command and himself had been included in that capitulation. Liberated on parole, he repaired to the seat of Government to report the causes of the disaster, and the failure of the campaign. He was immediately appointed a colonel in the regular army, and, soon after, promoted to the rank of brigadier-general, having in the meantime been elected major-general of the Ohio volunteers. On being exchanged and released from parole, he again repaired to the frontier, and joined the army for the recovery of Michigan. Being at that time without a command, he served and distinguished himself as a volunteer aide-de-camp to General Harrison at the battle of the Thames. He was appointed by President Madison, in October, 1813, Governor of Michigan. His position combined, with the ordinary duties of chief magistrate of a civilized community, the immediate management and control, as superintendent, of the relations with the numerous and powerful Indian tribes in that region of country. He conducted with success the affairs of the Territory under embarrassing circumstances. Under his sway peace was preserved between the whites and the treacherous and disaffected Indians, law and order established, and the Territory rapidly advanced in population, resources, and prosperity. He held this position till July, 1831, when he was, by President Jackson, made Secretary of War. In the latter part of 1836 President Jackson appointed him Minister to France, where he remained until 1842, when he requested his recall, and returned to this country. In January, 1845, he was elected by the Legislature of Michigan to the Senate of the United States; which place he resigned on his nomination, in May, 1848, as a candidate for the Presidency by the political party to which he belonged. After the election of his opponent (General Taylor) to that office, the Legislature of his State, in 1849, re-elected him to the Senate for the unexpired portion of his original term of six years. When Mr. Buchanan became President, he invited General Cass to the head of the Department of State, which position he resigned in December, 1860. He devoted some attention to literary pursuits, and his writings, speeches, and State papers would make several volumes; among which is one entitled "France, its King, Court, and Government," published in 1840. He died in Detroit, June 17, 1866, and will long be remembered as the most eminent and successful statesman of Michigan.

CHANDLER, ZACHARIAH.——Born in Bedford, New Hampshire, December 10, 1813; received an academical education; was bred a merchant, and was eminently successful in that business in Detroit; was mayor of Detroit, Michigan, in 1851; defeated candidate for Governor of Michigan in 1852; and a Senator in Congress from Michigan, having succeeded Senator Cass in that capacity, and taking his seat in the Thirty-fifth Congress, serving as a member of the Committee on the District of Columbia, and chairman of the Committee on Commerce. He was re-elected to the Senate in 1863, for the term ending in 1869, serving on the Committees on Revolutionary

Claims and on Mines and Mining, and again as chairman of the Committee on Commerce. He took a special interest in all measures for the suppression of the rebellion; and was a member of the National Committee appointed to accompany the remains of President Lincoln to Illinois; also a delegate to the Philadelphia "Loyalists' Convention" of 1866. In 1869 he was again re-elected to the Senate for the term ending in 1875.

CHAPMAN, WILLIAM.——He was born in Charles county, Maryland, January 22, 1810, and graduated at the West Point Academy in 1831. The first two years of his military life were spent at Fort Mackinaw, and in 1841 he was returned to that post, and remained about five years, when he was promoted to the rank of captain; after which he was stationed at Fort Howard on Green Bay, and which place has ever since been his nominal residence. Prior to his last service in Michigan he was attached to the Black Hawk expedition in 1832; was an assistant instructor of infantry tactics at the West Point Academy from 1832 to 1833; and adjutant of the 5th infantry. Just before the breaking out of the war with Mexico he was in military occupation of Texas, and having at once gone to the field, was engaged in the battles of Palo Alto, Resaca-de-la-Palma, Monterey, Vera Cruz, Cherubusco, Molino del Rey, and Chepultepec; and he was also present at the capture of San Antonio and the City of Mexico. For gallant and meritorious conduct at these various places he received two promotions. After the war with Mexico he was in active service in New York, Texas, Florida, Utah, New Mexico, and various parts of the Indian Territory; and on the breaking out of the rebellion, he served with honor with the Army of the Potomac at Yorktown, Malvern Hill, Harrison's Landing, Manassas, and for meritorious services at Bull Run received another promotion, that of brevet colonel. In 1863 he was retired from active service for disability, resulting from long and faithful service, and disease contracted in the line of duty. He was subsequently on special duty in Washington, and member of a Board for examining officers for promotion in the army; since which time he has been unemployed at his residence on Green Bay.

CHARLEVOIX, PETER FRANCIS XAVIER DE.——He was born at St. Quentin in 1682, educated as a Jesuit, and in 1721, under the auspices of the French Government, made a tour through the Great Lakes, and down the Illinois and Mississippi rivers to New Orleans. He spent a considerable time within the Territory now known as Michigan, and described in language of rare beauty many phases of its scenery. After his return to France he published a description of his travels, and also a general history of New France, both of which works were eminently successful in the original as well as in manifold English translations. He died in 1761.

CHIPMAN, HENRY.——He was born in Vermont in 1785, and after receiving a liberal education, adopted the profession of law. When quite young he went to South Carolina, and was engaged in the practice of the profession in that State until 1824, when he was appointed by President Monroe a Judge of the United States for the Territory of Michigan, when he removed to Detroit, and from which time until his death, which occurred about two years since, in Detroit, he was one of the most influential, cultivated, and distinguished citizens of the State. In a letter which Governor Woodbridge wrote to the compiler a few years before his death, he spoke of Judge Chipman as a first-class man, and one with whom it had been a pleasure to be associated on the bench; and the qualities which characterized Judge Chipman cannot, perhaps, be better expressed than in his own language, addressed to the compiler, when speaking of Governor Woodbridge:—"In his politics he was a disciple of the Washington school, whose principles he had imbibed in early life from his association with the founders of the Republic and framers of the Federal Constitution. He was truly national and conservative in his views and feelings, and always a devoted friend of the Union. He could never stoop to play the political partisan for his own advancement, but always carried his political opinions as parts of his private conscience and personal integrity, and never allowed a difference of political opinion to interfere with his social relations or public duties."

Chipman, John S.——He was born in Vermont, graduated at Middlebury College in 1823, and was a Representative in Congress from Michigan from 1845 to 1847. He subsequently went to California, as we have been told, and we have been unable to procure any further particulars of his history.

Christiancy, Isaac P.——He was born in Johnstown, New York, in March, 1812; received a common-school and academical education, which he fought for single-handed; when thirteen years of age became the main support of his father's family, and followed school teaching for their support. In 1835 he began the study of law; in 1836 he removed to Michigan and settled in Monroe; there completed his legal studies with Robert McClelland, and in which place he has since resided, practicing his profession uninterruptedly from 1838 to 1857. From 1841 to 1846 he was Prosecuting Attorney for Monroe county; in 1848 he became interested in the Free Soil party, and attended the Buffalo Convention of that year; in 1849 he was elected to the State Senate; in 1852 he consented to be the candidate of the Free Soil party for Governor, although he knew there was no hope of election at that time; and he was a prime mover in the political combination of 1854, which resulted in the organization of the Republican party, which was not only born in Michigan, but received its name at a convention held in the city of Jackson. He was a delegate to the Philadelphia Convention of 1856, which nominated Fremont for the Presidency; he then purchased the Monroe *Commercial*, which had been a Democratic paper down to that time, and became its editor; was an unsuccessful candidate for the United States Senate, (made so by his party,) and in 1857 he was elected a Judge of the Supreme Court of the State, and in 1865 was re-elected for eight years by the unanimous vote of all parties. He was, of course, a zealous supporter of the war for the Union, and performed some service on the staff of General A. A. Humphrey, as well as that of General G. A. Custer.

Clark, Robert.——He was born in Washington county, New York, and was of Scotch descent; was a member of the Assembly of that State from

1812 to 1815; a representative in Congress from New York from 1819 to 1821, and a delegate to the State Constitutional Convention held in the latter year. He subsequently adopted the medical profession, and settled in Monroe, Michigan Territory, and by President Monroe was appointed Register of the Land Office for the Second Land District of said Territory. He held the office from 1823 to 1832, and during the entire period his intimate friend, Charles James Lanman was the Receiver of Public Moneys. He carried on an extensive farm, was partial to horticulture, and an orchard which he planted and kept in splendid condition for many years had the reputation of being the most extensive and beautiful in the whole Territory.

Clark, Samuel.——He was born in New York, and was a Representative in Congress from New York from 1833 to 1835; on removing to Michigan was elected a Representative in Congress from that State from 1853 to 1855. He was a resident of Kalamazoo, where he died October 2, 1870.

Cocker, Benjamin F.——He was born in England, and came to this country about the year 1850; is the Professor of Philosophy in the University of Michigan, a Doctor of Divinity, and is the author of a work on "Christianity and the Greek Philosophy," which has acquired a high reputation. He revisited his native land about a year ago, and returned to the duties of his position in the University fortified with much new information, to be used for the benefit of the students who attend his lectures.

Cole, Henry S.——He was a native of Canandaigua, New York, and removed from that place to Detroit in 1827 or 1828. He was a man of culture, a lawyer by profession, to which he was devoted, and in which he was successful, and distinguished for his rapid dispatch of business. He was the successor of Judge Fletcher as Attorney-General of the Territory of Michigan, a courteous and popular man; and he died in Detroit in 1836, universally lamented. He had two brothers—Thomas G. and Joseph C.—who were both honorably identified with Michigan as Territory and State.

Cole, Thomas G.——He was born in Canandaigua, New York, and emigrated to the Territory of Michigan about the year 1830, locating at Monroe, on the River Raisin. He was a talented and active business man and a most courteous gentleman; was one of the first in projecting and carrying forward to successful termination the Detroit, Monroe, and Toledo Railroad; and was a Director and for some years Superintendent of the Michigan Southern Railroad. It was chiefly through his agency and liberality that the *Monroe Gazette* was established in 1846, and which the present writer had the honor of editing for a few months after its commencement. He died at Monroe in 1860. He had a brother, Joseph C. Cole, who was at one time postmaster at Monroe, and a man of much literary culture; and another brother, Henry S. Cole, who was long a leading lawyer in Detroit.

COMIS, EZRA.——He was elected a member of the Michigan Legislature from Calhoun county in 1836, and was the first Speaker chosen under the State Constitution, and he had previously been a member of the Convention which formed the said Constitution. He was also a general in the militia service; reputed a man of talents and strict integrity. Died in Detroit in February, 1837.

COMSTOCK, DARIUS.——He was of Quaker parentage, and one of the original contractors of the Erie Canal, and a number of the locks at Lockport were constructed under his supervision. Having made a fortune in that capacity he emigrated to Michigan, purchased an extensive tract of land in Lenawee county, and founded the village and now the flourishing city of Adrian. He was a worthy and sagacious man, and took an active part in developing the resources of the State, throughout the length and breadth of which his name was synonymous with prosperity and enterprise.

COMSTOCK, O. C.——He was born in New York in 1784; received a good education, and prepared himself to officiate as a Baptist preacher; was elected to the New York Assembly in 1810 and 1812; and was a Representative in Congress from that State from 1813 to 1819. He subsequently officiated as Chaplain of the National House of Representatives; and having, after sojourning for a time in Illinois, taken up his residence at Marshall, Michigan, remained there until his death, which occurred on the 11th January, 1860.

CONANT, SHUBAEL.——He was for a great many years one of the most influential, cultivated, and enterprising citizens of Detroit, and did much by his sagacity as a merchant to promote the prosperity of the city and State. He emigrated to the West from Massachusetts; had a brother, who resided on the River Raisin, at Monroe, who was a prominent physician, and also a man of ability and refinement. Mr. Shubael Conant was a man of rare judgment, by the exercise of which he acquired a handsome property, and stood high as a man of character and benevolence, always taking a deep interest in the welfare of Detroit and the entire State of Michigan. As early as the year 1819 he established, in conjunction with two other Detroit citizens, the first grain and saw-mills in the town of Pontiac. He was never married, and died in Detroit in 1865 or '66, leaving a name which will always be kindly remembered by the older citizens of the State. The writer regrets that he cannot be more particular in his notice, but if pleasant personal recollections were suited to this place he would have no trouble iu writing an entire essay. And this remark holds true in regard to nearly all the pioneer citizens whom it is his pleasure to mention in this volume.

CONGER, JAMES L.——He was born in New Jersey, and, on removing to Michigan, was elected a Representative in Congress from 1851 to 1853. Of his later history the compiler has been unable to obtain any particulars.

CONGER, OMAR D.——He was born in Cooperstown, Otsego county, New York, in 1818; removed with his father, who was a clergyman, to Huron county, Ohio, in 1824; graduated in 1842 at the Western Reserve College; from 1845 to 1847 he was employed in the Geological Surveys of Lake Superior; and in 1848 he settled at Port Huron, Michigan, in the practice of law. In 1850 he was elected Judge of St. Clair county; was a Senator in the State Legislature from 1855 to 1859, during the latter year serving as President *pro tem.*; was a Delegate to the Baltimore Convention of 1864; also a Presidential Elector at the ensuing election in 1865, and messenger from Michigan to carry the vote to Washington; in 1866 he was a member of the State Constitutional Convention; and in 1868 he was elected a Representative from Michigan to the Forty-first Congress, serving on several committees, but especially the Committee on Commerce. He resides at Port Huron, and was re-elected to the Forty-second Congress.

COOLEY, THOMAS M.——He was born at Attica, New York, January 6, 1824; studied law in Palmyra; removed to Michigan in 1843; completed his legal studies at Adrian, where he was admitted to the bar in 1846; and spent the two following years practicing his profession in Tecumseh, after which he settled permanently in Adrian. In 1857 he was appointed by the Legislature to compile the General Statutes of Michigan, which were duly published in two volumes; in 1858 he was appointed Reporter of the Supreme Court, held the position until 1864, and published eight volumes of Reports: in 1850 he was made Jay Professor of Law in the University of Michigan, which office he holds at the present time; in 1866 he published a Digest of Michigan Reports; and in 1868 (through Little, Brown & Co.) a "Treatise on the Constitutional Limitations which rest upon the Legislative Power of the States of the American Union," which work has been eminently successful. In 1864 he was elected a Justice of the Supreme Court by 17,000 majority, and in 1869 re-elected by a majority of more than 30,000 for the term which ends in 1878. Notwithstanding the pressure of his public duties, he has found time to prepare for early publication a new edition of Blackstone; and among the important cases which have been decided since he went upon the bench are, first, one declaring the Military Suffrage Act unconstitutional; and another declaring Railroad Subscriptions void—both of which have been extensively discussed by the public at large. The present residence of Judge Cooley is in Ann Arbor.

COOPER, GEORGE B.——Born at Long Hill, Morris county, New Jersey, June 6, 1808; received a good common-school education; removed to Michigan in 1830; served in the two Houses of the State Legislature; served two terms as State Treasurer of Michigan; held the position of Postmaster at Jackson for eleven years, which he resigned when chosen Treasurer; and was elected a Representative from Michigan to the Thirty-sixth Congress. His seat, however, was contested by William A. Howard, and before the close of the first session the latter was admitted.

CRAPO, HENRY H.——He was born in Dartmouth, Mass., May 24, 1804; resided for many years in New Bedford, from which place he removed to Michigan in 1857; became extensively engaged in the manufacture and sale of lumber; was for a time Mayor of Flint, where he resided; served in the State Senate; and was twice elected Governor of the State—in 1864 and 1866—performing important services during the progress of the Rebellion, all of which the reader will find fully set forth in that portion of this volume devoted to the part which Michigan took in the war for the Union. Died in Flint, July 23, 1869.

CRARY, ISAAC E.——He was born in Preston, New London county, Connecticut; received a good English education, and then graduated at an eastern College; adopted the profession of law, and removed to the Territory of Michigan; was there appointed a General of Militia; was elected a Delegate to Congress from the Territory in 1835 and 1836; was a Delegate to the State Constitutional Convention of 1835, and drew up the article which passed into a law creating the office of *Superintendent of Public Instruction;* also a Regent of the State University in 1837; and was a Representative in Congress from that State from the time of its admission into the Union in 1836 to 1841. He also edited at one time the *Democratic Expounder.* He was a member of the Legislature, and chosen Speaker of the Lower House in 1846. He died in Marshall, Michigan, May 8, 1854. A debate which he had on the floor of Congress with Thomas Corwin has passed into the history of parliamentary novelties.

CUSTER, GEORGE A.——He was born in New Rumley, Harrison county, Ohio, December 5, 1839, but as he identified himself with Michigan—first, by commanding her famous brigade of cavalry, and secondly, by becoming the son-in-law of one of her leading citizens—Daniel S. Bacon—we submit the following particulars with pleasure: After acquiring a good education, he became a school-teacher, and having been appointed to the West Point Academy, he graduated at that institution in 1861. He was first assigned to duty in the 2d United States cavalry, formerly commanded by R. E. Lee; reported himself for duty to General Scott the day before the battle of Bull Run; served on the staff of General Kearney; was with the Army of the Potomac, and when General McClellan was relieved, he was mustered out as a Captain and Aid-de-Camp. He then became a personal Aid to General Pleasanton, and for meritorious services was made a Brigadier-General of volunteers, and assigned to the command of the Michigan brigade, which distinguished itself at Gettysburg. He participated in the battle of the Wilderness, and for his services in the Shennandoah Valley he was complimented in an order of the War Department. He was a warm personal friend and important assistant of General Sheridan, who, although ten years his senior, when once in trouble on the field of battle, sighed for the help of "old Custer;" and in a letter to Mrs. Custer, accompanying the table, sent as a present, on which were signed the terms of surrender of the Virginia army, under General R. E. Lee, he said: "No person was more instrumental in bringing about this most desirable result than your most gallant husband." General Custer was promoted to the rank of Major-General of volunteers; accompanied General Sheridan to the Department of the Gulf after the war; was on important duty in Texas; and in 1866 was mustered out of the volunteer service and returned to resume his position in the regular army. It is said of him that he never lost a gun or color, but captured more guns, flags, and prisoners than any other General not an army commander. After the war he was sent as a delegate to the Union Convention of Philadelphia, and also to the Soldiers' Convention of Cleveland, since which time he has taken no part in politics.

DABLON, CLAUDE.——He was a Jesuit missionary, a personal friend and companion of Father Marquette, and an account of his labors on the Upper Lakes is contained in the *Jesuit Relation* of 1671. He was Superior of the Missions in that region, and an earnest and hard-working man. He took part in an expedition for the survey of Lake Superior, which resulted in a valuable and curious map of the region, and made this report in regard to the copper mines: "A day's journey from the head of the lake on the south side there is a rock of copper, weighing from six hundred to eight hundred pounds, lying on the shore, where any who pass may see it;" and he further speaks of the great copper boulders found in the bed of the river Ontonagan. His principal fields of operation as a missionary were at the Saute de Ste. Marie and at the head of Green Bay. He was the man who said that the region of Green Bay was an earthly paradise, but that the way to it was as difficult as the path to heaven—alluding to the rapids of Fox river. With regard to the name of Michigan, he wrote it *Mitchiganon;* and in speaking of the success which had attended his labors as a missionary, in conjunction with those of Allouez and Marquette, he rejoiced that his holy faith was established among the Indian tribes; and he had "good hope that they would soon carry it to the famous river called the Mississippi, and perhaps even to the South Sea."

DESNOYERS, PETER.——He was born in France in 1773; came from Paris to America in 1790; lived at Gallipolis a number of years, and afterwards in Pittsburg, from which place he removed to Detroit in August, 1796, where he resided until his death. In consequence of his loyalty as an American citizen, he received a donation of land on the river Detroit, under an act of Congress passed in 1807; was subsequently United States Marshal for the Territory; also, State Treasurer in 1839; and during his long residence in Detroit was considered one of the most influential men of the city, as well as a leading spirit among the French population.

DEWEY, JAMES STODDARD.——He was born in Broome county, New York, December 21, 1832; removed with his father to Lapeer county, Michigan, in 1838; and he was educated at the Miami University, in Ohio, where his uncle, Dr. O. N. Stoddard, was Professor of Chemistry and the Natural Sciences. After graduating in 1858, he returned to Michigan, and settled in Pontiac; for about one year he was an assistant principal in a Union School; next studied law, and, on being admitted to the bar, was clerk in the office of Judge M. E. Crofoot, and became his partner in business, continuing that connection until 1863. In 1864 he was elected City Justice of Pontiac; in 1866 he was elected Judge of the Circuit Court for the Sixth Circuit, to fill the unexpired term of Judge Sandford M. Green, resigned, and was subsequently re-elected for the full term of six years from the 1st of January, 1870, in which position he still continues.

Dobbins, Daniel.——He was born in Mifflin county, Pennsylvania, July 5, 1776, and visited Lake Erie with a party of surveyors as early as 1796. He was with General Wayne, at Presque Isle, at the time of his death, and became a resident of that locality, where he was distinguished as a navigator of the Great Lakes. He was at Mackinaw with his vessel, the *Salina*, when that place was captured by the British in 1812, and though taken prisoner, was paroled. He was again made a prisoner at Detroit, and again paroled, but now unconditionally. He was very efficient in fitting out the squadron at Erie, and was in the expedition, under Commodore Sinclair, that attempted to retake Mackinaw. After the war he was in command of a vessel called the *Washington*, and in 1816 conveyed troops in her to Green Bay, she having been the first vessel built by civilized man that entered that harbor. Having a commission in the navy as captain, he was ordered to sea in 1826, when he resigned his position, but remained in the employ of the Government. In 1829 President Jackson appointed him commander of a Revenue Cutter, and he finally retired from the service in 1849; and he died February 29, 1856. He was held in high repute by Commander Perry, whom he greatly assisted in his operations on Lake Erie; and a small cluster of islands in Green Bay is known by his name.

Doty, James D.——He was born in New York, and after preparing himself for the bar, removed to Michigan, where, for many years he took part in the affairs of the State. He was for many years United States Judge for Northern Michigan, also, Superintendent of Indian Affairs. From 1839 to 1841 he was a Delegate to Congress from the Territory of Wisconsin; Governor of the Territory from 1841 to 1844; and a Representative to Congress from 1849 to 1853. In 1864 he was appointed by President Lincoln Governor of Utah, of which Territory he had previously been Treasurer; and he died there in 1865, leaving in Michigan a large number of attached friends.

Driggs, John F.——Was born in Kinderhook, New York, March 3d, 1813; was apprenticed to a mechanical business connected with building in New York city, and was a master-mechanic until 1856; in 1844 he was appointed Superintendent of the New York Penitentiary, holding the office one year; settled in East Saginaw, Michigan, in 1856; was President of that village in 1858; during the two following years he was a member of the Michigan Legislature; and in 1862 he was elected a Representative from Michigan to the Thirty-eighth Congress, and was a member of the Committee on the Public Lands; re-elected to the Thirty-ninth Congress, serving on the Committees on Invalid Pensions, Mines and Mining, and Public Lands. He was also a delegate to the Philadelphia "Loyalists' Convention" of 1866, and re-elected to the Fortieth Congress.

Duffield, George.——He was born in Strasburg, Lancaster county, Pennsylvania, July 4, 1794, his father and grandfather having both been honorably identified with the history of his native State. He graduated at the University of Pennsylvania in 1811; subsequently studied four years at the Theological Seminary of New York; in 1815 he was called to the

Presbyterian Church in Carlisle, Pennsylvania, where he remained a number of years; next spent two years as Pastor of the Fifth Presbyterian Church of Philadelphia; one year at the Broadway Tabernacle in New York; and in 1838 he removed to Michigan and became the Pastor of the First Presbyterian Church of Detroit. From that time until his death, on the 26th of June, 1868, he continued in that relation, having for an assistant for three years the Rev. William A. McCorkle. A full review of his life, it has been said, would embrace a large share of the history of the Presbyterian Church in the United States for 30 years, and include many educational and scientific questions of the same period and would fill volumes. He always took an interest in the State University, and was twice appointed a Regent of the same. For well nigh the third of a century he was a bright and shining light in the religious world; he was distinguished for his industry; without neglecting the prime business of his life, that of preaching the truths of the Bible, he devoted much attention to agriculture and geology, and made himself master of nine languages besides his own; he was a true patriot, and sent two of his sons to the battle-field during the war for the Union. During the entire period of his residence in Michigan he identified himself with all the educational and religious interests of his adopted State and the beautiful city in which he lived; and on the second day before his death, and while delivering an address before the Young Men's Christian Association, he was stricken down by paralysis, and prepared himself to pass away to that rest which is the certain inheritance of the true Christian.

DUROCHER, LAURENT.——He was the son of a French Canadian, and born at the Mission of St. Genevieve, in Missouri, in 1786. He received a good collegiate education in Montreal, and in 1805 settled at Frenchtown, on the River Raisin. At the beginning of the war in 1812 he joined the army of General Hull, and after his surrender rendered important services to the Government. When the county of Monroe was organized in 1818 he was chosen county clerk, and held the office about twenty years. He was for six years a member of the Territorial Council, and was a member, in 1835, of the Convention which framed the first Constitution of the State. He also served in the Legislature, was a justice of the peace, probate judge, circuit clerk, and clerk of the city of Monroe, where he died on the 21st of September, 1861. He was an accomplished gentleman in his manners, and during his long public life was the great legal authority among the French population on the River Raisin.

In this connection, and for the want of a better place, we may notice the earlier French settlers on the River Raisin. These French families did not number over fifty, and among the most conspicuous were those of Bourdeaux, Duval, Beaubien, Couture, Nadeau, Bannac, Cicot, Campau, Jobien, Godfroy, Lassalle, Corsenau, Labodee, Robert, Lacroix, Loranger, Sancomb, Fourniet, Ferry, (who had served in the Revolution,) and Dauzette, who was for many years the leading physician of that section of country. As one who knew them well has written to us, "they were all among the first settlers; most of them originally from France, brave, patriotic, and ready always to make any sacrifice for the country, and during the war of 1812 true and faithful, and of great service to the American army, not only as fighting men, but as pioneers and spies, under the most trying circumstances, during the whole war."

EDMUNDS, JAMES M.——He was born in Niagara county, New York, August 23, 1810; received a common school and academical education. From 1826 until 1831 he was a school teacher, and in the latter year he removed to Michigan and became a merchant at Ypsilanti. He took an interest in the schools of that place, and was for ten years an inspector of schools, holding also a number of other local positions. In 1839 he was elected to the State Senate; in 1846 to the Lower House; and in 1847 he was the Whig candidate for Governor, but not elected. He was a member of the Constitutional Convention of 1851; in 1853 he removed to Detroit and entered extensively into the lumbering business, extending his operations to Saginaw and Tuscola counties. From 1857 to 1861 he was Comptroller of Detroit, which office he resigned to become Commissioner of the General Land Office in Washington; resigning that position in 1866 he was chosen Postmaster of the United States Senate, which he resigned in 1869, to accept the office of Postmaster of Washington city, which he still holds. From 1855 to 1861 he was Chairman of the Republican State Central Committee of Michigan; President of the Michigan Soldiers' Relief Association in Washington city from its organization in 1861; and he was also President of the National Council of the Union League of America from its organization in 1862 to 1869, when he retired from the position.

ELLIS, EDWARD D.——He was a descendant of the Puritans; emigrated at an early day from New England to the Territory of Michigan, and for a great many years was a resident of Monroe, on the River Raisin, where he printed and edited a newspaper. He was a man of culture and expansive views, and we regret that we cannot give the particulars of his life. This fact, however, we happen to remember. He was a member of the Convention which formed the first Constitution of the State. When a barren enactment was under discussion for establishing libraries in all the townships in the State without any provision either to secure books or sustain the libraries, it was Mr. Ellis who proposed and carried through the idea that *all fines* imposed for the violation of the penal laws throughout the State, and all sums assessed for the non-performance of military duty, should be set aside as a fund for the support of said libraries. The idea was original with him, and has frequently been mentioned to his credit.

EVANS, EDWARD P.——He was born in New York December 8, 1834; his father having been born in Wales, and by profession a Presbyterian minister. He removed to Michigan in 1850, and graduated at the State University in 1854. For a year afterwards he had charge of an academy in Mississippi, and was then appointed a professor in Carroll College, Wisconsin. In 1858 he visited Europe, and studied in the various German Universities of Gottingen, Berlin, and Munich; spent ten months in Italy and a winter in Paris and London, and in 1862 was appointed Professor of Modern Languages and Literature in the University of Michigan. Besides writing for the North American Review and many other leading periodicals, he published in 1866 a translation of the *Life and Works of Lessing;* in 1867 a translation of the "*First Historical Transformations of Christianity;*" and in 1869 an original work on German Literature in the German language.

EMMONS, H. H.——He was born in New York, and after acquiring the rudiments of a good education at the common-schools, he became an assistant in his father's office, who was the editor of a paper; he studied law, and was admitted to the bar of that State, and soon afterwards settled in Detroit, where his father had already located himself as a lawyer, and with whom he became associated in the practice of their profession about the year 1840. In 1843 his father died, and in the year following Joseph A. Van Dyke became his law partner; and although devoted to his profession, in which he had an extensive practice, he paid some attention to politics; acquired distinction during a period of commotion in Detroit by defending the *right* of an *American* Protestant clergyman to preach against Catholicism, Irish repeal, temperance, or secret societies, or whatever he conscientiously believed to be injurious to the welfare—temporal or eternal—of his fellow-citizens. In 1853 his health became somewhat impaired by application to business, and he partially retired from active professional life, although his services have been in frequent demand by the railroad companies of the State, whose business he had made a specialty. Early in 1870 he was appointed by the President Circuit Judge for the State of Michigan.

EVANS, MUSGROVE.——For what little we can communicate in regard to this worthy man we are indebted to an old friend. He emigrated to Michigan from Philadelphia about the year 1823, and was a Quaker by education and principle, and though mild and unpretending in manner, he possessed great physical endurance, had a large and full heart, and nerves of steel. He was a surveyor by profession, was for a long time in the employ of a French nobleman, who owned land in the Black river country of New York. He was, in conjunction with Wolcott Lawrence and Charles James Lanman, the founder of Tecumseh, and gave it its name, and was its first postmaster. From a letter that we have seen, written in 1824, the settlement of Tecumseh was chiefly concentrated around his own log cabins, in which his good wife had to provide for eight children and thirty-six hired men. He had two sons, who were led by the spirit of adventure to the Republic of Texas, both of whom were killed at the battle of the Alamo, and it is a singular fact that, after he had lost his wife, he emigrated to Texas, and died of a fever in the land where his children had perished in battle many years before. He was intimately identified with the early history of Michigan, and will always be remembered with respect by those he left behind.

FARMER, JOHN W.——He was a kinsman, we believe, of the eminent antiquarian, John Farmer, of New Hampshire, and was the publisher of several maps of the States of Michigan and Wisconsin. His sectional map of those States alone is sufficient to give him a high reputation, and it is worthy of note that it was engraved by his own hand. He died in Detroit, March 24, 1859.

FASQUELLE, JEAN LOUIS.——He was born in France, in 1808, and removed to the United States in 1834, engaging in educational pursuits. He was honored with the degrees of F.B. and LL.D., and was Professor of

Modern Languages and Literature in the University of Michigan from 1846 to 1862, performing for two years the additional duties of Librarian of the University. In 1854 he published in New York a new method for learning the French language, thirty thousand copies of which were issued in England; and he was also the author of the following productions, viz: "Telemaque, with Notes and Grammatical References," "The Colloquial French Reader," "Dumas's Napoleon, with Notes," and a "General and Idiomatical Dictionary of the French and English Languages." His works have all been eminently successful. Died in Michigan.

FELCH, ALPHEUS.——Born in Limerick, York county, Maine, September 28, 1806. He graduated at Bowdoin College, and adopted the law as a profession. He emigrated to Michigan when quite young; was a member of the State Legislature in 1836 and 1837; was appointed Bank Commissioner of Michigan in 1838, and resigned in 1839; for a short time in 1842 was Auditor-General of the State, but relinquished that position for a seat on the bench of the Supreme Court of Michigan; in 1845 he was elected Governor of Michigan, and having resigned in 1847, was elected a Senator in Congress for six years. He was appointed by President Pierce one of the Commissioners to settle Land Claims in California, under the act of Congress and the treaty of Guadalupe Hidalgo, in March, 1853; the business of which commission was closed by disposing of all the cases before it in March, 1856, since which time he has lived in retirement in Ann Arbor. He was also a delegate to the "Chicago Convention" of 1864.

FENTON, WILLIAM M.——He was one of the earlier emigrants to the county of Genesee, in Michigan, and after taking a leading part in founding the village of Fentonville, which bears his name, resided there and at Flint for many years, engaged in the practice of law, and holding a number of the more important local offices. In 1848 he was elected Lieutenant-Governor of the State, and re-elected in 1850 and 1851. At the commencement of the rebellion he became a member of the State Military Board, and during the war took a prominent part in organizing the 8th infantry of volunteers, which he commanded, and led over such a number of the battlefields of the country, that it came to be known as the "Wandering Regiment," and whose services will be found recorded in the preceding pages.

FERRY, THOMAS W.——He was born in Mackinaw, Michigan, June 1, 1827; was self-educated, and bred to pursuits of business. In 1850 he was elected to the Lower House of the State Legislature; to the State Senate in 1856; for eight years he was an active member of the Republican State Committee; was a delegate at large to the Chicago Convention of 1860, and was one of the vice presidents; was appointed in 1863 Commissioner, for Michigan, of the Soldiers' National Cemetery at Gettysburg; and in 1864 he was elected a Representative from Michigan to the Thirty-ninth Congress, serving on the Committees on the Post Office and Post Roads, the Militia, and the War Debts of the Loyal States. He was also a delegate to the Loyalists' Convention held in Philadelphia in 1866; was re-elected to the Fortieth Congress, serving on the Committee on Naval Affairs; and also re-elected to the Forty-first Congress. He resides in Grand Haven; and was re-elected to the Forty-second Congress.

FERRY, WILLIAM M.——He was born in Granby, Massachusetts, September 8, 1796; graduated at Union College, New York, in 1817, and after studying theology with Gardiner Spring, he went as a missionary of the Presbyterian Church to Mackinaw, where he located himself in 1821. He there established a school for white and Indian children, in which he labored unceasingly for a period of twelve years. His health having failed him, he purchased land in the Grand River Valley, where, with others, he founded a settlement, and became extensively engaged in the manufacture of lumber. His business was so extensive that he shipped to market in one year not less than fifteen million feet. He died at Grand Haven December 30, 1866 or '67, and left bequests for benevolent objects amounting to one hundred and twenty thousand dollars.

FITCH, CHAUNCEY W.——He was born in New York, and graduated at Middlebury College, in Vermont. He was subsequently a student in the Theological Seminary at Alexandria, Virginia, from 1825 to 1828. During a part of that period he was a teacher of languages in the Military Gymnasium of Georgetown, District of Columbia; and he was a professor in Kenyon College, Ohio, from 1829 to 1838. In the latter year he removed to Michigan, and became the principal in the Detroit Branch of the University of Michigan, in which position he continued until 1841; in 1842 he took charge of the Female Seminary in Detroit; and while holding these several positions, he performed the duties of Rector in various churches until 1863. In that year he was appointed hospital chaplain in the volunteer army of the United States; and as post chaplain, with the rank of captain, he was on duty in the vicinity of Detroit until the close of the rebellion.

FITZGERALD, THOMAS.——He was a lawyer by profession; served with credit in the war of 1812, under General Harrison; was appointed a Regent of the State University in 1837; and in 1848 and 1849 was a Senator in Congress from Michigan under the appointment of the Governor. A few years before entering Congress he was appointed a commissioner to inquire into the condition of the wild-cat banks, and his perseverance and industry effectually caused a winding up of these discreditable institutions. Died at Niles, Michigan, March 25, 1855. Although not a brilliant man, he was an honest politician and a true patriot.

FLETCHER, WILLIAM A.——He was a native of Massachusetts, where he was for some years engaged in mercantile pursuits, and settled in Michigan about the year 1820. He subsequently studied law, and was for many years one of the most successful lawyers in Detroit, filling with credit for a time the office of Attorney-General for the Territory. In 1835, on the adoption of the first State Constitution, he was appointed Chief Justice of the Supreme Court, and was employed by the Legislature to prepare the first codification of the laws. The "Revised Statutes" of Michigan, published in 1838, were his work, and the Legislature made very few changes in his draft of them. On leaving the bench in 1842, he returned to the practice of his profession, and died in Ann Arbor about the year 1855. He was reputed a man of high character and ability, and of strict integrity.

FRASER, ALEXANDER D.——He was born in Inverness, Scotland, January 20, 1796, and was educated at the Inverness Academy. In 1813 he began the study of law; two years afterwards he removed to Edinburgh, and prosecuted his studies in the office of the Writer to the Signet, and attended the law lectures of the University; and in 1819 he sailed for America and landed at Savannah, Georgia; came to the bar in Alabama, where he spent two years, and then removed to Vincennes, Indiana. He practiced his profession for two years in Indiana and Illinois; and in 1823 he arrived at Detroit, after a journey performed on horseback and in canoes, where he permanently settled, and with which place and the State of Michigan he has always been honorably identified. He was long a useful and active member of the bar, engaged in many important cases, but perhaps the most important was that known as the "Great Conspiracy Trial" of 1850, in which the Michigan Central railroad was plaintiff, and Mr. Fraser the prosecuting counsel, and the result of which trial was the conviction of twelve men, who, with others, had plotted the destruction of the railroad company. In 1856, while engaged in arguing an important case in the Supreme Court, he instantaneously lost the use of his right eye, by *amaurosis*, which compelled him to give up, excepting on special occasions, the practice of his profession. Under the advice of his physician, he soon decided to travel, and embarked for Europe, through which he travelled extensively. Always absorbed in the duties and studies of his profession, he had but little time or inclination to hold office; but in 1832 he was appointed Attorney for the city of Detroit; in 1836 and 1839 he was Recorder of the city, and in 1855 he was appointed one of the Board of Water Commissioners, in which he continues to this day, and the duties of which he discharges gratuitously. By common consent, he is to-day looked upon by his colleagues at the bar as the leading lawyer of Michigan; and as he is a man of much reading and culture outside of his profession, he has probably done as much as any other man to foster and perpetuate the history of the State of Michigan and the city of Detroit, where he is universally respected and venerated.

FRIEZE, HENRY S.——He is at the present time Acting President of the University of Michigan, Professor of Latin and Latin Literature in the same, a Doctor of Laws, and the author of several volumes connected with classical literature. Some years ago he visited Europe, and brought home for the University a fine collection of maps and books. Further particulars the compiler has been unable to procure.

GALINEE.——He was a priest of St. Sulpice, a companion of the discoverer La Salle, and the very first Frenchman or white man who is recorded to have visited the site of Detroit in 1670. After parting from La Salle at the head of Ontario, he and a fellow priest, named Dollier, coasted the southern shore of Lake Erie, and entered the Detroit river. At one of their camping places their altar service was washed into the lake, and this calamity was attributed directly to the Evil One; and it so happened that, on reaching Detroit, they stumbled upon a stone image, which Galinee believed to be a representation of the Devil, whereupon, in his exasperation, he demolished the image, and, with the help of his *coureurs des bois*, buried the fragments in the river. This man prepared a map of the Great Lakes, (the second ever attempted, for Champlain attempted one in 1632,) and, according to his map, he seems not to have known the fact that Michigan was a peninsula.

GOODWIN, DANIEL.——He was one of the early emigrants to the Territory of Michigan, where he settled himself in the practice of the legal profession. He was for many years the United States District Attorney for Michigan; subsequently appointed a District Judge; served repeatedly in the State Legislature; was President of the Constitutional Convention of 1850; appeared for the People in the great trial of 1851, known as the Railroad Conspiracy Case; and is at the present time Judge of the Circuit Court for the Northern Peninsula of Michigan.

GORDON, J. WRIGHT.——He was the Lieutenant-Governor of Michigan on the ticket with William Woodbridge, and when the latter resigned to accept a seat in the United States Senate, he became the acting Governor. He was an accomplished gentleman of ability and high character, but after leaving the public service his health became impaired, and he visited South America, and died at Pernambuco, from the effects of an accidental fall from a balcony in December, 1853. His place of residence was Marshall. In 1840 the Whigs had possession of the State, and when they came to nominate a candidate for the Senate they were divided between Woodbridge and Gordon, but the latter received the regular nomination. The night before the joint meeting of the Legislature was to be held for the election of Senator, while Mr. Gordon was enjoying a supper with his friends, a combination of Whigs and Democrats was made, by which it was agreed that they would support Mr. Woodbridge. The next morning the joint meeting was held, and Mr. Gordon, as Lieutenant-Governor, presided. The first name called was that of a noted Democrat, and he was heard to repeat the name of Woodbridge. The Whigs were astounded, and their candidate was defeated. The whole scene was one of intense interest, and was long laughed over by the politicians of Michigan.

GRANGER, BRADLEY F.——He was born in New York, and elected a Representative from Michigan to the Thirty-seventh Congress, serving on the Committee on Revolutionary Pensions. Further information the compiler has not been able to obtain.

GRANT, ULYSSES S.——As President Grant spent about four years of his military life in Michigan and at the post of Detroit, it is our duty as well as pleasure to introduce his name in the present record. The period in question was from the close of the Mexican war until his departure for Oregon, when he was brevet Captain of the fourth infantry; and if ever there was any doubt as to the attachment of the people of Michigan for him it was most satisfactorily settled when, after the Rebellion, he revisited Detroit, and was received with the greatest enthusiasm. He was born in Point Pleasant, Clermont county, Ohio, April 27, 1822. Although originally named Hiram Ulysses, the Congressman who nominated him for the West Point Academy gave his name, by mistake, as Ulysses S., and by that name has he ever been recognized. He graduated at the Military Academy in 1843, and as Second Lieutenant was assigned to the fourth infantry. He continued in the army from that time for eleven years, and participated in most of the battles of the Mexican war excepting Buena Vista, serving under Generals Scott and Taylor, and receiving two brevets for gallantry at Molino del Rey and Chapultepec. While serving in Oregon, in 1852, he was promoted to the rank of Captain. In 1854 he resigned his commission and settled near St. Louis on a farm; in 1859 he was a real-estate agent in St. Louis; and early in 1860 he removed to Galena, Illinois, where he joined his father and a brother in the manufacture of leather. When the Rebellion commenced he raised and took command of a company of volunteers, and before the close of 1861 he had command as Colonel of the Twenty-first Illinois Regiment, and was made a Brigadier-General of Volunteers; in 1862 he was promoted to the rank of Major-General of Volunteers, from which time his military history is to be traced in his achievements at Fort Donelson, Shiloh, Corinth, Iuka, Vicksburg, and Chattanooga in the West and South, and at the Wilderness, Spottsylvania, Cold Harbor, and Petersburg, in Virginia, culminating in the surrender of General Robert E. Lee on the 9th of April, 1865. It was on the 4th of July, 1863, that he was appointed by President Lincoln Major-General in the regular army, and he was appointed Lieutenant-General March 2, 1864, receiving this commission directly from the hands of the President; and the full title of *General* was conferred upon him July 25, 1866. After the close of the Rebellion he took command of the armies of the United States, with his headquarters at Washington. In December, 1863, Congress passed a joint resolution thanking him and the soldiers who fought under him for their gallant services and awarding him a gold medal. On the 12th of December, 1867, he was appointed by President Johnson Secretary of War *ad interim*, in the place of E. M. Stanton, suspended, which position he held until the November following, when the Senate refused to sanction the suspension of Mr. Stanton; and by the "Republican National Convention" of 1868, held in Chicago, he was nominated by acclamation for the office of President of the United States for the term beginning in 1869, and was duly elected. For his subsequent history the reader is referred to the records of the General Government.

GRATIOT, CHARLES.——He was born in the Territory of Missouri of French extraction, and educated at the West Point Academy, which he left in 1804. He served as a Captain and as Chief of Engineers in the army of General Harrison in 1812 and 1813, and in 1828 he was promoted to the rank of Brigadier-General for meritorious services and general good conduct; but he subsequently had some trouble with the Government, and under an act of Congress was dismissed from the service in 1838. As a part of his military duties were performed on the soil of Michigan, and as he was honored by having his name given to one of the fortifications of the State and also to one of its counties, it was thought proper to mention him in this connection.

GRAVES, BENJAMIN F.——He was born in Monroe county, New York, October 18, 1817; received a good education; and having studied law was admitted to the bar of that State in 1841. In May, 1843, he removed to Michigan and settled at Battle Creek, where he has ever since resided. In 1857 he was elected Judge of the Circuit Court for the fifth circuit, for the term of six years, having previously filled the same position by appointment from Governor Bingham for about one year, in the place of Abner Pratt, resigned. In 1863 he was re-elected for a second term of six years, but resigned in 1866; and in 1867 he was elected a Justice of the Supreme Court for the term of eight years, and is still in office.

GREGORY, JOHN MILTON.——He was born in Sand Lake, Rensallaer county, New York, July 6, 1822; received a common-school and academical education; and after teaching for awhile he entered Union College, whence he was graduated in 1846. He then studied law, but gave up that profession and became a Preacher in the Baptist Church; after much experience as a teacher in New York he removed to Detroit in 1852, and continued the same labor; in 1854, in conjunction with Professors A. S. Welch and E. O. Haven, he established the Michigan Journal of Education, which he edited for five years; in 1859 he was elected Superintendent of Public Instruction, in which position he served with great usefulness for six years; and he published a Compend of School Laws, as well as many addresses on topics connected with the educational interests of Michigan. In 1866, without his knowledge, he was appointed Regent and President of the State Industrial University of Illinois, to which institution he has been devoted down to the present time. In 1869 he visited Europe, and the extensive observations he made among the educational institutions of the Old World have tended greatly to enhance his usefulness in the laborious duties he has in charge.

GREENLY, WM. L.——He was born in Hamilton, Madison county, New York, September 18, 1813; graduated at Union College, Schenectady, in 1831; studied law and came to the bar in 1834; settled in Adrian, Michigan, in October, 1836; was a State Senator from 1837 to 1839; was elected Lieutenant-Governor of the State in 1845; became acting Governor by the resignation of Governor Felch (on account of his election to the United States Senate) in February, 1847; and was subsequently a justice of the peace for twelve years.

HALL, NORMAN J.——He was born in New York in 1837; appointed from Michigan to the West Point Academy, where he graduated in 1859; was assigned to the artillery service, and on duty in Virginia and South Carolina. In 1861 he was made First Lieutenant of the 5th artillery, and served on the Upper Potomac; was with General Hooker's division on the

Lower Potomac; on engineer duty in Virginia; and was a staff officer in the Peninsula campaign. In 1862 he was chosen Colonel of the 7th infantry, Michigan volunteers; was made Captain by brevet in 1862 for gallantry at Antietam, and before the close of the year a Major by brevet for services at Fredericksburg. In 1863 he was brevetted Lieutenant Colonel of volunteers for heroic conduct at Gettysburg, and during the same year was assigned as Captain to the 5th artillery, regular army. In 1864 he was discharged from the volunteer service for disability, and in 1865 was on duty in Boston as a mustering officer. Not long afterwards he was "retired from active service for disability resulting from long and faithful services and disease contracted in the line of duty." From 1865 until 1867 he resided in Massachusetts, and died in Brooklyn, New York, May 26, 1867.

HAMTRAMCK, JOHN FRANCIS.——He was a resident of Northern New York when the Revolution commenced, and served as a Captain in the Continental army. He was made a Major in the United States army in 1789, and promoted to be Lieutenant-Colonel in 1793; had command of the left wing of General Wayne's army at the battle of Maumee in 1794; was subsequently promoted to the rank of Colonel, and died in Detroit, where, in the grounds attached to the Roman Catholic Church of St. Anne, is to be found inscribed upon his monument a touching tribute to his memory, from which we gather the following additional particulars: That he was Colonel of the 1st United States regiment of infantry and commandant of Detroit and its dependencies; that he died April 11, 1803, in the 46th year of his age; that he was a true patriot and a soldier before he was a man; an active participator in the dangers, difficulties, and honors of the Revolutionary war; and that for his heroism he was thanked by General Washington; the monument having been erected as a grateful tribute to his merit and worth by the officers who had the honor to serve under his command.

HAND, GEORGE E.——He was born in East Guilford, now Madison, Connecticut, August 16, 1809; graduated at Yale College in 1829; and removing to Michigan, located in Detroit, and studied law with William A. Fletcher, with whom he became associated in business. In 1835 he was appointed Judge of Probate for Wayne county; in 1844, Injunction Master for Eastern Michigan; and in 1846 he was the sole representative of Detroit in the Legislature, taking an active part in preparing the Revised Statutes of that year, and introducing the resolution for selling the public works of the State, of which the Central and Southern railroads were the principal; and also prepared and proposed the present charters of those roads, and negotiated their final sale—the policy adopted by him having been of great service to the State. In 1853 he was appointed United States Attorney for Michigan, which office he held until 1857. He was one of the founders, and afterwards the President of the Detroit Young Men's Society; and also participated in founding the Bar Society of Detroit, and was for many years its President. He was a warm personal friend of Lewis Cass, and was chairman of the Democratic State Convention in 1848 when the General became a candidate for the Presidency. He has always been devoted to his profession, and has long been recognized as a prominent and influential member of the Detroit bar.

HARDING, FISHER AMES.——He was born in Dover, Massachusetts, in 1811; graduated at Harvard University in 1833; studied law with Daniel Webster, and in 1835 removed to Chicago for the purpose of following his profession. In 1837 he settled in Detroit; in 1841 he was elected to the State Legislature and bore a conspicuous part in public affairs; and in the same year he became an associate editor with Morgan Bates, of the Detroit *Daily Advertiser*, in which position he remained until his death, which occurred in Detroit, August 4, 1846.

HARRINGTON, DANIEL B.——In the spring of 1819 this worthy man arrived at Detroit from Ohio with his father, Jeremiah Harrington, and several friends, for the purpose of hunting and trapping in the wilds of Michigan. They travelled in a bateau, and, while obtaining supplies at Detroit, they called on the Governor, who told them not to go into the Indian country until he had made a certain treaty with them during the summer. They took his advice, and tarried until September on the site of Port Huron, when they visited the Valley of the Saginaw, where they spent the winter. The only white men then living in that region were Louis Campau and his brother, and John B. Cushway, all of them Indian traders, whose cabins stood on the site of the present Saginaw City. Mr. Harrington again visited the Saginaw Valley in 1834, travelling over-land. At that time there was only one house this side of Flint, and only a bridle-path to the Saginaw Valley. A man named Bonnell kept what he called a tavern where Saginaw City now stands, and there were, he thinks, about a dozen white residents living there. That was the only settlement on the river. He again visited the Valley in 1869 for the purpose of attending a railroad convention, and he found his old camping ground the centre of an immense commercial business, with a population of nearly thirty thousand souls. Mr. Harrington's present residence is Port Huron, and the story of his adventures in the wilds of Michigan would make an interesting volume.

HARRISON, WILLIAM HENRY.——Was born in Charles county, Virginia, February 9, 1773; was educated at Hampden Sydney College, and afterwards studied medicine. He received from Washington a military commission in 1791, and fought under Wayne in 1792. After the battle of Miami Rapids he was made Captain, and placed in command of Fort Washington. In 1797 he was appointed Secretary of the Northwest Territory, and in 1799 and 1800 he was a delegate to Congress. Being appointed Governor of Indiana, he was also a Superintendent of Indian Affairs, and negotiated thirteen treaties. He gained a great victory in the battle of Tippecanoe, November 7, 1811. In the war with Great Britain he was commander of the Northwest Army, and was distinguished in the defence of Fort Meigs and the victory of the Thames, and, in conjunction with Oliver H. Perry, rendered important services to the Territory of Michigan at Detroit. From 1816 to 1819 he was a Representative in Congress from Ohio; a Presidential elector in 1821 and 1825, and from 1825 to 1828 a United States Senator. In 1828 he was Minister to the Republic of Colombia, and on his return, he resided upon his farm at North Bend, Ohio. In 1840 he was elected President of the United States by 234 votes out of 294, and inaugurated March 4, 1841. He died in the Presidential Mansion, April 4, 1841. A sketch of his life was prepared by himself for Hon. James Brooks.

HARTSUFF, GEORGE L.——He was born in New York, but having become a citizen of Michigan, he was appointed in 1848 a cadet at West Point from that State, which has always been his nominal home. After graduating, in 1852, he was assigned to duty in New York, Texas, and Florida; in 1853 in the Topographical Department; in 1855 he was wounded in a fight with the Indians at Fort Drane, in Florida; in 1859 and 1860 he was stationed at Mackinaw; and after serving with credit through the whole war for the Union, from 1861 to 1866, he attained the rank of Major-General in the United States Army. He was present at the defence of Fort Pickens; Chief of Staff under General Rosecrans in Western Virginia; engaged in the affair at Carnifax Ferry; on special duty in the War Department; served on the Rappahannock and in Northwestern Virginia; was present at the battles of Cedar Mountain, Manassas, South Mountain, and Antietam, where he was wounded; was member of a board to revise rules and prepare a code for the government of armies; commanded 23d army corps in Kentucky and Tennessee; was at the battle of Petersburg; was Adjutant-General of the Military Division of the Gulf; and was next assigned to the command of the 5th Military Division, including Louisiana and Texas, where he is on duty at the present time.

HAVEN, ERASTUS O.——He was born in Boston, Massachusetts, in 1820; graduated at the College of Middletown, Connecticut, in 1842; in 1843 he became an instructor in the New York Amenia Seminary, and became its Principal in 1846; from 1848 to 1853 he was pastor, successively, over three churches in New York; from 1853 to 1854 Professor of Latin, and from 1854 to 1856 Professor of Rhetoric and English Literature in the University of Michigan, and from 1856 to 1863 editor of *Zion's Herald*, in Boston, the organ of New England Methodism, during which period he was a member of the State Board of Education and a Senator in the State Legislature. In 1863 he was made President of the University of Michigan, which position he held until 1869, when he resigned and became President of the Northwestern University, located in Chicago. He is both a Doctor of Divinity and a Doctor of Laws, and by his untiring and enlightened devotion to the cause of education, both in Massachusetts and Michigan, he has won a high position in the hearts of the people of both States, and would seem now to be accomplishing great good for the people of Illinois.

HENNEPIN, LOUIS.——He was born in Flanders, in 1640, and became a Recollet friar. He embarked for Quebec in 1675, and spent the next seven years among the Indian tribes of the Great Lakes and the Valley of the Mississippi. He was for a time the right hand man of La Salle during his sojourn in the Michigan country, but subsequently turned against the great explorer; he gave it as his opinion that the Detroit river was more beautiful than the Niagara, and also, "that those who will one day have the happiness to possess this fertile and pleasant strait, will be very much obliged to those who have shown them the way." The earliest description of the Falls of Niagara was from his pen; he named the river St. Francis in Canada, and was the discoverer of Lake Pepin and the Falls of St. Anthony. Although not considered a reliable writer, he published a number of books bearing upon his exploits and adventures in the wilds of America, which have been immensely popular. Indeed, not less than twenty editions of his travels were published in French, English, German, Italian, and Spanish. In 1697 he was refused permission to return to Canada, and became a citizen of Holland; also, figured at the Court of William III., of England; and, although he adopted the secular habit, he always added to his signature the title of "Missionary Recollet and Apostolic Notary." He died in Holland about the year 1700.

HENRY, ALEXANDER.——He was born in New Jersey in 1740; in 1760 he accompanied the expedition of General Amherst, and was present at the reduction of Fort Levi, on Lake Ontario, and the surrender of Montreal. After the conquest of Canada he became a fur-trader, and spent sixteen years as such (from 1760 to 1776) in the country of the Great Lakes, and in 1809 he published an account of his adventures at Mackinaw and his travels in Canada and the Indian Territories. He died in 1824. In his book are to be found some good descriptions of life and scenery along the more northern shores of Michigan.

HORNER, JOHN T.——He was born in Virginia, and in September, 1835, he was appointed by President Jackson Secretary of the Territory of Michigan, to which duties were very soon added those of Acting Governor of the same; but a few months after the State Constitution was ratified by the people, he was appointed Secretary of the newly-organized Territory of Wisconsin, beyond which point, unfortunately, we have not been able to pursue his career. His appointment to a leading position in Michigan, at a time when political feeling ran high, was very distasteful to the people of the State; and so unpopular was the new appointee, that in some instances he was treated with personal discourtesy, which probably accounts for his ephemeral residence within the limits of Michigan.

HOSFORD, ORAMEL.——He was born in Thetford, Orange county, Vermont, May 7, 1820; graduated at Oberlin College, Ohio, in 1843; was appointed Professor of Mathematics and Philosophy in Olivet College, Michigan, in 1846, to the duties of which position, as well as those of his clerical profession, as a clergyman of the Congregational Church, he was constantly devoted, in the town of Olivet, until 1864, when he was elected to the honorable and highly responsible office of Superintendent of Public Instruction for the State of Michigan, which he continues to retain. His annual reports have won for him the good opinion of all the people of Michigan who feel an interest in the cause of education; and a revised edition of the *School Laws of Michigan, with Notes and Forms*, was published by authority of the State in 1869, a copy of which is furnished to each district, township, and county officer in the State who may be concerned in the administration of the school laws.

HOUGHTON, DOUGLASS.——He was born in Troy, New York, September 21, 1809, and was educated for the medical profession at the Rensselaer

Institute in his native place, where he graduated in 1829. The following year he was appointed Assistant Professor of Chemistry and Natural History in the Institute; and while occupying this position he went to Detroit, by request of the citizens, to deliver a course of lectures on scientific subjects. In 1831 he was licensed to practice as a physician; and in the same year was appointed surgeon and botanist to the expedition sent out by the Government to explore the sources of the Mississippi river, and made an able and valuable report. On his return he settled in Detroit, and practiced his profession until 1837, when he was appointed Geologist for the State. From that time until his death he continued faithfully to discharge his laborious duties, and accomplished much towards developing the resources of the State, especially in attracting attention to its mineral wealth. In 1842 he was elected Mayor of Detroit; and, from its organization, was one of the professors of the University. He was also a member of the National Institute in Washington, of the Boston Society of Natural History, and an honorary member of the Royal Antiquarian Society of Copenhagen, and of many other scientific and literary associations. He was drowned in Lake Superior, near the mouth of Eagle river, during a violent storm, October 13, 1845, and his death was a great public loss, especially to the State of Michigan.

HOWARD, JACOB M.——He was born in Shaftsbury, Vermont, July 10, 1805; was educated at the Academies of Bennington and Brattleborough, and at Williams' College, where he graduated in 1830; studied law, and taught in an academy in Massachusetts for a time; removed to Michigan in 1832, and came to the bar of that Territory in 1833; in 1838 he was a member of the Legislature of the State; from 1841 to 1843 he was a Representative in Congress from Michigan; in 1851 he appeared for the people in the great legal trial known as the Railroad Conspiracy Case, in Michigan; in 1854 he was elected Attorney-General of the State, twice re-elected, and serving in all six years; and in 1862 he was elected a Senator in Congress, in the place of K. S. Bingham, deceased, for the term ending in 1865, serving as chairman of the Committee on the Pacific Railroad, and a member of the Committees on Military Affairs, the Judiciary, and Private Land Claims. He was re-elected a Senator in Congress for the term commencing in 1865 and ending in 1871, serving on the Library Committee, and those on Claims, Private Land Claims, the Library, the Special Joint Committee on the Rebellious States, and as chairman of that of Ordnance. He received from Williams' College, in 1866, the degree of LL.D., and was a delegate to the Philadelphia "Loyalists' Convention" of the same year. As an author, he published in 1847 a translation from the French of the *Secret Memoirs of the Empress Josephine.* He drew up the platform of the first convention ever held of the Republican party, in 1854, and is said to have given it its name.

HOWARD, WILLIAM A.——He was born in Vermont; graduated at Middlebury College in 1839; and, having taken up his residence in Michigan, was elected a Representative from that State to the Thirty-fourth and Thirty-fifth Congresses, and was a member of the Committee on Ways and Means. In 1851 he appeared for the defendants in the famous legal trial known as the Railroad Conspiracy Case. Having contested the seat of G.

B. Cooper in 1860, he became a Representative in the Thirty-sixth Congress, serving as a member of the Select Committee of Thirty-three. In 1861 he was appointed by President Lincoln postmaster at Detroit. He was also a delegate to the Philadelphia "Loyalists' Convention" of 1866. In 1869 he was appointed by President Grant Minister to China, but declined the position.

HULL, WILLIAM.——He was born in Derby, Connecticut, June 24, 1753; graduated at Yale College in 1772; came to the bar in 1775, but soon entered the Revolutionary army as a Captain; was rapidly promoted, and became Inspector of the army under Baron Steuben; was present at the battles of White Plains, Trenton, Princeton, Stillwater, Saratoga, Monmouth, and Stony Point, and for his services at Morrisiana he received the thanks of Washington. Two years after his surrender he was tried by court-martial and sentenced to be shot, but on account of his age and public services the sentence was remitted by President Madison, by whom he had been made commander-in-chief. It is now agreed among historians that his reasons for giving up Detroit to the British General Brock were not founded in cowardice or disloyalty. In 1824 he published a series of letters in vindication of himself, and died at Newton, Massachusetts, November 29, 1825.

HUMPHREY, LEVI S.——He was born in Vermont, and was among the earliest emigrants to Michigan after it became an organized Territory. He was for many years the Stage Coach King of the Lake Country, and probably did more than any other man to improve the breed of horses in the Northwest, and at one time he commanded great influence as a politician. He was for some years engaged in mercantile pursuits with Daniel S. Bacon; was a member of the State Legislature; was one of the Commissioners to locate the Southern and Central Railroads of Michigan; and he was connected with the Government as Register of the Land Office at Monroe, and as United States Marshal for the District of Michigan. Was afterwards a contractor on the Great Western and Grand Trunk Railroads in Canada, and subsequently returned to his old residence in Monroe, Michigan, where he died in 1869. Those who knew him personally can never forget his imposing personal appearance (for his stature was uncommonly large) as well as his gentle manners and kind heart.

HUNT, HENRY I.——He emigrated from New York to Detroit at an early date; was a citizen of that place prior to the surrender of Hull, and a witness of the exciting events of that day; he held a commission as colonel of militia, and was on intimate terms of friendship with General Cass. His profession was that of a merchant, in which he occupied a high rank; and in 1826 he was elected Mayor of the city of Detroit, and died in that year before the expiration of his term of office. Col. Thomas L. McKenney mentions the fact in his "Tour to the Lakes" that he had seen "few men in his life who possessed more of the confidence and affection of those who knew him, and that the feeling of regret at his death was universal."

HUNT, JAMES B.——He was a native of New York, and for many years law partner with Michael Hoffman. He removed to Michigan about the time of its admission into the Union, and was soon called to responsible public trusts. He was a member of Congress from Michigan from 1843 to 1847. He died in Pontiac, Michigan, August 15, 1857, aged 58 years.

JOGUES, ISAAC.——He was born in Orleans, France, in 1607; and before he had attained his thirtieth year we find him laboring among the Huron Indians as a Jesuit missionary, and visiting what was called the Tobacco Nation, north of Lake Erie. In 1641 he, with Charles Raymbault, passed along the shore of Lake Huron northward, entered the strait through which Lake Superior discharges itself, pushed on as far as the Saute de Ste. Marie, and preached the Faith to two thousand Ojibwas and other Algonquins there assembled. Not long afterwards, in his great zeal to convert the Indians, he visited Quebec for the purpose of obtaining necessary supplies for his mission, when he fell into an ambuscade, was taken prisoner by the Iroquois, with whom he was compelled to travel through Lake George to the Mohawk Towns, where he was cruelly tortured, but from which he finally made his escape, and, going down the Hudson to Manhattan, sailed from that place to France in 1664. On reaching Paris he was the lion of the hour, and having been summoned into the presence of the Queen, Anne of Austria, she bent and kissed his mutilated hands, while the ladies of the Court thronged around to do him homage because of his sufferings while a slave of the Mohawks. But these courtly honors were not in keeping with his simple tastes, and he soon returned again to the wilderness. The eventful story of his life may be found in the Jesuit Relation of 1643. He was a finished scholar, and might have acquired distinction in literature, but he preferred the trials and dangers of a missionary life, for which he was physically unsuited. A number of books were written of which he was the hero, and one was published from his own pen entitled *Novum Belgium*.

JOHNSON, FRANKLIN.——He was born in Vermont; received a legal education; and became a resident of Monroe, Michigan, in 1835, with which place he was intimately and honorably identified during the remainder of his life. While constantly engaged in practicing his profession, he found time to fill a variety of public positions. He was at one time Attorney for the city of Monroe; also Prosecuting Attorney for the State, and Judge of Probate, and lastly, Judge of the Circuit Court for the First District of Michigan for six years. He always maintained a high position at the bar, and it is said that his decisions as Circuit Judge were very seldom reversed by the Supreme Court. He died in Monroe October 11, 1870.

JOHNSON, OLIVER.——He was a native of Falley Cross-Roads, Massachusetts, and emigrated to Michigan in 1816; and having located himself on the River Raisin, was long a successful merchant and trader in furs. In 1825 he was appointed Judge of Probate, and held the office a number of years. He was a man of superior talents; possessed great energy of character; was a dignified gentleman in his bearing; a leader in all benevolent and Christian enterprises; and did much to advance the cause of religion in the new settlements by his able advocacy and active friendship. He was a Presidential Elector in 1857. He died in Monroe several years ago, and left a son, Charles G. Johnson, who has for many years been a prominent citizen and a banker in that city. His father-in-law, Henry Disbrow, was a man of the same high character, and was for many years a leading authority throughout the valley of the River Raisin in all matters appertaining to horticulture and agriculture.

JOHNSON, RICHARD M.——He was born in Kentucky in 1780, and died at Frankfort November 19, 1850. In 1807 he was chosen a Representative in Congress from Kentucky, which post he held until 1813. In 1813 he raised a volunteer regiment of cavalry of one thousand men to fight the British and Indians on the Lakes, and, during the campaign that followed, served with great credit under General Harrison as Colonel of that regiment. He greatly distinguished himself at the battle of the Thames, and the chief Tecumseh is said to have been killed by his hand; and for this reason we have thought it proper to introduce him in this collection of sketches. In 1814 he was appointed Indian Commissioner by President Madison. He was again Representative in Congress from 1813 to 1819. In 1819 he went from the House into the United States Senate to fill an unexpired term; was re-elected to the House, and remained there until 1837, when he became Vice President, and as such presided over the Senate. At the time of his death he was a member of the Kentucky Legislature, and he died from a second attack of paralysis. He was a kind-hearted, courageous, and talented man.

JOHNSTON, JOHN.——He was born near the Giant's Causeway in Ireland in 1763, and his connections were of the highest character on the score of social position, intellectual culture, and wealth. He emigrated to the United States during the Presidency of Washington, and was wont to boast that he had shaken him by the hand. After enduring many vicissitudes in Canada, he settled at the Saute de Ste. Maria in 1793, where he continued to reside until his death. He was a leading frontier merchant for more than forty years, and although far removed from the comforts of civilization, there was always a refined and cultured atmosphere about his modest home. In 1814 his property was plundered by the Americans, through the instrumentality of personal enemies or rivals in trade; and in consequence of that he re-visited Ireland, sold his patrimonial estate, and thus obtained a new start in the world. He did much as a writer upon Indian history; had a well-descended Indian woman for his wife, who, in her own person did so much for the American cause that General Cass called her his friend and a benefactress; and it was the eldest daughter of that woman, a lovely girl who was sent to Europe to be thoroughly educated, who subsequently became the wife of the historian of the Indians, Henry R. Schoolcraft.

JOLIET, LOUIS.——He was born in Quebec in 1645; educated for the Jesuit Priesthood; but soon renouncing the cowl and vestments, became a fur-trader and an explorer. He was designated by Talon, the intendant of Canada, about the year 1672, as a suitable person to explore the copper mines of Lake Superior, and although the expedition which he performed was unsuccessful as a speculation, it resulted in the production of one of the first maps of that region of country. He was subsequently sent by Frontenac to discover the Mississippi, and with La Salle and Marquette participated, to some extent, in accomplishing the discovery. On his return, he lost all his papers while passing down the rapids of the St. Lawrence, above Montreal, and could only make a verbal report to the Government. As a return for his services, he was presented with the Island of Anticosta, in the Gulf of St. Lawrence, where he settled with his family, built a fort, and continued his old employment of trading with the Indians. When the British came into power, his possessions were all confiscated, and he was sent as a prisoner to Quebec, where he is supposed to have died about the year 1737.

JONES, DE GARMO.——He was one of the earliest settlers in Detroit, and as a merchant was for many years a prominent actor in all the important business enterprises of the city and State. It was through his sagacity and means that the plaster-beds on the Grand river were first brought to light. He was a man of culture, and although nothing of a politician, he was elected Mayor of Detroit in 1839, and died in that city, at a good old age in 1846. His son, bearing the same name, served with credit as an officer during the rebellion, and is now a resident of Detroit.

JONES, GEORGE W.——Born at Vincennes, Indiana, and graduated at Transylvania University, Kentucky, in 1825. He was bred to the law, but ill health prevented him from practicing. He was Clerk of the United States District Court in Missouri, in 1826; served as an Aid-de-camp to General Henry Dodge in the Black Hawk war; was chosen Colonel of Militia in 1832; subsequently Major-General; also Judge of a County Court; in 1835 was elected a Delegate to Congress from the Territory of Michigan, and served two years; in 1839 was appointed by President Van Buren, Surveyor General of the Northwest; was removed in 1841 for his politics, but re-appointed by President Polk, and remained in the office until 1849; in 1848 he was elected a United States Senator from Iowa for six years, and re-elected in 1852 for six years, officiating as Chairman of the Committees on Pensions, and on Enrolled Bills, and as a member of the Committee on Territories. At the conclusion of his last term he was appointed, by President Buchanan, Minister to New Granada. In 1861 he was charged with disloyalty, and imprisoned in Fort Warren.

JOUETT, C.——All that the compiler happens to know in regard to this person is, that in 1803, he was an Indian agent for the General Government, and was located in Detroit. He deserves mention in this place, however, if, for no other reason, because he wrote an account of the condition of Detroit and the surrounding country, in the year above-named, which will be found printed in the *American State Papers*, and is of great value to all persons interested in the early history of Michigan.

KEARSLEY, JONATHAN.——He was born in Pennsylvania, and entered the army as a First Lieutenant in 1812; was made an Adjutant in 1813; served with distinction in 1814, in the defence of Fort Erie, in which he was severely wounded, having lost a leg, and for which he was promoted to the rank of Captain, and that of Major by Brevet; and he retired from the military service in 1815. In 1817 he was appointed a Collector of Internal Revenue in Pennsylvania; in 1820 he was appointed by President Monroe Receiver for the Land Office at Detroit, which highly responsible position he held until 1847; in 1829 he was elected Mayor of Detroit; was four times appointed a Regent of the State University; and after a long career of usefulness and honor, and lamented by a large circle of friends, he died in Detroit in 1855.

KELLOGG, FRANCIS W.——Born in Worthington, Hampshire County, Massachusetts, May 30, 1810; received a limited education, and, having removed to Michigan, entered into the business of lumbering. He served in the Legislature of Michigan, and was elected a Representative from that State to the Thirty-sixth Congress, serving as a member of the Committee on Invalid Pensions; was re-elected to the Thirty-seventh Congress, serving on the Committees on Public Lands, and on Expenditures in the Post Office Department; and was also re-elected to the Thirty-eighth Congress, and was a member of the Committee on Military Affairs. He performed the remarkable task of raising six regiments of cavalry during the rebellion. In 1865 he was appointed, by President Johnson, Collector of Internal Revenue for Alabama; and subsequently elected to Congress from that State.

KINGSBURY, JACOB.——He was born in Connecticut, in 1755, and entered the United States army as a lieutenant in 1789; removed to the western frontier about the commencement of the present century, and was for many years on duty at Detroit and Mackinaw, and subsequently at Belfontaine, then at the mouth of the Mississippi river, at Fort Adams on the same river, and at New Orleans. He rose, by regular course, to the rank of Inspector General, and for gallant services performed on the Ohio river in 1791, he was highly complimented by General Josiah Harmar. He retired from the army in 1815, and took up his residence in Missouri, where he died in 1837. He was the father of Julius J. B. Kingsbury, the worthy son of a distinguished father; and Harmar's handsome letter to the former, as well as an original drawing, made by him of Detroit as it appeared in 1800, are among the historical treasures of the compiler of this volume.

KINGSBURY, JULIUS J. B.——He was the son of General Jacob Kingsbury, and born in Connecticut in 1801; and educated at West Point, where he graduated in 1823. The first eight years of his official life as Second Lieutenant were spent at Fort Brady and Fort Gratiot, in Michigan; in 1831 he was made a First Lieutenant and stationed at Fort Niagara, New York; was on the "Black Hawk Expedition" in 1831, and also stationed at Fort Dearborn, Illinois; in 1833 he was again returned to Fort Brady, and also stationed at Saute de Ste. Marie and Mackinaw; and in 1837 he was made a Captain, and after some service in Florida, Maine, and New York, was returned for the third time to Fort Brady in 1845. He served with distinction in the Mexican war, participating in the siege of Vera Cruz, the battles of Cerro Gordo, of Contreras, Churubusco, Molino del Rey, and in the capture of the City of Mexico, and for his gallant and meritorious conduct, he was made a Brevet Major in 1847, and full Major in 1849. In the latter year he went to California, and after remaining there three or four years on frontier duty, he tired of his profession, and was dismissed from the army for absence from duty without authority. He died in Washington city, June 26, 1856.

KIRKLAND, CAROLINE M.——As this accomplished woman spent two years in Detroit and nearly another year in the interior of Michigan, and as her experiences in the West resulted in not less than three popular books associated with Michigan, a notice of her in this place is most appropriate. Her maiden name was Stansbury, and she was born in the city of New York. On becoming the wife of William Kirkland, himself an author of repute, she lived for some years in Geneva, New York; then settled in Michigan; and in 1843 she returned to her native city. Her books respecting Michigan were published under the assumed name of Mary Clavers, and entitled *"A New Home; Who'll Follow?"* *"Forest Life;"* and *"Western Clearings."* They made their appearance in 1839, 1842, and 1846; in the latter year she published an edition of *Edmund Spencer's Writings;* in 1847 became the editress of the *Union Magazine;* in 1848 she visited Europe and published *Holidays Abroad;* in 1852 she published two gift books, and in 1853, the Book of the Home Circle. Subsequently her pen was somewhat idle, although her productions were always popular, but none of them as much so as those associated with Michigan. She died April 6, 1864.

KNAGGS, JAMES.——He was born at Roche de Bout, on the river Maumee, about the year 1780, and from early life was familiar with the woods and their savage inhabitants. During the war of 1812 he rendered the Government important aid as a volunteer soldier and Indian fighter; and soon after Wayne's campaign he settled at Frenchtown and became a farmer. In 1811 he established a regular ferry at the Huron river, on the road between Frenchtown and Detroit, with only Indians for his neighbors. These, excited against all Americans by British emissaries, were very troublesome, and Knaggs had frequent and desperate conflicts with them. On one occasion he thrashed an Indian for some misconduct, and when a brother of the vagabond came at midnight to avenge the insult, a struggle ensued, which resulted in the breaking of every bone in the body of the Indian by means of a club. He was a leading man among the "Raisin men," who were called by General Harrison "the best troops in the world," and with them he was engaged in the various conflicts near Detroit, and under Colonel Richard M. Johnson, was present at the battle of the Thames, and was the man who identified the body of Tecumseh, with whom he had been acquainted. He performed a great many brave and patriotic deeds as a spy, scout, ranger, and general fighter; and a British officer named McGreggor, whom he had captured and carried to Hull's camp, subsequently offered a reward of five hundred dollars for his head. He was the youngest of five brothers, all of whom were active in the military service, while one of them was killed at Chicago, and another captured and carried to Halifax. Knaggs' mother lived near Frenchtown at the time of the battle there, and was one of those whom Proctor ordered away. She was then in her eightieth year, and having been robbed of her clothing, thinly clad, she proceeded in an open *traineau* and reached Detroit in safety. When asked how it happened that she did not perish, she replied, "My spunk kept me warm." The noted son of this worthy woman died in Detroit on the 23d of December, 1860.

KNIGHT, HENRY C.——He was born in East Bethlehem, Washington County, Pennsylvania, September 3, 1817; graduated at Jefferson College, Canonsburg, in 1836; and after spending one year at the Yale Law School, he removed in 1837 to Michigan, and continued his legal studies. On being admitted to the bar in 1839, he settled in Pontiac, where he remained until 1848. From that time until 1853 he was devoted to teaching in a classical school, and to the ministry, when his health became impaired, and he settled in Detroit, and resumed the practice of his profession. He was a useful member of the Board of Education for several terms, and one of the foremost of that body in caring for the wants of the children of Detroit, and furthering the cause of education generally; and he was for ten years the much-beloved Superintendent of the Sabbath School, attached to the Fort Street Presbyterian Church. He was twice elected to the Councils of Detroit as Alderman; was a Regent of the State University for nearly four years; and also Prosecuting Attorney for Wayne County, which last two positions he held at the time of his death, which occurred in Detroit March 26, 1867. When in the Council of Detroit, he was the Republican candidate for President of that body; and although there were two hundred ballots cast, extending through a period of two months, a tie vote prevented his election. Taken as a whole, his life was highly useful and honorable, and his name will long be treasured with respect by the bar as well as the citizens of Detroit.

LAHONTAN, BARON.——He was a native of France; bred a soldier; emigrated to Canada in his sixteenth year; and was for several years in command of a fort in Northern Michigan, chiefly at Michilimackinac. He spent about eleven years, from 1683 to 1694, in explorations along the St. Lawrence and in the country of the Great Lakes. He published the result of his adventures and observations in Paris, and some of his views so offended the Government of France he was obliged to take up his residence in Holland. He subsequently removed to England; and his letters from the wilderness, which had been revised by Count Frontenac, were "done into English," and with much information, omitted in the original French edition, were published in London in 1735. The work contained a number of maps, which have an interest for lovers of history. He cherished a strong animosity toward the Government of France; and in speaking of his letters in the English edition, he says they were "addressed to an old bigoted relation of mine, who fed on devotion, and dreaded the influence of the court." When in the employ of the French, he gloried in the title of "Lord Lieutenant of the French Colony at Placentia, in Newfoundland." In his work there are no less than four chapters devoted to affairs in and about Michilimackinac; and the place and date of his death are unknown. In the preceding pages his name is misprinted *Lahonton.*

LANMAN, CHARLES.——Born in Monroe, Michigan, June 14, 1819, and was the son of Charles James Lanman; received an Academical education in Plainfield, Connecticut; was a clerk in the house of Suydam, Jackson & Co., New York, from 1835 to 1845, when he revisited his birth place, and for a few months edited the *Monroe Gazette;* was associate editor in 1846 of the *Cincinnati Chronicle,* with Edward D. Mansfield; and after making a canoe tour of the Mississippi and through Lake Superior, returned to New York, and was associated as a writer with *The Daily Express.* In 1848 he visited Washington, and became a writer and travelling correspondent of the *National Intelligencer*; and while residing in Georgetown, D. C., continued in the service of that journal until the death of its editors, Gales & Seaton. As an amateur, he paid some attention to art, and travelled extensively throughout the United States. In Washington, he held the positions of Librarian of the War Department, Librarian of Copyrights in the State Department, and Private Secretary of Daniel Webster, Librarian of the Interior Department, and Librarian of the House of Representatives. Besides writing for the Press and the Magazines at home, in 1857 he became the American correspondent of the *Illustrated London News,* and in 1869 of the *London Athenæum.* As an author he has published the following: *Essays for Summer Hours,* three editions; *A Summer in the Wilderness; A Tour to the River Saguenay,* republished in England; *Letters from the Alleghany Mountains; Occasional Records of a Tourist; Private Life of Daniel Webster,* republished in England; *Adventures in the Wilds of America,* made from previous publications, printed in two volumes, and republished in England, with introductory letters from Washington Irving; *Dictionary of Congress,* six editions, three of them published by the General Government; *Life of William Woodbridge;* and as editor he has published *Prison Life of Alfred Ely,* and two volumes of *Sermons,* by Rev. Octavius Perinchief.—[*Abridged from Allibone's Dictionary of Authors.*

LANMAN, CHARLES JAMES.——He was the son of James Lanman, formerly a Judge and Senator in Congress, and born in Norwich, Connecticut, June 5, 1795. He graduated with honors at Yale College in 1814; studied law with his kinsman, Roger Griswold, as well as with his father; and was admitted to the bar early in 1817, in New London. Soon afterwards he was invited by Henry Clay to settle in Kentucky, but decided to seek his fortune in the Territory of Michigan, on the invitation of his friends, Wm. Woodbridge and Lewis Cass. He made the journey from Buffalo to Detroit chiefly on horse back. Joining Mr. Woodbridge in his law office, he began the practice of his profession, and while riding the circuit, he visited Frenchtown, on the River Raisin, (now called Monroe,) where he permanently settled. In that place he held many local positions, such as Attorney for the Territory, Judge of Probate, Colonel of Militia, and he was also Inspector of Customs, and Postmaster of Frenchtown. In 1823 President Monroe appointed him Receiver of Public Moneys for the District of Michigan, and he was re-appointed by President Adams, holding the office eight years. In those early days specie was the only currency in vogue, and the receipts of silver alone, in one year amounted to a hundred thousand dollars, which had to be transmitted to Detroit, through the wilderness, on pack horses; and it is worth mentioning, that when he visited Washington twenty-five years afterwards, he was officially informed that there was a handsome balance of money due him by the United States Treasury on account of his services as Receiver. He was one of the founders of Tecumseh, Michigan; was a Commissioner to locate the county seats of many of the leading counties in the State, including Ionia, Kent, and Clinton; was the Surveyor, and once the sole owner of the land where now stands the city of Grand Rapids; while the same is true of several other flourishing towns in the State. Although not a practical farmer, at one period of his life, he indulged his agricultural tastes by carrying on one or two farms, and he was among the very first to introduce into Michigan, from Kentucky and Virginia, the best breeds of blooded horses. In 1835, from family considerations, he returned to Norwich. During the financial revulsion of 1837 he lost the bulk of his property, all of which was located in Michigan; and in 1838 he was elected Mayor of Norwich; was subsequently President of the Norwich Water-Power Company; and at the conclusion of that service he lived chiefly in retirement. In 1862, lured by early recollections, and because of his intense love of the scenery and air of the ocean, he came to New London to reside; died in this city July 25, 1870, and was buried among his kindred in Norwich.—[*Abridged from a New London paper.*

LANMAN, JAMES H.——He was the son of James Lanman, of Connecticut, and born in Norwich, in that State, December 4, 1812. He was educated at Washington, now Trinity College, Hartford; and having studied law at Harvard College, came to the bar, and for a few years practiced his profession in Norwich and New London, and also for a short time in Baltimore, Maryland. A short time before Michican became a State, he visited it on a tour of pleasure, by invitation of his brother, J. Lanman, and having become interested in the country and people, he spent one or two years there, and then, under authority of the new State, published in 1839, his *History of Michigan.* Two years afterwards he prepared and published an abridgment of this work in Harper's Family Library, and which, with the author's consent, has been freely used in the first part of the present volume. He was also a contributor to the National Portrait Gallery, the North American and American Quarterly Reviews, and the Jurist, and for several years was the leading writer for Hunt's Merchant's Magazine, to which he contributed a large number of highly useful and important articles connected with the commerce of the country. Of late years he has lived in retirement in his native town.

LARNED, CHARLES.——He was born in Pittsfield, Massachusetts; educated at Williams' College in that State; and in 1811 he emigrated to Kentucky, where he became a law student in the office of Henry Clay. In 1813 he joined the army of General Harrison as an officer, on its way to the Lake country, and was present at the battle of the Thames. At the close of the war he settled in Detroit, and for many years, was one of the most active lawyers in that place, and a most influential citizen. His professional learning was highly respectable, but his great strength lay in his eloquence before a jury. Here, as Senator Howard informed the writer, he was highly distinguished—recognized by all his associates as an ingenious and powerful advocate in a contested case, depending upon close analysis of testimony, and an appeal to the feelings. On such occasions he showed great power, and his eloquence was enhanced by the imposing appearance of his person, and the wonderful *music of his voice.* Another tribute to his ability will be found in the "Life of William Woodbridge." He died in Detroit many years ago. He was a cousin, we believe, of General Benjamin F. Larned, and left a son, who is a well known lawyer in Detroit.

LARNED, BENJAMIN F.——He was born in Massachusetts; entered the army as an Ensign in 1813; rose within one year to the rank of First Lieutenant, and as such, served with honor at the battle of Fort Erie, under General Gaines, and for his gallant conduct was made a Captain; soon after, he entered the Paymaster's service; in 1847 was made Deputy Paymaster General, and in 1854 became the Paymaster General, serving his country in that capacity for many years with rare fidelity. A large proportion of his early official life was spent in Michigan, and among the older citizens of Detroit will always be remembered with peculiar gratification. Charles Larned, long a prominent lawyer of Detroit, was a relative of his, (we believe his cousin,) and he had two sons in the army, one of whom distinguished himself as an officer at the battle of Chepultepec in Mexico. He died in Washington City, September 6, 1862, lamented by a large circle of friends.

LA SALLE, ROBERT CAVELIER.——He was born at Rouen, France, in 1643, came of a wealthy family and was highly educated. He arrived in Canada in 1666, obtained a grant of land which he named *Le Chine*, by way of commemorating his pet idea that he was to discover a new pathway across the continent to China. In 1670 he started upon his discoveries, spent much of his time on the soil of Michigan, and discovered the Ohio and Illinois rivers. He arrived at Detroit in 1679, in his sailing vessel called the Griffin, which was the first craft of the kind that ever plowed the waves of Lake Erie. Her burthen was sixty tons, and she carried five guns. As a reward for his first explorations, La Salle was made a nobleman; he subsequently performed two important exploring expeditions; and in 1687 was assassinated on Trinity river in Texas. The filling up of this man's life, constitutes one of the most romantic and interesting chapters of bold exploits and wild adventure, blended with disappointments and hardships, which can anywhere be found. He spent 800,000 francs of his own money, on his various expeditions, and died with debts amounting to 100,000 livres. His purpose was an inspiration, and he clung to it with a certain fanaticism of devotion. It was the offspring of an ambition vast and comprehensive, yet acting in the interest both of France and civilization. The family bearing the same name, which settled on the River Raisin, at a later day, was allied to that of the great discoverer.

LAUGHTON, JOHN B.——He was born in Detroit, Michigan, but having at an early day, taken up his residence on the Canadian side of the Detroit river, he has always been a British subject. He was a member of the Kent Militia in 1812; and from Sandwich he saw the white flag which proclaimed the surrender of Detroit. He was then in his twenty-second year. He was afterwards engaged in the affair of Long Woods, in Canada; also at the battle of Chippewa, where he lost a brother; and at Niagara, where he was captured and taken as a prisoner to Greenbush, opposite Albany. At the present writing he is one of the oldest residents of Sandwich.

LAWRENCE, WOLCOTT.——He was born in Berkshire county, Massachusetts, in 1786, and was among the earliest settlers on the River Raisin, arriving there in 1816, where he was for many years an able and successful lawyer, for which profession he had prepared himself before leaving Massachusetts. There were times, however, when the law business was stagnant, and then it was that he turned some attention to the manufacture of flour. He served a number of terms in the State Legislature; held the office of Judge; and during his long and very active career, worked quite as hard for the public weal as for his own advantage, and he died at Monroe in April, 1843. One of his daughters, who was the first American child born in Monroe, became the wife of Alpheus Felch, and he left a number of sons, one of whom served with credit in the army during the late rebellion; while another, Edwin Lawrence, became a Judge of the Circuit Court of the State. By his ability and high moral character he exerted a happy influence upon the community, where he was always highly honored. He participated with Musgrove Evans and Charles J. Lanman in founding the town of Tecumseh, in 1824; and in conjunction with Daniel S. Bacon, erected the first frame house ever built in Monroe.

LEFEVERE, PETER PAUL.——He was born in Roulers, Belgium, near Ghent, in May, 1804; after passing through a course of theological studies he offered himself to the American mission, and was ordained a Roman Catholic priest at St. Louis in 1831; after laboring in that region for eight years he visited Europe, and in 1841 was appointed Bishop of Zela *in part*, coadjutor administrator of the diocess of Detroit, and was consecrated in November of that year. His administration as Catholic Bishop of Michigan extended through a period of twenty-eight years, until his death in Detroit, March 4, 1869. His immediate predecessor as Bishop was Fredric Rese, who held the office from 1833 to 1840; while the administration of Gabriel Richard (elsewhere mentioned in this volume) extended back to the year 1799; and the successor of Bishop Lefevere was C. H. Borgess, who entered upon his duties in May, 1870. The work accomplished by Bishop Lefevere, for his church was perhaps more extensive, but not more important than that performed by Bishop Richard. Leaving out of view the See of Marquette, it appears that within the diocess of Detroit there are now one hundred and sixty organized parishes, in the city itself, not less than eight churches, and among the institutions founded by the late Bishop are the following: St. Mary's Hospital, the Michigan State Retreat, the College of Lourain, together with several orphan asylums, convents, academies and schools, while his administration of the merely temporal affairs of the church within the State became pre-eminently successful. In his day he traversed the State from one extremity to another, making long journeys in his cause, and administering to the spiritual wants of his people among the Indian tribes and miners of Lake Superior. By way of showing his disinterested character, it has been said of him, that his death brought no profit to his kindred.

LEWIS, WILLIAM.——He was born in Virginia, and entered the army from that State as a Captain in 1791; was with General St. Clair in his expedition against the Indians on the Miami; and resigned his commission in 1797. On the renewal of hostilities in 1812 he took charge of a Kentucky regiment of volunteers as Lieutenant-Colonel; was with General Winchester in his operations in Michigan; and served with credit in the action against the British and Indians at Frenchtown, in 1813, but was unfortunate in being taken prisoner, with General Winchester and Major Madison, and transported to Quebec, where he was retained until 1814, when a general exchange of prisoners took place. He was subsequently on duty in Arkansas, and died near Little Rock, January 17, 1825.

LEACH, DE WITT C.——Born in Clarence, Erie County, New York, November 23, 1822. He was self-educated; bred a farmer; chosen a member of the Michigan Legislature in 1849 and 1850, and a member of the Convention to revise the State Constitution in 1850; he was also State Librarian in 1855 and 1856, and was elected a Representative to the Thirty-fifth Congress from Michigan, serving as a member of the Committee on Revisal and Unfinished Business; also elected to the Thirty-sixth Congress, serving on the Committee on Indian Affairs. After leaving Congress he was appointed an agent for the Indians of Michigan, and subsequently published some interesting papers on the soil, climate, and productions of the northern part of the Lower Peninsula of Michigan.

LONGYEAR, JOHN W.——He was born in Shandaken, Ulster county, New York, October 22, 1820; received a good academic education; removed to Michigan in 1844; studied law, and came to the bar in 1846; and was elected a Representative from Michigan to the Thirty-eighth Congress, serving on the Committee on Commerce, and as Chairman of the Committee on Expenditures on the Public Buildings. Re-elected to the Thirty-ninth Congress, serving on the same committees; he was also a Delegate to the Philadelphia "Loyalist's Convention" of 1866. In 1870 he was appointed by President Grant United States Judge for the Southern District of Michigan.

LOOMIS, CYRUS O.——He was educated for the bar; and when the rebellion commenced was practicing his profession in Cold Water. As already stated in this volume, he greatly distinguished himself as an officer of artillery; and what proved to be one of the most heroic fighting batteries of the war was honored with his name. He rose to the rank of Brigadier-General; and the writer regrets that he cannot give the particulars of his life.

LOVELL, LOUIS S.——He was born in Grafton, Windham County, Vermont, November 15, 1816; after due preparation he entered Middlebury College, where he graduated in 1832; and then he went South and taught school until 1838. He then read law in Springfield, Vermont, and also in New York City, and removed to the West in 1841, locating himself in

Ionia, Michigan. He was admitted to the bar in 1842; and in 1849 he was appointed by President Taylor Register of the General Land Office at Ionia, which he held until the accession of President Pierce. In 1857 he was elected Circuit Judge of the Eighth Judicial Circuit of Michigan for six years; re-elected in 1863 for a second term; and in 1869 was re-elected for a third term, the party opposed to him declining to make any nomination. Although earnestly devoted to his judicial duties, he finds time to participate in the local affairs of his town, and is Vice President of the First National Bank of Ionia, where he resides.

LYON, LUCIUS.—He was born in Vermont, but emigrated to Michigan when quite a young man; devoted himself for a number of years to the business of surveying the wild lands of the Territory; was a Delegate in Congress from that Territory, during the years 1833, 1834, and 1835; appointed a Regent of the State University in 1837; was a Senator in Congress from the State of Michigan from 1836 to 1840; and a Representative in Congress from 1843 to 1845. His last public position was that of Surveyor-General in the North-west. Died at Detroit, September 25, 1851. He left a son who served in the army during a part of the Rebellion, and subsequently became honorably identified with the Press of Detroit; and before entering Congress he had himself edited the *Democratic Expounder* in Marshall.

MACK, STEPHEN AND ANDREW.—The first of these worthy men located himself in Detroit as early as the year 1799, and was the pioneer merchant of the town. Soon after his arrival, he erected with true Yankee enterprise a shanty in the heart of the place, and spread out his goods to the admiring gaze of thronging customers. He was an Englishman by birth, and had performed military duty. In 1819 he participated with other Detroit citizens in building the first grain and saw mills in Pontiac. He was the father, as we have been informed, of Andrew Mack, who was bred a seaman, was a Superintendent of Light Houses, Collector of Customs for the Port of Detroit for many years, and in 1834 was elected Mayor of the city for the unexpired term of Charles C. Trowbridge, who had resigned. He died in 1854 at an advanced age.

MACOMB, ALEXANDER.—He was the son of William Macomb, a fur merchant in Detroit, where he was born on the third of April, 1782. On his mother's side he was descended from the Navarre family of the River Raisin. After receiving a good education in New Jersey, was a member of the "New York Rangers," a volunteer corps raised in 1779; was on the staff of General North in the Revolution; subsequently made himself useful as a dragoon; he was with General Wilkinson in the South-west; was for a time connected with West Point, where he compiled a treatise on martial law; became a Captain in 1805; a Major in 1808; had command of an artillery corps in 1812; and after many creditable exploits won special honor at the battle of Plattsburg for which he received the thanks of Congress with a gold medal. After the war, he was stationed at Detroit for many years; in 1821 he was made Chief Engineer of the Army, and removed to Washington; and in 1835 he was elevated to the position of Commander-in-Chief of the Army of the United States. He died in Washington June 25, 1841; was buried with military honors, (all of which he deserved,) in the Congressional Cemetery, and his resting place was soon marked by a handsome marble manument. He was a pure and accomplished gentleman, as well as an able officer, and had unnumbered friends in the National Metropolis as well as the State of his nativity. He was the author of a "Treatise on Martial Law and Courts Martial as practiced in the United States," published in 1809.

MACOMB, WILLIAM H.——He is the son of Alexander Macomb, and was born in Detroit, Michigan. In 1834 he was appointed a Midshipman in the Navy from New York; became a Passed-midshipman in 1840; and a Lieutenant in 1847. After continuous service in several parts of the world for nine years, he was attached to the *Portsmouth* frigate, and participated in the capture of the Barrier Forts, in the Canton river in 1856, when he was made a Lieutenant; in 1859 he had command of the steamer *Metacomet* on the Brazil station; in 1860 he was transferred to the steamer *Pulaski;* in 1862 he sailed in the *Genessee* of the blockading squadron; was made Commander in 1862, and performed much arduous duty at Port Hudson; and during the years 1864 and '65, he had command of the steamer *Shamrock*, and for gallantry on the coast of North Carolina, was advanced several numbers in the Navy Register. After the war, he was stationed at the Philadelphia Navy Yard, and in 1869, was attached to the Squadron in European waters.

MADISON, GEORGE.——He was born in Virginia in 1763, and while quite a mere boy, was a good soldier in the Revolution. He commanded a company under General St. Clair in the Northwest, and was wounded; was Lieutenant of a company of mounted volunteers, under Major John Adair of Kentucky; was wounded in an attack upon the Indians at Fort St. Clair in 1792; was a Major of Kentucky volunteers under General Winchester, and with Colonel Lewis in the battle with the British and Indians at Frenchtown, and also in the defeat on the River Raisin in 1813, when he was captured, and with Winchester and Lewis sent a prisoner to Quebec; but was released in 1814. He was for many years Auditor of public accounts in Kentucky. In 1816 he was nominated for the office of Governor, and was so popular and beloved, that his opponent withdrew in the heat of the canvass, and he was duly elected; but died on the 14th of October of the same year at Paris, in Kentucky.

MAYHEW, IRA.——He was born in Ellesburgh, Jefferson County, New York, in 1814; after receiving a classical education, he became a school teacher in 1832; in 1836 he visited Newfoundland for the benefit of his health; on his return in 1837 became Principal of Adam's Seminary; in 1841 Superintendent of the Jefferson County schools; and in 1843 he removed to Michigan, and took charge of the Monroe Branch of the State University. In 1845 he was elected Superintendent of Public Instruction; in 1848 received the degree of M. A. from Middletown University; and in

1850 he published a work entitled "Means and Ends of Universal Education;" in 1851 a work on Practical Book-keeping, which went through sixty editions in ten years. In 1853 he was appointed President of Albion College; in 1854 he was again elected Superintendent of Public Instruction, and, altogether, held the office for eight years; in 1860 he established what was called the Albion Commercial College; in 1862 he was appointed Collector of Internal Revenue for the United States; and then tiring of that kind of employment, resigned the position, and returned to the management of his Commercial College, in which he is still engaged.

MARQUETTE, JACQUES.——He was born at Laon, France, in 1637; in his seventeenth year he joined the order of Jesuits; and in 1666 was sent as a missionary to Canada. Having a taste for language, he soon acquired a knowledge of six Indian dialects, and in 1668 entered upon his duties in the country of the Great Lakes. Mackinaw and La Pointe, on Lake Superior, were each his home for a time, after which he accompanied Joliet in his discoveries, visiting the Illinois and Mississippi rivers, preaching in far-off Arkansas, and founding a mission at Kaskaskia; and having died on his return from these extensive labors on the river which now bears his name, he was, after some delay, buried with much ceremony on the Island of Mackinaw. The ruling idea of his mind was an extravagant affection for the Virgin Mary, and this peculiarity, blended with his many noble qualities as a man, won the sympathy of those who knew him, and made him a universal favorite. A journal of his adventures, and a map of the Northwest which he designed, have been published and found useful and interesting to the historical writers of this country. The date of his death was May 18, 1675, and it is said that his last words, were expressive of his gratitude to Heaven, because he was about to die in peace, a Jesuit, a missionary, and alone.

MARTIN, GEORGE.——He was born in Middlebury, Vermont, in 1825; acquired a good education, and having adopted the profession of law, removed to Michigan and settled at Grand Rapids. After holding a number of local positions of honor and trust, he was elected a Judge of the Supreme Court of the State, and was for several years the Chief Justice. He died in Detroit, December 15, 1867.

MASON, STEVENS THOMSON.——He was the son of General John Mason of Kentucky, but was born in Virginia in 1812. When nineteen years of age he was appointed Secretary of the Territory of Michigan, performing also the duties of Governor, and when the State was admitted into the Union, he was elected its first Governor, and re-elected to the position in which he served with credit to himself, and to the advantage of the people. He died January 4, 1843.

MAY, JAMES.——He was a native of England and settled in Detroit in 1778. The compiler regrets that he cannot furnish the particulars of this judicial pioneer, who was for many years honorably identified with the early history of Michigan. He was a Colonel of Militia; was appointed Chief Justice of the Court of Common Pleas about the year 1800; held the office for seven years; and died in January, 1829. A good portrait of him may be found in the "Early History of Michigan," by E. M. Sheldon. When the American Flag was hauled down, by order of Hull when he surrendered Detroit, Colonel May got possession of the flag, and keeping it in a safe place until the arrival of General Harrison, he hoisted it again to the breeze. An account which was published from his pen, respecting the condition of Detroit in 1778, is a document of very great interest and value.

MEIGS, RETURN J.——He was born in Middletown, Connecticut, in 1765; graduated at Yale College; and adopted the profession of law, which he began to practice in his native town. In 1802 he was chosen Chief Justice of the Supreme Court of Connecticut; in 1804 President Jefferson appointed him commandant of United States troops and militia in Upper Louisiana, and soon afterwards he became one of the Judges of that Territory. In 1807 he was commissioned a Judge in the Territory of Michigan, which he resigned in 1808, and was elected Governor of Ohio, which election was declared invalid, as he had not resided the required time in the new State. He was at once chosen a Senator in Congress, where he served from 1808 to 1810; and he was Governor of Ohio from 1810 until 1814, and by his cooperation with General Harrison, did much to help the American cause in Michigan against the operations of the British. In 1814 he was appointed to take charge of the General Post Office Department in Washington, where he remained until 1823, and in which position his services were important. He died at Marietta, Ohio, March 29, 1825. His singular name is accounted for as follows: When his mother was a girl, and had discarded her lover, Jonathan Meigs, she suddenly repented her conduct, and running to the door, called out, "Return Jonathan! Return Jonathan!" He did return, and they were married, and their first child they thought proper to identify with this domestic joke.

MCARTHUR, DUNCAN.——He was born in Duchess County, New York, in 1772. When he was eight years of age he removed with his father to Pennsylvania, and at the age of eighteen he volunteered in defence of the frontier settlement of Ohio against the Indians. He studied surveying, and acquired great wealth in the business of buying and selling lands in addition to surveying them. In 1805 he was a member of the Legislature, and in 1806 was appointed Colonel, and in 1808 Major-General of Militia. He performed valuable services during the war of 1813, especially within the limits of Michigan, in which he held a General's commission, and although elected to Congress in 1812, declined leaving his command; in 1815 was again a member of the Legislature; in 1816 was appointed Commissioner to conclude treaties with the Indians; from 1817 to 1819 was in the Legislature, and Speaker of the House in 1815. He was a Representative in Congress from Ohio from 1823 to 1825, and in 1830 was chosen Governor of the State, which position he held until 1833, and while in that service met with an accident, from the effects of which, he never recovered.

McCLELLAND, ROBERT.——Born in Franklin county, Pennsylvania, in 1807. He graduated at Dickinson College; practiced law for a year or so in Pittsburg, and in 1833 removed to Michigan, and established himself at Monroe, where his practice for many years was particularly successful. He served for several years in the Legislature of that State, and was a Representative in Congress from 1843 to 1849. He was Governor of Michigan in 1852 and 1853; and in 1853 was appointed Secretary of the Interior Department by President Pierce, the duties of which position he performed with recognized ability until 1857. He subsequently settled in Detroit and practiced his profession there. In 1870 he made a visit to Europe for the benefit of his health.

McCOSKRY, SAMUEL ALLEN.——He was born in Carlisle, Pennsylvania, November 9, 1804, and was the son of Dr. Samuel A. McCoskry, an eminent physician of that place, and grandson of the celebrated Dr. Nisbet, called by the trustees of Dickinson College to be its first President. After receiving the ordinary school education, he was appointed a cadet in the United States Military Academy, and numbered among the five distinguished cadets of the first year; he resigned in the Spring of his second year, and entered Dickinson College. He passed through the regular course in two years and three months, and was numbered fourth in his class. After he was graduated he read law, and was admitted to the bar in his native town when twenty-one years of age. At the close of his first year at the bar he was appointed Deputy Attorney General of the County of Cumberland, which office he held two years. He remained at the bar six years, and then became a candidate for Holy Orders in the Episcopal Church, and studied Divinity under Bishop Onderdonk, of Pennsylvania. At the close of one year he was ordained a Deacon, and was called as the Rector of Christ Church, Reading, Penn. He received Priest's orders during that rectorship, which continued one year. He was then called to St. Paul's Church, Philadelphia, where he remained two years. He was appointed first Bishop of Michigan by the House of Bishops, and was consecrated in St. Paul's Church, Philadelphia, July 9, 1836. He was also called to St. Paul's Church, in Detroit. He entered upon his duties as Bishop and Rector, and held the latter office twenty-seven years. As the fund for the office of Bishop was thought sufficient for his support, he resigned the rectorship, and devoted his energies to the Episcopal office. He had originally four clergymen in his diocess, but now there are eight parishes in Detroit alone, including missionary stations, and seventy-four clergymen in the diocess, and eighty-one parishes. The Right-Reverend Bishop is not only a Doctor of Divinity, but also a Doctor of Laws, the latter conferred upon him by the University of Oxford.

McKENNEY, THOMAS LORRAINE.——He was born at Hopewell, near Chestertown, Maryland, March 21, 1785; received a good education at Washington College, in Chestertown, and was bred a merchant, which business he followed in Georgetown, D. C. In 1816 he was appointed by President Madison Superintendent of Indian affairs; in 1824 he was appointed to preside over the Bureau of Indian Affairs, then for the first time organized in connection with the War Department; and in 1826 he was appointed a special commissioner with Lewis Cass to negotiate an important treaty with the Chippeway Indians at Fond du Lac, in the Territory of Michigan. In 1827 he published a "Tour to the Lakes," with illustrations, in which are many graphic sketches of Michigan life and scenery; and he also originated and published in conjunction with James Hall, "History of the Indian Tribes," a very splendid work, in three folio volumes, and illustrated with one hundred and twenty colored Indian portraits. He also published in 1846 two additional volumes, "Memoirs, Official and Personal, with Sketches of Travel among the Northern and Southern Indians." He was at one time a Colonel in the militia, or regular army, and that was the title by which he was generally known. In his manners and accomplishments he was a gentleman of the Old School; and his personal appearance was so imposing that the famous artist, Charles Loring Elliott, requested him to sit for his picture, when was produced one of the most superb portraits ever painted in this country, and which is now in the possession of James C. McGuire, of Washington. Colonel McKenney died in New York City February 19th, 1859. In 1823 an effort was made by interested parties to injure his fair fame; and a speech or defence that he made before a committee of Congress greatly increased his reputation for ability; and that his enemies were unsuccessful was proven by his continuance in the public service in a higher sphere than that he had previously occupied.

McKenzie, Alexander.——This man was a native of Inverness in Scotland; spent the greater part of his life as a fur-trader in the wilds of Canada; and in 1801 he published, in London, an extensive work entitled "Voyages from Montreal, on the River St. Lawrence through the Continent of America, to the Frozen and Pacific Oceans, in the years 1789 and 1793." For his services as an explorer, and for discovering the great river which bears his name, he received a title from his Government; but with all the honors showered upon his head, he did not scruple, on one occasion, to visit Detroit, dressed and painted like a common savage, for the purpose of instigating the neutral Indians to become the allies of his Government, and the enemies of the American Republic. He played the part of a savage so well, that he partially succeeded in his trickery; and he died as Sir Alexander McKenzie in 1820.

McKnight, Sheldon.——He was the founder of the Detroit *Free Press* in 1829, which soon became, and has ever continued, to be the leading organ of the Democratic party in the State of Michigan. He was at one time Postmaster of Detroit for several years; reputed a man of ability; and prior to his death, was engaged in the Lake Superior shipping interest, and constructed the marine railway at the Saute de Ste. Marie, over which the first vessels that ever navigated Lake Superior were transported. Died at Washington, D. C., in July, 1860.

McLean, John.——As his judicial powers extended over the State of Michigan, from the time it was admitted into the Union until his death, it is entirely proper that his services should be recorded in this volume. He was born in Morris County, New Jersey, in 1785. Four years after his birth his father emigrated with his family to Virginia, whence he removed to Kentucky, and finally settled in the State of Ohio. Here the son received a scanty education; and, having determined to pursue the legal profession, he engaged at the age of eighteen to write in the Clerk's office at Cincinnati, in order to maintain himself, by devoting a portion of his time to that labor, while engaged in his studies. In 1807 he was admitted to the bar, and entered upon the practice of the law at Lebanon, Ohio. In 1812 he became a candidate to represent his district in Congress, and was elected by a large majority. He professed the political principles of the Democratic party, being an ardent supporter of the war, and of President Madison's administration. In 1814 he was again elected to Congress by a unanimous vote—a circumstance of rare occurrence—and remained a member of the House of Representatives until 1816, when, the Legislature of Ohio having elected him a Judge of the Supreme Court of the State, he resigned his seat in Congress at the close of the session. He remained six years upon the Supreme Bench of Ohio. In 1822 he was appointed Commissioner of the General Land Office by President Monroe; and in 1823 he became Postmaster-General. In the year 1829 he was appointed by President Jackson, a Justice of the United States Supreme Court, after he had refused the offer of the War and Navy Departments. He entered upon the discharge of his judicial duties at the January term of 1830, and died in Cincinnati, April 4, 1861.

MILLER, DAN B.——He was a native of New York, and among the earliest emigrants to the Territory of Michigan, and settled in Monroe in 1823. As a merchant and a devoted friend of the Protestant Episcopal Church, he exercised an important influence for many years in the village and city of Monroe, where he held the office of Receiver of Public Moneys for the General Land Office for several years, and where he died in 1850, lamented by a large circle of devoted friends. He left two sons, Van Horne and Sidney, the first a resident of Monroe, and the second a lawyer in Detroit.

MINTY, ROBERT H. G.——He was born in Mayo, Ireland, December 4, 1831; entered the British army in 1849 as an Ensign; served five years in the West Indies, Honduras, and on the coast of Africa; in 1853 he retired from the English service and came to America. When the rebellion commenced he was a citizen of Michigan; joined the Third Cavalry as Major, at Grand Rapids, in 1861, and soon became Lieutenant-Colonel; he next became Colonel of the Fourth Cavalry, and afterwards commanded a brigade; and, as will be seen in the preceding pages, acquited himself with great ability on many battle-fields. The fact that it was his regiment which captured Jefferson Davis, will long be remembered by the people of Michigan, but that exploit was only one, of very many, that the regiment performed in its long and arduous career.

MIZNER, JOHN K.——He was born in New York, but appointed from Michigan to the West Point Academy, where he graduated in 1856. His first service was rendered at Carlisle, Pennsylvania; in 1857 he was assigned to the Second Dragoons as Second Lieutenant; and was on duty in Kansas and the neighboring frontiers. In 1861 he was appointed a Captain in the Second Cavalry; in 1862 was made Colonel of the Third Cavalry of Michigan; was made Major in 1862 for services at the battle of Corinth; and in 1863 Brevet Lieutenant-Colonel, for heroic conduct at Panola, Mississippi. In 1865 he was appointed a Brigadier-General by brevet of volunteers, for his meritorious services during the rebellion. In 1866 he was mustered out of the volunteer service; and was subsequently assigned to duty on the frontiers and in Nebraska, according to his Rank in the Regular Army.

MORRELL, GEORGE.——He was born in Lenox, Massachusetts, in 1786; graduated at Williams' College; was a United States Judge for the Territory of Michigan; subsequently an Associate Justice, and in 1842 Chief Justice of the Supreme Court of the State; and died in Detroit in March, 1845.

MOSELEY, JONATHAN OGDEN.——Born at East Haddom, Middlesex County, Connecticut; was a graduate of Yale College in 1780; and a Representative in Congress, from his native State, from 1805 to 1821. He subsequently removed to Michigan, with which he became identified in all his family and business interests, and died at Saginaw, in that State, September 9, 1839, aged seventy-seven years.

MUNDY, EDWARD.——He was among the earlier emigrants to the Territory of Michigan, and a lawyer by profession. He was the first Lieutenant-Governor of the State under the first State Constitution in 1835 and 1836, and again held the same office from 1837 to 1840; in 1847 he was chosen Attorney-General, which office he only held until 1843, when he was made an Associate Justice on the Supreme Bench; and from 1844 until 1848 he was Regent, by appointment, of the State University. He died in Detroit in 1851.

NAVARRE, PETER.——He was the grand-son of Robert Navarre, a French officer who came to America in 1745 and settled at Detroit, where he was born in 1790. In 1807 the whole family removed to the mouth of the Maumee. At that time, the widow of Pontiac was living there with her son *Otussa*. She was very old, and held in great reverence. Navarre was at the Prophet's town on the Wabash with a French trader, when General Harrison arrived there, just before the battle of Tippecanoe, but escaped. He joined Hull's army at the Maumee Rapids, was with him at Detroit, and after the surrender, returned to the Raisin and enlisted in Colonel Anderson's regiment. He was there when Brock was ordered to surrender, but was afterwards compelled to go with the British as a guide up the Maumee, where he deserted and joined Winchester's army. He was an eye witness of the massacre at the River Raisin. After that he and two brothers, Francois and Antoine, were employed as scouts, and performed excellent service, he, himself, having been one of the most trusty of Harrison's guides and scouts. The brothers were for many years among the most respectable inhabitants living in the valley of the River Raisin. As late as 1867 the subject of this notice was still living on the Maumee, in the enjoyment of a peaceful old age.

NEWBURY, OLIVER.——He was a native of Connecticut, as we have been informed, and emigrated to Michigan about the year 1816, locating in Detroit, where he was for many years a successful merchant. But it was as a builder of steamboats that he was chiefly known, and it was on account of the splendor of his vessels and the number of lines that he established, extending throughout the length of all the Great Lakes, that he became popularly known as "the steamboat king." He was a plain man in his life and manners, and his business sagacity and abilities were of the highest order. He was a man of indomitable enterprise, and far-seeing in his business calculations. It was said of him that for many years he carried all his business papers in his hat, and was rarely seen uncovered. He was never married, and was the brother of Walter Newbury, long a prominent citizen of Chicago; and he died many years ago in Detroit, leaving a name that was universally respected throughout the State.

NOBLE, CHARLES.——He was born in Williamstown, Massachusetts, and emigrated to the Territory of Michigan in 1818, locating at Frenchtown, on the River Raisin. Having received a liberal education, he adopted the profession of law, and was for nearly half a century one of the most influential citizens in that part of the country, where he held a great number of public positions of a local character. In 1824 he was appointed Prosecuting Attorney, and held the office several years; was also Postmaster of Monroe, a County Judge, Register of Probate, and Fund Commissioner for the State. In 1825 and '26 he was a member of the Legislative Council; was largely interested in the Michigan Southern Railroad, one of its projectors, and at one time President of the Company. In 1850 he received from President Taylor the appointment of Surveyor of the Territory northwest of the Ohio, holding the position until the close of President Fillmore's term. Most of the country about the Upper Lakes, including the copper and iron regions, were surveyed and brought into market under his administration of the office, besides much of the Lower Peninsula; it was during that time, also, that the solar compass was brought into general use, and adopted by the Government. To speak in general terms, he was always deeply interested in the settlement, growth, and prosperity of Michigan; in its schools and other institutions of learning, and in the moral and religious character of its people; and as a leading man on the River Raisin, he took an active part in all the canals and roads, and in every enterprise connected with the well being and prosperity of Monroe and the State generally. He was followed to the West by a number of brothers, all of whom were honorably identified with the State of Michigan as legislators or business men. In this connection we may remark that the early Anglo-Saxon settlers of Michigan, who congregated on the River Raisin, as a body of men were uncommonly intelligent and cultivated, and exceedingly enterprising. However much they might differ, practically or otherwise, on general subjects, they were always alive to the interests of Monroe, and in that particular always acted as a unit, and lost no political or other influence to which perfect unanimity of thought and action would entitle them. They possessed a commanding influence in the Legislature, and all over the State, and for many years went by the *soubriquet* of the "*Independent State of Monroe.*"

NOBLE, DAVID A.——He was born in Massachusetts; liberally educated; adopted the profession of law; and on removing to Michigan was elected a Representative in Congress from that State from 1853 to 1855. Has always been a successful practitioner at the bar. He is the brother of Charles Noble, mentioned in the preceding notice.

NOBLE, LOUIS LEGRAND.——He was born in Otsego County, New York, in 1812; in 1824 he removed with his parents to the Territory of Michigan, who located themselves on the River Huron, where his poetical sensibilities were stimulated by the beauty of the scenery with which he was surrounded. He was educated chiefly at the General Theological Seminary, in New York, and in 1840 was ordained a minister of the Protestant Episcopal Church. The several parishes over which he has presided were, first, in Elizabeth City, North Carolina; second, Catskill, New York; third, Chicago, Illinois; and lastly, in Hudson City, New Jersey. He published an Indian poem entitled *Ne-mah-min* about the year 1842, the scenes of which are laid in Michigan; in 1857 he published a volume of miscellaneous poems; and his best productions are *The Cripple Boy*, *A Ballad of the Ottawas*, and *Lines to a Flying Swan in the Vale of the Huron*, all of which are associated with the State in which he spent his boyhood. He is also the author of the *Life of Thomas Cole*, the famous landscape painter, and also of a delightful volume entitled "*After Icebergs with a Painter*," which commemorates a voyage that he made to Labrador with another famous landscape painter, Frederick E. Church. Mr. Noble's attachment to Michigan is so strong that he frequently visits the State, where members of his family still continue to reside. That he is a true poet, and fully appreciates the grandeur and beauty of the forests of Michigan, may be readily seen by the following extract from the "*Groves of the River Huron*:"

"O, I am glad you still are hand in hand
In the grand round of solitude! I joy
That yet in your magnificence ye move
With the rich summer garlanded; and feel
Ye bear for me a welcome on your brows.
For I have loved you from a very boy
With a most tender and unfailing love;
Nay, of your beauty spoken with a zeal
That has begotten many a wish to come
And kindle cottage fires beneath your green.
And here I own that I have never gone
Beyond the reach of your broad shadows; never
Beyond the music of your rustling; never
Beyond the music of your dropping dews.
Your image has pursued me to the waves,
Fleecing the rocks with whiteness; to the clouds,
Fleecing the mountain summits with their snow.
I own it here, you have possess'd me so,
So cooled and shaded me in feverish dreams,
So haunted me, and with my feelings wrought,

In gardens, city parks, and walks embowered,
That I no less could do than seek once more
Your presence and your blessing. I am here,
Thou Gothic forest, to be young again.
A benison, ye venerable forms,
O shed upon me from your outspread hands!
O bless me with my boyhood! Be to me
All that ye were!"

NORVELL, JOHN.——He was bred a printer; was for a time the editor of a newspaper in Philadelphia; was appointed by President Jackson Postmaster of Detroit; and having become identified with the Territory of Michigan, became one of the Senators in Congress from the new State, having served in that capacity from its admission into the Union until 1841. He was also for several years Attorney for the State, in which position he acquitted himself with ability; and in 1837 was appointed a Regent of the State University. He died of apoplexy in April, 1850.

OLNEY, EDWARD.——He was born in Moreau, Saratoga County, New York, July 24, 1827; when six years of age he removed with his father to Michigan, who soon afterwards settled in Ohio as a farmer. He received a common school education, under many disadvantages; for several years, before becoming of age, he studied Latin, and was engaged in teaching; he next devoted his attention to the study of Greek and French, and had charge of the Perrysburg Union School; in 1853 he received from Madison University, in New York, the degree of A. M., and shortly afterward removed to Kalamazoo, in Michigan, and was made Professor of Mathematics in the Literary Institute of that place; taught for ten years in the Kalamazoo College, and for a time edited the Michigan Christian Herald; and in 1863 he received, without personal knowledge or solicitation, the appointment of Professor of Mathematics in the University of Michigan. He is the author of a Mathematical Series, the first of which has been published and pronounced eminently successful.

PALMER, A. B.——He was born in Richfield, Otsego County, New York, October 6, 1815, and was the son of Benjamin Palmer, a worthy farmer, who was made blind by an accident four years before the birth of his son. He received an academical education, attended lectures at the Fairfield Medical College, and graduated at the College of Physicians and Surgeons of Western New York; in 1838 he removed to Michigan and settled in Tecumseh, where he practiced his profession for twelve years; between the years 1847 and 1850 he attended the Hospitals of New York and Philadelphia; in the latter year he removed to Chicago, where he remained seven years, during which period, in 1854, however, he delivered a course of Medical Lectures in the University of Michigan, and in which he has been a Professor of two important departments down to the present time. From 1852 to 1859 he was the Editor of the Peninsula "*Journal of Medicine*" and "*Independent Medical Journal;*" in 1859 he visited Europe; and when the rebellion commenced in 1861 he volunteered his services and was appointed a Surgeon in the army, and in that capacity, when his duties as a Professor would allow, served during the whole war. In 1864 he was appointed a Professor in the Berkshire Medical College, Massachusetts, and subsequently to a similar position in the Medical School of Maine, associated with Bowdoin College; has been a prominent member and Vice President of the American Medical Association; and his long connection with the University of Michigan is the best proof that his services have been highly valued. During his residence in Chicago he had much to do with the cholera, and published a pamphlet upon the subject, which went through several editions and was highly commended; and he has, besides his many lectures, written a number of reports on questions connected with his profession.

PARKMAN, FRANCIS.——As this distinguished author has done much to illustrate the history of Michigan by his writings, we must claim the privilege of inserting his name in the present record. He was born in Boston, September 16, 1823, and resides in that city. Soon after leaving Harvard College, about twenty-five years ago, he conceived the idea of writing the history of France and England in North America. The determined manner in which he began his work inspired commendation at the time, and his subsequent success may well be considered a satisfactory reward. He made summer tours into the wilds of Canada and the region of the Great Lakes; cast a thought upon the legal profession, but gave it the cold shoulder; visited Europe, and then made a pilgrimage over the prairies and among the mountains westward of the Mississippi river, and gave the public a charming book of personal adventures. This last frolic over, he then entered upon the chosen business of his life with decided earnestness. He threw aside the "sandal shoon," and, taking up his pen, began to explore the published and unpublished records bearing upon his subject, and was so persevering in his labors as seriously to impair his health. Indeed, he was well nigh losing his sight altogether, and for several protracted periods was compelled to suspend his labors. But he continued the battle, revisited Europe, delved into the archives of France, and may to-day be congratulated on having accomplished much the largest proportion of his self-assigned task, by the publication of four volumes. The first issued of these productions was the "History of the Conspiracy of Pontiac," and while it may be read and enjoyed as a separate work, will hereafter be considered as a kind of sequel to the fellow volumes. Of these, three have already been published, viz: the "Pioneers of France in the New World," the "Jesuits in North America in the Seventeenth Century," and the "Discovery of the Great West;" and the idea of the author, which includes the achievements of both France and England on this continent, will not be completed until the publication of several additional volumes.

PARSONS, ANDREW.——He was born in Hoosaac, Renssalear County, New York, July 22, 1817; brought up on a farm in Oswego County; received a common school education, and became a teacher in his sixteenth year; removed to Michigan in 1835 and became a teacher in Ann Arbor; was County Clerk of Shiawasse County from 1836 to 1838; was subsequently County Register for eight years, and also a Prosecuting Attorney; was elected to the State Senate in 1846; was for a time a Regent of the University of Michigan, by election, from 1852 to 1854; was elected Lieutentant-Governor of the State in 1852, and on the resignation of Robert McClellan in 1853 he became the Acting Governor, which office he held until 1854. He was next elected to the Legislature, but returning home at the end of the first session in very feeble health, he died in June of that year, lamented by many friends.

PECK, GEORGE W.——He was born in New York about the year 1818; removed to Michigan, and was a member of the Legislature of that State in 1846 and 1847, serving as Speaker during the latter year; was afterwards chosen Secretary of State; and was a Representative in Congress from Michigan, from 1855 to 1857.

PENNIMAN, EBENEZER JENCKES.——He was born in Lansingburgh, New York; when thirteen years of age was apprenticed to the business of printing, in the office of the "New Hampshire Sentinel," at Keene; when eighteen years of age he purchased his indentures, and entered upon mercantile pursuits in the City of New York; removed to Michigan in 1835, and was elected a Representative from that State to the Thirty-Second Congress.

PERRAULT, JOHN BAPTISTE.——He was born in Lower Canada, 1759, and belonged to one of the oldest families in Quebec. After receiving a collegiate education in that city, he visited Montreal on business for his father, when he was smitten with a love of wild life, and in 1783 became a bourgeois. He went to what was then the metropolis of the Indian trade, Michilimackinac, and after some primary trips to the Illinois, he chose the Lake country as the theatre of his life and adventures, and there passed nearly sixty years. He died at Saute de Ste. Marie on the 12th November, 1844; and a sketch of his career was published by Henry R. Schoolcraft in 1853.

PERRY, OLIVER HAZARD.——As this man, during his brief but splendid career in the West, did as much as any other to secure the people of Michigan in their civil and political rights, it would not be proper to omit his name in this place. He was born in Newport, Rhode Island, in 1785; entered the Navy as a Midshipman in 1798; served in the Tripolitan war; was made a Master-commandant in 1812, and in the following year he was appointed to the command of the squadron on Lake Erie, where, as already related in this volume, he triumphed over the British and restored peace to the people of Michigan, and won imperishable renown. For this service he was promoted to the rank of Captain, received the thanks of Congress and of the State of Pennsylvania. After the war he sailed to the Mediterranean under Decatur; was subsequently on duty in the West Indies, and in August, 1820, he was attacked with the yellow fever, which in a few days closed his bright career of honor at the age of thirty-five.

PIERCE, JOHN D.——He was born in New Hampshire, February 18, 1797; brought up in Massachusetts, were he remained until his twentieth year; and was educated at Brown University in Rhode Island, with money saved chiefly from presents and his own earnings. After graduating with honors in 1822, he became Principal of an Academy in New England, and at the end of a year entered the Seminary at Princeton, where he studied theology for one year. In 1824 he settled in Oneida County as Pastor of a Congregational Church, where he remained until 1830; spent another year in New England as Principal of Goshen Academy in Connecticut, and took up his residence in Michigan in 1831. In 1847 he was elected to the State Legislature; re-elected in 1848; and was a member of the State Constitutional Convention of 1850. While in the Legislature he secured the passage of bills for Homestead Exemptions, and for the Protection of Women in their Rights of Property, which were the first of that character passed in any of the States. Of Lectures and Addresses on Educational, Theological, and Historical subjects, he has published a goodly number; and during the two years that he was Superintendent of Public Instruction, he edited and published the *Journal of Education*. He also edited at one time the *Democratic Expounder*, at Marshall. By general consent the credit has been awarded to him of having been the author of the Michigan Free School System, and he will long be remembered by the children and youth of the State, as one who had wisely and earnestly labored to promote their welfare. As a preacher he has accomplished much good in various parts of the State; his last public position was that of Superintendent of Public Schools in Washtenaw County; and he is a resident of Ypsilanti.

PITCHER, ZINI.——He was born in Washington County, New York, April 12, 1797; received a common-school and academical education; at the age of twenty he began the study of medicine in Vermont, and in 1822 received the degree of M. D. from Middlebury College; and shortly afterwards he was appointed by President Monroe Assistant Surgeon in the United States Army, and promoted to full Surgeon by President Jackson, in which position he continued until 1836, when he became a permanent citizen of Michigan. While in the army he saw much service in the far Southwest, the South, and the Southeast, as well as in the country of the Great Lakes. In 1835 he became the President of the Army Medical Board; from 1837 to 1852 he was a Regent of the University of Michigan; took an active part in the organization of its Medical Department, and was made Professor of the Emeritus chair of that institution; in 1839 he was appointed a visitor to West Point; in 1840, '41, and '43, he was Mayor of the City of Detroit; and from 1848 to 1867 he was the physician and surgeon to St. Mary's Hospitol in Detroit, and also of the United States Marine Hospital. During all these years he did not neglect his engagements as a private practitioner, but found time to prepare various professional and literary papers for publication, and to attend the annual meetings, at least nine of them, of the American Medical Association, and was President of the meeting held in Detroit. He was also elected an honorary member of the New York and Rhode Island Medical Societies, corresponding member of the Philadelphia Academy of Natural Science, of the New York Lyceum of Natural History, also of the New York and Minnesota Historical Societies, and a Trustee of the Michigan State Asylum. He is still living in Detroit, with the growth and prosperity of which he has now been honorably identified foı more than a third of a century.

PHELPS, WILLIAM W.——He was born in Oakland County, Michigan, June 1, 1826; he graduated at the University of Michigan in 1846; studied law, and was admitted to the bar in 1848; and edited a Democratic newspaper in Oakland County, from 1851 to 1855. In 1852 and 1853 he held the office of Commissioner for his native County, performing the duties of Judge at Chambers; in 1854 was appointed, by President Pierce, Register of the United States Land Office at Red Wing, in Minnesota; and in 1857 he was elected a Representative to the Thirty-fifth Congress, from that State, and was a member of the Committee on Mileage. In 1860 he assumed the editorship of the "*Red Wing Sentinel.*"

PONTIAC.——He was born in the year 1720 on the Ottawa river, but early settled near Michilimackinac, and was an ally of the French in the Northwest. He made his appearance as an historical character by stopping Robert Rogers on his way to Detroit. He was the head chief of the Ottawa nation, but he held a kind of despotic sway over the Ojibway and Pottawattomie nations, the whole of whom had their camps on the soil of Michigan. As his principal deeds are chronicled in the first part of this work, and as Francis Parkman has made him the subject of an admirable volume, our allusions to him will be brief. His intellect was strong and capacious; he possessed a commanding energy, and was as crafty as any of his race; and though capable of acts of magnanimity, he was a thorough savage, treacherous and cruel. His faults, however, were those of his race; and they cannot eclipse his nobler qualities, the great powers and heroic virtues of his mind. He was the first Indian who ever issued such things as promissory notes, which were written upon birch bark, signed with the figure of an otter, which was his totum, and all of which notes he faithfully redeemed. From the year 1760, when he first met Robert Rogers on the shores of Lake Erie, until he left the Lake country in 1769, he exerted an influence and performed deeds of barbaric heroism which have seldom been equalled; and it was in the latter year, when he was on a visit to St. Louis, that he was murdered in cold blood near that town, by a savage enemy of the Illinois tribe, who had been bribed for that purpose by a not less savage English trader named Williamson. Over the grave of Pontiac, says Parkman, more blood was poured out in atonement, than flowed from the hecatombs of slaughtered heroes on the corpse of Patroclus; and the remnant of the Illinois who survived the carnage remained for ever after sunk in utter insignificance.

PORTER, AUGUSTUS S.——Born in Canandaigua, New York, January 18, 1798; graduated at Union College in 1818; studied law as a profession, and practiced for twenty years in Detroit, Michigan, of which city he was chosen Mayor in 1838. He was a Senator in Congress from Michigan from 1840 to 1845; and in 1848 he removed to Niagara Falls, the residence of his father, where he has since lived in retirement. He was also a Delegate to the Philadelphia "National Union Convention" of 1866.

PORTER, GEORGE B.——He was a native of Lancaster, Pennsylvania; received a liberal education, and adopted the profession of law; was an active and thorough business man; served as Governor of the Territory of Michigan from 1831 to 1834, and died in the latter year, leaving behind him troops of friends and a bright reputation.

PROCTOR, HENRY A.——He was born in Wales in 1787, and entered the British army when quite young. On the breaking out of the war of 1812, he was dispatched to Amherstburg by General Brock to prevent the landing of General Hull, whom he defeated at that place and at Brownstown. He was the man whom the Americans charged with sanctioning the massacre on the River Raisin in 1813, after the defeat of General Winchester, and for which conduct he was made a Brigadier-General by his Government. For his subsequent conduct at the battle of the Thames, he was court-martialed, and suspended from rank and pay for six months. He commanded again during the war; was promoted to the rank of Lieutenant-General; and died at his seat in Wales in 1859.

RANSOM, EPAPHRODITUS.——He was born in Massachusetts; received a collegiate education; and having studied law, was admitted to the bar in his native State. He removed to Michigan about the time that it became a State, and settled at Kalamazoo; he served a number of years in the Legislature; was Judge of the Supreme Court, where his field of labor was very extensive; and subsequently, taking a special interest in the building of plank roads in his section of country, he became involved, and in that manner lost the bulk of his property. He resigned his Judgeship in 1845; and his term of service as Governor of the State was from 1847 to 1849; and he afterwards made himself useful to the State by acting as President of the Michigan Agricultural Society. By President Buchanan he was appointed Receiver of the Land Office for one of the districts of Kansas, and died there before the expiration of his term. He was a man of sound sense, and left a worthy reputation in Michigan. He was on several occasions appointed a regent of the State University.

REYNOLDS, ROBERT.——He was born in Detroit about the year 1788; was Deputy Assistant Commissary General in the British army in the war of 1812, and was at the taking of Detroit. He also participated in the battle of the Thames; was subsequently stationed at Burlington Heights, on Lake Ontario; and then took up his residence near Amherstburg, on the Detroit River. He knew both Proctor and Tecumseh well, and never scrupled to denounce the conduct of the former while on the Michigan frontier, as shameful, and fully justifying the condemnation of the noted Indian warrior.

RICE, HENRY M.——He was born in Vermont November 29, 1816; and having emigrated to Michigan when it was a Territory, was a resident of Kalamazoo during the greater part of his early manhood. Much of his life was spent among the Indian tribes of the North-western States; in 1840 he was appointed a Sutler in the army; was employed as a commissioner in making many Indian treaties of great importance; in 1853 he was elected a Delegate to Congress from Minnesota; re-elected in 1855, and was active in securing the passage of the act authorizing the people of Minnesota to form a State constitution; and in 1857, he was elected a Senator in Congress for the term of six years, serving on the Committees on Indian Affairs and Post Offices and Post Roads. He was also a Delegate to the Philadelphia National Union Convention of 1866, since which time he has been devoted to his private affairs.

RICE, R. N.——He was born in Boston, Massachusetts, May 30, 1814; received a Public School education, and engaged in mercantile pursuits in Concord of that State, where he remained until 1844. In that year he engaged in the service of the Fitchburg Railroad Company, where he remained until 1846; when he removed to Michigan and became Disbursing Officer of the Michigan Central Railroad, and after occupying that position for two years, he became Master of Transportation, or what is now styled Assistant General Superintendent; and in 1855 he was appointed the General Superintendent, in which position he continued until 1867, when he resigned. It would thus appear that Mr. Rice was connected, in a prominent manner, with the vital business interests of Michigan for about twenty years. The gross receipts of the Michigan Central for one month in 1846, when he joined the company, amounted to $14,000 on 143 miles; while the receipts for the corresponding month in 1867, when he left the company, amounted to $300,000 on 269 miles, and the earnings of some of the fall months of the same year, amounted to nearly half a million of dollars. According to Henry M. Flint, in his *History of Railroads*, the admirable and successful management of the Michigan Central Railroad, is due, in a great measure, to the personal exertions and experience of its late General Superintendent.

RICHARD, GABRIEL.——He was born at Saintes, France, October 15, 1764; was educated at Angiers; received orders as a Priest at Paris in 1791; was made Vicar-General of the order of Sulpitians; came to America in 1792; was for a time Professor of Mathamatics in St. Mary's College, Maryland; subsequently labored as a Missionary in Illinois, and settled at Detroit in 1798. In 1809 he visited Boston, and took a printing press to Detroit, where he started a Journal called the *Michigan Essay*, which was not successful; he then published several Roman Catholic books and the Laws of the Territory, all in French; in 1812 he was taken prisoner by the British, and, after his release, finding his people destitute, purchased wheat at his own expense and distributed freely among them. During his ministry it became his duty, according to the rules of the Church, to excommunicate one of his parishioners who had been divorced from his wife. The unhappy husband prosecuted him for defamation of character, and obtained a verdict of one thousand dollars. This money the Priest could not pay, and he was consequently imprisoned in the common jail; but just before this event in 1823, he had been elected a delegate to Washington, and he went directly from his prison to the floor of Congress. He wrote several languages, and was a man of superior ability and rare benevolence; and died in Detroit, September 13, 1832, universally lamented.

RICHARDSON, ISRAEL B.——He was born in Fairfax, Vermont, in 1819; appointed from Michigan to the West Point Academy, where he graduated in 1841; as a Lieutenant was on duty in Florida, Missouri, and Louisiana; served in the war with Mexico, and was with General Taylor at the battles of Palo Alto and Resaca; with General Scott at Vera Cruz, Puebla, and Molino del Rey; in 1851 he was promoted to the rank of Captain, and assigned to duty in Mexico and Texas; and in 1855 he resigned his commission in the army, and settled as a farmer in Pontiac, Michigan. On the breaking out of the rebellion, he took an active interest in military affairs; organized, and took to the field as Commander the Second Infantry of Michigan; was soon transferred to the command of a Brigade; served with distinction in the Virginia-Peninsula Campaign, and was made a Brigadier, and soon afterwards a Major-General of Volunteers; and having been wounded at the battle of Antietam, Maryland, died from his wounds at Sharpsburg, November 3, 1862. He was a brave and able officer, and his loss was deeply lamented by the army.

ROBERTS, E. J.——He was born in New York and bred a printer; after publishing and conducting a paper at Rochester for some years, he removed to Michigan, and was long associated with the newspaper press of Detroit; he was a Delegate to the Constitutional Convention of 1850; subsequently settled in the Lake Superior Region, where he carried on an extensive business; served a number of years in the State Legislature; and after a long, useful, and honorable life, died many years ago.

ROBERTS, ROBERT E.——He settled in Detroit as early as 1827, and has been intimately identified with the progress of that city down to the present time. In 1855, for the gratification of his old friends, he published a small volume entitled "Sketches of the City of Detroit," which abounds in original information gathered from his long experience. Possessing a taste for letters and the arts, he has long been foremost among those who take pleasure in fostering the public taste. When the water-works of Detroit were projected, he took a special interest in the important enterprise, was made Secretary of the Board which had them in charge, and has ever since devoted himself to bringing them to their present perfection.

ROBERTSON, JOHN.——He was born in Banffshire, Scotland, January 2, 1814, and educated at one of the best schools in that section of country. He preferred a military profession, and desired to enter the British army, but was opposed in this by his uncle, the late Sir John Forbes, of London, through whose influence he expected to obtain a commission. In place of a position in the army, his uncle secured for him an appointment in the General Post Office in Edinburgh, and in 1829 he entered that Office. Disappointed at not getting into the army, and disliking the confinement of that office, he left it in 1833. Making up his mind fully for a military life, he concluded to immigrate to the United States and enter the army. Arriving at Montreal, he started on foot for the nearest American rendezvous, which he reached at Burlington, Vermont, where, on the 2d of July, 1833, he entered as a private in the United States Army. In the spring of 1834 he was sent to the 5th United States Infantry, stationed at Fort Howard, Green Bay, then in Wisconsin Territory. Soon after joining the regiment he was appointed a non-commissioned officer, and served the most part of six years as Quartermaster-Sergeant and Sergeant-Major of the regiment. After his term of service expired, he was engaged in the Quartermaster and Commissary Departments at Prairie du Chien, and went with the regiment from that post to Detroit in 1840. Soon after arriving at Detroit he was employed by Brady & Trowbridge, merchants of that city, and a few years afterwards went with one of the partners to Mexico, and engaged in mercantile business connected with the United States army, and remained there about eighteen months. Returning to Detroit, he rejoined Mr. Trowbridge, and a few years later became his partner, the two doing business as commission merchants, under the firm of C. A. Trowbridge & Co. In March, 1861, he was appointed by Governor Blair, Adjutant-General of the State, serving in that capacity throughout the war of the Rebellion, and has held the office until the present time. He has been identified with the militia and State troops of Michigan for about twenty years, and received his first commission as a Lieutenant of Independent State troops from Governor Bingham, in November, 1855.

ROGERS, RANDOLPH.——According to a statement already made in these pages, this eminent sculptor was born in Michigan, and in early life was a resident of the State; but Henry T. Tuckerman, in his book of American artists, gives Virginia as the native State of the sculptor. At any rate he is performing a great work, commemorative of the patriotism of Michigan, and for that reason he must be noticed here. He abandoned mercantile pursuits in early life, and turned his attention to sculpture. After a few years of study in Rome, he returned to this country and made his mark by the exhibition of "*Nydia, the Blind Girl of Pompeii,*" "*A Boy and Dog,*" and other similar productions. Returning to Rome, he made a statue of *John Adams,* designed bas-reliefs for the bronze doors of the new Capitol extension in Washington, also a monumental work entitled *The Angel of the Resurrection,* and occupied himself in furnishing the designs for the *Washington Monument in Richmond, Virginia,* which work had been commenced by the lamented Crawford. Among his more popular productions may be mentioned one entitled *Ruth* and another called *Isaac.* In 1867, and while engaged upon a monumental work for the State of Rhode Island, he received an order from the citizens of Michigan for the design and building of the elaborate and costly monument already described in this volume, to be erected in Detroit in memory of the heroes who lost their lives in defending their country from the assaults of the late Rebellion.

ROGERS, ROBERT.——He was a native of New Hampshire; a sturdy and adventurous soldier; commanded a body of provincial rangers, and stood in high repute as a partisan officer, whose chief theatre of action was in the region of Lake George; and for a time he was Governor of Michilimackinac. To him was entrusted the expedition which was sent out by General Amherst, after the surrender of Michigan by France to England in 1759, and his first meeting with Pontiac and subsequent services in the

Northwest will be found duly recorded in another part of this volume. He subsequently served in Algiers; at the opening of the war of Independence he returned to his country, espoused the British cause and received a Colonel's commission from the Crown; was proscribed by the act of New Hampshire in 1778, and died in obscurity. Besides a work entitled "A Concise Account of North America," he published a Journal of his Expedition to Detroit, when he took possession of the ports of Michigan; and also a drama entitled "Ponteach, or the Savages of America." The name of "Roger's Rangers" has passed into history, and a prominent mountain on Lake George bears his name to this day.

ROMEYN, THEODORE.——He was born in Hackinsack, New Jersey, in August, 1810, and is descended from the Knickerbocker stock of that region; educated at Rutger's College; and studied law with Peter D. Vroom and Samuel L. Southard in New Jersey, and with Benjamin F. Butler in Albany, coming to the bar in 1832. In the summer of 1835 he visited Michigan on a tour of pleasure, going in a Mackinaw boat as far as Lake Superior with a party of ladies, and in the spring of 1836 he returned and settled in Detroit. After remaining in that city for twelve years in the constant practice of his profession, and uniformly declining all proffers of office, he removed to New York city in 1848, and in 1858 he again became a resident of Detroit, to which he is bound by many endearing associations, and where he expects to spend the remainder of his days. Although brought up in the Democratic school of politics, he was an earnest supporter of President Lincoln, and of the war for the Union, and in consequence of his popularity as a speaker, was frequently called upon to deliver speeches of encouragement or welcome to the troops assembled in Detroit during the war. Among his more notable successes as a lawyer may be mentioned, first, his efforts, single-handed, to prove the unconstitutionality in both the State and Federal courts of the general banking laws of the State, which resulted in so much financial disaster many years ago; secondly, his efforts in bringing about a change in the policy of the General Government respecting the locating of public lands in the mineral region of Lake Superior, under what were called "*Mineral leases,*" which he maintained were invalid; and although his legal services in behalf of the State and country have been recognized as important, he has never asked or received a single dollar in the way of compensation for such services. His declared hostility to what was known as the "wild cat banks," naturally raised a great deal of opposition to him personally; and when he subsequently thought proper to accept a commission from the contracting parties in New York for negotiating an important loan in that city for the benefit of the State, he was subjected to much further animosity; but these unhappy and semi-political differences have been well nigh forgotten, and all men acquainted with the history of those times, acknowledge that his course in the whole transaction was only fair and honorable.

ROWLAND, THOMAS.——He was born in Ohio; served as a Major of Infantry under General Hull, in 1813 and '14; and retired from the army in 1815, locating in Detroit. He held the position of Secretary of the Territory of Michigan; was subsequently appointed United States Marshal for the Detroit district; was appointed Postmaster of that city by General Harrison; was also elected Secretary of State in 1840, and died in Detroit in August, 1848. He was a man of culture and highly esteemed, and in 1819 he read a paper before the Detroit Lyceum on Hull's Campaign, which has frequently been quoted with commendation.

RUCKER, DANIEL H.——He was born on Grosse Isle, Detroit River, and was a resident of Michigan, when appointed, in 1837, a Second Lieutenant in the Light Dragoons, and subsequently performed much official duty within the limits of the State. In 1838 he became an assistant in the Subsistence Department of the Army; in 1844 a First Lieutenant; and a Captain in 1847. He served in the Mexican war, and had command of a squadron at the battle of Buena Vista, and for his gallantry and meritorious conduct he was breveted a Major. In 1849 he was transferred to the Quartermaster's Department, with which he has ever since been connected, and in which, during the Rebellion, he performed at Washington an immense amount of the most arduous labor. Although holding the rank of Colonel in the army, he was made a Brigadier-General, and also a Major-General by brevet, for diligent and faithful services during the late Rebellion. After the war he was made Chief Quartermaster for the District of the East, with his headquarters at Philadelphia; but was subsequently assigned to similar duty in the North-west, with his headquarters at Chicago.

SCHOOLCRAFT, HENRY ROWE.——He was born in Albany, New York, March 28, 1793; educated at Middlebury College; in 1817 he visited the West, and published a work entitled "A View of the Lead Mines of Missouri;" in 1820 he was appointed geologist of the exploring expedition, under General Cass, to Lake Superior and the head of the Mississippi, and published an account of it in 1821; made a second tour to the West, and published "Travels in the Central Portions of the Mississippi Valley;" in 1822 he was appointed an Indian agent for the Northwest; from 1828 to 1832 he was a member of the Territorial Legislature of Michigan; in the former year founded the Michigan Historical Society at Detroit, and in 1831 the Algic Society; in 1832 he made another expedition to the West, and discovered the source of the Mississippi, of which he published an account in 1834; in 1836 he made an Indian treaty, which secured sixteen million acres of land to the United States; removed to New York City in 1841; visited Europe in 1842; published, by authority of the State of New York, in 1848, "*Notes on the Iroquois;*" about that time published a book of Indian legends, entitled "*Algic Researches;*" commenced the publication in 1850 for the Government, of "*Historical Information Respecting the History, Condition, and Prospects of the Indian Tribes of the United States,*" which resulted in six quarto volumes, illustrated by Captain Seth Eastman; and after many years of suffering from rheumatic affections, which he bore with rare Christian fortitude, he died at his residence in Washington City December 10, 1864. The total number of his publications, as his widow informed the writer, was thirty-one; and as the historian of the American Indians, he will always be considered the leading authority. While he did not aspire to the title of poet, he nevertheless wrote verses occasionally; and one of his poems, because of its association with Michigan and the fate of its aborigines, may with propriety be appended to this notice. It is entitled *Geehale, an Indian Lament:*

The black-bird is singing on Michigan's shore,
As sweetly and gaily as ever before;
For he knows to his mate he at pleasure can hie,
And the dear little brood she is teaching to fly.
The sun looks as ruddy and rises as bright,
And reflects o'er the mountains as beamy a light
As it ever reflected, or ever expressed,
When my skies were the bluest, my dreams were the best.
The fox and the panther, both beasts of the night,
Retire to their dens on the gleaming of light;
And they spring with a free and sorrowless track,
For they know that their mates are expecting them back.
Each bird and each beast it is bless'd in degree;
All nature is cheerful, all happy but me.

I will go to my tent and lie down in despair;
I will paint me with black, and will sever my hair;
I will sit on the shore, where the hurricane blows,
And reveal to the God of the tempest my woes.
I will weep for a season on bitterness fed,
For my kindred are gone to the hills of the dead;
But they died not by hunger, or lingering decay,
The steel of the white man hath swept them away.

This snake-skin, that once I so sacredly wore,
I will toss with disdain on the storm-beaten shore;
Its charms I no longer obey or invoke,
Its spirit has left me, its spell is now broke.
I will raise up my voice to the source of the light,
I will dream on the wings of the blue-bird at night;
I will speak to the spirits that whisper in leaves,
And that minister balm to the spirit that grieves;
And will take a new Manitou—such as shall seem
To be kind and propitious in every dream.

O, then I shall banish these cankering sighs,
And tears shall no longer gush salt from my eyes.
I shall wash from my face every cloud-colored stain;
Red, red shall alone on my visage remain!
I will dig up my hatchet and bend my ash bow,
By night and by day I will follow the foe;
Nor lakes shall impede me, nor mountains, nor snows,
His blood can alone give my spirit repose.

They came to my cabin when heaven was black,
I heard not their coming, I knew not their track;
But I saw by the light of their blazing fusees
They were people engendered beyond the big seas.
My wife and my children—O spare me the tale!
For who is there left that is kin to Geehale?

SIBLEY, EBENEZER S.——He was the son of Solomon Sibley, and born in Ohio; entered the West Point Academy from Michigan and was graduated in 1827; as Second Lieutenant in the Artillery he served at Fort Monroe in Virginia, Fort Independence in Massachusetts, Fort Moultrie in South Carolina, and then on Engineer duty until 1834, when he was made First Lieutenant. In 1836 he was in the Florida war; in 1837 and 1838, on Indian duty, and as aid to General Brady; from 1838 to 1840 he was on duty at Savannah, Georgia; was again in the Florida war from 1840 to 1842; also as Captain on duty in Maine, Massachusetts, and Texas; served in the Mexican war, and was present at the battle of Buena Vista, and for gallant conduct was appointed a Major by brevet in 1848; from 1848 to 1851 he was on duty in Detroit; and after service in New Mexico and Kansas, he became an Assistant in the Quartermaster's Department at Washington in 1856, with the title of Staff Major; and from 1861 to 1864 he was Principal Assistant and Deputy Quartermaster General, with the rank of Lieutenant-Colonel of Staff. He resigned his Commission in the army in 1864, since which time he has been the Vice President of two important mining companies of Lake Superior.

SIBLEY, HENRY H.——He was the son of Solomon Sibley, and born in Detroit in 1811; spent much of his early life on the Northwestern frontier; and was for many years an Indian trader in the employ of the American Fur Company at Mackinaw and at Fort Snelling. From 1849 to 1853 he was a Delegate to Congress from the Territory of Minnesota; and having witnessed its progress from a wilderness to an organized State, he was elected in 1857 its first Governor, serving until 1858. He was a Brigadier-General of volunteers during the great Rebellion; commanded an expedition against the Indians in 1863, and was subsequently breveted a Major-General of volunteers. He was also a Delegate to the Cleveland "Soldiers' Convention" of 1866; and in 1867 was appointed a visitor to the West Point Academy.

SIBLEY, SOLOMON.——He was born in Sutton, Massachusetts, October 7, 1769. He studied law, and removed to Ohio in 1795, establishing himself first at Marietta, and then at Cincinnati, in the practice of his profession. He removed to Detroit in 1797, and in 1799 was elected to the first Territorial Legislature of the Northwestern Territory. In 1819 he took part in what was called the "Pontiac Mill Company," which erected the first flouring and saw mills in that town. He was a Delegate to Congress from the Territory of Michigan, from 1820 to 1823; in 1824 he was appointed Judge of the Supreme Court, and held the office until 1836, when he resigned in consequence of increasing deafness. He died at Detroit, April 4, 1846. He was universally respected for his talents and manifold virtues. He left three sons, two born in Detroit, Michigan, and all of whom have conferred honor upon the family name as public men.

SHEARMAN, FRANCIS W.——He was born in Vernon, Oneida County, New York; graduated at Hamilton College in that State, in his nineteenth year; soon afterwards removed to Michigan and settled at Detroit; and was for a time an assistant of Henry R. Schoolcraft when engaged in making treaties with the Indians. He subsequently studied law, and after his admission to the bar, became a resident of Marshall, about the year 1840. Besides a variety of local positions of honor and trust, he was elected to the Legislature, and was for some years Superintendent of Public Instruction; and although always devoted to his profession, he officiated for several years as Editor of the "*Democratic Expounder*" in Marshall. In 1852 he published a very useful work on the System of Public Instruction, and the Primary School Laws of Michigan. He is still a citizen of Marshall.

SHELDON, ELECTRA M.——With the personal history of this lady, the writer is unacquainted, but he does know that she has reflected honor upon herself and the State of Michigan with her pen. While editing a literary periodical in Detroit, in 1853, she commenced the publication of such facts as she could obtain concerning the early history of Michigan. General Cass took an interest in her enterprise, and presented her with a mass of interesting documents bearing upon her studies, which he had obtained in Paris. These, with her own materials, she worked up into a valuable work, which she published in 1856, entitled "The Early History of Michigan, from the first settlement to 1815." In 1860 Mrs. Sheldon published another work entitled "The Clevelands; showing the influence of a Christian Family in the New Settlements."

SHELDON, JOHN P.——He was the founder, in 1817, of the *Detroit Gazette*, which continued to flourish until 1830, when the office was burned and the paper suspended. During the term of William Woodbridge upon the bench, a man named John Reed was tried in the court before a jury and found guilty, and in noticing the case, Mr. Sheldon was very severe upon the court, declared that he had a perfect right to print his own opinion, and uttered the curious boast that he had "scourged one set of Judges off the Bench, and most of them out of the Territory." For this assault he was himself tried and fined five hundred dollars, which sum, although abundantly able, he refused to pay, and consequently suffered a short imprisonment.

SMITH, HENRY.——He was born in New York; graduated at the United States Military Academy in 1815, and at once appointed a Third Lieutenant of Artillery; in 1816 he was made a Second Lieutenant of Infantry, serving in the Garrison at Greenbush from 1816 to 1819. During the four following years he was on Quartermaster's duty at Sackett's Harbor and Plattsburgh, New York; Green Bay, in Wisconsin; Fort Brady, in Michigan; and Fort Smith, in Arkansas; from 1823 to 1826, as a First Lieutenant, he served on the Staff of General Scott; and during the following ten years he was stationed at Jefferson Barrack, in Missouri; served as a Captain in the Black Hawk war, and was present at the battle of Bad Axe, and also served as an Engineer, resigning his commission in 1836. From 1836 to 1840 he was a Civil Engineer in the service of the United States, superintending harbor improvements on Lake Erie; was a member of the Michigan Legislature in 1837 and 1840; Disbursing Agent for the Indian Department in 1838; Major-General of the Michigan Militia from 1841 to 1846; and Mayor of Monroe in the latter year. In 1847 he was reappointed in the Army with the rank of Major, performing quartermaster's duty at Detroit and in the war with Mexico, and died at Vera Cruz, July 24, 1847. He always took a special interest in the public affairs of Michigan, and left a large circle of friends.

SMITH, JOSEPH R.——He was born in New York, and graduated at the West Point Military Academy in 1823. As a Lieutenant he served at Saute de Ste. Marie from 1823 to 1825; in 1826 was assigned to Topographical duty in New York and on the frontiers; was stationed at Fort Mackinaw from 1832 to 1833; at Fort Brady from 1833 to 1835; after which he was sent to Florida, and for his services there and elsewhere, he was promoted to the rank of Captain. He took an active part in the war with Mexico; was present at the siege of Vera Cruz, the battles of Cerro Gordo, Oka Laka, Contreras, and Churubusco, in which he was twice wounded, and for his gallant and meritorious services was appointed Brevet Major in 1847. In 1851 he was promoted to the rank of Major of the Seventh United States Infantry, and was absent from duty on sick leave from 1851 to 1862. In 1861 he was retired for disability from wounds received in battle; but as the Rebellion progressed he was again called upon and performed much important duty as Mustering and Disbursing officer in Michigan, as Military Commander of the District of Michigan, as Commissary of Musters in the Northern Department, and the Department of Ohio and of the Great Lakes. In 1865 he was made a Brevet-Colonel for meritorious services during the Rebellion; and shortly afterwards was breveted Brigadier-General for "long and faithful services" in behalf of his country.

SPRAGUE, WILLIAM.——He was born in Rhode Island, and, removing to Michigan, was a Representative in Congress from that State, from 1849 to 1851; and died soon afterwards.

STANLEY, J. M.——He was born in Canandaigua, New York, in 1814; spent his boyhood chiefly in Buffalo; removed to Michigan in 1834, and in the following year commenced his profession of Portrait Painting in Detroit; between the years 1837 and 1839 he resided in Chicago and Galena, painting much among the Indians at Fort Snelling; subsequently practiced his art in New York, Philadelphia, Baltimore and Troy; in 1842 travelled extensively over the western prairies, painting the portraits, in full costume, of leading chiefs around Fort Gibson, in Texas and New Mexico; crossed the Rocky Mountains with the Kearney and Emory Expeditions, and after performing much important labor for the Government in California, he visited Oregon, travelled extensively along the Columbia River, taking sketches and painting pictures of many varieties, in great numbers; after which he spent more than a year in the Sandwich Islands, and in 1851 settled in Washington City, where he resided until 1863, when he returned to Detroit, where it is likely he will spend the remainder of his days. For several years, a chief attraction of the Smithsonian Institution in Washington, was a very extensive collection of Indian Portraits and miscellaneous pictures, painted by Mr. Stanley, but they were unfortunately destroyed by fire. As a delineator of Indian character he has never had a superior in this country, and among his historical paintings are several of great interest depicting events in the history of Michigan, which have been reproduced in chromo-lithograph. Admirable portraits from his pencil, of distinguished men, are to be fond in all parts of the country.

STEVENS, HESTOR L.——He was born in Lima, Livingston County, New York, in October, 1803; received a good English and classical education;

adopted the profession of law; was for several years connected with the press in Rochester; and having taken up his residence in Michigan, was elected a Representative in Congress from that State from 1853 to 1855. Died in Georgetown, D. C., May 7, 1864.

St. Clair, Arthur.——He was born in Edinburgh; was a Lieutenant under General Wolfe, and subsequently settled in Pennsylvania, where he became a naturalized citizen. At the commencement of the Revolution he joined the American Army; and in 1777 was appointed a Major General, and served with distinction. In 1783 he was elected President of the Cincinnati Society of his adopted State; was a delegate to the Continental Congress from 1785 to 1787, and in the latter year was chosen President of that body. He was afterwards appointed Governor of the Northwest Territory, which then included Michigan, and in 1790 he commanded an army against the Miami Indians. He resigned his commission as Major General in 1792, and the closing years of his life were passed in obscurity and poverty. He died in 1818; and although some of his military acts caused much discussion, he was honored by having his name affixed to one of the counties of the State; but the beautiful lake which borders the Detroit region of Michigan was so named by the early missionaries on account of the purity of its waters, and not, as many suppose, after the General.

Stoughton, William L.——He was born in New York March 20, 1827; studied law, and, on coming to the bar, settled in Sturges, Michigan, in 1851; from 1856 to 1860 he was a Prosecuting Attorney; in 1861 he was appointed by President Lincoln United States District Attorney for Michigan, which he soon resigned; he then entered the volunteer army as Lieutenant-Colonel, was promoted a Colonel, and commanded in all the operations of his regiment until wounded at Atlanta. During the war he was breveted a Brigadier-General for "gallantry in the field," and after the war he was breveted a Major-General. He had the credit of firing the first gun at Chickamauga; commanded a brigade at Mission Ridge, and in the Atlanta campaign; and lost a leg by a cannon-ball at Rupp's Station, in front of Atlanta. In 1866 he was elected Attorney-General of Michigan, and in 1868 a Representative from that State to the Forty-first Congress, serving on the Committees on Military Affairs and Revolutionary Pensions. He resides in Sturgis, and was re-elected to the Forty-second Congress.

Strickland, Randolph.——He was born in Danville, Steuben County, New York, February 4, 1823; received a common school education and engaged in teaching; removed to Michigan in 1844, and studied law; came to the bar in 1849; was Prosecuting Attorney for Clinton County in 1852, 1854, 1856, 1858, and 1862; was elected to the State Senate in 1861 and 1862; was a Provost Marshal from 1863 to 1865; member of the State Republican Committee; a Delegate to the National Conventions of 1856 and 1868; and was elected a Representative from Michigan to the Forty-First Congress, serving on the Committees on Invalid Pensions, and Mines and Mining. He resides in St. John.

STRICKLAND, WILLIAM P.——He was born in Pittsburg, Pennsylvania, in 1809; was educated at the Athens University of Ohio; entered the Methodist ministry in 1832; was for four years agent of the American Bible Society; and was subsequently associate editor of the *Christian Advocate and Journal* in New York city. He is also a Doctor of Divinity; and is the author of an interesting and useful work entitled *Old Mackinaw; or the Fortress of the Lakes and its Surroundings*, published in 1860; and also of *A History of the American Bible Society*, published in 1849; *A History of the Missions of the Methodist Episcopal Church*, 1850; *Manual of Biblical Literature*, 1853; and *Light of the Temple*, 1854. He has been an extensive contributor to the leading periodicals of the country, and is recognized as a man of ability.

STUART, CHARLES E.——He was born in Columbia County, New York, November 25, 1810, and adopted the profession of law. He was a member of the Michigan Legislature in 1842; a Representative in the Thirtieth and Thirty-Second Congresses; and was elected in 1853, for six years, a Senator in Congress, serving as Chairman of the Committee on Public Lands. He was also a Delegate to the Philadelphia National Union Convention of 1866.

STUART, DAVID.——He was born in New York, and was a Representative in Congress from Michigan, from 1853 to 1855.

SUTHERLAND, JABEZ G.——He was born in Onondaga County, New York, October 6, 1825; removed with his Father to Michigan in 1836, and has ever since resided in the Counties of Genesee and Saginaw. He studied law, and came to the bar in 1848; in 1849 he settled in Saginaw City, and was made Prosecuting Attorney for that County; he was a Delegate to the Constitutional Convention of 1850, and it was through his efforts that the Counties of Tuscola, Saginaw, Midland, Montcalm, and Newaygo, were named as entitled to one Representative each in the Legislature, without regard to the number of their inhabitants. In 1853 he was elected to the State Legislature; during the next ten years, was wholly devoted to the practice of his profession, with unusual success; in 1858 he was the unsuccessful Democratic candidate for the office of Attorney-General; in 1863 he was elected Circuit Judge of the Tenth Circuit, and re-elected to the same position in 1869 without opposition. His Circuit was for a time the largest in the State, and the character of the business important, and his written decisions would fill many volumes. He was also a Delegate to the Constitutional Convention of 1867. In August, 1870, he was nominated for Congress by the Democrats,. with the help of the Republicans, and contrary to his will, and at the election in November, was elected to the Forty-Second Congress.

SWAYNE, NOAH H.——As the successor of John McLean, and because of his judicial connection with the State of Michigan, we submit the following particulars respecting Mr. Justice Swayne. He was born in Culpepper

County, Virginia, December 27, 1804. While performing the duties of a clerk in an Apothecary store in Alexandria, he acquired the rudiments of an English and classical education, and prepared himself for the Medical profession. He soon began the study of law, however, at Warrenton, and immediately after his admission to the bar in 1824, he removed to Ohio and settled at Coshocton. In 1829 he was elected to the Legislature of that State; in 1830 he was appointed by President Jackson, United States District Attorney for Ohio, holding the position nine years, and residing in Columbus. In 1834 he was chosen Judge of the Court of Common Pleas, but declined the office. In 1836 he was again elected to the State Legislature, and took a leading part in organizing Institutions or Asylums for the benefit of the Blind, the Lunatic, and the Deaf and Dumb of the State; and in 1861 he was appointed by President Lincoln a Justice of the Supreme Court of the United States, his District comprehending the States of Ohio, Michigan, Kentucky, and Tennessee.

SWEET, WILBER.——He was born in Vermont in 1760; served as a boy in the Army of the Revolution, and as a soldier throughout the entire war of 1812; settled in Michigan in 1818; became an active member of the Church when in the eighty-third year of his age; and died at Kalamazoo, August 19, 1857.

TAPPAN, HENRY PHILIP.——He was born in Rhinebeck, early in the present century; graduated at Union College in 1825; was for two years pastor of the Dutch Reformed Church in Schenectady; in 1828 became Pastor of the Congregational Church at Pittsfield, Massachusetts, which position he resigned in 1831, and visited the West Indies; was a Professor in the University of New York from 1832 to 1838; subsequently devoted himself to literary pursuits; in 1851 and again in 1853, he visited Europe; in 1852 he was again invited to the New York University, (which Institution he left by resignation,) but declining that offer, became Chancellor of the University of Michigan, in which position he remained for many years, when his connection with it was broken off, and he again visited Europe. His publications are as follows: *Freedom of the Will, Doctrine of the Will, Elements of Logic, University Education,* and *A Step from the New World to the Old World.* It was through his personal efforts that a first class Astronomical Observatory was established in connection with the University, the necessary funds having been obtained from liberal citizens of Detroit.

TECUMSEH.——He was born in Ohio on the Sciota River, about the year 1770; was for many years engaged in predatory incursions against the white inhabitants of the Northwest, and to a considerable extent in the Territory of Michigan; and in 1806, as elsewhere mentioned in this volume, he matured the project of a Confederacy of all the Indian tribes in the Lake country, for the extermination of the white race in that region. The battle of Tippecanoe, fought November 7, 1811, in which General Harrison defeated the brother of Tecumseh, more generally known as the Prophet, completely annihilated the hopes of the barbarian brothers. Tecumseh was not present at this battle. During the war with Great Britain, he was an ally of King George; had under his command about two thousand fellow Indians, and held the rank of Brigadier-General. He was present with his forces in several engagements, and was killed by Colonel Richard M. Johnson in the battle of Moravian Towns, October 5, 1813. He has been made the hero of many poems and tales, and was a warrior of much renown; and his life was written by Benjamin Drake. Henry J. Morgan, in his work on *Celebrated Canadians*, makes the remark that the Provinces of Canada might have been lost to the British Crown, had it not been for such "brave and devoted men" as Tecumseh and his brother, the Prophet.

THURBER, JEFFERSON G.——He was born in 1807, and become a resident of Monroe, Michigan, in 1833. He was a lawyer by profession, and earnestly devoted to its practice; was a Prosecuting Attorney for the State; Judge of Probate for Monroe County; a Presidential Elector in 1849; also served as a Representative and a Senator in the State Legislature; was Speaker of the House in 1852; and filled all those positions with honor to himself and the State. He died in Monroe, May 6, 1857, leaving a bright reputation.

TONTI, HENRI DE.——He came to Canada from Italy, where he had been an officer in the military service, as an assistant to La Salle, but spent more time in the Michigan country than did his chief. He was on duty at Detroit, Mackinaw, and the Saute de Ste. Marie; explored Lakes Huron and Michigan, as well as the rivers Illinois and Mississippi; and he was so deeply attached to La Salle that he served him as Captain from 1678 for a long time without pay. By all those with whom he was associated his services were highly appreciated. When La Salle died he happened to be in the North, and seized with a desire to rescue his remains, he attempted a journey to the Southwest, which only terminated in disaster. Having in early life lost one of his hands in a military exploit in Italy, he subsequently used an iron hand, which he kept gloved, and all his exploits in America as an explorer and fur-trader were performed under that disadvantage. It is said, however, that he would occasionally knock an Indian's tooth out of his head with great ease, which gave him the reputation of being a "medicine man." For some years there was a blight resting upon his reputation because of the rascalities of his brother, Alphonse de Tonti, who long commanded at Detroit. He wrote an account of his adventures in America, which was published after his death, but when and where he died is unknown. During a portion of his career in America he served as a Captain, under Cadillac, the founder of Detroit. His name is printed Tonty as well as Tonti, but the latter style would seem to be more in keeping with the Italian language.

TROWBRIDGE, CHARLES C.——He was born in Albany, New York, December 29, 1800, and was the son of Luther Trowbridge, who served with credit as an officer in the Revolutionary War from Massachusetts, but subsequently settled in New York. When twelve years of age he became a clerk with Horatio Ross, of Oswego, New York, where he remained until 1819, when he removed to the Territory of Michigan, and settled in Detroit, with which he has ever since been intimately identified. From 1819 to 1825 he held various positions of trust under Thomas Rowland and Lewis Cass. With the latter he was on the most intimate terms of friendship, and in many negotiations with the Indians he was vested by the Governor with large discretion; and because of his acquaintance with various Indian dialects, he was enabled to render important assistance to the Government in negotiating treaties. When General Cass became Secretary of War he invited Mr. Trowbridge to take a leading position in that Department; but his disinclination for office compelled him to decline the offer. In 1825 he was appointed Cashier of the Bank of Michigan, at that time the only bank north of Cincinnati and west of Rochester, and held the position for ten years; he was Mayor of Detroit in 1834, when the city suffered from cholera, and the duties of the office were performed with great danger and discomfort; in 1837 he was the Whig candidate for Governor of Michigan, and was defeated by a small majority; in 1839 he became President of the Bank of Michigan, and so continued during its existence; from 1844 to 1854 he was President of the Michigan State Bank; in 1853 he became the Secretary, Treasurer, and Resident Director of the Detroit and Milwaukee Railroad Company; and in 1863 he was elected President of the Company, which position he still holds. During the summer of 1870 he visted Europe. With regard to the part he has taken in projecting and promoting works of public interest, of charity and benevolence, and of religious importance connected with the State of Michigan, there is but one opinion among the people, and that is altogether honorable to his mind and heart.

TROWBRIDGE, ROWLAND E.——Was born in Elmira, New York, June 18, 1821; removed with his parents to Michigan when a mere child; graduated at Kenyon College, Ohio, in 1841; has been devoted all his life to the business of farming; was elected to the Senate of Michigan in 1856 and 1858; and in 1860 was elected a Representative from Michigan to the Thirty-seventh Congress, serving on the Committee on the Post Office and Post Roads. He was also re-elected to the Thirty-ninth Congress, serving on the Committees on Revolutionary Claims and Agriculture. He was also a Delegate to the Philadelphia "Loyalists' Convention" of 1866, and was re-elected to the Fortieth Congress, serving as Chairman of the Committee on Agriculture. He is a nephew of C. C. Trowbridge, one of the most prominent citizens of Detroit.

TROWBRIDGE, WILLIAM P.——He was born in Michigan, and appointed from that State to the West Point Academy, where he graduated in 1848. He was assigned to the Corps of Engineers, and had charge of the Observatory at West Point. In 1849, as Lieutenant, he was assigned to duty in the Coast Survey; engaged in making Primary Triangulations on the coasts of Maine and Virginia; in 1854 was promoted to First Lieutenant, and assigned to surveying duties on the Pacific coast. In 1856 he resigned his commission in the Army; was Professor of Mathematics in the University of Michigan in 1856 and 1857; was made an A. M. by the Rochester (New York) University; and from 1857 until 1861 was a scientific assistant to Professor Bache on the coast survey. From 1861 until 1865 he was engaged in superintending, as Engineer, the public works in the harbor of New York, viz: at Willett's Point, Fort Schuyler, and Governor's Island. Since 1865 he has held the position of Vice President of the extensive Novelty Works in New York.

TRUMBULL, JOHN.——As this eminent author and jurist was the father-in-law of William Woodbridge, and spent the last six years of his life as a citizen of Michigan, he comes into our present record with strict propriety. He was born in Connecticut in 1750, and graduated at Yale College at a very early age. In 1772 he published the first part of his poem, entitled *The Progress of Idleness*. In the following year he was admitted to the bar in Connecticut, and removing to Boston, continued his legal studies in the office of John Adams. He returned to Connecticut in 1774, and commenced the practice of his profession in New Haven. The first part of *McTingal* was published in Philadelphia in 1775; but in 1782 the poem was completed and published in Hartford, where the author at that time resided. More than thirty editions of this work were published in his life time. In 1789 he was appointed State Attorney for the County of Hartford, and in 1801 a Judge of the Superior Court of Errors, which position he held until 1819. In 1825 he removed to Detroit and resided with his daughter, Mrs. Woodbridge, and he died at Spring Wells in May, 1831.

TURNER, JOSIAH.——He was born in New Haven, Addison County, Vermont, September 1, 1811; received an academical education at Middlebury and St. Albans in that State; studied law with his uncle, Hon. Bates Turner, and was admitted to the bar in 1833, in St. Alban's County, where he commenced the practice of his profession. In 1840 he emigrated to Michigan and settled in Howell, Livingston County, where he resumed his profession; in 1857 he was appointed a Justice of the Supreme Court of the State by the Governor, and shortly afterwards was elected by the people Circuit Judge of the Seventh Judicial Circuit for six years, and in 1863 re-elected for the same time. In 1869 he was again re-elected, by both political parties, for a third term of six years, and without any opposition. He removed from Howell to Owasso in 1860; was chosen Mayor of that city in 1864 for two years; and he was a member of the State Contitutional Convention of 1867. With such a record to stand upon, it were superfluous to add that Judge Turner has been a popular and highly influential citizen of the State.

TYLER, MOSES COIT.——He was born in Griswold, New London county, Connecticut, in 1835; was taken to Michigan by his parents while yet an infant, and they settled first in Calhoun county, and afterwards in Detroit; he graduated at Yale College in 1857; studied theology at Andover, and in 1860 was engaged in the ministry at Poughkeepsie, New York; left the ministry in 1862 on account of his health, and visited Europe. During his stay abroad he lectured on topics connected with the civil war; wrote occasionally for English and American periodicals; returned to this country in 1867, and lectured throughout the Northern States; and during that year he was appointed Professor of the English Language and Literature in the University of Michigan, which position he continues to hold. In 1869 he published a volume of Essays on physical culture, entitled "The Brownville Papers," and has been connected editorially with the New York *Independent*, and a writer for various periodicals. He has frequently been invited to accept of honorable positions outside of Michigan, but has preferred to cast in his lot with the State to which he is bound by many old associations.

UPSON, CHARLES.——Born in Southington, Hartford county, Connecticut, March 19, 1821; received a good English education; removed to Michigan in 1845; studied law, and came to the bar in 1847; in 1849 and 1850 was County Clerk for St. Joseph county; in 1853 and 1854 was Prosecuting Attorney for the same; in 1855 and 1856 held the office of State Senator; in 1861 and 1862 he was Attorney-General for Michigan, and was elected a Representative from Michigan to the Thirty-eighth Congress, serving on the Committee on Elections and Unfinished Business. Re-elected to the Thirty-ninth Congress, serving on the Committees on Elections, and Revolutionary Pensions. He was also a Delegate to the Philadelphia "Loyalists' Convention" of 1866; and was re-elected to the Fortieth Congress, and made Chairman of the Committee on Expenditures in the Navy Department. In 1870 he was elected Judge of the Circuit Court for the Fifteenth District of Michigan.

VAN DYKE, JAMES A.——He was born in Mercersburg, Franklin County, Pennsylvania, in December, 1813; received his education at Madison College, which he entered in 1828; studied law at Chambersburg, and also at Hagerstown, in Maryland; and after spending one year in Baltimore, removed to Detroit. In that city he was associated with A. D. Frazer, C. W. Whipple, E. B. Harrington, and H. H. Emmons in the practice of his profession. In 1840 he was appointed Prosecuting Attorney for the County of Wayne; in 1843 and 1844 he was chosen an Alderman in the Councils of Detroit; in 1847 he was elected Mayor of the City; was a member of the Board of Commissioners of the Detroit Water Works; also an active fireman, and President of the Fire Department of the city for five years; he also held a number of other local positions of honor and trust, and died May 7, 1855; and having for many years been a prominent member of the Bar at Detroit, the honors which were paid to his memory by that body were in keeping with his many virtues as a man of high character and ability. An interesting tribute to his memory was published in Detroit in 1856. He acquired special distinction in what was known as the railroad conspiracy case of 1851.

WALBRIDGE, DAVID S.——Born in Bennington, Vermont, July 30, 1802; received his education from the common schools of that vicinity; devoted himself to the various employments of the farmer, the merchant, and the miller; removed to Michigan in 1842, and was elected a Representative in Congress from that State in 1854, and served as such until 1857. He lived at Kalamazoo, and died in that place June 15, 1868.

WALDRON, HENRY.——He was born in Albany, New York, October 11, 1819; graduated at Rutger's College, New Brunswick, New Jersey, in July, 1836; became a civil engineer by profession, and settled in Michigan; was elected to the Legislature of Michigan in 1843; and served as a Representative in Congress during the years 1855, '56, '57, and '58, and was a member of the Committee on Mileage. He was re-elected to the Thirty-sixth Congress, serving on the Committee on Territories. He subsequently held a number of local positions of honor and trust in the First Congressional district; took a prominent part in organizing troops during the Rebellion; and in 1870 was re-elected to the Forty-second Congress.

WALKER, CHARLES IRISH.——He was born in Otsego county, New York, April 25, 1814; received a common school education, and was afterwards a merchant's clerk; and in 1836 removed to Michigan, and settled at Grand Rapids, where he was engaged in the purchase, for others, of real estate. In 1839 he began the study of law; in 1840 he was elected to the State Legislature; in 1841 went to New England to complete his legal studies; and having come to the bar in Vermont, spent about ten years in that State practicing his profession. In 1851 he returned to Michigan, and settled in Detroit; and in 1857 he aided in reviving the Historical Society of Michigan, and became its Corresponding Secretary, delivering occasional addresses on the early history of the State. On the organization of the Law Department in the University of Michigan in 1859, he was appointed Professor of Law, which honorable position he still holds, the school over which he presides being considered one of the most successful and largest in the Union. In 1867 he was appointed by the Governor to fill a vacancy in the Judgeship of the third judicial circuit, which office, after serving one term, he resigned, and returned to the more lucrative employment of practicing his profession.

WALK-IN-THE-WATER.——He was a Huron of the Wyandot tribe. His Indian name was My-ee-rah, and he was one of the most active Chiefs with Tecumseh in the beginning of the war of 1812. He was friendly to the United States, and offered his services to Hull, but, the humane impulses of that General, together with his instructions from the Government, would not allow him to employ savages. He was leader and orator of the Wyandots on the American side of the Detroit river, but was forced by circumstances to join the British at Malden. His heart, however, was not with them, and he was active in persuading various tribes to remain neutral. The British took measures to counteract this influence, and a council was convened at Malden, wherein he vindicated his conduct in a speech, which, was called by his enemies "American talk," but it resulted in the separation of Tecumseh and the Prophet, with two Wyandot Chiefs, who openly joined the British; while Walk-in-the-Water and his associates declined to remain with them. He with many of his followers deserted from Proctor at Chatham, Canada West. He was at the battles of the River Raisin and Thames, and, at the latter, he with his sixty warriors offered their services to Harrison conditionally; which he declined, and they returned to the Detroit river. His residence at Maguaga was on the land afterwards owned by John Biddle, and on which he built his farm houses. His *totem* or arms, was a turtle. He died about the year 1817.

WATSON, JAMES C.——While living upon a farm in Michigan, with his mother, he conceived the idea of obtaining an education at the University of the State, and after many difficulties, went through a course of studies and was duly graduated. He was subsequently made Professor of Astronomy in that Institution, which position he still holds. He is the author of a work on Comets, and another on Theoretical Astronomy; and has acquired distinction in the scientific world as the discoverer of several new planets; and in 1870, the French Academy of Sciences awarded to him the Astronomical prize for his important discoveries.

WAYNE, ANTHONY.——He was born in Easttown, Chester County, Pennsylvania, in 1746. In 1773 he was elected a Representative in the General Assembly, where he took an active part against the claims of Great Britain. In 1775 he entered the army as a Colonel, and in the battle at Three Rivers in 1776, received a wound in the leg, and at the close of the campaign was made a Brigadier-General. In the battles of Brandywine, Germantown, and Monmouth, and especially at Stony Point, he greatly distinguished himself, receiving a wound in his head. In 1781 he led the Pennsylvania line to form a junction with Lafayette in Virginia, and participated in the capture of Cornwallis. After that he conducted the war in Georgia, with equal success, receiving from that State, through its Legislature, a valuable farm as a reward for his services, upon which he retired after the war. In 1787 he was a member of the Convention for framing the Federal Constitution; and he served as a Representative in Congress from Georgia, in 1791, but his seat was successfully contested by James Jackson, and vacated by a resolution of the House. In 1792, he was again called into military service, and succeeded St. Clair, in the command of the Northwest Territory, and so became identified with the Territory of Michigan. In 1794, at the battle of the Miami, he gained a complete victory over the Indians, won the name of "Mad Anthony," and in 1795 he concluded a lasting treaty with the hostile tribes of the Northwest, and subsequently attained the rank of Major-General. It was whilst returning from the Upper Lake country, that he had an attack of gout, of which he died in a hut at Presque Isle, Harbor of Erie, in 1796, and was temporaily buried there; but in 1809 his remains were removed to St. David's Church, in Chester County, Pennsylvania, where a monument recalling the patriotic achievements of his life was placed over his grave, to mark the resting place of a true warrior and patriot. That his services on the frontier, were appreciated by Michigan, is proven by the name which distinguishes its wealthiest and most populous county.

WELCH, ADONIJA S.——He was born in East Hampton, Connecticut, in 1821; removed to Michigan in 1839, and graduated at the University of that State in 1846; studied law, but preferred teaching, and had charge of a High School at Jonesville; visited California in 1849; and on his return was Principal of the Normal School of Michigan for four years; in 1865 he removed to Florida, and in 1868 he was elected a Senator in Congress from that State for the term ending in 1869, serving on the Committees on Agriculture, and Post Offices and Post Roads.

WHEELOCK, JULIA S.——As England had her Florence Nightingale in the Crimean war, so had the State of Michigan her Julia Wheelock amid the battle-fields of Virginia, and of this noble heroine we submit the following: On the 10th of September, 1862, while engaged in school teaching in the township of Ionia, Michigan, she heard the sad news that her soldier brother, Orville Wheelock, had been wounded at Bull Run; and in less than five days from that time she stood beside his grave in the city of Alexandria. Then it was that she resolved to remain in this strange land, and endeavor, God being her helper, to do for others as she fain would have done for her brother. A field of labor soon presented itself, which she gladly entered, and to which she devoted all her energies from September, 1862, until July, 1865. Her acts of kindness and words of Christian comfort during that period, soothed the anguish of many a poor soldier in his dying hour, and became a part of the unwritten history of Michigan, which the heroic soldiers of that State, still living, will ever remember with heart-felt gratitude. During the period in question she kept a Journal for her own pleasure and not for publication; but in 1870 she was induced by her friends to revise it for the press, and thus came into existence "*The Boys in White; the Experience of a Hospital Agent in and Around Washington.*" Of this book, we have only to say that it is written with ability and in good taste, abounds in passages of rare interest and pathos, and is calculated to give the reader an exalted idea of the truly noble and unselfish authoress and heroine. We have only to add that, for her services during the war, she never asked nor received any compensation, and that for two years thereafter she was a suffering invalid.

WENDELL, J. A. T.——He was of Scotch parentage, born on the Island of Mackinaw, and has always resided there. After acquiring a good education, he turned his attention to mercantile pursuits, and for many years has been a prime mover in developing the commerce of the more Northern Lakes. He served for many sessions in the two Houses of the State Legislature; and was the Democratic candidate for Lieutenant-Governor of Michigan, but failed of election. He visited Europe a few years ago, and has travelled much over the United States, but has not yet found any place strong enough to allure him from his Island home in the North.

WHISTLER, WILLIAM.——By his long residence and military service in the North-west, and also by family ties, Colonel Whistler has long been identified with Michigan. He entered the Army as a Lieutenant in 1801; distinguished himself at the battle of Maguago in 1812, and was at once promoted to the rank of Captain; in 1822 he was appointed a Major by brevet for ten years' faithful service; made a full Major in 1826; Lieutenant-Colonel in 1834; and full Colonel in 1845. His subsequent career was equally honorable. His father, John Whistler, Jr., was an Army officer, and a citizen of Michigan Territory, and was wounded at the battle of Maguago in 1812, and died in 1813. His grandfather, John Whistler, was a soldier in the British Army, served also in the Army of the United States, and died in 1827. His brother, George W. Whistler, was educated at West Point, and after leaving the Army obtained distinction as an engineer in the service of Russia, and died at St. Petersburgh in 1849.

WHITING, HENRY.——He was born in Massachusetts, and entered the United States Army as Cornet in the Light Dragoons, in 1808, and was on duty in Michigan for many years, and always took an interest in the Territory and State. He was a man of reflection and literary culture, a writer for the reviews, and by his occasional discourses, threw much light on the history of the Lake country. As a Lieutenant and Aid to General Boyd, he was present at the capture of Fort George, in Canada, in 1813, and for his gallantry on that occasion he was breveted a Captain. He was also Aid to General Macomb in 1815, and in 1817 was made a Captain; in 1824 he was breveted Major for ten years' service; in 1834 he became a Lieutenant-Colonel; in 1838 Deputy Quartermaster General, with the rank of Colonel; in 1846 he was made an Assistant Quartermaster-General; served in Mexico under General Taylor as Chief Quartermaster; was breveted a Brigadier-General in 1847 for gallant and meritorious service at Buena Vista; in 1858 he was elected a Regent of the University of Michigan; and died in St. Louis, Missouri, September 16, 1851. He had a son, Henry M. Whiting, who served with honor in the war with Mexico, became a Lieutenant of Artillery, and died at Fort Brown, Texas, October 8, 1853, aged thirty-two years.

WHITING, GEORGE L.——He was a printer and a man of rare culture, long honorably identified with the interests of Michigan, and in 1829 established the Detroit *Weekly Advertiser*, which appeared as a daily newspaper in 1835, and after a long and useful career, was consolidated in 1862 with *The Tribune*, and is still published under the title of *Advertiser and Tribune.* In 1834, Mr. Whiting, in conjunction with Stephen Wells, published a small volume, entitled *Historical and Scientific Sketches of Michigan*, which was made up of interesting papers prepared by Lewis Cass, H. R. Schoolcraft, John Biddle, and Henry Whiting. He also published in Detroit two books in the Ottawa language; first, *The Ottawa Prayer Book or Anamie Misinaigan*, in 1842; and, second, *The Indian Book or Anicinabek Amisinahikaniwa*, in 1830.

WHIPPLE, CHARLES W.——He was born in New York, and was among the earliest emigrants to Michigan from the East, and for many years was well known throughout the State as a faithful officer and jurist. He was frequently elected to the State Legislature, and in 1836 and 1837 was Speaker of the House of Representatives. He held various positions of trust and honor, having long been Judge of the Supreme Court, and a member of the Convention of 1850 which framed the present Constitution of the State. He died at Detroit, October 25, 1856.

WHITTELSEY, HENRY M.——He was born in Connecticut, August 12, 1821; studied law in New York City, and was admitted to the bar in 1845; removed to Michigan in 1854, and located in Detroit, where he held various positions connected with the Fire Department, Young Men's Society, State Military Board, and the Light Guard of the City. He was an officer in the School of Instruction at Fort Wayne, where were instructed the officers of the first five regiments furnished by Michigan for the suppression of the Rebellion, and subsequently rendered important services as a mustering officer. In 1860 he was elected Register for Wayne County; in 1861, Captain and Acting-Quartermaster of Volunteers; in 1865, with the rank of Colonel, he was associated with the army of Georgia as Chief-Quartermaster; subsequently served on similar duty in Mississippi, and also in the Freedmen's Bureau in Washington City; he was promoted in regular gradation to the rank of Colonel, and made a Brigadier-General by brevet; and was mustered out of the military service in 1867. According to the records of the War Department, his services as an officer were highly appreciated by a number of the leading General Commanders, and he was recommended for a position in the Regular Army. In 1870, after having acquired much experience in the affairs of the Metropolis, he was elected Comptroller of the City of Washington. He is connected with the distinguished Whittlesey family of Ohio, although the name is spelled differently.

WILCOX, ORLANDO B.——He was born in Detroit, Michigan, about the year 1826; and graduated at the West Point Academy in 1846. He took an active part in the war with Mexico, as a Lieutenant of Artillery, and remained in the United States service until about 1854, when he resigned and entered upon the practice of law, to the study of which, in a quiet way, he had previously devoted some attention. Prior to the Rebellion he took a lively interest in organizing the Militia of Michigan, and when hostilities commenced, he offered his sword to the State and was appointed Colonel of the First Infantry, and his regiment was the first to report for service at Washington from the West. He was in command at Alexandria just before the battle of Bull Run, and participated in that battle, in which he was wounded and taken prisoner, and as such remained in Richmond about fifteen months. When General Lorenzo Thomas was negotiating with the Confederate officer Robert Ould, for the exchange of prisoners, he made a special request in behalf of Colonel Wilcox, to which, in a day or two, the Confederate assented. He soon afterwards returned to the army and participated in many of the engagements in Virginia, and was subsequently promoted to the rank of Brevet Brigadier and Brevet Major-General of Volunteers, for gallant and meritorious services at Spottsylvania and Petersburg. He was mustered out in 1866 and appointed an Assessor of Internal Revenue at Detroit, but again re-appointed in the army; and at the present writing, 1870, he is Colonel of the Twelfth United States Infantry, and stationed on Angel Island, Bay of San Francisco, California. As an author he published in 1856, "*Shoepack Recollections—A Way-side Glimpse of American Life,*" and in 1857, another work entitled "*Foca, an Army Memoir, by Major March.*"

WILKINS, ROSS.——He was born in Pennsylvania; educated for the bar in that State; and removed to the West at an early day, with a Commission in his pocket from President Jackson, as a Federal Judge for the Territory of Michigan. In 1837, and on several subsequent occasions, he was appointed a Regent of the State University. Aside from exerting much influence in his judicial capacity, he has always taken an interest in the public affairs of the State; and he presided over the first war-meeting held in Detroit after the commencement of the Rebellion. He was many years ago appointed a Circuit Judge, and remained in office until the summer of 1870, when he voluntarily retired from the Bench, and is now resting from his long judicial labors in the City of Detroit.

WILKINSON, MORTON S.——Born in Skeneateles, Onondaga County, New York, January 22, 1819; received an Academical education, working occasionally upon his father's farm; in 1837 he visited Michigan, but pushed on to Illinois, where he was engaged for two years in the railroad business; returned to his native town, studied law, and on being admitted to the bar removed to Michigan again, and settled at Eaton Rapids. In 1847 he removed to Minnesota, and in 1849, when that Territory was organized, he was elected to the Legislature, and he drafted the code of laws for that Territory; in 1859 he was elected a Senator in Congress for the term ending in 1865, serving as Chairman of the Committee on Revolutionary Claims, and as a member of the Committee on Indian Affairs. He was also a Delegate to the Baltimore Convention of 1864, and to the Philadelphia "Loyalists' Convention" of 1866.

WILLIAMS, ALPHEUS S.——He was born in Saybrook, Connecticut, September 20, 1810; and after graduating at Yale College in 1831, spent two years travelling in Europe. In 1836 he settled in Detroit, where he began the practice of law; was Judge of Probate for Wayne County from 1840 to 1844; was next elected Recorder of Detroit, after having been defeated as a candidate for Mayor; and from 1843 to 1847 he was the editor and proprietor of the Detroit *Daily Advertiser*. As a Lieutenant Colonel he served through the Mexican war, and in 1849 he was appointed by President Taylor Postmaster of Detroit, holding the office until 1853. On the breaking out of the Rebellion he was appointed a Major General of Michigan Volunteers, and also President of the State Military Board. He subsequently received from President Lincoln the appointment of Brigadier General in the national army, and was in active service on the Upper Potomac and in Shenandoah Valley; was for a time in command of General Bank's division at Winchester; commanded a division under General Pope at Cedar Mountain, on the Rappahannock, and at Manassas; after the battle of South Mountain, succeeded General Banks as Corps Commander, and commanded the twelfth corps at Antietam, and also took an active and leading part in the battles of Chancellorsville, Gettysburg, and the Atlanta campaign. Was with General Sherman in his "march to the sea," and at Savannah he was breveted a Major-General for gallant and meritorious services in the Georgia campaign. He was subsequently assigned to duty in Arkansas, and was mustered out of the service in 1866. Soon after, he was appointed one of several commissioners to examine and adjust the military claims of Missouri. In 1866 he was nominated for Governor of Michigan, but not elected; and was then appointed Minister Resident to the Republic of San Salvador, in Central America, in which position he remained until 1869, when he returned to Detroit and to private life.

WILLIAMS, JOHN R.——He was one of the earliest settlers in Detroit; a merchant by occupation, and for many years took a leading part in all the enterprises calculated to promote the prosperity of Michigan and its largest city. He was elected Mayor of Detroit on six different occasions; the first time in 1824, and the last time in 1846; and he died in 1854, universally lamented by his fellow-citizens of all parties.

WILLIAMS, THOMAS.——He was born in New York in 1815, but subsequently becoming a citizen of Michigan, where he resided many years, and was appointed from that State a cadet at West Point, where he graduated in 1837. He was at once assigned to duty in the Fourth Artillery, serving in Florida, in New York, and in Michigan, with headquarters at Detroit, until 1840; during the latter year he was Professor of Mathematics at West Point, and was again transferred to Michigan; from 1844 until 1850 he was an Aid-de-camp to General Scott, and was present with him at Vera Cruz, Cerro Gordo, Cherubusco, and at the City of Mexico, and for his gallant and meritorious services he received two promotions, the second being that of Major for gallantry at Chepultepec. From 1850 until 1852 he was again on duty in Michigan, headquarters at Mackinaw; and from 1852 until 1858 he was on duty in Florida and on the Western frontiers. He entered the war for the Union as Major of the Fifth Artillery, and for his services in Virginia and Pennsylvania he was made a Brigadier General of Volunteers, and after important services in the Carolinas, the Gulf States, and on the Lower Mississippi, he was killed in battle at Baton Rouge August 5, 1862. His last words, uttered to an Indiana regiment just before he fell, were these: "*Boys, your field officers are all gone; I will lead you.*" He was a soldier of rare bravery and high character, and was deeply lamented by all who knew him. Although General Robertson speaks of him as a native of Michigan, the records of the War Department mention New York as his native State.

WILLIAMS, WILLIAM G.——He was born in Philadelphia in 1801; spent his boyhood in England, and went through a course of studies at Exeter; graduated at the West Point Academy in 1824; spent two years in Paris, studying his profession; as a Second Lieutenant of Infantry he served ten years on topographical duty; as First Lieutenant he surveyed the site for a fort in the river Delaware; as Brevet Captain of Staff in the Topographical Engineers, he surveyed the route for a ship-canal around the Falls of Niagara in 1835 and '36, performing similar service on Lake Champlain, at Charleston, South Carolina, and at Cincinna i, Ohio; in 1837 he went upon a military reconnoissance to the country of the Cherokees; in 1838 he attained the rank of Captain of Engineers, and during the eight following years he was engaged in making triangulations and constructing harbor works on Lake Erie, was Superintendent of Survey of the North-western Lakes, and of the boundary between the States of Wisconsin and Michigan, and in the latter State he spent much of his time making his headquarters at Detroit. He served under General Taylor in the war with Mexico as Chief of Engineers, and at the battle of Monterey, in 1846, he was mortally wounded, and died at that place September 21, 1846. His dying words were, "Tell my friends that I fell while in the advance, and in the performance of my duty." His literary and scientific acquirements were of a high order, and he also possessed an uncommon taste for the fine arts, and was an adept in painting; and he was very popular among his brother officers in the old army.

WINCHELL, ALEXANDER.——Born in East, Dutchess County, New York, December 31, 1824; after acquiring a primary education, he taught school for one or two years, and prepared himself for college; graduated at Amenia Seminary in 1844; in 1847 he also graduated at the Wesleyan University; then became a teacher of Natural Sciences in Pennington Seminary, New Jersey; also in the Amenia Seminary; in 1851 assumed the charge of a Seminary in Eutaw, Alabama; was made President of the Masonic University in Selma of the same State in 1853; before the close of that year he was appointed Professor of Physics and Engineering in the University of Michigan; was transferred to the Chair of Geology, Zoology and Botany, in 1855; in 1859 became the editor of the *Journal of Education*, &c.; in 1866 was made a Professor in the Kentucky University; was made an L.L. D. by the Wesleyan University in 1867; and in 1869 was appointed Director of the Geological Survey of Michigan. He declined a number of appointments that were tendered to him; made a number of presents of Scientific Collections to various institutions; and is a member of nearly all the Scientific Academies in America, and of several in Europe. He published in various journals more than two hundred scientific papers, and is the author of the following works, viz: The First Biennial Report on the Geology of Michigan; Report on the Grand Traverse Region; a Geological Map of Michigan; Genealogy of the Winchell Family; and Sketches of Creation. As to his miscellaneous publications, they are sufficiently numerous to make many volumes, and all of them are upon subjects of vital interest to the students and lovers of nature, in many of its departments.

WINCHESTER, JAMES.——Although the military career of this officer was inglorious, it is our duty to mention him among those who have been identified with the Territory of Michigan. He was born in Maryland in 1756; entered the Army as a Colonel from Tennessee, in March, 1812; was made a Brigadier-General in March, 1813, and had command of a detachment under General Harrison, and, as stated in the preceding pages, met with great disaster on the River Raisin in January, 1813, when he was compelled to surrender to the British forces, and became a prisoner and was carried into Canada and confined for about a year in Quebec, with his subordinate officers, Colonels Wm. Lewis and George Madison. He was subsequently on duty in Mobile, Alabama, under General Jackson. In March, 1815, he resigned his commission in the Army, and after living in retirement in Tennessee, died there July 27, 1826.

WING, AUSTIN E.——He was born in Hampshire County, Massachusetts; was a Delegate to Congress from the Territory of Michigan, from 1828 to 1832; resided at Monroe, and was for many years a leading man in all its local affairs, holding among other positions that of United States Marshal for the Southern District of Michigan. He was also twice appointed a Regent of the State University. He died at Cleveland, Ohio,

August 25, 1849. He was the father of Talcott E. Wing, a well-known lawyer of Monroe; and the brother of Warner Wing, long a leading lawyer of the State, and also a resident of Monroe.

WING, WARNER.——He was born in Marietta, Ohio, September 19, 1805; graduated at the Northampton Law School, Massachusetts, and removed to the Territory of Michigan in 1817. He settled on the River Raisin, where he lived for many years, actively engaged in practicing the profession of law in which he was eminently successful; was Judge of the Circuit Court from 1845 to 1856, during which period it was identical with the Supreme Court. Of all the trials over which he presided as Judge, the most important, perhaps, was that commonly known as the *Railroad Conspiracy Case*, in 1851, on which occasion, according to the universal opinion, he acquitted himself with very rare ability. The proceedings of this trial were published in a volume of more than eight hundred and fifty pages, and form a curious episode in the history of railroads, and of the State of Michigan. At the present time Judge Wing is the Attorney for the Michigan Southern and Northern Indiana Railroad Company, which position he has held for about fourteen years.

WISNER, MOSES.——He was born in Aurelieus, Cayuga County, New York, in 1818; received a good education; removed to Michigan in 1839, and settled upon a farm near the town of Atlas, Lapeer County; in about a year afterwards he removed to Pontiac, and studied law; coming to the bar in 1842. In 1843 he was appointed Prosecuting Attorney for Lapeer County; but in 1844 resumed the practice of his profession, and continued in it until 1858, when he was elected Governor of the State. In 1862 he was appointed a Colonel in the Volunteer Army, and was assigned to the command of the Michigan Twenty-second; and while on his way to the seat of war, he was prostrated by sickness in Lexington, Kentucky, where he died, January 5, 1863. He was a candidate for Circuit Judge in 1852, but was defeated; took little interest in politics, was a man of fine mind, a good friend, and most worthy citizen.

WITHERELL, BENJAMIN F. H.——He was the son of James Witherell, and was during all his mature life identified with the Territory and State of Michigan. He was a lawyer by profession, long a successful practitioner in Detroit, and held a prominent judgeship for many years. He was called by his intimate friends a "Walking Historical Dictionary of Detroit," and published a series of Historical Recollections, of great value and interest; and his death was lamented as a public calamity. His last judicial position was that of Judge of the Third Circuit Court. He took an active interest in all public affairs during the Rebellion, and was the originator, and chosen President of the Soldiers' and Sailors' Monument Association when organized; and it was while deeply engaged in maturing its plans that he died in Detroit, June 26, 1867, giving to the patriotic work the last hours of his life. He was also appointed, on several occasions, a Regent of the State University.

WITHERELL, JAMES——In 1808, the small but highly cultivated society of Detroit was made happy by the advent of James Witherell. He was a native of Vermont, received a liberal education, and adopted the profession of law. From 1798 to 1803 he served in the Legislature of Vermont; the two following years, as a county Judge; was a State Councellor from 1803 to 1807; was elected to Congress in the latter year, but before the expiration of his term, was appointed a Federal Judge in the Territory of Michigan, in which position he continued until 1828, when he was appointed Secretary of the Territory; and he resided in Detroit until his death, which occurred in that City, January 9, 1838. He was a man of strong native powers of mind, always took a special interest in the local affairs of Detroit, and left to his accomplished son, long a prominent lawyer in Detroit, a valuable collection of papers bearing upon the history of that city and the State of Michigan. An admirable portrait of him may be found in Sheldon's "Early History of Michigan."

WITHEY, SOLOMON L.——He was born in St. Albans, Vermont, April 21, 1820; removed to Ohio in 1835, where he obtained a good English education; and in 1838 he removed to Michigan and located at Grand Rapids. In 1839 he began the study of law, and came to the bar in 1844; and becoming a partner of the late Chief Justice Martin, continued with him until he was called to the bench, and in practice until 1863. In 1848 he was elected Judge of Probate, and held the office four years; in 1860 he was elected to the State Senate, and took an active part in promoting effective legislation for putting down the Rebellion; and he was appointed by President Lincoln United States District Judge for the western district of Michigan, in which office he still continues. During the illness of Judge Willson, of Northern Ohio, he held the United States Courts at Cleveland; and for a year preceding the resignation of Judge Wilkins he presided over the courts of Eastern Michigan. In December, 1869, he received from President Grant a commission as Judge of the Sixth United States Judicial Circuit; but his duty to his family compelled him to decline the honor. For that position he was warmly supported by the leading members of the bar in Michigan and Northern Ohio, and of all political parties, and that fact alone made him reluctant to decline. In the way of local positions, we may add that Judge Withey is President of the First National Bank of Grand Rapids. He is a man of culture; and as a citizen, a lawyer and judge occupies a leading position in the State.

WOODBRIDGE, WILLIAM.——Born in Norwich, Connecticut, August 20, 1780; and his father becoming one of the earliest emigrants to the Northwest Territory, he removed to Marietta in 1791. He received his earliest education in Connecticut; studied law at Litchfield, Connecticut, and was admitted to the bar in Ohio in 1806. In 1807 he was elected to the Assembly of Ohio; in 1808 was Prosecuting Attorney for his county, which office he held until 1814, and during the same period he was also a member of the State Senate. In 1814 he received from President Madison, unexpectedly, the appointment of Secretary of the Territory of Michigan, and removed to Detroit; and in 1819 he was elected the first Delegate from Michigan to Congress, where he was very active in promoting the interests of his constituents. In 1828 he was appointed Judge of the Supreme Court of Michigan Territory, and held the office four years; in 1835 he was a member of the Convention called to form a State Constitution; in 1837 he was elected to the State Senate of Michigan; in 1839 he was chosen Governor of the State; and he was a Senator in Congress from 1841 to 1847. He was a working member on many important committees, and his reports and speeches were numerous; and Daniel Webster, in a note to his speech in defence of the Ashburton Treaty, attributed to Mr. Woodbridge the first suggestion that was ever made to him for inserting in that treaty a provision for the surrender of fugitives, under certain circumstances, upon the demand of foreign governments. For many years before his death he lived in retirement at Detroit, devoting himself to his books and the pleasures of horticulture, for which he had a special fondness. Died October 20, 1861. In 1867 a small volume was published, entitled the "Life of William Woodbridge," from the pen of the compiler of this work. Among the many opinions expressed of Governor Woodbridge by leading men, soon after his death, were the following: That he was an eminent jurist and constitutional lawyer; the oldest and most distinguished member of the Detroit bar; eminently a man of principle and honor; a faithful and honored public servant; had a highly cultivated and refined taste, and left to his children the rich legacy of a spotless name.

WOODWARD, AUGUSTUS B.——He was a native of Virginia; emigrated to Michigan in 1805, when he was appointed a judge of the Territory, which honorable position he held until 1824. He was the author of a "Code of Laws," which bears his name. In 1824 he was appointed a Judge for the Territory of Florida, and died there after a service of three years. He was the man, moreover, who, in 1812, had a resolution adopted in the Legislature prohibiting the wearing of apparel made from English goods. The colleagues of Judge Woodward on the bench were Frederick Bates and John Griffin, in regard to whom the writer has been unable to obtain any biographic particulars. We have seen it stated that Judge Woodward, in conjunction with John Steward and William W. Harwood, founded the town of Ypsilanti in 1825; but if he went to Florida in 1824, the statement cannot be true.

FOURTH PART.

MISCELLANEOUS RECORDS.

MISCELLANEOUS RECORDS.

THE CENSUS OF MICHIGAN IN 1870.

(Officially furnished for this work by the Census Bureau.)

In the preceding pages the Compiler has submitted two or three paragraphs respecting the Census of Michigan for 1870, which were obtained from local authorities, or from the Marshals of the United States, before making their final reports to the Government. It is now his privilege, however, through the kindness of the Superintendent of the Census Bureau, Mr. Francis A. Walker, to lay before the reader a statement of the population of the State, respecting the authenticity of which there cannot be any doubt. In doing this, the population of each County will be given for 1870, in regular order, with a corresponding column exhibiting the population of the same Counties in 1860; and there will also be added to this list, the leading cities of the State, with the number of their inhabitants, exclusive of the suburbs or villages which may be identified with them:

Counties.	1860.	1870.
Alcona,	185	696
Allegan,	16,087	32,106
Alpena,	290	2,756
Antrim,	179	1,985
Barry,	13,853	22,202
Bay,	3,164	15,900
Benzie,	No report.	2,184
Berrien,	22,378	35,104
Branch,	20,981	26,226
Calhoun,	29,564	36,569
Cass,	17,721	21,094
Charlevoix,	No report.	1,724
Cheboygan,	517	2,196
Chippewa,	1,603	1,689
Clare,	No report.	366
Clinton,	13,916	22,845
Crawford, (no report.)		
Delta,	1,172	2,441
Eaton,	16,476	25,172
Emmett,	1,149	1,211
Genesee,	22,498	33,900
Gladwin,	14	No report.
Grand Traverse,	1,286	4,443
Gratiot,	4,042	11,810
Hillsdale,	25,675	31,684
Houghton,	9,234	13,879
Huron,	3,165	9,049
Ingham,	17,435	25,268
Ionia,	16,682	27,679
Iosco,	175	3,163
Isabella	1,443	4,113
Jackson,	26,671	36,050
Kalamazoo,	24,646	32,054
Kalcasca,	No return.	424
Kent,	30,716	50,403
Keewenaw,	No report.	4,205
Lake,	No report.	548
Lapeer,	14,754	21,345
Leelenaw,	2,158	4.816
Lenawee,	38,112	45,596
Livingston,	16,851	19,336
Mackinaw,	1,938	1,716
Macomb,	22,843	27,616
Manitou,	1,042	891
Manistee,	975	6,074
Marquette,	2,825	14,234
Mason,	831	3,264
Mecosta,	970	5,643
Menominee,	No report.	1,892
Midland,	787	3,285
Missaukee,	No report.	130
Monroe,	21,593	27,483
Montcalm,	3,968	13,629
Montmorency, (no report.)		
Muskegon,	3,947	14,895
Newaygo,	2,760	7,294
Oakland,	38,261	40,867
Oceana,	1,816	7,222

Counties.	1860.	1870.	Counties.	1860.	1870.
Ogemaw,	No report.	12	Schoolcraft, (not known to be complete)	78	799
Ontonagon,	4,568	2,845	Shiawassee,	12,349	20,858
Osceola,	27	2,093	St. Joseph,	21,262	26.276
Oscoda,	No report.	70	Tuscola,	4,886	13,714
Otsego, (no report.)			Van Buren,	15,224	28,828
Ottawa,	13,215	26,649	Washtenaw,	35,686	41,434
Presque Isle,	26	355	Wayne,	75,547	119,041
Roscommon, (no report.)			Wexford,	No report.	650
Saginaw,	12,693	39,097			
Saint Clair,	26,604	36,661			
Sanilac,	7,599	14,562	Total population,	749,113	1,184,310

POPULATION OF LEADING CITIES.

Cities.	1860.	1870.	Cities.	1860.	1870.
Detroit,	45,619	79,580	Battle Creek,	3,509	5.831
Grand Rapids,	8,085	16,507	Ypsilanti,	3,955	5,478
Jackson,	4,799	11,400	Flint,	2,950	5,386
East Saginaw,	3,001	11,350	Lansing,	3,074	5,241
Kalamazoo,	6,070	9,181	Monroe,	3,892	5,086
Adrian,	6,213	8,438	Marshall,	3,736	4,925
Saginaw,	1,699	7,460	Pontiac,	2,575	4,867
Ann Arbor,	5,097	7,363	Niles,	2 826	4,630
Muskegon,	1,450	6,002	Coldwater,	2,905	4,381
Port Huron,	4,371	5,973			

STATE OFFICERS OF MICHIGAN FROM 1836 TO 1870.

GOVERNORS.

Territorial Governors: William Hull, 1805; Lewis Cass, 1814; George B. Porter, 1829; Stevens T. Mason, 1834; J. T. Horner *ex officio*, 1835.

State Governors: Stevens T. Mason, 1836; William Woodbridge, 1840; J. Wright Gordon (Acting,) 1841; John S. Barry, 1842; Alpheus Felch, 1846; William L. Greenly (Acting,) 1847; Epaphroditus Ransom, 1848; John S. Barry, 1850; Robert McClelland, 1852; Andrew Parsons (Acting,) 1853; Kinsley S. Bingham, 1855; Moses Wisner, 1859; Austin Blair, 1861; Henry H. Cropo, 1865; and Henry P. Baldwin, 1869, re-elected and now in office.

LIEUTENANT GOVERNORS.

Edward Mundy, 1835; J. Wright Gordon, 1840; Origen D. Richardson, 1842; William L. Greenly, 1847; William M. Fenton, 1848; William L. Greenly, 1849; William M. Fenton, 1851; Andrew Parsons, 1853; George A. Coe, 1855; Edmund B. Fairfield, 1859; James Birney, 1861; Joseph R. Williams (Acting,) 1861; Henry T. Backus (Acting,) 1862; Charles S. May, 1863; Ebenezer O. Grosvenor, 1865; Dwight May, 1867; and Morgan Bates, 1869, re-elected and now in office.

SPEAKERS OF THE HOUSE OF REPRESENTATIVES.

Ezra Convis, 1835; Charles W. Whipple, 1836; Kinsley S. Bingham, 1838; Henry Acker, 1840; Philo C. Fuller, 1841; Kinsley S. Bingham, 1842; Robert McClelland, 1743; Edwin H. Lathrop, 1844; Alfred H. Hanscom, 1845; Isaac E. Crary, 1846; George W. Peck, 1847; Alexander W. Buel, 1848; Leander Chapman, 1849; Silas G. Harris, 1850; Jefferson G. Thurber, 1851; Daniel G. Quackenboss, 1853; Cyrus Lovell, 1855;

Byron G. Stout, 1857; Henry A. Shaw, 1859; Dexter Mussey, 1861; Sullivan M. Cutcheon, 1863; Gilbert E. Read, 1865; P. Dean Warner, 1867; and Jonathan J. Woodman, 1869.

SECRETARIES OF STATE.

Keutzing Pritchette, 1835; Randolph Manning, 1838; Thomas Rowland, 1840; Robert P. Eldridge, 1842 to 1846; Gideon O. Whittemore, 1846; George W. Peck, 1848; George Redfield, 1850, (resigned April 11, 1850;) Charles H. Taylor, 1850 to 1852; William Graves, 1852; John McKinney, 1854 to 1858; Nelson G. Isbell, 1858; James B. Porter, 1860 to 1866; Oliver L. Spaulding, 1866 to 1871; Daniel Striker, 1871.

STATE TREASURERS.

Henry Howard, 1836–9; Peter Desnoyer, 1839; Robert Stuart, 1840; George W. Jermain, 1841; John J. Adam, 1842; George Redfield, 1845; George B. Cooper, 1846–50; Banard Whittemore, 1850–4; Silas M. Holmes, 1854–8; John McKinney, 1858; John Owen, 1860–6; Ebenezer O. Grosvenor, 1866–71; Victory P. Collier, 1871.

ATTORNEYS GENERAL.

Daniel Le Roy, 1836; Peter Morey, 1837–41; Zephaniah Platt, 1841; Elon Farnsworth, 1843; Henry N. Walker, 1845; Edward Mundy, 1847; George V. N. Lothrop, 1848–51; William Hall, 1851–4; Jacob M. Howard, 1854–60; Charles Upson, 1860; Albert Williams, 1862–66; William L. Stoughton, 1863; Dwight May, re-elected, and now in office, 1868–71.

AUDITORS GENERAL.

Robert Abbott, 1836–9; Henry Howard, 1839; Eurotas P. Hastings, 1840; Alpheus Felch, 1842; Henry, L. Whipple, (to fill vacancy,) 1842; Charles G. Hammond, 1842–5; John J. Adam, 1845; Digby V. Bell, 1846–8; John J. Adam, 1848–50; John Swegles, jr., 1850; John Swegles, 1852; Whitney Jones, 1854–8; Daniel L. Case, 1858; Langford G. Berry, 1860; Emil Anneke, 1862–6; William Humphrey, re-elected and now in office, 1866–71.

THE JUDICIARY OF THE STATE OF MICHIGAN IN 1870.

Circuit Court of the United States.—Sixth Circuit, Noah H. Swayne, of Ohio; H. H. Emmons, of Michigan.

District Court of Michigan.—John W. Longyear, of Lansing; Solomon L. Withey, of Grand Rapids.

Supreme Court of Michigan.—James V. Campbell, Detroit, Chief Justice; Isaac P. Christiancy, Monroe; Benjamin F. Graves, Battle Creek; Thomas M. Cooley, Ann Arbor.

Circuit Court of Michigan.—Daniel L. Pratt, Hillsdale; David Blackman, Cassopolis; Jared Patchin, Detroit; Samuel Higby, Jackson; George Woodruff, Marshall; James S. Dewey, Pontiac; Josiah Turner, Owosso; Louis S. Lovell, Ionia; Charles R. Brown, Kalamazoo; Jabez G. Sutherland, Saginaw City; Daniel Goodwin, Detroit; James O'Grady, Marquette; Jonathan G. Ramsdell, Traverse City; A. H. Giddings, Newaygo; Charles Upson, Coldwater; William T. Mitchell, Port Huron.

PRESIDENTIAL ELECTORS OF MICHIGAN FROM 1837 TO 1869.

1837—Martin Van Buren, elected. Vice President, Richard M. Johnson.—Daniel LeRoy, William H. Hoeg, David C. McKinstry.

1841—William Henry Harrison, elected. Vice President, John Tyler.—Thomas J. Drake, H. G. Wells, J. Van Fossen.

1845—James K. Polk, elected. Vice President, George M. Dallas.—Lewis Beaufait, George Redfield, P. S. Paulding, Charles P. Bush, Samuel Axford.

1849—Zachary Taylor, elected. Vice President, Millard Fillmore.—John S. Barry, L. M. Mason, Rix Robinson, J. G. Thurber, William T. Howell.

1853—Franklin Pierce, elected. Vice President, William R. King.—John S. Barry, D. J. Campau, A. Edwards, William McCauley, Salmer Sharpe, John Stockton.

1857—James Buchanan, elected. Vice President, John C. Breckinridge.—F. C. Beaman, O. Johnson, H. Chamberlain, W. H. Whitney, C. H. Miller, Thomas J. Drake.

1861—Abraham Lincoln, elected. Vice President, Hannibal Hamlin.—Hezekiah G. Wells, Rufus Hosmer, George W. Lee, Edward Dorsch, Philetus Hayden, Augustus Coburn.

1865—Abraham Lincoln, re-elected. Vice President, Andrew Johnson.—Robert R. Beecher, Marsh Giddings, Thomas D. Gilbert, O. D. Conger, F. Walldorf, George W. Back, Christian Eberbach, J. Eugene Tenney.

1867—Ulysses S. Grant, elected. Vice President, Schuyler Colfax.—Charles M. Crosswell, John Burt, William Daeltz, Charles W. Chisbee, Charles T. Gorham, Byron M. Cutcheon, Giles Hubbard, Michael T. C. Pleasner.

OFFICERS OF THE UNIVERSITY OF MICHIGAN FROM 1837 TO 1870.

Presidents of the Board of Regents.

Until the adoption of the Revised Constitution, the Governor of the State was *ex-officio* President of the Board. That instrument conferred upon the Regents the power, and under it their duty, to elect a President of the University, who should be *ex-officio* President of their Board. Under this power, the first President was chosen in 1852:

Stevens T. Mason, 1837; William Woodbridge, M. A., 1840; James Wright Gordon, M. A., 1841; John S. Barry, 1842; Alpheus Felch, 1846; William L. Greenly, 1847; Epaphroditus Ransom, 1848; John S. Barry, 1850; Rev. Henry Philip Tappan, D. D. LL. D., 1852; Rev. Erastus Otis Haven, D. D. LL. D., 1863 to 1869.

Regents Ex-officio.

Until the Revised Constitution took effect, the Lieutenant-Governor, the Chancellor, and the Justices of the Supreme Court, for the time being, were *ex-officio* members of the Board of Regents:

Lieutenant Governors.—Edward Mundy, 1837; J. Wright Gordon, 1840; Origen D. Richardson, 1842; William L. Greenly, 1846; William M. Fenton, 1848 to 1852.

Chancellors.—Elon Farnsworth, 1837; Randolph Manning, 1842; Elon Farnsworth, 1846 to 1847, when the office was abolished.

Justices of the Supreme Court.

From 1837: William A. Fletcher, Chief Justice; resigned 1842. George Morrell, Associate Justice; promoted, 1842. Epaphroditus Ransom, Associate Justice. Charles W. Whipple, Associate Justice; appointed, 1837. George Morrell, Chief Justice; from 1842, *vice* Fletcher. Alpheus Felch, Associate Justice; from 1842, *vice* Morrell.

From 1843: Epaphroditus Ransom, Chief Justice; resigned, 1845. Charles W. Whipple, Associate Justice; promoted, 1848. Alpheus Felch, Associate Justice; resigned, 1845. Daniel Goodwin, Associate Justice; resigned, 1846. Charles W. Whipple, Chief Justice; from 1848, *vice* Ransom. Warner Wing, Associate Justice; from 1845, *vice* Felch. George Miles, Associate Justice; from 1846, *vice* Goodwin. Sanford M. Green, Associate Justice; from 1848, *vice* Whipple. Edward Mundy, Associate Justice; from 1848—new appointment.

From 1850: Charles W. Whipple, Chief Justice; Warner Wing, Associate Justice; Sanford M. Greene, Associate Justice; Abner Pratt, Associate Justice; Edward Mundy, Associate Justice; died 1851. George Martin, Associate Justice; from 1851, *vice* Mundy.

Regents by Appointment.

From the organization of the University till 1852, the Regents were appointed by the Senate, on the nomination of the Governor, to hold office for four years, three being appointed annually:

John Norvell, 1837; Ross Wilkins, M. A., 1837; John J. Adam, 1837; Lucius Lyon, 1837; Isaac E. Crary, M. A., 1837; Thomas Fitzgerald, 1837, (resigned in 1837;) John F. Porter, (*vice* T. Fitzgerald, 1837, resigned in 1838;) Jonathan Kearsley, M. A., 1838, (*vice* J. F. Porter;) Samuel Denton, M. D., 1827; Gideon O. Whittemore, 1827; Michael Hoffman, 1827, (resigned in 1838;) Gurdon C. Leach, 1838, (*vice* M. Hoffman;) Zina Pitcher, M. D., 1837; Henry R. Schoolcraft, LL. D., 1837; Robert McClelland, 1837, (resigned in 1837;) Seba Murphy, 1837, (*vice* R. McClelland, resigned in 1839;) Joseph W. Brown, 1839, (*vice* Murphy, resigned in 1840;) Daniel Hudson, M. D., 1840, (*vice* J. W. Brown;) John J. Adam, 1838, (resigned in 1840;) John Norvel, 1838, (resigned in 1839;) Ross Wilkins, M. A. 1838.

Charles C. Trowbridge, 1837, (*vice* J. Norvell;) Michael A. Patterson, M. D., 1840; (*vice* J. J. Adam;) Lucius Lyon, 1839, (resigned in 1839;) Jonathan Kearsley, M. A., 1839; Isaac E. Crary, M. A., 1839; Rev. George Duffield, D. D., 1839, (*vice* L. Lyon;) William Draper, M. A., 1840; Francis J. Higginson, M. D., 1840, (resigned in 1841;) Samuel W. Dexter, M. A., 1840, (resigned in 1841;) Rev. Oliver C. Comstock, A. M. M. D., 1841, (*vice* S. W. Dexter, resigned in 1843;) John Owen, 1841, (*vice* F. J. Higginson;) Lewis Cass, LL. D., 1843, (*vice* O. C. Comstock;) Zina Pitcher, M. D., 1841; Martin Kundig, M. A., 1841; George Goodman, 1841, (resigned in 1843;) Dewitt C. Walker, 1843, (*vice* G. Goodman, resigned in 1844;) Rev. Robert R. Kellogg, M. A., 1844, (*vice* D. C. Walker;) Rev. Andrew M. Fitch, 1842; Randolph Manning, 1842, (resigned in 1842;) Rev. Elisha Crane, 1842; William A. Fletcher, 1842, (*vice* R. Manning;) Jonathan Kearsley, 1843; Isaac E. Crary, 1843, (resigned in 1843;) Rev. Marvin Allen, 1843; Alexander H. Redfield, M. A., 1844, (*vice* J. E. Crary;) Edward Mundy, 1844; John Owen, 1844; Rev. George Duffield, D. D., 1844; Zina Pitcher, M. D., 1845; Austin E. Wing, M. A., 1845;

Minot T. Lane, 1845; Rev. Charles C. Taylor, M. A., 1846; Rev. Elijah H. Pilcher, M. A., 1846; Elon Farnsworth, M. A., 1846; Jonathan Kearsley, 1847; Alexander H. Redfield, M. A., 1847; Rev. Marvin Allen, 1847; Rev. John G. Atterbury, M. A., 1848; Justus Goodwin, M. A., 1848; Benjamin F. H. Witherell, 1848; Zina Pitcher, M. D., 1849; Austin E. Wing, M. A., 1849, (resigned in 1850;) Edwin M. Cust, M. A., 1849, (resigned in 1849;) Epaphroditus Ransom, 1850, (*vice* E. M. Cust;) Rev. Gustavus L. Foster, 1850, (*vice* A. E. Wing;) Robert McClelland, 1850; Elon Farnsworth, M. A., 1850; Rev. Elijah H. Pilcher, 1850; Jonathan Kearsley, 1851; Alexander H. Redfield, M. A., 1851; Rev. Marvin Allen, 1851.

The amended Constitution of 1851 provided for the election of a Regent in each Senatorial District, to hold office for the period of six years.

Regents by Election.

From 1852 to 1857, 1st District, Michael A. Patterson, M. D; 2d District, Edward S. Moore; 3d District, Elon Farnsworth; 4th District, James Kingsley; 5th District, Elisha Ely; 6th District, Charles H. Palmer, M. A.; 7th District, Andrew Parsons, (deceased 1854;) Henry Horatio Northrop, M. A., (*vice* A. Parsons;) 8th District, William Upjohn, M. D.

From 1858 to 1863, 1st District, Benjamin L. Baxter; 2d District, J. Eastman Johnson; 3d District, Levi Bishop; 4th District, Donald McIntyre; 5th District, E. Lakin Brown; 6th District, George W. Pack, (resigned in 1858;) Henry Whiting, (*vice* G. W. Pack;) 7th District, Luke H. Parsons; 8th District, Rev. John Van Vleck, (resigned in 1858;) Oliver L. Spaulding, (*vice* J. Van Vleck;) 9th District, William M. Ferry, 1858; 10th District, George Bradley, 1858.

By an amendment of the Constitution, adopted in 1862, it was provided that eight Regents should be elected in 1863, to enter upon their office in 1864; two for two years, two for four years, two for six years, and two for eight years; and that at every election of a Justice of the Supreme Court thereafter, there should be elected two Regents for eight years. In accordance with this provision, the following were elected, and the term of their office was determined by lot, according to law.

Edward C. Walker, re-elected, term expires 1865; George Willard, re-elected, term expires 1865; Thomas D. Gilbert, re-elected, term expires 1867; Thomas J. Joslin, term expires 1867; Henry C. Knight, term expires 1869; Hiram A. Burt, Joseph Estabrook, term expires 1869; J. Eastman Johnson, term expires 1869; Alvah Sweetser (deceased 1864,) term expires 1871; Syrus M. Stockwell, M. D., of Port Huron, term expires 1871; James A. Sweezey, term expires 1871; Walker, Willard, Gilbert, and Burt have been re-elected; Jonas H. McGowan, elected in 1870, term expires 1878.

Secretaries.

Charles W. Whipple, 1837; Anthony Ten Eyck, 1839; James Valentine Campbell, M. A.; Eben N. Wilcox, 1845; O. W. Moore, 1852; Edward R. Chase, 1853; Prof. Alexander Winchell, M. A., 1854; John Livingston Tappan, M. A., 1856; Daniel Leonard Wood, M. A., 1858.

Treasurers.

Charles C. Trowbridge, 1837; John Norton, Jr., 1838; H. K. Sanger, 1839; A. H. Sibley, 1841; John J. Adam, 1844; Digby V. Bell, 1846; John J. Adam, 1848; John M. Chase, 1851; Henry Wolsey Welles, 1859; Volney Chapin, 1860; Donald McIntyre, 1864.

Librarians.

Rev. Henry Colclazer, 1837; Prof. George Palmer Williams, LL. D., 1845; Prof. Abram Sager, M. D., 1848; Prof. Andrew Ten Brook, M. A., 1850; Prof. Daniel D. Whedon, D. D., 1851; Prof. Louis Fasquelle, LL. D., 1852; John Livingston Tappan, M. A., 1856; Datus Chase Brooks, M. A., 1863.

Superintendents of Public Instruction.

John D. Pierce, 1838; Franklin Sawyer, Jr., 1841; Oliver C. Comstock, M. D., 1843; Ira Mahew, M. A., 1845; Francis W. Shearman, M. A. 1849; Ira Mayhew, M. A., 1855; John M. Gregory, M. A., 1858; Oramel Hosford, 1865.

Presidents of the University.

Rev. Henry Philip Tappan, D. D., LL. D., 1852; Rev. Erastus Otis Haven, D. D., LL. D., 1863 to 1869.

I. Department of Literature, Science, and the Arts.

Professors.

Asa Gray, M. D., Botany and Zoology, 1838 to 1842.
Douglass Houghton, M. A., M. D., Chemistry and Mineralogy, 1838 to 1845.
Rev. George Palmer Williams, LL. D., Ancient Languages, 1841.
Rev. Joseph Whiting, M. A., Ancient Languages, 1841 to 1845.
Rev. George Palmer Williams, LL. D., Mathematics and Physics, 1841 to 1852.
Abram Sager, M. D., Botany and Zoology, 1842 to 1850.
Rev. Edward Thomson, D. D., LL. D., Moral and Intellectual Philosophy, 1843 to 1844.
Rev. Andrew Ten Brook, M. A., Moral and Intellectual Philosophy, 1844 to 1851.
Rev. John Holmes Agnew, D. D., Ancient Languages and Literature, 1845 to 1852.
Rev. Daniel D. Whedon, D. D., History and Rhetoric, 1845 to 1852.
Silas Hamilton Douglass, M. A., M. D., Chemistry and Mineralogy, 1846 to 1848.
Louis Fasquelle, LL. D., Modern Languages and Literature, 1846 to 1862.
Silas Hamilton Douglass, M. A., M. D., Chemistry, Geology, and Mineralogy, 1848 to 1855.
Rev. William S. Curtis, D. D., Moral and Intellectual Philosophy, 1851 to 1852.
Rev. Henry Philip Tappan, D. D., LL. D., Philosophy, 1852 to 1863.
Rev. George Palmer Williams, LL. D., Natural Philosophy and Mathematics, 1852 to 1854.
James Robinson Boise, M. A., Ancient Languages, Greek Language and Literature, 1852.
Rev. Erastus Otis Haven, D. D., LL. D., Latin Language and Literature, 1852 to 1854.
Alvah Bradish, M. A., Fine Arts, 1852 to 1863.
Rev. George Palmer Williams, LL. D., Mathematics, 1854 to 1863.
Alexander Winchell, M. A., Physics and Civil Engineering, 1854 to 1855.
Rev. Charles Fox, M. A., Theoretical and Practical Agriculture, 1854.
Francis Brunnow, Ph. D., Astronomy and Director of the Observatory, 1854 to 1858.
Rev. Erastus Otis Haven, D. D., LL. D., History and English Literature, 1854 to 1856.
Henry Simmons Frieze, M. A., Latin Language and Literature, 1854.
Silas Hamilton Douglass, M. A., M. D., Chemistry and Mineralogy, 1855.
Alexander Winchell, M. A., Geology, Zoology, and Botany, 1855.
William G. Peck, M A., Physics and Civil and Mining Engineering, 1855 to 1857.
William P. Trowbridge, M. A., Mathamatics, 1856 to 1857.
Andrew Dickson White, M. A., History and English Literature, 1857.
Francis Brunnow, Ph. D., Director of the Observatory, 1859 to 1860.
Devolson Wood, M. A., Physics and Civil Engineering, 1859 to 1860.
James Craig Watson, M. A., Astronomy, 1859 to 1860.
Devolson Wood, M. A., Civil Engineering, 1860.
James Craig Watson, M. A., Physics, 1860 to 1863.
Francis Brunnow, Ph. D., Astronomy and Director of the Observatory, 1860 to 1863.
Thomas McIntyre Cooley, Constitutional Law, 1861.
Edward Payson Evans, Ph. D., Modern Languages and Literature, 1863.
Rev. Erastus Otis Haven, D. D., LL. D., Rhetoric and English Literature, 1863.

Rev. Lucius Delison Chapin, M. A., Moral and Intellectual Philosophy, 1863.
James Craig Watson, M. A., Astronomy and Director of the Observatory, 1863.
Rev. George Palmer Williams, LL. D., Physics, 1863.
Edward Olney, M. A., Mathematics, 1863.

Assistant Professors.

Datus Chase Brooks, M. A., Rhetoric and English Literature, 1857 to 1863.
John Emery Clark, M. A., Mathematics, 1857 to 1859.
Alfred Du Bois, M. A., Chemistry, 1857 to 1863.
Devolson Wood, M. A., Civil Engineering, 1857 to 1859.

Instructors.

Jonathan Beach, 1843 to 1845.
Silas Hamilton Douglass, M. A., M. D., Chemistry, 1844 to 1846.
Burrett A. Smith, B. A., 1845 to 1847.
Alfred Du Bois, M. A., Chemistry, 1855 to 1857.
Datus Chase Brooks, M. A., Rhetoric and English Literature, 1856 to 1857.
James Craig Watson, M. A., Assistant in the Observatory, 1857 to 1859.
Adam Knight Spence, M. A., Greek, 1858 to 1859.
Fitch Reed Williams, B. A., Latin, 1858 to 1860.
James Craig Watson, M. A., Mathematics, 1859 to 1860.
Adam Knight Spence, M. A., Greek and French, 1859 to 1860.
Cleveland Abbe, B. A., Physics and Civil Engineering, 1859 to 1860.
Adam Knight Spence, M. A., Greek, Latin, and French, 1860 to 1863.
Preston B. Rose, Chemistry, 1861 to 1863.
Charles Kendall Adams, M. A., History, 1862 to 1863.
William H. Bruckner, Chemistry, 1862 to 1863.
Edward Payson Evans, Ph. D., Modern Languages and Literature, 1862 to 1863.
Adam Knight Spence, M. A., Greek and French, 1863.
Charles Kendall Adams, M. A., History and Latin, 1863.
Albert Benjamin Prescott, M. D., Chemistry, 1863.
Henry Sylvester Cheever, B. A., Chemistry, 1863.
Dexter Valverd Dean, Chemistry, 1863.
Allen Jeremiah Curtis, M. A., Rhetoric and Mathematics, 1863.
Elmore Horton Wells, B. S., Civil Engineering, 1864.

II.—Department of Medicine and Surgery.

Professors.

Silas Hamilton Douglass, M. A., M. D., Materia Medica, Pharmacy, and Med. Jurisprudence, 1848 to 1850.

Abram Sager, M. A., M. D., Theory and Practice of Medicine, 1848 to 1850.

Moses Gunn, M. A., M. D., Anatomy, 1848 to 1850.

Abram Sager, M. A., M. D., Obstetrics and Diseases of Women and Children, 1850 to 1854.

Moses Gunn, M. A., M. D., Anatomy and Surgery, 1850 to 1852.

Samuel Denton, M. D., Theory and Practice of Medicine and Pathology, 1850 to 1860.

Silas Hamilton Douglass, M. A., M. D., Chemistry, Pharmacy, and Medical Jurisprudence, 1850.

Jonathan Adams Allen, M. A., M. D., Therapeutics, Materia Medica, and Physiology, 1850 to 1854.

Zina Pitcher, M. D., (Emeritus,) Institutes of Medicine and Obstetrics, 1851.

Moses Gunn, M. A., M. D., Surgery, and Lecturer on Anatomy, 1852 to 1854.

Alonzo Benjamin Palmer, M. A. M. D., Anatomy, 1852 to 1854.

Abram Sager, M. A., M. D., Obstetrics and Physiology, 1854 to 1860.

Moses Gunn, M. A., M. D., Surgery, 1854.

Alonzo Benjamin Palmer, M. A., M. D., Materia Medica, Therapeutics, and Diseases of Women and Children, 1854 to 1860.

Corydon La Ford, M. A., M. D., Anatomy, 1854 to 1869.

Edmund Andrews, M. A., M. D., Comparative Anatomy, 1854 to 1855.

Alfred Dubois, M. A., (Assistant Professor,) Chemistry, 1857 to 1863.

Abram Sager, M. A., M. D., Obstetrics, and Diseases of Women and Children, 1860.

Alonzo Benjamin Palmer, M. A., M. D., Pathology, and Practice of Medicine and Materia Medica, 1860 to 1861.

Corydon La Ford, M. A., M. D., Anatomy and Physiology, 1860.
Thomas McIntyre Cooley, Medical Jurisprudence, 1860.
Alonzo Benjamin Palmer, M. A., M D., Pathology, and Practice of Medicine, 1861.
Samuel Glasgow Armor, M. D., Institutes of Medicine and Materia Medica, 1861.

Instructors.

Edmund Andrews, M. A., M. D., Demonstrator, and Assistant Lecturer on Anatomy, 1851 to 1854.
Edmund Andrews, M. A., M. D., Demonstrator of Anatomy, 1854 to 1855.
Charles P. Tanner, M. D., Demonstrator of Anatomy, 1855 to 1857.
Alfred Dubois, M. A., Assistant to the Prefessor of Chemistry, 1865 to 1857.
Albert Miller Helmer, M. D., Demonstrator of Anatomy, 1857 to 1858.
William Lewitt, M. D., Demonstrator of Anatomy, 1858.
Preston B. Rose, M. D., Assistant in Chemistry, 1861.
William H. Bruckner, Assistant in Chemistry, 1862 to 1863.
Albert Benjamin Prescott, M. D., Assistant in Chemistry, 1863.
Henry Sylvester Cheever, B. A., Assistant in Chemistry, 1863.
Dexter Valverd Dean, Assistant in Chemistry, 1863.

III. Department of Law.

Professors.

James Valentine Campbell, M. A., Marshall Professor of Law, 1859.
Charles Irish Walker, Kent Professor of Law, 1859.
Mharles McIntyre Cooley, Jay Professor of Law, 1859.

TRUSTEES OF MICHIGAN COLLEGES IN 1870.

Adrian College.—Trustees, L. G. Berry, Adrian; J. S. Thrap, Adrian; W. S. Wilcox, Adrian; John Redman, Pittsburg, Pa.; C. Springer, Zanesville, Ohio; James Mayall, Princeton, Illinois; T. J. Finch, Springfield, Ohio; John Fordyce, Cambridge, Ohio; R. R. Beecher, Adrian, President; John J. Gillispie, Pittsburg, Pa., Treasurer; Peter Low, Adrian; R. Rose, Jeffersonville, Ohio; G. B. McElroy, Secretary.

Albion College.—Trustees, B. F. Coeker, Ann Arbor; David Preston, Detroit; S. W. Walker, Detroit; Jacob Anderson, Albion; A. M. Fitch, Albion, Treasurer; J. S. Smart, Adrian; M. A. Daugherty, Albion; William Bort, Niles; James W. Sheldon, Albion, President; Seth Reed, Romeo; William H. Brockway, Albion; Orlando C. Gale, Albion; J. L. G. McKown, Albion, President *ex-officio*.

Hillsdale College.—Trustees, Horace Blackmar, Hillsdale; John Corey, Fayette; George T. Day, D. D., Dover, N. H.; Ransom Dunn, Hillsdale; Samuel B. Philbrick, Chester, Ohio; Lawrens B. Potter, Lansing; Henry E. Whipple, Hillsdale; Samuel D. Bates, Marion, O.; Ebenezer O. Grosvenor, Hillsdale; David H. Lord, M. D., Hillsdale; Chauncy Reynolds, Hillsdale; S. F. Smith, Berlin, Wisconsin; Nicholas Vineyard, Hillsdale; Henry Waldron, Hillsdale; Jeremiah Baldwin, Hillsdale; Daniel M. Graham, D. D., Chicago; Frederick Fowler, Reading; Spencer J. Fowler, Hillsdale; James Calder, D. D., Hillsdale; Charles B. Mills, Vassar; Linus S. Parmalee, Reading; Daniel Beebee, Hillsdale; Henry J. King, Hillsdale; Charles T. Mitchell, Hillsdale; William Calder, Harrisburg, Pa.; David L. Rice, Hillsdale; Lewis J. Thompson, Hillsdale; J. W. Winsor, Hillsdale; Oscar E. Baker, Wilton, Indiana; John P. Cook, Hillsdale; Daniel Dunakin, Homer; Frederick M. Holloway, Fayette; Caleb C. Johnson, Hillsdale; Leonard Olney, Hillsdale; and Daniel L. Pratt, Hillsdale.

Kalamazoo College.—Trustees, Kendall Brooks, D. D., President; H. L. Wayland, D. D., Secretary; Caleb Van Husan, Treasurer; T. L. R. Jones; E. B. Smith; F. W. Wilcox; B. P. Russell; Caleb Eldred, Jr.; F. S. Hamilton; N. S. Burton; D. D.; L. D. Palmer; E. G. Huntington; John Antisdell; A. Owen; L. H. Trowbridge; Isaac W. Lamb; D. L. Latourette; Martin Wilson; Caleb Ives; A. E. Mather; H. L. Morehouse; Geo. Ingersoll; S. Cornelius, D. D.; Silas Bailey; J. S. Boyden, H. Stanwood; Charles Cooper; Latham Hall; S. Haskell; D. Putnam; H. C. Briggs; E. Curtiss; G. S. Chase; and E. J. Fish.

Olivet College.—Trustees: Nathan J. Morrison, D. D., President; Henry Bates, Canton, Ill; James S. Hoyt, Port Huron; Calvin Clark, Marshall; Newell Avery, Detroit; Herbert A. Reed, Marshall; J. L. Patton, Greeneville; Oramel Hosford, Olivet;

Samuel F. Drury, Olivet; Thomas Jones, Augusta; Philo R. Hurd, Romeo; James B. Porter, Lansing; Serens W. Streeter, Union City; O. Hitchcock, Kalamazoo; Fitz. L. Reed, Olivet; Philo Parsons, Detroit; Albertus L. Greene, Olivet; Addison Ballard, D. D., Detroit; Willard Davis, Vermontville; Franklin Moore, Detroit; William Hogarth, D. D, Detroit; Wolcott B. Williams, Charlotte; Jesse W. Hough, Jackson; Latham Hull, Kalamazoo; M. S. Sweet, Grand Rapids.

Hope College.—As a notice of this institution was omitted in its proper place, a summary of its history and condition is submitted as follows: It is located in Holland City, Ottawa County; is under the control of the Reformed (Dutch) Church, and was incorporated in 1866. It was established as an Academy about the year 1850, by Rev. A. C. Van Raalte, the founder of the Holland Colony. Its grounds are sixteen acres in extent, and its buildings, though comfortable, are temporary in their character.

At the close of 1869, it had an endowment fund of about $50,000, and the work of increasing this was in progress. At present the Board of Education of the Reformed Church also furni hes the chief part of the sum needed for the salaries of the professors, and expends about $1,000 per annum for the support of candidates for the ministry. A similar board of the Hollandish churches contributes about $3,000 per annum for the support of students under its care.

The Departments already organized are three, viz: Preparatory, Academic, and Theological. In the Preparatory Department or Grammer school, are four classes, which, in November, 1869, contained 72 pupils. The Academic Department has the customary classes, Freshmen, Sophomore, Junior, and Senior, which embraced in November, 1869, 25 students. The first class received the degree of A. B., in 1866, and of A. M. in 1869; and from this Department have been sent four classes, numbering together twenty-two graduates, of whom seventeen are either in the ministry or preparing for it. The Theological Department ushered its first class, a class of seven, into the ministry in June, 1869. It had in November last nine members, distributed into Junior, Middle, and Senior classes. Thus the whole number of students for the year 1869–'70, was 106. From the college printing house is issued a weekly religious newspaper in the Hollandish language. The following persons comprise the faculty of the institution:

Albertus C. Van Raalte, D. D., Professor of Evangelistic Theology.

Philip Phelps, D. D., Professor of Exegetical Theology, and of Mental and Moral Philosophy.

Cornelius E. Crispell, D. D., Professor of Didactic and Polemic Theology, and of Mathematics and Natural Philosophy.

Peter J. Oggel, A. M, Lector in Sacred Rhetoric and Pastoral Theology, and Professor of Sacred Literature.

T. Romeyn Beck, A. M., Lector in Biblical Criticism and Philology, and Professor of Latin and Greek.

Charles Scott, A. M., Lector in Ecclesiastical History and Government, and Professor of Natural History and Chemistry.

Cornelius Doesberg, Tutor in Modern Languages. William A. Shields, A. M., Tutor.

The General Synod of the Reformed Church in America, is the ultimate Board of Trustees exercising its trust, at first through its Board of Education alone, but since the incorporation of the College principally by means of a Board of Superintendents, whose corporate title is The Council of Hope College. The following is the list of its officers:

Albertus C. Van Raalte, D. D., Holland, Mich., President.

John S. Joralmon, Fairview, Ill., Vice President.

Abel T. Stewart, Holland, Mich., Secretary.

Peter J. Oggel, Holland, Mich., Treasurer.

John L. See, D. D., New Brunswick, N. J., Corresponding Secretary of the Board of Education.

Philip Phelps, D. D., Holland, Mich., President of the College.

In the past the great effort of the friends of this Institution has been to build up its Theological Department, but it is proposed to form new departments as soon as practicable, and measures have been taken to add a Primary and a Female Department at an early day.

State Board of Agriculture.—Hezekiah G. Wells, of Kalamazoo, President; David Carpenter, of Blissfield; Abraham C. Prutzman, Three Rivers; S. O. Knapp, Jackson; Oramel Hosford, Olivet; J. Webster Chiles, Ypsilanti. His Excellency H. P. Baldwin and T. C. Abbott, President of the College, *ex-officio;* Sanford Howard, Secretary; Joseph Mills, Lansing.

BOOKS CONNECTED WITH THE TERRITORY AND STATE OF MICHIGAN.

Agassiz, Louis.—Lake Superior, Its Physical Character. Boston, 1850.

American State Papers.—Volumes on Indian Affairs and Public Lands. Washington, 1832.

Andrews, Israel D.—Colonial and Lake Trade. Washington, 1852.

Baraga, Frederick.—The Ottawa Prayer Book. Detriot, 1842.

Bishop, Levi.—Teuchsa Grondie, a Poem. Albany, 1870.

Blois, J. T.—Gazeteer of Michigan. Detroit, 1840.

Bryant, William C.—Letters of a Traveller. New York, 1851.

Burt, W. A., and Hubbard B.—Geography of the South Shore of Lake Superior. Detroit, 1846.

Carver, Jonathan.—Travels Through North America in 1766–8. London, 1779. A mutilated copy of this work was published in New York a few years ago as Travels in Wisconsin.

Charlevoix, Father.—Travels Through Canada. London, 1763.

Clark, Charles F.—Michigan State Gazeteer. Detroit, 1863.

Colton, George H.—Tecumseh; or the West Thirty Years Since. New York, 1842.

Cooley, Thomas M.—Digest of Michigan Reports. Detroit, ——.

Cooper, J. Fennimore.—Oak Openings; a novel, the scene of which is laid in Kalamazoo County, Michigan. New York, 1848.

Copway, George.—Traditional History of the Ojibway Nation. Boston, 1851.

Darby, William.—A Tour from New York to Detroit. New York, 1819.

Dejean.—The Missionary; A Vocabulary of French and Ottawa Words. Detroit, 1830.

Disturnell, John.—The Great Lakes and their Commerce. New York, 1863.

Drake, Benjamin.—Life of Tecumseh and his Brother, the Prophet. Cincinnati, 1841.

Farmer, John.—Michigan and Ouisconsin Territories. New York, 1830.

Farmer, J. W.—Map of Southern Michigan; also, Sectional Map of Wisconsin and Michigan. New York, 1856.

Ferris, J.—States and Territories of the Great West. New York, 1856.

Flint, Henry M.—The Railroads of the United States. Philadelphia, 1868.

Foster, J. W.—The Physical Geography of the Mississippi Valley. Chicago, 1869.

Fuller, Margaret S.—Summer on the Lakes. Boston, 1856.

Hennepin, Louis—Travels in Canada, Paris, ——.

Henry, Alexander.—Travels and Adventures in Canada. London, 1809.

Historical Society of Michigan. Discourses by Lewis Cass, Henry R. Schoolcraft, Henry Whiting, and John Biddle. Detroit 1834.

Hoffman, Charles Fenno.—A Winter in the West, 2 vols. New York, 1835.

Jameson, Anna.—Winter Studies and Summer Rambles, 3 vols. London, 1838.

Kane, Paul.—Wanderings of an Artist Among the Indians of North America. London, 1859.

Kirkland, Caroline M.—A New Home; Who'll Follow; Forest Life; and Western Clearings. New York, 1839, 1842, and 1846.

Kohl, J. G.—Kitchi Gami; Wanderings Around Lake Superior. London, 1860.

La Hontan, Baron.—Voyages to North America, 2 vols. London, 1703.

Lanman, Charles.—A Summer in the Wilderness. New York. 1847. Life of William Woodbridge. Washington, 1867. The Red Book of Michigan. Detroit, 1871.

Lanman, James H.—History of Michigan, Civil and Topographical. New York, 1839. Abridgement of the same. New York, 1843.

Lossing, Benson J.—Field Book of the War of 1812. New York, 1868.

Mac Afee, Robert B.—History of the Late War in the Western Country. Lexington, Kentucky, 1816.

McKenney, Thomas L.—Tour to the Lakes. Baltimore, 1827.

Noble, Louis Le Grand.—Miscellaneous Poems. Philadelphia and New York, 1842 and 1857.

Parkman. Francis.—Conspiracy of Pontiac. Boston, 1851. Jesuits in North America. Boston, 1867.

Roberts, Robert E.—Sketches of the City of Detroit. Detroit, 1855.

Rogers, Robert.—Journal of an Expedition to Detroit. London, ——.

Roosevelt, Robert B.—Superior Fishing. New York, 1865.

Schooley, Augustus C—Among the Wolverines. Chicago, 1869.

Schoolcraft, Henry R.—Journal of Travels Through the American Lakes to the Sources of the Mississippi River. Albany, 1821. The Rise of the West, and other poems. Detroit, 1827. Algic Researches, 2 vols. New York, 1839. Personal Memoirs from 1812 to 1842. Philadelphia, 1851. Life and Character of Lewis Cass. Albany, 1848. See also Miscellaneous Discourses and Lectures on the Minerals, Indians, and History of Michigan.

Shearman, Francis W.—System of Public Instruction and the Primary School Laws of Michigan. Lansing, 1852.

Sheldon, E. M.—Early History of Michigan. New York, 1830.

St. John, J. R.—Lake Superior Country and the Copper Mines. New York, 1826.

Strickland, W. P.—Old Mackinaw. Philadelphia, 1853.

Tanner, H. S.—Map of Michigan and Wisconsin. Philadelphia, 1846.

Tour of the American Lakes. Anonymous. London, 1833.

Van Fleet, J. A.—Old and New Mackinac. Ann Arbor, 1870.

Wheelock, Julia S.—The Boys in White. New York, 1870. Appended to this work is a Poem by U. J. Baxter.

Whitney, George L.—Historical and Scientific Sketches of Michigan. Detroit, 1834.

Winchell, Alexander—Reports on the Geology of Michigan, and also on the Grand Traverse Region. Lansing, 1870.

Young, William T., Life of Lewis Cass, Philadelphia, 1853.

Zeisberger, David—His Life and Times as a Western Pioneer and Apostle of the Indians. Philadelphia, 1870.

To the above should be added the long list of documents, published by authority of the State, bearing on all its natural and industrial resources, which are not only numerous, but of great value.

NEWSPAPERS OF MICHIGAN, WITH THEIR PUBLISHERS, IN 1870.

Also, the character of the papers, and in what year established.

Adrian Times and Expositor, daily and weekly, Applegate & Fee, 1838.
Adrian Journal, weekly, J. Cross, 1867.
Adrian Michigan Teacher, monthly, Payne, Whitney, & Co., 1865.
Albion Mirror, weekly, L. W. Cole, 1856.
Albion Recorder, weekly, Reed & Bissell, 1868.
Allegan Democrat, weekly, Oscar Hare, 1867.
Allegan Journal, weekly, D. C. Henderson, 1856.
Allegan Star, monthly, W. W. Vosburg, 1867.
Alpena Pioneer, weekly, A. C. Tefft, 1863.
Ann Arbor Democrat, weekly, H. E. H. Bower, 1868.
Ann Arbor Michigan Argus, weekly, E. B. Pond, 1845.
Ann Arbor Peninsula Courier, weekly, R. A. Beal, 1861.
Ann Arbor Chronicle, bi-weekly, University Students, 1869.
Battle Creek Advent Review, weekly, Adventist's Publishing Company, 1850.
Battle Creek Journal, weekly, George Willard & Co., 1851.
Battle Creek Youth's Instructor, semi-monthly, G. H. Bell, 1852.
Battle Creek Health Reformer, monthly, W. C. Gauge, 1866.
Battle Creek Real Estate Reporter, monthly, A. Hitchcock & Co., 1868.
Bay City Journal, weekly, Wilson & Bryce, 1864.
Bay City Saginaw Valley News, weekly, Republican Association, 1870.
Bay City Signal, weekly, Kennedy & Worden, 1864.
Benton Harbor Palladium, weekly, J P. Thresher, 1868.
Big Rapids Pioneer, weekly, Charles, Gay & Co., 1862.
Bronson Herald, weekly, T. M. & C. C. Babcock, 1867.
Buchanan Advent Christian Times, weekly, Publishing Association, 1864.
Buchanan Record, weekly, D. A. Wagner, 1857.
Buchanan Christian Proclamation, monthly, D. A. Wagner, 1868.
Buchanan Advent, quarterly, W. L. Himes, 1869.
Burr Oak Democrat, weekly, E. B. Dewey, 1869.
Caro Tuscola Advertiser, weekly, H. G. Chapin, 1868.
Cassopolis National Democrat, weekly, C. C. Allison, 1850.
Cedar Springs, Wolverine Clipper, weekly, Maze & Sellers, 1869.
Centerville Republican, weekly, H. Egabroad & Co., 1869.
Charlevoix Sentinel, weekly, W. A Smith, 1869.
Charlotte Argus, weekly, J. V. Johnson & Co., 1855.

Charlotte Republican, weekly, Saunders & Trash, 1853.
Chesaning Banner, weekly, Publishing Company, 1869.
Clinton Standard, weekly, D. B. Sherwood, 1870.
Coldwater Republican, weekly, Bowen, Dunham & Moore, 1866.
Coldwater Sentinel, weekly, F. V. Smith, 1864.
Constantine Mercury, weekly, L. F. Hull, 1845
Corunna Shiawassee American, weekly, John N. Ingersoll, 1855.
Decatur Republican, weekly, E. A. Blackman, 1867.
Detroit Abend Post, daily and weekly, Augustus Marxhausen, 1867.
Detroit Advertiser and Tribune, daily, tri-weekly, and weekly, Advertiser and Tribune Company, 1829.
Detroit Free Press, daily, tri-weekly, and weekly, Free Press Company, 1832.
Detroit Michigan Journal, daily, C. Marxhausen, 1855.
Detroit, Michigan Volksblatt, daily and weekly, M. Cramer & Co., 1853.
Detroit Post, daily, tri-weekly, and weekly, Daily Post Company, 1866.
Detroit Union, daily and weekly, Union Printing Company, 1865.
Detroit Anti-Roman Advocate, weekly, Mederic Lanctot, 1870.
Detroit Commercial Advertiser, weekly, W. H. Burk, 1861.
Detroit Journal of Commerce, weekly, J. T. Gradwell, 1865.
Detroit, Michigan Farmer, weekly, Johnstone & Gibbons, 1869.
Detroit, Peninsular Herald, weekly, Temperance Association, 1863.
Detroit American Observer, monthly, Edwin A. Lodge, 1864.
Detroit Mechanic and Inventor, monthly, Publishing Association, 1867.
Detroit, Review of Medicine and Pharmacy, monthly, G. P. Andrews, 1866.
Dexter Leader, weekly, A. McMillan, 1869.
Dowagiac Republican, weekly, Henry C. Buffington, 1857.
East Saginaw Courier, weekly, S. S. Pomeroy, 1858.
East Saginaw Enterprise, daily and weekly, publisher not known to Compiler, 1855.
Eaton Rapids Journal, weekly, Frank C. Culley, 1865.
Elk Rapids, Traverse Bay Eagle, weekly, Sprague & Spencer, 1864.
Escanawba Tribune, weekly, E. P. Lott, 1869.
Fenton Gazette, weekly, W. H. H. Smith, 1865.
Fentonville Independent, weekly, H. N. Jennings, 1868.
Fentonville Christian Home, quarterly, O. E. Fuller, 1869.
Flint, Genesee Democrat, weekly, Jenny & Fellows, 1848.
Flint Globe, weekly, A. L. Aldrich, 1866.
Flint, Wolverine Citizen, weekly, F. H. Rankin, 1850.
Grand Haven Herald, weekly, Henry S. Chubb, 1869.
Grand Haven News, weekly, John H. Mitchell, 1859.
Grand Haven Union, weekly, L. M. S. Smith, 1861.
Grand Ledge Independent, weekly, B. F. Saunders, 1870.
Grand Rapids Democrat, daily and weekly, M. H. Clark & Co., 1862.
Grand Rapids Eagle, daily and weekly, A. B. Turner & Co., 1844.
Grand Rapids Sun, daily, R. A. Marvin & Co, 1869.
Grand Rapids Industrial Journal, weekly, Labor Union Publishing Company, 1867.
Grand Rapids Vrijheid's Banier, weekly, Verberg & Co., 1868.
Grass Lake Reporter, weekly, Andrew Allison, 1867.
Greenville Independent, weekly, E. F. Grabill, 1854.
Hart Oceana Journal, weekly, J. Palmeter, 1869.
Hastings Banner, weekly, George M. Dewey, 1854.
Hastings Home Journal, weekly, Gibson Brothers, 1868.
Hillsdale Democrat, weekly, Wm. H. Tallman, 1859.
Hillsdale Standard, weekly, H. B. Rowlson, 1846.
Holland De Hollander, weekly, W. Benjaminse, 1850.
Holland De Hope, weekly, Hope College, 1866.
Holland, Der Wachter, semi-monthly, C. Vorst, 1866.
Holly Register, weekly, Henry Jenkins, 1865.
Houghton Portage Lake Gazette, weekly, H. McKenzie, 1859.
Howell Livingston Democrat, weekly, Jos. T. Titus, 1857.
Howell Livingston Republican, weekly, J. D. Smith & Co., 1855.
Hudson Gazette, weekly, Wm. T. B. Schermerhorn, 1858.
Hudson Post, weekly, C. W. Stevens, 1862.
Ionia Sentinel, weekly, Taylor & Stevenson, 1866.
Ithaca Gratiot Journal, weekly, Daniel Taylor, 1866.
Ithaca School Journal, monthly, Daniel Taylor, 1868.

Jackson Citizen, daily and weekly, O'Donnell, Hilton, & Smith, 1849.
Jackson Patriot weekly, Carlton and Van Antwerp, 1844.
Jonesville Independent, weekly, James I. Dennis, 1848.
Kalamazoo Telegraph, daily and weekly, Telegraph Company, 1868.
Kalamazoo Gazette, weekly, Joseph Lomax, 1862.
Kalamazoo Present Age, weekly, Spiritual Publishing Company, 1868.
Kalamazoo Bill Poster, monthly, McCarthy & Whipple, 1869.
Kalamazoo Freemason, monthly, Chapin & Rix, 1869.
Lansing State Democrat, weekly, J. W. Higgs, 1866.
Lansing State Republican, weekly, W. S. George & Co., 1855.
Lapeer Clarion, weekly, S. J. Tomlinson, 1857.
Lawton Tribune, weekly, J. H. Wickwire, 1869.
Leslie Herald, weekly, Jas. H. Ford & Co., 1869.
Lexington Sanilac Jeffersonian, weekly, Nims & Beach, 1853.
Lowell Journal, weekly, Morris & Smith, 1865.
Luddington Record, weekly, Geo. W. Clayton, 1867.
Manchester Enterprise, weekly, M. D. Blosser, 1867.
Manistee Times, weekly, S. W. Fowler, 1865.
Manistee Tribune, weekly, John E. Rostall, 1864.
Marquette Mining Journal, weekly, A. P. Swineford, 1868.
Marquette Plain Dealer, weekly, J. C. Buchanan, 1867.
Marshall Expounder, weekly, Chastain Mann, 1836.
Marshall Statesman, weekly, Burgess & Lewis, 1839.
Mason News, weekly, K. Kittredge, 1859.
Menominee Herald, weekly, A. R. Bradbury, 1863.
Midland City Cheek, weekly, W. H. H. Bartram, 1869.
Monroe Commercial, weekly, D. H. Hamilton, 1840.
Monroe Monitor, weekly, E. G. Morton, 1862.
Mount Clemens Press, weekly, John Trevidick, 1864.
Mount Clemens Monitor, weekly, W. T. and C. H. Lee, 1863.
Mount Pleasant Enterprise, weekly, I. A. Fancher, 1864.
Muskegon Chronicle, weekly, Geo. C. Rice, 1869.
Muskegon Enterprise, weekly, I. Ransom Sanford, 1869.
Muskegon News and Reporter, weekly, F. Weller, 1868.
Newaygo Republican, weekly, E. O. Shaw, 1856.
Niles Democrat, weekly, A. J. Shakespear, 1839.
Niles Republican, weekly, L. A. Duncan, 1866.
North Lansing Enterprise, weekly, Willis F. Cornell, 1868.
Northville Record, semi-monthly, Samuel H. Little, 1869.
Ontonagon Miner, weekly, Thomas J. Lasier, 1855.
Otsego Record, weekly, H. E. J. Clute, 1869.
Ovid Register, weekly, J. W. Fitzgerald, 1866.
Owosso Press, weekly, J. H. Champion & Co., 1862.
Owosso Crusader, monthly, A. B Wood, Jr., 1870.
Parma Advertiser, monthly, James Hammell, 1869.
Paw-Paw Northerner, weekly, Thomas O. Ward, 1856.
Paw-Paw Press, weekly, J. W. Van Fossen, 1844.
Pentwater Times, weekly, Palmeter & Dresser, 1861.
Pontiac Gazette, weekly, Rann & Turner, 1844.
Pontiac Jacksonian, weekly, D. H. Solis, 1836.
Port Austin News, weekly, V. W. Richardson, 1861.
Port Huron Commercial, weekly, Talbot & Son, 1849.
Port Huron Press, weekly, Boynton & Young, 1858.
Port Huron Times, weekly, J. H. Stone, 1869.
Portland Advertiser, weekly, Joseph W. Bailey, 1867.
Quincy Times, weekly, Times Company, 1868.
Reading Review, weekly, R. W. Lockhart, ——.
Saginaw Republican, weekly, F. A. Palmer, 1858.
Saginaw Saginawian, weekly, George F. Lewis, 1869.
St. Clair Republican, weekly, Wands & Ross, 1857.
St. John's Independent, weekly, Corbet & Estes, 1866.
St. John's Republican, weekly, D. M. Phillips, 1854.
St. Joseph Herald, weekly, H. W. Guerensey, 1866.
St. Joseph Traveller, weekly, A. L. Aldrice, 1859.
St. Louis Gazette, weekly, H. E. Church, 1869.

St. Louis Advocate, monthly, A. D. Rust, 1869.
Laramie Standard, weekly, Spencer & Wilson, 1870.
Saugatuck Commercial, weekly, George Sherwood & Co., 1869.
Schoolcraft News, weekly, V. C. Smith, 1869.
Shepardsville Advance, weekly, Shepard & Brass, 1869.
South Haven Sentinel, weekly, William E. Stewart, 1867.
Spring Lake Independent, weekly, John Lee, 1869.
Stanton, Montcalm Herald, weekly, E. R. Powell, 1867.
Sturgis Journal, weekly, G. W. Wait, 1861.
Tawas City Gazette, weekly, Charles S. Helbourn, 1868.
✓ Tecumseh Herald, weekly, C. M. Burlingame, 1849.
Tecumseh Raisin Valley Record, weekly, Chapin & Page, 1866.
Three River's Reporter, weekly, W. H. Clute & Co., 1860.
Traverse City Herald, weekly, D. C. Leach, 1858.
Vassar Pioneer, weekly, Alexander Trotter, 1857.
Wenona Herald, weekly, James B. Teneyck, 1869.
Whitehall Forum, weekly, Benjamin Frank, 1869.
Ypsilanti Commercial, weekly, C. R. Pattison, 1864.

THE POST OFFICES OF MICHIGAN IN 1870.

Official and brought down to October 1, 1870; *those marked with a * are Money-Order Offices.*

Abscota, Calhoun
Acme, Grand Traverse
Ada, Kent
Adamsville, Cass
Addison, Lenawee
Adrian,* (*c. h.*) Lenawee
Ætna, Newaygo
Akron, Tuscola
Alabaster, Iosco
Alamo, Kalamazoo
Alaska, Kent
Albion,* Calhoun
Alcona, Alcona
Algansee, Branch
Algodon, Ionia
Algonac, St. Clair
Alice, Oceana
Allegan,* (*c. h.*) Allegan
Allen, Hillsdale
Allendale, Ottawa
Allens, Eaton
Alma, Gratiot
Almena, Van Buren
Almira, Benzie
Almont, Lepeer
Alpena,* (*c. h.*) Alpena
Alpine, Kent
Alto, Kent
Alton, Kent
Alverson, Ingham
Amadore, Sanilac
Amber, Mason
Amboy, Hillsdale
Amsden, Montcalm
Ann Arbor,* (*c. h.*) Washtenaw
Antrim City, Antrim
Arcadia, Manistee
Arenac, Bay
Argentine, Genesee
Arland, Jackson
Arlington, Van Buren
Armada, Macomb
Ashland, Newaygo
Ashley, Kent
Assyria, Barry
Athens, Calhoun
Athlone, Monroe
Atlas, Genesee
Atwood, Antrim
Au Gres, Bay
Augusta, Kalamazoo
Aurelius, Ingham
Au Sable, Iosco
Austerlitz, Kent
Austin, Oakland
Averill's Station, Midland
Avery, Berrien
Bad River, Gratiot
Bainbridge, Berrien
Baldwin's Mills, Jackson
Baltimore, Barry
Bangor, Van Buren
Baraga, Houghton
Barnard, Charlevoix
Barryville, Barry
Barton, Newaygo
Base Lake, Washtenaw
Batavia, Branch
Bates, Osceola
Bath, Clinton
Battle Creek,* Calhoun
Bay City,* (*c. h.*) Bay
Bear Lake, Manistee
Bear Lake Mills, Van Buren
Bear River, Emmett
Beaver Creek, Gratiot
Bedford, Calhoun
Belle River, St. Clair
Belleville, Wayne
Bellevue,* Eaton
Belmont, Kent
Bengal, Clinton
Bennington, Shiawassee
Benona, Oceana
Benton, Washtenaw
Benton Harbor,* Berrien
Benzonia, (*c. h.*) Benzie
Berlin, Ottawa
Berrien Centre, Berrien
*Berrien Springs** (*c. h.*) Berrien
Bertrand, Berrien
Berville, St. Clair
Bethel, Branch
Betsey Lake, Grand Traverse
Big Beaver, Oakland
Big Creek, Mecosta
Big Prairie, Newaygo
Big Rapids,* (*c. h.*) Mecosta
Big Spring, Ottawa
Birch Run, Saginaw
Birmingham, Oakland
Blackberry Ridge, Oceana
Black Lake, Muskegon
Blair, Barry
Blendon, Ottawa
Blissfield, Lenawee
Bloomer Centre, Montcalm
Bloomingdale, Van Buren
Blue Lake, Muskegon
Bluffton, Muskegon
Blumfield, Saginaw
Blumfield Junction, Saginaw
Bostwick Lake, Kent
Bowen's Mills, Barry
Bowne, Kent

Boyne, Charlevoix
Bradley, Allegan
Brady, Kalamazoo
Brandon, Oakland
Breedsville, Van Buren
Bridgeport Centre, Saginaw
Bridgeton, Newaygo
Bridgeville, Gratiot
Brighton, Livingston
Brockway, St. Clair
Brockway, Centre, St. Clair
Bronson's Prairie Branch
Brookfield, Eaton
Brooklyn,* Jackson
Brookside, Oceola
Brown's Mills, Muskegon
Brownstown, Wayne
Brownsville, Cass
Buchanan,* Berrien
Buel, Sanilac
Buena Vista, Saginaw
Bunker Hill, Ingham
Burch's, Kent
Burdickville, Leelenaw
Burlington, Calhoun
Burnip's Corners Allegan
Burns, Shiawassee
Burnside, Lapeer
Burr Oak,* St. Joseph
Bushnell Centre, Montcalm
Butler, Branch
Byron, Shiawassee
Byron Centre, Kent
Cady, Macomb
Caledonia, Kent
Caledonia Station, Kent
California, Branch
Calumet, Houghton
Calvin, Cass
Cambria Mills, Hillsdale
Cambridge, Lenawee
Camden, Hillsdale
Campbell, Ionia
Can, Huron
Canandaigua, Lenawee
Cannonsburgh, Kent
Canton, Wayne
Capac, St. Clair
Carleton, Muskegon
Carlisle, Eaton
Caro,* (*c. h.*) Tuscola
Carrollton, Saginaw
Carson City, Montcalm
Cascade, Kent
Casco, St. Clair
Caseville, Huron
Casnovia, Kent
Cass, Hillsdale
Cass Bridge, Saginaw
Cass City, Tuscola
Cassopolis,* (*c. h.*) Cass
Cato, Montcalm
Cedar Creek, Barry
Cedar Dale, Sanilac
Cedar Fork, Menomonee

Cedar Run, Grand Traverse
Cedar Springs, Kent
Central Lake, Antrim
Centre, Eaton
Centreville, (*c. h.*) St. Joseph
Ceresco, Calhoun
Charlevoix, (*c. h.*) Charlevoix
*Charlotte** (*c. h.*) Eaton
Cheboygan, (*c. h.*) Cheboygan
Chelsea, Washtenaw
Cheasaning, Saginaw
Cheshire, Allegan
Chester, Eaton
Chickaming, Berrien
China, St. Clair
Chippewa Lake, Mecosta
Church's Corners, Hillsdale
Clarence, Calhoun
Clarendon Centre, Calhoun
Clarksburgh, Marquette
Clarkston, Oakland
Clay Bank, Oceana
Clay Hill, Wexford
Clayton, Lenawee
Clear Water, Antrim
Clifford, Lapeer
Climax Prairie, Kalamazoo
Clinton, Lenawee
Clio, Genesee
Clyde Mills, St. Clair
Cob Moo Sa, Oceana
Cody's Mills, Kent
Cohoctah, Livingston
Cold Water,* (*c. h.*) Branch
Colfax, Mason
Coloma, Berrien
Colon, St. Joseph
Columbia, Jackson
Columbiaville, Lapeer
Columbus, St. Clair
Commerce, Oakland
Comstock, Kalamazoo
Concord, Jackson
Conner's Creek, Wayne
Constantine, St. Joseph
Convis Centre, Calhoun
Cook's Station, Newaygo
Cooper, Kalamazoo
Coopersville, Ottawa
Copper Falls Mine, Keweenaw
Copper Harbor, Keweenaw
Coral, Montcalm
Cortland Centre, Kent
Corunna,* (*c. h.*) Shiawassee
County Line, Eaton
Covert, Van Buren
Cracow, Huron
Crapo, Osceola
Crawford, Isabella
Creswell, Antrim
Croton,* Newaygo
Crystal, Montcalm
Dallas, Clinton
Dalton's Corners, Wayne

Danby, Ionia
Dansville, Ingham
Davisburgh, Oakland
Davison, Genesee
Davisville, Sanilac
Dayton, Berrien
Dearbornville, Wayne
Decatur, Van Buren
Deckerville, Sanilac
Deer Creek, Livingston
Deerfield, Lenawee
Delroy, Wayne
Delta, Eaton
Denmark, Tuscola
Dennison, Ottawa
Denton, Wayne
Denver, Newaygo
Detour, Chippewa
Detroit,* (*c h.*) Wayne
De Witt, Clinton
Dexter, Washtenaw
Disco, Macomb
Dorr, Allegan
Douglas, Allegan
Dowagiac,* Cass
Drayton Plains, Oakland
Dryden, Lapeer
Dundee, Monroe
Dunningville, Allegan
Du Plain, Clinton
Eagle, Clinton
Eagle Harbor, Keweenaw
Eagle River, (*c h.*) Keweenaw
East Dayton, Tuscola
East Gilead, Branch
East Leroy, Calhoun
Eastmansville, Ottawa
East Milan, Monroe
Easton, Ionia
East Saginaw,* Saginaw
East Tawas, Iosco
East Traverse Bay, Gr. Traverse
Eaton Rapids, Eaton
Eau Claire, Berrien
Ecorse, Wayne
Eden, Ingham
Edenville, Midland
Edgerton, Kent
Edinburgh, Hillsdale
Edwardsburgh, Cass
Elgin, Genesee
Elk, Saginaw
Elklake, Lapeer
Elkland, Tuscola
Elk Rapids, (*c. h.*) Antrim
Ellington, Tuscola
Elm, Wayne
Elm Hall, Gratiot
Elmira, Eaton
Elsie, Clinton
Emmett, St. Clair
Empire, Leelenaw
Englishville, Kent
Ensley, Newaygo

Erie, Monroe
Esconawba,* (*c. h.*) Delta
Essex, Clinton
Eureka Clinton
Evart, Osceola
Exeter, Monroe
Fairfield, Lenawee
Fair Grove, Tuscola
Fair Haven, St. Clair
Fairview, Mason
Fallasburgh, Kent
Farmers, Sanilac
Farmer's Creek, Lapeer
Farmington, Oakland
Fawn River, St. Joseph
Fayette, Delta
Felt's Ingham
Fenn's Mill's, Allegan
Fentonville,* Genesee
Ferris, Montcalm
Ferrysburgh, Ottawa
Filer City, Manistee
Fillmore, Barry
Fitchburgh, Ingham
Five Lakes, Lapeer
Fleming, Livingston
Flint,* (*c. h.*) Genesee
Florence, St. Joseph
Flower Creek, Oceana
Flowerfield, St. Joseph
Flushing, Genesee
Forest City, Muskegon
Forest Hill, Gratiot
Forestville, Sanilac
Fork, Mecosta
Forrester, Sanilac
Fort Gratiot, St. Clair
Four Towns, Oakland
Fowlerville, Livingston
Franciscoville, Jackson
Frankenlust, Saginaw
Frankenmuth, Saginaw
Frankfort, Benzie
Franklin, Oakland
Fraser, Macomb
Fredonia, Washtenaw
Fremont, Shiawassee
Fremont Centre, Newaygo
Frontier, Hillsdale
Fruitport, Muskegon
Fulton, Kalamazoo
Gagetown, Tuscola
Gaines' Station, Genesee
Gainesville, Kent
Galesburgh,* Kalamazoo
Galien, Berrien
Ganges, Allegan
Garden, Delta
Geary, Clinton
Genesee Village, Genesee
Geneva, Lenawee
Genoa, Livingston
Georgetown, Ottawa
Gibralta, Wayne
Gilead, Branch
Gilford, Tuscola
Girard, Branch
Glass River, Shiawassee
Glen Arbor, Leelenaw
Glendale, Van Buren
Glen Haven, Leleenaw
Golding, Oceana
Good Harbor, Leelenaw
Goodland, Lapeer
Goodrich, Genesee
Graafschap, Allegan
Grafton, Monroe
Grand Blanc, Genesee
Grand Haven,* (*c. h.*) Ottawa
Grand Ledge, Eaton
Grand Rapids,* (*c. h.*) Kent
Grandville, Kent
Grant, Kent
Grass Lake,* Jackson
Grattan, Kent
Gravel Run, Washtenaw
Greenbush, Alcona
Greenfield, Wayne
Greenland, Ontonagon
Green Oak, Livingston
Greenville,* Montcalm
Greenwood Furnace, Marquette
Groveland, Oakland
Gull Lake, Barry
Gun Marsh, Allegan
Hadley, Lapeer
Hamburgh, Livingston
Hamilton, Allegan
Hamlin, Monroe
Hammond, Kent
Hancock, Houghton
Hanley, Ottawa
Hanover, Jackson
Hansen, Oceana
Harris Creek, Kent
Harrisville, (*c. h.*) Alcona
Hart,* (*c. h.*) Oceana
Hartford, Van Buren
Hartland, Livingston
Hartwellville, Shiawassee
Harvey, Marquette
Harwood, Muskegon
Hasler, Lapeer
Hastings,* (*c. h.*) Barry
Hazelton, Shiawassee
Hazelgreen, Shiawassee
Hemlock City, Saginaw
Henrietta, Jackson
Hersey, (*c. h.*) Osceola
Hesperia, Oceana
Hickory Corners, Barry
Highland, Oakland
Hilliard's, Allegan
Hillsdale,* (*c. h.*) Hillsdale
Holland,* Ottawa
Holly,* Oakland
Holt, Ingham
Home, Newaygo
Homer, Calhoun
Homestead, Benzie
Hooker, Van Buren
Hopkins Allegan
Hopkins Station, Allegan
Houghton,* (*c. h.*) Houghton
Howard, Muskegon
Howard City, Montcalm
Howardsville, St. Joseph
Howell, (*c. h.*) Livingston
Hubbardston, Ionia
Hudson,* Lenawee
Hughesville, Saginaw
Humboldt, Marquette
Hunter's Creek, Lapeer
Huron City, Huron
Huron Station, Wayne
Ida, Monroe
Imlay, Lapeer
Indian Creek, Kent
Indian Town, Mason
Inkster, Wayne
Inland, Benzie
Ionia,* (*c. h.*) Ionia
Irving, Barry
Isabella City, Isabella
Ishpeming, Marquette
Ithaca,* (*c. h.*) Gratiot
Jackson,* (*c. h.*) Jackson
Jamestown, Ottawa
Jay, Saginaw
Jeddo, St. Clair
Jefferson, Hillsdale
Jeffersonville, Cass
Jersey, Oakland
Johnston, Barry
Jonesville,* Hillsdale
Josco, Livingston
Joyfield, Benzie
Kalamazoo,* (*c. h.*) Kalamazoo
Kalamo, Eaton
Kawkawlin, Bay
Keelersville, Van Buren
Keene, Ionia
Kelloggsville, Kent
Kelly's Corners, Lenawee
Kendall, Van Buren
Kenockee, St. Clair
Kensington, Oakland
Kiddville, Ionia
Kinderhook, Branch
Kipp's Corners, Genesee
La Fayette, Gratiot
La Grange, Cass
Lainsburgh, Shiawassee
Lake Linden, Houghton
Lake Mill, Van Buren
Lake Port, St. Clair
Lake Ridge, Lenawee
Laketon, Berrien
Lakeview, Montcalm
Lakeville, Oakland
Lambertville, Monroe
Lamont, Ottawa
Lamotte, Sanilac

L'Ance, Houghton
Langston, Montcalm
LANSING,* Ingham
Lapeer (*c. h*) Lapeer
La Salle, Monroe
Lawrence,* Van Buren
Lawton,* Van Buren
Leland, Leelenaw
Leoni, Jackson
Leonidas, St. Joseph
Leslie, Ingham
Lexington,* (*c. h.*) Sanilac
Liberty, Jackson
Lima, Washtenaw
Lincoln, (*c. h.*) Mason
Linden, Genesee
Lisbon, Ottawa
Litchfield,* Hillsdale
Little Prairie Ronde, Cass
Little Traverse, (*c. h.*) Emmett
Locke, Ingham
London, Monroe
Lowell, Kent
Ludington,* Mason
Lynn, St. Clair
Lyons,* Ionia
Lyon's Mill, Clinton
Mackinaw,* (*c. h*) Mackinac
Macomb, Macomb
Macon, Lenawee
Madison, Livingston
Mahopac, Oakland
Manchester, Washtenaw
Manistee,* (*c. h.*) Manistee
Manlius, Allegan
Maple, Ionia
Maple Grove, Barry
Maple Hill, Montcalm
Maple Rapids, Clinton
Mapleton, Grand Traverse
Marathon, Lapeer
Marcellus, Cass
Marengo, Calhoun
Marine City,* St. Clair
Marion, Livingston
Marlette, Sanilac
Marquette,* (*c. h.*) Marquette
Marshall,* (*c. h.*) Calhoun
Marshville, Oceana
Martin, Allegan
Martinsville, Wayne
Marysville, St. Clair
Mason,* (*c. h.*) Ingraham
Matherton, Ionia
Mattawan, Van Buren
Mattison, Branch
May, Tuscola
Mayfield, Grand Traverse
Meade, Macomb
Mead's Mills, Wayne
Meadville, Barry
Mecosta, Mecosta
Medina, Lenawee
Melville, Leelenaw
Memphis,* Macomb
Mendon, St. Joseph
Menomonee,* (*c. h.*) Menomonee
Merrillsville, St. Clair
Metamora, Lapeer
Micham, Leelenaw
Michigan Centre, Jackson
Middletown, Ingham
Middleville,* Barry
Midland,* (*c. h.*) Midland
Milan, Washtenaw
Mile Creek, Muskegon
Milford,* Oakland
Millbrook, Mecosta
Millburgh, Berrien
Mill Creek, Kent
Millington, Tuscola
Milo, Barry
Milton, Macomb
Minden, Sanilac
Mitchell, Antrim
Model City, Cass
Moline, Allegan
Monroe,* (*c. h.*) Monroe
Monroe Centre, Gr. Traverse
Montague,* Muskegon
Monterey, Allegan
Montrose, Genesee
Morenci, Lenawee
Morgan, Marquette
Morganville, Hillsdale
Morley, Mecosta
Moscow, Hillsdale
Mosherville, Hillsdale
Mottville, St. Joseph
Mount Clemens,* (*c. h.*) Macomb
Mount Morris Station, Genesee
Mount Pleasant,* (*c. h.*) Isabella
Mount Vernon, Macomb
Mud Creek, Eaton
Muir, Ionia
Mundy, Genesee
Mungerville, Shiawassee
Munising, Schoolcraft
*Muskegon** (*c. h.*) Muskegon
Nahma, Delta
Nankin, Wayne
Napoleon, Jackson
Nashville,* Barry
Negaunee, Marquette
Nelson, Kent
Nelsonville, Charlevoix
Newark, Gratiot
Newaygo,* (*c. h.*) Newaygo
New Baltimore, Macomb
New Boston, Wayne
New Buffalo,* Berrien
Newburgh, Cass
Newbury, Tuscola
New Casco, Allegan
New Haven, Macomb
New Haven Centre, Gratiot
New Home, Montcalm
New Hudson, Oakland
Newport, Monroe
New River, Huron
New Salem, Allegan
Newton, Calhoun
New Troy, Berrien
Niles,* Berrien
Noble Centre, Branch
North Adams, Hillsdale
North Aurelius, Ingham
North Branch, Lapeer
North Byron, Kent
North Eagle, Clinton
North Farmington, Oakland
North Irving, Barry
North Newberg, Shiawassee
North Plains, Ionia
Northport,* (*c. h.*) Leelenaw
North Raisinville, Monroe
North Star, Gratiot
North Unity, Leelenaw
North Vernon, Shiawassee
Northville, Wayne
Norvell, Jackson
Norwalk, Manistee
Norwood, Charlevoix
Novi, Oakland
Nunico, Ottawa
Oak, Wayne
Oakfield, Kent
Oak Grove, Livingston
Oak Hill, Oakland
Oakland, Oakland
Oakley, Saginaw
Oakville, Monroe
Oakwood, Oakland
Ogden Centre, Lenawee
Oceola Centre, Livingston
Ogemaw, Iosco
Ohio Mill, Ottawa
Okemos, Ingham
Old Mission, Grand Traverse
Olive, Clinton
Olivet,* Eaton
Omena, Leelenaw
Onondaga, Ingham
Onota, Schoolcraft
Ontonagon (*c. h.*) Ontonagon
Oporto, St. Joseph
Ora Labor, Huron
Orange, Ionia
Orangeville, Branch
Orangeville Mills, Barry
Orion, Oakland
Orleans, Ionia
Ortonville, Oakland
Oshtemo, Kalamazoo
Osseo, Hillsdale
Ossineke, Alpena
Otisco, Ionia
Otisville, Genesee
Otsego, Allegan
Ottawa Lake, Monroe
Otter Creek, Jackson

Overisel, Allegan
Ovid,* Clinton
Owosso,* Shiawassee
Oxford, Oakland
Pack's Mills, Sanilac
Paint Creek, Washtenaw
Palmyra, Lenawee
Palo, Ionia
Pa-Pa-Me, Oceana
Paris, Mecosta
Park, St. Joseph
Parkville, St. Joseph
Parma,* Jackson
Parshallville, Livingston
Partello, Calhoun
Patterson's Mills, Ionia
Pavilion, Kalamazoo
Paw Paw,* (*c. h.*) Van Buren
Peck, Sanilac
Penn Mine, Keweenaw
Pent Water, Oceana
Perrinsville, Wayne
Perry, Shiawassee
Petersburgh, Monroe
Pettysville, Livingston
Pewamo, Ionia
Phoenix, Keweenaw
Pierson, Montcalm
Pinckney, Livingston
Pine Creek, Calhoun
Pine Grove, Tuscola
Pine Grove Mills, Van Buren
Pine Hill, Sanilac
Pine River, Lake
Pine Run, Genesee
Pinnebog, Huron
Pipestone, Berrien
Pittsburg, Shiawassee
Pittsford, Hillsdale
Plainfield, Livingston
Plainwell, Allegan
Plank Road, Wayne
Platte, Benzie
Pleasant, Kent
Pleasanton, Manistee
Pleasant Valley, Berrien
Plymouth, Wayne
Pokagon, Cass
Pompei, Gratiot
Ponama, Newaygo
Pontiac,* (*c. h.*) Oakland
Pool, Lapeer
Portage, Kalamazoo
Port Austin, (*c. h.*) Huron
Port Cresent, Huron
Porter, Midland
Port Hope, Huron
Port Huron,* St. Clair
Portland, Ionia
Port Sanilac, Sanilac
Port Sheldon, Ottawa
Portsmouth, Bay
Pottamie, Ottawa
Pottersville, Eaton
Prairieville, Barry
Prospect Lake, Van Buren
Pulaski, Jackson
Quincy,* Branch
Quinn, Macomb
Raisin Centre, Lenawee
Randall, Saginaw
Ransom, Hillsdale
Ravenna, Muskegon
Rawsonville, Wayne
Ray Centre, Macomb
Raynold, Montcalm
Reading, Hillsdale
Red Bridge, Ingham
Redford, Wayne
Reed, Oceana
Richfield, Genesee
Richland, Kalamazoo
Richmond, Macomb
Richmondville, Sanilac
Richville, Tuscola
Ridgeway, Lenawee
Rienza, Mecosta
Riga, Lenawee
Riley, Clinton
Riley Centre, St. Clair
River Raisin, Washtenaw
Riverton, Mason
Rives Junction, Jackson
Roberts' Landing, St. Clair
Robinson, Ottawa
Rochester, Oakland
Rock Falls, Huron
Rockford,* Kent
Bockland, Ontonagon
Rollin, Lenawee
Rollo, Iosco
Rome, Lenawee
Romeo,* Macomb
Romulus, Wayne
Rootville, Antrim
Rose, Oakland
Roseville, Macomb
Round Lake, Branch
Rowland, Isabella
Roxana, Eaton
Royal Oak, Oakland
Ruby, St. Clair
Rural Vale, Lapeer
Saginaw,* (*c. h.*) Saginaw
Saint Charles, Saginaw
Saint Clair,* (*c. h.*) St Clair
Saint James,* (*c. h.*) Manitou
Saint John's,* (*c. h.*) Clinton
Saint Joseph,* Berrien
Saint Louis, Gratiot
Salem, Washtenaw
Saline, Washtenaw
Salt River, Isabella
Salzburgh, Bay
Sand Beach, Huron
Sand Lake, Kent
Sandstone, Jackson
Saranac, Ionia
Satterlee's Mills, Mecosta
Saugatuck,* Allegan
Saute de Ste. Marie, (*c. h.*) Chippewa
Sawyer, Berrien
Schoolcraft, Kalamazoo
Scio, Washtenaw
Sebewa, Ionia
Sebewaing, Huron
Secillia, Calhoun
Seneca, Lenawee
Shave Head, Cass
Shelby, Oceana
Shepardsville, Clinton
Sheridan, Montcalm
Sherman, (*c. h.*) Wexford
Sherwood, Branch
Sidney, Montcalm
Silver Creek, Allegan
Sitka, Newaygo
Six Corners, Ottawa
Skinner, Bay
Slocum's Grove, Muskegon
Smith's Corners, Oceana
Smith's Creek, St. Clair
Smithville, Wayne
Smyrna. Ionia
Sodus, Berrien
Solon, Leelenaw
Somerset, Hillsdale
South Boston, Ionia
South Butler, Branch
South Camden, Hillsdale
South Cass, Ionia
South Climax, Kalamazoo
Southfield, Oakland
South Georgetown, Ottawa
South Haven, Van Buren
South Jackson, Jackson
South Lyon, Oakland
South Riley, Clinton
South Saginaw, Saginaw
South Wright, Hillsdale
Sparta Centre, Kent
Spencer Creek, Antrim
Spencer's Mill, Kent
Spring Arbor, Jackson
Spring Brook, Gratiot
Spring Creek, Oceana
Springfield, Oakland
Spring Lake, Ottawa
Spring Mills, Oakland
Springport, Jackson
Springville, Lenawee
Stanton, (*c. h.*) Montcalm
Stebbinsville, Oceana
Stella, Gratiot
Stockbridge, Ingham
Stony Creek, Washtenaw
Stony Run, Oakland
Strait's, Lake, Oakland
Strickland, Isabella
Stronach, Manistee
Sturgis,* St. Joseph
Summerton, Gratiot
Summerville, Cass
Summit, Washtenaw

Sumner, Gratiot
Sunfield, Eaton
Sutton's Bay, Leelenaw
Swan Creek, Saginaw
Swartz Creek, Genesee
Sylvan, Washtenaw
Tallmadge, Ottawa
Tamarack, Montcalm
Tawas City,* (*c h.*) Iosco
Taylor Centre, Wayne
Taymouth, Saginaw
Tecumseh,* Lenawee
Tekonsha, Calhoun
Thetford Centre, Genesee
Thomas, Oceana
Thornton, St. Clair
Thornville, Lapeer
Three Oaks,* Berrien
Three Rivers,* St. Joseph
Tipton, Lenawee
Tompkins, Jackson
Torch Lake, Antrim
Traverse City,* (*c. h.*) Grand Traverse
Trent, Muskegon
Trenton, Wayne
Trostville, Saginaw
Troy, Oakland
Turnersport, Manistee
Tyre, Sanilac
Tyrone, Livingston
Unadilla, Livingston
Union, Cass
Union City, Branch
Union Pier, Berrien
Unionville, Tuscola
Utica,* Macomb
Vandalia, Cass
Vassar,* (*c. h.*) Tuscola
Ventura, Ottawa
Vergennes, Kent
Vermontville, Eaton
Vernon, Shiawassee
Verona Mills, Huron
Vickeryville, Montcalm
Victor, Clinton
Victory, Mason
Vincent, St. Clair
Volinia, Cass
Vriesland, Ottawa
Wacousta, Clinton
Wahjamega, Tuscola
Wakeshma, Kalamazoo
Waldenburgh, Macomb
Wales, St. Clair
Wallaceville, Wayne
Walled Lake, Oakland
Warren, Macomb
Washington, Macomb
Waterford, Oakland
Waterloo, Jackson
Watertown, Tuscola
Watervliet, Berrien
Watrousville, Tuscola
Watson, Allegan
Waverly, Van Buren
Wayland,* Allegan
Wayne, Wayne
Weare, Oceana
Webberville, Ingham
Webster, Washtenaw
Weesaw, Berrien
Wellsville, Lenawee
Wenona, Bay
West Campbell, Ionia
West Casco, Allegan
West Geneva, Van Buren
West Haven, Shiawassee
West Leroy, Calhoun
West Milan, Monroe
West Novi, Oakland
West Ogden, Lenawee
Weston, Lenawee
Westphalia, Clinton
West Windsor, Eaton
Wexford, Wexford
Wheatland Centre, Hillsdale
Wheeler, Gratiot
Whiteford Centre, Monroe
Whitehall, Musketon
White Lake, Oakland
White Oak, Ingham
White Pigeon, St. Joseph
White Rock, Muskegon
Whitesburgh, Genesee
Whitmore Lake, Washtenaw
Williams, Bay
Williamsburgh, Grand Traverse
Williamstown, Ingham
Williamsville, Cass
Windsor, Eaton
Winfield, Ingham
Winn, Isabella
Wiota, Isabella
Wood Lake, Montcalm
Woodland, Barry
Wood's Corners, Ionia
Woodstock, Lenawee
Worth, Tuscula
Wyandotte, Wayne
Yankee Spring, Barry
Yew, Wayne
York, Washtenaw
Yorkville, Kalamazoo
Ypsilanti,* Washtenaw
Yuba, Grand Traverse
Zeeland, Ottawa
Zilwaukee, Saginaw

CONSTITUTION OF THE STATE OF MICHIGAN.

ARTICLE I.

BOUNDARIES.

The State of Michigan consists of, and has jurisdiction over, the territory embraced within the following boundaries, to wit: Commencing at a point on the eastern boundary line of the State of Indiana, where a direct line drawn from the southern extremity of Lake Michigan to the most northerly cape of the Maumee Bay shall intersect the same—said point being the north-west corner of the State of Ohio, as established by act of Congress, entitled "An act to establish the northern boundary line of the State of Ohio, and to provide for the admission of the State of Michigan into the Union upon the conditions therein expressed," approved June fifteenth, one thousand eight hundred and thirty-six; thence with the said boundary line of the State of Ohio till it intersects the boundary line between the United States and Canada in Lake Erie; thence with said boundary line between the United States and Canada through the Detroit river, Lake Huron and Lake Superior to a point where the said line last touches Lake Superior; thence in a direct line through Lake Superior to the mouth of the Montreal river; thence through the middle of the main channel of the said river Montreal to the head waters thereof; thence in a direct line to the center of the channel between Middle and South Islands, in the Lake of the Desert; thence in a direct line to the southern shore of Lake Brule; thence along said southern shore, and down the river Brule to the main channel of the Menomonee river; thence down the center of the main channel of the same to the center of the most usual ship channel of the Green Bay of Lake Michigan; thence through the center of the most usual ship channel of the said bay to the middle of Lake Michigan; thence through the middle of Lake Michigan to the northern boundary of the State of Indiana, as that line was established by the act of Congress of the nineteenth of April, eighteen hundred and sixteen; thence due east with the northern boundary line of the said State of Indiana to the north-east corner thereof; and thence south with the eastern boundary line of Indiana to the place of beginning.

ARTICLE II.

SEAT OF GOVERNMENT.

Section 1. The seat of government shall be at Lansing, where it is now established.

ARTICLE III.

DIVISION OF THE POWERS OF GOVERNMENT.

Section 1. The powers of government are divided into three departments: the legislative, executive, and judicial.

Sec. 2. No person belonging to one department shall exercise the powers properly belonging to another, except in the cases expressly provided in this constitution.

ARTICLE IV.

LEGISLATIVE DEPARTMENT.

Section 1. The legislative power is vested in a Senate and House of Representatives.

Sec. 2. The Senate shall consist of thirty-two members. Senators shall be elected for two years, and by single districts. Such districts shall be numbered from one to thirty-two inclusive; each of which shall choose one senator. No county shall be divided in the formation of senate districts, except such county shall be equitably entitled to two or more senators.

Sec. 3. The House of Representatives shall consist of not less than sixty-four, nor more than one hundred members. Representatives shall be chosen for two years, and by single districts. Each representative district shall contain, as nearly as may be, an equal number of white inhabitants, and civilized persons of Indian descent, not members of any tribe, and shall consist of convenient and contiguous territory. But no township or city shall be divided in the formation of a representative district. When any township or city shall contain a population which entitles it to more than one representative, then such township or city shall elect, by general ticket, the number of representatives to which it is entitled. Each county hereafter organized, with such territory as may be attached thereto, shall be entitled to a separate representative when it has attained a population equal to a moiety of the ratio of representation. In every county entitled to more than one representative, the board of supervisors shall assemble at such time and place as the legislature shall prescribe, and divide the same into representative districts, equal to the number of representatives to which such county is entitled by law, and shall cause to be filed in the offices of the secretary of state and clerk of such county, a description of such representative districts, specifying the number of each district, and the population thereof, according to the last preceding enumeration.

Sec. 4. The legislature shall provide by law for an enumeration of the inhabitants in the year eighteen hundred and fifty-four, and every ten years thereafter, and at the first session after each enumeration so made, and also at the first session after each enumeration by the authority of the United States, the legislature shall re-arrange the senate districts, and apportion anew the representatives among the counties and districts, according to the number of white inhabitants, and civilized persons of Indian descent, not members of any tribe. Each apportionment and the division into representative districts, by any board of supervisors, shall remain unaltered until the return of another enumeration.

Sec. 5. Senators and representatives shall be citizens of the United States, and qualified electors in the respective counties and districts which they represent. A removal from their respective counties or districts shall be deemed a vacation of their office.

Sec. 6. No person holding any office under the United States [or this State,] or any county office, except notaries public, officers of the militia, and officers elected by townships, shall be eligible to or have a seat in either house of the legislature; and all votes given for any such person shall be void.

Sec. 7. Senators and representatives shall, in all cases, except treason, felony, or breach of the peace, be privileged from arrest. They shall not be subject to any civil process during the session of the legislature, or for fifteen days next before the commencement and after the termination of each session. They shall not be questioned in any other place for any speech in either house.

Sec. 8. A majority of each house shall constitute a quorum to do business; but a smaller number may adjourn from day to day, and compel the attendance of absent members, in such manner and under such penalties as each house may prescribe.

Sec. 9. Each house shall choose its own officers, determine the rules of its proceedings, and judge of the qualifications, elections, and returns of its members; and may, with the concurrence of two-thirds of all the members elected, expel a member. No member shall be expelled a second time for the same cause, nor for any cause known to his constituents antecedent to his election. The reason for such expulsion shall be entered upon the journal, with the names of the members voting on the question.

Sec. 10. Each house shall keep a journal of its proceedings, and publish the same, except such parts as may require secrecy. The yeas and nays of the members of either house, on any question, shall be entered on the journal at the request of one-fifth of the members elected. Any member of either house may dissent from and protest against any act, proceeding, or resolution which he may deem injurious to any person or the public, and have the reason of his dissent entered on the journal.

Sec. 11. In all elections by either house, or in joint convention, the votes shall be given *viva voce*. All votes on nominations to the senate shall be taken by yeas and nays, and published with the journal of its proceedings.

Sec. 12. The doors of each house shall be open, unless the public welfare require secrecy. Neither house shall, without the consent of the other, adjourn for more than three days, nor to any other place than where the legislature may then be in session.

Sec. 13. Bills may originate in either house of the legislature.

Sec. 14. Every bill and concurrent resolution, except of adjournment, passed by the legislature, shall be presented to the governor before it becomes a law. If he approve, he shall sign it; but if not, he shall return it, with his objections, to the house in which it originated, which shall enter the objections at large upon their journal, and reconsider it. On such reconsideration, if two-thirds of the members elected agree to pass the bill, it shall be sent, with the objections, to the other house, by which it shall be reconsidered. If approved by two-thirds of the members elected to that house, it shall become a law. In such case, the vote of both houses shall be determined by yeas and nays, and the names of the members voting for and against the bill shall be entered on the journals of each house respectively. If any bill be not returned by the governor within ten days, Sundays excepted, after it has been presented to him, the same shall become a law, in like manner as if he had signed it, unless the legislature, by their adjournment, prevent its return, in which case it shall not become a law. The governor may approve, sign, and file in the office of the secretary of State, within five days after the adjournment of the legislature, any act passed during the last five days of the session; and the same shall become a law.

Sec. 15. The compensation for the members of the legislature shall be three dollars a day for actual attendance, and when absent on account of sickness, for the first sixty days of the session of the year one thousand eight hundred and fifty-one, and for the first forty days of every subsequent session, and nothing thereafter. When convened in extra session, their compensation shall be three dollars a day for the first twenty days, and nothing thereafter; and they shall legislate on no other subjects than those expressly stated in the governor's proclamation, or submitted to them by special message. They shall be entitled to ten cents, and no more, for every mile actually travelled, going to and returning from the place of meeting, on the usually travelled route; and for stationery and newspapers, not exceeding five dollars for each member during any session. Each member shall be entitled to one copy of the laws, journals, and documents of the legislature of which he was a member, but shall not receive, at the expense of the State, books, newspapers, or other perquisites of office not expressly authorized by this constitution.

Sec. 16. The legislature may provide by law for the payment of postage on all mailable matter received by its members and officers during the sessions of the legislature, but not on any sent or mailed by them.

Sec. 17. The President of the Senate and the Speaker of the House of Representatives shall be entitled to the same per diem compensation and mileage as members of the legislature, and no more.

Sec. 18. No person elected a member of the legislature shall receive any civil appointment within this State, or to the Senate of the United States, from the governor, the governor and senate, from the legislature, or any other State authority, during the term for which he is elected. All such appointments, and all votes given for any person so elected for any such office or appointment, shall be void. No member of the legislature shall be interested, directly or indirectly, in any contract with the State, or any county thereof, authorized by any law passed during the time for which he is elected, nor for one year thereafter.

Sec. 19. Every bill and joint resolution shall be read three times in each house before the final passage thereof. No bill or joint resolution shall become a law without the concurrence of a majority of all the members elected to each house. On the final passage of all bills the vote shall be by yeas and nays, and entered on the journal.

Sec. 20. No law shall embrace more than one object, which shall be expressed in its title. No public acts shall take effect or be in force until the expiration of ninety days from the end of the session at which the same is passed, unless the legislature shall otherwise direct, by a two-thirds vote of the members elected to each house.

Sec. 21. The legislature shall not grant nor authorize extra compensation to any public officer, agent, or contractor, after the service has been rendered or the contract entered into.

Sec. 22. The legislature shall provide by law that the furnishing of fuel and stationery for the use of the State, the printing and binding the laws and journals, all blanks, paper and printing for the executive departments, and all other printing ordered by the legislature, shall be let by contract to the lowest bidder or bidders, who shall give adequate and satisfactory security for the performance thereof. The legislature shall prescribe by law the manner in which the State printing shall be executed, and the accounts rendered therefor, and shall prohibit all charges for constructive labor. They shall not rescind nor alter such contract, nor release the person or persons taking the same, or his or their sureties, from the performance of any of the conditions of the contract. No member of the legislature nor officer of the State shall be interested, directly or indirectly, in any such contract.

Sec. 23. The legislature shall not authorize, by private or special law, the sale or conveyance of any real estate belonging to any person, nor vacate nor alter any road laid out by commissioners of highways, or any street in any city or village, or in any recorded town plat.

Sec. 24. The legislature may authorize the employment of a chaplain for the State prison; but no money shall be appropriated for the payment of any religious services in either house of the legislature.

Sec. 25. No law shall be revised, altered, or amended by reference to its title only; but the act revised, and the section or sections of the act altered or amended, shall be re-enacted and published at length.

Sec. 26. Divorces shall not be granted by the legislature.

Sec. 27. The legislature shall not authorize any lottery, nor permit the sale of lottery tickets.

Sec. 28. No new bill shall be introduced into either house during the last three days of the session without the unanimous consent of the house in which it originates.

Sec. 29. In case of a contested election, the person only shall receive from the State per diem compensation and mileage, who is declared to be entitled to a seat by the house in which the contest takes place.

Sec. 30. No collector, holder, nor disburser of public moneys, shall have a seat in the legislature, or be eligible to any office of trust or profit under this State, until he shall have accounted for and paid over, as provided by law, all sums for which he may be liable.

Sec. 31. The legislature shall not audit nor allow any private claim or account.

Sec. 32. The legislature, on the day of final adjournment, shall adjourn at twelve o'clock at noon.

Sec. 33. The legislature shall meet at the seat of government on the first Wednesday in February next, and on the first Wednesday in January of every second year thereafter, and at no other place or time, unless as provided in this constitution.

Sec. 34. The election of senators and representatives, pursuant to the provisions of this constitution, shall be held on the Tuesday succeeding the first Monday of November, in the year one thousand eight hundred and fifty-two, and on the Tuesday succeeding the first Monday of November of every second year thereafter.

Sec. 35. The legislature shall not establish a State paper. Every newspaper in the State which shall publish all the general laws of any session within forty days of their passage, shall be entitled to receive a sum not exceeding fifteen dollars therefor.

Sec. 36. The legislature shall provide for the speedy publication of all statute laws of a public nature, and of such judicial decisions as it may deem expedient. All laws and judicial decisions shall be free for publication by any person.

Sec. 37. The legislature may declare the cases in which any office shall be deemed vacant, and also the manner of filling the vacancy, where no provision is made for that purpose in this constitution.

Sec. 38. The legislature may confer upon organized townships, incorporated cities and villages, and upon the board of supervisors of the several counties, such powers of a local, legislative, and administrative character as they may deem proper.

Sec. 39. The legislature shall pass no law to prevent any person from worshipping Almighty God according to the dictates of his own conscience, or to compel any person to attend, erect, or support, any place of religious worship, or to pay tithes, taxes, or other rates, for the support of any minister of the gospel or teacher of religion.

Sec. 40. No money shall be appropriated or drawn from the treasury for the benefit of any religious sect or society, theological or religious seminary, nor shall property belonging to the State be appropriated for any such purposes.

Sec. 41. The legislature shall not diminish or enlarge the civil or political rights, privileges, and capacities, of any person on account of his opinion or belief concerning matters of religion.

Sec. 42. No law shall ever be passed to restrain or abridge the liberty of speech or of the press; but every person may freely speak, write, and publish, his sentiments on all subjects, being responsible for the abuse of such right.

Sec. 43. The legislature shall pass no bill of attainder, *ex-post facto* law, or law impairing the obligation of contracts.

Sec. 44. The privilege of the writ of habeas corpus remains, and shall not be suspended by the legislature, except in case of rebellion or invasion the public safety require it.

Sec. 45. The assent of two-thirds of the members elected to each house of the legislature shall be requisite to every bill appropriating the public money or property, for local or private purposes.

Sec. 46. The legislature may authorize a trial by a jury of a less number than twelve men.

Sec. 47. The legislature shall not pass any act authorizing the grant of license for the sale of ardent spirits or other intoxicating liquors.

Sec. 48. The style of the laws shall be, "The people of the State of Michigan enact."

ARTICLE V.

EXECUTIVE DEPARTMENT.

Section 1. The executive power is vested in a governor, who shall hold his office for two years. A lieutenant governor shall be chosen for the same term.

Sec. 2. No person shall be eligible to the office of governor or lieutenant governor, who has not been five years a citizen of the United States, and a resident of this State two years next preceding his election; nor shall any person be eligible to either office who has not attained the age of thirty years.

Sec. 3. The governor and lieutenant governor shall be elected at the times and places of choosing the members of the legislature. The person having the highest number of votes for governor or lieutenant governor, shall be elected. In case two or more persons shall have an equal and the highest number of votes for governor or lieutenant governor, the legislature shall, by joint vote, choose one of such persons.

Sec. 4. The governor shall be commander-in-chief of the military and naval forces, and may call out such forces to execute the laws, to suppress insurrections, and to repel invasions.

Sec. 5. He shall transact all necessary business with officers of government, and may require information, in writing, from the officers of the executive department, upon any subject relating to the duties of their respective offices.

Sec. 6. He shall take care that the laws be faithfully executed.

Sec. 7. He may convene the legislature on extraordinary occasions.

Sec. 8. He shall give to the legislature, and at the close of his official term, to the next legislature, information by message of the condition of the State, and recommend such measures to them as he shall deem expedient.

Sec. 9. He may convene the legislature at some other place, when the seat of government becomes dangerous from disease or a common enemy.

Sec. 10. He shall issue writs of election to fill such vacancies as occur in the senate or house of representatives.

Sec. 11. He may grant reprieves, commutations, and pardons, after convictions, for all offenses except treason and cases of impeachment, upon such conditions, and with such restrictions and limitations, as he may think proper, subject to regulations provided by law, relative to the manner of applying for pardons. Upon conviction for treason, he may suspend the execution of the sentence, until the case shall be reported to the legislature at its next session, when the legislature shall either pardon, or commute the sentence, direct the execution of the sentence, or grant a further reprieve. He shall communicate to the legislature, at each session, information of each case of reprieve, commutation, or pardon granted, and the reasons therefor.

Sec. 12. In case of the impeachment of the governor, his removal from office, death, inability, resignation, or absence from the State, the powers and duties of the office shall devolve upon the lieutenant governor for the residue of the term, or until the disability ceases. When the governor shall be out of the State in time of war, at the head of a military force thereof, he shall continue commander-in-chief of all the military force of the State.

Sec. 13. During a vacancy in the office of governor, if the lieutenant governor die, resign, be impeached, displaced, be incapable of performing the duties of his office, or absent from the State, the president *pro tempore* of the senate shall act as governor, until the vacancy be filled, or the disability cease.

Sec. 14. The lieutenant governor shall, by virtue of his office, be president of the senate. In committee of the whole he may debate all questions; and when there is an equal division, he shall give the casting vote.

Sec. 15. No member of congress, nor any person holding office under the United States, or this State, shall execute the office of governor.

Sec. 16. No person elected governor or lieutenant governor, shall be eligible to any office or appointment from the legislature, or either house thereof, during the time for which he was elected. All votes for either of them, for any such office, shall be void.

Sec. 17. The lieutenant [governor,] and president of the senate *pro tempore,* when performing the duties of governor, shall receive the same compensation as the governor.

Sec. 18. All official acts of the governor, his approval of the laws excepted, shall be authenticated by the great seal of the State, which shall be kept by the secretary of State.

Sec. 19. All commissions issued to persons holding office under the provisions of this constitution, shall be in the name and by the authority of the people of the State of Michigan, sealed with the great seal of the State, signed by the governor, and countersigned by the secretary of State.

ARTICLE VI.

JUDICIAL DEPARTMENT.

Section 1. The judicial power is vested in one supreme court, in circuit courts, in probate courts, and in justices of the peace. Municipal courts of civil and criminal jurisdiction may be established by the legislature in cities.

Sec. 2. For the term of six years, and thereafter until the legislature otherwise provide, the judges of the several circuit courts shall be judges of the supreme court, four of whom shall constitute a quorum. A concurrence of three shall be necessary to a final decision. After six years, the legislature may provide by law for the organization of a supreme court, with the jurisdiction and powers prescribed in this constitution, to consist of one chief justice and three associate justices, to be chosen by the electors of the State. Such supreme court, when so organized, shall not be changed or discontinued by the legislature for eight years thereafter. The judges thereof shall be so classified that but one of them shall go out of office at the same time. Their term of office shall be eight years.

Sec. 3. The supreme court shall have a general superintending control over all inferior courts, and shall have power to issue writs of error, habeas corpus, mandamus, quo warranto, procedendo, and other original and remedial writs, and to hear and determine the same. In all other cases it shall have appellate jurisdiction only.

Sec. 4. Four terms of the supreme court shall be held annually, at such times and places as may be designated by law.

Sec. 5. The supreme court shall, by general rules, establish, modify, and amend the practice in such court and in the circuit courts, and simplify the same. The legislature shall, as far as practicable, abolish distinctions between law and equity proceedings. The office of master in chancery is prohibited.

Sec. 6. The State shall be divided into eight judicial circuits; in each of which the electors thereof shall elect one circuit judge, who shall hold his office for the term of six years, and until his successor is elected and qualified.

Sec. 7. The legislature may alter the limits of circuits, or increase the number of the same. No alteration or increase shall have the effect to remove a judge from office. In every additional circuit established, the judge shall be elected by the electors of such circuit, and his term of office shall continue, as provided in this constitution for judges of the circuit court.

Sec. 8. The circuit courts shall have original jurisdiction in all matters, civil and criminal, not excepted in this constitution, and not prohibited by law; and appellate jurisdiction from all inferior courts and tribunals, and a supervisory control of the same. They shall also have power to issue writs of habeas corpus, mandamus, injunction, quo warranto, certiorari, and other writs necessary to carry into effect their orders, judgments and decrees, and give them a general control over inferior courts and tribunals within their respective jurisdictions.

Sec. 9. Each of the judges of the circuit courts shall receive a salary payable quarterly. They shall be ineligible to any other than a judicial office during the term for which they are elected, and for one year thereafter. All votes for any person elected such judge for any office other than judicial, given either by the legislature or the people, shall be void.

Sec. 10. The supreme court may appoint a reporter of its decisions. The decisions of the supreme court shall be in writing, and signed by the judges concurring therein. Any judge dissenting therefrom, shall give the reasons of such dissent in writing, under his signature. All such opinions shall be filed in the office of the clerk of the supreme court. The judges of the circuit court, within their respective jurisdictions, may fill vacancies in the office of county clerk and of prosecuting attorney; but no judge of the supreme court, or circuit court, shall exercise any other power of appointment to public office.

Sec. 11. A circuit court shall be held at least twice each year in every county organized for judicial purposes, and four times in each year in counties containing ten thousand inhabitants. Judges of the circuit court may hold courts for each other, and shall do so when required by law.

Sec. 12. The clerk of each county organized for judicial purposes, shall be the clerk of the circuit court of such county, and of the supreme court when held within the same.

Sec. 13. In each of the counties organized for judicial purposes, there shall be a court of probate. The judge of such court shall be elected by the electors of the county in which he resides, and shall hold his office for four years, and until his successor is elected and qualified. The jurisdiction, powers and duties of such court shall be prescribed by law.

Sec. 14. When a vacancy occurs in the office of judge of the supreme, circuit, or probate court, it shall be filled by appointment of the governor, which shall continue until a successor is elected and qualified. When elected, such successor shall hold his office the residue of the unexpired term.

Sec. 15. The supreme court, the circuit and probate courts of each county, shall be courts of record, and shall each have a common seal.

Sec. 16. The legislature may provide by law for the election of one or more persons in each organized county, who may be vested with judicial powers, not exceeding those of a judge of the circuit court at chambers.

Sec. 17. There shall be not exceeding four justices of the peace in each organized township. They shall be elected by the electors of the townships, and shall hold their offices for four years, and until their successors are elected and qualified. At the first election in any township, they shall be classified as shall be prescribed by law. A justice elected to fill a vacancy shall hold his office for the residue of the unexpired term. The legislature may increase the number of justices in cities.

Sec. 18. In civil cases, justices of the peace shall have exclusive jurisdiction to the amount of one hundred dollars, and concurrent jurisdiction to the amount of three hundred dollars, which may be increased to five hundred dollars, with such exceptions and restrictions as may be provided by law. They shall also have such criminal jurisdiction, and perform such duties as shall be prescribed by the legislature.

Sec. 19. Judges of the supreme court, circuit judges, and justices of the peace, shall be conservators of the peace within their respective jurisdictions.

Sec. 20. The first election of judges of the circuit courts shall be held on the first Monday in April, one thousand eight hundred and fifty-one, and every sixth year thereafter. Whenever an additional circuit is created, provision shall be made to hold the subsequent election of such additional judges at the regular election herein provided.

Sec. 21. The first election of judges of the probate courts shall be held on the Tuesday succeeding the first Monday of November, one thousand eight hundred and fifty-two, and every fourth year thereafter.

Sec. 22. Whenever a judge shall remove beyond the limits of the jurisdiction for which he was elected, or a justice of the peace from the township in which he was elected, or by a change in the boundaries of such township shall be placed without the same, they shall be deemed to have vacated their respective offices.

Sec. 23. The legislature may establish courts of conciliation, with such powers and duties as shall be prescribed by law.

Sec. 24. Any suitor in any court of this State shall have the right to prosecute or defend his suit, either in his own proper person or by an attorney or agent of his choice.

Sec. 25. In all prosecutions for libels, the truth may be given in evidence to the jury; and if it shall appear to the jury that the matter charged as libelous is true, and was published with good motives and for justifiable ends, the party shall be acquitted. The jury shall have the right to determine the law and the fact.

Sec. 26. The person, houses, papers, and possessions of every person shall be secure from unreasonable searches and seizures. No warrant to search any place or to seize any person or things shall issue without describing them, nor without probable cause, supported by oath or affirmation.

Sec. 27. The right of trial by jury shall remain, but shall be deemed to be waived in all civil cases, unless demanded by one of the parties, in such manner as shall be prescribed by law.

Sec. 28. In every criminal prosecution the accused shall have the right to a speedy and public trial by an impartial jury, which may consist of less than twelve men in all courts not of record; to be informed of the nature of the accusation; to be confronted with the witnesses against him; to have compulsory process for obtaining witnesses in his favor, and have the assistance of counsel for his defense.

Sec. 29. No person, after acquittal upon the merits, shall be tried for the same offense; all persons shall, before conviction, be bailable by sufficient sureties, except for murder and treason, when the proof is evident or the presumption great.

Sec. 30. Treason against the State shall consist only in levying war against [it,] or in adhering to its enemies, giving them aid and comfort. No person shall be convicted of treason unless upon the testimony of two witnesses to the same overt act, or on confession in open court.

Sec. 31. Excessive bail shall not be required; excessive fines shall not be imposed; cruel or unusual punishment shall not be inflicted, nor shall witnesses be unreasonably detained.

Sec. 32. No person shall be compelled, in any criminal case, to be a witness against himself, nor be deprived of life, liberty, or property, without due process of law.

Sec. 33. No person shall be imprisoned for debt arising out of or founded on a contract, express or implied, except in cases of fraud or breach of trust, or of moneys collected by public officers, or in any professional employment. No person shall be imprisoned for a militia fine in time of peace.

Sec. 34. No person shall be rendered incompetent to be a witness on account of his opinions on matters of religious belief.

Sec. 35. The style of all process shall be: "In the name of the people of the State of Michigan."

ARTICLE VII.

ELECTIONS.

Section 1. In all elections every white male citizen, every white male inhabitant residing in the State on the twenty-fourth day of June, one thousand eight hundred and thirty-five; every white male inhabitant residing in this State on the first day of January, one thousand eight hundred and fifty, who has declared his intention to become a citizen of the United States, pursuant to the laws thereof, six months preceding an election, or who has resided in this State two years and six months, and declared his intention as aforesaid; and every civilized male inhabitant of Indian descent, a native of the United States, and not a member of any tribe, shall be an elector and entitled to vote; but no citizen or inhabitant shall be an elector, or entitled to vote at any election, unless he shall be above the age of twenty-one years, and has resided in this State three months, and in the township or ward in which he offers to vote, ten days next preceding such election.

Sec. 2. All votes shall be given by ballot, except for such township officers as may be authorized by law to be otherwise chosen.

Sec. 3. Every elector, in all cases except treason, felony, or breach of the peace, shall be privileged from arrest during his attendance at election, and going to and returning from the same.

Sec. 4. No elector shall be obliged to do military duty on the day of election, except in time of war or public danger, or attend court as a suitor or witness.

Sec. 5. No elector shall be deemed to have gained or lost a residence by reason of his being employed in the service of the United States, or of this State; nor while engaged in the navigation of the waters of this State or of the United States, or of the high seas; nor while a student of any seminary of learning; nor while kept at any alms-house or other asylum at public expense; nor while confined in any public prison.

Sec. 6. Laws may be passed to preserve the purity of elections, and guard against abuses of the elective franchise.

Sec. 7. No soldier, seaman, nor marine in the army or navy of the United States shall be deemed a resident of this State in consequence of being stationed in any military or naval place within the same.

Sec. 8. Any inhabitant who may hereafter be engaged in a duel, either as principal or accessory before the fact, shall be disqualified from holding any office under the constitution and laws of this State, and shall not be permitted to vote at any election.

ARTICLE VIII.

STATE OFFICERS.

Section 1. There shall be elected at each general biennial election a secretary of State, a superintendent of public instruction, a State treasurer, a commissioner of the land office, an auditor general, and an attorney general, for the term of two years. They shall keep their offices at the seat of government, and shall perform such duties as may be prescribed by law.

Sec. 2. Their term of office shall commence on the first day of January, one thousand eight hundred and fifty-three, and of every second year thereafter.

Sec. 3. Whenever a vacancy shall occur in any of the State offices, the governor shall fill the same by appointment, by and with the consent of the Senate, if in session.

Sec. 4. The secretary of State, State treasurer, and commissioner of the State land office shall constitute a board of State auditors, to examine and adjust all claims against the State not otherwise provided for by general law. They shall constitute a board of State canvassers to determine the result of all elections for governor, lieutenant governor, and State officers, and of such other officers as shall by law be referred to them.

Sec. 5. In case two or more persons have an equal and the highest number of votes for any office, as canvassed by the board of State canvassers, the legislature in joint convention shall choose one of such persons to fill such office. When the determination of the board of State canvassers is contested, the legislature in joint convention shall decide which person is elected.

ARTICLE IX.

SALARIES.

Section 1. The governor shall receive an annual salary of one thousand dollars; the judges of the circuit court shall each receive an annual salary of one thousand five hundred dollars; the State treasurer shall receive an annual salary of one thousand dollars; the auditor general shall receive an annual salary of one thousand dollars; the superintendent of public instruction shall receive an annual salary of one thousand dollars; the secretary of State shall receive an annual salary of eight hundred dollars; the commissioner of the land office shall receive an annual salary of eight hundred dollars; the attorney general shall receive an annual salary of eight hundred dollars. They shall receive no fees or perquisites whatever, for the performance of any duties connected with their offices. It shall not be competent for the legislature to increase the salaries herein provided.

ARTICLE X.

COUNTIES.

Section 1. Each organized county shall be a body corporate, with such powers and immunities as shall be established by law. All suits and proceedings by or against a county shall be in the name thereof.

Sec. 2. No organized county shall ever be reduced by the organization of new counties to less than sixteen townships, as surveyed by the United States, unless, in pursuance of law, a majority of electors residing in each county to be affected thereby shall so decide. The legislature may organize any city into a separate county, when it has attained a population of twenty thousand inhabitants, without reference to geographical extent, when a majority of the electors of a county in which such city may be situated, voting thereon, shall be in favor of a separate organization.

Sec. 3. In each organized county there shall be a sheriff, a county clerk, a county treasurer, a register of deeds, and a prosecuting attorney, chosen by the electors thereof, once in two years, and as often as vacancies shall happen, whose duties and powers shall be prescribed by law. The board of supervisors in any county may unite the offices of county clerk and register of deeds in one office, or disconnect the same.

Sec. 4. The sheriff, county clerk, county treasurer, judge of probate, and register of deeds, shall hold their offices at the county seat.

Sec. 5. The sheriff shall hold no other office, and shall be incapable of holding the office of sheriff longer than four in any period of six years. He may be required by law to renew his security from time to time, and in default of giving such security, his office shall be deemed vacant. The county shall never be responsible for his acts.

Sec. 6. A board of supervisors, consisting of one from each organized township, shall be established in each county, with such powers as shall be prescribed by law.

Sec. 7. Cities shall have such representation in the board of supervisors of the counties in which they are situated, as the legislature may direct.

Sec. 8. No county seat once established shall be removed until the place to which it is proposed to be removed shall be designated by two-thirds of the board of supervisors of the county, and a majority of the electors voting thereon shall have voted in favor of the proposed location, in such manner as shall be prescribed by law.

Sec. 9. The board of supervisors of any county may borrow or raise by tax one thousand dollars, for constructing or repairing public buildings, highways or bridges; but no greater sum shall be borrowed or raised by tax for such purpose in any one year, unless authorized by a majority of the electors of such county voting thereon.

Sec. 10. The board of supervisors, or, in the county of Wayne, the board of county auditors, shall have the exclusive power to prescribe and fix the compensation for all services rendered for, and to adjust all claims against, their respective counties; and the sum so fixed or defined shall be subject to no appeal.

Sec. 11. The board of supervisors of each organized county may provide for laying out highways, constructing bridges, and organizing townships, under such restrictions and limitations as shall be prescribed by law.

ARTICLE XI.

TOWNSHIPS.

Section 1. There shall be elected annually, on the first Monday of April, in each organized township, one supervisor, one township clerk, who shall be, *ex-officio*, school inspector, one commissioner of highways, one township treasurer, one school inspector, not exceeding four constables, and one overseer of highways for each highway district, whose powers and duties shall be prescribed by law.

Sec. 2. Each organized township shall be a body corporate, with such powers and immunities as shall be prescribed by law. All suits and proceedings by or against a township shall be in the name thereof.

ARTICLE XII.

IMPEACHMENTS AND REMOVALS FROM OFFICE.

Section 1. The house of representatives shall have the sole power of impeaching civil officers for corrupt conduct in office, or for crimes and misdemeanors; but a majority of the members elected shall be necessary to direct an impeachment.

Sec. 2. Every impeachment shall be tried by the senate. When the governor or lieutenant governor is tried, the chief justice of the supreme court shall preside. When an impeachment is directed, the senate shall take an oath or affirmation truly and impartially to try and determine the same according to the evidence. No person shall be convicted without the concurrence of two-thirds of the members elected. Judgment in case of impeachment shall not extend further than removal from office; but the party convicted shall be liable to punishment according to law.

Sec. 3. When an impeachment is directed, the house of representatives shall elect from their own body three members, whose duty it shall be to prosecute such impeachment. No impeachment shall be tried until the final adjournment of the legislature, when the senate will proceed to try the same.

Sec. 4. No judicial officer shall exercise his office after an impeachment is directed, until he is acquitted.

Sec. 5. The governor may make a provisional appointment to fill a vacancy occasioned by the suspension of an officer until he shall be acquitted, or until after the election and qualification of a successor.

Sec. 6. For reasonable cause, which shall not be sufficient ground for the impeachment of a judge, the governor shall remove him on a concurrent resolution of two-thirds of the members elected to each house of the legislature; but the cause for which such removal is required, shall be stated at length in such resolution.

Sec. 7. The legislature shall provide by law for the removal of any officer elected by a county, township or school district, in such manner and for such cause as to them shall seem just and proper.

ARTICLE XIII.

EDUCATION.

Section 1. The superintendent of public instruction shall have the general supervision of public instruction, and his duties shall be prescribed by law.

Sec. 2. The proceeds from the sales of all lands that have been or hereafter may be granted by the United States to the State, for educational purposes, and the proceeds of all lands or other property given by individuals, or appropriated by the State for like purposes, shall be and remain a perpetual fund, the interest and income of which, together with the rents of all such lands as may remain unsold, shall be inviolably appropriated and annually applied to the specific objects of the original gift, grant or appropriation.

Sec. 3. All lands, the titles to which shall fall from a defect of heirs, shall escheat to the State; and the interest on the clear proceeds from the sales thereof, shall be appropriated exclusively to the support of primary schools.

Sec. 4. The legislature shall, within five years from the adoption of this constitution, provide for and establish a system of primary schools, whereby a school shall be kept without charge for tuition, at least three months in each year, in every school district in the State; and all instruction in said schools shall be conducted in the English language.

Sec. 5. A school shall be maintained in each school district at least three months in each year. Any school district neglecting to maintain such school, shall be deprived for the ensuing year of its proportion of the income of the primary school fund, and of all funds arising from taxes for the support of schools.

Sec. 6. There shall be elected in each judicial circuit, at the time of the election of the judge of such circuit, a regent of the university, whose term of office shall be the same as that of such judge. The regents thus elected shall constitute the board of regents of the University of Michigan.

Sec. 7. The regents of the university, and their successors in office, shall continue to constitute the body corporate, known by the name and title of "The Regents of the University of Michigan."

Sec. 8. The regents of the university shall, at their first annual meeting, or as soon thereafter as may be, elect a president of the university, who shall be *ex-officio* a member of their board, with the privilege of speaking, but not of voting. He shall preside at the meetings of the regents, and be the principal executive officer of the university. The board of regents shall have the general supervision of the university, and the direction and control of all expenditures from the university interest fund.

Sec. 9. There shall be elected at the general election in the year one thousand eight hundred and fifty-two, three members of a State board of education, one for two years, one for four years, and one for six years; and at each succeeding biennial election there shall be elected one member of such board, who shall hold his office for six years. The superintendent of public instruction shall be *ex-officio* a member and secretary of such board. The board shall have the general supervision of the State normal school, and their duties shall be prescribed by law.

Sec. 10. Institutions for the benefit of those inhabitants who are deaf, dumb, blind, or insane, shall always be fostered and supported.

Sec. 11. The legislature shall encourage the promotion of intellectual, scientific and agricultural improvement; and shall, as soon as practicable, provide for the establishment of an agricultural school. The legislature may appropriate the twenty-two sections of salt spring lands now unappropriated, or the money arising from the sale of the same, where such lands have been already sold, and any land which may hereafter be granted or appropriated for such purpose, for the support and maintenance of such school, and may make the same a branch of the university, for instruction in agriculture and the natural sciences connected therewith, and place the same under the supervision of the regents of the university.

Sec. 12. The legislature shall provide for the establishment of at least one library in each township; and all fines assessed and collected in the several counties and townships for any breach of the penal laws, shall be exclusively applied to the support of such libraries.

ARTICLE XIV.

FINANCE AND TAXATION.

Section 1. All specific State taxes, except those received from the mining companies of the upper peninsular, shall be applied in paying the interest upon the primary school, university, and other educational funds, and the interest and principal of the State debt in the order herein recited, until the extinguishment of the State debt, other than the amounts due to educational funds, when such specific taxes shall be added to, and constitute a part of the primary school interest fund. The legislature shall provide for an annual tax, sufficient, with other resources, to pay the estimated expenses of the State government, the interest of the State debt, and such deficiency as may occur in the resources.

Sec. 2. The legislature shall provide by law a sinking fund of at least twenty thousand dollars a year, to commence in eighteen hundred and fifty-two, with compound interest at the rate of six per cent. per annum, and an annual increase of at least five per cent., to be applied solely to the payment and extinguishment of the principal of the State debt, other than the amounts due to educational funds, and shall be continued until the extinguishment thereof. The unfunded debt shall not be funded or redeemed at a value exceeding that established by law in one thousand eight hundred and forty-eight.

Sec. 3. The State may contract debts to meet deficits in revenue. Such debts shall not in the aggregate at any one time exceed fifty thousand dollars. The moneys so raised shall be applied to the purposes for which they were obtained, or to the payment of the debts so contracted.

Sec. 4. The State may contract debts to repel invasion, suppress insurrection, or defend the State in time of war. The money arising from the contracting of such debts shall be applied to the purposes for which it was raised, or to repay such debts.

Sec. 5. No money shall be paid out of the treasury, except in pursuance of appropriations made by law.

Sec. 6. The credit of the State shall not be granted to, or in aid of, any person, association or corporation.

Sec. 7. No scrip, certificate, or other evidence of State indebtedness shall be issued, except for the redemption of stock previously issued, or for such debts as are expressly authorized in this constitution.

Sec. 8. The State shall not subscribe to, or be interested in, the stock of any company, association, or corporation.

Sec. 9. The State shall not be a party to, or interested in, any work of internal improvement, or engaged in carrying on any such work, except in the expenditure of grants to the State of land or other property.

Sec. 10. The State may continue to collect all specific taxes accruing to the Treasury under existing laws. The legislature may provide for the collection of specific taxes from banking, railroad, plank road, and other corporations hereafter created.

Sec. 11. The legislature shall provide an uniform rule of taxation, except on property paying specifie taxes; and taxes shall be levied on such property as shall be prescribed by law.

Sec. 12. All assessments hereafter authorized shall be on property at its cash value.

Sec. 13. The legislature shall provide for an equalization by a State board in the year one thousand eight hundred and fifty-one, and every fifth year thereafter, of assessments on all taxable property, except that paying specific taxes.

Sec. 14. Every law which imposes, continues, or revives a tax, shall distinctly state the tax, and the object to which it is to be applied; and it shall not be sufficient to refer to any other law to fix such tax or object.

ARTICLE XV.

CORPORATIONS.

Section 1. Corporations may be formed under general laws, but shall not be created by special act, except for municipal purposes. All laws passed pursuant to this section may be altered, amended, or repealed.

Sec. 2. No banking law, or law for banking purposes, or amendments thereof, shall have effect until the same shall, after its passage, be submitted to a vote of the electors of the State, at a general election, and be approved by a majority of the votes cast thereon at such election.

Sec. 3. The officers and stockholders of every corporation or association for banking purposes, issuing bank notes or paper credits to circulate as money, shall be individually liable for all debts contracted during the time of their being officers or stockholders of such corporation or association.

Sec. 4. The legislature shall provide by law for the registry of all bills or notes issued or put in circulation as money, and shall require security to the full amount of notes and bills so registered, in State or United States stocks bearing interest, which shall be deposited with the State treasurer for the redemption of such bills or notes in specie.

Sec. 5. In case of the insolvency of any bank or banking association, the bill-holders thereof shall be entitled to preference in payment, over all other creditors of such bank or association.

Sec. 6. The legislature shall pass no law authorizing or sanctioning the suspension of specie payments by any person, association, or corporation.

Sec. 7. The stockholders of all corporations and joint stock associations shall be individually liable for all labor performed for such corporation or association.

Sec. 8. The legislature shall pass no law altering or amending any act of incorporation heretofore granted, without the assent of two-thirds of the members elected to each house; nor shall any such act be renewed or extended. This restriction shall not apply to municipal corporations.

Sec. 9. The property of no person shall be taken by any corporation for public use without compensation being first made or secured in such manner as may be prescribed by law.

Sec. 10. No corporation, except for municipal purposes, or for the construction of railroads, plank roads, and canals, shall be created for a longer time than thirty years.

Sec. 11. The term "corporation," as used in the preceding sections of this article, shall be construed to include all associations and joint stock companies having any of the powers or privileges of corporations not possessed by individuals or partnerships. All corporations shall have the right to sue and be subject to be sued in all courts in like cases as natural persons.

Sec. 12. No corporation shall hold any real estate hereafter acquired for a longer period than ten years, except such real estate as shall be actually occupied by such corporation in the exercise of its franchises.

Sec. 13. The legislature shall provide for the incorporation and organization of cities and villages, and shall restrict their powers of taxation, borrowing money, contracting debts, and loaning their credit.

Sec. 14. Judicial officers of cities and villages shall be elected, and all other officers shall be elected or appointed at such time and in such manner as the legislature may direct.

Sec. 15. Private property shall not be taken for public improvements in cities and villages without the consent of the owner, unless the compensation therefor shall first be determined by a jury of freeholders, and actually paid or secured in the manner provided by law.

Sec. 16. Previous notice of any application for an alteration of the charter of any corporation shall be given in such manner as may be prescribed by law.

ARTICLE XVI.

EXEMPTIONS.

Section 1. The personal property of every resident of this State, to consist of such property only as shall be designated by law, shall be exempted to the amount of not less than five hundred dollars, from sale on execution or other final process of any court, issued for the collection of any debt contracted after the adoption of this constitution.

Sec. 2. Every homestead of not exceeding forty acres of land, and the dwelling house thereon, and the appurtenances, to be selected by the owner thereof, and not included in any town plat, city, or village; or instead thereof, at the option of the owner, any lot in any city, village, or recorded town plat, or such parts of lots as shall be equal thereto, and the dwelling house thereon, and its appurtenances, owned and occupied by any resident of the State, not exceeding in value fifteen hundred dollars, shall be exempt from forced sale on execution, or any other final process from a court, for any debt contracted after the adoption of this constitution. Such exemption shall not extend to any mortgage thereon lawfully obtained; but such mortgage or other alienation of such land by the owner thereof, if a married man, shall not be valid without the signature of the wife to the same.

Sec. 3. The homestead of a family, after the death of the owner thereof, shall be exempt from the payment of his debts, contracted after the adoption of this constitution, in all cases during the minority of his children.

Sec. 4. If the owner of a homestead die, leaving a widow, but no children, the same shall be exempt, and the rents and profits thereof shall accrue to her benefit during the time of her widowhood, unless she be the owner of a homestead in her own right.

Sec. 5. The real and personal estate of every female, acquired before marriage, and all property to which she may afterwards become entitled by gift, grant, inheritance, or devise, shall be and remain the estate and property of such female, and shall not be liable for the debts, obligations, or engagements of her husband, and may be devised or bequeathed by her as if she were unmarried.

ARTICLE XVII.

MILITIA.

Section 1. The militia shall be composed of all able bodied white male citizens between the ages of eighteen and forty-five years, except such as are exempted by the laws of the United States or of this State; but all such citizens, of any religious denomination whatever, who, from scruples of conscience, may be adverse to bearing arms, shall be excused therefrom, upon such conditions as shall be prescribed by law.

Sec. 2. The legislature shall provide by law for organizing, equipping, and disciplining the militia, in such manner as they shall deem expedient, not incompatible with the laws of the United States.

Sec. 3. Officers of the militia shall be elected or appointed, and be commissioned in such manner as may be provided by law.

ARTICLE XVIII.

MISCELLANEOUS PROVISIONS.

Section 1. Members of the legislature, and all officers, executive and judicial, except such officers as may by law be exempted, shall, before they enter on the duties of their respective offices, take and subscribe the following oath or affirmation: "I do solemnly swear (or affirm,) that I will support the Constitution of the United States and the constitution of this State, and that I will faithfully discharge the duties of the office of ——— according to the best of my ability." And no other oath, declaration, or test, shall be required as a qualification for any office or public trust.

Sec. 2. When private property is taken for the use or benefit of the public, the necessity for using such property, and the just compensation to be made therefor, except when to be made by the State, shall be ascertained by a jury of twelve freeholders, residing in the vicinity of such property, or by not less than three commissioners, appointed by a court of record, as shall be prescribed by law.

Sec. 3. No mechanical trade shall hereafter be taught to convicts in the State prison of this State, except the manufacture of those articles of which the chief supply for home consumption is imported from other States or countries.

Sec. 4. No navigable stream in this State shall be either bridged or dammed without authority from the board of supervisors of the proper county, under the provisions of law. No such law shall prejudice the right of individuals to the free navigation of such streams, or preclude the State from the further improvement of the navigation of such streams.

Sec. 5. An accurate statement of the receipts and expenditures of the public moneys shall be attached to and published with the laws, at every regular session of the legislature.

Sec. 6. The laws, public records, and the written judicial and legislative proceedings of the State shall be conducted, promulgated, and preserved in the English language.

Sec. 7. Every person has a right to bear arms for the defence of himself and the State.

Sec. 8. The military shall, in all cases, and at all times, be in strict subordination to the civil power.

Sec. 9. No soldier shall, in time of peace, be quartered in any house without the consent of the owner or occupant, nor in time of war, except in a manner prescribed by law.

Sec. 10. The people have the right peaceably to assemble together, to consult for the common good, to instruct their representatives, and to petition the legislature for redress of grievances.

Sec. 11. Neither slavery, nor involuntary servitude, unless for the punishment of crime, shall ever be tolerated in this State.

Sec. 12. No lease or grant hereafter of agricultural land for a longer period than twelve years, reserving any rent or service of any kind, shall be valid.

Sec. 13. Aliens who are, or who may hereafter become, *bona fide* residents of this State, shall enjoy the same rights in respect to the possession, enjoyment, and inheritance of property, as native born citizens.

Sec. 14. The property of no person shall be taken for public use without just compensation therefor. Private roads may be opened in the manner to be prescribed by law; but in every case the necessities of the road and the amount of all damage to be sustained by the opening thereof, shall be first determined by a jury of freeholders; and such amount, together with the expenses of proceedings, shall be paid by the person or persons to be benefited.

Sec. 15. No general revision of the laws shall hereafter be made. When a reprint thereof becomes necessary, the legislature in joint convention shall appoint a suitable person to collect together such acts and parts of acts as are in force, and without alteration, arrange them under appropriate heads and titles. The laws so arranged shall be submitted to two commissioners appointed by the governor, for examination, and if certified by them to be a correct compilation of all general laws in force, shall be printed in such manner as shall be prescribed by law.

ARTICLE XIX.

UPPER PENINSULA.

Section 1. The counties of Mackinaw, Chippewa, Delta, Marquette, Schoolcraft, Houghton, and Ontonagon, and the islands and territory thereunto attached, the islands of Lakes Superior, Huron, and Michigan, and in Green Bay, and the Straits of Mackinaw and the River Ste. Marie, shall constitute a separate judicial district, and be entitled to a district judge and district attorney.

Sec. 2. The district judge shall be elected by the electors of such district, and shall perform the same duties and possess the same powers as a circuit judge in his circuit, and shall hold his office for the same period.

Sec. 3. The district attorney shall be elected every two years by the electors of the district, shall perform the duties of prosecuting attorney throughout the entire district, and may issue warrants for the arrest of offenders in cases of felony, to be proceeded with as shall be prescribed by law.

Sec. 4. Such judicial district shall be entitled at all times to at least one senator; and until entitled to more by its population, it shall have three members of the house of representatives, to be apportioned among the several counties by the legislature.

Sec. 5. The legislature may provide for the payment of the district judge a salary not exceeding one thousand dollars a year, and of the district attorney not exceeding seven hundred dollars a year; and may allow extra compensation to the members of the legislature from such territory, not exceeding two dollars a day during any session.

Sec. 6. The elections for all district and county officers, State senator or representatives, within the boundaries defined in this article, shall take place on the last Tuesday of September in the respective years in which they may be required. The county canvass shall be held on the first Tuesday in October thereafter, and the district canvass on the last Tuesday of said October.

Sec. 7. One-half of the taxes received into the treasury from mining corporations in the upper peninsula, paying an annual State tax of one per cent., shall be paid to the treasurers of the counties from which it is received, to be applied for township and county purposes, as provided by law. The legislature shall have power, after the year one thousand eight hundred and fifty-five, to reduce the amount to be refunded.

Sec. 8. The legislature may change the location of the State prison from Jackson to the upper peninsula.

Sec. 9. The charters of the several mining corporations may be modified by the legislature, in regard to the term limited for subscribing to stock, and in relation to the quantity of land which a corporation shall hold; but the capital shall not be increased, nor the time for the existence of charters extended. No such corporation shall be permitted to purchase or hold any real estate, except such as shall be necessary for the exercise of its corporate franchises.

ARTICLE XX.

AMENDMENT AND REVISION OF THE CONSTITUTION.

***Section* 1. Any amendment or amendments to this constitution may be**

proposed in the senate or house of representatives. If the same shall be agreed to by two-thirds of the members elected to each house, such amendment or amendments shall be entered on their journals respectively, with the yeas and nays taken thereon, and the same shall be submitted to the electors at the next general election thereafter; and if a majority of the electors qualified to vote for members of the legislature voting thereon, shall ratify and approve such amendment or amendments, the same shall become part of the constitution.

Sec. 2. At the general election to be held in the year one thousand eight hundred and sixty-six, and in each sixteenth year thereafter; and also at such other times as the legislature may by law provide, the question of a general revision of the constitution shall be submitted to the electors qualified to vote for members of the legislature; and in case a majority of the electors so qualified, voting at such election, shall decide in favor of a convention for such purpose, the legislature, at the next session, shall provide by law for the election of delegates to such convention. All the amendments shall take effect at the commencement of the political year after their adoption.

SCHEDULE.

That no inconvenience may arise from the changes in the constitution of this State, and in order to carry the same into complete operation, it is hereby declared, that

Section 1. The common law, and the statute laws now in force, not repugnant to this constitution, shall remain in force until they expire by their own limitations, or are altered or repealed by the legislature.

Sec. 2. All writs, actions, causes of action, prosecutions and rights of individuals and of bodies corporate, and of the State, and all charters of incorporation, shall continue; and all indictments which have been found, or which may hereafter be found, for any crime or offense committed before the adoption of this constitution, may be proceeded upon as if no change had taken place. The several courts, except as herein otherwise provided, shall continue with the like powers and jurisdiction, both at law and in equity, as if this constitution had not been adopted, and until the organization of the judicial department under this constitution.

Sec. 3. That all fines, penalties, forfeitures, and escheats accruing to the State of Michigan under the present constitution and laws, shall accrue to the use of the State under this constitution.

Sec. 4. That all recognizances, bonds, obligations, and all other instruments entered into or executed before the adoption of this constitution, to the people of the State of Michigan, to any State, county or township, or any public officer or public body, or which may be entered into or executed under existing laws "to the people of the State of Michigan," to any such officer or public body, before the complete organization of the departments of government under this constitution, shall remain binding and valid; and rights and liabilities upon the same shall continue, and may be prosecuted as provided by law. And all crimes and misdemeanors and penal actions, shall be tried, punished and prosecuted, as though no change had taken place, until otherwise provided by law.

Sec. 5. A governor and lieutenant governor shall be chosen under the existing constitution and laws, to serve after the expiration of the term of the present incumbent.

Sec. 6. All officers, civil and military, now holding any office or appointment, shall continue to hold their respective offices, unless removed by competent authority, until superseded under the laws now in force, or under this constitution.

Sec. 7. The members of the senate and house of representatives of the legislature of one thousand eight hundred and fifty-one shall continue in office, under the provisions of law, until superseded by their successors, elected and qualified under this constitution.

Sec. 8. All county officers, unless removed by competent authority, shall continue to hold their respective offices until the first day of January, in the year one thousand eight hundred and fifty-three. The laws now in force as to the election, qualification, and duties of township officers shall continue in force until the legislature shall, in conformity to the provisions of this constitution, provide for the holding of elections to fill such offices, and prescribe the duties of such officers respectively.

Sec. 9. On the first day of January, in the year one thousand eight hundred and fifty-two, the terms of office of the judges of the supreme court under existing laws, and of the judges of the county courts, and of the clerks of the supreme court, shall expire on the said day.

Sec. 10. On the first day of January, in the year one thousand eight hundred and fifty-two, the jurisdiction of all suits and proceedings then pending in the present supreme court shall become vested in the supreme court established by this constitution, and shall be finally adjudicated by the court where the same may be pending. The jurisdiction of all suits and proceedings at law and equity, then pending in the circuit courts and county courts for the several counties shall become vested in the circuit court of the said counties and district court of the upper peninsula.

Sec. 11. The probate courts, the courts of justices of the peace, and the police court authorized by an act entitled "an act to establish a police court in the city of Detroit," approved April second, one thousand eight hundred and fifty, shall continue to exercise the jurisdiction and powers now conferred upon them respectively, until otherwise provided by law.

Sec. 12. The office of State printer shall be vested in the present incumbent until the expiration of the term for which he was elected under the law then in force; and all the provisions of the said law relating to his duties, rights, privileges, and compensation, shall remain unimpaired and inviolate until the expiration of his said term of office.

Sec. 13. It shall be the duty of the legislature, at their first session, to adapt the present laws to the provisions of this constitution, as far as may be.

Sec. 14. The attorney general of the State is required to prepare and report to the legislature, at the commencement of the next session, such changes and modifications in existing laws as may be deemed necessary to adapt the same to this constitution, and as may be best calculated to carry into effect its provisions; and he shall receive no additional compensation therefor.

Sec. 15. Any territory attached to any county for judicial purposes, if not otherwise represented, shall be considered as forming part of such county, so far as regards elections for the purpose of representation.

[Sections 16, 17, 18, 19, 20, and 21, referring to the mode of voting for the new constitution, are omitted, not having any direct connection with the instrument.]

Sec. 22. Every county except Mackinaw and Chippewa, entitled to a representative in the legislature, at the time of the adoption of this constitution, shall continue to be so entitled under this constitution; and the county of Saginaw, with the territory that may be attached, shall be entitled to one representative; the county of Tuscola, and the territory that may be attached, one representative; the county of Sanilac and the territory that may be attached, one representative; the counties of Midland and Arenac, [Bay,] with the territory that may be attached, one representative; the county of Montcalm, with the territory that may be attached thereto, one representative; and the counties of Newaygo and Oceana, with the territory that may be attached thereto, one representative. Each county having a ratio of representation and a fraction over, equal to a moiety of said ratio, shall be entitled to two representatives, and so on above that number, giving one additional member for each additional ratio.

Sec. 23. The cases pending and undisposed of in the late court of chancery, at the time of the adoption of this constitution, shall continue to be heard and determined by the judges of the supreme court. But the legislature shall, at its session in one thousand eight hundred and fifty-one, provide by law for the transfer of said causes that may remain undisposed of on the first day of January, one thousand eight hundred and fifty-two, to the supreme or circuit court, established by this constitution, or require that the same may be heard and determined by the circuit judges.

Sec. 24. The term of office of the governor and lieutenant governor shall commence on the first day of January next after their election.

Sec. 25. The territory described in the article entitled "Upper Peninsula," shall be attached to and constitute a part of the third circuit for the election of a regent of the university.

Sec. 26. The legislature shall have authority, after the expiration of the term of office of the district judge first elected for the upper peninsula, to abolish said office of district judge and district attorney, or either of them.

Sec. 27. The legislature shall, at its session of one thousand eight hundred and fifty-one, apportion the representatives among the several counties and districts, and divide the State into senate districts, pursuant to the provisions of this constitution.

Sec. 28. The terms of office of all State and county officers, of the circuit judges, members of the board of education, and members of the legislature, shall begin on the first day of January next succeeding their election.

Sec. 29. The State, exclusive of the upper peninsula, shall be divided into eight judicial circuits, and the counties of Monroe, Lenawee, and Hillsdale, shall constitute the first circuit; the counties of Branch, St. Joseph, Cass, and Berrien, shall constitute the second circuit; the county of Wayne shall constitute the third circuit; the counties of Washtenaw, Jackson, and Ingham, shall constitute the fourth circuit; the counties of Calhoun, Kalamazoo, Allegan, Eaton, and Van Buren, shall constitute the fifth circuit; [the] counties of St. Clair, Macomb, Oakland, and Sanilac, shall constitute the sixth circuit; the counties of Lapeer, Genesee, Saginaw, Shiawassee, Livingston, Tuscola, and Midland, shall constitute the seventh circuit; and the counties of Barry, Kent, Ottawa, Ionia, Clinton, and Montcalm shall constitute the eighth circuit.

Done in convention, at the capital of the State, this fifteenth day of August, in the year of our Lord one thousand eight hundred and fifty, and of the independence of the United States the seventy-fifth.

D. GOODWIN, *President.*

AMENDMENTS TO THE CONSTITUTION.

On the 8th of November, 1870, the people of Michigan voted upon the ratification of four amendments to the State constitution, as follows: *First,* an amendment striking out the word "white" wherever it occurs in the organic law; *Second,* authorizing the board of supervisors of any county to borrow or raise by tax two thousand dollars, for constructing or repairing public buildings, highways, or bridges, but no greater amount without the sanction of the electors of such county; *Third,* an amendment for increasing the salaries of the State executive and judicial officers; and *Fourth,* an amendment authorizing the legislature to pass laws establishing certain charges on the railroads of the State, prohibiting running contracts between railroad companies with certain discriminations, also prohibiting the consolidation of stock, property, or franchises between parallel or competing lines of railroads without due notice to stockholders, and finally, that the legislature may provide by law for the payment by counties, townships, and municipalities of the State, of all bonds or other obligations heretofore issued in aid of railroads, subject to the will of the electors of each county. As the concluding page of this volume is passing through the press, it is quite impossible to ascertain the official result of the election on these amendments; but according to the latest newspaper reports, they have all been defeated excepting the two articles, placing railroad tariffs under the control of the legislature, and forbidding the consolidation of competing lines of railroads, and perhaps the amendment on suffrage.